SOUTHERN MASSACHUSETTS CEMETERY COLLECTION

Volume Two

Susan Salisbury

HERITAGE BOOKS
2012

HERITAGE BOOKS
AN IMPRINT OF HERITAGE BOOKS, INC.

Books, CDs, and more—Worldwide

For our listing of thousands of titles see our website
at
www.HeritageBooks.com

Published 2012 by
HERITAGE BOOKS, INC.
Publishing Division
100 Railroad Ave. #104
Westminster, Maryland 21157

Other Heritage Books by the author:
Descendants of Walter Cook
My Family: Lariviere-Morin
Southern Massachusetts Cemetery Collection: Volumes 1 and 2
The Darlings of Mendon, Massachusetts
The Thayers of Mendon, Massachusetts
The Wheelocks of Mendon, Massachusetts

International Standard Book Numbers
Paperbound: 978-0-7884-0570-9
Clothbound: 978-0-7884-9435-2

Due to the widespread problem of cemetery vandalism, I have undertaken the task of preserving, in part, as many cemeteries as possible. With each worn and toppled stone, a portion of our past disappears. Every year the memory of more and more of the brave men and women who gave their lives during the Revolutionary and Civil Wars vanishes. Let this, Southern Massachusetts Cemetery Collection, Volume 2, as in Volume 1, stand in dedication to those long forgotten.....

S. Salisbury
May 1996

About the Author

Susan Salisbury, Publisher & Editor of the Salisbury Newsletter, and an avid genealogist since 1978, has undertaken the monumental task of preserving old cemeteries. In Volume II, she has continued the never ending task, spreading a little further across the state of Massachusetts.

Susan, her husband of twenty seven-years, and their daughter live in a small New England town in southern Massachusetts.

Introduction

Welcome to Southern Massachusetts Cemetery Collection Volume 2. As with Volume 1, I continue to compile our precious resources of the past (pre-1950) with the hope of preserving this information for future generations. Within the pages of this book, I have recorded, as accurately as possible, a list of cemeteries and those buried within, by towns and then by readable names, including dates and inscriptions from each stone. However, here in New England where much of our country's history began, the ravages of time have not always been kind. The continued exposure to rain, snow and wind have left many stones broken and scattered or worn beyond readability. So much has already been lost. The current problem of vandalism is playing a greater role in our lost past daily. So upon myself I set the task of recording with great care, the inscriptions on those tombstones still standing for the next generation of genealogists. Many of our fine ancestors who worked, fought, and died while creating the legacies that we have come to appreciate as the United States of America are among those buried in our local cemeteries. In honor of these individuals this book is dedicated.

SS

Table of Content

Newell Cemetery
West Street
South Attleborough, Massachusetts

Slack, Lucy, w/o Samuel Slack, d 10 Dec 1848 aged 79 yrs
Slack, Samuel, s/o Captain Samuel Slack, d 15 Nov 1845 aged 76 yrs
Slack, Mary, w/o Samuel Slack, d 27 Dec 1811 aged 39 yrs
Slack, Lucy, w/o Samuel Slack, d 10 Dec 1849 aged 79 yrs
Slack, Captain Samuel, d 5 June 1806 aged 68 yrs
Slack, Ruth, w/o Captain Samuel Slack, d 14 Aug 1815 aged 75 yrs
Slack, Welcome, b 12 Feb 1811, d 21 Dec 1875
Slack, Maria, b 5 Dec 1803, d 23 March 1882
Slack, Samuel, s/o Samuel & Mary Slack, d 7 June 1863 aged 52 yrs
Slack, Benjamin, s/o Samuel & Ruth Slack, d 3 Jan 1815 aged 48 yrs
Slack, Adah, d/o Samuel & Ruth Slack, d 9 Dec 1821 aged 46 yrs
Jillson, Albert J., b 2 Oct 1837, d 6 Nov 1926
Rounds, Susan B., w/o Albert J. Jillson, b 19 June 1838, d 26 Aug 1918
Robinson, Asahel H., b 5 Oct 1810, d 11 June 1898
Robinson, Lucy D., w/o Asahel H. Robinson, b 14 Nov 1816, d 3 Dec 1893
Robinson, Lewis A., d 18 Nov 1883 aged 47 yrs
Robinson, Sarah A., w/o Lewis A. Robinson, d Dec (can't read)
Robinson, Dr. Stephen, d 27 Sept 1833
Breck, Francis MD, b 16 March 1838, d 14 March 1906
Breck, Helen, w/o Dr. Francis Breck, b 16 May 1843, d 22 Jan 1833
Walcott, Otis, s/o Lyman & Julia Brown, d 24 Sept 1837 aged 7 mos
Slack, Ruth, b April 1810, d Oct 1894
Newell, Jabez, d 5 April 1849 aged 68 yrs 3 mos
Newell, Lydia, w/o Jabez Newell, d 7 June 1854 aged 74 yrs
Newell, Emma, w/o Jabez Newell, d 6 June 1804 aged 21 yrs
Spencer, Eunice R., w/o Jonathan N. Spencer of Pawtucket, RI, & d/o
    Jabez & Eunice Newell, d 1 Oct 1825 aged 22 yrs
Davis, Deacon Aaron, d 4 Jan 1820 aged 88 yrs
Davis, Margaret, w/o Deacon Aaron Davis, d 14 Feb 1816
Robinson, Sarah, w/o Elijah Robinson, d 26 May 1789 aged 51 yrs
Robinson, Elijah, d 14 April 1799 aged 71 yrs
Robinson, George, d 19 Aug 1812 aged 86 yrs
Slack, William, s/o George & Ruth Slack, b 17 Oct 1772, d 26 May 1840
Robinson, George, b 31 Oct 1770, d 19 Sept 1825

Gay, Jabez, d 19 Aug 1809 aged 28 yrs

Gay, Candace, w/o Jabez Gay, d 28 Aug 1871 aged 87 yrs

Gay, Jabez J. R., d 21 Jan 1883 aged 73 yrs 5 mos 24 days

Slack, Ella, w/o Jabez J. R. Gay & d/o Samuel Slack, d 20 June 1844 aged
38 yrs 1 mo 21 days

Gay, Candace, d/o Jabez J. R. & Ella Gay, d 19 April 1867 aged 28 yrs 4
mos 20 days

Stimpson, Alexander, d 18 May 1850 aged 75 yrs

Stimpson, Lucy, w/o Alexander Stimpson, d 19 July 1845 aged 68 yrs

Jillson, Willard, b 3 July 1806, d 8 Jan 1886

Jillson, Eliza M., w/o Willard Jillson, d 18 May 1877 aged 73 yrs 3 mos 5
days

Shaw, William, b 15 Sept 1830, d 28 April 1920

Shaw, Angeline B., w/o William P. Shaw, b 20 Nov 1829, d 20 Feb 1897

Shaw, Evelyn H., b 29 Sept 1852, d 29 March 1858

Read, Ezra, b 5 July 1773, d 15 April 1852

Read, Mary, w/o Ezra Read, b 8 Oct 1770, d 28 Sept 1851

Shaw, Charles W., b 16 June 1863, d 1 April 1893

Lane, Bethiah, w/o Deacon Ebenezer Lane, d 10 Jan 1787 aged 70 yrs

Rogerson, Dr. Robert, d 1 April 1806 aged 49 yrs

Rogerson, Lucy, w/o Dr. Robert Rogerson, d 4 March 1807 aged 38 yrs

Ide, Amanda Shepard, b 21 April 1829, d 20 Jan 1920

Wheelock, Jemina W., w/o Ebenezer Ide & d/o Philitus Wheelock, d 16
June 1845 Smithfield, RI aged 47 yrs

Read, Joel Esq., d 27 Jan 1837 aged 83 yrs

Read, Chloe, w/o Joel Read Esq., d 3 March 1826 aged 68 yrs

Ide, Bebee, w/o Captain Jacob Ide & formerly w/o Ezra Barrows, d 11
May 1831 aged 57 yrs

Barrows, Simeon, d 15 Feb 1816 aged 65 yrs

Barrows, Anna, d 28 Feb 1819 aged 48 yrs

Davis, Eunice, d/o Dea. Aaron & Hannah Davis, d 1 Feb 1816 aged 58 yrs

Robinson, Nathaniel, d 17 Aug 1771

Barrows, Benjamin, d 20 Feb 1801 aged 84 yrs

Barrows, Hannah, w/o Benjamin Barrows, d 1876

Barrows, Lydia, d 22 May 1792 aged 47 yrs

Peck, Daniel, d Nov 1750 aged 65 yrs

May, Catherine E., d/o Tilly & Hannah May, d 19 Dec 1878

May, Tilly C., (can't read)

Weld, Habjah, M.A., b 2 Sept 1762, d 14 May 1782

Weld, Mary, w/o Habjah Weld, M.A., d 7 Jan 1799

Barrows, Huldah, w/o William Barrows, d 6 Nov 1777 aged 26 yrs
Nutting, Jonathan, d 1731
Whipple, Jeremiah, d 14 May 1721 aged 38 yrs
Barrows, John, d 17 Dec 1795 aged 43 yrs
Barrows, Eleanor, w/o William Barrows, d 26 Feb 1801 aged 66 yrs
Barrows, Priscilla, w/o John Barrows, d 17 Feb 1801 aged 84 yrs
Barrows, William, d 17 Dec 1795 aged 43 yrs
Foster, John, d 29 Dec 1759
Foster, Margaret, w/o John Foster, d 4 Nov 1761
Barrows, Selinda, d 3 Dec 1851
Hunt, Joseph W., d 6 Jan 1825 aged 74 yrs
Hunt, Abigail, w/o Joseph W. Hunt, d 26 May 1810 aged 54 yrs
Hunt, Charlotte, d/o Joseph & Abigail Hunt, d 15 Oct 1805 aged 16 yrs
Hunt, Deacon Richard, d 21 Aug 1864 aged 82 yrs
Hunt, Ann, w/o Deacon Richard Hunt, d 7 April 1849 aged 67 yrs
Hunt, Richard Baxter, b 5 Nov 1816, d 7 Jan 1898
Hunt, Edward Warren, b 3 Nov 1819, d 7 July 1897
Hunt, Caroline Frances, w/o Edward Warren Hunt, b 2 Aug 1823, d 21
    March 1902
Bullock, Richard, d 15 June 1832 aged 72 yrs
Bullock, Mary, w/o Richard Bullock, d 27 Oct 1833 aged 56 yrs 2 mos
Bullock, Julia Augusta, d/o Richard & Mary Bullock, d 20 July 1839 aged
    45 yrs
Proal, George V., 1859-1917
Proal, Inez E., w/o George V. Proal, 1869-1915
Bullock, Sophia, d/o Richard & Hannah Bullock, d 17 Sept 1817 aged 31
yrs
Bullock, Corles, s/o Richard & Hannah Bullock, d 29 Nov 1812 aged 23
yrs
Cushman, Lt. Jacob, d 4 Nov 1802 aged 28 yrs
Cushman, Richard, d 16 Nov 1814 aged 32 yrs
Cushman, Lucy, w/o Richard Cushman, d 22 Nov 1854 aged 70 yrs
Cushman, Samuel, d 16 Oct 1822 aged 78 yrs
Cushman, Caroline, d/o Samuel & Rebecca Cushman, d 27 June 1846
Daggett, Thomas, d 19 Aug 1807 aged 76 yrs
Daggett, Sibel, w/o Thomas Daggett, d 7 Jan 1810 aged 80 yrs
Jillson, Daniel, d 26 May 1826 aged 77 yrs
Jillison, Mehetable, w/o Daniel Jillson, d 27 May 1834 aged 85 yrs
Jillson, Samuel, d 14 June 1834 aged 60 yrs
Bowen, Uriel Jr., b 6 Oct 1803, d 21 May 1843

Withington, Laura M., d/o Thomas & Lydia Withington, b 29 June 1793, d 6 Oct 1860

Hewes, Betsey, w/o Elijah Hewes & d/o Samuel & Margaret Tingley, b 8 Oct 1753, d 25 July 1838

Tingley, Eunice, d/o Samuel & Margaret Tingley, b 10 March 1751, d 20 Dec 1831

Tingley, Samuel, s/o Samuel & Hannah Tingley, b 4 July 1714, d 15 Oct 1784

Cushman, Rebecca, w/o Samuel Tingley & d/o Jacob & Elizabeth Cushman, d 6 Dec 1790 aged 30 yrs

Tingley, Samuel, s/o Samuel & Margaret Tingley, b 17 Oct 1752, d 21 March 1846

Tingley, Amy, w/o Samuel Tingley, d 1 May 1858 aged 86 yrs

Tingley, Louisa Everett, d/o Samuel & Amy Tingley, b 2 Nov 1796, d 4 Sept 1866

Holmes, Hannah, d 28 Nov 1870 aged 77 yrs

Holmes, Hannah, w/o Samuel Holmes, d 12 March 1794 aged 38 yrs

Holmes, Asenath, w/o Samuel Holmes, d 21 Sept 1810 aged 30 yrs

Holmes, Samuel, d 19 April 1808 aged 30 yrs

Jillson, Abel, d 27 May 1862 aged 78 yrs

Jillson, Mary, w/o Abel Jillson, d 18 Sept 1825 aged 41 yrs

Jillson, Polly, w/o Abel Jillson & formerly w/o David Jillson, d 4 Oct 1870 aged 79 yrs

Jillson, David, d 28 Nov 1824 aged 35 yrs

Jillson, Rebekah, w/o David Jillson, d 9 Dec 1821 aged 30 yrs

Wellman, Ezra, d 4 April 1869 aged 87 yrs

Wellman, Hetty, w/o Ezra Wellman, d 20 July 1870 aged 88 yrs

Read, Nathan, b 22 Oct 1771, d 14 Oct 1858

Read, Sally, w/o Nathan Read, d 1 April 1830 aged 62 yrs

Draper, Alonzo, d 10 March 1846 aged 43 yrs

Draper, Mary, w/o Paul Draper, d 8 March 1816

Tingley, Thomas, d 9 Jan 1809 aged 77 yrs

Tingley, Martha, w/o Thomas Tingley, d 22 Nov 1805 aged 74 yrs

Draper, Horace, only s/o Fisher & Hannah Draper, d 8 Jan 1823 aged 25 yrs

Wellman, Nancy, d/o Lot & Marcy Wellman, d 14 June 1827 aged 28 yrs

Wellman, Elijah, d 20 June 1790 aged 58 yrs

Wellman, Rhoda, d 16 Dec 1836 aged 76 yrs

Wellman, Rachel, d/o Elijah Wellman, d 16 Jan 1816 aged 37 yrs

Bucklen, Else, w/o Barak Bucklen, d 13 Dec 1732 aged 62 yrs

Draper, Stephen, d 15 March 1825 aged 84 yrs
Draper, Elizabeth, w/o Stephen Draper, d 28 March 1800 aged 64 yrs
Morris, Andrew, 1869-1927
Wilson, Edith, w/o Andrew Morris, 1876-1958
Pidge, Sarah, d 1826
Pidge, Desire, d/o David & Amy Pidge, d 14 Dec 1806 aged 21 yrs
Read, Abigail, w/o Artemus Read, d 26 Nov 1860 aged 67 yrs
Read, Artemus, d 12 Jan 1826 aged 39 yrs
Read, Thomas, d 7 Sept 1817 aged 69 yrs
Read, Rachel, w/o Thomas Read, d 1823
Hall, John, d 2 Oct 1820 aged 46 yrs
Hall, Mary, w/o John Hall & formerly w/o Barney Davis, d 2 Nov 1838
    aged 59 yrs
Hall, Benjamin, d 1857
Hall, Ruana, w/o Benjamin Hall, d 25 Jan 1867 aged 71 yrs
Gatewood, Adam, b 15 Aug 1824, d 11 Dec 1893
Gatewood, Hannah, w/o Adam Gatewood, b 31 July 1826, d 25 Feb 1896
Butler, Nancy J., w/o H. F. Butler, b 3 Sept 1862, d 15 March 1908
Howard, Mary V., w/o Nathan Howard, b 1 Jan 1847, d 11 March 1903
Cary, George W., 1852-1913
Cary, Edith M., w/o George W. Cary, 1853-1928
Chace, John C., b 31 Dec 1820, d 6 Nov 1894
Eddy, Sarah, w/o John C. Chace, d 1 July 1885
Eldridge, Horace, b 20 Oct 1859, d 10 Jan 1922
Eldridge, Warren, b 11 Nov 1818, d 31 July 1884
Hathaway, Helen, w/o Warren Eldridge, b 3 June 1820, d 14 Nov 1901
Evans, Sallie H., b 8 Dec 1855, d 4 Feb 1941
Stanley, Daniel D., d 18 June 1886 aged 50 yrs 5 mos 1 day
Stanley, Nancy D., w/o Daniel D. Stanley, d 12 Nov 1867
Stanley, Jabez G., 1871-1957
Coggsell, Mary, d 15 May 1865 aged 27 yrs 1 mo 15 days
Coggsell, Thomas, d 15 March 1872 aged 48 yrs
Cain, George, d 20 Jan 1790 aged 50 yrs
Yates, Sarah, w/o Thomas Yates, d 10 May 1789 aged 87 yrs
Yates, Thomas, d 10 May 1788 aged 77 yrs
Campbell, Margaret, d 20 Oct 1870 aged 71 yrs
Campbell, Matthew, d 15 Sept 1867 aged 72 yrs
Peck, Jeremiah, d 26 April 1846 aged 82 yrs 6 mos
Peck, Elizabeth, w/o Jeremiah Peck, d 20 Feb 1846 aged 72 yrs 7 mos 11
    days

Draper, Prudence, d 12 April 1853 Providence, RI aged 64 yrs

Draper, Charlotte, d 22 Aug 1848 Thompson, CT 64 yrs

Draper, Isaac, d 17 July 1824 aged 88 yrs

Draper, Chloe, w/o Isaac Draper, d 4 April 1828 aged 82 yrs

Draper, Ebenezer, b 12 Feb 1771, d 2 July 1852

Capron, Sally, w/o Ebenezer Draper, b 9 Jan 1772, d 3 Feb 1860

Draper, Chloe T., d/o Ebenezer & Sally Draper, b 26 Feb 1809, d 9 Sept 1884

Carpenter, Nathan, d 3 Sept 1814 aged 48 yrs

Carpenter, Lucinda, w/o Nathan Carpenter, d 26 Feb 1831 aged 58 yrs

Tingley, Captain Timothy, d 9 March 1816 aged 48 yrs

Tingley, Eunice, w/o Captain Timothy Tingley, d 26 May 1839 aged 60 yrs

Tingley, Eunice S., d/o Captain Timothy & Eunice Tingley, d 19 Feb 1835 aged 19 yrs

Draper, Fisher, d 18 May 1839 aged 74 yrs

Draper, Hannah, w/o Fisher Draper, d 24 June 1843 aged 76 yrs

Draper, Hannah M., youngest d/o Fisher & Hannah Fisher, d 19 April 1832 aged 25 yrs

White, Eliphalet, 1766-1840

White, Bethania, w/o Eliphalet White, 1762-1848

White, Deronza, 1801-1866

White, Catherine A., w/o Deronza White, 1807-1840

White, Harriet T., w/o Deronza White, 1807-1843

White, Almira, w/o Deronza White, 1817-1904

Titus, John, d 21 July 1825 aged 48 yrs

Titus, Betsey, w/o John Titus, d 22 Oct 1844 aged 64 yrs

Richard, Joseph Anthoine, A native of Ginaseries, France, b 24 June 1748, d 23 Dec 1825

Haven, John, d 15 April 1828 aged 71 yrs

Haven, Abigail, w/o John Haven, d 27 Feb 1850 aged 86 yrs

Haven, Amelia, d/o John & Abigail Haven, d 24 March 1874 aged 78 yrs 3 mos

Fuller, Stephen, d 23 March 1832 aged 89 yrs 10 mos

Fuller, Elizabeth, w/o Stephen Fuller, d 8 Aug 1808 aged 55 yrs

King, William W., d 16 July 1883 aged 64 yrs

King, Philena C., w/o William W. King, d 8 April 1885 aged 63 yrs

Hunt, Rev. Samuel, d 23 July 1878 aged 68 yrs

Hunt, Abby B., w/o Rev. Samuel Hunt, d 24 April 1862

Hunt, Samuel, b 9 Feb 1842 Natick, MA, d 8 July 1877 Phoenix, Arizona

Hunt, Mary Agnes, d/o Rev. Samuel Hunt, b 21 Aug 1839, d 24 Nov 1903

Hunt, Abby Charlotte, d/o Rev. Samuel & Mary Foster Hunt, b 19 Nov 1845, d 26 Jan 1937

Todd, James, 1831-1897

Gils, Elizabeth, w/o James Todd, 1834-1907

Hunt, Elist, b 22 May 1847, d 9 Sept 1883

Hunt, Stella May, w/o Elist Hunt, b 28 April 1848, d 29 March 1885

Hunt, Carlos F., s/o Elist & Stella Hunt, b 21 Nov 1875, d 3 June 1954

Hunt, Stella May, d/o Elist & Stella Hunt, b 7 Dec 1878, d 26 Feb 1952

Todd, William, 1834-1908

Todd, Harvey, 1895-1899

Riding, Margaret, w/o William Riding, d 5 Jan 1907 aged 78 yrs

Pierce, Nathan, b 1 Dec 1824, d 20 May 1899

Seekell, Mary A., w/o Nathan Pierce, b 23 July 1830, d 21 Dec 1924

Pierce, Abby A., b 28 Oct 1830, d 28 Nov 1899

Pierce, Nathan, d 10 May 1847 aged 47 yrs 3 mos

Pierce, Maria, w/o Nathan Pierce, d 28 March 1863 aged 60 yrs 11 mos 8 days

Pierce, Ellis Perry, s/o Nathan & Maria Pierce, d 2 April 1864 aged 21 yrs 5 mos 25 days

Jillson, Lewis Alton, 1853-1916

Baker, Ellen M. M., w/o Lewis Alton Jillson, 1856-1934

Jillison, Nellie J., d/o Lewis & Ellen Jillson, 1890-1977

Jillson, Arnold, b 15 April 1808, d 20 May 1888

Cushman, Nancy B., b 23 Sept 1827, d 26 Nov 1922

Jackson, William A., b 8 Aug 1845, d 30 April 1904

Jillson, Myra J., b 12 Feb 1827, d 24 April 1900

Williams, Laura M., b 23 Jan 1818, d 5 Dec 1902

Bowens, Emma P., d/o Edward & Mary Bowens, d 5 Feb 1873 aged 80 yrs

Bowens, Adaline E., d/o Edward & Mary Bowens, d 8 Oct 1868 aged 69 yrs

Smith, Harriet, d 10 Dec 1886 aged 80 yrs

Fuller, Mary, w/o Nathan Fuller, d 20 April 1875 aged 75 yrs

Fuller, Nathan, d 27 May 1857 aged 65 yrs

Fuller, Andrew, d 11 Jan 1851 aged 22 yrs

Fuller, Phylina, d 25 July 1858 aged 17 yrs

Knowles, Henry, d 17 March 1863 aged 66 yrs

Knowles, Nancy, w/o Henry Knowles, d 29 Nov 1874 aged 78 yrs

Knowles, John Brainerd, s/o Henry & Nancy Knowles, d 20 Aug 1846 aged 41 yrs 8 mos 19 days

Knowles, Ann Virginia, d/o Henry & Nancy Knowles, d 8 Aug 1833 aged
    2 yrs 9 mos

Day, Dexter, d 15 March 1871 aged 85 yrs

Day, Lydia M., w/o Dexter Day, ...

Ackerman, Frederick, 1812-1885

Ackerman, Rosina, w/o Frederick Ackerman, 1830-1914

Day, Loammi, d 30 Nov 1827 aged 70 yrs

Day, Mary, w/o Loammi Day, d 14 Feb 1825 aged 76 yrs

Day, Rachel, d 1723

Day, Anna, w/o Lt. Eliphaz Day, d 24 Oct 1802 aged 59 yrs

Day, Eunice, 2nd w/o Lt. Eliphaz Day, d 21 June 1825 aged 75 yrs

Newell, Jacob, d 13 Feb 1779 aged 75 yrs

Newell, Sarah, w/o Jacob Newell, d 4 Oct 1779 aged 72 yrs

Ide, Captain Harvey, d Aug 1857 aged 60 yrs

Ide, Mary, w/o Captain Harvey Ide, d 25 Feb 1845 aged 16 yrs

George, Harriot, d/o William & Nancy George, d 22 May 1870 aged 72
    yrs

George, Lydia M., d/o William & Mary George, d 22 Dec 1841 aged 49
    yrs

George, William, d Aug 1836 aged 75 yrs

George, Nancy, w/o William George, d 17 Oct 1804 aged 45 yrs

Haskins, Marcus A., b 24 April 1829, d 23 July 1896

Haskins, Eleona C., w/o Marcus A. Haskins, b 26 May 1829, d 24 Dec
    1890

George, Preston M., d 10 June 1855 aged 45 yrs

Morse, Charles, d 28 July 1831 aged 64 yrs 9 mos 5 days

Morse, Sabra, w/o Charles Morse, d 27 Aug 1846 aged 73 yrs

Morse, C. Hanson, 1815-1832

Bosworth, Sabra, w/o C. Hanson Morse, 1815-1900

Marsh, Lois F., d 21 March 1838 aged 24 yrs

George, Joshua, w/o William George, d 27 Jan 1795 aged 23 yrs

Jackson, Nancy, d/o Joseph & Elizabeth Jackson, d 17 March 1795 aged
    29 yrs

George, Joanna, w/o Preston George, d 19 Aug 1792 aged 23 yrs

Stanley, Seneca M., 1804-1877

Stanley, Mary A., 1811-1896

George, Margaret, w/o Joshua George, d 17 Feb 1735 aged 55 yrs

Tyler, Samuel, d Sept 1796

Tyler, Captain Ebenezer, d 29 Jan 1811 aged 71 yrs

Tyler, Hannah, w/o Captain Ebenezer Tyler, d 18 Sept 1822 aged 79 yrs

Morse, Sarah, d/o Henry & Mary Morse, d 27 Jan 1801
Sadler, Charles O., d 8 Feb 1889 aged 24 yrs
Sadler, Walter B., d 2 Oct 1825 aged 69 yrs
Sadler, Minnie, w/o Walter B. Sadler, d 22 Nov 1885 aged 26 yrs
Sadler, Melissa D., w/o George W. Sadler, d 15 Feb 1911 aged 78 yrs
Whitehill, Alfred P., 1876-1940
Gay, Sarah E., w/o Alfred P. Whitehill, 1874-1965
Whitehill, Clara A., 1870-1960
Whitehill, Phily J., 1886-1942
Coupe, Ernest J., 1909-....
Whitehill, Helen B., w/o Ernest J. Coupe, 1910-1989
Whitehill, Rev. John, 1833-1921
Permenter, Elizabeth A., w/o Rev. John Whitehill, 1842-1890
Read, Captain Daniel, d 22 Feb 1801 aged 85 yrs
Read, Ichabod, d 27 Nov 1784 aged 77 yrs
Read, Elizabeth, w/o Ichabod Read, d 1 April 1823 aged 92 yrs
Read, Ichabod, s/o Ichabod & Elizabeth Read, d 3 June 1748 aged 13 yrs
Read, Patience, d/o Ichabod & Elizabeth Read, d 1823
Read, Barbara, d/o Thomas & Rachel Read, d 9 Jan 1809 aged 25 yrs
Newell, Samuel, d 31 March 1830 aged 83 yrs
Newell, Abigail, w/o Samuel Newell, d 29 May 1805 aged 55 yrs
Ide, John, d 25 Nov 1781 aged 72 yrs
Robin, Captain Samuel, d 2 Nov 1826 aged 98 yrs
Robins, Susan, w/o Captain Samuel Robin, d 7 June 1820 aged 80 yrs
Parker, Daniel W., 1847-1887
Peck, Josephine, w/o Daniel W. Parker, 1847-1938
Parker, Alfred A., 1883-1883
Parker, Albert M., 1883-1891
Parker, Henry A., 1878-1937
Martin, Amey W., 1813-1893
Titus, Simeon, d 11 Sept 1811 aged 72 yrs
Titus, Hannah, w/o Simeon Titus, b 2 July 1745, d 17 Dec 1805
Newell, Ephraim, d 26 April 1782 aged 67 yrs
Newell, Anna, w/o Ephraim Newell, d 19 Sept 1791
Newell, Anna, d/o Ephraim & Anna Newell, d 17 Aug 1808 aged 63 yrs
Ide, Amos, d 5 Feb 1810
Ide, Huldah, w/o Amos Ide, d Oct 1789
Ide, Hannah, w/o Amos Ide, d 19 Oct 1839 aged 93 yrs 11 mos 12 days
Ide, Amos, d 24 March 1846 aged 60 yrs
Ide, Sarah, w/o Amos Ide, d 23 Dec 1845 aged 81 yrs

Ide, Sarah, d/o Amos & Sarah Ide, b 19 Dec 1796, d 19 Dec 1871
Ide, Ira, s/o Amos & Sarah Ide, d 6 May 1859 aged 57 yrs
Newell, William Coffin, d 6 May 1828 aged 23 yrs
McKenzie, Peter, b 2 June 1857 Scotland, d 3 May 1885
Robinson, Ezekiel, d 3 Sept 1803 aged 69 yrs
Robinson, Hannah, w/o Ezekiel Robinson, d 19 Oct 1802 aged 60 yrs
Robinson, Cynthia S., w/o Ezekiel Robinson, d 26 Feb 1860 Norfolk,
    Virginia
Robinson, Martha, d/o Ezekiel & Elizabeth Robinson, d 26 Jan 1808 aged
    70 yrs
Robinson, Ezekiel, d 4 Oct 1819 aged 46 yrs
Robinson, Samuel, b 12 Dec 1810, d 8 March 1850
Wilder, Rev. John, d 12 Feb 1836 aged 77 yrs
Wilder, Esther, w/o Rev. John Wilder, d 19 Jan 1811 aged 42 yrs
Wilder, Esther, d/o Rev. John & Esther Wilder, d 17 July 1808 aged 18
    yrs
Wilder, Betsey Brown, d 29 March 1868 Worcester, MA
Wilder, Julia Green, d 14 May 1859 Lowell, MA aged 64 yrs
Phillips, Betsey T., 1819-1899
Blake, Eliab F., d 16 Oct 1852 aged 49 yrs
Blake, Abigail E., w/o Eliab F. Blake, d 9 Dec 1860 aged 51 yrs
Blake, Charlotte J., d/o Eliab & Abigail Blake, d 21 Aug 1852 aged 17 yrs
Guild, Lewis, d 27 July 1866 aged 84 yrs
Guild, Sally, w/o Lewis Guild, d 27 May 1849 aged 60 yrs 7 mos
Read, Deacon Levi, d 6 April 1853 aged 91 yrs
Read, Nancy W., w/o Deacon Levi Read, d 16 Jan 1864 aged 85 yrs
Read, Levi Albert, s/o Dea. Levi & Nancy Read, d 1 Sept 1825 aged 11
    yrs
Read, Cynthia M., d/o Dea. Levi & Nancy Read, d 14 May 1836 aged 24
    yrs
Harris, Ellen, d/o M. C. & Eunice S. Harris, d 16 March 1923 aged 79 yrs
Ingraham, Ann Eliza, w/o Caleb Bowen, b 18 Dec 1801, d 24 Jan 1887
Harris, Eunice S., d/o M. G. Harris of Sparta, Georgia, & d/o Lemuel &
    Betsey Ingraham, d 17 Aug 1844 aged 25 yrs
Ingraham, Lemuel, d 26 April 1849 aged 73 yrs
Ingraham, Nancy, w/o Lemuel Ingraham, d 29 Dec 1807 aged 28 yrs
Ingraham, Betsey, w/o Lemuel Ingraham, d April 1856
Read, Clement O., b 7 Aug 1802, d 16 Sept 1879
Read, Anna, w/o Clement O. Read, d 6 June 1843 aged 34 yrs
Buffum, Lydia, w/o Clement O. Read, b 28 Jan 1815, d 10 April 1897

Read, Bertha, d/o Clement & Lydia Read, b 14 Aug 1854, d 8 May 1867
Read, Orin A., b 9 July 1814 Attleborough, MA, d 15 June 1898
    Providence, RI
Read, Ellen, w/o Orin A. Read, b 31 Dec 1814 England, d 21 June 1904
    Providence, RI
Read, Russell, b 26 July 1792, d 7 Feb 1816
Read, Susan, w/o Russell Read, b 6 Dec 1792, d 7 April 1852
The 2 stones in next row of cemetery read:
Read, Russell, d 7 Feb 1816 aged 24 yrs
Barrows, Susan, w/o Russell Read, b 6 Oct 1792, d 7 April 1852
Field, Almira, d/o Ebenezer & Miriam Field, d 5 Oct 1823 aged 26 yrs
Field, John, d 4 May 1824 aged 84 yrs
Field, Hannah, w/o John Field, d 22 March 1799 aged 24 yrs
Field, Joseph, d 13 Oct 1853 aged 82 yrs
Field, Sarah, w/o Joseph Field, d 12 Sept 1861 aged 66 yrs
Field, Chloe, w/o Joseph Field, d 22 Sept 1833 aged 72 yrs
Field, Josiah, s/o Joseph & Chloe Field, d 24 Feb 1821 aged 28 yrs
Gay, Captain Jabez, d 8 Oct 1793 aged 36 yrs
Bacon, Catherine, w/o Captain Jabez Gay, d 29 Nov 1835 aged 76 yrs
Gay, Lucinda, d/o Jabez & Catheirne Gay, d 14 July 1780
Ide, Jacob, d 17 Aug 1834 aged 82 yrs
Ide, Lydia, w/o Jacob Ide, d 25 Dec 1814 aged 59 yrs
Ide, Parley, s/o Jacob & Lydia Ide, d 15 July 1810 aged 28 yrs
Ide, Captain Jacob, d 2 June 1777 aged 54 yrs
Ide, Sarah, w/o Captain Jacob Ide, d 1 Jan 1809 aged 89 yrs
Stearns, Lydia, d/o Capt. John & Rebecca Stearns, d 22 Feb 1822 AE 73
    yrs
Stearns, Captain John, d 15 Aug 1792 aged 84 yrs
Stearns, Mary, w/o Captain John Stearns, d 16 Nov 1795 aged 77 yrs
Stearns, Rebekah, w/o Captain John Stearns, d 17 March 1856 aged 41
    yrs
Tingley, Otis, d 6 Oct 1843 aged 38 yrs
Tingley, Anjanette B., w/o Otis Tingley, d 10 Feb 1874 aged 60 yrs
Sadler, Clarissa K., 3rd w/o Thomas D. Sadler, d 14 Dec 1868 aged 61 yrs
Sadler, Sarah L., 2nd w/o Thomas D. Sadler, d 27 Nov 1841
Sadler, Thomas D., d 15 Dec 1878 aged 84 yrs
Bradford, Hon. Peres Esq.,d 19 June 1746 aged 52 yrs
Bradford, Abigail, w/o Hon. Peres Bradford Esq., d 15 Nov 1746
Lathrop, Samuel Pierce, 1828-1903
Springer, Elizabeth, w/o Samuel Pierce Lathrop, 1831-1887

11

Fuller, Noah, d 25 Feb 1832
Fuller, Amos, d 27 Aug 1851
Fuller, Frank B., 1853-1913
Fuller, Clare E., 1859-1922
Fuller, Caleb, d 22 Feb 1853 aged 84 yrs
Fuller, Caleb, b 12 Nov 1812, d 24 Jan 1882
Fuller, Selina, w/o Caleb Fuller, b 24 May 1826, d 25 Oct 1889
Wilson, Joseph M., 1835-1904
Wilson, Mary A., w/o Joseph M. Wilson, 1842-1924
Wilson, Fred, s/o Joseph M. & Mary A. Wilson, 1864-1889
Fuller, Noah, d 10 Aug 1776 AE 74 yrs
Fuller, Rebekah, w/o Noah Fuller, d 10 May 1806 AE 62 yrs
Fuller, Kenez, d 2 July 1847 aged 65 yrs 3 mos 10 days
Widing, Edwin, 1852-1927
Wilding, Mary, w/o Edwin Wilding, 1851-1931
Hughes, May E., 1893-1924
Allen, Benjamin, d 9 Jan 1808 aged 87 yrs
Fletcher, Alexander C., 1866-1909
Fletcher, Matilda, w/o Alexander C. Fletcher, 1864-1936
Minnard, James C., d 6 March 1835 aged 45 yrs
Minnard, James, s/o James C. Minnard, d 13 March 1825 aged 1 yr 2 mos
    27 days
Allen, Josiah, d 28 Dec 1830 aged 75 yrs
Allen, Elizabeth, w/o Josiah Allen, d 19 Jan 1844 aged 82 yrs
Robbins, Ezekiel, d 16 Jan 1816 AE 84 yrs
Robbins, Lydia, w/o Ezekiel Allen, d 16 Oct 1816 AE 86 yrs
Titus, Robert, s/o Samuel & Chloe Titus, d 14 Oct 1807 aged 17 yrs
Fletcher, Alexander C., 1866-1909
Fletcher, Matilda, w/o Alexander C. Fletcher, 1864-1936
Titus, Chloe, w/o Samuel Titus, d 15 Nov 1825 aged 56 yrs
Titus, Otis T., b July 1797, d 7 June 1883
Titus, Celistina W., w/o Otis T. Titus, b 18 July 1801, d 30 Nov 1854
Capron, Elisha, d 18 Oct 1808 aged 71 yrs
Capron, Abigail, w/o Elisha Capron, d 2 July 1832 aged 90 yrs
Worcester, Walter E., 1873-1943
Worcester, Carrie L., w/o Walter E. Worcester, 1877-1933
Worcester, Carleton F., 1900-1973
Mchalik, John P., 1905-1983
Roy, Irene M., w/o John P. Mchalik, 1910-1972

Cushman, Rev. Richard, A missionary at St. Marc, Hayti, d 9 June 1849 aged 30 yrs

Cushman, Captain Samuel, b 23 Nov 1785, d 3 Nov 1864

Cushman, Sophia, w/o Captain Samuel Cushman, b 4 April 1791, d 10 April 1864

Cushman, Samuel, s/o Captain Samuel & Sophia Cushman, d 10 May 1826 aged 9 mos

Cushman, Deacon Robert, b 17 Sept 1821, d 17 Aug 1891

Draper, Louisa, w/o Deacon Robert Cushman, b 22 July 1822, d 18 Feb 1907

Cushman, Josephine, d 28 Oct 1863 aged 4 yrs

Cushman, Louisa, d 29 Nov 1932 aged 71 yrs

Cushman, Deacon George, d 11 March 1866 aged 38 yrs

Cushman, Sarah J., w/o Deacon George Cushman, d 11 Aug 1897 aged 64 yrs

Cushman, George Jr., s/o Deacon George & Sarah J. Cushman, d 21 Jan 1863 aged 4 days

White, Damon, d 8 Sept 1884 aged 86 yrs 5 mos 8 days

White, Melancy T., w/o Damon White, d 17 July 1875 aged 74 yrs 13 days

White, Albert A., d 28 Feb 1905 aged 78 yrs 1 mo 24 days

White, Melissa A., w/o Albert A. White, 1841-1931

White, Eliphalet, 1832-1912

Tennant, Edward, 1864-1938

Tennant, Louisa E., w/o Edward Tennant, 1864-1922

Wellman, Edmond, s/o Nelson & Laura A. F. Wellman, d 17 Sept 1872 aged 22 yrs

Perry, John, 1801-1879

Perry, Cynthia, w/o John Perry, 1807-1866

Perry, Joseph W., s/o John & Cynthia Perry, 1836-1924

Perry, Elizabeth A., d/o John & Cynthia Perry, 1837-1856

Perry, Mary E., d/o John & Cynthia Perry, 1839-1922

Perry, Lydia, d/o John & Cynthia Perry, 1843-1927

Read, Albert Miller, b 27 Feb 1826, d 19 June 1905

Mason, Margaret, w/o Albert Miller Read, b 20 Nov 1831, d 13 Jan 1900

Read, Daniel, b 14 Feb 1795, d 3 March (BROKEN)

Newell, Arthur I., 1866-1954

Newell, Emma F. Abbey, w/o Arthur I. Newell, 1873-1936

Newell, Elisha A., 1904-1979

King, J. Irma, w/o Elisha A. Newell, 1908-1989

Barrows, Lydia, w/o John Thomson, b 10 Oct 1813, d 24 Dec 1860

Barrows, Benjamin, d 7 March 1832 aged 80 yrs

Barrows, Leah, w/o Benjamin Barrows, d 17 Oct 1835 aged 81 yrs

Barrows, Benjamin, s/o Benjamin & Leah Barrows, d 22 Jan 1822 aged 19 yrs

Barrows, Comfort, b 2 Feb 1786, d 18 March 1865

Barrows, Lucy, w/o Comfort Barrows, d 21 Dec 1815 aged 38 yrs

Blake, Mela, w/o Comfort Barrows, b 29 July 1791, d 14 Nov 1836

Saunders, Sylvia, w/o Comfort Barrows & d/o Jeremiah Petrie, b 12 Dec 1792, d 9 Dec 1882

Barrows, Hiram, b 5 Sept 1790, d 4 Oct 1852 aged 62 yrs

Barrows, Maria, w/o Hiram Barrows, d 14 Nov 1839 aged 51 yrs

Barrows, Mary W., d/o Hiram & Maria Barrows, d 23 March 1845 aged 25 yrs

Barrows, Melinda G., d/o Hiram & Mary Barrows, d 1868

Barrows, Charles Augustus, s/o Hiram & Mary Barrows, d 7 May 1853 aged 21 yrs

Barrows, Sanford L., b 5 Sept 1837, d 9 May 1860

Barrows, Leonard, b 23 April 1789, d 31 Dec 1887

Barrows, Hannah B., w/o Leonard Barrows, b 10 Aug 1803, d 20 Aug 1857

Crocker, Susannah, w/o Benjamin Bowen, 1820-1909

Patterson, Joseph, 1850-1898

Bowen, Lydia Augusta, w/o Joseph Patterson, 1852-....

Ide, Hartford, b 9 Nov 1797, d 11 April 1878

Ide, Mary T., w/o Hartford Ide, b 29 March 1798, d 26 Dec 1867

Ide, Harriet F. A., d/o Hartford & Mary T. Ide, b 31 Jan 1842, d 3 March 1846

Ide, Mary P., d/o Hartford & Mary T. Ide, b 11 March 1824, d 23 Aug 1899

Ide, George F., 1833-1924

Ide, Lucy, w/o George F. Ide, 1835-1924

Tucker, John, d 28 Feb 1893

Tucker, Nancy, w/o John Tucker & d/o Asa & Cynthia Allen, d 2 Dec 1850 aged 44 yrs

Allen, Asa, d 19 Feb 1868 aged 91 yrs 6 mos

Allen, Cynthia E., w/o Asa Allen, d 9 Jan 1861 aged 91 yrs 10 mos

Draper, James O., b 25 June 1818, d 14 Oct 1891

Draper, Gamabel Bradford, 1831-1915

Draper, Ebenezer 2nd, b 14 Jan 1784, d 25 May 1852

Draper, Paul, d 25 April 1885 aged 74 yrs
Draper, Maria, w/o Paul Draper, (can't read)
Barrows, Aaron, d 31 Oct 1856 aged 52 yrs
Morris, Evaline, w/o Aaron Barrows, d 22 May 1871 aged 55 yrs
Barrows, Milton, b 3 Jan 1802, d 10 April 1861
Child, Mary A., w/o Milton Barrows, b 23 July 1806, d 24 Dec 1891
Barrows, Alfred, d 8 March 1866 aged 66 yrs
Barrows, Louisa, w/o Alfred Barrows, d 21 Jan 1895 aged 29 yrs
Barrows, Arthur, d 1 Feb 1895 aged 51 yrs
Guild, Samuel, 1795-1878
Barrows, Clarissa, w/o Samuel Guild, 1797-1869
Guild, Rebecca Maria, d/o Samuel & Clarissa Guild, 1827-1830
Guild, Samuel, s/o Samuel & Clarissa Guild, b 2 Aug 1832, d 18 Nov
    1832
Guild, Rebecca, d/o Samuel & Clarissa Guild, 1830-1917
Barrows, Mary, d/o Milton & Rebecca Barrows, d 16 Jan 1852 aged 53
    yrs
Barrows, Henry H., s/o Aaron & Evelyn Morris, 1839-1908
Barrows, Aaron, d 21 Dec 1801 aged 58 yrs
Barrows, Mary, w/o Aaron Barrows, d 16 Feb 1847 aged 100 yrs 7 days
Robinson, Ann E., w/o Milan H. Robinson, b 1 Jan 1827, d 6 Sept 1877
Stanley, J. Herbert, b 10 Dec 1811, d 15 March 1894
Draper, Cornelia, w/o J. Herbert Draper, b 9 Oct 1816, d 27 Oct 1901
Brown, Della M., b 19 Sept 1838, d 20 Nov 1919
Robinson, Hannah, 1846-1910
Robinson, Lewis O., b 26 Sept 1823, d 10 Sept 1903
Bowen, Frances M., w/o Lewis O. Robinson, b 22 March 1830, d 17 Nov
    1894
Whiting, David E., b 13 April 1801, d 16 Nov 1883
Whiting, Florentina, w/o David E. Whiting, b 21 April 1803, d 14 June
    1886
Barnes, Alonzo, 1825-1890
Barnes, Susan, w/o Alonzo Barnes, 1830-1904
Barnes, Ida W., d/o Alonzo & Susan Barnes, 1858-1910
Atwood, Deacon Abner, b 5 March 1825, d 23 Nov 1908
Draper, Lydia A., w/o Deacon Abner Atwood, b 22 Sept 1827, d 4 Nov
    1906
Brown, Jesse C., b 21 Feb 1835, d 25 Oct 1925
Draper, Hannah M., w/o Jesse C. Brown, b 4 Sept 1833, d 22 Aug 1899
Titus, William H., 1840-1917

Titus, Frank S., 1835-1911

Titus, Hiram W., 1800-1871

Titus, Anna S., w/o Hiram W. Titus, 1802-1827

Titus, Lucy B., 1812-1878

Wellman, David B., b 10 Aug 1808, d 31 Dec 1893

Wellman, Betsey, w/o David B. Wellman, b 12 Jan 1808, d 28 June 1892

Bacon, Betsey, w/o Lemuel May & d/o Major Ebenezer Bacon, d 9 July 1810 aged 24 yrs

Wilder, Eliza W., w/o Lemuel May Esq., & d/o Rev. John Wilder, d April 1831 AE 36 yrs

May, Lemuel Augustus, b 214 Dec 1816, d March 1862

Titus, Hortense B., 1856-1887

Wood, Jonathan, d 16 Sept 1861 aged 82 yrs

Wood, Betsey, w/o Jonathan Wood, d 23 Jan 1864 aged 84 yrs

Robinson, Daniel H., 1839-1901

Robinson, Clara E., 1850-1913

Robinson, Daniel O., 1884-1889

Horton, James, b 13 Oct 1813, d 9 Nov 1881

Horton, Abby B., w/o James Horton, b 28 March 1817, d 29 March 1903

Champlin, Mary A., b 20 Feb 1837, d 7 April 1894

Walker, Ezra, d 25 Oct 1862 aged 62 yrs

Walker, Mary R., w/o Ezra Walker, d 23 April 1855 aged 61 yrs

Phillips, Charles, b 7 Dec 1832, d 15 Dec 1921

Phillips, Ellen, w/o Charles Phillips, b 22 Nov 1831, d 22 Dec 1895

Phillips, Mary S., b 4 June 1810, d 7 April 1885

Walker, William J., d 17 Jan 1861 aged 27 yrs

Walker, Eunice, d/o Ezra & Martha Walker, d 17 Jan 1884 aged 71 yrs

Woodcock, J. Daggett, d 9 Oct 1871 aged 62 yrs

Woodcock, Candace, w/o J. Daggett Woodcock, d 24 June 1855 aged 42 yrs

Jillson, William, 1775-1844

Robinson, Betsey, w/o William Jillson, 1775-1805

Cushman, Betsey, w/o William Jillson, 1779-1849

Haskins, Abijah, d 28 April 1863 aged 60 yrs 22 days

Haskin, Cordelia A., w/o Abijah Haskins, d 10 May 1830 aged 21 yrs 4 mos 7 days

Haskins, Caroline, w/o Abijah Haskins, d 8 Dec 1866 aged 57 yrs 1 mo 2 days

Morse, Nelson, b 27 Sept 1798, d 23 Dec 1854

Morse, Eliza B., w/o Nelson Morse, d 25 Jan 1882 Lowell, MA

Tingley, Nathan, d 10 Nov 1798 Providence, RI
Tingley, Lucy, w/o Nathan Tingley, d 15 Jan 1816 aged 69 yrs
Tingley, Araimah, b 23 Oct 1775, d 26 May 1822 Providence, RI
Tingley, Hartford, d 23 March 1852 aged 64 yrs
Tingley, Nathan, b 19 Sept 1784, d 6 April 1832
Ginston, James, b 18 Nov 1831, d 22 Aug 1913
Batchelor, Sarah, w/o James Ginston, b 31 Dec 1832, d 21 Nov 1929
Ginston, Mary Elizabeth, 1868-1933
Newell, Jabez, d 17 April 1875 aged 80 yrs
Maxcy, Susan, w/o Jabez Newell, d 19 Sept 1865 aged 70 yrs
Carpenter, Rosetta, d 24 Feb 1882 aged 87 yrs
Kranska, Anna, w/o Jason Kranska & d/o Stephen & Elizabeth Draper, d
    22 Jan 1803 aged 33 yrs
Draper, George, 1801-1876
Lee, Harriet, w/o George Draper, 1800-1891
Draper, H. Anna, d/o George & Harriet Draper, 1842-1845
Draper, Dwight, s/o George & Harriet Draper, 1830-1845
Tiffany, Edward P., b 17 Oct 1835, d 8 Feb 1911
Tiffany, Mary L., w/o Edward P. Tiffany, b 30 Dec 1836, d 13 Sept 1900
Tiffany, William S., b 16 Oct 1868, d 12 May 1938
Tiffany, Johnny, s/o Edward & Mary Tiffany, d 1 April 1868 aged 9 yrs
Phillips, Samuel, b 1 June 1798, d 16 Sept 1865 aged 67 yrs
Phillips, Emeline, w/o Samuel Phillips, d 1887
Travers, Sabin L., d 30 Nov 1885 aged 79 yrs 21 days
Skinner, Christopher E., b 14 Feb 1803, d 9 April 1890
Skinner, Mahala B., w/o Christopher E. Skinner, b 21 Feb 1836, d 15 Nov
    1879
Allen, Elizabeth, w/o Christopher E. Skinner & d/o Josiah & Rowena
    Allen, d 27 March 1854 aged 33 yrs 1 mo 9 days
Allen, Josiah, d 26 April 1864 aged 80 yrs
Tingley, Rowena, w/o Josiah Tingley, d 15 June 1874 aged 87 yrs
Henry, William, s/o Welcome & Nancy Henry, d 28 July 1846 aged 14 yrs
    10 mos
Skinner, Jesse C., b 9 Oct 1868, d 12 May 1948
Skinner, Mary F., w/o Jesse C. Skinner, b 22 Dec 1869, d 31 Jan 1930
Barrows, Nancy Elenora, d/o Carlos & Cynthia Carrows, b 16 April 1838,
    d 31 Jan 1892
Barrows, Carlos, b 8 Dec 1807, d 5 June 1885
Barrows, Cynthia, w/o Carlos Barrows, b 26 Aug 1810, d 17 May 1896
Draper, George Lee, b March 1832, d 5 Oct 1901

Barrows, Henrietta E., w/o George Lee Draper, b 30 Aug 1842, d 13 March 1925

Bruce, Samuel H., b 13 April 1824, d 4 Jan 1886

Bruce, Sarah C., w/o Samuel H. Bruce, d 2 July 1876 aged 49 yrs 2 mos 19 days

Bruce, Martha D., w/o Samuel H. Bruce, 1824-1869

Bruce, Clara M., d/o Samuel & Martha Bruce, d 9 June 1916 aged 66 yrs 9 mos 24 days

Norton, William, d 15 Dec 1877 aged 55 yrs

Norton, Mary Ann, w/o William Norton, d 8 Jan 1874 aged 49 yrs

Bruce, Benjamin T., d 2 Jan 1878 aged 34 yrs

Bruce, Abbie W., w/o Benjamn T. Bruce, d 18 June (BROKEN)

Fuller, Welcome, d 13 March 1853

Fuller, Polly, w/o Welcome Fuller, d 15 Aug (BROKEN)

Ebert, Christian G., 1833-1909

Roches, Catherine H., w/o Christian G. Ebert, 1841-1912

Guild, Margaret E., 1893-1926

Mahler, Ernest H., s/o Henry C. & Mary Y. Mahler, b 20 Oct 1887, d 19 Nov 1898

Coupe, William, 1834-1920

Munroe, William C., 1902-1961

Sadler, Phyliss W., w/o William C. Munroe, 1896-1988

Johnson, Charles W., 1894-1974

Sadler, Olive T., w/o Charles W. Johnson, 1894-1969

Allen, H. Bradford, 1846-1931

Sweetland, Robert W., 1881-1907

Landry, Alina B. Allen, w/o Robert W. Sweetland, 1881-1920

Landry, David L., 1889-1966

Bucklin, Granville Earl, 1900-1903

Newell, Frank B., d 6 Feb 1875 Santa Barbara, California

Newell, Samuel, d 19 July 1881

Newell, Catherine, w/o Samuel Newell, d 23 Dec 1836 aged 34 yrs

Newell, Charles M., d 5 March 1864 aged 34 yrs

Newell, Anna E., w/o Charles M. Newell, d 1 April 1893 aged 61 yrs

Smalley, Keziah E., w/o Frank B. Newell, 1835-1921

Ingraham, Otis, d 26 Sept 1869 aged 75 yrs 16 days

Ingraham, Lydia, w/o Otis Ingraham, d 9 June 1813 aged 46 yrs

Ingraham, L. Marie, 1819-1902

Booth, Mary M., d/o Edward & Susan M. Booth, d 18 April 1833 aged 64 yrs

Foster, William F., 1833-1916

Foster, Harriet M., 1837-1917

Foster, Ida, 1858-1868

Foster, Eugene L., 1876-1882

Fuller, Edward S., b 18 Dec 1869, d 1 March 1891

Fuller, Catherine, b 21 April 1837, d....

Fuller, Lemuel, b 7 Aug 1826, d 19 Jan 1881

Fuller, Mary C., d/o Edward & Eliza W. Fuller, b 15 July 1839, d 5 Dec 1875

Fuller, Eliza W., d 17 Jan 1893

Fuller, Edward, d 18 Dec (Can't read)

Fuller, Doct. Lemuel, d 7 Dec 1858 aged 81 yrs

Brightman, Charles W., 1868-1932

Sharp, Edith I., w/o Charles W. Brightman, 1862-1925

Martyn, Ellen M., d/o Carlos & Nancy Barrows, d 18 Aug 1882 aged 65 yrs

Martyn, Susan M., w/o Edward Booth, d 29 Nov 1870 Chicago, Illinois AE 32 yrs

Coupe, Ellen Martyn, b 25 May 1825, d 18 Feb 1904

Salbey, David W., 1901-1953

Roddell, Avis M., w/o David W. Salbey, 1904-1992

Carpenter, C. Ray, 1895-1971

Esten, Benjamin R., b 15 Jan 1866, d 26 Dec 1924

Bastow, Ellen, w/o Benjamin R. Esten, b 7 July 1876, d 25 March 1919

Esten, Randall, b 17 Feb 1817, d 26 Feb 1902

Esten, Sarah P., w/o Randall Esten, b 18 Oct 1817, d 6 Jan 1894

Esten, Richard B., MD, 1855-1925

Upton, Rose I., w/o Dr. Richard B. Esten, 1869-1973

Esten, Isabelle U., 1889-1950

Duckworth, George, 1834-1898

Duckworth, Eliza Olive, w/o George Duckworth, 1837-1898

Bruce, John, b 10 Oct 1798, d 25 Oct 1886

Bruce, Rebecca B., w/o John Bruce, b 6 Feb 1805, d 2 Aug 1885

Chace, Barton,.....

Chace, Miriam T., w/o Barton Chace, d 20 Oct 1870 aged 74 yrs

Chace, Samuel B., s/o Barton & Miriam T. Chace, d 19 Oct 1876 aged 38 yrs

Carpenter, Nathan B., 1832-1928

Moore, Maria P., w/o Nathan B. Carpenter & d/o Joel & Abigail Moore, 1834-1893

Carpenter, Mabel M., 1869-1958
Bastow, Rev. F. William, 1898-1956
Allen, Gladys E., w/o Rev. F. William Bastow, 1898-1983
Bastow, Frederick A., s/o Rev. F. William & Gladys E. Bastow, 1936-1987
Clarkson, B. Matthew, b 25 Jan 1850, d 6 Jan 1919
Grover, Mary Clarkson, b 7 April 1877, d 27 June 1923
Groves, Maria, b 27 Sept 1882, d 21 Sept 1899
Cass, Maria, d 10 April 1804 aged 80 yrs
Clarkson, Jessie I., b 1 Nov 1887, d 26 Aug 1906
Clarkson, Walter, 1884-1972
Dickey, Elizabeth, w/o Walter Clarkson, 1882-1964
Cass, Annie, w/o B. M. Clarkson, b 11 Dec 1850, d 24 July 1898
Esten, Richard S., 1890-1984
Brown, Lorinda, w/o Richard S. Esten, 1883-1976
Esten, Richard Stewart, Jr., 1919-1923
Guild, Charles, d 1 Sept 1816 aged 18 yrs
Guild, Ebenezer, d 10 April 1847 aged 83 yrs
Guild, Mary, w/o Ebenezer Guild, d 8 April 1840 aged 68 yrs
Guild, William Crane, b 9 July 1809, d 23 Nov 1893
Guild, Almira F., w/o William Crane Guild, b 9 Aug 1808, d 15 March 1875
Newell, Samuel, d 11 July 1842 aged 61 yrs
Newell, Philena, w/o Samuel Newell, d 22 July 1844 aged 69 yrs
Tyler, Thankful, w/o Lt. Moses Tyler, d 25 Aug 1816 aged 83 yrs
Tyler, Moses, d 9 Oct 1804 aged 83 yrs
Tyler, Patience, w/o Moses Tyler, d 15 Nov 1756 aged 32 yrs
Hunt, Daniel H., 1885-1969
Johnson, Ruth A., w/o Daniel H. Hunt, 1886-1913
Sherman, Ruby S., 1886-1932
Palmer, Annie E., 1862-1919
Norwood, Wilbur A., 1881-1950
Currie, Hannah M., w/o Wilbur A. Norwood, 1877-1958
Williams, George M., 1852-1916
Smith, Emma L., w/o George M. William, 1872-1959
Williams, Charles M., 1904-1919
Norlund, Thomas L., 1900-1985
Williams, Evangeline S., w/o Thomas L. Norlund, 1899-1991
Morris, Ross, 1878-1940
Morris, Stuart E., 1908-1926

Morris, Henry A., 1868-1908
Knowles, George F., 1834-1905
Knowles, Mary M., w/o George F. Knowles, 1852-1916
Knowles, Mark N., s/o George F. & Mary M. Knowles, 1876-1877
Orr, James R., 1888-1955
Orr, Gladys R., 1891-1978
McCulloch, William, b 29 Jan 1852, d 21 Nov 1867
Esten, Susan R., b 3 Jan 1865, d 9 June 1949
Sadler, Herbert A., 1860-1931
Knight, Grace E., w/o Herbert A. Sadler, 1875-1951
Clarke, Buelah Sadler, d/o Herbert A. & Grace E. Sadler, 1903-1983
Firth, Edwin, 1838-1913
Kesketh, Annie, w/o Edwin Firth, 1862-1955
Howe, Ruth Ann, 1920-1922
Howe, Edwin Smith, 1918-1924
Brown, William D., 1839-1927
Brown, Phebe A., w/o William D. Brown, 1848-1912
Marsland, John, 1863-1942
Marsland, Anne E., w/o John Marsland, 1860-1911
Marsland, Lucy E., w/o John Marsland, 1880-1959
Marsland, John Jr., 1918-1983
Brown, William E., 1870-1931
Gardner, Herbert T., 1879-1948
Heywood, Annie G., w/o Herbert T. Gardner, 1879-1941
Thomas, Henry Binmore, 1866-1917
Thomas, Lena, w/o Henry Binmore Thomas, 1869-1957
Gardner, Donald Ross, 1892-1968
Quinney, Margaret, w/o Donald Ross Gardner, 1888-1985
Ross, Margaret, b 23 Oct 1850, d 6 Jan 1939
Arnold, Nelson, 1850-1924
Arnold, Annie, w/o Nelson Arnold, 1855-1937
Wheeler, Welcome H., 1842-1933
Wheeler, Ellen F., w/o Welcome H. Wheeler, 1849-1905
Wheeler, Edith G., 1874-1957
French, Minnie E., 1879-1918
Gray, Joseph, 1854-1916
Fife, Margaret, w/o Joseph Gray, 1857-1936
Francis, Joseph, 1833-1891
Francis, Martha Ann, w/o Joseph Francis, 1838-1911
Francis, Inogene, 1880-1986

Robbins, Mary, 1814-1882
Coupe, Elsie J., 1885-1983
Estes, Hersey, b 2 May 1833, d 8 Feb 1916
Aiken, Mary A., w/o Hersey Estes, b 16 March 1840, d 1 May 1907
Allen, George W. Jr., 1887-1941
Allen, Grace M., w/o George W. Allen Jr., 1885-1973
Nicherson, Edgar B., 1854-1919
Orr, Mary A., w/o Edgar B. Nickerson, 1852-1915
Nickerson, Chester J., 1878-1957
Nickerson, Ira B., 1890-1973
Stevenson, Mabel R., w/o Ira B. Nickerson, 1893-1967
Holmes, Leander, 1848-1919
Duckworth, Margaret E., w/o Leander Holmes, 1858-1916
Holmes, Oliver C., 1843-1929
Marsden, Joseph, 1873-1930
Holmes, Maria L., w/o Joseph Marsden, 1878-1958
Holmes, John F., 1885-1959
Knight, Mary Holmes, 1882-1960
Anderson, Julia A. Thayer Buttrick, 1842-1920
Horton, Augustus, 1845-1931
Horton, Hannah, w/o Augustus Horton, 1849-1924
Lawder, Robert J., 1861-1925
Lawder, Jennie, w/o Robert J. Lawder, 1862-1933
Southwick, Chester A., 1890-1961
Southwick, Nettie A., w/o Chester A. Southwick, 1891-1961
Shields, George, 1852-1929
Shields, Flora, 1853-1928
Shields, Maria M., 1875-1919
Shields, Alexander W., 1884-1956
Shields, William G., 1888-1962
Carpenter, Lester E., b. 1899, d 29 Nov 1991
Hopkins, L. Elora, w/o Lester E. Carpenter, 1899-1980
Carpenter, George C., 1875-1930
Holmes, Eliza J., w/o George C. Carpenter, 1880-1968
Carpenter, Howard, s/o George C. & Eliza J. Carpenter, 1901-1921
Richard, William, 1864-1947
Richard, Mary A., w/o William Richard, 1866-1940
Richard, William Norman, s/o William & Mary Richard, 1896-1920
Richard, Elsie, d/o William & Mary Richard, 1887-1891
Richard, Walter Morgan, s/o William & Mary Richard, 1904-1928

Richards, William N., 1922-....
Richards, Eunice M., w/o William N. Richards, 1925-1956
Dennett, Frederick T., 1878-1952
Dennett, Ella May, w/o Frederick T. Dennett, 1876-1967
Dennett, Ellen M., 1909-1974
McGee, James, 1885-1955
Allen, George W., 1858-1931
Allen, Nellie T., w/o George W. Allen, 1862-1923
Cheetham, Joseph H., ...
Cheetham, Elizabeth, w/o Joseph H. Cheetham,.....
Lewis, Leroy E., 1877-1938
Heywood, Mary A., w/o Leroy E. Lewis, 1877-1937
Titus, Hiram, 1873-1959
Titus, Mabel, 1876-1963
Titus, Phyliss, 1898-1966
Titus, John A., 1876-1949
Adams, James, 1867-1950
Todd, Elizabeth E., w/o James Adams, 1870-1939
Atwood, Annie A., d/o James & Elizabeth Adams, 1895-1948
Faulkner, Olive B., d/o James & Elizabeth Adams, 1897-1986
Wilbur, Frank Elliott, 1870-1922
Adams, Isabelle, w/o Frank Elliott Wilbur, 1862-1935
Adams, Susan E., 1874-1942
Armitage, John R., 1873-1927
Armitage, Elizabeth A., w/o John R. Armitage, 1874-1943
Armitage, Joseph C., s/o John & Elizabeth Armitage, 1899-1930
Holden, Alfred J., 1872-1957
William, Susannah J., w/o Alfred J. Holden, 1873-1943
Holden, E. Stanley, 1902-1926
Orr, Maria, w/o James W. Orr, 1864-1942
Orr, James W., 1860-1945
Bristol, Eliza Jane, w/o Edgar S. Bristol, d 1946
Bristol, Emily H., 1815-1887
Bristol, Charles L., 1843-1895
Bristol, Emma L., 1848-1933
Bristol, Edgar S., 1845-1914
Bristol, Ellen Francis, w/o Edgar S. Bristol, 1852-1898
Orr, Emery H., 1876-1914
Orr, Clifford H., 1898-1953
Orr, George W., 1865-1948

Orr, Mary, w/o George W. Orr, 1880-1971
Orr, Mary J., 1858-1932
Jellison, Frank, 1854-1920
Orr, James, 1831-1907
Orr, Rachel W., w/o James Orr, 1830-1904
Orr, Ellen F., 1863-1928
Orr, Elizabeth, 1867-1950
Orr, William P., 1878-1958
Orr, Bertha F., w/o William P. Orr, 1877-1945
Darey, George O., 1882-1947
Jellison, Ada M., w/o George O. Darey, 1883-1946
Rhodes, Thomas, 1895-1932
Sadler, Thomas G., 1871-1948
Wilson, Mary, w/o Thomas G. Sadler, 1873-1931
Francis, Mabel, w/o Thomas G. Sadler, 1883-1969
Sadler, Thomas G. Jr., 1895-1977
Tarbox, Fay, w/o Thomas G. Sadler, 1892-1984
Sadler, Mary Helen, 1923-1932
Read, Dorothy B., 1912-1976

North Purchase Cemetery
Rte 152
Attleborough, Massachusetts

This cemetery is mostly recent burials, I recorded the older stones only.

Sinclair, John H., 1877-1942
Sinclair, Jennie C., w/o John H. Sinclair, 1878-1949
Sinclair, Mildred L., d/o John & Jennie Sinclair, 1905-1927
Gereck, Edward, d 1940
Gereck, Harriet, w/o Edward Gereck, d 1930
Clarke, Joshua W., MD, 1870-....
Arnold, Alice A., w/o Dr. Joshua Clarke, 1865-1938
Reese, Mary Clarke, 1914-1929
Reese, John A., MD, 1885-1947
Reese, Taylor B., w/o Dr. John A. Reese, 1889-1967

Rounseville, Lucius H., 1865-1940
Frederick, Ida M., w/o Lucius H. Rounseville, 1867-1930
Rounseville, Chester O., 1894-1923
Rounseville, Atherton H., 1897-1961
Limerick, Virginia R., 1916-1967
Greenwood, James N., 1870-1929
Greenwood, Margaret, w/o James N. Greenwood, 1876-1947
Greenwood, Thomas, 1867-1939
Greenwood, Martha J., w/o Thomas Greenwood, 1872-1954
Lovenbury, Harry, 1904-1967
Lovenbury, Martha, w/o Harry Lovenbury, 1904-1989
Fuller, Sadie, w/o George Fuller, 1896-1987
Neval, Edwin H., 1869-1926
White, Alice M., w/o Edwin H. Neval, 1869-1929
Neval, Linwood S., 1894-1943
Grant, Helen A., w/o Linwood S. Neval, 1896-1950
White, Archie E., 1873-1928
Hodges, William M., 1855-1952
Hodges, Nellie B., w/o William M. Hodges, 1855-1929
Hodges, Harold W., 1890-1975
Hogdes, Helen M., w/o Harold W. Hodges, 1895-1937
Haley, William, 1876-1929
Barnhill, Flora L., w/o William Haley, 1881-1969
Barnhill, Emma M., 1885-1972
Seeton, Lola Brown, 1890-1956
Seeton, John W., 1877-1944
MacLellan, Ella M., w/o John W. Seeton, 1885-1977
Thurber, Eva M., 1893-1930
Barlow, Leroy, 1898-1945
Barlow, Irene C., 1901-1978
Wilde, Eben, 1866-1929
Rhodes, Estelle, w/o Eben Wilde, 1876-1945
Vallette, John H., 1874-1929
Vallette, Nellie F., 1874-1934
Tyndall, Calvin, 1880-1938
Hinds, Abbie, w/o Calvin Tyndall, 1888-1978
Tyndall, Bradford, 1915-1951
White, Alexander, 1868-1940
Guild, Mary L., w/o Alexander White, 1873-1953
White, Raymond B., s/o Alexander & Mary White, 1891-1945

White, Earl Russell, MD, 1894-1968

Watson, William James, b 17 Sept 1869, d 2 Dec 1939

Watkins, Marjorie Marilyn, w/o William James Watson, b 28 Feb 1897, d....

Watkins, Frederick Lyman, b 17 May 1873, d 29 Dec 1948

Wells, Ada, w/o Frederick Lyman Watkins, b 1 March 1873, d 15 Nov 1945

Olson, John Alfred, 1875-1950

Lundin, Bertha A., w/o John Alfred Olson, 1877-1939

Olson, Robert O., 1902-1989

Kendall, Louise, w/o Robert O. Olson, 1903-1991

Anderson, John E., 1863-....

Anderson, A. Lillian, w/o John E. Anderson, 1862-1934

Anderson, Effie I., 1891-1936

McMann, Sidney, 1858-1941

Luther, Carl D., 1889-1969

McMann, Ella M., w/o Carl D. Luther, 1889-1960

Anderson, Charles, 1871-1940

Anderson, Johanna M., w/o Charles Anderson, 1879-1957

Kendall, Frank K., 1879-1946

Chase, Florence E., w/o Frank K. Kendall, 1890-1984

Sherman, I. Edwrin, 1882-1959

Kendall, Mabel E., w/o I. Edwin Sherman, 1882-1965

Kendall, Mary H., 1857-1953

Swift, Levi Pratt, 1873-1943

Holmes, Annie Mary, w/o Levi Pratt Swift, 1875-1950

Swift, Howard Mann, 1890-1973

Clitheroe, Elsie M., w/o Howard Mann Swift, 1901-1982

Mathewson, Charles O., 1883-1946

Godfrey, Lillie H., w/o Charles O. Matthewson, 1882-1963

Bosworth, Linneus M., 1863-1945

Bosworth, Annie G., 1872-1940

Oldham, Marie B., 1860-1943

Spatcher, George I., 1902-1981

Dovey, Sidney W., 1873-1954

Dovey, Lillian E., w/o Sideny W. Dovey, 1896-....

Gusten, George M., 1874-1939

Keil, Josephine R., w/o George M. Gusten, 1879-1979

Harrington, Frances J., 1907-1982

Hall, Anson Louis, 1920-....

Richardson, Jean Elizabeth, w/o Anson Louis Hall, 1922-1955
Richardson, Roger King, 1909-....
Richardson, Deborah, w/o Roger King Richardson, 1911-....
Sargeant, William J., b 25 Oct 1871, d 18 Dec 1948
Wilde, Mary, w/o William J. Sargeant, b 6 May 1871, d 8 March 1936
Weeman, William O., 1862-1938
Crowe, Ella F., w/o William O. Weeman, 1868-1946
Weeman, Clarence E., 1893-1963
Aldrich, Irene, w/o Clarence E. Weeman, 1896-1988
Veazer, Elmer M., 1885-1945
Lee, Emma H., w/o Elmer M. Veazer, 1874-1951
Veazer, Bryon M., 1913-1972
Brown, Hazel P., w/o Bryon M. Veazer, 1912-1989
Young, Leith, 1882-1958
Brennan, Florence, w/o Leith Young, 1883-1958
Moberg, Carl E., 1872-1942
Wikman, Emma S., w/o Carl E. Moberg, 1871-1965
Young, Albert L., 1877-1965
Llewellyn, Clara, w/o Albert L. Young, 1876-1946
Young, Albert F., 1914-1958
Bowen, Terrence F., 1888-1943
Ellis, Verna L., w/o Terrence F. Bowen, 1888-1987
Sweet, Frank R., b 31 Oct 1880, d 27 May 1936
Pitman, Harriet E., w/o Frank R. Sweet, b 27 Sept 1883, d 1 June 1931
Sweet, William Otis, b 11 March 1919, d 27 Nov 1975
Bowater, Florence A., w/o Sidney W. Dovey, 1869-1940
Brewer, John C., 1884-1954
MacLeod, Mary, w/o John C. Brewer, 1881-1958
Elsbree, William M., 1873-1941
Mosher, Susie A., w/o William M. Elsbree, 1873-1941
Elsbree, Milton, s/o William M. & Susie A. Elsbree, 1903-1972
Nicholson, Mary J., w/o Milton M. Elsbree,....
Sanborn, Captain Roscoe G., 1880-1940
MacLeod, Grace, w/o Capt. Roscoe Sanborn, 1884-1960
Thomas, Walter J., 1878-1946
Snead, Florence, w/o Walter J. Thomas, 1880-1954
Perry, William S., 1885-1946
Perry, Margaret, w/o William S. Perry, 1888-1976
Fales, Lewis A., 1873-1946
Gonia, Annie G., w/o Lewis A. Fales, 1871-1950

Fales, Evelyn, w/o Robert C. Smith, 1899-1953
Smith, Robert, 1901-1982
Larsen, Engval, 1864-1982
Richards, Anna R. (Richardson), 1864-1943
Feid, Jeralin (Richards), 1900-1986

Woodlawn Cemetery
North Main Street
Attleborough, Massachusetts

Wetherell, Lester, 1886-1969
Angell, Gladys, w/o Lester Wetherell, 1886-1970
Stanhope, Virginia, 1910-1933
Baker, George Cornelius, b 24 July 1881, d 20 Jan 1956
Reed, Hazel Laurette, w/o George Cornelius Baker, b 23 Sept 1892, d 11
    Sept 1957
Argus, Herman A., 1867-1920
Argus, Arno, 1886-1928
Hanson, Anna Maria, 1843-1920
Knowles, Thomas, 1873-1920
Benjamin, Ina, w/o Thomas Knowles, 1876-1961
Crathorne, Harry, 1848-1908
Crathorne, Catherine, w/o Harry Crathrone, 1849-1926
Matteson, Muriel L., 1904-1949
Matteson, Catherine, 1879-1968
Sheldon, Joseph A., 1851-1920
Sherlock, Maria, w/o Joseph A. Sheldon, 1850-1928
Murto, Christina A., 1869-1921
Sandberg, Sven, 1835-1921
Sandberg, Severina, w/o Sven Sandberg, 1852-1922
Dexter, Everett O., 1863-1941
Dexter, Flora M., w/o Everett O. Dexter, 1854-1922
Moore, A. Estella A., 1872-1970
Smith, William E. S., 1876-....
Quinn, Rose E., w/o William E. S. Smith, 1880-1909
Barnard, Maude, w/o William E. S. Smith, 1889-1941

Smith, William E., 1907-1951
Collingwood, Fred H., 1867-1920
Collingwood, Lenora A., w/o Fred A. Collingwood, 1862-1941
Collingwood, Harold W., 1891-1956
Collingwood, Ethel, 1893-1974
Bergevine, Edna M., 1912-1923
Bowen, Claude L., 1871-1921
Davis, Cora L., w/o Claude L. Bowen, 1872-1931
Bowen, Emily A., 1895-1950
Trafton, J. Inez, 1869-1932
Walker, Howard, 1859-1933
Taylor, Hannah, w/o Howard Walker, 1856-1922
Walker, Harold C., 1886-1948
Pink, Agnes M., w/o Harold C. Walker, 1890-1985
Walker, Dana W., 1912-1960
John, Donald, 1866-1925
MacDonald, Harriet, w/o Donald John, 1867-1902
Eldon, Agnes, 1892-1922
Robinson, Henry D., b 17 Feb 1835, d 23 Nov 1932
Sanborn, Sarah, w/o Henry D. Robinson, b 6 Feb 1839, d 16 Feb 1922
Pima, Alice, 1862-1930
Pima, Grace R., 1893-1955
Moe, Bergy S., 1873-1955
Moe, Ellemina, w/o Bergy S. Moe, 1873-1922
MacKennon, Herbert O., 1872-1950
MacKennon, Flora, w/o Herbert O. MacKennon, 1874-1940
MacKennin, Gordon M., 1907-1969
MacKennon, Raymond H., 1913-1973
Bronson, Gladys M., 1905-....
Howarth, James, 1853-1935
Johnson, Sara M., w/o James Howarth, 1853-1926
Coe, Edward M., 1868-1945
Howarth, Florence M., w/o Edward M. Coe, 1874-1964
Sanford, Lester C., 1882-1930
Sanford, M. Beatrice , w/o Lester C. Sanford, 1881-1920
Dix, George G., 1890-1977
Smith, Elmer S., 1875-1955
Tucker, M. Edith, w/o Elmer S. Smith, 1878-1961
Smith, Irma Waitee, d/o Elmer & M. Edith Smith, 1911-1932
Makepeace, David E., 1848-1934

Johnson, Almira, w/o David E. Makepeace, 1850-1941
Kershaw, Joseph, 1872-1942
Makepeace, Lulu E., w/o Joseph Kershaw, 1873-1960
Webb, Charles H., 1877-1932
Sadler, Irma, w/o Charles H. Webb, 1880-1963
MacKnight, Adam S., MD, 1858-1929
Patton, Sarah L., w/o Dr. Adam S. MacKnight, 1855-1927
Snitko, Nicky, 1848-1949
Lamond, Clara, 1856-1927
William, John, 1875-1941
MacIvop, Hattie E., w/o John William, 1881-1977
Dix, Walter G., 1858-1941
Dix, C. Lizzie, w/o Walter G. Dix, 1859-1947
Hewitt, Arthur R., 1862-1927
Hewitt, Mary L., w/o Arthur R. Hewitt, 1864-1940
Paul, Arthur H., 1856-1921
Pillsbury, Aravesta H., w/o Arthur H. Paul, 1859-1946
Lamond, Daniel, 1886-1950
McLane, Florence E., w/o Daniel Lamond, 1890-1947
Sadler, Frank H., 1853-1933
Newell, Alice, w/o Frank H. Sadler, 1854-1943
Bottomley, Ada Sadler, 1878-1967
Richardson, Henry Bliss, 1853-1920
Carnes, Lucy G., w/o Henry Bliss Richardson, 1852-1930
Guild, Charles A., 1876-1961
MacLeod, Nellie M., w/o Charles A. Guild, 1874-1967
Wilmarth, George O., 1849-1920
Austin, Emma F., w/o George O. Wilmarth, 1854-1943
Wilmarth, Maude E., w/o Edward Morse, 1884-1979
Battenshall, Joseph Ward, MD, 1842-1922
Battenshall, Mary, w/o Dr. Joseph Ward Battenshall, 1854-1928
Battenshall, Jesse W., MD, 1893-1945
Battenshall, Frances, w/o Dr. Jesse W. Battenshall, 1892-1984
Goff, Nathan E., 1861-1920
Goff, Elizabeth, w/o Nathan E. Goff, 1867-1955
Goff, James W., 1889-1954
Philbrick, Margaret, w/o James W. Goff, 1894-1966
Brown, Amelia D., w/o Percy Brown, 1892-1951
Brown, Percy, 1897-1963
Neval, Henry, 1882-1951

Goff, Mabel, w/o Henry Neval, 1893-1964
Lawton, Abel, 1839-1921
Buckley, Margaret, w/o Abel Lawton, 1841-1929
Lawton, Sophia, d/o Abel & Margaret Lawton, 1868-1915
Dyer, Samuel, 1891-1952
Dexter, Alice Everett, w/o Samuel Dyer, 1891-1986
Money, John W., b 22 Jan 1891, d 18 June 1965
Dexter, Ethel L., w/o John W. Money, b 17 April 1893, d 3 Jan 1970
Brown, Marcus, 1821-1906
Brown, Lucy N., w/o Marcus Brown, 1824-1913
Brown, Martha A., 1850-1935
Brown, George L., 1862-1942
Brunner, Emma, 1890-1919
Robbins, Charles May, b 1 May 1856, d 13 Sept 1929
Pratt, Lucie Brigham, w/o Charles May Robbins, d 15 July 1906
Swent, Minnie Alice, w/o Charles May Robbins, b 1 Feb 1875, d 27
   March 1961
MacDonald, Robert B., 1845-1929
MacDonald, Lydia B., w/o Robert B. MacDonald, 1848-1915
Chace, S. Howard, 1871-1934
Chace, Alice M., 1878-1952
Betts, Rev. Jacob, b 1 March 1852 Middleboro, Nova Scotia, d 8 April
   1908 Fall River, MA
Canfield, Margaret L., w/o Rev. Jacob Betts, b 8 June 1852 Wallace, Nova
   Scotia, d 26 Nov 1926
Adams, Daniel M., 1852-1915
Adams, Louisa H., w/o Daniel M. Adams, 1852-1933
Smith, James, 1861-1949
Smith, Mabel A., w/o James Smith, 1869-1955
Smith, James H., s/o James & Mabel Smith, 1889-1917
Stone, Samuel M., 1872-1957
Baer, Tilda, w/o Samuel M. Stone, 1887-1974
Stone, Samuel M. Jr., 1910-1980
Benson, Septimus, 1868-1926
Benson, Annie M., 1873-1956
Benson, Richard O., 1908-1986
Cannon, Arlene S., w/o Richard O. Benson, 1909-1990
Carpenter, J. Perry, 1847-1914
Carpenter, Mary I, w/o J. Perry Carpenter, 1848-1932
Carpenter, Fred L., 1879-1938

Bottomley, John, b 2 April 1846, d 10 Aug 1918

Taylor, Mary A. B., w/o John Bottomley, b 5 Dec 1845, d 21 June 1933

Bottomley, Arthur, s/o John & Mary Bottomley, b 20 June 1875, d 22 April 1962

Bottomley, Frances T., d/o John & Mary Bottomley, b 16 Dec 1871, d 4 May 1962

White, Howard E., 1876-1960

Weadick, Elizabeth M., w/o Howard E. White, 1877-1965

Rich, Joshua A. L., 1840-1919

Rich, Susan C., w/o Joshua A. L. Rich, 1843-1940

Rich, Herbert Lowell, ...

Grover, Stillman R., 1849-1917

Ashley, Theodora A., w/o Stillman R. Grover, 1852-1917

Grover, Edgar L., s/o Stillman R. & Theodora A. Grover, 1819-1880

Blois, Fred A., 1885-1918

Cook, George E., 1921-1946

Cook, Goerge, 1872-1949

Pierce, Frances Brooks, 1861-1942

Pierce, Barbara, 1916-1918

Perry, Jabez H., 1888-1967

Grover, Esther E., w/o Jabez H. Perry, 1887-1945

Norwood, William, 1857-1925

White, Mary J., w/o William Norwood, 1858-1927

Fiske, Louis T., 1874-1954

MacLeod, Catherine, w/o Louis T. Fiske, 1879-1940

Fiske, Charles Oliver, 1898-1917 France, PVT Co 1 101st Inft

Angell, Thomas H., 1861-1925

Angell, Charlotte, w/o Thomas H. Angell, 1868-1924

Angell, Cyril M., s/o Thomas & Charlotte Angell, 1895-1918 France

Ives, George H., d 9 Sept 1892 aged 22 yrs

Rhodes, Ann M., 1853-1932

Rhodes, Charles M., b 30 Dec 1838, d 14 Feb 1902

Rhodes, Anna F., w/o Charles M. Rhodes, b 16 Sept 1846, d 3 Nov 1885

Rhodes, Freddie C., s/o Charles & Anna Rhodes, b 8 Oct 1873, d June 1874

Rhodes, John A., s/o John Rhodes, d 18 Feb 1817 aged 12 yrs 1 mo 2 days

White, Daniel D. Jr., 1884-1939

Pinkert, Annie, w/o Daniel D. White Jr., 1879-1939

White, Daniel D., 1853-1921

Staples, Carrie E., w/o Daniel D. White, 1856-1945

Rogers, James H., 1885-1962
LeBurn, Edith M., w/o James H. Rogers, 1900-1981
Rud, Isabell, 1849-1931
Rud, Alfred J., 1890-1959
Whallen, Theresa, w/o Alfred J. Rud, 1890-1968
McNerney, James M., 1846-1930
McNerney, Rebecca Jane, w/o James M. McNerney, 1853-1920
Wells, Harold H., b 9 Oct 1880, d 10 Nov 1916
Slade, Irene Wells, b 26 Sept 1885, d 9 March 1966, buried at sea
Candelet, Robert J., 1885-1958
Horne, Bessie M., w/o Robert J. Candelet, 1888-1948
Horne, J. John, 1852-1916
Hanway, Mary, w/o J. John Horne, 1849-1925
Horne, Walter P., 1884-1945
Dredge, Ellen I, w/o Walter P. Horne, 1889-1945
Ellis, Joseph R., 1891-1940
Ellis, Harry G., 1900-1972
Johnson, Emil L., b 28 Sept 1881, d 1 May 1942
Johnson, Bertha L., w/o Emil L. Johnson, b 28 Feb 1887, d 24 Feb 1929
Hall, Ruth M., w/o Emil L. Johnson, b 19 Sept 1900, d 29 April 1963
Megquier, Mary J. (Hixon), 1842-1917
Megquier, Vivian E., 1880-1918
Girrell, John W., 1854-1917
Megquier, Gertrude M., w/o John W. Girrell, 1864-1951
MacDonald, Nan L., w/o Howard C. Gay, 1891-1920
Gay, Howard C., 1888-1976
Wells, Jason L., b 4 Nov 1852, d 22 Oct 1917
Wells, Jane M., b 9 Dec 1856, d 7 July 1946
Carpenter, Elsie Wells, b 3 June 1887, d 21 Jan 1942
Hayes, Jeremiah, 1882-....
Briggs, Frances L., w/o Jeremiah Hayes, 1878-1945
deCastro, Ralph E., 1874-1919
Fisher, Margaret L., w/o Ralph E. deCastro, 1878-1949
de Castro, Elsie A., 1900-1987
Vose, Howard N., 1884-1920
Stevens, Philomine M. Vose, 1883-1952
Burns, Harold, 1908-1987
Burns, Roberta Vose, w/o Harold Burns,....
Ellis, Joseph B., 1864-1946
Sheldon, Ella A., w/o Joseph B. Ellis, 1863-1917

Stoddard, Mildred S., w/o Joseph B. Ellis, 1889-1953
Watkins, T. Leslie, 1859-1937
Watkins, Cora G., w/o T. Leslie Watkins, 1860-1917
Watkins, Hattie M., w/o T. Leslie Watkins, 1858-1953
McLane, Eugene F., 1859-1947
McLane, Lucy C., w/o Eugene F. McLane, 1862-1918
McLane, Albert M., 1900-1900
McLane, Chester E., 1887-1952
Barton, Frederick T., 1861-1950
Fairbanks, Sarah, w/o Frederick T. Barton, 1863-1917
Barton, Frederick R., s/o Frederick & Sarah Barton,1883-1925
Barton, Albert F., s/o Frederick & Sarah Barton, 1885-1943
Barton, Walter R., s/o Frederick & Sarah Barton, 1887-1956
Bruce, Minnie, w/o Walter R. Barton, 1871-1943
Cummings, Frank A., 1861-1924
Cummings, Nellie L., w/o Frank A. Cummings, 1875-1966
Gabler, Irene R., 1893-1967
Wheelock, Godfrey, b 1804, d Sept 1878
Wheelock, Rebecca, w/o Godfrey Wheelock, b 1813, d July 1900
Lawton, Abigail Bell, w/o Godfrey Wheelock, & d/o Sebray & Elizabeth
    Lawton, b 27 Dec 1801, d 12 March 1863
Bronson, John Richard Jr., s/o John & Catherine Bronson, b 8 Nov 1854,
    d 12 Aug 1856
Bronson, John Richard Jr., s/o John & Catherine Bronson, b 2 May 1857,
    d 14 Sept 1861
Bronson, John R., MD, b 5 June 1828, d 9 May 1900
Wheelock, Catherine F., w/o Dr. John R. Bronson, b 4 Nov 1829, d 14
    April 1916
Bronson, Emma M., b 27 April 1853, d 28 March 1939
Barney, Ralph A., 1864-1935
Cole, Retta G., w/o Ralph A. Barney, 1866-1939
Barney, Waldo E., 1893-1952
Pierce, Mabel I., w/o Waldo E. Barney, 1894-1984
Barney, Rosamond, 1897-1973
Mason, Noah, d 14 Sept 1882 aged 76 yrs
Mason, Harriet W., w/o Noah Mason, d 7 Aug 1880 aged 72 yrs
Mason, Calvin H., s/o Noah & Harriet Mason, d 18 July 1841 aged 2 yrs
Mason, Caroline F., d/o Noah & Harriet Mason, d 8 March 1844 aged 1
    yrs
Mason, Fisher N., s/o Noah & Harriet Mason, d 8 Oct 1846 aged 9 yrs

Low, David L., b 5 April 1855, d 1 July 1933

Beers, Ella F., w/o David L. Low, b 5 March 1853, d 13 Nov 1916

Low, C. Gertrude, b 29 April 1882, d 28 Nov 1957

Wilmarth, Herbert G., b 22 Dec 1846, d 5 Jan 1926

Wilmarth, Clara R., b 28 Jan 1859, d 2 June 1864

Wilmarth, Harrison, 1814-1873

Wilmarth, Sarah A., w/o Harrison Wilmarth, 1810-1881

Wilmarth, Lemira B., 1839-1847

Davis, Richard William, 1819-1975

Whitney, Cora M., w/o Richard William Davis, 1876-1963

Ferguson, Donald Davis, 1942-1942

Lincoln, Mary A., 1830-1865

Capron, Frank Edgar, d 13 Jan 1889 aged 44 yrs

Fisher, Tisdall, b 12 April 1837, d 21 May 1880

Fisher, Fannie B., w/o Tisdall Fisher, b 20 Nov 1845, d 28 Sept 1881

Fisher, Nellie, d/o Tisdall & Fannie Fisher, b 29 Sept 1866, d 16 Sept 1868

Fisher, Alice B., d/o Tisdall & Fannie B. Fisher, b 13 July 1865, d 21 May 1905

Gruninger, Captain Lawrence, d 9 Nov 1867 aged 50 yrs

Gruninger, Alice B., w/o Captain Lawrence Gruninger, d 4 Aug 1902 aged 74 yrs

Cushman, Heman, d 4 Feb 1866 aged 79 yrs

Cushman, Deborah, w/o Heman Cushman, d 10 April 1859 aged 79 yrs

MacDonald, Edward, 1856-1923

MacDonald, Ray Allen, 1889-1926

Sherman, Inez M., 1885-1926

MacDonlad, Edward, 1890-1951

Claflin, Daniel B., b 24 July 1825, d 4 July 1905

Claflin, Julia M., w/o Daniel B. Claflin, b 28 Aug 1838, d 10 Feb 1919

Claflin, Daniel, b 23 June 1792, d 10 July 1850

Claflin, Lita A., w/o Daniel Claflin, b 8 March 1797, d 6 April 1883

Claflin, Caroline E., d/o Daniel & Lita B. Claflin, b 23 Oct 1830, d 15 May 1833

Claflin, Ellen A., d/o Daniel & Lita B. Claflin, b 29 Aug 1843, d 18 Dec 1873

Adams, Ephraim, 1834-1872

Capron, Isabel, w/o Ephraim Adams, 1836-1914

Adams, Oscar M., s/o Ephraim & Isabel Adams, 1864-1898

Adams, Francis A., 1870-1948

Wilcox, Henry Allen, RI PVT 3 Corps Art Park, d 6 April 1930
Briggs, Charles H., 1837-1888
Coan, Sarah N., w/o Charles H. Briggs, 1838-1887
Elliot, William L., 1853-1927
Sanford, Mary W., w/o William L. Elliot, 1865-1939
Holden, Dr. Charles S., 1856-1932
Sanford, Caroline E., w/o Dr. Charles S. Holden, 1850-1947
Stabbs, Alice Holden, 1886-1962
Briggs, Wheaton, d 10 Aug 1869 aged 60 yrs 6 mos 5 dys
Briggs, Sylvia, w/o Wheaton Briggs, 1816-1886
Briggs, Arthur F., d 9 May 1871 aged 25 yrs 4 mos 3 days
Smith, Jennie F., w/o Daniel Smith, b 31 May 1846, d 3 Jan 1912
Crandall, Dr. Edwin L., d 6 March 1887 aged 44 yrs 11 mos 1 day
Martin, Dr. Alfred, d 16 June 1880 aged 72 yrs 8 days
Martin, Bebe, w/o Dr. Alfred Martin, d 21 July 1885 aged 78 yrs 1 mo 21
    days
Marble, Robert P., 1850-1929
Marble, Ida Evelyn, w/o Robert P. Marble, 1858-1882
Marble, Walter B., s/o Robert P. & Ida Evelyn Marble, 1877-1945
Marble, Mary Willetta, w/o Robert P. Marble, 1859-1928
Savery, Job B., b 24 Jan 1841, d 3 Oct 1886
Luther, James W., b 24 June 1841, d 12 May 1921
Briggs, Sarah A., w/o James W. Luther, b 29 July 1843, d 26 June 1885
Horton, Edwin J., b 10 Nov 1838, d 12 June 1880
Horton, R. Adelaide, w/o Edwin J. Horton, b 23 Dec 1841, d 24 Aug
    1920
Horton, Edwin J. Jr., b 23 June 1869, d 22 Dec 1878
Horton, Raymond M.,....
McGregor, Una, w/o Raymond M. Horton, 1875-1954
Horton, Gideon Jr., d 16 Dec 1886 aged 46 yrs 3 mos
Horton, Helen F., d 28 Aug 1885 aged 42 yrs 7 days
Blaney, Samuel C., 1858-1920
Peterson, Fannie E., w/o Samuel C. Blaney, 1861-1934
Blaney, W. H., 1848-1935
Martland, Alice E., w/o W. H. Blaney, 1849-1880
Emerson, Annie D., w/o W. H. Blaney, 1865-1943
Blake, James E., 1851-1927
Sturdy, Ella J., w/o James E. Blake, 1854-1941
Walker, William, b 2 March 1824, d 9 Oct 1899
Bliss, Lydia A., w/o William Walker, b 28 Dec 1828, d 27 Jan 1896

Bliss, Herbert F., b 12 Feb 1855, d 29 Nov 1929

Reed, Louisa P., w/o Herbert F. Bliss, b 27 Sept 1857, d 19 June 1921

Walker, Albert, b 29 June 1834, d 5 Sept 1904

Sweet, Clara, w/o Albert Walker, b 30 July 1837, d 7 Nov 1899

Clark, Major Herbert A., b 22 Feb 1859, d 16 Feb 1903

Horton, James J., b 19 Oct 1841, d 22 July 1900

Clark, Emily H., w/o James J. Horton, b 23 Nov 1845, d 5 June 1920

Horton, Major Everett S., b 15 June 1836, d 3 June 1911

Fremont, Eliza D., w/o Maj. Everett S. Horton, b 25 Jan 1836, d 28 Nov 1931

Kendall, Gertrude Horton, b 29 May 1876, d 18 Dec 1928

Kendall, Walter M., 1884-1956

Cudworth, Laura, w/o David Cudworth, b 14 April 1800, d 4 Dec 1881

Cudworth, David, b 22 Aug 1811, d 17 Dec 1890

Sanford, Caleb, 1812-1884

Sanford, Ellen M., w/o Caleb Sanford, 1822-1906

Lincoln, Stephen T., b 23 Sept 1819, d 23 Dec 1904

Lincoln, Elizabeth, w/o Stephen T. Lincoln, b 4 March 1815, d 12 Jan 1890

Briggs, William H., b 6 Aug 1820, d 1 Sept 1895

Nichols, Hannah P., w/o William H. Briggs, b 6 Oct 1821, d 16 Dec 1890

Whitman, George L., b 18 Oct 1837, d 15 Feb 1919

Winter, Marilla L., w/o George L. Whitman, b 12 May 1839, d 24 April 1929

Whitman, George E., b 14 Aug 1860, d 21 Feb 1888

Whitman, Hattie M., b 16 May 1867, d 12 June 1946

Bullock, Edwin B., 1843-1927

Bullock, Carrie S., w/o Edwin B. Bullock, 1849-....

Short, Mace Burt, b 15 Feb 1827, d 19 Aug 1903

Wheaton, Nancy Burr, w/o Mace Burt Short, b 10 March 1824, d 24 March 1914

Short, Phillip, b 18 Sept 1796, d 16 Aug 1861

Burt, Matilda Lincoln, w/o Phillip Short, b 21 Feb 1801, d 15 Dec 1862

Manchester, Richard D., b 19 March 1853, d 26 July 1917

Manchester, Leuella E., w/o Richard D. Manchester, b 4 Dec 1865, d 17 June 1943

Bradford, Soramus Standish, b 24 Nov 1854, d 3 Jan 1903

Andrews, Hattie E., w/o Soramus S. Bradford, b 7 July 1855, d 9 May 1920

Bradford, Hattie Lola, d/o Soramus & Hattie Bradford, b 2 May 1877, d 13 July 1877

Bradford, Hattie E., w/o Craig C. Pope, b 28 Sept 1880, d 18 Feb 1904

Cole, Seneca, 1842-1916

Brown, Minerva Jane, 1846-1886

Bowen, Elizabeth Carpenter, 1867-1962

Cole, Elizabeth Blanding, 1901-....

Handy, George W., 1832-1895

Gammons, Elizabeth, w/o George W. Handy, 1839-1917

Handy, Bertha E., 1870-1876

Smith, Abraham L., 1861-1955

Handy, Stella A., w/o Abraham L. Smith, 1868-1943

Smith, Lincoln A., 1891-1918

Denzer, Margaret, w/o Lincoln A. Smith, 1871-1929

Handy, Willard A., 1905-1925

Chase, Clarence J., 1896-1975

Handy, Gladys, w/o Clarence J. Chase, 1898-1983

Prince, Benjamin D., 1848-1923

Prince, Stella F., w/o Benjamin D. Prince, 1856-1881

Parker, Warren, 1841-1923

Parker, Annie, w/o Warren Parker, 1844-1935

Parker, Albert C., 1866-1938

Parker, Annie M., w/o Albert C. Parker, 1867-1063

Heywood, Joseph, 1839-1925

Campbell, Sarah A., w/o Joseph Heywood, 1842-1918

Heywood, Allee, d/o Joseph & Sarah A. Heywood, b 9 Jan 1875, d 16 Sept 1875

Heywood, Joseph J., 1877-1962

Melvin, Marcella C., w/o Joseph J. Heywood, 1882-1948

Heywood, George E., 1882-1979

Lamond, Clara Maude, w/o George E. Heywood, 1884-1975

Seibert, Frederick H., 1845-1883

Sweet, Eleanor Amanda, w/o Frederick H. Seibert, 1845-1929

Seibert, Edith Howard, d/o Frederick & Eleanor Seibert, 1874-1875

Seibert, Inez Helena, d/o Frederick & Eleanor Seibert, 1869-1885

Rothwell, Richard, 1823-1886

Heywood, Ann, w/o Richard Rothwell, 1819-1878

Campbell, John, 1815-1881

Rogers, Ann S., d/o John Campbell, 1819-1892

Cummings, Edgar A., 1842-1935

Lee, Martha W., w/o Edgar A. Cummings, 1844-1916
Cummings, Arthur B., 1873-1956
Courtney, Gertrude M., w/o Arthur B. Cummings, 1874-1952
Cummings, John C., 1841-1930
Curtis, Addie M., w/o John C. Cummings, 1849-1926
MacDonald, Richard M., 1850-1948
Jones, Mary B., w/o Richard M. MacDonald, 1852-1934
Blackinton, Virgil, 1872-1941
Blackinton, Ida M., w/o Virgil Blackinton, 1878-1945
MacDonald, George E., 1890-1964
MacDonald, Eva, w/o George E. MacDonald, 1886-1962
Smith, N. Justin, 1837-1912
Smith, Ophelia F., w/o N. Justin Smith, 1838-1885
Smith, Fannie E., w/o N. Justin Smith, 1867-1949
Smith, Leland B., 1893-1975
Smith, Ruth P., w/o Leland B. Smith, 1893-1952
Robbins, Freeman, 1837-1924
Crosby, Dora, w/o Freeman Robbins, 1842-1886
Robbins, Seth, 1802-1885
Higgins, Eunice, w/o Seth Robbins, 1799-1883
Hoffman, Robert H., 1834-1909
Batson, Emma F., w/o Robert H. Hoffman, 1838-1902
Ingraham, Ezra R., b 13 May 1805, d 23 June 1896
Hunt, Julia R., w/o Ezra R. Ingraham, b 2 April 1821, d 28 July 1908
Wetherell, Charles H., b 13 Dec 1839, d 16 Oct 1896
Wetherell, Annie M., w/o Charles H. Wetherell, b 7 June 1848, d 23 Oct
   1937
Wetherell, Fannie L., b 14 Oct 1871, d 17 July 1872
Sweet, Amos, 1805-1877
Thrasher, Mary, w/o Amos Sweet, 1815-1837
Thrasher, Sarah, w/o Amos Sweet, 1810-1898
Wilkinson, Sarah Helena, 1841-1877
Vedder, Helena Sweet, 1871-1892
Sweet, Frank S., 1849-1912
Sweet, Frankie, s/o Frank S. Sweet, 1880-1881
Bliss, Charles Edwin, b 8 Feb 1837, d 1 April 1908
Newcomb, Sarah H., w/o Charles Edwin Bliss, b 21 July 1836, d 7 May
   1920
Newcomb, Deacon Joseph M., b 9 Nov 1808, d 17 Jan 1891

Newcomb, Hannah K., w/o Deacon Joseph M. Newcomb, b 27 Aug 1809, d 18 Nov 1886

Newcomb, J. Herbert, d 27 Sept 1863 aged 21 yrs 8 mos

Newcomb, Otis C., d 10 Nov 1865 aged 26 yrs 10 mos

Newcomb, Ella C., d 18 April 1868 aged 19 yrs 5 mos

Bliss, Mary Herbert,. d 28 Dec 1864 aged 4 yrs 9 mos

Bliss, Clinton Edwin, d 24 Aug 1894 aged 24 yrs 8 mos 25 days

Bliss, Ernest M., 1871-1913

MacDonald, William A., 1842-1927

Richardson, Maria A., w/o William A. MacDonald, 1847-1913

Lyle, Alexander, 1851-1934

Lyle, Mary, w/o Alexander Lyle, 1852-1933

Lyle, Frederick H., 1892-....

Lyle, Florence B., w/o Frederick H. Lyle, 1892-1922

Paine, Elijah M., 1807-1852

Morse, Mary A., w/o Elijah M. Paine, 1809-1884

Fisher, William M., 1828-1891

Paine, M. A. Frances, w/o William M. Fisher, 1832-1911

Fisher, Gertrude Moore, d/o William & M. A. Fisher, 1857-1864

Lamb, Florence F., 1854-1921

Fisher, Elwood J., 1862-1935

Goff, Hattie E., w/o Elwood J. Fisher, 1864-1937

Fisher, Marshall E., s/o Elwood & Hattie Fisher, 1889-1962

Burgess, Edith H., w/o Marshall E. Fisher, 1895-1991

Richardson, H. Nelson, d 31 Jan 1879 aged 66 yrs 3 mos 19 days

Dean, Mary, w/o H. Nelson Richardson, b 1 July 1814, d 12 March 1893

Richardson, William E., b 3 Feb 1853, d 30 April 1921

Richardson, Orville P., b 11 Sept 1825, d 12 April 1888

Johnson, Eliza A., w/o Orville P. Richardson, b 2 Aug 1829, d 10 Nov 1900

Johnson, Andrew, b 6 Aug 1784, d 7 May 1863

Parmenter, Betsey, w/o Andrew Johnson, b 20 July 1792, d 22 Jan 1876

Johnson, George P., b 24 Aug 1834, d 9 Sept 1864 Andersonville, Georgia

Woodward, Maria L., w/o William B. Woodward, d 18 April 1881 aged 54 yrs

Woodward, Henry Bradford, s/o William B. & Caroline Woodward, b 26 Nov 1843, d 14 June 1862 Patterson Park Hospital, Baltimore, Maryland aged 18 yrs 6 mos 10 days

Woodward, Elizabeth Adeline, w/o Henry D. Spaulding, & d/o William B. & Caroline E. Woodward, b 20 Jan 1841, d 5 Aug 1863 Sullivan, New Hampshire aged 22 yrs 6 mos 16 days

Shaw, William P., d 14 Oct 1879 aged 45 yrs

Shaw, Susan E., w/o William P. Shaw, d 25 Oct 1904 aged 70 yrs

Jones, Hiram, b 15 Jan 1816, d 13 Dec 1873

Hunt, Fanny J., w/o Hiram Jones, b 7 March 1819, d 3 March 1857

Jones, George G., s/o Hiram & Fanny Jones, b 9 Jan 1851, d 17 May 1871

Thayer, Mary A., w/o Hiram Jones, b 12 Aug 1834, d 28 May 1928

Walker, Esther J., d 9 Aug 1886 aged 59 yrs

Withington, William D., 1822-1863

Withington, Laura J., w/o William D. Withington, 1819-1899

Bowen, Louisa, b 15 Sept 1829, d 13 Nov 1887

Danforth, Nancy, w/o Edward Richardson, b Feb 1811, d 16 Oct 1893

Hammond, William B., 1819-1888

Hammond, Sophia A., w/o William B. Hammond, 1822-1870

Hammond, Henry M., 1845-1909

Hammond, Ellen M., w/o Henry M. Hammond, 1843-1914

Hammond, Edward A., 1848-1928

Hammond, Josephine L., w/o Edward A. Hammond, 1856-1934

McMurray, David, 1858-1940

McMurray, Frances L., w/o David McMurray, 1865-1921

McMurray, Bessie E., w/o David McMurray, 1887-1933

Solomon, Dr. S. Augusta, 1854-1931

Lee, Alvin F., b 22 Nov 1843, d 29 March 1937

Lee, Ida M., w/o Alvin F. Lee, b 21 Nov 1848, d 11 Oct 1901

Lee, George F., 1872-1951

Lee, Luella K., w/o George F. Lee, 1878-....

Richards, Earl L., 1828-1896

Richards, Minerva A., w/o Earl L. Richards, 1830-1864

Richards, Marion L., w/o Earl L. Richards, 1846-1920

Richards, Clarence E., 1856-1935

Richards, Agnes, w/o Clarence E. Richards, 1860-1884

Richards, Josephine T., w/o Clarence E. Richards, 1859-1956

Philbrook, Charles, 1887-1947

Philbrook, Marion A., w/o Charles Philbrook, 1889-1985

Luther, John W., 1942-1938

Luther, Amelia J., w/o John W. Luther, 1849-1939

Luther, Effie M., 1872-1898

Luther, Lewis C., 1870-1956

Luther, Ada B., 1873-1924

Hodges, Gardner C., b 25 Dec 1816, d 25 Feb 1897

Hodges, Bebe W., w/o Gardner C. Hodges, b 10 Oct 1813, d 28 Aug 1904

Hodges, Howard B., s/o Gardner C. & Bebe W. Hodges, b 20 April 1846, d 17 July 1848

Hodges, Josephine, d/o Gardner C. & Bebe W. Hodges, b 20 Dec 1839, d 10 July 1858

Hodges, Orville O., s/o Gardner C. & Bebe W. Hodges, b 28 April 1842, d 29 Sept 1862

Hodges, Howard C., s/o Gardner C. & Bebe W. Hodges, b 27 July 1856, d 5 Oct 1876

Martin, Sarah B., w/o Alcott Hardon, b 31 March 1818, d 10 Sept 1899

Bourne, Stephen, b 4 May 1783, d 7 Feb 1867

Bourne, Nancy, w/o Stephen Bourne, b 7 June 1787, d 25 March 1868

Chace, Atwood B., 1875-1940

Stone, Grace E., w/o Atwood B. Chace, 1874-1959

Chace, William H., 1910-1993

Wales, Abigail T., 1833-1912

Wales, Josephine, 1836-1867

Wales, Alice M., 1862-1938

Wales, Edward N., 1857-1933

Wales, Eliza Boice, 1862-1943

Wales, Mabel Doris, 1859-1929

Wales, Alice M., 1860-1938

Wales, Perry Howe, 1922-1961

Wales, Marion L., 1897-1962

Hamilton, Joseph, d 30 Sept 1860 aged 49 yrs

Hamilton, James, d 14 May 1887 aged 67 yrs

Hamilton, Margaret, d 3 July 1899 aged 87 yrs

Hamilton, Ann M., d 21 Oct 1843 aged 11 yrs

Hamilton, John, d 12 May 1862 aged 79 yrs

Hamilton, Nancy, d 18 Sept 1846 aged 67 yrs

Thompson, Clelland, d 28 Aug 1872 aged 62 yrs

Thompson, Abbie F., b 12 May 1846 Attleborough, MA, d 20 Sept 1919 Dorchester, Ma

Sweet, Charles O., 1848-1928

Cooper, Elizabeth J., w/o Charles O. Sweet, 1848-1922

Sweet, Ervin V., 1870-1947

Purdy, Bertha A., w/o Ervin V. Sweet, 1876-1947

Wallace, Elliot M., 1843-1867, A member of Co H 40th Mass Reg

Hawkins, Lewis O., 1833-1885
Hawkins, Margaret, w/o Lewis O. Hawkins, 1835-1909
Hawkins, Mary E., d/o Lewis & Margaret Hawkins, 1855-1864
Hawkins, Jennie, d/o Lewis & Margaret Hawkins, 1863-1864
Gardner, Nicholas E., 1842-1904
Gardner, Mary S., w/o Nicholas E. Gardner, 1847-1919
Gardner, Grace E., 1870-1870
Hawkins, Albert L., 1825-1882
Hawkins, Charlotte M., w/o Albert L. Hawkins, 1827-1897
Rawson, Saloma, 1801-1890
Pike, Eugene C., 1841-1911
Pike, Catherine, w/o Eugene C. Pike, 1840-1896
Pike, Charles A., 1864-1933
Pike, Addie E., w/o Charles A. Pike, 1865-1907
Hawkins, David P., 1850-1937
Bullock, Ella E., w/o David P. Hawkins, 1853-....
Baker, John H., 1836-1892
Baker, Frances S., 1843-1919
Stanton, Henry L. Sr., b 28 Sept 1849, d 6 Jan 1923
Stanton, Sarah E., w/o Henry L. Stanton Sr., d 14 Oct 1903 aged 45 yrs
Stanton, William E., b 17 May 1830, d 9 Sept 1876
Stanton, Harriet A., w/o William E. Stanton, b 25 Jan 1830, d 16 Dec 1894
Madison, Jessie W., b 18 Sept 1880, d 31 Dec 1904
Stanton, Charles E., b 4 Jan 1886, d 21 Sept 1906
Eddy, Josephine, w/o Charles H. Eddy, d 28 Nov 1887 aged 38 yrs
Eddy, Charles H., d 2 April 1930 aged 78 yrs
Stanton, Marietta, w/o Charles H. Eddy, b 25 Nov 1855, d 13 Oct 1943
Luther, William J., 1862-1959
Niles, Minnie H., w/o William J. Luther, 1862-1945
Luther, Warren B., 1888-1909
Clark, Albert H., 1897-1959
Clark, Helen D., w/o Albert H. Clark, 1895-1976
Dean, George Asa, b 2 May 1835, d 4 Aug 1900
Richardson, Betsey B., w/o George Asa Dean, b 8 Dec 1835, d 30 Oct 1908
Thacher, John, b 4 Nov 1828, d 17 Feb 1911
Bullock, Ida, w/o John Thacher, b 14 Nov 1845, d 22 Dec 1893
Jewett, Harriet, w/o John Thacher, b 9 March 1855, d 26 March 1904
Metcalf, Samuel Wilde, b 17 June 1822, d 20 Dec 1892

Partridge, Eliza J., w/o Samuel Wilde Metcalf, b 21 April 1829, d 2 Dec 1914

Metcalf, Eldora L., w/o George B. Fitts, b 25 Sept 1846, d 7 March 1915

Metcalf, Helen P., b 6 April 1850, d 11 March 1919

Metcalf, Louis P., b 9 Dec 1861, d 8 Dec 1930

MacDonald, Florence A., w/o Louis P. Metcalf, b 22 Feb 1873, d 12 April 1938

Metcalf, Edward O. Sumner, b 22 June 1854, d 5 July 1855

Smith, Laura Marsh, w/o Harvey Wool Smith, 1832-1914

Smith, Harvey Leigh, 1870-1910

Sweet, Lou Castline, 1874-1962

Seagrave, Joseph M., b 15 Aug 1871, d 3 April 1931

Smith, Lucy G., w/o Joseph M. Seagrave, b 21 April 1872, d 30 Dec 1955

Smith, Eunice E., b 15 Aug 1859, d 14 Jan 1947

Smith, Caroline E., b 6 Feb 1875, d 13 May 1957

Williams, Lawrence D., 1898-1969

Monroe, George A., b 5 April 1846, d 3 March 1926

Cole, Mary A., w/o George A. Monroe, b 4 April 1848, d 5 Jan 1931

Monroe, Mary A., d/o George A. & Mary A. Monroe, b 12 May 1839, d 6 April 1892

Monroe, George A., s/o George A. & Mary A. Monroe, b 1 Sept 1874, d 29 Sept 1901

Monroe, Leslie M., s/o George A. & Mary A. Monroe, b 4 Feb 1877, d 25 March 1953

Monroe, Sophia A., w/o Leslie M. Monroe, b 7 Sept 1875, d 9 Aug 1956

Thacher, John J., 1878-1931

Richardson, Orville Pratt, b 5 June 1851, d 23 March 1920

Smith, Bertha King, w/o Orville Pratt Richardson, b 8 Jan 1856, d 24 May 1915

Howard, John A., b 27 Jan 1825, d 2 Sept 1907

King, Elizabeth W., w/o John A. Howard, b 21 Feb 1828, d 9 July 1907

Cobb, Charles I., 1848-1918

Smith, Myra D., w/o Charles I. Cobb, 1848-1936

Smith, C. Adin, 1860-1944

Mathewson, Carra E., w/o C. Adin Smith, 1860-1938

Smith, Ruel H., 1888-1971

Riley, Ethel M., w/o Ruel H. Smith, 1890-1987

Williams, Jesse Everett, 1858-1910

Smith, Irma B., w/o John Laing Gibb, b 25 Aug 1882, d 3 July 1909

Smith, Earl B., b 6 April 1858, d 22 Aug 1914

Wolfenden, Fannie E., w/o Earl B. Smith, b 26 Dec 1856, d 14 March
1891

Carnes, William, b 16 April 1823, d 10 Sept 1905

Guild, Frances Adelaide, w/o William Carnes, b 5 April 1827, d 12 Oct
1903

Hayward, Henry L., b 18 Nov 1832, d 30 Dec 1933

Marble, Lloyd P., 1828-1908

Wyatt, Eliza B., w/o Lloyd P. Marble, 1826-1898

Thompson, Francis C., 1886-1912

Thompson, Elmer A., 1878-1902

Thompson, Frederick R., 1876-1895

Thompson, Samuel P., 1840-1913

Thompson, Mary D., w/o Samuel P. Thompson, 1849-1916

Hayward, Charles E., b 28 Aug 1824, d 4 May 1886

Wheelwright, Charlotte, w/o Charles E. Hayward, b 15 July 1825, d 17
Aug 1892

Hayward, Walter E., b 28 Dec 1858, d 30 July 1909

Lyon, Margaret, w/o Walter E. Hayward, b 13 Oct 1862, d 3 Aug 1933

Hayward, Charles E., b 10 Sept 1896, d 19 Dec 1980

Hill, Frederick H., 1874-1946

Wolfenden, John W., b 12 Dec 1849, d 18 Nov 1908

Wolfenden, Emma A., w/o John W. Wolfenden, b 16 July 1854, d 2
March 1939

Wolfenden, Robert, b 12 Dec 1824, d 29 May 1933

Wolfenden, Mary, w/o Robert Wolfenden, b 19 July 1825, d 29 July 1888

Wolfenden, Oscar, b 10 Feb 1852, d 16 April 1932

Wolfenden, Annie B., w/o Oscar Wolfenden, b 5 March 1855, d 14 Dec
1913

Tiffany, Eben C., b 18 May 1833, d 25 May 1891

Read, Jane, w/o Eben C. Tiffany, b 1 Nov 1829, d 7 Nov 1906

Beers, Courtland L., 1828-1870

Sisson, Harriet N., w/o Courtland L. Beers, 1825-1908

Beers, Leonora P., 1850-1922

Capron, Virgil Henry, 1816-....

Dunbar, Nancy, w/o Virgil Henry Capron, 1815-1897

Capron, Virgil Henry Jr., 1849-1950

Capron, May Elizabeth, d/o Virgil H. & Nancy Capron, 1842-1881

Capron, Selina Huntington, d/o Virgil H. & Nancy Capron, 1857-1891

Cooper, Alvin N., 1858-1952

Simpson, Carrie B., w/o Alvin N. Cooper, 1866-1939

Steward, Frank M., 1848-1894

Cook, Martha A., w/o Frank M. Steward, 1848-1928

Christersen, Carl V. J., 1866-1925

Steward, Ethel E., w/o Carl Christersen, 1879-1957

Carpenter, Jesse Lafayette, d 28 Aug 1895 aged 50 yrs 11 mos 25 days

Lincoln, Angelia A., w/o Jesse Lafayette Carpenter, 1844-1937

Carpenter, Mary E., 1875-1948

Carpenter, Jesse, 1869-1948

Carpenter, Lila A., w/o Jesse Carpenter, 1871-1964

Adams, George Albert Esq., b 3 April 1850, d 3 Aug 1902

Adams, Clara J., w/o George Albert Adams Esq., b 22 Aug 1849, d 30 Oct 1930

Adams, Mary S., b 21 Aug 1872, d 8 Dec 1939

Adams, Charles S., b 6 March 1878, d 26 May 1895

Williams, Douglas, 1845-1908

Williams, Abbie D., w/o Douglas Williams, 1850-1919

Williams, Edward D., 1874-1894

Williams, Abbie D., 1886-1906

Cobb, William R., b 4 Aug 1844, d 9 July 1921

Cobb, R. Josephine, w/o William R. Cobb, b 28 Oct 1843, d 6 July 1921

Cobb, Thomas A., b Aug 1842, d May 1895

Cobb, S. Josephine, w/o Thomas A. Cobb, b 5 Dec 1844, d 19 Nov 1927

Cobb, Amaziah Vinton, b 31 July 1849, d 19 Nov 1928

Simmons, Mary, w/o Amaziah Vinton Cobb, b 16 Sept 1847, d 16 Feb 1925

Cobb, Bertha Vinton, b 12 Aug 1873, d 24 Feb 1965

Cobb, Albert, 1812-1892

Tabor, Susan, w/o Albert Cobb, 1813-1902

Cobb, Mary Durfee, b May 1838, d May 1914

Simpson, William C., b 26 Aug 1836, d 29 May 1894

Bean, Lizzie M., w/o William C. Simpson, b 11 June 1836, d 28 March 1911

Simpson, George Irving, 1869-1907

Simpson, Julia, w/o George I. Simpson, ...

Cole, Perle R., 1875-1953

Pappas, Nicholas H., Sr., 1880-1962

Pappas, Bertha, w/o Nicholas H. Pappas Sr., 1885-1970

Pappas, Harry N., s/o Nicholas & Bertha Pappas, 1921-1922

Cole, Samuel, 1843-1928

Cole, Arvilla A., w/o Samuel Cole, 1848-1914

Fuller, Emma E., d/o Samuel & Arvilla Cole, 1873-1890
Thomas, Emma Sweet, 1851-1919
Eden, John, 1850-1931
Eden, Margaret, w/o John Eden, 1849-1911
Eden, Robert Wolfenden, 1880-1899
Eden, Edith F., w/o John Eden, 1877-1959
Eden, Edwin R., 1885-1939
Slade, Abbee J., 1853-1925
Slade, Caleb, 1852-1938
Slade, Emerson A., 1876-1949
Slade, Alice R., 1878-1961
King, William L., 1860-1934
Gillmore, Annie E., w/o William L. King, 1862-1949
Gillmore, Ernest D., 1860-1944
Crawford, Annie S., w/o Ernest D. Gillmore, 1862-1921
Lamond, Nettie M., w/o Ernest D. Gillmore, 1880-1957
Hardon, Alcott, b 22 April 1820, d 7 July 1902
Moore, Marion F., w/o Thomas Moore, 1868-1928
Bliss, Rodolphus, d 26 Aug 1888 aged 59 yrs
Bliss, Lydia S., w/o Rodolphus Bliss, b 27 Oct 1825, d 11 Feb 1891
Bliss, Lydia C., d/o Rodolphus & Lydia S. Bliss, b 5 Jan 1849, d 5 Aug
    1886
Bliss, Martin, d 29 March 1864 aged 69 yrs
Bliss, Sophia, w/o Martin Bliss, d 4 Jan 1880 aged 84 yrs
Carpenter, William, d 28 Nov 1875 aged 84 yrs
Carpenter, Sabina, w/o William Carpenter, d 27 May 1858 aged 55 yrs
Griffin, Peleg, 1802-1866
Griffin, Lucy A., w/o Peleg Griffin, 1805-1942
Griffin, Sarah G., 1851-1895
Griffin, Oliver P., 1827-1895
Griffin, Mary E., w/o Oliver P. Griffin, 1833-1915
Curien, George W., d 28 July 1844
Curien, Abbee F., w/o George W. Curien, d 26 Feb 1893 aged 78 yrs
Curien, Abbie Ann, w/o George W. Curien, d 11 Feb 1869 aged 30 yrs
Curien, George W., d 13 May 1905 aged 67 yrs
Kelly, Ensign E., d 3 Jan 1897 aged 76 yrs
Kelly, Betsey D., w/o Ensign E. Kelly, d 15 June 1894 aged 72 yrs
Kelly, Sarah S., w/o Ensign E. Kelly, d 4 Nov 1869 aged 46 yrs 4 days
Benton, James Edward, b 3 Dec 1824, d 1 Feb 1893
Benton, Jane Marie, b 3 Oct 1835, d 8 April 1911

Benton, Edward Augustus, b 11 Sept 1855, d 7 Sept 1894

Benton, Ella Read, b 19 Jan 1857, d 15 March 1935

Bliss, George Nelson, d 24 Feb 1886 aged 60 yrs

Bliss, Lucia Smith, d 3 Jan 1912 aged 88 yrs

Bliss, Walter S., d 28 Dec 1855 aged 5 yrs 16 days

Bliss, Lucia C., d 18 Jan 1856 aged 6yrs 7 mos

Bliss, Frederick, d 23 Dec 1873 aged 30 yrs 14 days

Bliss, Hannah B., w/o Frederick Bliss, d 30 Oct 1878 aged 31 yrs 5 mos
12 days

Treen, James H., 1853-1930

Sloman, Georgianna M., w/o James H. Treen, 1861-1958

Hall, William D., 1885-1982

Sloman, Mary E., w/o William D. Hall, 1885-1981

Harding, Moses E., 1830-1876

Seavey, Abbie J., w/o Moses E. Harding, 1836-1914

Harding, Annie Louise, d/o Moses & Abbie Harding, 1871-1886

Dean, James B., b 2 Sept 1816, d 10 April 1891

Dean, Hepsey, w/o James B. Dean, b 2 March 1814, d 11 March 1898

Babcock, Frank J., 1851-1935

Babcock, Geoege W., 1849-1928

Murphy, Mary, w/o George W. Babcock, 1847-1868

Maddox, Dora, w/o George W. Babcock, 1858-1934

Cushman, Peter, d 19 May 1896 aged 65 yrs 5 mos

Barnes, Loring W., d 25 Oct 1905 aged 71 yrs 6 mos

Barnes, Julia A., d 18 July 1906 aged 76 yrs 5 mos 8 days

Barnes, Clarence W., s/o Loring & Julia Barnes, d 31 May 1892 aged 38
yrs 3mos 11 days

Barnes, Charles L., s/o Loring & Julia Barnes, 1858-1924

Daggett, Ernestine Rose, d/o John M. & Ernestine B. Daggett, b 14 Oct
1872, d 26 Feb 1873

Bishop, Naman, d 30 Jan 1817 aged 35 yrs

Bishop, Lydia, w/o Naman Bishop, d 19 Jan 1875 aged 80 yrs

Foster, James S., d 30 July 1875 aged 66 yrs

Foster, Abigail, w/o James S. Foster, d 1 Feb 1876 aged 69 yrs

Makenson, Charles E., 1846-1908

Wilmarth, Harriet M., w/o Charles W. Makenson, 1843-1915

Manchester, William S., 1862-1932

Manchester, Sara B., w/o William S. Manchester, 1869-1959

Bacheler, Judson H., s/o Origen & Charlotte W. Bacheler, d 4 Sept 1849
aged 1 yr 7 days

Bacheler, Origen, d 14 March 1848 aged 48 yrs
Bacheler, Charlotte W., w/o Origen Bacheler, d 15 Feb 1895 aged 83 yrs
Capron, Herbert Simmons, 1853-1900
Capron, Herbert Wallace, 1882-1918
Capron, Josie Allen, 1886-1890
Gage, Charles Irving, 1869-1931
Carpenter, Luella, 1863-1933
Parmenter, Mary F., 1866-1951
Parmenter, Charles E., 1873-1956
Parmenter, Adella M., w/o Charles E. Parmenter, 1877-1929
Parmenter, Grace M., w/o Charles E. Parmenter, 1883-1968
Sharp, Henry A., 1871-1950
Sharp, Cora F., w/o Henry A. Sharp, 1878-1958
Adams, Rev. John Q., b 1828 Warren, RI, d 1909
Phinney, Mary J., w/o Rev. John Q. Adams, b 1829 Cumberland, RI, d
   1913
Adams, Charles A., 1854-1905
Adams, Anna M., w/o Charles A. Adams, 1854-1913
Adams, Louis E., s/o Charles A. & Anna M. Adams, 1876-1884
Carpenter, Gerald F., 1907-1917
Carpenter, Alice B., 1876-1969
Carpenter, Frank I., 1872-1930
Carpenter, Charles E., 1840-1929
Carpenter, Martha A., w/o Charles E. Carpenter, 1836-1910
Nerney, William, 1851-1938
Wetherell, Emma I., w/o William Nerney, 1852-1929
Carr, Araminta A., 1855-1959
Berthold, Elden G., 1903-1968
Baker, Charles Reed, DMD, b 15 Aug 1919, d 26 Jan 1988
Goddard, Helen Marie, w/o Charles Reed Baker, ...
Blackburn, William A., 1889-1959
Blackburn, Fanny M., w/o William A. Blackburn, 1893-1955
Blackburn, Russell Carlton, 1914-1922
Berthold, Herman L., 1905-1958
Taylor, Thomas, 1872-1952
Taylor, Mabel L., 1885-1972
Cobb, Edwin Everett, 1849-1940
Shepard, Annie Delia, w/o Edwin Everett Cobb, 1851-1932
Cobb, George Lamont, s/o Edwin Everett & Annie Delia Cobb, 1869-1925

Cobb, Frederick Shepard, s/o Edwin Everett & Annie Delia Cobb, 1871-1940
Lincoln, William S., 1826-1884
Bliss, Ann Sophia, w/o William S. Lincoln, 1826-1866
Burt, Caroline E., w/o William S. Lincoln, 1824-1910
Lincoln, Frederick W., 1853-1927
Shaw, Ermina G., w/o Frederick W. Lincoln, 1856-1938
Pratt, Gustavus, 1880-....
Lincoln, Helen L., w/o Gustavus Pratt, 1885-1960
Rich, Samuel W., 1820-1886
Rich, Pamelia C., 1820-1902
Holbrook, Marion R., 1880-1884
Rich, Samuel A., 1846-1911
Cobb, Z. F., 1846-1891
Cobb, Olava S., w/o Z. F. Cobb, 1858-1890
Cobb, Ellis F., s/o Z. F. & Olava S. Cobb, 1884-1900
Edwam, Harold B., 1894-1920
Edwam, Fannie H., w/o Harold B. Edwam, 1882-1961
Williams, Otis, 1827-1906, A member of Co H 7th Mass Vols
Thurber, Francis W., b 15 May 1844, d 2 Aug 1907
Thurber, Sarah E., w/o Francis W. Thurber, b 3 May 1853, d 15 Sept 1892
Thurber, Charles W., 1874-1941
Thurber, Louis M., 1884-1955
Carnes, William L., 1854-1923
Coyle, Margaret, w/o William L. Carnes, 1857-1887
Carnes, Frances A., 1878-1954
Hall, Ephraim R., b 8 Aug 1822, d Dec 1868
Hall, Elizabeth A., w/o Ephraim R. Hall, 1825-1907
Sweeney, George A., 1852-1914
Bowman, Mary E., w/o George A. Sweeney, 1856-1938
Sweeney, George Jr., 1881-1952
Brett, Grace V., w/o George Sweeney Jr., 1880-1914
Bowman, Genevieve, w/o George Sweeney Jr., 1889-1990
Newell, Olney P., b 4 May 1842, d 14 June 1903
Newell, Elizabeth L., w/o Olney P. Newell, b 11 Oct 1842, d 7 March 1929
MacKenzie, Daniel D., 1855-1886
MacKenzie, Sarah E., w/o Daniel D. MacKenzie, 1858-1919
MacKenzie, Edwin C., 1885-1904

Silboug, Jacob, b 16 July 1835, d 9 April 1890
Bancroft, Etta, w/o Jacob Silboug, b 15 Aug 1831, 26 Oct 1921
Silboug, Carrie Etta, b 16 June 1857, d 6 Dec 1937
Broadbent, James, 1865-1937
Broadbent, Elizabeth A., 1872-1942
Broadbent, Hugh, 1895-1943
McIsaac, Veronica, 1897-1926
McIsaac, James A., 1898-1968
Holbrook, Horace R., 1850-1928
Holbrook, Mary P., 1852-1921
Holbrook, Elizabeth, 1877-1964
Smith, Tom, 1896-1973
Holbrook, Minnie, w/o Tom Smith, 1889-1971
Sumner, Alice, w/o George W. Bemis, b 2 Nov 1861, d 17 Oct 1889
Lee, Rhoda Hack, 1789-1885
Lee, George W., 1834-1914
Lee, Harriet E., w/o George W. Lee, 1835-1926
Lee, George E., , s/o George & Harriet Lee, 1859-1928
Lee, Jennie I., 1870-1889
West, Benjamin G., d 14 Dec 1849 aged 27 yrs 2 mos 20 days
West, Henry Rubbele, s/o Benjamin G. & Mary M. West, d 6 Oct 1848
    aged 6 mos
Manchester, Richard O., d 2 Feb 1836 aged 36 yrs 8 mos
Manchester, Hannah, w/o Richard O. Manchester, d 29 March 1875 aged
    74 yrs 11 mos
Gardner, Merton B., 1884-1938
Gardner, Charles M., 1848-1911
West, Mary G., w/o Charles M. Gardner, 1849-1907
Bright, Edwin, b 10 Dec 1845, d 15 July 1910
Bright, Ida C., w/o Edwin T. Bright, b 18 Feb 1853, d 29 Sept 1922
Snell, Charles W., 1828-1904
Snell, Helen M., w/o Charles W. Smith, 1834-1903
Snell, Charles E., s/o Charles W. & Helen M. Snell, 1854-1870
Claflin, Patta, w/o Noah Claflin, d 28 Aug 1796 aged 25 yrs 4 mos 14
    days
Claflin, Noah Jr., s/o Noah & Hannah Claflin, d 11 April 1835
Claflin, Noah, d 11 Aug 1825 aged 91 yrs
Claflin, Keziah, w/o Noah Claflin, d 17 Oct 1788 aged 56 yrs
Claflin, Hannah, d/o Noah & Keziah Claflin, d 1 Oct 1802 aged 39 yrs
Dean, Lawrence E., 1876-1932

Dean, Percy A., 1887-1939
Dean, Lyman W., b 22 Feb 1805, d 7 March 1891
Dean, Maryett I., w/o Lyman W. Dean, b 31 May 1807, d 4 Dec 1892
Capron, Leprelette, b 25 July 1807, d 2 Feb 1883
Pierce, Candace, w/o Leprelette Capron, b 3 July 1813, d 10 Oct 1898
Capron, Henry K., b 26 Feb 1846, d 6 Sept 1890
Capron, Frank H., b 18 Aug 1849, d 10 March 1931
Nunes, Anna D., w/o Frank H. Capron, b 11 Nov 1864, d 22 Oct 1910
Capron, Gracie M., b 31 July 1890, d 19 June 1893
Lee, Eugene B., 1857-1946
Lee, Ella L., w/o Eugene B. Lee, 1862-1925
Lee, William T., 1832-1876
Lee, Patience M., w/o William T. Lee, 1838-1918
Lee, George A., s/o William T. & Patience M. Lee, 1872-1877
Bromeley, Samuel, b 10 Aug 1816, d 13 June 1891
Bromeley, Nancy, w/o Samuel Bromeley, b 26 June 1818, d 22 June 1893
Bromeley, Adelaide N., d/o Samuel & Nancy Bromeley, b 22 Feb 1841, d
    29 June 1842
Dean, Inez E., 1887-1951
Dean, Allen M., 1909-1966
Parmenter, Henry P., b 1 Nov 1856, d 27 March 1943
Chadwick, Viola G., w/o Henry P. Parmenter, b 26 March 1857, d 5 Feb
    1911
Gilligan, John H., 1850-1920
Parmenter, Mary E., w/o John H. Gilligan, 1854-1932
Gardner, Sarah, w/o William D. Gardner, d 25 Dec 1883 aged 60 yrs
Chadwick, Lurad H., b 29 Aug 1835, d 10 Nov 1902, A member of Co H
    40th Reg Mass Vols
Manchester, Henry R., 1853-1897
Morrison, Mary E., w/o Henry R. Manchester, 1865-1953, buried at North
    Purchase Cemetery
Manchester, Lydia I., w/o Henry R. Manchester, d 27 Dec 1882 aged 29
    yrs
Wetherell, Frederick A., 1854-1935
Chadwick, Eudora I., w/o Frederick A. Wetherell, 1859-1913
Wetherell, Mabel E., d/o Frederick & Eudora Wetherell, 1889-1957
Chadwick, Sarah, w/o Lurad H. Chadwick, b 2 March 1838, d 9 May
    1886
Titus, George L., 1842-1907
Titus, Sarah, w/o George L. Titus, 1842-1903

Titus, Grace E., d/o George & Sarah Titus, 1870-1873
Titus, George E., 1880-1972
Titus, Mary S., w/o George E. Titus, 1879-1921
Brown, Susie Titus, 1875-1962
Carpenter, Earle B., 1898-1972
Hall, Irene S., w/o Earle B. Carpenter, 1899-1986
White, William C., 1836-1916
Bishop, Rachel, w/o William C. White, 1839-1915
White, Laura A., 1861-1902
White, F. Howard, 1875-1881
Gardner, Waitee, d 28 April 1901 aged 70 yrs
Gardner, Mary A., w/o Waite Gardner, d 16 Dec 1882 aged 56 yrs
Smith, Stephen T., d 11 March 1904 AE 81 yrs 3 mos 21 days
Smith, Sarah A., w/o Stephen T. Smith, d 3 Feb 1882 AE 61 yrs 6 mos
Babcock, Hartford Sweet, 1821-1898
Barrows, Lydia, w/o Hartford Sweet Babcock, 1820-1885
Babcock, Lydia B., 1857-1914
Babcock, Alice A., 1847-1926
Babcock, Elvira E., 1854-1945
Clemence, Thomas, 1847-1916
Clemence, Emma E., w/o Thomas Clemence, 1853-1920
Babcock, Abbott H., 1849-1924
Fisher, Eva L., w/o Abbott H. Babcock, 1853-1914
Babcock, Cyrus W., 1851-1925
Leethem, Annie V., w/o Cyrus W. Babcock, 1857-1926
Parker, Edward W., b 1 May 1851, d 23 Sept 1913
Fisher, Etta L., w/o Edward W. Parker, b 6 April 1857, d 1 May 1923
Adams, George R., 1840-1926
Fisher, Hattie E., w/o George R. Adams, 1843-1919
Thayer, John J., d 7 May 1909 aged 76 yrs 5 mos 19 days
Thayer, Margery R., w/o John J. Thayer, d 23 Feb 1877 aged 30 yrs 24
    days
Thayer, Mary, w/o John J. Thayer, d 25 July 1881 aged 34 yrs 5 mos 2
    days
Carter, William G., 1858-1931
Carter, Elizabeth M., w/o William G. Carter, 1867-1928
Leonard, Charles I., 1856-1946
Leonard, Caroline M., w/o Charles I. Leonard, 1859-1929
Leonard, Edgar B., 1891-1984
Leonard, Grace, w/o Edgar B. Leonard, 1890-1987

Chase, B. Franklin, b 5 June 1852, d 13 Jan 1885

Pierce, Patience C., w/o W. L. Pierce, b 18 May 1817, d 13 Aug 1897

Chilson, Jonathan D., b 6 Jan 1847, d 20 Dec 1928

Shepard, Jane E., w/o Jonathan D. Chilson, b 6 Oct 1847, d 18 June 1900

Baldwin, Mary, w/o Jonathan D. Chilson, b 25 Jan 1862, d 22 Dec 1938

Chilson, Maude Shepard, d/o Jonathan D. & Mary Chilson, b 7 Jan 1884, d 24 July 1885

Barrows, Mary P., w/o Wheaton Barrows, 1818-1892

Metcalf, Ella M., 1847-1907

Barrows, Wheaton, d 4 Nov 1874 aged 57 yrs 5 mos 14 days

Blackinton, Charles A., 1828-1916

Blackinton, Harriet A., 1829-1906

Blackinton, Josiah A., 1861-1864

Blackinton, Caroline E., 1863-1864

Blackinton, Frank F., 1858-1936

Davidson, Emma B., 1865-1951

Davidson, Emma N., 1889-1932

Chatterton, Alfred, 1885-1963

Rushlow, Elizabeth M., w/o Alfred Chatterton, 1887-1974

Jones, Thelma E., d/o Alfred & Elizabeth Chatterton, 1911-1964

Gilmore, George R., 1816-1882

Barrows, Emeline, w/o George R. Gilmore, 1817-1892

Gilmore, William H., 1850-1912

Lane, Anna W., w/o William H. Gilmore, 1857-1917

Chatterton, Charles R., 1859-1934

Chatterton, Margaret J., w/o Charles R. Chatterton, 1858-1940

Chatterton, Gertrude Emma, d/o Charles R. & Margaret J. Chatterton, 1883-1904

Parmenter, Captain Charles, 1756-1850

Rounds, Elizabeth, w/o Capt. Charles Parmenter, 1758-1854

Ross, Edgar S., 1858-1894

Watts, Abby, 1804-1882

Parmenter, Caleb E., 1838-1929

Watts, Abby J., w/o Caleb E. Parmenter, 1836-1890

Parmenter, Esther, d/o Caleb E. & Abby J., Parmenter, 1863-1892

Webber, Cyrus, 1806-1878

Fuller, Joanna R., w/o Cyrus Webber, 1821-1899

Fuller, Susan E., sister of Joanna R. Fuller, 1819-1904

Nye, Fred Cudworth, b 27 Feb 1859, d 27 Nov 1920

Carter, Niles Leach, b 12 July 1865 South Hope, Maine, d 29 Aug 1931

Carter, Marion Williams Pierce, b 24 May 1865, d 9 Sept 1946

Morse, Donald C., b 30 March 1892, d 27 March 1965

Benton, Gladys F., w/o Donald C. Morse, b 22 Oct 1896, d 14 Sept 1987

Perry, Herbert L., 1866-1953

Perry, Emma S., w/o Herbert L. Perry, 1865-1945

Perry, Clara Mildred, d/o Herbert & Emma Perry, 1891-....

Perry, Laura Isabel, d/o Herbert & Emma Perry, 1898-1920

Perry, Herbert Lincoln Jr., s/o Herbert & Emma Perry, 1903-1958

Perry, Nahum, 1840-1915

Perry, Clara J., w/o Nahum Perry, 1837-1908

Watkins, Albion H., b 20 June 1846, d 17 April 1913

Watkins, Mary R., w/o Albion Watkins, b 5 Dec 1842, d 10 Feb 1913

Capron, Sumner E., d 10 Jan 1890 aged 83 yrs 8 mos

Capron, Sabra A., w/o Sumner E. Capron, d 29 Jan 1868 aged 61 yrs 2 mos

Capron, Juline, d/o Sumner E. & Sabra A. Capron, d 1 Sept 1836 aged 6 mos 2 days

Capron, Anna Judson, d/o Sumner E. & Sabra A. Capron, d 13 Jan 1841 aged 1 yrs 5 mos

Everett, Chester S., 1881-1945

Bearse, William F., 1877-1960

Everett, Florence A., w/o William F. Bearse, 1878-1962

Harris, Ralph, b 5 Jan 1827, d 25 Jan 1879

Harris, Elizabeth, w/o Ralph Harris, b 5 Jan 1830, d 24 March 1888

Clifford, James W., 1851-1895

Clifford, Annie E., w/o James W. Clifford, 1857-1921

Mellor, George, 1831-1912

Harris, Emma, w/o George Mellor, 1836-1912

Belcher, Charles W., 1830-1898

Belcher, Cynthia C., w/o Charles W. Belcher, 1830-1913

Belcher, Mary A., d/o Charles & Cynthia Belcher, 1854-1958

Belcher, Cora E., d/o Charles & Cynthia Belcher, 1858-1922

Belcher, Charles W., s/o Charles & Cynthia Belcher, 1861-1937

Belcher, Rose Avery, d/o Charles & Cynthia Belcher, 1890-1916

Pearce, Gilbert D., b 16 Dec 1809, d 13 April 1882

Pearce, Eliza, w/o Gilbert D. Pearce, d 14 Aug 1877 aged 53 yrs

Pearce, Fannie Blanding, d/o Gilbert D. & Eliza Pearce, d 30 May 1879 aged 19 yrs

Pearce, Sarah Frances, d/o Gilbert & Eliza Pearce, d 14 July 1877 aged 29 yrs

Perry, Orim F., d 16 Jan 1869 aged 38 yrs 8 mos
Perry, Adeline M., w/o Orim Perry, d 23 April 1912 aged 79 yrs
Capron, Daniel H., d 28 Aug 1878 aged 50 yrs 8 mos
Capron, Lydia J., w/o Daniel H. Capron, d 9 Dec 1926 aged 92 yrs 9 mos
Athorne, Madeline W., 1889-1970
Woodley, Edward W., d 18 Dec 1925 aged 72 yrs 5 mos
Capron, Marion, w/o Edward W. Woodley, b 26 Oct 1867, d 5 Jan 1936
Price, Amy A., d 19 June 1866 aged 21 yrs 6 mos
LeBaron, Frederick L., d 2 April 1912
LeBaron, Adelaide J., w/o Frederick LeBaron, d 21 Aug 1924
Colburn, Edson M., 1830-1867
Engley, Arvilla A., w/o Edson M. Colburn, 1831-....
Engley, John, 1789-1857
Cutting, Lucy, w/o John Engley, 1790-1858
Engley, Abbie, d/o John & Lucy Engley, 1819-1821
Blackinton, Davis A., 1830-...
Engley, Lemire, w/o Davis A. Blackinton, 1826-1916
Blackinton, Lora Etta, d/o Davis & Lemira Blackinton, 1854-1959
Hoyle, William, 1890-1982, Master Silver Smith
Angevine, Alice M., w/o William Hoyle, 1890-1972
McCarthney, Samuel, 1860-1907
McCarthney, Ella E., w/o Samuel McCarthney, 1861-1916
McCarthney, Alice M., 1885-1945
McCarthney, Bertram F., 1884-1950
Walton, Charles A., 1869-1906
Purdy, Ellen M., w/o Charles A. Walton, 1872-1947
Durfee, Morris, 1813-1905
Durfee, Ariadna, w/o Morris Durfee, 1828-1886
Durfee, Lula, d/o Morris & Ariadna Durfee, 1851-1924
Marble, Walter E., 1858-1941
Marble, Ariadna D., w/o Walter E. Marble, 1864-1955
Marble, Gertrude M., 1887-1979
Japson, Nels, 1872-1912
Pearson, Thilda, w/o Nels Japson, 1870-1954
Sweeney, William Ellis, 1883-1957
Sweeney, Leonilda Orup, 1884-1973
Scott, Grace E., 1881-1884
Linnell, Henry B., d 30 July 1922
Linnell, Fannie I., w/o Henry B. Linnell, d 2 May 1910
Linnell, Harry A., 1872-1927

Barrett, Eli, 1874-1905

Metters, Annie, w/o Eli Barrett, 1879-1955

Burnham, Algie G., 1883-1943

Barrett, Myrtle, 1904-1905

Simmons, Dorothy Burnham, 1912-1933

Barrett, Beverly, 1927-1928

Edwards, Peter, 1838-1896

Martin, Ann, w/o Peter Edwards, 1835-1915

Edwards, John W., 1858-1918

Robinson, Mary A., w/o John W. Edwards, 1856-1917

Edwards, Joseph, s/o John & Mary Edwards, 1882-1901

Edwards, Mary, d/o John & Mary Edwards, 1891-1891

Jewett, James N., b 11 Nov 1941, d 31 Oct 1981

Engley, Orlando S., 1828-1907

Allen, Abbie J., w/o Orlando Engley, 1844-1908

Engley, Addie F., d/o Orlando & Abbie Engley, 1865-1870

Engley, Charles A., s/o Orlando & Abbie Engley, 1867-1887

Capron, Dennis, d 30 Dec 1884 aged 82 yrs 2 mos 7 days

Capron, Louisa C., w/o Dennis Capron, d 18 March 1879 aged 71 yrs 10
  mos

Kelley, George J., 1872-1951

Blake, Musa, w/o George J. Kelley, 1873-1903

Kelley, Walter L. Jr., 1876-1951

Capron, Harford A., b 10 Oct 1828, d 30 March 1908

Capron, Rhoda P., w/o Harford A. Capron, b 13 May 1829, d 1 Feb 1912

Carpenter, Shepard W., b 23 Jan 1833, d 18 May 1898

Carpenter, Eliza J., w/o Shepard W. Carpenter, b 10 Jan 1831, d 5 Feb
  1923

Carpenter, Daniel E., s/o Shepard & Eliza J. Carpenter, 1862-1890

Capron, Addison, b 1 Jan 1808, d 8 May 1871

Worsly, Mary A., w/o Addison Capron, b 29 June 1814, d 25 Feb 1900

Crandall, George N., b 28 Oct 1819, d 17 Aug 1902

Crandall, Maria S., w/o George N. Crandall, d 14 Jan 1856 aged 32 yrs

Crandall, Frances A., w/o George N. Crandall, b 22 June 1833, d 26 May
  1925

Capron, Joseph W., b 24 Sept 1802, d 13 March 1895

Capron, Adeline B., w/o Joseph W. Capron, b 3 Jan 1807, d 8 March
  1872

Capron, Cynthia B., w/o Joseph W. Cparon, 1831-1924

Nye, Annette C., b 21 June 1861, d 1 March 1885

Nye, Thomas R., b 6 May 1858, d 2 Jan 1888
Nye, Herbert S., b 16 March 1867, d 27 April 1888
Nye, Russell B., b 8 March 1830, d 12 Oct 1893
Cudworth, Sarah N., w/o Russell B. Nye, b 9 Nov 1829, d 13 April 1909
Nye, Evelina, b 20 March 1828, d 15 Dec 1886
Wilmarth, D. Edwin, d 14 May 1894 aged 31 yrs
Wilmarth, Elizabeth J., d 18 Oct 1927 aged 69 yrs
Wilmarth, Henry P., d 14 May 1944 aged 74 yrs
Nye, Thomas S., 1826-1908
Wales, Louisa T., 1838-1871
Nye, Mary Chloe, 1870-1871
Wilmarth, William D., d 6 March 1882 aged 44 yrs
Mann, Susan Josephine, w/o William D. Wilmarth, d 15 Oct 1893 aged
    56 yr
Bates, Charles R., 1856-1916
Bates, Annie C., w/o Charles R. Bates, 1857-1932
Bates, Howard T., 1878-1941
Bates, Joseph M., 1880-1954
Bates, Kate E., w/o Joseph M. Bates, 1886-1968
Bates, Joseph M., 1833-1906
Bates, Sarah L., w/o Joseph M. Bates, 1835-1922
Bates, Mary L., 1861-1905
Bates, Frank M., 1868-1916
Engley, Willard A., 1856-1921
Webber, Bessie H., w/o Willard A. Engley, 1864-1943
Theobald, Norman C., 1909-1970
Theobald, Florence B., 1873-1965
Theobald, Jean C., 1873-1952
Sanford, Edward, MD, b 10 March 1825, d 5 Feb 1913
Moores, Charles A., MD, 1847-1935
Capron, Edith, w/o Dr. Charles A. Moores, 1858-1935
Mason, Frederick G., 1858-1935
Carpenter, Mabel W., w/o Frederick G. Mason, 1858-1949
Carpenter, Frank W., 1866-1938
Carpenter, Gertrude W., w/o Frank W. Carpenter, 1872-1928
Carpenter, Alberta R., w/o Frank W. Carpenter, 1874-1971
Williams, Israel N., d 27 Dec 1878 aged 71 yrs 7 mos
Williams, Nancy, w/o Israel N. Williams, d 20 April 1891 aged 77 yrs 4
    mos 7 days
Draper, Charles T., 1845-1918

Staples, Frances M., w/o Charles T. Draper, 1846-1932
Draper, Rory E., 1873-1967
Hawes, Elsie J., w/o Rory E. Draper, 1875-1946
Draper, Carroll W., 1878-1966
Lajoie, Marie, w/o Carroll W. Draper, 1885-1954
Draper, Harold, 1904-1994
Belot, Barbara H., w/o Harold Draper, 1917-1985
Carpenter, Arthur B., b 14 Nov 1839, d 17 May 1912
Carpenter, Harriet A., w/o Arthur B. Carpenter, b 8 April 1846, d 20 Sept 1914
Carpenter, Zenas B., d 16 Jan 1878 aged 75 yrs
Carpenter, Lucinda I., w/o Zenas B. Carpenter, 1805-1895
Luther, Alvah C., 1855-1931
Campbell, Alice, w/o Alvah C. Luther, 1857-1951
Luther, John Dalziel, 1884-1939
Tiffany, Joseph Osmond, d 27 Dec 1902 aged 67 yrs 11 mos
French, Caroline, w/o Joseph Osmond Tiffany, d 28 June 1925 aged 94 yrs 11 mos
Tiffany, Joseph A., d 27 Dec 1868 aged 66 yrs 3 mos 1 days
Tiffany, Laura B., b 22 Aug 1846, d 15 April 1899
Tiffany, William H., b 17 May 1838, d 10 June 1904
Carpenter, Lydia, w/o William H. Tiffany, b 2 Feb 1834, d 25 July 1916
Luther, Nathan C., d 9 Jan 1890 aged 71 yrs
Luther, Clarissa E., w/o Nathan C. Luther, d 10 March 1909 aged 86 yrs
Luther, Emma E., d/o Nathan & Clarissa Luther, d 16 Aug 1935 aged 88 yrs
Mason, Frederick, 1857-1944
Blanchard, Josephine, w/o Frederick Mason, 1863-1884
Stanley, Clara A., w/o Frederick Mason, 1861-1943
Stanley, Lyman M., 1832-1906
Staples, Mary A., w/o Lymn M. Stanley, 1835-1918
Spear, William A., d 21 Feb 1871 aged 37 yrs
Spear, Arthur B., d 2 April 1865 aged 30 yrs
Spear, Charlotte C., 1834-1915
Bailey, Enoch, d 11 Aug 1861 aged 72 yrs
Bailey, Charlotte C., w/o Enoch Bailey, d 6 May 1885 aged 85 yrs
Parmenter, Horatio D., 1828-1912
Parmenter, Adeline L., w/o Horatio Parmenter, b 30 Oct 1829, d 20 Jan 1898
Carpenter, Philip M., 1845-1929

Carpenter, Harriet E., w/o Philip M. Carpenter, d 6 May 1919
Carpenter, Eben, s/o Philip & Harriet Carpenter, d 10 Dec 1878 aged 6 yrs
Bigelow, Gertrude L., d/o Philip & Harriet Carpenter, 1870-1939
Carpenter, Eben, d 25 July 1882 aged 78 yrs
Carpenter, Louisa W., w/o Eben Carpenter, d 20 Dec 1914 aged 108 yrs
Carpenter, Hannah F., d/o Eben & Louisa W. Carpenter, d 30 Aug 1889 aged 48 yrs
Carpenter, Isabella W., d/o Eben & Louisa W. Carpenter, d 15 March 1913 aged 71 yrs
Guyot, Arthur F., b 30 April 1878, d 2 Feb 1936
Guyot, Rhoda May, b 9 Aug 1882, d 7 Aug 1950
Guyot, Gladys Ruth, b 16 July 1910, d 18 Aug 1925
Stetson, Fred J., 1849-1919
Steson, Emily S., w/o Fred J. Stetson, 1851-1929
Bacon, Ebenezer, 1815-1900
Bacon, Lucretia M., w/o Ebenezer Bacon, 1820-1912
Bacon, Idlyne L., 1853-1902
Bacon, George M., 1843-1917
Bodman, Phyliss, 1909-1909
Bodman, Harriet J., 1883-1945
Bodman, Bertha L., 1892-1952
Bodman, Ivan F., 1891-1962
Bodman, Ralph H., 1883-1969
Bodman, Henry A., 1831-1893
Bodman, Sarah M., w/o Henry A. Bodman, 1833-1891
Cash, George Stewart, 1870-1980
Cash, Odessa D., w/o George Stewart Cash, 1870-1926
Cash, Cyril G., 1893-1946
Guild, Arthur A., 1868-1928
deCastro, Lillian, w/o Arthur A. Guild, 1863-1936
Briggs, John Shaw, 1851-1942
Perry, Alice Emma, w/o John Shaw Briggs, 1851-1906
Ballou, Albert E. M., 1869-1911
Ballou, Carrie E., w/o Albert E. M. Ballou, 1871-1933
McLane, Eliza A., 1831-1916
McLane, James H., 1864-1938
Thurber, Arthur S., 1862-1938
Briggs, Lydia R., w/o Arthur S. Thurber, 1860-1920
Thurber, Edwin A., 1884-1939

Cook, John W., 1854-1926
Cook, Sarah J., 1855-1925
Hyde, Karl H., 1868-1952
Hyde, Amy E., w/o Karl H. Hyde, 1872-1940
Heather, Henry Gillen, 1851-1922
Heather, Mary A., w/o Henry Gillen Heather, 1856-1941
Heather, George Alfred, s/o Henry G. & Mary A. Heather, 1880-1880
Heather, Everett Lester, s/o Henry G. & Mary A. Heather, 1882-1916
Heather, William Osborn, s/o Henry G. & Mary A. Heather, 1881-1919
Heather, Clarence, s/o Henry G. & Mary A. Heather, 1889-1932
Clark, George W., d 16 Aug 1864 Deep Run, Virginia, A member of Co
    H 24th Reg Mass Vols Inf
Clark, Eliza Ann, w/o George W. Clark, 1841-1901
Vetter, Julia K., 1859-1912
Vetter, Louis J., 1888-1963
Holmes, Mary D., w/o Louis J. Vetter, 1891-1928
Holbrook, Harry R., 1874-1958
Marrs, Lida, w/o Harry R. Holbrook, 1874-1966
Cody, Marion H., d/o Harry & Lida Holbrook, 1899-1952
Colby, Herbert O., 1872-1954
Underwood, Maud A., w/o Herbert O. Colby, 1873-1953
Linkletter, George Palmer, 1860-1936
Hall, Harriet Rollin, w/o George Palmer Linkletter, 1871-1951
Sears, Albert E., 1885-1936
Tooker, Caroline F., w/o Albert E. Sears, 1887-1947
Fargo, Edwin A., 1867-1934
Tooker, Sarah Olive, w/o Edwin A. Fargo, 1875-1952
Taylor, George L., b 20 Oct 1863, d 27 Nov 1938
Moore, Mertie A., w/o George L. Taylor, b 25 Sept 1864, d 5 June 1919
Currie, Malcolm, 1858-1919
Currie, Lydia, w/o Malcoln Currie, 1856-1950
Osgood, George Endicott, 1854-1930
Osgood, Helen Frances, w/o George Endicott Osgood, 1851-1919
Linkletter, Sylvester, 1905-1976
Billington, Amy, w/o Sylvester Linkletter, 1901-1979
Smith, Ezra Sheldon, 1868-1934
Sweet, Dorothy, w/o Ezra Sheldon Smith, 1870-1947
Smith, Ezra Sheldon Jr., 1905-1967
Fernandez, Virginia R., w/o Ezra Sheldon Smith Jr., 1908-1970
Billington, Charles, d 1935

Billington, Eliza, w/o Charles Billington, d 1923
Miller, Annie M., 1861-1921
Miller, Mary L., 1883-1928
Gladden, Carrie W., 1876-1952
Briggs, Walter Emerson, DMD, b 16 Feb 1883, d 10 Feb 1959
Anderson, Edna Olivia, w/o Walter Emerson Briggs, DMD, b 31 Dec
    1885, d 27 Nov 1987
Briggs, Seth Richardson, 1847-1934
Shepard, Martha A. K., w/o Seth Richardson Briggs, 1857-1928
Johnston, Tom, b 13 Sept 1872, d 26 March 1947
McKim, Lena E., w/o Tom Johnston, b 22 Dec 1881, d 24 Nov 1965
Fleet, Elizabeth H., 1841-1918
Douglass, J. Edward, 1875-1949
Fleet, Lillian R., w/o J. Edward Douglass, 1876-1955
Macomber, Albert, 1860-1931
Macomber, Ada M., w/o Albert Macomber, 1862-1939
Macomber, Alice J., 1888-1973
Stewart, Malcolm, 1863-1939
Bears, Louisa, w/o Malcolm Stewart, 1874-1931
Scott, Charles M., 1899-1931
Scott, Alice A., w/o Charles Scott, 1900-1982
Schambach, Velma I., d/o Charles & Alice A. Scott, 1926-1989
Grant, Campbell C., 1861-1925
Fleming, Flora, w/o Campbell C. Grant, 1863-1940
Nixon, Charles, 1864-1934
Nixon, Emma, w/o Charles Nixon, 1863-1928
Nixon, William P., 1882-1968
Packer, Harriet E., w/o Willia, P. Nixon, 1889-1972
Padelford, Arthur W., 1875-1927
Padelford, S. Jennie, w/o Arthur W. Padelford, 1874-1961
Kiff, Leroy, 1894-1965
Kiff, Lillian P., w/o Leroy Kiff, 1897-1988
MacIntosh, Frederick W., 1881-1963
Simms, Margaret A., w/o Frederick W. MacIntoah, 1879-1942
Bath, William H., 1889-1919
Mowry, Mary, w/o William H. Bath, 1884-1917
Mowry, Lester M., 1882-1955
Wheeler, Lillian A., w/o Lester M. Mowry, 1895-1934
Mowry, Joseph D., Jr., 1918-1983
Gustafson, Marica F., w/o Joseph D. Mowry Jr.,......

Wilmarth, Frederic C., 1871-1935
Chase, Mabel J., w/o Frederic C. Wilmarth, 1875-1956
Wilmarth, Louis R., 1899-1962
Rogers, Lois E., w/o Louis R. Wilmarth, 1898-1990
Wilmarth, Mildred E., 1901-1995
Keeler, Charles Pierson, b 29 Aug 1860, d 10 March 1921
Bullock, Ada Bullock, w/o Charles Pierson Keeler, b 20 Jan 1862, d 10
    Oct 1956
Bliss, Hazel L., w/o Harry Steel, 1901-1923
Bliss, Francis E. Sr., 1852-1921
Barber, Mary E., w/o Frances E. Bliss Sr., 1858-1914
Bliss, Francis E. Jr., 1876-1946
Debow, Gertrude B., w/o Francis E. Bliss Jr., 1875-1912
Wilmarth, Daniel B., 1832-1920
Wilmarth, Anna E., w/o Daniel B. Wilmarth, 1843-1922
Wilmarth, Fred B., s/o Daniel B. & Anna E. Wilmarth, 1861-1926
Coles, William E., 1867-1956
Smith, Mary F., w/o William E. Coles, 1865-1930
Coles, Chester E., 1889-1974
McKim, Mabel E., w/o Chester E. Coles, 1891-1974
Mathewson, Charles W., 1856-1935
James, Lillian B., w/o Charles W. Mathewson, 1860-1912
Clulee, Stephen J., 1859-1929
Bates, Addie L., w/o Stephen J. Clulee, 1860-1932
Clulee Ernest R., 1879-1921
Clulee, Roland C., 1881-1881
Benson, Muriel Read, d/o Rufus & Rachel Read, b 24 Aug 1903, d 9 Dec
    1978
Read, Rufus Curtis, b 22 March 1874, d 9 Feb 1961
Wilmarth, Rachel, w/o Rufus Curtis Read, b 26 Jan 1879, d 20 Jan 1912
Wilmarth, Edith M., w/o Rufus Curtis Read, b 10 Nov 1890, d 29 Jan
    1948
Fisher, John M., 1850-1920
Horton, Hannah S., w/o John M. Fisher, 1842-1936
Leonard, William, 1854-1926
Bullock, Sarah, w/o William Leonard, 1849-1920
Bullock, Ida A., 1860-1942
Bullock, William G., b 17 April 1820, d 3 Nov 1894
Parmenter, Marie, w/o William G. Bullock, b 14 July 1820, d 29 Jan 1900
Smith, Daniel H., 1835-1913

Smith, Abbie J., w/o Daniel H. Smith, 1834-1913

Palmer, Alexander, b 2 June 1851, d 16 April 1927

Palmer, Lillas M., w/o Alexander Palmer, b 7 Aug 1856, d 16 Jan 1927

Palmer, Ella M., d/o Alexander & Lillas M. Palmer, b 13 March 1877, d 10 May 1879

Mattson, Sandra E. W., b 25 Oct 1874, d 10 Feb 1913

Purdy, John H., 13 April 1833, d 11 June 1915

Purdy, Ann, w/o John H. Purdy, b 6 March 1831, d 11 April 1915

Patterson, Charles Perry, b 24 Oct 1858, d 25 June 1913

Marshall, Mary A., w/o Charles Perry Patterson, b 6 May 1870, d 10 Oct 1945

Patterson, Marshall D., b 13 July 1890, d 20 Jan 1919

Patterson, Charles A., b 18 May 1893, d 2 June 1989

Jillson, Mildred O., w/o Charles A. Patterson, b 2 July, d 14 Sept 1968

Perry, Jabez, 1846-1937

Holt, Mary, w/o Jabez Perry, 1854-1915

Tobett, John L., 1841-1916, A member of Co H 7th Mass Vol Inf

Tobett, Martha, w/o John L. Tobett, 1841-1927

Crosby, Alfred D., 1871-1937

Tobett, Marion I., w/o Alfred D. Crosby, 1870-1932

Cochrane, Samuel Henry, 1866-1937

Allen, Ada Galleson, w/o Samuel Henry Cochrane, 1862-1920

Smith, Willim D., 1854-1917

Cameron, Belle C., w/o William D. Smith, 1856-1935

MacDonald, Laura C., 1870-1928

Packard, Hiram R., 1855-1928

Rowe, Mary E., w/o Hiram R. Packard, 1862-1927

Packard, Hiram R. Jr., 1893-....

Peterson, Gladys M., w/o Hiram R. Packard Jr., 1895-1925

Cooper, Herbert A., 1897-1958

Cooper, Earl P., 1899-1984

Umer, Ruth J., w/o Earl P. Cooper, 1899-1990

Banks, S. Helen, w/o Samuel L. Hale, 1846-1920

Hale, Sarah E., w/o L. H. Rounseville, 1880-....

Aubrey, George R., 1865-1928

Aubrey, Margaret J., w/o George R. Aubrey, 1868-1933

Crosby, Arthur Nelson, 1887-1919, A member of Co A 36th M. G. Batt

Whitmarsh, Louis W., 1864-1914

Bliss, Isabel C., w/o Louis W. Whitmarsh, 1866-1933

Sweet, George Orsen, b 22 March 1878, d 24 Feb 1914

Kingston, Annie M., w/o George Orsen Sweet, b 26 Sept 1879, d 1 March 1926

Call, Wallace W., 1850-1912

Stackpole, Ida L., w/o Wallace W. Call, 1855-1917

Hancock, Annie C., 1834-1912

Hulbowan, Mary H., 1854-1917

Gingras, Edmond H., 1884-1948

Gray, Lula A., w/o Edmond H. Gingras, 1887-1967

O'Brien, Robert D., b 1 June 1838, d 11 Nov 1906

Canfield, Augusta, w/o Robert D. O'Brien, b 6 March 1838, d 12 July 1923

Fergueson, Elizabeth G., 1862-1937

Guild, Hattie E., 1872-1960

Amesbury, Charles H., 1867-1957

Amesbury, Vianna A., w/o Charles H. Amesbury, 1872-1958

Amesbury, Samuel J., b 6 July 1831, d 1 Jan 1904

Amesbury, Ann F., w/o Samuel J. Amesbury, b 15 Aug 1835, d 7 Feb 1915

Amesbury, Samuel E., 1860-1938

Amesbury, Ellen C., w/o Samuel E. Amesbury, 1868-1950

Amesbury, Ruth C., b 23 Nov 1904, d 28 Jan 1914

Gibb, George Sweet, b 16 Sept 1916, d 19 April 1989

Ballou, Ruth W., w/o George Sweet Gibb, b 8 June 1918, d 4 Feb 1949

Nolan, Elizabeth R., b 7 April 1921, d 30 May 1976

Holton, Hilma B., b 27 March 1918, d....

Chapman, Martin L., 1854-1935

Chapman, Hortense C., w/o Martin L. Chapman, 1858-1936

Chapman, William, s/o Martin & Hortense C., 1885-1904

Sweeney, Lucy S., 1889-1985

Sweeney, Edward A., b 15 June 1853, d 25 Feb 1922

Ellis, Hannah, w/o Edward A. Sweeney, b 25 Jan 1851, d 6 Feb 1904

Hawkins, Orlando W., 1859-1929

Kelley, Minnie, w/o Orlando W. Hawkins, 1856-1909

Hawkins, Sarah Selina, d/o Orlando & Minnie Hawkins, 1887-1887

Hawkins, Robert Earl, s/o Orlando & Minnie Hawkins, 1885-1904

Hawkins, Bertha May, d/o Orlando & Minnie Hawkins, 1888-1981

Mason, George A., b 12 Feb 1834, d 7 March 1931

Cushman, Mary A., w/o George A. Mason, b 31 July 1836, d 27 Aug 1913

Mason, William H., b 18 Jan 1860, d 17 Aug 1946

Rollen, John J., 1844-1915

Rollen, Sarah M., w/o John J. Rollen, 1862-1948

Eggleston, Oscar Hale, b 9 Oct 1877, d 19 Sept 1966

Sweet, Ada, w/o Oscar Hale Eggleston, b 23 March 1874, d 17 Feb 1955

Sweet, Benjamin Franklin, b 23 July 1840, d 25 Dec 1909

Dow, Mary Allen, w/o Benjamin Franklin Sweet, b 15 Aug 1839, d 1 Feb 1916

Simmons Family.....

Dean, Albert O., 1835-1882. A member of Co H 24th Reg Mass Vols

Daggett, Sarah, w/o Albert O. Dean, 1834-1907

Thurber, William N., b 25 Dec 1806, d 22 June 1884

Thurber, Mary, w/o William N. Thurber, b 13 Oct 1807, d 4 March 1885

Bliss, Florella, w/o Draper Parmenter, b 8 Oct 1805, d 28 Dec 1875

Lincoln, Henry O., b 20 Aug 1839, d 23 May 1900

White, Walter E., b 3 Jan 1849, d 18 Aug 1893

Hoit, Ellen E., w/o Walter E. White, b 8 Jan 1857, d 24 April 1942

Mathewson, John, 1822-1894

Mathewson, Eunice S., w/o John Mathewson, 1827-1894

Wilbur, Caroline M., 1832-1917

White, Frank E., 1878-1945

Newell, Florence A., w/o Frank E. White, 1880-1967

White, Howard E., s/o Frank & Florence White, 1904-1959

Claflin, Albert F., 1839-1924

Hardon, Anna F., w/o Albert F. Claflin, 1846-1926

Fogg, Reginald Dean, 1881-1906

Goff, Gilbert A., 1839-1909

Goff, Sarah M., w/o Gilbert A. Goff, 1842-1873

Ballou, Halsey, b 10 May 1826, d 26 May 1894

Ballou, Ardelia M., w/o Halsey Ballou, d 2 April 1888 aged 57 yrs

Drake, Hattie A., w/o Howard Drake, d 14 March 1895 aged 64 yrs

Drake, David, d 25 March 1862 aged 75 yrs

Drake, Susan, w/o David Drake, d Sept 1824 aged 29 yrs

Drake, Howard, 1824-1922

Drake, Augusta E., w/o Howard Drake, d 2 March 1881 aged 52 yrs

Brigg, Edward E., 1839-1926

Brigg, Adeline M.,w/o Edward E. Brigg, 1854-1928

Brigg, Charles E., s/o Edward E. & Adeline M. Brigg, d 30 April 1891 aged 22 yrs

Brown, William, 1856-1931

Halliday, Ella, w/o William Brown, 1859-1924

Taylor, George A., b 4 May 1846, d 1 May 1918
Weatherhead, Alice G., w/o George A. Taylor, b 5 Feb 1848, d 4 April
    1912
Taylor, Forrest C., 1880-1969
Taylor, Ethel E., 1877-1928
Taylor, Elenor E., 1897-1941
Ryder, Capt. Josiah F., 1836-1920
Prence, Chloe A., w/o Capt. Josiah F. Ryder, 1844-1919
Smith, Aaron Thomas, 1860-1917
White, Jarvis E., 1882-1953
White, Nettie, w/o Jarvis E. White, 1886-1947
Kent, Harry P., 1859-1929
Barney, Etta F., w/o Herry P. Kent, 1863-1951
Kent, Ralph P. MD, 1880-1943
Kent, Eva L., w/o Dr. Ralph P. Kent, 1882-1967
Kent, Earl B., 1888-1926
Kent, Ralph Jr., 1912-1956
Kingman, Fred F., 1867-1930
Kingman, Ella M., 1867-1938
Read, Deacon Noah, d 2 Dec 1778 AE 60 yrs
des Jardins, Charles B., 1831-1912, 1st Lieutenant Co I 7th Mass Regt
Capron, Mary E., w/o Charles B. desJardins, 1847-1887
Shaw, Joseph B., b 7 June 1859, d 8 Feb 1913
Crawford, Margaret, w/o Joseph B. Shaw, b 7 Aug 1866, d 14 March
    1909
Crawford, M. Ida, w/o John E. Conway, 1875-1900
Wilkinson, Edgar A., 1862-1916
Roberts, William T., 1863-1950
Roberts, Hattie A., w/o William T. Roberts, 1873-1967
Inman, Rory Winfield, b 25 June 1886, d 5 Feb 1964
Humes, Marybelle W., w/o Rory Winfield Inman, b 30 Sept 1891, d 29
    July 1974
Holmes, George T., b 6 Feb 1833, d 17 Oct 1909
Leach, Emily, w/o George T. Holmes, b 6 May 1838, d 10 June 1982
White, Jason, d 11 Oct 1826 AE 33 yrs
White, Lucy H., w/o Jason White, d 25 June 1829
Lee, James, d 5 May 1863 aged 78 yrs
Walton, Amos, d 13 Feb 1851 aged 66 yrs
Walton, Polly, w/o Amos Walton, d 21 March 1852 aged 54 yrs

Walton, Charles Edwards, s/o Amos & Polly Walton, d 23 Nov 1832 aged 8 mos 23 days

Walton, Susan Maria, w/o Amos Walton, d 11 Dec 1862 aged 32 yrs

Brown, Andrew, d 3 Sept 1814 AE 69 yrs

Brown, Sarah, w/o Andrew Brown, d 28 Aug 1826 AE 81 yrs

Walton, Deacon Amos, d 6 Feb 1811 AE 63 yrs

Walton, Jerusha, w/o Deacon Amos Walton, d 23 July 1835 AE 84 yrs

Walton, Jerusha, d/o Deacon Amos & Jerusha Walton, d 22 April 1842 aged 64 yrs

Richardson, Enos, 1797-1873

Holley, Richmond, b 1 Aug 1846, d 3 Dec 1910

Holley, Harriet C., w/o Richmond Holley, b 26 Sept 1839, d 14 July 1913

Holley, Alonzo I., s/o Richmond & Harriet Holley, b 17 May 1868, d 16 Sept 1868

Holley, Albert, s/o Richmond & Harriet Holley, b 27 May 1877, d 15 Aug 1877

Holley, Harry, s/o Richmond & Harriet Holley, b 7 Dec 1875, d 25 Jan 1915

Richardson, Daniel, d 11 March 1857 aged 92 yrs

Rochardson, Chloe, w/o Daniel Richardson, d 24 March 1816 AE 57 yrs

Richardson, Lydia, w/o Daniel Richardson, d 21 Nov 1835 AE 71 yrs

Richardson, Lt. Daniel, d 24 Dec 1817 AE 75 yrs

Richardson, Sarah, w/o Lt. Daniel Richardson, d 15 June 1820 AE 74 yrs

Tyler, Ebenezer Esq., s/o John & Anna Tyler, & Grandson of Ebenezer & Catherine Tyler, d 15 Oct 1827 Pawtucket, RI AE 67 yrs

Dean, Catherine, w/o Ebenezer Tyler Esq., & d/o Deacon Daniel Dean, d 5 March 1834 aged 64 yrs

Sweet, John, d 26 Sept 1754 AE 59 yrs

Ide, Jemima, w/o Josiah Ide & formerly w/o John Sweet, d 28 Oct 1813 AE 86 yrs

Sweet, John, d 7 April 1762 AE 38 yrs

Sweet, Laurette, d/o Henry & Lucinda Sweet, b 21 May 1790, d 22 June 1869

Sweet, Henry, d 21 Feb 1828 AE 67 yrs

Greene, Nabbi, w/o Henry Sweet & d/o Rev. Roland Greene, d 11 June 1813 AE 67 yrs

Hall, David C., d 1917

Richardson, Henry W., 1859-1940

Sayles, Lucy, w/o Henry W. Richardson, 1857-1922

Richardson, Henry, 1826-1894

Westcott, Anna S., w/o Henry Richardson, 1830-1878
Richardson, Everett S., 1833-1897
Richardson, Sarah, w/o Everett S. Richardson, 1822-1881
Parmenter, Draper, b 26 Dec 1806, d 6 Oct 1886
Parmenter, Frederick A., 1868-1939
Thompson, Mary A. B., w/o Frederick Parmenter, 1871-1919
Collins, Jessie A., w/o Frederick Parmenter, 1886-1944
Thurber, Crawford A., 1845-1925
Thurber, Mary J., w/o Crawford A. Thurber, 1859-1911
Capron, Abby W., d 25 April 1871 aged 61 yrs
Lee, R. Henry, s/o Royal & Horatia N. Lee, d 26 Oct 1838, d 8 June 1872
Richardson, Benjamin S., 1884-1961
Frechette, Ida M., w/o Benjamin S. Richardson, 1883-1974
Richardson, Henry L., 1908-1968
Carlisle, Harry A., 1867-1942
Carlisle, Katherine C., w/o Harry A. Carlisle, 1866-1941
Horton, George W., b 8 Aug 1833, d 13 Sept 1905
Horton, Sarah J., w/o George W. Horton, b 9 Feb 1831, d 4 March 1919
O'Conner, James, 1853-1921
Woodward, Emily J., w/o James O'Conner, 1855-1947
Shattuck, Walton F., 1817-1907
Shattuck, Hittie L., w/o Walton F. Shattuck, 1823-1881
Aldrich, Welcome B., b 26 Sept 1843, d 2 Feb 1830
Aldrich, Amanda A., w/o Welcome B. Aldrich, b 30 June 1845, d 21 May
   1918
Aldrich, Merrill J., b 2 March 1869, d 23 Dec 1928
Aldrich, Carrie S., w/o Merrill J. Aldrich, b 29 July 1867, d 15 June 1939
Aldrich, Samuel R., b 20 March 1841, d 5 Sept 1910
Heritage, Lydia, w/o Samuel R. Aldrich, b 6 March 1851, d 27 Feb 1880
Aldrich, Effie May, b 18 June 1881, d 9 July 1881
Briggs, Arnold M., 1834-1902
Briggs, Elizabeth M., w/o Arnold M. Briggs, 1833-1889
Joslin, Henry L., 1832-1863
Perry, John W., 1886-1971
Perry, Mary I., w/o John W. Perry, 1890-1971
Bixby, Almira B., 1841-1918
Allen, Emma C., 1882-1952
Bird, John, b 26 Feb 1863, d 25 Dec 1938
Bartosch, Mary, w/o John Bird, b 17 June 1871, d 11 June 190
Bird, Harold G., s/o John & Mary Bird, b 24 Aug 1897, d 3 Sept 1920

Turner, Robert, 1817-1899

Turner, Isabella A., w/o Robert Turner, 1821-1891,

(**two stones further down in this section have these inscriptions**)

Turner, Robert, 1817-1899

Spinall, Isabella A., w/o Robert Turner, 1821-1891

Eddy, Rose Bully, 1870-156

McCrea, Sara Bulley, 1879-1968

Bulley, Frank, 1877-1952, A member of Co I 5th Regt. Spanish American War

Mott, Eugene A., d 27 Sept 1882 aged 36 yrs

Mott, Fannie B., w/o Eugene A. Mott, b 19 Sept 1848, d 14 March 1916

Matteson, James W., 1872-1939

Edwards, Florence M., 1879-1928

Fisher, Lillian E., 1876-1959

Fisher, Adella F., 1874-1960

Morse, Albert, b 2 May 1821, d 21 June 1896

Morse, Margaret G., w/o Albert Morse, b 18 Feb 1828, d 7 April 1894

Morse, Mary E., d/o Albert & Margaret G. Morse, b 28 March 1850, d 28 Nov 1866

Morse, George A., s/o Albert & Margaret G. Morse, b 17 April 1848, d 25 Jan 1872

Morse, Louisa L., d/o Albert & Margaret G. Morse, b 23 April 1853, d 19 Oct 1870

Morse, Alice M., d/o Albert & Margaret G. Morse, b 10 Sept 1864, d 22 Oct 1864

Morse, Annie G., d/o Albert & Margaret G. Morse, b 14 Dec 1865, d 2 Nov 1866

Morse, Elmer L., s/o Albert & Margaret G. Morse, b 20 Sept 1868, d 4 April 1892

Morse, Abbie L., s/o Albert & Margaret Morse, b 20 Sept 1857, d July 1858

Precious, James, 1869-1930

Precious, Sarah E., w/o James Precious, 1869-1933

Gay, Robert Malcolm, 1879-1964

Joslin, Lulu, w/o Robert Malcolm Gay, 1883-1946

Clegg, Joseph, 1878-1958

Benson, Annie, w/o Joseph Clegg, 1881-1967

Clegg, Ethel, d/o Joseph & Annie Clegg, 1903-1904

Clegg, Phyliss, d/o Joseph & Annie Clegg, 1907-1927

Inman, Lloyd Carleton, 1895-1918

Wood, Henry W., 1893-1927

Alcock, Annie, w/o Henry W. Wood, 1897-1921

Alcock, Emma, 1896-1920

Alger, Isaac A., 1890-1957

Swift, David A., 1838-1897

Hewin, Eleanor E., w/o David A. Swift, 1842-1903

Fisher, Howard E., 1865-1942

Jones, Ruth E., w/o Howard E. Fisher, 1866-1941

Donaldson, James, 1889-1953

Fisher, Harriet T., w/o James Donaldson, 1891-1967

Fisher, Emor T., b 20 Aug 1839, d 30 July 1895

Whitney, Harriet A., w/o Emor T. Fisher, b 7 April 1843, d 20 May 1910

Fisher, Benjamin F., b 12 March 1848, d 29 Jan 1891, A member of Co H 24th Reg Mass Vols

Adel, George, 1853-1910

Adel, Annie E., w/o George Adel, 1858-1902

Joslin, Frank L., 1959-....

Roberts, Loretta E., w/o Frank L. Joslin, 1854-1919

Joslin, Olive C., d/o Galen P. & Sarah Lee Joslin, d 12 May 1892

Claflin, Julius W., 1847-....

Claflin, Sarah, w/o Julius W. Claflin, 1841-1901

Bannister, Wilson, d 8 Nov 1900 aged 68 yrs 3 mos 8 days

Bannister, Ann, w/o Wilson Bannister, d 28 May 1898 aged 59 yrs 2 mos 5 days

Joslin, Henry L. Jr., b 12 Aug 1863, d 25 Sept 1897

Joslin, Mary W., w/o Henry L. Joslin, d 13 April 1925 aged 58 yrs

Vickery, William N., s/o Abdial & Julia A. Vickery, d 12 June 1869 aged 21 yrs

Fisher, Joel A., b 23 Dec 1841, d 8 Sept 1882

Fisher, Lucy, w/o Joel A. Fisher, d 27 Sept 1872

Broomhead, Walter H., 1883-1953

Hodge, James C., 1852-1906

Glynn, Catherine, w/o James C. Hodge, 1852-1923

Hodge, Mary A., 1877-1962

Hodge, Rhoda, 1880-1881

Hodge, Nellie, 1884-1886

Hodge, William C., 1882-1937

Godfrey, Emma, w/o William C. Hodge, 1882-1940

Huse, Albert, d 13 March 1887 aged 70 yrs

Franklin, Algena, w/o Benjiman Franklin, d 4 April 1882 aged 47 yrs 2 mos 20 days

Butters, Charles E., b 16 July 1854, d 15 Oct 1898

Daggett, Susan, w/o Harvey Daggett, d 29 Nov 1846 aged 36 yrs

Daggett, Harvey M., 1809-1886

Daggett, Nancy J., w/o Harvey M. Daggett, 1817-1900

Parsons, James B., d 1905

Daggett, Ella, w/o James B. Parsons, 1853-1901

Parsons, Carroll D., s/o James B. & Ella Parsons, 1885-1917

Grant, Walter J., 1856-1946

Grant, Edna J., w/o Walter J. Grant, 1863-1948

Hewitt, George L., 1849-1929

Hewitt, Annie E., w/o George L. Hewitt, b 2 Jan 1857, d 23 July 1926

Suttis, Minnie, 1879-1926

Blais, William, 1871-1942

Desaulniers, Evelina, w/o William Blais, 1876-1942

Briggs, James Elmer, 1862-1929

Briggs, Mary Emma, w/o James Elmer Briggs, 1857-1922

Boomer, B. Frank, d 27 Sept 1894 aged 48 yrs 12 days

Nina, Percy H., 1893-1962

Smith, Grace, w/o Percy H. Nina, 1892-1978

Pearce, Harold B., 1897-1978

Smith, Inez E., w/o Harold B. Pearce, 1896-1971

Rounds, Herbert F., 1844-1910

Rounds, Margaret M., w/o Herbert F. Rounds, 1842-1910

Whiting, Sila T., 1844-1903, A member of Co H 40th Mass Inf

Whiting, Barbara H., w/o Sila T. Whiting, 1843-1893

Chase, Hiram O., 1870-1945

Chase, Harriet E., w/o Hiram O. Chase, 1869-1946

Chase, Lloyd, 1896-1973

Mohr, Leonora, w/o Lloyd Chase, 1897-1977

Randall, George, 1845-1937

Randall, Emma M., w/o George Randall, 1848-1916

Fuller, Edward C., 1871-1929

Fuller, Sophia G., w/o Edward C. Fuller, 1871-1960

Fuller, Ada J. Taber., 1845-1925

Dean, Edward Nelson, 1840-1873

Tyler, Harriet, w/o Edward Nelson Dean, 1837-1908

Smith, Charlotte, sister of Edward N. Dean, 1887-1912

Dean, Reuben A., b 17 Jan 1829, d 3 May 1901

Dean, R. Allen, b 31 Dec 1887, d 6 March 1890

Rogers, Edwin F., d 28 Aug 1883 aged 32 yrs 4 mos

Blackington, Ella Rogers, w/o Edwin F. Rogers, b 3 Feb 1852, d 24 April 1919

Bullock, John O., b 8 March 1830, d 21 March 1882

Cutting, Martha F., w/o John O. Bullock, b 11 March 1838, d 29 Jan 1898

Hinds, Edward, b 22 Feb 1835, d 12 April 1902

Hinds, Hannah, w/o Edward Hinds, b 13 March 1839, d 21 Feb 1903

Hinds, Harry, s/o Edward & Hannah Hinds, b 11 May 1868, d 14 July 1890

Hinds, Clara, b 27 Feb 1870, d 5 Feb 1961

Hinds, Leonard, b 3 Feb 1878, d 8 Nov 1944

Harris, Robert E., 1839-1907, A member of Co's 4, 29, 40th Regt's of Civil War

Harris, Sarah, w/o Robert E. Harris, 1852-1924

Harris, George V., s/o Robert & Sarah Harris, 1882-1948

Harris, Vera E., w/o George V. Harris, 1888-1967

Taylor, William, 1877-1958

Taylor, Annie L., w/o William Taylor, 1877-1953

Jillson, Estelle, w/o George L. Jillson, b 7 Sept 1843, d 5 April 1887

Stanton, Frank B., b 10 Nov 1872, d 20 Aug 1928

Stanton, Hattie P., w/o Frank B. Stanton, b 26 May 1870, d 4 May 1941

Stanton, Harold B., s/o Frank B. & Hattie P. Stanton, 1905-1948

Humbold, Margaret M., 1872-1915

Evans, William H., 1851-1916

Evans, Anna J., 1859-1936

Evans, Luena S., 1882-1900

Evans, John W., 1884-1937

Dobson, Mary E., 1876-1940

Annis, Susan, 1844-1894

Wright, Philina E., 1902-1907

Williams, Albert, 1843-1939

Roberts, Deliah, w/o Robert T. Roberts, b 23 Aug 1862, d 1 Aug 1891

Jillson, William H., s/o George L. & Estelle Jillson, b 10 April 1871, d 28 March 1905

Hamlin, George W., b 10 May 1837, d 17 June 1877, A member of Co H 40th Reg Mass Vols

Hamlin, Maria L., w/o George W. Hamlin, b 29 Nov 1835, d 10 Oct 1921

Harvey, Charles H., 1881-1958

Harvey, Grace B., w/o Charles H. Harvey, 1884-1958

Harvey, C. Randall, 1905-1908

Kingman, Henry R., s/o Robert & Mary E. Kingman, d 24 March 1879 aged 23 yrs

Briggs, Mary E., w/o Robert C. Kingman, d 8 Feb 1886 aged 53 yrs

Moore, John T., 1837-1877

Moore, Minnie, w/o John T. Moore, 1835-1882

Darling, Edward A., 1863-1926

Moore, Jennie, w/o Edward A. Moore, 1860-1950

Slater, Edythe M., b 13 May 1875, d 15 March 1933

Shaw, John, b 15 May 1825, d 21 June 1890

Shaw, Paulina, w/o John Shaw, b 27 Oct 1827, d 3 Dec 1897

Slater, John, b 20 Dec 1842, d 19 Oct 1894

Slater, Mary J., w/o John Slater, b 21 Oct 1845, d 17 Dec 1925

Slater, Fred W., b 9 Oct 1872, d 29 Jan 1945

Slater, Evelyn M., w/o Fred W. Slater, b 15 Sept 1874, d 26 Feb 1929

Knight, Gertrude A. G., 1857-1943

Mason, Mary M. F., 1859-1947

White, George E., 1872-1955

White, Martha L., 1870-1932

White, Sarah A., 1843-1913

White, Isaac, 1825-1897

Patten, John F., 1861-1925

Patten, Eunice A., w/o John F. Patten, 1867-1929

Lander, Henry C., 1856-1925

Patten, Lois L., w/o Henry C. Lander, 1873-1944

Thayer, Lorenzo T., b 31 March 1829, d 16 Aug 1869, A member of Co G 47th Regt, Mass Vols

Clark, Mary P., w/o Lorenzo T. Thayer, b 25 May 1831, d 5 March 1904

Thayer, Herbert M., 1856-1927

Crosby, Stillman Y., 1844-1924

Crosby, Lilla F., w/o Stillman Y. Crosby, 1853-1928

Crosby, Mabel I., d/o Stillman & Lilla F. Crosby, 1877-1922

Crosby, Leander F., s/o Stillman & Lilla F. Crosby, 1872-1909

Crosby, Winfred A., 1874-1923

Hall, Uberto A., b 8 May 1860, d 22 June 1899

Cushman, Hiram, 1758-....

Amsden, Lucy M., w/o Hiram Cushman, 1852-1917

Martin, Daniel O., b 4 Feb 1864, d 7 Nov 1931

Martin, Alice E., w/o Daniel O. Martin, b 15 Dec 1863, d 28 Sept 1926

Martin, Daniel O. Jr., 1910-1933

Burlingame, Byron S., 1858-1930

Burlingame, Ada E., w/o Byron S. Burlingame, 1865-1950

Burlingame, Elmer E., 1886-1965

Bulringame, Jessie B., w/o Elmer E. Burlingame, 1884-1934

Robbins, Francis B., 1844-1910

Mason, Narzette F., w/o Francis B. Robbins, 1844-1936

Robbins, Ethel N., 1884-1957

Mason, Warren S., 1840-1886

Pond, Delia W., w/o Warren S. Mason, 1841-1870

Ballou, David M., 1865-1932

Gaboury, Melvina, w/o David M. Ballou, 1865-1955

Ballou, William A., 1839-1907

Ballou, Ella M., w/o William A. Ballou, 1847-1890

Bullock, George R., 1850-1928

Bullock, Clara, w/o George R. Bullock, 1853-1941

Bullock, Marion G., 1878-1903

Bullock, John W., 1873-1949

Bullock, Mabel E., w/o John W. Bullock, 1877-1955

Gatcomb, Isabel G., 1848-1927

Snell, George H., 1884-1928

Snell, Ida M., w/o George H. Snell, 1865-1933

Hayden, Savilla M., 1859-1915

Fuller, Charles L., 1833-1921

Dean, Harriet E., w/o Charles L. Fuller, 1832-1888

Fuller, Charlie B., s/o Charles L. & Harriet E. Fuller, 1863-1867

Trick, Mary, w/o Henry Watkins, b 21 Aug 1831, d 16 June 1890

Watkins, David Mundell, b 31 Jan 1866, d 25 Oct 1916

Babcock, Velema Worth, w/o David Mundell Waltkins, b 18 Sept 1875, d
    13 April 1956

Watkins, Frederick Mundell, s/o David Mundell & Velema Worth
    Watkins, b 26 March 1910, d 29 March 1972

Watkins, Mary Sprague, d/o David Mundell & Velema Worth Watkins, b
    29 Nov 1912, d 14 Jan 1977

Walden, Captain Samuel D., b 8 Oct 1828, d 19 Jan 1895

Carpenter, Henry L., b 22 Aug 1843, d 24 Sept 1892

Bliss, Chloe M., w/o Henry L. Carpenter, b 11 June 1844, d 5 Aug 1869

Walden, Harriet D., w/o Henry L. Carpenter, 1851-1922

Hopwood, James W., 1876-1905

Young, Annie B., w/o James W. Hopwood, 1879-1962

Young, L. Blanche, 1884-1965

Hopwood, James T., 1847-1911
Oddie, Sarah, w/o James T. Hopwood, 1847-1912
Olson, Ola S. F., 1861-1910
Olson, Johanna, w/o Ola S. F. Olson, 1863-1916
Tupper, Charles L., 1882-1910
York, Margaret M., w/o Charles L. Tupper, 1847-1907
Jackson, Charles A., 1909-1910
Jackson, Frederick, 1902-1910
Jackson, William H., 1905-1927
Becker, Emile J., 1843-1911
Diemer, Caroline P., w/o Emile J. Becker, 1853-1899
Becker, Louis C., 1891-1965
deWolfe, Marion, w/o Louis C. Becker, 1887-1978
Diemer, Pelegie, 1828-1900
Sommers, Fritz R. Sommers, 1863-1900
Sullivan, Josiah, d 15 Jan 1907 aged 60 yrs
Sullivan, Julia, w/o Josiah Sullivan, ...
Lassell, Ira N., 1855-1936
Mansfield, Nancy J. L., 1850-1899
Greene, William J., 1869-1931
Greene, Mary E., w/o William J. Greene, 1872-1948
Greene, Myrtle R., d/o William J. Greene, 1899-1900
French, Augustus M., 1854-1903
French, Josephine M., w/o Augustus M. French, 1856-1907
French, Grace M., 1888-1920
Anderson, E. Berger E., b 21 March 1877, d 21 Oct 1902
Henry, George F., 1866-1902
Henry, Mary E., w/o George F. Henry, 1866-1943
Halliday, Thomas J., 1860-1921
Halliday, Emma S., w/o Thomas J. Halliday, 1863-1936
Halliday, Rena M., d/o Thomas J. & Emma S. Halliday, 1887-1902
Crow, Bertha, w/o Alstyne J. Crow, 1874-1900
Burrows, Thomas M., 1851-1914
Burrows, Mary J., w/o Thomas M. Burrows, 1856-1941
Burrows, Inez G., 1880-1898
Burrows, Stanford D., 1878-1906
Burrows, Eva L., 1885-1916
Burrows, Raymond E., 1899-1920
Enbom, Henry A., 1863-1944
Enbom, Josephine W., w/o Henry A. Enbom, 1865-1901

Enbom, Carlton H., 1890-1914

Hillside Cemetery
Orchard Street...Rte. 152
Attleboro, Massachusetts

Daniels, Julian C., 1867-1941
Daniels, Pauline P., w/o Julian C. Daniels, 1865-1950
Wiggin, Harriet P., 1847-1926
Mason, James B., 1823-1881
Mason, Sarah S., w/o James B. Mason, 1826-1912
Carpenter, Chester H., 1888-1960
Lapham, Lillian G., w/o Chester H. Carpenter, 1888-1926
Carpenter, Helen Lee, 1888-1981
Mason, Andrew S., 1856-1936
Mason, Hattie L., w/o Andrew S. Mason, 1860-1929
Lange, Joseph, 1859-1923
Lange, Emma W., w/o Joseph Lange......
Wildes, Harriet S., w/o William O. Wildes, 1887-1924
Shaw, Edward C., 1852-1948
Shaw, Mary M., w/o Edward C. Shaw, 1854-1919
Downing, Isabelle, 1860-1936
Downing, Joseph, 1856-1939
Carpenter, John H., 1863-1933
Pierce, Harriet E., w/o John H. Carpenter, 1867-1944
Carpenter, Raymond D., 1894-1916
Carpenter, Raymond D., 1916-1921
Blanchard, Levi C., 1879-1926
Blanchard, Hattie L., w/o Levi C. Blanchard, 1879-1957
Blanchard, Bertha, d/o Levi C. & Hattie L. Blanchard, 1903-1926
Kenyon, Archibald, 1875-1959
Kenyon, Jessie M., w/o Archibald Kenyon, 1880-1932
Wight, Charles A., 1865-1929
Wight, Elizabeth A., w/o Charles A. Wight, 1869-1953
Annis, James, 1858-....
Annis, Alice E., w/o James Annis, 1861-1925

Holbrook, George D., 1856-1916
Holbrook, Ella L., 1865-1943
Kirkby, Rev. William, 1840-1911, Pastor of the Hebronville Methodist
Episcopal Church from 1904-1910
Ross, Clara Ann, 1851-1919
O'Mara, Richard, 1871-1912
O'Mara, Ida R., w/o Richard O'Mara, 1873-1951
Sheldon, Clinton H., 1887-1958
Sheldon, Clara A., w/o Clinton H. Sheldon, 1897-1965
Tierney, Martin J., 1871-1944
Tierney, Minnie D., w/o Martin J. Tierney, 1875-1940
Swan, Howard M., 1889-1952
Tierney, Ethel M., w/o Howard M. Swan, 1906-1974
Nurnberger, Rosina, 1838-1912
Farrington, George S., 1868-1912
Farrington, George S., 1868-1925
Farrington, Christina R., w/o George S. Farrington, 1863-1952
Burdick, Joel, b 13 Feb 1825, d 10 April 1902
Lyon, Mebcelia E., w/o Joel Burdick, b 21 March 1828, d 18 March 1916
Goghreaurn, William H., b 30 March 1867, d 10 Nov 1929
Bauer, Christopher, 1864-1929
Bauer, Johanna, w/o Christopher Bauer, 1867-1931
Bauer, Christopher J. W., s/o Christopher & Johanna Bauer, 1905-1968
Stafford, Charles H., 1863-1944
Stafford, Julia C., w/o Charles H. Stafford, 1871-1931
Stafford, Ruth, 1898-1946
Stafford, Grace H., 1900-1970
Maine, Samuel F., 1862-1955
Kenney, Adella N., w/o Samuel F. Maine, 1860-1913
Atwell, Edna L., w/o Samuel F. Maine, 1864-1943
Sturtevant, George, b 5 Aug 1842, d 25 Aug 1916
Hicks, Angeline, w/o George Sturtevant, b 23 Jan 1843, d 26 April 1919
Sturtevant, George Edward, b 20 Oct 1871, d 8 April 1957
Rodgers, Mina Estella, w/o George Edward Sturtevant, b 13 Jan 1873, d 4
Jan 1963
Kirkby, Albert Farwell, 1875-1923
Pearson, Ernest Kirkby, 1908-1979
Bigelow, Ethel M., b 15 May 1885 Holland, Vermont, d 23 July 1945
Attleboro, MA
Bachand, Clara, 1868-1950

Bachand, Louis P., 1868-1951
Turner, Ruth J., 1914-1971
Turner, Ralph, 1912-1982
Kulaga, Zygmund, 1921-1972
Kulaga, Elaine G., w/o Zygmund Kulaga, 1825-1971
Desorsiers, Napoleon J., 1921-1985
Salisbury, Roland, 1930-....
Gousie, Marie J., w/o Roland Salisbury, 1926-1978
Salisbury, Robert E., 1923-....
Murphy, Catherine A., w/o Robert E. Salisbury, 1945-1992
Salisbury, Richard, 1956-1989
Smith, Marilyn J., 1945-1990
Salisbury, Donald L., Cpl US Army, Korea, b 22 June 1933, d 2 Sept
    1988
Lange, Danielle M., grand-daughter of Donald L. Salisbury, 1988-1989
Bott, Frederick, 1871-1941
Bott, Kate A., w/o Frederick Bott, 1873-1952
Bott, Kathryn A., 1900-1969
Carlosn, Axel N., 1870-1953
Carlosn, Hannah M., w/o Axel N. Carlson, 1867-1945
Carlson, Carl E., s/o Axel N. & Hannah M. Carlosn, 1891-1963
Whitehead, Thomas H., 1892-1958
Duff, Sarah J., w/o Thomas H. Whitehead, 1893-1984
Fuller, Benjamin F., 1895-1964
Borden, Hazel, w/o Benjamin F. Fuller, 1894-1962
Hanson, Henry, 1881-1938
Hanson, Mary R., w/o Henry Hanson, 1880-1941
Burdick, Lewis C., 1867-1931
Burdick, Eva M., w/o Lewis C. Burdick, 1872-1960
Wood, Henry W., 1864-1942
Swan, Evelyn J., w/o Henry W. Wood, 1868-1958
Wood, Chester F., 1895-1970
Wilmarth, Percy O., 1881-1937
Wilmarth, Ada, 1882-1966
Claflin, Cornelius, s/o Capt. Rufus Claflin, d 12 April 1836 aged 23 yrs
Claflin, Hannah, w/o Rufus Claflin, d 23 April 1885 aged 75 yrs
Dexter, Candace, w/o William Dexter & d/o Rufus Claflin, d 20 May
    1838 aged 28 yrs
Sklebes, Jacob, 1846-1924

Claflin, Horace, s/o Comfort F. & Anna Claflin, d 11 Aug 1845 aged 24 yrs

Claflin, Rachel, d/o Comfort F. & Anna Claflin, d 6 June 1829

Claflin, Comfort F., d 15 Sept 1847 aged 61 yrs

Claflin, Anna, w/o Comfort Claflin, d 30 March 1833 aged 51 yrs

Wilmarth, Ebenezer, d 24 Jan 1828 AE 89 yrs

Claflin, Nehemiah, d 5 Jan 1820 AE 77 yrs

Claflin, Mehetable, w/o Nehemiah Claflin, d 4 June 1840 aged 95 yrs 6 mos 23 days

Parkinson, Wilfred, 1909-1956

Stevens, Borden F., 1870-1956

Pike, Hannah F., d Dec 1831 AE 24 yrs

Pike, William W., d 3 Jan 1832 aged 58 yrs

Fuller, Joshua, b 9 Sept 1801, d 4 April 1888

Fuller, Sarah B., w/o Joshua Fuller, d 16 Feb 1881 aged 75 yrs 8 mos

Fuller, Manly J., d 20 May 1914 aged 84 yrs

Andrew, William, 1824-1902

Andrew, Elizabeth, w/o William Andrew, 1837-1871

Russell, Richard, 1877-1944

Russell, Margaret, w/o Richard Russell, 1879-1973

Russell, Richard Jr., 1922-1932

Pitas, Margaret Russell, 1912-1934

Hathaway, Lester L., 1913-1979

Russell, Jane O., w/o Lester L. Hathaway, 1914-1975

Patterson, Willis J., s/o Jerome Patterson, 1875-1942

Hoxie, Jennie Helena, 1870-1951

Hoxie, Charles Alfred, 1867-1941

Hagan, Clifton F., 1885-1949

Gross, Bertha M., w/o Clifton F. Hagan, 1886-1953

Gross, Erwin E., 1882-1963

Kellough, Nellie, w/o Erwin E. Gross, 1888-1971

Hughes, Harold J., 1894-1954

Weeks, Edith G., w/o Harold J. Hughes, 1900-1974

Fletcher, William, 1885-1958

Broadley, Sarah, w/o William Fletcher, 1888-1968

Nadow, Elmer E., 1901-1956

Nadow, Bernice E., 1903-1988

Rice, Chauncey F., 1894-1958

Rice, Nellie, w/o Chauncey F. Rice, 1895-19..

London, Wallace R., 1882-1961

London, Edith M., 1888-1969
Dickerson, Winfred S., 1901-1959
Ploeltner, Viola M., w/o Winfred S. Dickerson, 1903-1990
Yates, Alice, d 8 Sept 1887 aged 77 yrs
Broomhead, Charles, 1846-1915
Strapp, Samuel A., 1881-1940
Goff, William N., 1856-1927
Goff, Sarah F., w/o William N. Goff, 1861-1930
Goff, Henry N., 1882-1883
Goff, Flora M., 1886-1967
Goff, William H., b 3 July 1826, d 11 June 1870
Goff, Cynthia B., w/o William H. Goff, b 9 May 1825, d 31 March 1890
Goff, Cynthia A., b 2 Jan 1853, d 26 March 1859
Makepeace, Mehitable W., w/o Jason T. L. Makepeace, b 13 Oct 1827, d 6
    July 1872
Read, William F., b 9 July 1845, d 20 July 1894
Read, William W., 1817-1896
Read, Sarah F., w/o William W. Read, 1823-1907
Trimm, Mary E., 1839-1902
Trimm, Lottie C., 1875-1898
Claflin, Alfred, d 24 March 1876 aged 68 yrs
Claflin, Betsey, w/o Alfred Claflin, d 13 July 1882 aged 72 yrs
Holbrook, Frederick, 1874-1932
Caswell, S. Alice, w/o Frederick Holbrook, 1878-1974
Holbrook, Gertrude, 1900-1901
Holbrook, Bernice A., 1905-1910
Johnson, John, 1842-1924
Cox, Rebecca, w/o John Hohnson, 1838-1917
Weymouth, Mary E., 1878-1970
Oswald, John, 1836-1926
Graham, Mary, w/o John Oswald, 1842-1902
Oswald, William, s/o John & Mary Oswald, 1875-1885
Parker, Raymond E., 1889-1942
Atwell, Ethel J., w/o Raymond E. Parker, 1893-1981
Bates, James, 1829-1914
Bates, Sarah, w/o James Bates, 1833-1914
Wilson, Daniel, 1851-1930
Wilson, Susan, 1839-1919
Roder, John, 1875-1941
Barney, Jason M., 1854-1932

Barney, Jessie, w/o Jason M. Barney, 1844-1920
Amos, William W., 1881-1923
Amos, Esther L., w/o William W. Amos, 1887-1979
Coburn, John Henry, b 22 Jan 1832, d 14 Aug 1900
Coburn, Maria Louise, w/o John Henry Coburn, b 8 July 1839, d 29 June 1899
Holbrook, Ezekiel, d 20 March 1871 aged 74 yrs
Holbrook, Caroline M., w/o Ezekiel Holbrook, d 22 Aug 1879 aged 80 yrs
Bicknell, Japheth D., 1831-1907
Holbrook, Julia A., w/o Japheth D. Bicknell, 1836-1917
Holbrook, John, d 1 April 1866 aged 42 yrs
Holbrook, Maria M., w/o John Holbrook, d 15 Sept 1859 aged 31 yrs 1 mo
Holbrook, Caroline M., d/o John & Maria M. Holbrook, d 16 Oct 1859 aged 1 yr 8 mos 3 days
Holbrook, Franklin R., b 27 July 1852, d 22 Feb 1912
Holbrook, Josephine, w/o Franklin R. Holbrook, b 4 Feb 1874, d 5 Aug 1898
Holbrook, Cora E., w/o F. Everett Holbrook, b 24 Sept 1874, d 23 July 1901
French, Ella F., w/o Herbert French, 1855-1876
French, Sebia, s/o Herbert & Cora E. French, 1876-1877
Wilmarth, P. Capron, 1815-1898
Robinson, Harriet A., w/o P. Capron Wilmarth, 1820-1906
Wilmarth, Isabella R., 1855-1872
Ray, Annie L., 1854-1914
Cook, Francis A., b 4 Sept 1830, d 1 Aug 1895
Cook, Mary A., w/o Francis A. Cook, b 2 June 1831, d.....
Hoyt, William J., d 15 June 1881 aged 78 yrs
Hoyt, Edith, w/o William J. Hoyt, d 12 March 1886 aged 78 yrs
Parker, Rev. Lowell, d 25 July 1878 aged 66 yrs
Parker, Mary M., w/o Rev. Lowell Parker, d 26 April 1887 aged 77 yrs
Fuller, Warren A., 1839-1925
Fuller, Elizabeth A., w/o Warren A. Fuller, 1840-1932
Bowen, Walter C., b 20 Aug 1858, d 10 Dec 1876
Bowen, Sarah C., 1855-1900
Blanchard, Levi J., d 14 Oct 1865 aged 43 yrs
Wilcox, Ruth, w/o Levi J. Blanchard & d/o Jonathan & Mary Wilcox, d 11 July 1859 aged 33 yrs
Blanchard, John R., b 4 Dec 1852, d 3 June 1889

Thurber, Bertha A., w/o John R. Blanchard & d/o J. C. & Mary A. Thurber, b 29 March 1851, d 22 March 1887

Allen, John Jay, b 17 Dec 1843, d 16 Feb 1920

Allen, Eunice Josephine, w/o John Jay Allen, b 12 Oct 1843, d 27 Feb 1908

Bowen, Isabell F., b 24 Oct 1846, d 20 April 1862

French, Milton J., b 13 Sept 1825, d 4 July 1881

Claflin, Oren E., 1859-1859

Claflin, Ellen M., 1852-1879

Claflin, George E., 1841-1885

Claflin, Albert, 1807-1884

Claflin, Lydia, 1811-1873

Slater, Robert, 1840-1892, A member of Co H 3rd Mass Vols

Slater, Elizabeth, w/o Robert Slater, 1840-1926

Slater, Lizzie, d/o Robert & Elizabeth Slater, 1875-1880

Eldridge, Hiram, 1814-1888

Eldridge, Caroline, 1812-1885

Eldridge, Mary F., 1841-1865

Eldridge, Carrie C., 1843-1884

Eldridge, George F., 1848-1867

Eldridge, Lizzie T., w/o Dexter E. Newell, b 28 Jan 1846, d 11 Dec 1898

Simpson, Joseph E., 1844-1917

Bistos, Harriet L., w/o Joseph E. Simpson, 1848-1928

Smith, Noyes, d 18 April 1885 aged 74 yrs

Smith Emily, w/o Noyes Smith, d 11 Feb 1887 aged 85 yrs

Smith, Emily A., d/o Noyes & Emily A. Smith, d 20 Aug 1925 aged 71 yrs

Fuller, Jonathan, d 3 July 1863 aged 74 yrs

deGoeg, William, 1872-1935

Simpson, Harriet P., w/o William de Geog, 1868-1957

Atwell, E. Jennie Groves, 1867-1889

Atwell, Elmer W., 1861-1937

Atwell, Sarah E. Bates, 1868-1936

Atwell, Violette, 1895-1895

Wilmarth, George A., 1826-1888

Bowen, Harriet, w/o George A. Wilmarth, 1833-1914

Bournn, Leafa, w/o Eli Bourn, d 3 Dec 1827 aged 41 yrs

Bourn, Eunice, d/o Eli & Leafa Bourn, b 30 Sept 1819, d 25 May 1903

Bourn, Lydia I., d/o Eli & Leafa Bourn, b 12 Jan 1815, d 7 May 1900

Bourn, Eliza, d/o Eli & Leafa Bourn, b 28 Oct 1812, d 20 Nov 1887

Corey, Ada Carpenter, b 14 March 1862, d 15 Oct 1928

Carpenter, Henry, b 11 Sept 1830, d 19 Nov 1919

Carpenter, Mary J., w/o Henry Carpenter, b 19 June 1833, d 3 Jan 1914

Carpenter, Everett H., s/o Henry & Mary J. Carpenter, d 30 July 1858 aged 8 mos

Carpenter, Willard A., s/o Henry & Mary J. Carpenter, d 26 March 1868 aged 4 mos

Carpenter, Marion M., d/o Henry & Mary J. Carpenter, d 4 Aug 1869 aged 4 mos

Carpenter, Willie M., s/o Henry & Mary J. Carpenter, d 22 Aug 1875 aged 8 mos

Carpenter, Alden, 1826-1865

Woodcock, Charles, d 6 Sept 1841 aged 47 yrs

Woodcock, Jane, w/o Charles Woodcock, d 14 Dec 1878 aged 66 yrs

Thurber, Thomas W., 1858-1919

Thurber, Jennie B., w/o Thomas W. Thurber, 1860-1919

Thurber, Joseph C., b 7 Sept 1825, d 11 Dec 1900

Thurber, Mary A., w/o Joseph C. Thurber, b 17 June 1827, d 21 Feb 1908

Fuller, Lewis M., b 29 July 1803, d 22 Feb 1821

Moore, Sarah, b 27 Feb 1773, d 17 March 1859

Fuller, Freelove, b 2 Oct 1773, d 9 May 1862

Fuller, Annah, b 7 Oct 1775, d 19 Feb 1864

Fuller, Lewis C., 1841-1869

Fuller, Charles W., 1846-1909

Fuller, Mary A., 1844-1932

Bliss, Newman, d 22 Dec 1818 AE 51 yrs 11 mos 27 days

Bliss, Mary, w/o Newman Bliss, d 20 Dec 1831 AE 60 yrs 8 mos 23 days

Bliss, William, d 21 Feb 1803 AE 5 yrs 4 mos

Claflin, Sarah, w/o Sylvester Claflin, d 7 April 1863 aged 65 yrs 6 mos 11 days

Claflin, Mary, d 23 Jan 1863 aged 59 yrs 7 mos 16 days

Smith, William H., 1840-1919

Smith, Ardelia, w/o William H. Smith, 1840-1912

Smith, Ellen B., w/o William H. Smith, 1877-1919

Perry, John, d 27 Jan 1873 aged 63 yrs

Perry, Caroline, w/o John Perry, d 5 July 1883 aged 73 yrs

Mott, Charles Bosworth, s/o Bradford & Mary J. Mott, d 5 Nov 1871 aged 24 yrs

Mott, Charles E., 1871-1944

Geisee, Emma, w/o Charles E. Mott, 1877-1975

Mott, Bradford C., d 21 Oct 1884 aged 69 yrs

Mott, Mary Jane, w/o Bradfrod C. Mott, d 7 Jan 1874 aged 53 yrs

Mott, Lucy J., d/o Bradford & Mary Jane Mott, d 10 April 1866 aged 21 yrs 8 mos 16 days

Bailey, Robert, 1863-1911

Pollock, Jean, w/o Robert Bailey, 1872-1934

Cunningham, Ernest M., 1898-1966

Bailey, Mildred J., w/o Ernest M. Cunningham, 1902-1993

Corey, Martin V., d 31 Dec 1876 aged 40 yrs

Fuller, Deacon Noble P., d 23 Aug 1873 aged 70 yrs

Guild, George W., 1837-1907

Guild, Nancy A., w/o George W. Guild, 1837-1907

Stafford, Mary C., w/o John B. Stafford, d 3 Sept 1892 aged 59 yrs

Patten, Adin Jr., b 28 July 1832, d 11 June 1870

Patten, Nathaniel, b 18 Aug 1826, d 5 Sept 1905

Barber, Manly P., 1834-1919

Barber, Hannah, w/o Manly Barber, 1839-1917

Joy, Jennette B., w/o Charles F. Joy, 1861-1917

Allen, Lucy J., d/o Benjamin & Lucy Allen, d 17 Jan 1862 aged 16 yrs

Bourn, Clarissa T., w/o Albert Bourn, d 26 Dec 1849 aged 39 yrs

Bowen, Uriel, d Dec 1811

Bowen, Sally, w/o Uriel Bowen, d 19 April 1823 AE 54 yrs

Bowen, Deborah, w/o Uriel Bowen, d 12 June 1849 aged 62 yrs

Carpenter, Molly, w/o Lemuel Carpenter, d 10 Aug 1815 Seekonk, MA AE 66 yrs

Carpenter, Benjamin of Seekonk, MA., d 26 Jan 1819 AE 55 yrs 2 days

Carpenter, Lerviah, w/o Benjamin Carpenter, d 29 Jan 1828 AE 60 yrs 5 mos

Carpenter, Zachariah, d 1 Oct 1775 AE 41 yrs

Carpenter, Hannah, w/o Zachariah Carpenter, d 20 April 1790 AE 50 yrs

Fuller, Frederick, d 2 Oct 1820 AE 50 yrs

Atwell, Allen E., b 6 Jan 1828, d 27 Sept 1884

Atwell, Sarah J., w/o Allen E. Atwell, b 8 Aug 1830, d 7 Dec 1892

Tiffany, Eunice Weld, d/o William & Betsey Tiffany, d 11 Sept 1823 AE 35 yrs

Tiffany, William, d 2 Nov 1789 AE 29 yrs 5 mos

Tiffany, Captain Ebenezer, d 30 Oct 1807 AE 74 yrs

Tiffany, Molly, w/o Captain Ebenezer Tiffany, d 18 Sept 1825 AE 87 yrs

Tiffany, James, d Oct 1776 AE 79 yrs

Tiffany, Elizabeth, w/o James Tiffany, d 1 Aug 1796 AE 92 yrs

Bassett, Miranda, d 29 March 1850 aged 56 yrs

Tiffany, Captain Joseph, d 13 Dec 1850 aged 87 yrs

Tiffany, Charlotte, w/o Captain Joseph Tiffany, d 30 Jan 1842 aged 78 yrs

Hutchins, Jerusha, w/o David Thurber, d 23 Aug 1798 AE 74 yrs

Hutchins, David, d 4 Oct 1794

Wilmarth, Parley, d 16 Oct 1851 aged 61 yrs

Wilmarth, Mary S., w/o Parley Wilmarth, d 10 Sept 1882 aged 97 yrs

Wilmarth, Albert A., s/o Parley & Mary S. Wilmarth, d 8 Nov 1821 aged 1 yr 7 mos 21 days

Wilmarth, Ann Maria, w/o George H. Wilmarth, d 10 Sept 1850 aged 23 yrs

Claflin, Alfred, d 26 Nov 1861 aged 58 yrs

Claflin, Harriet N., w/o Alfred Claflin, d 24 May 1850 aged 34 yrs

Fuller, Rhoda, w/o Abiel Fuller, d 7 Jan 1843 aged 63 yrs

Bowen, Anjennette, w/o Charles H. Rounds, b 27 Feb 1848, d 25 Nov 1904

Bowen, Benjamin, b 9 Nov 1811, d 28 Feb 1879

Bowen, Leafa, w/o Benjamin Bowen, b 28 Nov 1819, d 31 Dec 1898

Allen, Squire, 1796-1848

Allen, Eleanor, 1795-1881

Witherell, Joseph A., 1812-1853

Allen, Albert, 1827-1832

Allen, Esther, 1830-1832

Thurber, Albert D., 1818-1891

Thurber, Harriet R., 1819-1908

Thurber, Albert A., 1840-1884

Fuller, Fanny H., d/o Abial & Rhoda Fuller, d 31 Aug 1838 aged 21 yrs

Claflin, Hartford, d 4 June 1844 aged 66 yrs

Wilmarth, Sally Claflin, d 17 Dec 1868 aged 87 yrs 11 mos

Fuller, Jaduthan, d 20 Sept 1900 aged 78 yrs

Fuller, Sally C., w/o Jaduthan Fuller, d 31 Dec 1886 aged 63 yrs

Guild, Harmon L., b 9 Oct 1815, d 13 Jan 1884

Guild, Marinda C., w/o Harmon L. Guild, b 24 July 1814, d 29 Sept 1886

Witherell, Joseph, d 7 May 1863 aged 78 yrs 5 mos 19 days

Streeter, John F., 1838-1923

Guild, Ellen M., w/o John F. Streeter, 1840-1920

Streeter, Willis H., 1858-1935

Claflin, Sylvester N., d 18 Nov 1847 aged 33 yrs

Claflin, Sylvester, d 30 Jan 1847 aged 70 yrs 6 mos 8 days

Claflin, Hannah, w/o Sylvester Claflin, d 26 Nov 1832 aged 54 yrs

Claflin, Alfred, b 23 Feb 1784, d 4 Feb 1859

Claflin, Chloe, w/o Alfred Claflin, d 16 Sept 1863 aged 79 yrs

Claflin, Eliza A., d/o Alfred & Chloe Claflin, b 28 Dec 1818, d 28 Sept 1819

Claflin, Horace C., s/o Alfred & Chloe Claflin, b 26 Sept 1820, d 21 Oct 1821

Bauer, Albert J., 1892-1960

Platt, Dorothy M., w/o Albert J. Bauer, 1912-1993

Droun, Sears L., Mass Tec 5 Co 320 Inf Rec WWII, b 16 July 1923, d 14 Aug 1963

Salisbury, Charles H., 1880-1965

Card, Mary A., w/o Charles H. Salisbury, 1898-1970

Knowlton, Clifton E., 1922-1965

Lawton, Frederick Henry, 1891-1966

Taylor, Bertha, w/o Frederick Henry Lawton, 1894-1981

Jacques, Gilbert A., 1934-1938

Ross, Charles W., 1851-1938

Ross, Lizzie M., w/o Charles W. Ross, 1862-1945

Ross, Frank K., 1885-1956

Fischbach, John W., 1866-1936

Fischbach, Mary Agnes, w/o John W. Fischbach, 1858-1945

Cooper, Thomas, d 11 Oct 1835 aged 27 yrs

Bruster, Maria, w/o John D. Peacock & d/o John Bruster, b 10 April 1859 Mensworth, Yorksihre, England, d ....

Babcock, Charlotte, w/o Stephen Babcock, d 4 June 1838 aged 56 yrs

Carpenter, Hannah, d 19 May 1873 aged 74 yrs 25 yrs

Carpenter, Captain Jonathan, d 28 March 1833 aged 38 yrs

Carpenter, Lephe, w/o Capt. Jonathan Carpenter, d 23 May 1832 aged 36 yrs

Carpenter, Lephe, d/o Captain Jonathan & Lephe Carpenter, d 1 July 1828 aged 10 mos 10 days

Carpenter, Benjamin, d 23 July 1832 aged 31 yrs

Carpenter, Esther, w/o Remember Carpenter, d 9 Oct 1858 aged 83 yrs

Carpenter, Nancy, d/o Remember & Esther Carpenter, d 12 Oct 1858 aged 38 yrs

Carpenter, Betsey, d/o Remember & Esther Carpenter, d 14 Oct 1858 aged 65 yrs

Miller, Edward F., d 4 Feb 1893 aged 61 yrs 5 mos 24 days

Miller, Minerva, d 9 Feb 1893 aged 59 yrs 3 mos

Miller, Francis Eugene, s/o Edward & Minerva Miller, d 20 April 1865
  aged 17 yrs 1 mo 16 days
Roder, John, 1845-1907
Roder, Barbara, w/o John Roder, 1845-1936
Roder, Anna, 1884-1899
Roder, Anthony, 1891-1946
Read, Nathaniel, d 16 Dec 1835 aged 76 yrs
Bourn, Captain Stephen, d Oct 1814
Bourn, Susanna, w/o Captain Stephen Bourn, d 17 Aug 1829 aged 65 yrs
Freeman, William, d 25 March 1804 aged 45 yrs
Freeman, Molly, w/o William Freeman, d 12 March 1848 aged 82 yrs
Freeman, Welcome, d 2 March 1855 aged 62 yrs
Freeman, Joanna, d 8 March 1793 AE 30 yrs
Martin, Erastus, d 19 July 1839 aged 36 yrs
Martin, Job, d 28 Nov 1833 aged 87 yrs
Martin, Susanna, w/o Job Martin, d 6 may 1829 AE 79 yrs
Gardner, Nancy, d 13 Aug 1886 aged 100 yrs 18 days
Freeman, Hannah Marilla, 1845-1929
Freeman, Stella Louise, d/o Ezra R. & Stella M. Freeman, d 19 Aug 1861
  aged 25 yrs
Freeman, Ezra R., d Aug 1888 aged 58 yrs
Warren, Hannah, w/o Ezra R. Freeman, d 22 June 1889
Washburn, Stella, w/o Ezra R. Freeman, d July 1811
French, Ezra W., b 7 Ocrt 1825, d 29 Sept 1872
French, Alice M., w/o Ezra W. French, b 15 April 1825, d 26 May 1857
French, Walter B., s/o Ezra W. & Alice M. French, b 9 Feb 1848, d 22
  Feb 1868
Fuller, Suky, w/o Capt. Ezra A. French & d/o Deacon Ebenezer Fuller, d
  28 Aug 1852 aged 60 yrs
French, Captain Ezra A., d 7 Feb 1863 aged 72 yrs 7 mos 2 days
Specht, Nicholas J., b 21 Sept 1831, d 23 Nov 1906
Specht, Christof, 1879-1918
Specht, Jackob, 1872-1930
Bauer, Lorenz J., 1879-1899
Read, Daniel, d 29 April 1855 aged 71 yrs
Read, Anna, w/o Nathaniel Read, d 1 Sept 1840 aged 86 yrs
Read, Fanny, d/o Nathaniel & Anna Read, d Sept 1813 aged 22 yrs
Read, Bathsheba, d/o Nathaniel & Anna Read, d 16 Jan 1833 aged 35 yrs

Briggsville Burial Ground
Park Street
Attleboro, Massachusetts

Wilmarth, Lt. Daniel, d 17 Feb 1769 AE 54
Wilmarth, Jonathan, d 20 Jan 1752 AE 26
Wilmarth, Jonathan, d 4 Sept 1756 AE 67
Wilmarth, Bulah, d 14 Feb 1770 AE 79
Wilmarth, Elizabeth, d 21 Sept 1824 AE 82
Wilmarth, Moses, d 16 Nov 1759 AE 68
Wilmarth, Jonathan, d 1756
French, Thomas, d 2 June 1746
French, Christopher, d 1755
Blandin, Rachel, w/o Lamech Bladin, d 28 Feb 1812
Blandin, Lamech, d 22 March 1774 AE 51

Solomon Burial Yard
Solomon Street
Attleboro, Massachusetts

Solomon, Dr. James.....
Solomon, William D., d 19 Jan 1842
Solomon, Cornelia F., d 1836
Solomon, Rebecca F.........

Town Hall
Hickory Road
North Attleboro, MA 02760

Walker Cemetery
William Street
Dighton, Massachusetts

Walker, Mary, (can't read)

Walker, John, s/o Nathan & Sarah Walker, wounded Petersburg, VA, on
12 July 1864, d David's Island Hospital, New York, 27 July 1864 aged
19 yrs 7 days

Walker, Deacon Nathan, d 27 Nov 1896 aged 86 yrs 10 mos 19 days

Walker, Sarah G., w/o Deacon Nathan Walker, d 28 Sept 1877 aged 50
yrs 10 mos

Walker, Henry, d 17 May 1849 aged 64 yrs

Walker, Mary, w/o Henry Walker, d 13 Aug 1855 aged 70 yrs 8 mos 1 day

Walker, John G., s/o Henry & Polly Walker, d 29 June 1832 aged 17 yrs

Walker, George Henry, s/o Joseph B. & Elizabeth W. Walker, d 16 Oct
1849 aged 1 yr 5 mos 17 days

Walker Lot
Walker Street
Dighton, Massachusetts

Walker, Harold, 1886-1938

Bradshaw, Mabel L. Walker, w/o Harold Walker, 1888-1978

Walker, N. Allen, 1847-1935

Hayman, Anna L., w/o N. Allen Walker, 1851-1920

Walker, Nehemiah, d 9 Nov 1886 aged 72 yrs 6 mos

Walker, Emily A., w/o Nehemiah Walker, d 14 Jan 1896 aged 79 yrs 5
mos 9 days

Walker, Jasper, s/o Nehemiah & Emily A. Walker, d 23 Feb 1876 aged 20
yrs 7 mos 20 days

Horton, Nathan H., d 3 March 1892 aged 51 yrs 5 mos 15 days

Walker, Charlotte A., w/o Nathan H. Horton & d/o Nehemiah & Emily A.
Walker, d 28 March 1880 aged 35 yrs 5 mos 8 days

Walker, Alonzo, s/o Nehemiah & Emily A. Walker, b 1 Nov 1848, d 17
    Sept 1849
Walker, Elijah B., s/o Nehemiah & Emily A. Walker, d 9 Feb 1880 aged
    31 yrs 3 mos 9 days
Walker, Mary F., w/o Earl B. Guild, b 7 Dec 1851, d 30 Jan 1911
Walker, Jeffie A., s/o Elijah & Mary F. Walker, d 13 Dec 1879 aged 3 yrs
Walker, Homer, s/o Elijah & Mary Walker, d 18 Jan 1879 aged 11 days
Walker, Howard, s/o Elijah & Mary F. Walker, d 17 Sept 1879 aged 8
    mos 9 days

Briggs Lot
Wellington Street
Dighton, Massachusetts

Briggs, Ebenezer, d 20 Nov (BROKEN)
Briggs, Nancy, w/o Ebenezer Briggs, d 12 Aug 1883 aged 77 yrs
Briggs, Emma E., d/o Ebenezer & Nancy Briggs, d 2 Oct 1891 aged 42
    yrs
Briggs, John, d 26 Oct 1880 aged 83 yrs
Briggs, Sophia, w/o John Briggs, d 17 March 1868 aged 64 yrs
Briggs, Charles H., s/o John & Sophia Briggs, d 27 Dec 1864 aged 37 yrs
Dean, B. Leonard, 1841-1907
Briggs, Julia E., w/o B. Leonard Dean, 1843-1920
Briggs, Sarah P., d 13 March 1912 aged 76 yrs
Briggs, Samuel, d 25 Feb 1867 aged 86 yrs
Briggs, Mary, w/o Samuel Briggs, d 26 Nov 1823
Briggs, Avis R., d 18 Sept 1882 aged 86 yrs 1 mo 7 days
Briggs, Harriet, b 13 June 1839, d 1 Aug 1887
Briggs, Clarissa A., d 2 April 1851 aged 58 yrs
Briggs, Eliakim, d 27 Sept 1852 aged 86 yrs
Briggs, Elizabeth, w/o Eliakim Briggs, d 27 Aug 1842 aged 75 yrs
Briggs, Julia, d/o Eliakim & Elizabeth Briggs, d March 1828
Levin, Catherine, w/o William Y. Levin, d 27 Oct 1882 aged 75 yrs
Briggs, Fanny, w/o William Y. Levin & d/o Eliakim & Elizabeth Briggs,
    b 7 May 1804, d 23 May 1841
Briggs, David, b 4 Aug 1803, d 25 Oct 1887

Briggs, Hannah H., w/o David Briggs, b 23 Nov 1805, d 18 March 1894

Briggs, Orren, s/o David & Hannah H. Briggs, d 22 Dec 1832 aged 2 yrs 5 mos

Merrelle, Harriet M., 1859-1947

Briggs, Raymond F., 1880-1882

Briggs, H. Walter, 1855-1937

Cole, Polly, w/o Constant Cole, d 1 June 1846 aged 53 yrs 11 mos 11 days

West Dighton Congregational Church Cemetery
Wellington Street
Dighton, Massachusetts

Horton, Herbert W., 1853-1937

Goff, Lillian W., w/o Herbert W. Horton, 1852-1922

Goff, Benjamin, 1801-1866

Pettis, Rebecca, w/o Benjamin Goff, 1811-1867

Goff, Charles, 1813-1877

Goff, Priscilla, w/o Charles Goff, 1810-1857

Goff, Truman, 1819-1841

Paull, Emeline, w/o Truman Goff, 1815-1888

Bliss, Joshua, 1842-1937

Goff, Nancy E., w/o Joshua Bliss, 1846-1913

Goff, Henry N., 1823-1890

Francis, Ardella M., w/o Henry N. Goff, 1827-1884

Goff, Eudora J., d/o Henry N. & Ardella M. Goff, 1853-1854

Goff, Jane L., d/o Henry & Ardella Goff, 1861-1867

Goff, Lillas W., d/o Henry & Ardella Goff, 1852-1922

Peck, Otis, d 9 March 1853 aged 49 yrs 11 mos 24 days

Peck, Mary A., w/o Otis Peck, d 20 Jan 1864 aged 43 yrs

Peck, Sybil, d 11 Sept 1878 aged 90 yrs 10 mos 21 days

Goff, Levi, d 23 Nov 1824 aged 80 yrs

Goff, Hannah, w/o Levi Goff, d 13 May 1812 aged 70 yrs

Goff, Judith, w/o Levi Goff, d 9 Sept 1831 aged 79 yrs

Goff, Elder Enoch, Organizer of this Church in 1772 & the Pastor until his death on 6 March 1810 AE 70 yrs

Goff, Deborah, w/o Elder Enoch Goff, d 15 Oct 1816 aged 76 yrs

Chase, Simpson, b 9 Aug 1799, d 8 May 1855

Chase, Rebecca, w/o Simpson Chase, b Dec 1801, d 8 Oct 1868

Westcoat, Richard M., d 19 Feb 1880 aged 68 yrs

Westcoat, Rebecca C., w/o Richard M. Westcoat, d 26 Feb 1846 aged 32 yrs

Westcoat, Levira H., w/o Richard M. Westcoat, d 27 Feb 1882 aged 66 yrs

Lesure, William E., b 15 May 1784, d 8 July 1861

Lesure, Elizabeth, w/o William E. Lesure, b 18 Oct 1778, d 6 Feb 1859

Macker, Charles, d 31 Aug 1854

Macker, Nancy, w/o Charles Macker, d 25 Dec 1842 aged 95 yrs

Wheeler, Job, d 10 July 1853 aged 81 yrs

Wheeler, Patience, w/o Job Wheeler, d 29 Aug 1847

Wheeler, Emily Jane, d/o Leonard & Lavina W. Wheeler, d 15 Oct 1853 aged 16 yrs 7 mos 5 days

Andrews, Etta Amelia, w/o Duawon O. Andrews, d 2 April 1854

Wheeler, Walker, d 26 Nov 1846 aged 67 yrs

Wheeler, Anna, w/o Walker Wheeler, d 1876

Maker, Philly P., 1807-1890

Maker, Clarissa W., w/o Philly P. Maker, d 26 Oct 1861

Lesure, Hannah, 1803-1898

Horton, Eldora A., 1864-1904

Wheeler, John S., s/o Walker & Anna Walker, d 4 Aug 1868 aged 51 yrs

Westcoat, Charles E., 1855-1922

Westcoat, Henry M., d 13 Sept 1889 aged 56 yrs 14 days

Westcoat, Betsey Emeline, w/o Henry M. Westcoat, d 25 Nov 1878 aged 35 yrs 19 days

Westcoat, Truman, s/o Henry M. & Betsey E. Westcoat, d 9 May 1881 aged 20 yrs 3 mos

Westcoat, Elenor B., d/o Henry M. & Betsey E. Westcoat, d 8 May 1881 aged 1 yr 5 mos

Westcoat, Richard, b 5 March 1866, d 1 Sept 1899

Westcoat, Charlotte, w/o Richard Westcoat, 1868-1920

Westcoat, Alvin T., 1858-1946

Westcoat, Etta P., w/o Alvin T. Westcoat, 1867-1964

Wheeler, John, d Oct 1824

Wheeler, Deborah, w/o John Wheeler, d 1824

Wheeler, Enoch, d 20 Feb 1832 aged 43 yrs

Goff, Enoch, d 14 June 1805 aged 33 yrs

Goff, Mary, w/o Enoch Goff, d 4 March 1858 aged 58 yrs 2 days

Goff, Benjamin, d 8 Nov 1832 aged 50 yrs

Goff, Elenor, w/o Benjamin Goff, d 9 April 1871 aged 84 yrs

Goff, Nancy, w/o Nathan Goff & d/o Hosea Horton, d 20 Jan 1824 AE 23 yrs

Horton, Constant, d 14 Feb 1825 AE 85 yrs

Horton, Aaron, d 1 June 1823 AE 51 yrs

Horton, Abigail, w/o Aaron Horton, d 13 Dec 1828 AE 49 yrs

Horton, Aaron, d 22 Aug 1878 aged 78 yrs 6 mos 15 days

Horton, Susan, w/o Aaron Horton, d 27 Sept 1846 aged 50 yrs

Horton, Joannah, w/o Shubael Horton, d 21 Jan 1856 aged 89 yrs

Horton, Shubael, d 16 Sept 1840

Pettis, Benjamin, d 16 March 1856 aged 75 yrs

Pettis, Sally, w/o Benjamin Pettis, d 6 Aug 1842 aged 61 yrs

Paull, James, 1791-1859

Paull, Betsey, 1790-1874

Paull, James A., 1814-1873

Paull, Eleanor, 1815-1867

Goff, Jesse J., d 1 Dec 1847 aged 25 yrs

Horton, James, b 10 Sept 1837, d 31 March 1907

Horton, Mary Asenath, w/o James Horton, b 30 June 1843, d 28 Jan 1915

Horton, George L., 1797-1866

Horton, Ann, w/o George L. Horton, 1795-1837

Horton, Patience B., w/o George L. Horton, 1801-1853

Goff, Jefferson, d 20 Sept 1829 aged 25 yrs

Goff, Asenath, w/o Jefferson Goff, d 22 July 1832 aged 26 yrs

Goff, Samuel, d 9 Sept 1827 aged 67 yrs

Goff, Nathan B., b 7 Sept 1800, d 23 July 1861

Goff, Hannah, w/o Nathan B. Goff (BROKEN)

Goff, Polly, w/o Nathan B. Goff, b 26 March 1801, d (BROKEN)

Goff, William A., b 29 June 1831, d 4 Feb 1862

Goff, Sybil A. P., d/o James & Deborah Goff, b 17 Sept 1826, d 19 Nov 1851

Wheeler, Leonard, d 25 Jan 1890 aged 81 yrs 6 mos 18 days

Wheeler, Lovina, w/o Leonard Wheeler, d 22 Feb 1891 aged 78 yrs 10 mos 22 days

Wheeler, Royal, d 21 March 1877 aged 82 yrs 11 days

Wheeler, Serena, w/o Royal Wheeler, b 28 Oct 1799, d 27 Oct 1873

Goff, Isaiah, d 30 July 1846 aged 53 yrs 2 mos

Goff, Adaline H., w/o Isaiah Goff, b 16 Aug 1807, d 22 March 1868

Goff, Pamela, w/o Isaiah Goff, d 9 Sept 1825 AE 25 yrs

Goff, Nathan D., s/o Nathan & Hannah Goff, d 19 Dec 1830

Goff, Ruth A., d/o Nathan & Hannah Goff, d 16 Aug 1825 aged 11 yrs 8 mos

McNally, Matthew P., 1829-1902

McNally, Mary, w/o Matthew P. McNally, 1840-1921

Horton, Shubael L., b 11 Oct 1823, d 6 June 1857

Westcoat, John, d 31 May 1815 aged 74 yrs

Westcoat, Cordelia, w/o John Westcoat, d 21 May 1849 aged 74 yrs

Wood, Lillis, w/o David Wood, d 5 July 1843

Wastcoat, Cornelius, d 3 Jan 1803 aged 74 yrs

Wastcoat, Sarah, w/o Cornelius Wastcoat, d 30 Oct 1791 aged 60 yrs

Wastcoat, Rebekah, w/o Cornelious Wastcoat, d 1 March 1786 aged 30 yrs

Westcoat, Richard Esq., d 19 Dec 1836 aged 60 yrs

Westcoat, Sibbel, w/o Richard Westcoat Esq., d 25 Sept 1814 aged 38 yrs

Westcoat, Hannah, w/o Richard Westcoat Esq., d 26 Feb 1864 aged 78 yrs

Westcoat, Martha, d/o Richard & Sibbel Westcoat, d 12 Feb 1847 aged 44 yrs

Paull, Peter W., d 17 Jan 1811 aged 51 yrs

Paull, Silence, w/o Peter W. Paull, d 7 May 1795 aged 34 yrs

Pierce, Rachel, w/o Nathaniel Pearce, d 5 Jan 1831 aged 69 yrs

Pearce, Royal, s/o Nathaniel & Rachel Pearce, d 8 Dec 1848 aged 24 yrs

Bowen, David, d 6 Dec 1816

Bowen, Jonathan, d 14 Feb 1843 aged 57 yrs

Bowen, Polly, w/o Jonathan Bowen, d 22 Feb 1849

Bowen, Eliza E., d/o Jonathan & Polly Bowen, d 15 Oct 1844

Bowen, Polly, d/o Jonathan & Polly Bowen, d 6 Sept 1846 aged 21 yrs

Paull, Peter W., d 19 Feb 1855 aged 40 yrs

Lee, Israel, d 28 Nov 1838 aged 71 yrs

Lee, Elizabeth, w/o Israel Lee, d 28 Jan 1837 aged 66 yrs

Goff, Sarah A., d/o Isaish & Adaline H. Goff, d 20 Sept 1851 aged 18 yrs

Cummings, Caroline E., b 15 Aug 1828, d 1 April 1900

Waterman, Asa, d 1 May 1861 aged 76 yrs 8 mos

Waterman, Hannah, w/o Asa Waterman, d 24 Jan 1841 aged 45 yrs

Bosworth, Elisha, d 22 Nov 1843 aged 89 yrs

Bosworth, Lydia, w/o Elisha Bosworth, d 24 Jan 1840 aged 84 yrs

Waterman, Abraham G., s/o Asa & Hannah Waterman, d 23 Oct 1840 aged 4 yrs 3 mos 3 days

Richards, Adaline, d 11 March 1904 aged 74 yrs

Bowen, Levi, d 21 March 1816 aged 32 yrs 2 mos

Bowen, Ruth, w/o Levi Bowen, d 21 Jan 1867 aged 80 yrs 8 mos

Witherell, Ephraim, b 24 March 1793, d 16 March 1835

Baker, Polly, w/o Ephraim Witherell, b 18 Jan 1799, d 7 Jan 1871 aged 71 yrs 11 mos 17 days

Wetherell, Rebecca, w/o Thomas B. Wetherell, b 25 April 1838, d 20 June 1873

Wetherell, Mary, d/o Ephraim & Polly Wetherell, d 23 Feb 1855 aged 20 yrs 20 days

Wetherell, Thomas B., b 30 Jan 1828, d 2 April 1900

Fish, Rebecca, w/o Thomas B. Wetherell, b 25 April 1838, d 30 June 1873

Pidge, Polly, w/o Benjamin Pidge, d 1 Nov 1847 aged 71 yrs

Witherell, Sally, d 31 Dec 1855 aged 83 yrs

Smith, Stephen, d 25 June 1899 aged 84 yrs

Francis, Ezekiel, d 13 Nov 1849 aged 66 yrs

Francis, Betsey, w/o Ezekiel Francis, d 12 June 1810 aged 22 yrs

Francis, Joanna, w/o Ezekiel Francis, d 4 April 1875 aged 84 yrs

Talbot, Deacon Seth, d 3 Feb 1857 aged 70 yrs

Talbot, Sally, w/o Deacon Seth Talbot, d 30 Aug 1857

Talbot, Mary, w/o Thomas Featherstone & d/o Deacon Seth & Sally Talbot, d 26 Oct 1851

Bliss, Lydia, d 2 Nov 1876 aged 85 yrs

Bliss, Olive, d 24 April 1874 aged 85 yrs

Bliss, Ardel, d 29 Aug 1831 aged 71 yrs

Bliss, Sybil, w/o Ardel Bliss, d 13 June 1850 aged 95 yrs

Bliss, Sarah P., d/o Ardel & Sybil Bliss, d 13 Jan 1804 aged 6 yrs

Vickorey, Robert, d 23 May 1827 aged 68 yrs

Vickorey, Ruth, w/o Robert Vickorey, d 27 Feb 1870 aged 90 yrs 1 mo 21 days

Paul, Captain Peter, b 20 March 1787, d 27 Oct 1851

Paul, Eunice, w/o Captain Peter Paul, b 29 May 1798, d (BROKEN)

Paul, Dilly, w/o Captain Peter Paul, d 14 Sept 1872 aged 28 yrs

Goff, Ephraim, d 23 Sept 1838

Goff, Anna, w/o Ephraim Goff, d 30 Aug 1837 aged 56 yrs

Horton, Benson, d 30 May 1875 aged 77 yrs 5 mos 6 days

Horton, Pamela, w/o Benson Horton, d 1 Sept 1861

Horton, Alfred A., b 27 Nov 1842, d ......

Horton, Sarah M., w/o Alfred A. Horton, b 13 March 1844, d 12 June 1913

Horton, Lucy S., w/o Alfred A. Horton, d 1 March 1875 aged 27 yrs 9 mos 9 days

Horton, Orrin N., b 21 June 1839, d 2 July 1913

Horton, Charlotte, w/o Orrin N. Horton, b 15 April 1843, d....

Horton, Wheeler, d 11 Nov 1857 aged 91 yrs

Horton, Lucretia, w/o Wheeler Horton, d 21 Dec 1855 aged 85 yrs 7 mos

Elliot, William W., d 18 April 1881 aged 21 yrs 26 days

Horton, Charlotte A., w/o George H. Horton, b 3 May 1851, d 13 Sept 1876

Goff, Zenas, d 25 Dec 1863 aged 80 yrs 7 mos 18 days

Goff, Nancy, w/o Zenas Goff, d 25 Nov 1866 aged 79 yrs

Lewis, Isaac, d 10 July 1872 aged 65 yrs

Lewis, Oshea Ann, w/o Isaac Lewis, d 13 Jan 1863 aged 53 yrs

Goff, Adoniram B., d 18 Nov 1925 aged 71 yrs 1 mo

Leonard, Sarah E., w/o Adoniriam B. Goff, d 21 July 1893 aged 34 yrs 1 mo 7 days

Goff, Louis Bliss Jr., 1928-1933

Horton, Charles A., 1835-1919

Wastcoat, Rebecca E., w/o Charles A. Horton, 1839-1860

Jackens, Lydia M., w/o Charles A. Horton, 1843-1919

Babbitt, Gideon A., 1859-1938

Sisson, Clara A., w/o Gideon A. Babbitt, 1862-1899

Babbitt, Bertha A., 1885-1908

Horton, Lindly, d 20 March 1904 aged 92 yrs 15 days

Horton, Adaline B., w/o Lindly Horton, d 18 Dec 1884 aged 63 yrs 2 mos 6 days

Horton, Fannie M., d/o Lindly & Adaline B. Horton, d 24 April 1878 aged 24 yrs

Horton, Esther A., d/o Lindly & Adaline B. Horton, d 17 Oct 1871 aged 21 yrs 2 mos

Horton, John H., s/o Lindly & Adeline B. Horton, d 23 May 1928 aged 72 yrs 1 mo 17 days

Williams, George O., b 19 Feb 1834, d 14 June 1884

Williams, Susan M., b 11 ov 1834, d 22 June 1911

Goff, Alpheus B., 1857-1903

Briggs, Emma A., w/o Alpheus B. Goff, & d/o David H. & Lillas Briggs, 1860-1881

McMaster, Eliza, w/o Alpheus B. Goff, 1862-1939

Williams, William P., 1839-1909

Horton, Nancy S., w/o William P. Williams, 1843-1914

Williams, Eva J., d/o William P. & Nancy S. Williams, b 6 April 1870, d 7 Dec 1892

Horton, Nelson, b 9 June 1821, d 5 June 1907

Horton, Caroline F., w/o Nelson Horton, b 1 March 1833, d 25 April 1865

Francis, Henry, 1809-1859

Francis, Nancy M., w/o Henry Francis, 1820-1896

Pettis, Aaron, 1792-1858

Pettis, Dorcas, w/o Aaron Pettis, 1794-1880

Wheeler, Shubael G., 1815-1877

Wheeler, Henrietta M., w/o Shubael G. Wheeler, 1824-1863

Wheeler, Elkanah A., s/o Shubael & Henrietta Wheeler, 1843-1863

Wheeler, Anna M., d/o Shubael & Henrietta Wheeler, 1852-1863

Wheeler, Sarah E., d/o Shubael & Henrietta Wheeler, 1858-1863

Wheeler, William W., s/o Shubael & Henrietta Wheeler, 1841-1863

Wheeler, Harriet, w/o William W. Wheeler, 1836-1893

Waterman, Robert S., b 14 Jan 1830, d 21 Jan 1876

Bliss, Elder Otis,....

Sheldon, Eliza A., 1818-1910

Sweet, Gardner G., A member of Co H 7th Regt RI Vols, b 20 Sept 1813, d 17 March 1874

Sheldon, George W., 1833-1907

Horton, Howard A., 1884-1930

Horton, Emma H., w/o Howard A. Horton, 1881-1964

Horton, Charles L., 1875-1966

Horton, Clara M., w/o Charles L. Horton, 1896-1921

Gorton, Rebecca, w/o Rufus Gorton, d 6 April 1899 aged 57 yrs

Gorton, Thomas E., s/o Rufus & Rebecca Gorton, d 25 July 1887 aged 29 yrs

Dunbar, Addie, w/o Frank M. Dunbar, d 25 Oct 1880 aged 17 yrs 16 days

Francis, E. G., d 2 March 1889 aged 74 yrs 1 mo 18 days

Francis, Lydia W., w/o E. G. Frances, d 26 June 1895 aged 74 yrs 10 mos 2 days

Francis, Seth T., d 1 June 1863 aged 6 yrs 7 mos 25 days

Francis, Amelia J., d 11 June 1863 aged 10 yrs 7 mos 8 days

Francis, Anna L., d 13 June 1863 aged 12 yrs 5 mos 9 days

Goff, Emerson W., 1848-1917

Wheeler, Clarebel, w/o Emerson W. Goff, 1854-1873

Sherman, Ida M., w/o Emerson W. Goff, 1856-1930

Goff, Chester E., 1883-1953

Goff, Andrew J., b 17 Sept 1843, d 25 March 1899

Goff, Ephraim, d 9 Jan 1872 aged 68 yrs 8 mos

Wheeler, Laura A., w/o Ephraim Goff, d 30 May 1888 aged 77 yrs 8 mos 11 days

Goff, Albert W., 1844-1891

Francis, Nancy M., w/o Albert W. Goff, 1849-1928

Goff, Sarah B., w/o Leonard Goff, 1808-1876

Goff, Ephraim N., b 25 July 1838, d 19 Feb 1908

Goff, Harriet J., w/o Ephraim N. Goff, b 23 Jan 1832, d 20 April 1865

Lizotte, Barbara E., b 7 Sept 1912, d 14 Sept 1985

Goff, William A., 1871-1934

Lewis, Juliane E., w/o William A. Goff, d 1952

Bliss, Abdial, d 6 March 1878 aged 92 yrs 1 mo 17 daus

Bliss, Charlotte, w/o Abdial Bliss, d 18 Nov 1874 aged 86 yrs 2 mos

Bliss, Seneca, d 12 Oct 1879 aged 85 yrs 8 mos

Francis, David W., 1841-1913

Francis, Elizabeth W., w/o David W. Francis, 1851-1880

Francis, Bradford, 1811-1866

Francis, Betsey, w/o Bradford Francis, 1808-1837

Francis, Abby, w/o Bradford Francis, 1805-1872

Francis, Betsey E., d/o Bradford & Abby Francis, 1844-1858

Brown, Benjamin, d 23 April 18..

Brown, Lydia, w/o Benjamin Brown, d 12 Nov 1877 aged 74 yrs

Olney, Merrell C., 1897-1963

Olney, Gertrude N., w/o Merrell C. Olney, 1906-1988

Olney, Charles E., 1872-1919

Goff, Truman N., b 31 Aug 1845, d 9 Feb 1916

Carey, Mary A., w/o Truman N. Goff, b 21 Jan 1842, d 6 June 1896

Goff, Benjamin F., b 15 Aug 1850, d 7 Nov 1913

Smith, Ernest H., 1885-1959

Smith, Mildred M., w/o Ernest H. Smith, 1899-1988

Wheeler, Jasper W., 1822-1892

Wheeler, Patty A. F., w/o Jasper W. Wheeler, 1824-1878

Wheeler, Frances J., s/o Jasper & Patty Wheeler, 1848-1928

Wheeler, Julia S., w/o Francis J. Wheeler, 1851-1935

Allen, Mae V., 1917-1968

Best, Jean R. Horton, 1912-1994

Chace, Mary A., w/o David W. Francis, b 5 Dec 1857, d 25 Oct 1943

Goff, George H., b 13 May 1846, d 3 Feb 1903

Goff, Sarah A., w/o George H. Goff, b 23 March 1851, d 27 March 1933

Harlow, John H., 1854-1928

Harlow, Nellie M., w/o John H. Harlow, 1856-1942

Harlow, Nellie A., d/o John & Nellie Harlow, 1882-1945
Harlow, Clifford N., s/o John & Nellie Harlow, 1884-1917
Duffy, William F., 1897-1967
Stuart, Florence, w/o William F. Duffy, 1898-1991
Zieba, Doris M., 1919-1970
Goff, Howard B., s/o George & Sarah A. Goff, b 28 Dec 1881, d 9 July 1904

Scott, Col. Saul B., d 27 Jan 1898 aged 88 yrs 6 mos 21 days

Scott, Susan P., w/o Col. Saul B. Scott, d 14 July 1886 aged 76 yrs 7 mos

Bassett, Oscar M., d 22 Aug 1901 aged 78 yrs 4 mos 17 days

Bassett, Caroline S., b 8 Jan 1828, d 5 Feb 1923

Bassett, Mary A., d 7 July 1870 aged 1 yr

Bassett, Walter S., d 10 Oct 1880 aged 8 yrs

Bassett, Clara M., w/o George Andrews, d 27 July 1902

Skyes, Elizabeth R., 1835-1911

Comey, William M., b 18 Feb 1840, d 16 Feb 1927, A member of Co E
2nd US Inf

Comey, Ophelia H., b 30 June 1842, d 11 May 1925

Comey, Frank Roy, b 12 Jan 1880, d 13 March 1898

Dalghren, Ernest F., 1876-1935

Marley, Ella F., w/o Ernest F. Dalghren, 1876-1956

Dalghren, Charles A., 1875-1941

Ledbury, Henry, b 26 Feb 1858, d 3 Jan 1938

Ledbury, Mary Louisa, w/o Henry Ledbury, b 7 Dec 1855, d 12 March
1907

Petty, Catherine M., w/o Henry Ledbury, b 15 Aug 1863, d 7 Jan 1935

Milbye, Lucy L., b 11 June 1884, d 21 June 1974

Ledbury, Arthur F., b 15 Nov 1881, d 24 Jan 1919

Hallam, Flora, w/o Arthur Ledbury, b 12 June 1883, d 29 Oct 1960

Ledbury, Albert V., s/o Arthur & Flora Ledbury, b 10 May 1911, d 29
Nov 1977

Blackwell, Thomas H., d 8 Jan 1877 aged 32 yrs 10 mos

Shepardson, James, d 8 March 1863 aged 74 yrs

Shepardson, Joseph E., 1824-1897

Shepardson, Hellen Cole, 1840-1904

Goodwin, William B., b 16 Feb 1910, d 7 June 1975

Johnson, Doris F., w/o William B. Goodwin, b 26 June 1913, d 12 Dec
1988

Stack, Robert T., b 7 March 1914, d 24 Jan ,1961

Stack, Beatrice F., w/o Robert T. Stack, b 12 Feb 1913, d 22 Sept 1989
Stack, Margaret E., 1880-1963
Dalghren, Albert J., 1845-1932
Dalghren, Matilda, w/o Albert J. Dalghren, 1848-1912
Stowers, Herbert Morrell, b 2 April 1854, d 6 Feb 1934
King, Elizabeth Eldora, w/o Herbert M. Stowers, b 22 Sept 1856, d 10 Oct 1925
Fisher, Rufus Albert, ...
Rhodes, Elizabeth A., w/o Rufus Albert Fisher, 1843-1909
Shepardson, John, d 4 Oct 1878 aged 78 yrs
Shepardson, Mary, w/o John Shepardson, d 5 April 1882 aged 88 yrs
Blandon, Thomas, d 17 Nov 1891 aged 68 yrs
Blandon, Lucy F., w/o Thomas Blandon, d 23 June 1872 aged 44 yrs
Blandon, Ella F., 1865-1935
Blandon, Cora M., 1858-1940
Comey, Ethel O., d 6 Dec 1877 aged 7 days
McCormick, Thomas, d 3 June 1882 aged 61 yrs 4 mos
Foster, Georgianna, d 9 March 1871 aged 3 yrs 10 mos 10 days
Kingsbury, Stephen, d 30 Jan 1856 aged 73 yrs
Kingsbury, Olive, w/o Stephen Kingsbury, d 30 Jan 1873 aged 84 yrs 6 mos
Torrey, John F., b 19 Feb 1833, d 13 May 1910
Torrey, Clara A., w/o John F. Torrey, b 10 Oct 1845, d 24 Jan 1879
Torrey, Mary J., w/o John F. Torrey, b 9 Jan 1851, d 29 March 1914
Tenney, John E., 1851-1933
Tenney, Mary, w/o John E. Tenney, 1853-1917
Daniels, T. Jefferson, 1826-1906
Hicks, Celia A., w/o T. Jefferson Daniels, 1824-1857
Billings, Mary E., w/o T. Jeferson, 1838-1922
Daniels, Cyrus, 1874-1875
Daniels, Dora E., 1879-1881
Howard, Henry M., 1868-1944
Howard, Hattie E., 1868-1964
Howard, Apollo F., d 25 Nov 1874 aged 67 yrs 10 mos 14 days
Howard, Caroline W., d 12 Feb 1904 aged 76 yrs 7 mos 5 days
Stark, Laura E., d 8 Sept 1859 aged 8 yrs
Howard, Franklin E., d 12 Jan 1874 aged 9 yrs
Ramsey, Robinson, d 6 Jan 1890 aged 75 yrs
Ramsey, Ann Jane, w/o Robinson Ramsey, d 10 Feb 1890 aged 65 yrs
Kingsbury, John H., 1819-1898

Kingsbury, Harriet S., w/o John H. Kingsbury, 1818-1919

Richardson, Elmira L., w/o John W. Richardson, d 18 May 1874 aged 34 yrs

Fisher, James, b 11 Aug 1794 Medway, MA, d 16 May 1886 Franklin, MA

Fisher, Lydia, w/o James Fisher, d 10 Dec 1866 aged 67 yrs

Wiggin, Shepard C., b 12 Aug 1821 Tuftonborough, New Hampshire, d 16 Jan 1862 Falmouth, Virginia, where his body now rests, A member of 35th Reg Mass Vols

Wiggins, Shepard G., d 28 May 1854 Medway, MA aged 31 yrs

Hardy, Eunice M., w/o Eliphat D. Hardy, d 28 May 1861 AE 63 yrs

Paine, Hiram, d 28 Nov (BROKEN) aged 41 yrs 8 mos

Paine, Rozina B., w/o Hiram Paine, d 28 Oct 1852 aged 49 yrs

Miller, Lewis L., d 20 Oct 1862 Georgetown, DC aged 22 yrs

Kingsbury, Horatio, 1812-1883

Gillmore, Adelia R., w/o Horatio Kingsbury, 1814-1898

Kingsbury, Abbie Maria, d/o Horatio & Adelia Kingsbury, 1840-1859

Richardson, Stephen, d 13 Nov 1890 aged 77 yrs 7 mos

Richardson, Eliza B., w/o Stephen Richardson, d 17 Oct 1844 aged 28 yrs 9 mos

Richardson, Mary, w/o Stephen Richardson, d 30 April 1883 aged 74 yrs

French, Robert F., 1876-1943

Kingsbury, Mary L., w/o Robert F. French, 1875-1951

Paine, Phila, w/o Lt. Alvah Paine, d 5 Feb 1818 aged 28 yrs

Paine, Arnold J., s/o Hiram & Rozina B. Paine, b 19 Aug 1847, d 22 Feb 1887

Weeman, Eli P., 1850-1935

Fisher, Isabell L., w/o Eli P. Weeman, 1856-1937

Fisher, Elmer M., 1873-1952

Fisher, Walter M., 1839-1918, A member of Vol Co C 45th Mass Inf & 3rd Heavy Art

Fisher, Alice J., w/o Walter M. Fisher, 1846-1930

Fisher, Walter, d 26 March 1890 aged 81 yrs

Fisher, Emily P., w/o Walter Fisher, d 28 March 1900 aged 86 yrs

Miller, Nathaiel, MD, b Rehoboth, MA, d 10 June 1830 Franklin, MA

Miller, Hannah, w/o Dr. Nathaniel Miller, b 29 May 1777, d 19 April 1840

Gill, Henry, d 13 Jan 1888 aged 64 yrs

Gill, Annie M., w/o Henry Gill, d 4 Jan 1895 aged 67 yrs

Gill, Henry Levitt, s/o Henry & Annie Gill, d 12 Oct 1850 aged 13 mos

Boyd, Col. John, d 27 July 1828 aged 90 yrs

Boyd, Hannah, w/o Col. John Boyd, d 9 Nov 1829

Paine, Ellen M., d/o Hiram & Rozina Paine, d 2 July 1841 aged 4 mos

Paine, Eva R., d/o Hiram & Rozina Paine, d 22 Dec 1843 aged 4 mos

Boyd, William B., d 27 July 1883 aged 82 yrs 10 mos

Boyd, Emeline C., w/o William B. Boyd, d 8 Feb 1868 aged 59 yrs

Boyd, Emeline C., d/o William & Emeline Boyd, d 11 May 1837 aged 6 yrs 9 mos

Miller, Emily, d 16 Jan 1884 aged 70 yrs

Miller, John W., d 8 March 1867 aged 65 yrs

Atwood, Harriet, w/o Samuel M. Bullard, b 28 March 1819, d 20 Oct 1892

Sanborn, John F., b 12 Feb 1843, d 22 Jan 1893, A member of Co A 22nd Regt Mass Vols

Bullard, Carrie A., w/o John Sanborn, b 1 July 1852, d 8 Sept 1918

Boyd, Martha W., d 13 April 1885 aged 87 yrs

Blanchard, Esther A., w/o William Blanchard, d 9 Jan 1851 aged 20 yrs 2 mos 25 days

Horton, Caleb M., s/o Jabez & Martha Horton, d Dec 1848 aged 37 yrs

Horton, Martha, w/o Jabez Horton & d/o Phily Martin, d 29 July 1824 aged 47 yrs

Boyd, Oliver D., b 8 June 1802, d 22 March 1862

Boyd., Maria L., w/o Oliver D. Boyd, d 10 Sept 1866 aged 64 yrs 3 mos

Cleaveland, Captain George P., d 8 Nov 1836 aged 36 yrs

Cleaveland, Lona, w/o Capt. George P. Cleaveland, d 19 March 1838 aged 50 yrs

Boyd, Rachel, w/o Amos H. Boyd, d 21 Dec 1880

Folsom, John S., b 12 Oct 1840, d 27 Aug 1907

Guild, Hermon, d 5 July 1860 aged 76 yrs 10 mos 21 days

Guild ,Melinda J., w/o Hermon Guild, d 28 May 1852 aged 56 yrs 7 mos 21 days

Guild, James A., b 17 May 1817, d 18 Dec 1891

Winn, Lucina P., w/o James A. Guild, b 5 Dec 1819, d 22 Feb 1900

Jordan, George A., d 4 April 1879 aged 57 yrs

Jordan, Sarah Louisa, w/o George A. Jordan, b 1 Feb 1820, d 23 Dec 1893

Fisher, John J., d 7 Feb 1876 aged 82 yrs

Fisher, Esther, w/o John J. Fisher, d 22 Dec 1828 aged 31 yrs

Hallam, Samuel, 1852-1911

Foley, Elizabeth, w/o Samuel Hallam, 1862-1926

Hartshorn, Edmund, d 13 Aug 1893 aged 82 yrs 10 mos

Hartshorn, Susan M., w/o Edmund Hartshorn, d 8 Oct 1880 aged 65 yrs 3 mos 19 days

Hartshorn, Frank Eugene, s/o Edmund & Susan Hartshorn, d 15 Aug 1846 aged 8 mos

Hartshorn, Herbert Austin, s/o Edmund & Susan Hartshorn, d 14 May 1848 aged 9 mos 19 days

Leonard, Harriette, w/o Arthur Leonard, b 4 March 1846, d 2 April 1902

Gould, Priscilla, b 16 Sept 1813, d 20 May 1877

Adams, Edna M., w/o Earl Bradford Guild, 1854-1896

Winn, Josephine L., only child of Otis & Lydia Winn, d 27 Aug 1854 aged 21 days

Hallam, Thomas, 1816-1902

Hallam, Eliza, w/o Thomas Hallam, 1820-1900

Harris, Elisha R., d 21 May 1891 aged 72 yrs 7 mos

Harris, Betsey, w/o Elisha R. Harris, b 3 April 1821, d 18 Oct 1887

White, Cyrus D., b 25 Aug 1827, d 26 April 1880

Jordan, Hartley D., d 5 Feb 1873 aged 20 yrs 9 mos

Jordan, Charles, d 6 Jan 1877 ged 71 yrs 3 mos

Wood, Horace A., d 8 Dec 1843 aged 29 yrs

Wood, Lucretia, w/o Horace A. Wood, d 6 Dec 1845 aged 23 yrs

Trulson, Andrew, b 20 March 1840, d 15 Oct 1909

Scott, Pardon E., d 17 Oct 1852 aged 30 yrs

Fisher, Harlow, b 1 Sept 1795, d 16 Jan 1874

Fisher, Ruth, w/o Harlow Fisher, d 21 Jan 1866 aged 72 yrs

Daniels, Lucretia D., w/o Amos Daniels, 1829-1884

Daniels, Abigail A., w/o William H. Daniels, d 6 Nov 1847 aged 30 yrs

Metcalf, Alfred H., b 7 April 1816, d 14 March 1890

Metcalf, Susannah B., w/o Alfred H. Metcalf, b 30 Dec 1817, d 12 March 1896

Winn, Otis H., d 6 March 1863 Alexandria, Virginia, aged 44 yrs 10 mos 6 days

King, Louisa, w/o Warren King, d 31 Dec 1857 aged 23 yrs

Richards, Sarah, d/o Amos & Mary Richards. b 9 June 1847, d 23 Aug 1849

Cook, Eliza A., d 18 April 1900 aged 45 yrs

Wood, Horace A., b 13 Sept 1859 aged 20 yrs 11 mos

Wood, Josiah O.C., d 14 Dec 1864 of wounds received at Malvan Hill, he d. at David's Island

Wood, Alonzo H., d 26 Nov 1881 aged 71 yrs 6 mos

Wood, Abigail B., w/o Alonzo H. Wood, d 6 May 1882 aged 75 yrs 7 mos

Metcalf, Whiting, b 31 Jan 1779, d 27 May 1870

Metcalf, Betsey, w/o Whiting Metcalf & d/o Ichabod & Chloe Dean, b 21 Sept 1781, d 5 Nov 1859

Richards, Martha H., d/o Jeremiah & Sarah Richards, d 10 June 1818 aged 19 yrs 6 mos

Richards, Eleanor, d/o Amos & Mary Richards, b 13 June 1832, d 13 June 1851

Littlefield, Elizabeth, d 30 Oct 1844 aged 66 yrs

Dorr, Emma F., d/o David & Helen Dorr, d 20 Oct 1852 aged 1 yr 10 mos

Buckley, James, 1838-1909

Buckley, Mary A., w/o James Buckley, 1849-1899

Connor, Olive, d/o Anthony & Sarah K. Connor, b 7 April 1870, d 6 Aug 1895

Holmes, George W., b 16 Oct 1876 England, d 28 May 1895

Clark, Simeon, d 14 April 1856 aged 73 yrs

Clark, Betsey, w/o Simeon Clark, d 12 May 1863, aged 78yrs

Clark, Dyar, d 7 April 1841 aged 71 yrs

Clark, Mary, w/o Dyar Clark, d 22 Feb 1842 aged 72 yrs

Clark, Nancy, d/o Dyar & Mary Clark, d 8 Jan 1833 aged 38 yrs

Metcalf, Eramus B., 1819-1908

Downs, Ann Sophia, w/o Eramus B. Metcalf, 1820-1866

Metcalf, Charles, s/o Eramus & Ann Sophia Metcalf, 1843-1854

Kingsbury, Doct. Samuel Allen, d 8 Oct 1821 aged 28 yrs

Kingsbury, Polly, w/o Capt. Ebenezer Kingsbury, d 15 Jan 1853 aged 79 yrs

Richards, Amos, d 11 Aug 1852 aged 51 yrs 11mos

Richards, Mary, w/o Amos Richards, d 20 Aug 1883 aged 77 yrs 10 mos 15 days

Sawyer, Carrie M., 1839-1923

Lawrence, Addison C., d 18 April 1881 aged 72 yrs

Lawrence, Alice, w/o Addison C. Lawrence......

Reid, Abner, 1828-....

Reid, Rebecca, w/o Abner Reid, 1835-1900

Reid, Emma R., d/o Abner & Rebecca Reid, 1871-1902

Whiting, Deacon Joseph, d 7 Nov 1826 aged 95 yrs

Whiting, Abigail, w/o Dea. Joseph Whiting, d 13 May 1824 aged 90 yrs

Ward, Clara Helen, 1847-1850

Ward, Edward L., 1824-1885

Ward, Mary F., w/o Edward L. Ward, d 5 Feb 1906

Ward, Herbert E., 1853-1932

Kingsbury, Abigail, w/o Capt. Stephen Kingsbury, d 31 Dec 1820 aged 56 yrs

Kingsbury, Capt. Stephen, d 16 Sept 1809 aged 56 yrs

Kingsbury, Horatio, d 31 July 1808 aged 29 yrs

Daniels, John H.R., b 16 Oct 1800, d 23 Sept 1870

Daniels, Louisa P., w/o John H.R. Daniels, d 30 Dec 1848 aged 70 yrs

Johnson, Samuel C., d 20 Aug 1822 aged 22 yrs

Fisher, Samuel, d 6 Oct 1800 aged 68 yrs

Lethbridge, Richard, d 8 May 1838 aged 81 yrs

Lethbridge, Jerusha, w/o Richard Lethbridge, d 2 July 1833 aged 74 yrs

Lethbridge, Samuel, d 22 Oct 1806 aged 84 yrs

Kingsbury, Ebenezer, d 1 July 1811

Pond, Nancy W., w/o Lewis Pond 2nd, d 13 Jan 1855 aged 66 yrs

Richardson, Eli, d 4 June 1827 aged 50 yrs

Richardson, Chloe, d 18 June 1856 aged 81 yrs

Richardson, Capt. Eli, d 24 April 1823 aged 77 yrs

Richardson, Mehitabel, w/o Capt. Eli Richardson, d 12 July 1837 aged 88 yrs

Bacon, Abigail, d 1807

Bacon, Chloe, d 1802

Daniels, Nathan, d 25 Nov 1841 aged 93 yrs

Daniels, Sarah, w/o Nathan Daniels, d 5 March 1838 aged 80 yrs

Daniels, Adams, d 1826 aged 69 yrs

Richardson, Ruth M., d 9 June 1884 aged 72 yrs

Breck, Mr. James, d 10 Nov 1822 aged 64 yrs

Breck, Judith, w/o James Breck, d 1 Nov 1841 aged 87 yrs

Richardson, John W., b 30 Dec 1774, d 15 Sept 1843

Richardson, Matilda K., w/o John W. Richardson, d 19 Jan 1859 aged 80 yrs

Richardson, Elisha, d 15 March 1798 aged 54 yrs

Richardson, Abigail, w/o Elisha Richardson, d 3 Oct 1827 aged 79 yrs

Pond, Martha, w/o Amie B. Pond, d 10 Jan 1836 aged 92 yrs

Pond, Amie B., d 6 April 1855 aged 65 yrs 4 mos

Fisher, Mary, w/o Jason Fisher, d 14 June 1804 aged 43 yrs

Fisher, Jason, d 29 April 1822 aged 62 yrs

Kingsbury, Ebenezer, d 12 Nov 1892 aged 84 yrs 2 mos

Breck, Anna, d 12 May 1877 aged 60 yrs 5 mos

Breck, Silas, b 13 July 1783, d 25 May 1875

Breck, Anne, w/o Silas Breck, b 8 May 1795, d 29 Aug 1849

Richardson, Elisha, d 14 June 1866 aged 75 yrs 10 mos

Richardson, Ruth, w/o Elisha Richardson, d 15 Oct 1827 aged 40 yrs
Blake, Harriet, w/o Elisha Richardson, d 21 Feb 1891 aged 95 yrs 1 mo 16 days
Fisher, David, b 23 May 1809, d 3 June 1886
Morse, Jason, d 10 July 1829 aged 68 yrs
Morse, Deacon Levi, d 13 Oct 1866 aged 69 yrs
Morse, Triphena, w/o Dea Levi F. Morse, d 4 Jan 1864 aged 62 yrs
Fisher, Hattie E., w/o R. A. Fisher & d/o A.T. & Harriet A. Lawrence, d 4 March 1875 aged 23 yrs
Fisher, Daniel, b 5 May 1764, d 17 Nov 1835
Fisher, Betsey, w/o Daniel Fisher, b 11 Jan 1778, d 26 Feb 1860
Fisher, Olive, w/o Jason Fisher, d 21 Jan 1836 aged 85 yrs
Metcalf, Abijah Whiting, s/o Whiting & Betsey Metcalf, b 17 Dec 1803, d 6 Sept 1839
Metcalf, Joanna W., w/o Abijah Whiting Metcalf & also w/o Hartford Leonard, b 21 Jan 1803, d 16 Sept 1884
Bullard, Cephas, d 21 Nov 1861 aged 71 yrs
Bullard, Sukey M., w/o Cephas Bullard, d 5 Feb 1861 AE 68 yrs
Sanger, Charles K., b 7 Dec 1829, d 10 April 1902
Fisher, Hezekiah, d 27 June 1809 aged 84 yrs
Fisher, Abigail, w/o Hezekiah Fisher, d 16 Jan 1788
Fisher, Daniel, b 31 Aug 1800, d 29 July 1870
Fisher, Sylvia D., w/o Daniel Fisher, b 3 April 1805, d 11 May 1863
Warfield, Ebenezer E., d 16 Dec 1848 aged 36 yrs
Warfield, Sarah M., d 29 Jan 1881 aged 67 yrs
Warfield, Mary E., d 12 Feb 1870 aged 27 yrs, buried in Turkey
Bacon, Deacon Joseph, d 6 May 1843 aged 80 yrs
Bacon, Ruth, d 17 Jan 1866 aged 89 yrs
Metcalf, Deacon James, d 19 July 1843 aged 86 yrs
Metcalf, Abigail, w/o Dea James Metcalf, d 3 Feb 1815 aged 58 yrs
Allen, Samuel, d 14 Jan 1866 aged 88 yrs
Allen, Rhoda M., w/o Samuel Allen, d 15 April 1862 aged 67 yrs
Allen, Julitta, w/o Samuel Allen, d 11 Oct 1848 aged 56 yrs
Howard, Huldah, d 10 Oct 1815 aged 30 yrs
Pease,Mary L., w/o A.D. Richardson, b Jan 1836 East Windsor, CT, d 4 March 1864
Bacon, Lt. Seth, d 24 Nov 1822 aged 86 yrs
Bacon, Timothy, d 6 June 1784
Bacon, Abigail, only child of Capt. Joseph & Chloe Bacon, d 10 Nov 1807 aged 20 yrs

Bullard, Catherine F., b 20 March 1830, d 16 Sept 1888
Bullard, Eliza A., w/o Charles K. Sanger, b 9 Oct 1832, d 30 May 1913

Union Street Cemetery
Union Street
Franklin, Massachusetts

Metcalf, William, d 28 June 1872 aged 82 yrs 3 mos
Gaskill, Sally, w/o William Metcalf, d 25 Feb 1885 aged 87 yrs 10 mos 23
    days
Metcalf, Dr. William Warren, s/o William & Sally Metcalf, d 18 Aug
    1870 aged 51 yrs 4 mos 6 days
Metcalf, Alfred G., d 12 July 1901 aged 76 yrs 1 mo 19 days
Gilmore, Charlotte A., w/o Alfred G. Metcalf, d 26 Dec 1898 aged 74 yrs
    10 mos 21 days
Metcalf, Evelyn Eudora, d/o Alfred & Charlotte Metcalf, d 20 May 1865
    aged 18 yrs 8 mos 4 days
Metcalf, Louisa A., b 30 Jan 1861, d 12 Aug 1945
Chilson, Orin, b 25 July 1799, d 16 Sept 1863
Chilson, Diadama, w/o Orin Chilson, b 5 May 1808, d 10 March 1888
Chilson, James O., b 28 March 1837, d 2 July 1919
Chilson, Melansa G., w/o James O. Chilson, b 4 Sept 1843, d 30 Sept
    1917
Hubbard, Nathaniel T., 1826-1880
Hubbard, Mary L., 1836-1922
Hubbard, Ethel D., 1876-1959
King, Martha Eliza, w/o Edwin H. King, b 6 April 1836, d 12 March
    1875
Thayer, Davis, b 11 Dec 1778, d 27 Dec 1863
Thayer, Betsey M., b 30 June 1782, d 11 Aug 1863
Thayer, Davis Jr., b 20 Oct 1816, d 21 June 1902
Thayer, Margaret G., w/o Davis Thayer Jr. d 18 Nov 1842 aged 23 yrs 11
    mos
Thayer, Mary M., w/o Davis Thayer Jr., b 23 July 1822, d 26 April 1896
Whiting, Herbert, s/o Mary & Davis Thayer, 1858-1908

Thayer, Mary Eliza, d/o Davis & Mary Thyaer, & w/o A. J. Gallison MD, 1862-1904

Thayer, Emery, 1818-1899

Thayer, Eliza, w/o Emery Thayer, 1823-1867

Thayer, Rev. William M., 1820-1898

Thayer, Rebecca W., w/o Rev. William M. Thayer, 1823-1912

Thayer, William Makepeace, s/o Rev. William & Rebecca Thayer, 1854-1855

Thayer, Emery Davis, s/o Rev. William & Rebecca Thayer, 1856-1861

Thayer, Emma L., d/o Rev. William & Rebecca Thayer, b July 1862, d Oct 1862

Whiting, William E., b 10 July 1824, d 30 Oct 1891

Whiting, Betsey, 1822-1899

Whiting, Joseph, d 8 March 1866 aged 66 yrs

Whiting, Zeolide, b 26 Oct 1804, d 17 May 1891

Whiting, Jannette, d 6 July 1858 aged 5 yrs 7 mos

Metcalf, Lewis Dudley, 1834-1908

Metcalf, Myrtilla M., 1837-1920

Metcalf, Bessie Bird, 1871-1876

Metcalf, Fred Dudley, 1864-1929

Metcalf, Rachel, 1804-1891

Leonard, Elijah, 1826-1900

Leonard, Casendana M., 1842-1921

Guild, Grace M., 1873-1896

Stebbins, Charles H., 1822-1879

Jenks, C. Ellen, w/o Charles H. Stebbins, 1825-1919

Daniels, Elvira L., b 2 July 1826, d 1 Aug 1896

Daniels, Sabin, b Oct 1822, d June 1887

Daniels, Ellen, w/o A.O. Moffett, b 25 Jan 1846, d 13 Nov 1911

Aldrich, Frederick, b 4 June 1846, d 13 Jan 1900

Mann, Emily F., w/o Frederick Aldrich, b 27 Dec 1845, d 4 Feb 1926

Russell, William S.,....

Russell, Minnie May, w/o William S. Russell, 1865-1892

Corbin, Daniel O., 1844-1916, A member of Co H 18th Regt Mass Vols

Newell, Anne B., w/o Daniel O. Corbin, 1846-1936

Corbin, Otis C., 1874-1947

Mellish, M. Maud, w/o Otis C. Corbin, 1874-1963

Hall, Thomas T., 1890-1984

Hall, Hortense R., 1893-1981

Noyes, Nellie R., 1872-1952

Noyes, Frank W., 1870-1950
Razee, Isaac E., 1837-1899
Razee, Sarah T., 1841-1906
Razee, Ora H., 1865-1938
Razee, Nellie A., 1867-1949
Razee, James E., 1862-1947
Hancock, Francis E., 1836-1914
Hancock, Hannah, w/o Francis Hancock, 1837-1923
Talbot, Henry A., 1859-1903
Talbot, Sarah F., w/o Henry A. Talbot, 1866-1933
Talbot, Esther F., 1896-1938
Hancock, Walter L., 1878-1952
Hancock, Eva M., w/o Walter L. Hancock, 1885-1943
King, George, MD, 1822-1902
Eddy, Lucy A., w/o Dr. George King, 1826-1905
King, Walter Lyman, s/o Dr. George & Lucy King, 1866-1867
King, Hattie Lucy, d/o Dr. George & Lucy King, 1869-1869
King, Theodore Dexter, s/o Dr. George & Lucy King, 1870-1873
King, Frances Eddy, 1862-1926
King, William, 1859-1859
King, Lucy Cadey, 1853-1864
King, George 2nd, 1864-1865
King, Georgianna, 1857-1867
Fisher, L. L., 1822-1904
Fisher, Louisa, w/o L. L. Fisher, 1830-1912
Squire, Rev. Salmon Ward, 1819-1895, 3rd Pastor of the Universalist
   Church of Franklin
Knight, Betsey Jane, w/o Rev. Salmon Ward Squire, 1824-1903
Metcalf, Rector Leonard, b 1545 Tellerford, England, d....
Metcalf, Michael B., s/o Rector Leonard Metcalf, 1586-1664, settled in
   Dedham, MA
Metcalf, Michael, 1620-1654
Metcalf, Eleazer, 1653-....
Metcalf, Jonathan, 1693-1791
Metcalf, Jonathan, 1725-1775
Metcalf, Eleal, 1759-1792
Metcalf, Preston, b 1791, d 15 Jan 1840
Hill, Lucretia, w/o Preston Metcalf, d 6 Jan 1879 aged 84 yrs
Metcalf, Lucretia, 1822-1915
Metcalf, Eleab, d 1830 aged 1 yr

Metcalf, Alfred, d 1832 aged 7 yrs
Metcalf, Timothy A., d 1832 aged 10 yrs
Metcalf, Erastus L., 1814-1901
Fisher, Emeline, w/o Erastus L. Metcalf, d 1873 aged 60 yrs
Swayer, Eliza H., w/o Erastus L. Metcalf, 1849-1931
Metcalf, Ernest L., 1881-1949
Metcalf, Edwina T., 1887-1968
Metcalf, Charles T., 1912-1970
Metcalf, Lorraine, 1908-1995
Metcalf, Herbert L., 1877-1948
Metcalf, Herbert L. Jr., 1906-1980
Davis, Gertrude Jane, w/o Edmund Davis & d/o Salmon & Jane Squire, b 13 March 1846, d 4 Nov 1869
Davis, Julius S., only child of Edmund & Gertrude J. Davis, b 19 Oct 1866, d 6 June 1870
Bacon, James, b 15 Sept 1807, d 8 Feb 1874
Bacon, Mary, w/o James Bacon, b 24 Nov 1813, d 31 Jan 1897
Bacon, Millie M., d/o James & Mary Bacon, d 11 July 1866 aged 27 yrs 9 mos 28 days
Bacon, Albert A., 1840-1918
Bacon, A. Lizzie, w/o Albert Bacon, 1843-1902
Bacon, Francis A., 1869-1951
Bacon, Nellie M., 1875-1954
Bickley, John H., 1851-1922
Bickley, Cecilia E., w/o John H. Bickley, 1852-1927
Bickley, Will P., 1874-1940
Plmpton, Alice M., 1864-1911
Bickley, Joseph H., 1853-1920
Humphreys, Mary J., 1836-1888
Daniels, Waldo, 1827-1886
Gilmore, Helen R., w/o Waldo Daniels, 1825-1920
Daniels, Harry A., 1872-1877
Daniels, Arvilla F., 1851-1935
Bowden, Mary L., w/o Arville F. Daniels, 1853-1874
Daniels, Myrtle R., 1853-1874
Campbell, Ella Daniels, 1849-1925
Percy, William G., 1820-1911
Percy, Minerva H., w/o William G. Percy, 1819-1876
Percy, John E., 1849-1914
Craig, Charles B., 1835-1911

Craig, Malvina J., 1834-1904
Craig, Gertrude A., 1877-1879
Craig, Georgette F., 1859-1936
Craig, E. Channing, 1873-1940
Arnold, Inez E., 1852-1913
Pond, Henry B., 1817-1855
Ware, Annie M., w/o Henry B. Pond, 1821-1879
Howe, W. H., 1842-1919
Howe, Alice, w/o W. H. Howe, 1852-1938
Fisher, Sarah H., w/o L. L. Fisher, 1824-1896
Howe, Ella, w/o W. H. Howe & d/o L. L. & S. H. Fisher, b 2 Aug 1849, d
    6 Dec 1876
Metcalf, Alberton, b 22 Sept 1851, d 28 April 1916
Gorton, Jennie S., w/o Alberton Metcalf, 1859-1963
Metcalf, Walter Alberton, 1879-1955
Hills, Sanford, b 16 July 1823, d 18 July 1904
Metcalf, Mary C., w/o Sanford Hills, b 1 Nov 1821, d 27 Nov 1884
Hills, Edward Sanford, s/o Sanford & Mary Hills, b 13 April 1854, d 18
    July 1855
Hills, Eudora Frances, d/o Sanford & Mary Hills, b 1 Dec 1846, d 9 Oct
    1869
Gowen, Deacon Charles, 1819-1898
Phills, Harriet N., w/o Deacon Charles Gowen, 1823-1902
Gowen, Luther, 1782-1864
Gowen, Elvira M., 1789-1822
Gowen, Polly H., 1791-1866
Gowen, Horace M., b 30 April 1822, d 2 Nov 1881
Gowen, Sarah M., w/o Horace M. Gowen, b 22 July 1828, d 4 Aug 1919
Daniels, Joseph Hill, d 1908 aged 81 yrs
Scott, Samantha, w/o Joseph Hill Daniels, d 1870 aged 40 yrs
Darling, Mayo C., 1829-1892
Cook, Lucy A., w/o Mayo Darling, 1830-1914
Darling, Harriet C., 1862-1865
Darling, Edward J., 1871-1931
Atwood, Jessie L., w/o Edward J. Darling, 1864-1902
Darling, Herbert E., 1872-1950
Darling, Kenneth A., 1899-1962
Darling, Dora B., 1887-1970
Emmons, Deliverance, w/o Rev. Nathaniel Emmons aged 36 yrs
Daniels, Albert E., b 25 Sept 1802, d 21 Sept 1887

Daniels, Olive, w/o Albert B. Daniels, 1808-1877
Ware, Eugene F., 1847-1913
Ware, Ada A., w/o Eugene F. Ware, 1851-1912
Ware, Leslie H., 1878-1947
Ware, Aurora D., w/o Leslie H. Ware, 1876-1943
Redpath, Andrew, 1863-1930
Redpath, Nellie, w/o Andrew Redpath, 1862-1931
Redpath, Percy C., 1884-1900
Redpath, Ruby P., 1886-1913
Cook, Herbert A., 1854-1953
Cook, Mary E., w/o Herbert A. Cook, 1860-1943
Cook, Gertrude D., 1884-1900
Cook, Hazel J., 1901-....
Clark, Deacon Alfred, b 19 July 1819, d 13 Sept 1887
Clark, Polly W., w/o Deacon Alfred Clark, b 15 Dec 1815, d 17 June 1903
Lucas, Pearl E., 1908-1927
Clark, Nathan, b 1812, d 11 Aug 1865 of wounds received in the Battle of
     the Wilderness, VA
Ballou, Julie E., d/o Thurston & Caroline Ballou, d 5 Nov 1857 aged 28
     yrs 11 mos 5 days
Ballou, Thurston, b 20 Nov 1803 Cumberland, RI, d 10 Dec 1886
Ballou, Caroline, w/o Thurston Ballou, b 28 Feb 1801, d 4 Feb 1888
Robinson, John, 1792-1855
Robinson, Jane, 1797-1855
Robinson, Rodger, 1822-1852
Pond, Hiram, 1798-1857
Pond, Joanna M., w/o Hiram Pond, 1799-1886
Pond, Addison N., 1836-1853
Pond, Almira L., 1842-1931
Hobigand, Martha N., w/o J.A. Hobigand, 1837-1895
Wales, Christina, d/o Mason & Electra Wales, d 21 Jan 1856 aged 27 yrs
Fairbanks, Molly, widow of Levi Fairbanks, d 23 March 1843 aged 73 yrs
King, George W., d 21 April 1875 aged 51 yrs
King, Albert N., d 24 Dec 1869 aged 41 yrs
Hartshorn, Gilbert, b 3 Sept 1818, d 22 May 1882
Haskill, Eleanor A., w/o Gilbert Hartshorn, b 5 Aug 1820, d 17 March
     1902
Hamant, Francis, 1881-1928
Hamant, Helen G., 1922-....
Snyder, Ruth H., 1889-1989

Snyder, Elizabeth, 1930-....
Pond, Timothy, d 24 May 1836 aged 41 yrs
King, Erepta, d 4 June 1871 aged 71 yrs
Pond, Justin, d 19 Oct 1842 aged 49 yrs
Pond, Ruth D., w/o Justin Pond, d 19 Feb 1847 aged 52 yrs
Haskill, Samuel, b 4 Aug 1793, d 6 May 1876
Pond, Amanda, w/o Samuel Pond, b 28 Nov 1798, d 31 Aug 1843
Newell, Hannah, w/o Samuel Pond, b 23 May 1801, d 23 Oct 1867
Gilmore, Mary, w/o John Pierce & d/o James & Elizabeth Gilmore, d 7
    Dec 1844 aged 83 yrs
Pierce, John, d 27 Aug 1829 aged 74 yrs
Ray, Gilbert Ruel, s/o George W. & Eliza A. Ray, d 11 July 1844 aged 12
    yrs 4 mos
Ray, Eliza Ann, w/o George W. Ray, d 7 June 1845 aged 38 yrs 9 mos 11
    days
Ray, Harriet Eliza, d/o George & Eliza Ray, d 8 Oct 1842 aged 10 mos
Gilmore, Nathan O., d 14 March 1879 aged 81 yrs 1 mo
Gilmore, Capt. Elbridge G., s/o Nathan & Nancy F. Gilmore, d at sea Oct
    1839 aged 30 yrs
Fisher, Nancy, w/o Nathan Gilmore, d 28 April 1862 aged 86 yrs
Gilmore, Capt. James W., s/o Nathan & Nancy Gilmore, d Aug 1836
    Texas aged 23 yrs
Ward, Chloe, d 27 Nov 1837 aghed 73 yrs 7 mos 29 days
Walker, John H., d 18 July 1875 aged 34 yrs 10 mos
Walker, Ruby F., d/o J. H. Emma Walker, d 9 July 1875 aged 1 yr
Walker, Mary Ann, d/o John & Emma Walker, d 27 Nov 1888 aged 20
    yrs 4 mos
Walker, Mattie E., d/o John & Emma Walker, d 8 Jan 1894 aged 29 yrs 5
    mos
Walker, Emma J., w/o John H. Walker, d 10 Dec 1907 aged 72 yrs
Whitaker, Richard, b 11 Feb 1801, d 7 Feb 1837
Whitaker, Mary Ann, w/o Hartford P. Leonard, d 25 Aug 1855 Wabansee,
    Kann, aged 23 yrs 5 mos 6 days
Gilmore, Mary Ann, w/o Richard Whitaker, b 2 June 1805, d 15 Jan 1896
Partridge, Phinehas, d 14 Dec 1845 aged 69 yrs
Partridge, Abigail, w/o Phinehas Partridge, d 24 May 1819 aged 42 yrs
Ware, Betsey E., w/o David Ware, 1815-1893
Ware, Ruth C., d Nov 1887
Ware, Daniel, d May 1842 aged 64 yrs

Thurfton, Mary, d/o Daniel & Bathsheba Thurfton, d 28 Sept 1821 aged
    14 yrs
Thurston, Daniel, d 13 Nov 1844 aged 61 yrs
Perry, Simeon, d 9 Sept 1835 aged 70 yrs
Nason, Charles M., 1829-1885, A member of Co A 35th Mass Vols
Newell, Sylvia A., w/o Charles M. Nason, 1831-1876
Nason, Oramel, 1851-1934
Gilmore, Joseph, d 6 Dec 1852
Gilmore, Maria, w/o Joseph Gilmore, d 27 Dec 1867 aged 78 yrs
Gilmore, David, d 19 Oct 1831 aged 99 yrs
Metcalf, Hanan, d 13 June 1843 aged 87 yrs
Metcalf, Prudence, w/o Hanan Metcalf, d 12 May 1840 aged 47 yrs
Metcalf, Abigail, w/o Hanan Metcalf, d 6 Nov 1841 aged 73 yrs
Fisher, Capt. Maxey, d 30 Aug 1865 aged 80 yrs
Blake, Abigail, w/o Capt. Maxey Fisher, d 28 Sept 1885 aged 82 yrs 7
    mos
Fisher, Maria Richardson, d/o Capt. Maxey & Abigail Fisher, d 9 Oct
    1885 aged 59 yrs 3 mos
Fisher, Martha E., d/o Capt. Maxey & Abigail Fisher, d 19 Aug 1843
    aged 12 yrs
Fisher, Emmons, d 31 Jan 1853 aged 22 yrs
Fisher, Sarah, b 17 Sept 1836, d 15 Sept 1854
Fisher, Jason, b 30 March 1787, d 10 July 1863
Fisher, Mary, w/o Jason Fisher, b 31 March 1789, d 5 June 1877
Fisher, Mary Adeline, d/o Jason & Mary Fisher, b 5 June 1815, d 10 April
    1816
Fisher, John Warren, s/o Jason & Mary Fisher, b 17 Jan 1817, d 17 June
    1821
Fisher, Ellen Maria, b 11 May 1818, d 29 March 1872
Fisher, Willard, d 14 Jan 1866 aged 69 yrs 10 mos
Fisher, Betsey R.W., w/o Willard Fisher, d 21 July 1847 aged 42 yrs
Cooke, Winslow, 1801-1883
Whiting, Ruth A., w/o Winslow Cooke, 1802-1859
Cooke, Lucy A., 1834-1840
Cooke, Mary H., 1843-1870
Cooke, Rena S., 1845-1881
Cooke, Jennie R., 1832-....
Whiting, Joseph, d 18 Dec 1811 aged 43 yrs
Daniels, Fisher, d 10 March 1874 aged 77 yrs 7 mos 8 days
Adams, Eunice, w/o Fisher Daniels, d 14 Oct 1827 aged 32 yrs 9 mos

116

Eames, Ann, w/o Fisher Daniels, d 16 Feb 1876 aged 74 yrs 10 mos
Blake, Solomon, d 29 Dec 1839 aged 59 yrs
Blake, Hannah M., w/o Solomon Blake, d 24 Nov 1856 aged 74 yr
Fisher, Sarah, w/o Caleb Fisher, d 11 Aug 1835 aged 61 yrs
Fisher, Joseph, d 26 Jan 1819 aged 78 yrs
Fisher, Susan, w/o Joseph Fisher, d 28 May 1842 aged 90 yrs
Fisher, Julia, d/o Joseph & Susan Fisher, d 6 Sept 1877 aged 96 yrs 6 mos
    4 days
Blake, Susan Day, only child of Solomon & Hannah Blake, d 25 March
    1824 aged 1yr 9 mos
Phipps, William, d 10 March 1872 aged 83 yrs
Phipps, Fanny, w/o William Phipps, d 23 Oct 1843 aged 51 yrs
Bodwell, Caroline E., b 13 Feb 1840, d 12 Aug 1916
Bodwell, Frederick, b 17 Feb 1836, d 8 July 1915
Bodwell, Mary E., b 15 Aug 1866, d Aug 1896
Ware, Philander, d 18 Nov 1841 aged 52 yrs
Mann, Thomas, d 20 June 1809 aged 52 yrs
Stanley, Rebecca, w/o Thomas Mann, d 19 March 1837 aged 76 yrs
Pond, Irena, d 28 Jan 1825 aged 35 yrs
Pond, Polly, w/o Jeremiah M. Pond, d 20 April 1863 aged 78 yrs 10 mos
    20 days
Pond, Jeremiah, d 2 June 1827 aged 46 yrs
Bassett, Capt. Rufus, d 20 Jan 1830 aged 53 yrs
Daniels, Nahum W., b 5 April 1800, d 23 Jan 1831 NY
Whiting, Lucy, w/o Nahum W. Daniels, b 3 Dec 1803, d 13 Nov 1869
Daniels, Lucy M., w/o Otis F. Metcalf, b 8 June 1824, d 4 Feb 1862
Daniels, Abigail C., b 12 Feb 1827, d 15 June 1840
Daniels, Abigail Clapp, d/o Nahum & Lucy Daniels, d 15 June 1840 aged
    14 yrs
Phipps, Lydia, w/o Jedediah Phipps, d 12 Jan 1834 aged 26 yrs
Phipps, Rhoda, w/o Jedediah Phipps, d 21 July 1831 aged 27 yrs
Ware, Samuel, d 16 May 1861 aged 77 yrs
Daniels, Sally, w/o Samuel Ware, d 30 Nov 1889 aged 100 yrs 6 mos
Ware, Sanuel, d 22 Oct 1829 aged 76 yrs
Ware, Mehitable, w/o Samuel Ware, d 4 March 1831 aged 76 yrs
Ware, Samuel G. s/o Samuel & Mehitable Ware, d 12 Oct 1826 aged 2 yrs
    7 mos 4 days
Ware, George, s/o Samuel & Mehitable Ware, d 25 Sept 1833 aged 6 mos
Gamble, William F., 1878-1927
Gamble, Bertha L., w/o William F. Gamble, ...

Pond, Louisa, w/o Alfred Pond, d 14 May 1845 aged 35 yrs
Pond, Alfred, b 31 March 1806, d 25 Jan 1848
Quilter, Henry, b 2 May 1870, d 8 Oct 1891
Cole, Nathan, d 11 Oct 1879 AE 76 yrs
Cole, Lucy A., w/o Nathan Cole, 1805-1887
Earl, Paul, d 20 March 1854 aged 23 yrs
Huntley, Lucy E., d 28 April 1920 AE 81 yrs
Hills, Harvey, d 20 June 1862 aged 60 yrs
Hills, Abigail E., w/o Harvey Hills, d 10 Feb 1845 aged 38 yrs
Hills, George H., s/o Harvey & Abigail Hills, d 19 Dec 1845 AE 14 mos
Hills, Mary E., w/o Harvey Hills, b 12 Dec 1816, d 23 Jan 1898
Richards, Abigail C., w/o Henry Richards, b 24 Oct 1812, d 27 June 1887
Gay, Charlotte B., d 2 Nov 1895 aged 83 yrs 9 mos
Nason, George W., b 11 Jan 1806, d 9 Nov 1868
Nason, Hannah G., w/o George W. Nason, b 19 July 1807, d 27 Aug 1880
Nason, Peacy S., w/o George W. Nason, b 17 Feb 1808, d 5 Nov 1886
Nason, Walter L., b 9 May 1860, d 12 Oct 1917
Grossley, Reuben, d 7 Oct 1867 aged 38 yrs 7 mos
Banks, Mary F., w/o Reuben Grossley, d 3 April 1890 aged 61 yrs 3 mos
Woodward, Joseph A., b 9 Sept 1823, d 14 May 1883
Woodward, Polly G., d 12 Sept 1861
Leach, Abigail, w/o Elias Ware, d 8 Sept 1862 aged 73 yrs
Thomas, Edgar A., d 4 July 1872 aged 16 yrs 8 mos 21 days
Languerand, Peter, 1864-19..
Languerand, Mary J., w/o Peter Languerand, 1845-1925
Farrington, Preston M., b 26 Sept 1825, d 24 April 1925
Farrington, Caroline Thayer, b 26 March 1823, d 14 March 1918
Morse, Horace S., b 17 Aug 1822, d 8 July 1911
Morse, Eliza J., w/o Horace S. Morse, b 3 June 1822, d 4 Sept 1876
Nolan, Dr. William B., d 4 Sept 1899 aged 82 yrs
Verry, Sally, w/o Dr. William B. Nolan, d 11 Feb 1896 aged 78 yrs
Bemis, Charles H., d 12 Feb 1865 aged 36 yrs
Bemis, Evelyn C., w/o Charles H. Bemis, d 24 July 1852 aged 19 yrs
Bemis, Henry, d 24 April 1900 AE 90 yrs
Bemis, Nancy, w/o Henry Bemis, d 19 May 1875 aged 68 yrs
Johnson, Nathaniel C., d 29 June 1863 aged 33 yrs
Johnson, Nancy Louisa, w/o Nathaniel C. Johnson, d 5 April 1900 aged
   65 yrs
Metcalf, Willis B., b 21 June 1869, d 16 June 1890
Allen, Mary W., w/o Amos H. Allen, d 3 April 1832 aged 32 yrs

Bullard, Elisha, d 11 Dec 1880 aged 87 yrs
Fisher, Rena, w/o Elisha Bullard, d 29 Sept 1864 aged 71 yrs
Dumas, P. Mary, 1861-1945
Bullard, Walter H., 1859-1908
Bullard, Henry C., s/o John & E. S. Bullard, d 21 Feb 1873 aged 40 yrs
Bullard, Martha, w/o Henry C. Bullard, d 4 March 1890 aged 58 yrs
Bullard, Emeline, 1827-1897
Richardson, E. T., 1818-1903
Bullard, Rena, w/o E.T. Richardson, 1829-1918
Farrington, Nathan., 1793-1879
Farrington, Julia, 1793-1865
Metcalf, Otis F., b 25 June 1820, d 30 March 1899
Metcalf, Lucy M., w/o Otis F. Metcalf, d 4 Feb 1862 aged 37 yrs 7 mos
Freeman, Amanda M., 1823-1895
Lewis, Edwin A., 1839-1888
Woodward, Annabelle Lewis, 1852-1943
Lewis, Mary Gamble, 1919-1956
Lewis, Edwin Ray, 1878-1963
Lewis, Margaret C., 1890-1973
Martin, T. L., 1854-1938
Martin, J. M., 1854-1918
Morse, A. H., 1819-1895
Morse, Deborah, w/o A. H. Morse, b 8 Nov 1821, d 27 Nov 1882
Greene, Martin, b 8 Jan 1791, d 27 May 1867
Greene, Lois H., w/o Martin Greene, b 7 Aug 1799, d 30 May 1881
Greene, Henry W., b 11 June 1856, d 25 June 1907
Fisher, Weston, b 20 Dec 1796, d 25 April 1869
Fisher, Margaret, b 5 April 1798, d 24 June 1883
Walker, Elmore H., 1821-1892
Johnson, Charles S., 1844-1918
Thayer, Isalene, w/o Charles S. Johnson, 1848-1922
Johnson, Royal T., 1876-1947
Wales, Herbert Linfield, 1869-1918
Reid, Bertha W., 1870-1944
Stewart, Beatrice W., 1909-1909
Rockwood, Edmund J., 1842-1915
Cook, Abbie W., w/o Edmund J. Rockwood, 1843-1913
Rockwood, Albert E., 1864-1906
Stearns, Elizabeth L., w/o Albert E. Rockwood, 1866-1901
Rockwood, Capt. Erastus, 1812-1864

Daniels, Mary A., w/o Capt. Erastus Rockwood, 1812-1842
Daniels, Walter, 1863-1929
Daniels, Annie, w/o Walter Daniels, 1869-1951
Conway, James T., 1859-1913
Conway, Eliza J., w/o James T. Conway, 1862-1960
Ledbury, Ida R., 1874-1950
Fisher, Adin, b 6 April 1800, d 17 May 1891
Fisher, Mary, w/o Adin Fisher, b 6 May 1805, d 24 March 1891
Fisher, Frank, s/o Adin & Mary Fisher, b 20 May 1852, d 11 Oct 1852
Spence, Thomas W., 1844-1929
Spence, Catherine, w/o Thomas W. Spence, 1847-1919
Spence, Hephzibah, w/o Thomas W. Spence, 1877-1949
Breck, Elias, b 9 May 1807 Medfield, MA, d 21 June 1884 Newport, RI
Mann, William, b 1819 Chesterfield, New Hampshire, d 1900 Franklin,
    MA
Metcalf, Sarah B., b 1827 Winthrop, Maine, d 1872 Franklin, MA
Whiting, Deacon Peter, d 9 Dec 1805 aged 60 yrs
Whiting, Lydia, w/o Deacon Peter Whiting, d 12 June 1794 aged 49 yrs
Fisher, Hon. Jabez Esq., d XV Oct MDCCCVI
Blake, Philly, d 16 Dec 1836 aged 90 yrs 10 mos
Blake, Beriah, w/o Philly Blake, d 23 May 1828 aged 76 yrs
Blake, Olive, w/o Philly Blake, d 7 Feb 1842 aged 90 yrs
Dean, Tryohena, d/o Seth & Edene Dean, d 7 Sept 1813 aged 29 yrs
Dean Ruth, d 5 June 1834
Hawes, Moses, d 8 March 1830 aged 77 yrs 4 mos
Hawes, Mary D., w/o Moses Hawes, 26 Feb 1820 aged 58 yrs
Whiting, Peter, d 14 July 1816 aged 40 yrs
Whiting, Anna, w/o Peter Whiting, d 25 March 1862 aged 81 yrs
Metcalf, Abigail, widow of Timothy Metcalf, d 31 Dec 1831 aged 68 yrs
Metcalf, Timothy, d 16 May 1816 aged 60 yrs
Nason, Jesse, d 24 May 1845 aged 69 yrs
Nason, Hannah, w/o Jesse Nason, d 27 Dec 1856 aged 80 yrs
Woodward, Preston, b 12 Aug 1801 Franklin, MA, d 6 June 1828
    Providence, NY
Nason, Elizabeth C., w/o Preston Woodward, b 15 Feb 1802 Walpole,
    MA, d 20 July 1878
Adams, Deacon Peter, b 3 April 1811, d 27 Feb 1890
Richardson, Clarissa D., w/o Deacon Peter Adams, b 16 Oct 1816, d 12
    Sept 1901
Adams, Deacon James, d 16 April 1830 aged 61 yrs

Adams, Lucy F., w/o Deacon James Adams, d 1 July 1878 aged 88 yrs 11 mos 11 days

Metcalf, Julia, d/o Calvin & Eunice Metcalf, d 7 Dec 1797 aged 3 days

Dean, Ebenezer, d 12 Aug 1800 aged 87 yrs

Dean, Hannah, w/o Ebenezer Dean, d 27 Sept 1807 aged 88 yrs

Dean, Capt. Ebenezer, d 15 Jan 1820 aged 81 yrs

Dean, Abigail, w/o Capt. Ebenezer Dean, d 8 Jan 1826 aged 84 yrs

Woodward, Nathan, d 29 Feb 1836 aged 78 yrs

Woodward, Anna, w/o Nathan Woodward, d 21 June 1808 aged 39 yrs

Woodward, Hannah, d 27 Sept 1838 AE 76 yrs

Woodward, Joseph, d 24 Feb 1778 AE 49 yrs

Whiting, Asa, d 22 Dec 1794 aged 64 yrs

Ware, Dianna, w/o Sanford Ware, d 21 Aug 1860 aged 75 yrs

Ware, Jefse, d 13 July 1813 aged 77 yrs

Fairbanks, Susanna, w/o Capt. Nathaniel Fairbanks, d 24 Sept 1791 aged 52 yrs

Atwood, Anna M., w/o J. Francis Atwood, 1824-1906

Makepeace, Mary, w/o William Makepeace Esq., d 27 July 1839 aged 67 yrs

Brooks, Julia A., w/o George W. Bacon, b 21 Aug 1831, d 15 June 1865

Brooks, Julian, b 6 May 1865, d 1 Nov 1865

Rockwood, Seth, d 17 Jan 1822 aged 69 yrs

Rockwood, Margaret, w/o Seth Rockwood, d 3 Sept 1848 aged 86 yrs

Hawes, Deacon Levi, d 9 May 1839 aged 75 yrs

Hawes, Pamelia, w/o Deacon Levi Hawes, d 4 Sept 1839 aged 75 yrs

Hawes, Mariah, w/o Jofiah Hawes, d 28 Aug 1779 aged 55 yrs

Hawes, Jofiah, d 28 Feb 1804 aged 80 yrs

Mann, Chloe, d 16 Jan 1848 aged 65 yrs

Mann, Patly, d 9 Jan 1879 aged 87 yrs

Baker, Capt. David, b 5 June 1789, d 11 Oct 1861

Baker, Lucy F. P., w/o Capt. David Baker, d 13 Aug 1874 aged 79 yrs 6 mos

Baker, Jemima, w/o Capt. David Baker, d 26 July 1845 aged 60 yrs

Baker, David P., b 9 June 1817, d 15 JAn 1887

Green, Lois, w/o David P. Baker, b 17 Aug 1825, d 6 Dec 1914

Mann, Eunice, d 30 March 1853 aged 74 yrs

Mann, Nathan, d 26 June 1818 aged 71 yrs

Mann, Eunice, w/o Nathan Mann, d 13 April 1835 aged 80 yrs

Hubbard, Sarah, w/o Joshua Hubbard, d 8 April 1844 aged 74 yrs

Blake, Marcy, d/o Ebenezer & Marcy Blake, d 26 July 1808 aged 32 yrs

Fisher, Whiting, b 3 Oct 1790, d 4 April 1873
Metcalf, Abigail, d 4 Oct 1870 aged 75 yrs
Metcalf, William H., d 22 July 1842 aged 88 yrs
Metcalf, Ruth, w/o William H. Metcalf, d 4 March 1823 aged 68 yrs
Fisher, Asa, d 23 Nov 1843 aged 86 yrs
Fisher, Rachel, d 4 March 1830 aged 72 yrs
Fisher, James, d 12 Oct 1814 aged 27 yrs
Fisher, Lewis, d 20 July 1811 aged 27 yrs
Adams, Nehemiah, d 14 Dec 1854 aged 81 yrs 11 mos
Adams, John Martin, s/o Nehemiah Adams, d 8 March 1808
Adams, Ward, b 23 Nov 1798, d 27 Oct 1865
Adams, Hannah, w/o Ward Adams, b 4 Jan 1804, d 16 April 1872
Everett, Dr. Abijah, d 2 Jan 1804 aged 47 yrs
Clark, Paul, d 14 March 1852 aged 81 yrs
Clark, Phebe, w/o Paul Clark, d 20 May 1829 aged 61 yrs
Adams, Daniel, d 3 Nov 1814 aged 26 yrs
Adams, Nancy, w/o Daniel Adams, d 26 Sept 1827 aged 47 yrs
Adams, Nancy R., d/o Daniel & Nancy Adams, d 15 March 1826 aged 21
    yrs
Metcalf, Milton, s/o Calvin & Eunice Metcalf, d 19 Aug 1809 aged 19 yrs
Fisher, Timothy, d 22 May 1814 aged 88 yrs
Fisher, Esther, d/o Timothy Fisher, d 5 Oct 1825 aged 54 yrs
Fisher, Rachel, w/o Timothy Fisher, d 7 Nov 1819 aged 87 yrs
McPhepson, Patty M., w/o James McPhepson, d July 1881 aged 79 yrs 10
    mos
Adams, John, d 30 May 1793 aged 78 yrs
Adams, Thaddeus, d 28 June 1827 aged 82 yrs
Adams, Rachel, w/o Thaddeus Adams, d 27 Sept 1823 aged 73 yrs
Rockwood, Benjamin, d 1 Oct 1812 aged 67 yrs
Rockwood, Anne, w/o Benjamin Rockwood, d 10 Jan 1842 aged 86 yrs
Baker, Erastus E., b 20 July 1825, d 9 July 1904
Bacon, Abbie M., w/o Erastus E. Baker, b 2 April 1829, d 17 Sept 1906
Bullard, Rachel, w/o Elijah Bullard, d 29 Sept 1851 aged 95 yrs
Ware, Susan, d 5 March 1833 aged 40 yrs
Ware, Phinehas, d 17 Jan 1826 aged 75 yrs
Ware, Susan, w/o Phinehas Ware, d 27 Sept 1817 aged 62 yrs
Metcalf, Asa, b 16 March 1754, d 29 Aug 1830
Metcalf, Melea, w/o Asa Metcalf, d 7 March 1832 aged 70 yrs
Thayer, Susanna, w/o Nathaniel Thayer, d 30 Jan 1788 aged 31 yrs
Metcalf, Ruth, w/o Asa Metcalf, d 7 July 1787 aged 28 yrs

Fisher, Levi, d 22 Oct 1844 aged 86 yrs

Fisher, Susanna, w/o Levi Fisher, d 27 May 1858 aged 84 yrs

Fisher, Mary, w/o Levi Fisher, d 31 March 1808 aged 46 yrs

Fisher, Sally, d 11 Oct 1873 aged 84 yrs 3 mos

Clark, Paul B., 1809-1894

Wheeler, Abigail, w/o Paul B. Clark, 1812-1862

Clark, Ellen M., d/o Paul B. & Abigail Clark, 1837-1846

Fisher, Willis, b 20 July 1783, d 1 Jan 1866, married 8 Feb 1810 to

Fairbanks, Caroline, b 26 Sept 1791, d 26 July 1858

Fisher, Milton, s/o Willis & Caroline Fisher, b 30 Jan 1811, d 20 April
1903

Fisher, George P., s/o Willis & Caroline Fisher, b 15 April 1813, d 7 June
1850

Fisher, Abigail B., d/o Willis & Caroline Fisher, b 9 May 1816, d 24
April 1862

Fisher, Charles W., s/o Willis & Caroline Fisher, b 3 Nov 1818, d 16 Sept
1819

Fisher, Charles F., s/o W. & Caroline Fisher, b 1 Nov 1820, d 17 July
1857

Fisher, Caroline F., d/o Willis Fisher, b 9 March 1823, d 29 July 1848

Fisher, Ellen M., d/o Willis & Caroline Fisher, b 22 Aug 1826, d 5 March
1851

Fisher, Julia, d/o Willis & Caroline Fisher, b 28 Feb 1831, d ....

Partridge, Asa, d 26 April 1858 aged 85 yrs

Partridge, Eliza F., w/o Asa Partridge, d Jan 1859

Partridge, Polly, w/o Asa Partridge, d 5 Dec 1848 aged 77 yrs

Partridge, Harriet Keith, d/o Eleazer & Hannah Partridge, d 15 Oct 1855
aged 24 yrs

Keith, Hannah, w/o Eleazer Partridge, d 3 June 1856 aged 58 yrs

Partridge, Eleazer, d 8 March 1850 aged 67 yrs

Partridge, Nancy, w/o Eleazer Partridge, d 9 Feb 1825 aged 89 yrs

Bullard, Rachel, d 22 Oct 1842 aged 47 yrs

Rockwood, Timothy, d 14 Dec 1841 aged 94 yrs

Rockwood, Sarah, w/o Timothy Rockwood, d 20 March 1829 aged 78 yrs

Bailey, Susanna, d 3 Oct 1836 aged 76 yrs

Pond, Mime, w/o Oliver Pond, d 18 Nov 1803 aged 32 yrs

Pond, Oliver, d 1812 aged 44 yrs

Pond, Erasmus, d 17 Oct 1828 aged 28 yrs

Smith, Remember, w/o Moses Smith & formerly w/o Oliver Pond, d 10
March 1854 aged 86 yrs

Pond, Goldsbury, b 28 Sept 1770, d 9 Dec 1866

Fisher, Priscilla, w/o Goldsbury Pond, b 15 April 1770 Medway, MA, d 11 April 1845

Pond, Albert D., s/o Goldsbury & Priscilla Pond, b 23 Feb 1830, d 12 April 1830

Pond, Richard V., s/o G. & Priscilla Pond, b 19 Sept 1831, d 3 Nov 1831

Pond,.Chloe E., d/o Goldsbury & Priscilla Pond, b 21 Sept 1832, d Nov 1837

Pond, Juline Orella, d/o Goldsbury & Priscilla Pond, & w/o Cyrus P. Crane, b 21 Dec 1842, d 26 Dec 1867 Jersery City, NJ

Hawes, Sally, w/o Jonathan Hawes, b 25 Jan 1772, d 12 May 1863

Woodward, Amos P., 1837-1917

Woodward, Charlotte M., w/o Amos P. Woodward, 1836-1896

Seavey, Harriet Elvira, 1821-1902

Gilmore, Philander S., 1807-1875

Gilmore, Nancy L., 1812-1898

Gilmore, Joseph, 1836-....

Gilmore, Nancy H., d/o Philander & Nancy Gilmore, d 31 May 1851 aged 19 yrs

Metcalf, Michael, d 3 June 1854 aged 52 yrs 10 mos

Daniels, Lois, w/o Henry Daniels, d 4 Oct 1796 aged 60 yrs

Daniels, Milcah, d 12 Sept 1819 aged 52 yrs

Walker, William, 1830-1913

Walker, Susan F., w/o William Walker, 1831-1911

Walker, Charles E., 1857-1918

Carpenter, Unity, w/o Job Carpenter, d 3 April 1809 Paxton, MA aged 31 yrs

Frost, Benjamin, d 25 June 1863 aged 54 yrs 5 mos 5 days

Fisher, Belinda A., w/o John H. Fisher, d 14 June 1851 aged 39 yrs

Gilmore, Alice, 1859-1859

Gilmore, Robert, 1788-1855

Gilmore, Rebecca, 1790-1870

Gilmore, Albert A., 1824-1826

Gilmore, Olive R., 1827-1844

Gilmore, Susan A., 1832-1854

Gilmore, William D., 1830-1865

Gilmore, Harriet M., w/o William D. Gilmore, 1835-1920

Hartmann, Edward F., 1851-1920

Hartmann, Elizabeth, w/o Edward F. Hartmann, 1855-1884

Hartmann, Rose, w/o Edward F. Hartman, 1854-1016

Cobb, Bessie J., d/o Henry G. & Betsey T. Cobb, A victim of the Calender
    Street fire, Providence, RI,d 21 Nov 1882 agd 15 yrs 10 mos 15 days
Hawes, Sally, d 27 March 1899 aged 87 yrs 8 mos 27 days
Hawes, Fanny, d 3 Jan 1896 aged 90 yrs 6 mos 10 days
Hawes, Jonathan, d 21 May 1854 aged 31 yrs
Wilson, Rebecca, d 28 April 1834 aged 78 yrs
Adams, Albert, b 22 Dec 1807, d 16 Nov 1868
Davis, John A., b 26 March 1819, d 30 Jan 1903
Brown, Martha P., w/o John A. Davis, b 5 March 1827, d 26 May 1876
Davis, Ellen Brown, d/o John & Martha Davis, d Jan 1864 aged 12 yrs
Lawrence, Joseph, d 20 Feb 1837 aged 80 yrs
Lawrence, Anna, w/o Joseph Lawrence, d 3 Dec 1846 aged 86 yrs
Adams, Simeon P., b 16 Nov 1809, d 21 Feb 1859
Adams, Harriet B., b 11 Nov 1807, d 7 Nov 1887
Nye, Caleb T., 1819-1893
Nye, Sophia B. C., w/o Caleb T. Nye, 1826-1892
Adams, Achsa P., b 4 March 1787, d 25 Jan 1868
Adams, Alpheus, b 22 Dec 1785, d 9 Jan 1852
Carter, Merrill E., b 14 March 1822, d 6 Jan 1901
Adams, Achsa, w/o Merrill E. Carter, b 2 Nov 1824, d 21 May 1900
Pond, Sally, w/o Jemotes Pond, d 20 Oct 1826 aged 50 yrs
Metcalf, Olive, w/o Deacon James Metcalf & former w/o Deacon Robert
    Gillmore, d 24 July 1846 aged 81 yrs
Hubbard, Joshua, d 1 Sept 1834 aged 59 yrs
Kingsbury, George D., 1830-1880
Kingsbury, Caroline M., 1804-1854
Allen, Samuel, 1724-1783
Smith, Abigail, 1724-1761
Pond, Emily, d 28 Sept 1880 aged 82 yrs 1 mo
Pond, Jemima, w/o Elihu Pond, d 3 Jan 1835 aged 66 yrs
Blake, Solomon, d 5 Jan 1824 aged 81 yrs
Blake, Sibel, d 10 March 1826 aged 91 yrs
Barnard, Charles, 1837-1910
Barnard, Hannah F., 1834-1895
Barnard, Charles N., s/o Charles & Hannah Barnard, 1867-192
Haven, Rev. Elias, d 10 Aug 1754 aged 41 yrs
Fairbanks, John, d 10 May 1754 aged 49 yrs
Alldis, Sarah, w/o Nathan Alldia, d 6 May 1773 aged 34 yrs
Mann, Abiel, d 24 April 1822 aged 70 yrs
Mann, Elias, d 27 Jan 1829 aged 74 yrs

Mann, Mary, w/o Elias Mann, d 27 June 1829 aged 75 yrs
Mann, Elias Watts, d 3 Sept 1829 aged 34 yrs
Wright, Jabez, d 2 Dec 1852 aged 76 yrs
Rockwood, Mehitable, w/o Jabez Wright & formerly w/o Willis Fisher
   Esq., b 12 March 1789, d 16 April 1874
Lawrence, Ebenezer, d 4 Oct 1796 aged 76 yrs
Lawrence, Seth, s/o Ebenezer Lawrence, d 5 Dec 1793 aged 36 yrs
Bacon, Thomas, d 15 May 1799 aged 75 yrs
Pond, Jabez, s/o Asa & Judith Pond, d 5 Sept 1778 aged 19 mos
Lawrence, David, d 26 Oct 1793 aged 82 yrs
Lawrence, Elizabeth, w/o David Lawrence, d 8 June 1799
Blake, Sally, w/o Elizas Baker, d 5 Jan 1832
Baker, Abijah, b 11 Aug 1749, d 20 April 1824
Parker, Esther, w/o Abijah Baker, d 12 May 1795 aged 41 yrs
Boyden, Phoebe, w/o Abijah Baker, d 19 Nov 1824 aged 71 yrs
Gould, William H., b 26 May 1827, d 8 April 1900
Gould, Marcy J., w/o William H. Gould, b 16 July 1832, d 26 Dec 1917
Lincoln, John, d 17 July 1769 aged 36 yrs
Clark, Samuel, 1783-1854
Clapp, Hannah, w/o Samuel Clark, 1783-1855
Gould, Alice Elizabeth, d/o William A. & Mary Gould, d 3 June 1870
Ockinton, William, d 1 Oct 1793 aged 90 yrs
Clark, Samuel, d 17 Jan 1822 aged 79 yrs
Clark, Esther, w/o Samuel Clark, d 2 June 1825 aged 78 yrs
Pond, Timothy, d 27 Oct 1776 aged 39 yrs
Gay, William G., d 31 Jan 1872 aged 56 yrs 7 mos
Gay, Susan A., w/o William G. Gay, d 12 Feb 1874 aged 50 yrs 4 days
Redpath, James W., b 24 March 1833 Turo, Nova Scotia, d 16 Aug 1873
Redpath, Annie L., w/o James W. Redpath, d 6 Aug 1926 aged 93 yrs 6
   mos 11 days
Clark, Erastus, 1803-1893
Lawrence, Elizabeth M., w/o Erastus Clark, 1822-1899
Wood, John, b 21 Oct 1856, d 11 March 1909 Founder & First Chief of
   Providence, RI division of Railroad Telegrapher
Hosie, Clara A., w/o John Wood, b 12 Sept 1858, d 4 Aug 1938
Hosie, George S., b 14 March 1830, d 22 April 1900
Morse, Hannah B., w/o George S. Hosie, b 4 April 1832, d 6 July 1923
Ferlayson, John S., 1854-1916
Corson, David W., 1839-1925
Corson, Hannah, w/o David W. Corson, 1834-1920

Corson, Fred W., 1873-1875
Gage, Horace, 1836-1917
Bryant, Ella, w/o Horace Gage, 1849-1929
Gage, Horace Jr., 1874-1874
Bright, Warren H., 1841-1907
Peary, Mary E., w/o Warren H. Bright, 1845-1886
Bright, Ina E., d/o Warren & Mary Bright, 1870-1871
Bright, Mabel, d/o Warren & Mary Bright, 1873-1875
Bright, Henry J., s/o Warren & Mary Bright, 1877-1904
Bright, Harry R., s/o Warren & Mary Bright, 1881-1952
Bright, Edna A., d/o Warren & Mary Bright, 1867-1958
Taylor, Herbert J., b 21 June 1853, d 29 April 1923
Taylor, Sarah J., b 26 Feb 1827, d 25 Oct 1914
Taylor, Cora E., w/o Leon C. Morse, 1856-1890
Ware, Frederic A., d 13 Sept 1875 aged 77 yrs 2 mos
Ware, Eliza, w/o Frederic A. Ware, d 15 Feb 1879 aged 52 yrs
Mann, William Addison, s/o William & Sarah B. Mann, 1857-1865
Mann, Ruth Buxton, 1763-1871
Mann, Diana, 1826-1875
Tourtellott, Gilbert C., 1841-1919
O'Connell, Ellen M., w/o Gilbert C. Tourtellott, 1840-1913
Davis, Fred L., 1863-1944
Fairbanks, Bertha, w/o Fred L. Davis, 1860-1944
Smith, William F., 1831-1872
Bright, Mary W., w/o William F. Smith, 1832-1910
Mann, William, 1819-1900
Smith, George C., 1860-1888
Fisher, David, 1847-1928
Fisher, Emma, w/o David Fisher, 1849-1915
Dauphinee, George D., 1899-1966
Dudley, Frank E., 1862-1953
Dudley, Rebecca J., w/o Frank E. Dudley, 1865-1914
Peary, Elmon S., b 4 March 1848, d 26 June 1888
Mann, Alexander, 1840-1886
Mann, Helen P., w/o Alexander Mann, 1840-1916
Peary, Samuel A., 1854-1914
Peary, Margaret E., 1869-1945
Peary, Grace Ellis, 1878-1900
Peary, Edmond D., 1880-1904
Mann, Samuel H., 1848-1931

Mann, Eleanor A., w/o Samuel H. Mann, 1853-1935
Benedict, Newton, 1830-1911
Corbett, James S., d 4 March 1886 aged 70 yrs
Stewart, Charles Washington, b 2 Feb 1814, d 17 March 1902
Stewart, Mary Hannah, w/o Charles Washington Stewart, b 19 June 1821,
    d 17 July 1914
Ackley, Louise G., 1880-1918
Parish, John B., 1895-1970
Deems, Beulah S., w/o John B. Parish, 1888-1968
Door, George B., 1835-1912
Adams, Sarah, w/o George B. Dorr, 1841-1903
Door, Mary Edith, d/o George & Sarah Door, 1870-1871
Door, Annie Blanche, d/o Geoege & Sarah Dorr, 1886-1886
Door, David Adams, s/o George & Sarah Door, 1881-1891
Door, Eugene H., s/o George & Sarah Door, 1875-1929
Atwood, Shadrach MD, b 17 May 1801, d 27 Sept 1888
Atwood, Ruth, w/o Dr. Shadrach Atwood, b 21 Feb 1802, d 7 Nov 1862
Atwood, Charlotte M., b 16 Aug 1840, d 28 July 1914
Newell, Frances A., b 8 Aug 1845, d 1 Aug 1894
Newell, Frederick A., b 8 Aug 1845, d 20 Sept 1910
Walden, Ida, w/o Frederick Newell, 1855-1931
Newell, Hiram, b 5 Aug 1806, d 19 May 1858
Newell, Clarissa, w/o Hiram Newell, b 8 April 1811, d 19 Sept 1861
Lowell, William H., 1842-1911, 1st Mass Cav
Lowell, Caroline A., w/o William H. Lowell, 1844-....
Harding, Russ Walker, b 13 Dec 1868, d 24 June 1938
Aldrich, Emily, w/o Russ Walker Harding, b 13 Aug 1882, d 30 Oct 1963
Sanborn, Marston, 1861-1934
Raymond, Ruth T., w/o Marston Sanborn, 1891-1970
Raymond, Wilfred, 1855-1953
Raymond, Ella T., 1858-1943
Mann, Alden T., 1861-1951
Smith Elise, w/o Alden T. Mann, 1867-1948
Mann, Helen, 1893-1894
Mann, Alden T. Jr., 1895-1966
Smith, Henry A., 1861-1935
Smith, Mary E., w/o Henry A. Smith, 1864-1944
Smith, Gladys E., 1890-1892
Greenwood, Alonzo S., 1854-1928
Richardson, Lilla M., w/o Alonzo Greenwood, 1853-1921

Greenwood, Cora M., 1877-1879
Gould, Albert W., 1859-1947
Gould, Mira B. 1870-1889
Gould, Nina B., 1868-1939
Vale, Evelyn M., 1895-1953
Barnes, Lucy M., 1839-1907
Quilter, Wenona E., 1862-1932
Hawkins, Elman A., 1843-1901
Chase, Mary E., w/o Elman E. Hawkins, 1845-1894
Hawkins, Frank E., 1874-1952
Hawkins, J. Agnes, w/o Frank E. Hawkins, 1878-1959
Hawkins, Walter E., 1916-1942
Hawkins, Frank E. Jr., 1920-1920
Hawkins, Harold L., 1901-1975
Hawkins, Annie A., w/o Harold L. Hawkins, 1899-1964
Kendrick, R. Frank, 1867-1928
Kendrick, Ada L., w/o R. Frank Kendrick, 1857-1944
Kendrick, Earl F., 1891-1895
Rose, James F., 1839-1919
Rose, Catherine, w/o James F. Rose, 1850-1919
Willard, Albert P., 1877-1933
Fales, Mary L., w/o Albert P. Willard, 1878-....
Fales, C. Elmer, 1869-1951
Cosseboom, Minnie B., 1870-1896
Cosseboom, Frances D., 1866-1904
Cosseboom, Amanda M., 1843-1927
Kilburn, Nellie J., 1845-1901
Heaton, Joseph H., b 26 Oct 1829, d 22 Aug 1897
Heaton, Ellen F., w/o Joseph H. Heaton, b 7 Aug 1833, d 16 Jan 1904
Heaton, Ella Flora, d/o Joseph & Ellen Heaton, b 4 April 1855, d 19 Oct
     1856
Heaton, Charles H., 1847-1916
Heaton, Annie M., w/o Charles H. Heaton, d 19 March 1879
Heaton, Sylvia, w/o Charles H. Heaton, d 3 Dec 1890 aged 35 yrs
Holmes, Arthur S., b 5 Oct 1873, d 22 Oct 1898
Holmes, Ida M., w/o Arthur S. Holmes, b 14 March 1875, d 3 Nov 1956
Reed, Eva Arlie, w/o Arthur S. Curtis, 1883-1908
Hosie, John P., b 9 May 1835, d 6 Feb 1910
Hosie, Jean S., w/o John P. Hosie, b 27 Nov 1839, d 27 Feb 1915

Taft, Daniel F., 1828-1864, Killed at Battle of Cold Harbor, A member of
  Co G 18th Mass Regt Vols
Taft, Ann Eliza, w/o Daniel F. Taft, 1827-1910
McFadden, Andrew J., d 14 Jan 1903 aged 52 yrs
McFadden, Kate J., w/o Andrew J. McFadden, d 22 Aug 1919
Partridge, George I., 1822-1912
Hancock, Harriet, w/o George I. Partridge, 1825-1908
Partridge, Charles H., s/o George & Harriet Partridge, 1860-1903
Partridge, Edmund F., s/o George & Harriet Partridge, 1845-1913
Guigon, Frank P., d 1899
Guigon, Nellie A., w/o Frank P. Guigon, d 1923
Hooper, William T., 1860-1932
Hooper, Henrietta J., w/o William T. Hooper, 1861-1943
Hooper, Ethel May, d/o William & Henrietta Hooper, 1879-1884
Hooper, Irene, d/o William & Henrietta Hooper, 1885-1886
Tufts, Fred L., 1871-1930
Tufts, Bessie I., w/o Fred L. Tufts, 1879-1926
Morse, Ethan Allen, b 24 Jan 1848, d 19 Sept 1924
Morse, Mary A., w/o Ethan Allen Morse, b 24 Aug 1847, d 30 June 1912
Scott, Ethel, 1888-1945
Briggs, W. Earle, 1895-1959
Briggs, Mary, w/o W. Earle Briggs, 1896-1952
Briggs, Ruth K., w/o W. Earle Briggs, 1904-1975
Briggs, Charles A., b 4 Aug 1871, d 13 Sept 1948
Briggs, Carrie R., w/o Charles A. Briggs, b 28 Aug 1868, d 23 Nov 1895
Briggs, Eva, w/o Charles A. Briggs, b 24 May 1874, d 28 March 1936
Willard, Emery E., 1871-1919
Wood, Lizzie Lincoln, w/o Emery E. Willard, 1867-1914
Buck, Lillian E. M., w/o Emery E. Willard, 1872-1961
Willard, Warren A. Sr., 1926-1983
O'Brien, Smith, 1861-1931
O'Brien, Mary, w/o Smith O'brien, 1877-1922
O'Brien, Lillian M., d/o Smith & Mary O'Brien, 1897-1926
Snodgrass, Joseph, 1866-1932
Snodgrass, Selina, w/o Joseph Snadgrass, 1874-1923
Carlson, Robert M., 1922-1925
Johnston, Russell H., 1900-1965
Johnston, Ethel S., w/o Russell H. Johnston, 1896-1972
Hutchinson, James P., 1888-1923
Hutchinson, Barbara D., 1921-....

Guild, Edwin A., 1844-1923
Adams, Amanda M., w/o Edwin A. Guild, 1844-1922
Guild, Gertrude M., 1871-1950
Guild, Walter R., 1875-1955
Guild, Bertha B., 1893-1967
Chute, Rupert James, d 19 Feb 1931
Osbourne, Emma, w/o Rupert James Chute, d 9 Feb 1921
Chute, Paul Jones, d 3 July 1930
Jacobs, Milan E., 1886-1922
Jacobs, Mary K., w/o Milan E. Jacobs, 1872-1957
Nason, Dr. O.C.B., 1858-1934
Nason, Medora T., w/o Dr. O.C.B. Nason, 1856-1923
Yankee, Gustave, 1839-1909
Yankee, Emily, w/o Gustave Yankee, 1834-1904
Yankee, Ausust H., w/o Gustave Yankee, 1861-1922
Yankee, Celcelia D., 1867-1941
Yankee, Emily C., 1900-1903
Carlosn, Robert O., 1892-1955
Carlson, Zaidee O., 1884-1949
Pond, Arthur A., 1858-1929
Pond, Annie L., w/o Arthur A. Pond, 1857-1937
Pond, Una E., 1885-1957
Straw, Fenton W., 1886-1925
Dexter, Clara C., w/o Fenton W. Straw, 1887-1980
Johnson, Wallace W., 1866-1935
Johnson, Emma L., w/o Wallace W. Johnson, 1875-1954
Ingalls, John W., 1869-1936
Blackstock, Isabelle, w/o John W. Ingalls, 1875-1926
Jeffery, Robert F., 1898-1975
Reed, Robert Stanley, 1888-1961
Abbott, Gladys, w/o Robert Stanley Reed, 1891-1959
Chilson, Austin B., 1861-1954
Grant, Carrie, w/o Austin B. Chilson, 1865-1959
Chilson, Stanley Grant, s/o Austin & Carrie Chilson, 1891-1972
Buchanan, Grace Chilson, w/o Martin Luther Buchanan & d/o Austin &
    Carrie Chilson, 1897-1992
Buchanan, Martin Luther, 1890-1973
Clark, Clinton Stearns, 18943-1970
Woodward, Dora, w/o Clinton Stearns Clark, 1897-1981
Bassett, Charles S., b 7 Aug 1834, d 2 April 1915

Bassett, Abbie C., w/o Charles S. Bassett, b 28 July 1839, d 31 Dec 1915

McDougall, Elizabeth S., d/o Charles S. & Abbie C. Bassett, b 16 Jan 1866, d 18 Dec 1922

Bassett, Harriet E., d/o Charles S. & Abbie C. Bassett, b 13 May 1867, d 1 Nov 1928

Sherman, Nelson T., 1866-1918

Waterman, Lottie M., w/o Nelson T. Sherman, 1872-1938

Tobey, George F., s/o James J. & Mary A. Tobey, 1871-1910

Daniels, Henry W., 1854-1913

Daniels, Freda E., 1859-1927

Tobey, Rev. James J., 1849-1903

Tobey, Mary A., w/o Rev. James J. Tobey, 1848-1901

Crafts, R. C., 1855-1932

Guild, Ada, w/o R. C. Crafts, 1858-1931

Clark, Charles E., 1844-1900

Clark, Margaret C., w/o Charles E. Clark, 1849-1888

Mason, George P., 1856-1914

Mason, Mary J., w/o George P. Mason, 1855-1946

Bullard, Rufus K., 1834-1894

Bullard, Celista A., w/o Rufus K. Bullard, 1838-1908

Howe, Benjamin F., 1876-1961

Stanley, William A., 1814-1904

Shaw, Olive A., w/o William A. Stanley, 1818-1892

Stanley, Mary E., d/o William & Olive Stanley, 1840-1840

Stanley, Abbie S., d/o William & Olive Stanely, 1845-1902

Stanley, Julette D., d/o William & Olive Stanley, 1848-1888 Colorado

Stanley, James A., s/o William & Olive Stanley, 1852-1852

Hubbard, Elisha, d 8 July 1853 aged 51 yrs 6 mos 22 days

Hubbard, Sabin, b 20 June 1823, d 8 March 1900

Sargeant, Alvira, w/o Sabin Hubbard, b 27 Feb 1826, d 12 July 1900

Redpath, William, 1859-1924

Redpath, Pheobe, w/o William Redpath, 1862-1934

Fleming, James F., 1879-1968

Fleming, Emily, d/o James F. Fleming, 1883-1928

Fleming, James F. Jr., 1913-1930

Mewton, Persis, b 24 March 1809, d 17 Dec 1827

Mewton, Abraham, b 12 Dec 1822, d 8 June 1831

Sargeant, Asa, b 3 Sept 1779, d 9 Jan 1868

Ball, Polly, w/o Asa Sargeant, b 25 Oct 1781, d 10 Oct 1856

Sargeant, Lorinda, d/o Asa & Polly Sargeant, b 30 Dec 1818, d 21 April 1860
Blake, Lydia, b 6 March 1836, d 11 Oct 1888
Morrell, William W., 1845-1907
Morrell, Lottie F., 1845-1932
Morrell, Herbert W., 1878-1952
McDougall. Charles, 1843-1904
McDougall, Julia A., w/o Charles McDougall, 1845-1905
Nye, Herbert W., 1847-1921
McCutchen, Anna I., w/o Herbert W. Nye, 1855-1940
Merrifield, Alvin T., 1820-1887
Merrifield, Harriet B., w/o Alvin T. Merrifield, 1826-1905
Merrifield, Albert L., 1867-1919
Ballou, Adin, b 29 Dec 1835, d 7 April 1885
Ballou, Harriet O., w/o Adin Ballou, b 17 Jan 1841, d 4 Dec 1891
Smith, Abner M., 1848-1914
Smith, Stella M., w/o Abner M. Smith, 1855-1935
Lougest, Charles A., MD, 1837-1907
Lougest, Frederica, w/o Dr. Charles A. Lougest, 1848-1925
MacKenzie, Helena, 18971-1941
Alexander, Betsey S., w/o Samuel Alexander & d/o Asa & Polly Sargeant, b 13 Dec 1802, d 11 July 1882
Black, George, b March 1805, d 11 July 1883
Sargeant, Polly, 1805-1863
Sargeant, Miranda, 1816-1861
Blake, Persis A., w/o A. Chase.....
Southa, Robert, 1851-1906
Southa, Margaret J., w/o Robert Southa, 1856-1900
Jordan, Samuel H., b 18 Oct 1845, d 29 Dec 1898
Jordan, Alice J. , w/o Samuel Jordan, b 28 Aug 1849, d 18 April 1917
Blanchard, C. Etta Jordan, 1891-1951
Jordan, John W., b 6 July 1854, d 20 May 1891
Tower, Jason, b 1824, d 23 Aug 1899
Tower, Mary E., 1848-1924
Tower, Electra R., ...
Sutherland, Alexander, 1868-1957
Sutherland, Lucy M, 1879-1941
Sutherland, Marion A., 1903-1903
Sutherland, George Heaton, 1917-1962
Warren, Van R., d 10 Jan 1892

Smith, James, 1865-1927

Smith, Minnie P., w/o James Smith, 1863-1904

Smith, Harriet A., 1880-1959

Jordan, Frank A., b 10 Oct 1869, d 31 March 1917

Fiske, Orrin F., 1849-1911

Bliss, Lizzie M., w/o Orrin F. Fiske, 1849-1895

Darling, Marcia C., w/o Orrin F. Fiske, 1852-1926

Field, Edith L., 1881-1894

Cochrane, I. Milton, 1852-1903

Booth, Harriet L., w/o I. Milton Cochrane, 1883-1907

Cochrane, Walter C., 1878-1896

Cochrane, Dana E., 1883-1907

Whiting, Martha B., b 7 Nov 1847, d 28 Aug 1854

Whiting, Harietta Eva, b. 18 Sept 1854, d 5 June 1874

Whiting, Alfred D., b 17 June 1849, d 10 Jan 1900

Whiting, Daniel P., b 24 March 1801, d 23 May 1893

Briggs, Lydia Adeline, w/o Daniel P. Whiting., b 18 Sept 1826, d 23 April 1891

Whiting, George R., b 24 March 1852, d 9 Feb 1934

Sprague, Mary Woodman, w/o George R. Whiting, b 28 June 1859, d 26 Jan 1911

Emerson, Waldo S., 1869-1952

Emerson, Mary A., w/o Waldo S. Emerson, 1873-1966

Sherman, Richard, 1867-1938

Bailey, Adeline J., b 22 Sept 1834, d 13 Jan 1919

Bailey, Hiram H., d 20 Aug 1889 aged 78 yrs

Woodward, Palmer A., 1867-1935

Woodward, Annie M., 1867-1843

Ruggles, Henry E., 1858-1926

Ruggles, Carrie E., w/o Henry E. Ruggles, 1859-1894

Weston, Lucy Maud, w/o Henry E. Ruggles, 1864-1948

Cotton, William A., 1859-1895

Cotton, Daniel C., 1831-1891

Cotton, Abby, w/o Daniel C. Cotton, 1834, 1902

Blake, Elias, d 3 March 1894 aged 79 yrs

Adams, Mary, w/o Elias Blake, & d/o William Adams, d 18 Dec 1881 aged 73 yrs

Rounds, Sylvanus C., d 12 March 1882

Rounds, Amanda A., w/o Sylvanus C. Rounds, d 30 Sept 1904

Knapp, James H., 1857-1932

Brackett, Lucy J., w/o James H. Knapp, 1856-1947
Knapp, Helen B., 1896-1989
Arnold, Austin William, 1870-1934
Arnold, Jayne, w/o Austin William Arnold, 1874-1957
Peden, John, 1862-1954
Peden, Elizabeth, w/o John Peden, 1862-1928
Forbes, James, 1884-1975
Forbes, Fannie P., w/o James Forbes, 1884-1974
Dana, William G., 1874-1934
Bassett, Agnes, w/o William G. Dana, 1881-1968
Dana, David Lincoln, 1947-1951
Woodward, Frank Ellsworth, 1862-1934
Campbell, Cynthia, w/o Frank Ellsworth Woodward, 1867-1949
Woodward, Nellie M., 1864-1940
Daniels, Mary A., 1862-1944
Smith, Charles E., 1853-1842
Lynds, Georgia M., w/o Charles E. Smith, 1875-1928
Smith, E. Leon, 1897-1963
Moore, Martin P., 1805-1879
Otis, Harriet, w/o Martin P. Moore, 1812-1878
Nicherson, John W., 1853-1934
Moore, Emma E., w/o John W. Nicherson, 1856-1928
Corey, Charles W., 1840-1921
Dyer, Sylvia M., w/o Charles W. Corey, 1829-1922
Tabor, Harrison P., b 10 Oct 1820, d 25 Feb 1888
Butler, Edward F., 1843-1920
Butler, Louise C., w/o Edward F. Butler, 1851-1923
Butler, Sarah F., 1870-1879
Butler, Edith M., 1875-1879
Butler, Etta M., 1877-1879
Hutchinson, Joseph T., 1848-1915
Hutchinson, Mary D., w/o Joseph T. Hutchinson, 1844-1923
Spear, William H., b 26 June 1828, d 2 Jan 1909
Holt, Annie E., w/o William H. Spear, b 22 June 1850, d 1922
Dana, Alfred Crapon, b 9 July 1836, d 14 Oct 1906
Gerry, Sarah A., w/o Alfred Capron Dana, b 25 Sept 1838, d 23 Feb 1917
Dana, Alfred W., 1872-1944
Dana, Lillian D., w/o Alfred W. Dana, 1872-1961
Bright, Elizabeth, w/o John W. Metcalf, d 18 Feb 1920
Metcalf, John, d 12 May 1884 aged 63 yrs 4 mos

Metcalf, Mary T., w/o John Metcalf, d 26 Dec 1866 aged 44 yrs 3 mos
Metcalf, Marion, d/o John & Mary Metcalf, d 3 April 1852 aged 3 yrs 8 mos
Metcalf, Mary Ann, d 21 Jan 1903
Metcalf, Bertha M., d/o John M. & Elizabeth Metcalf, d 19 Jan 1967
Harris, Electra, w/o James Jilson, d 11 Jan 1891 aged 85 yrs 5 mos
Cockell, Henry, 1865-1952
Jeffery, Martha A., w/o Henry Cockell, 1865-1913
Clark, Henry, 1846-1904
Pendleton, Minnie O., w/o Henry Clark, 1857-1890
Clark, Mercy, d/o Henry & Minnie Clark, 1846-1904
Freeman, James M., 1816-1899
Harris, Nancy L., w/o James M. Freeman, 1815-1843
Crandall, Mary G., w/o James M. Freeman, 1825-1900
Metcalf, Leroy Alfred, 1886-1960
Barber, Ethel A., w/o Leroy Alfred Metcalf, 1886-1950
Metcalf, William Sumner, 1858-1939
Heaton, Ida E., w/o William Simner Metcalf, 1852-1919
Warmell, Julia A., b 22 Feb 1835, f 3 March 1891
Woodman, George S., 1868-1954
Woodman, Minnie M., w/o Goerge S. Woodman, 1868-1953
Woodman, Erma E., w/o Allen T. Swan, 1892-1916
Field, Edward, b 3 June 1832, d 3 June 1889
Small, Paulina K., w/o Edward Field, b 1 Sept 1837, d 10 Sept 1912
Field, Henry W., d 1 June 1877 aged 20 yrs 8 mos 25 days
Field, Edward E., d 22 Dec 1929 aged 67 yrs 3 mos 21 days
Chapman, Elizabeth, 1839-1910
Chapman, Elisha P., 1838-1921
Stewart, Alice, 1819-1877
Stewart, Hamilton P., 1814-1897
Young, Rob Roy, 1816-1949
Young, Ethel May, w/o Rob Roy Young, 1876-1971
Smith, Francis N., d 22 Dec 1888 aged 48 yrs 11 mos
Smith, Abby J., w/o Francis N. Smith, 1844-1918
Clark, Brenton W., 1860-1944
Taber, Carrie, w/o Brenton W. Clark, 1866-1947
Daniels, Lucius W., 1839-1920
Daniels, Sarah D., w/o Lucius W. Daniels, 1840-1923
Daniels, Mary L., 1862-1923
Daniels, Hattie A., 1863-1934

Darling, Annice L., 1870-1879
Richardson, Fremont M., 1849-1916
Richardson, Henrietta, w/o Fremont M. Richardson,....
Richardson, William F., 1872-1909
Richardson, Harriet B., 1825-1879
Hatch, John D., 1856-1922
Hatch, Annie G., w/o John D. Hatch, '857-1937
Newell, Albert J., 1835-1938
Clark, Betsey W., w/o Albert J. Newell, 1842-1926
Dove, William, 1837-1902
MacDonald, Katie, C., w/o William Dove, 1845-1926
Dove, Francis B., s/o William & Katie Dove, 1872-1893
Hawes, Mary J., 1832-1914
Hawes, Nancy M., 1835-1929
Dove, Benjamin, 1803-1874
Laurence, Susan, w/o Benjamin Dove, 1810-1884
Dove, Samuel, s/o Benjamin & Susan Dove, 1832-1860
Chilson, Stillman R., 1841-1926
Chilson, Louise, w/o Stillamn R. Chilson, b 1 Aug 1847, d 5 April 1923
Hills, Joseph G., b 20 Sept 1822, d 16 Nov 1900
Hills, Mary A. B., w/o Joseph G. Hills, b 8 Jan 1835, d 27 May 1923
Brown, Lewis, d 17 Jan 1862 aged 75 yrs 6 mos 22 days
Brown, Susanna, w/o Lewis Brown, b 16 Sept 1791, d 22 Sept 1885
Halleburton, William J., d 5 Dec 1883 aged 73 yrs
Warden, Susan H., w/o George R., b 17 May 1836, d 28 Nov 1867
Hawes, Eugene D., 1849-1918
Howard, Annie, w/o Eugene D. Hawes, 1853-1909
Hawes, Nathaniel, 1815-1899
Hawes, Eliza Ann, w/o Nathaniel Hawes, b 6 Oct 1817, d 5 April 1878
Fairbanks, John L., b 27 Sept 1826, d 11 May 1900
Pond, Eliza, w/o John L. Fairbanks, b 12 June 1837, d 18 June 1907
Fairbanks, Clara Anna, d/o John L. & Eliza Fairbanks, b 4 Jan 1865, d 9 Dec 1966
Prince, Charles H., 1873-1936
Prince, Annie B., 1872-1962
Prince, Helen B., 1900-1992
Prince, Marion G., 1901-1925
Ribero, George F., 1873-1945
Bright, Elvira, w/o George F. Ribero, 1875-1965
Newell, Albert W., 1834-1895

Newell, Mary E., w/o Albert W. Newell, 1839-1902
Newell, James E., 1854-1896
Marden, Eliza, 1810-1883
Pike, Alonzo G., 1817-1896
Pike, Martha T., 1822-1884
Wales, Amos S., 1848-1921
Wales, Sarah Lovice, 1845-1909
Richardson, Wallace E., 1846-1913
Walker, Elizabeth J., w/o Wallace E. Richardson, 1850-1920
Snow, Florence Homer, 1883-1975
Brock, Albert L., 1840-1920, A member of Co C 21st Mass Vols
Brock, Mary J., w/o Albert L. Brock, 1850-1933
Brock, Arthur L., s/o Albert L. & Mary J.Brock, 1881-1881
Colson, George William, b 19 July 1889, d 19 Aug 1938
Burrington, Venila S., w/o George William Colson, b 5 Sept 1871, d 23
   June 1954
Trowbridge, Edwin, 1844-1896
Trowbridge, Flora, w/o Edwin Trowbridge, 1845-1920
Kingsbury, Martha B., 1843-1919
Metcalf, Edgar A., 1854-1936
Metcalf, Elizaebth H., w/o Edgar A. Metcalf, 1855-1949
Gay, Sally Ann, w/o Walter Gay, d 24 June 1881 aged 72 yrs 9 mos
Blake, George A., 1842-1902
Gay, Samuel E., 1825-1892
Gay, Sarah A., 1819-1894
Wadsworth, George F., d 21 Sept 1880 aged 36 yrs 7 mos
Foster, George Warren, 1841-1917
Foster, Hannah Amelia, w/o George Warren Foster, 1853-1931
Foster, Gertrude Louise, 1874-1878
Besse, Louisa M., w/o Milton G. Besse, b 24 Sept 1853, d 25 June 1881
Knowlton, Garland W., 1907-1911
Knowlton, F. Louise, 1907-1909
Knowlton, William E., 1873-1919
Knowlton, Catherine B., 1876-1928
Knowlton, William J. Jr., 1899-1927
Garland, Joseph H., 1811-1891
Garland, Lorinda Gracie, w/o Joseph H. Garland, 1821-1898
Knowlton, Ellen L., 1848-1931
Wales, William A., s/o Adelbert & Lizzie Wales, 1890-1920
Blake, Oramel B., b 2 Dec 1833, d 24 Dec 1907

Witshire, George, b 19 Sept 1865, d 27 May 1897
Faxon, James W., b 24 Oct 1835, d 25 June 1908
Faxon, Mary H., w/o James W. Faxon, b 11 Jan 1841, d 20 March 1908
Faxon, Louis P., 1869-1944
Candon, Emma G., d 23 March 1895
Cox, Annie R., d 18 Sept 1887
Faxon, Adeline L., b 2 Sept 1866, d 4 June 1886
Faxon, Annie M., 1876-1947
Stratton, Martha Woolford, d/o John & Sophia Stratton, b 25 Dec 1822, d
    25 Dec 1908
Sanderson, H. Arthur, 1859-1891
Ledbury, Francis H., b 30 Dec 1911, d 9 Feb 1987
Ballou, Phebe, w/o Barton Ballou, b 18 July 1833, d 26 July 1903
Cowell, Mary J. Adams, w/o Barton Balou, b 4 March 1836, d 25 June
    1907
Swanson, Wyman, 1850-1916
McMasters, William H., b 1 April 1830, d 23 Sept 1873
Swanson, Jane, 1839-1908
Palmer, Sophia J., b 23 June 1876, d 12 Oct 1959
Thayer, Elmer J., 1864-1911
Newcomb, Rose R., w/o Elmer J. Thayer, 1865-1905
Bourne, Samuel C., 1840-1932
Bourne, Evelyn E., w/o Samuel C. Bourne, 1843-1889
Lundborn, John A., 1848-1921
Lindborn, Ada C., 1869-1953
Fisher, Daniel W., 1842-1925
Ferguson, Josephine L., w/o Daniel W. Fisher, 1841-1912
Perrot, Jules E., 1880-1912
Perrot, Maria H., w/o Jules E. Perrot, 1866-1929
Perrot, Alice L., 1905-1905
Neilson, John, b 29 Sept 1860, d 21 Jan 1908
Neilson, Maud Isadora, w/o John Nielson, b 5 April 1864, d 19 April
    1917
Cleaveland, Charles, 1845-1907
Loose, Ottilee E., w/o Carl F. Loose, d 15 March 1907 aged 36 yrs
Loose, Carl F., 1869-1944
Davidson, Elizabeth, 1795-1881
Fiske, Mildred B., 1896-1896
Corbett, Abigail B., d 30 Sept 1910 aged 99 yrs
Fisher, David, 1812-1899

Fuller, Nancy C., w/o Davis Fisher, b 27 March 1816, d 2 March 1881
Gage, Aurilla M., w/o Nelson A. Gage, 1855-1897
Darling, Sadie L., b 29 June 1874, d 14 Oct 1955
Darling, Fenner, b 3 Nov 1829, d 10 Oct 1895
Darling, Sarah M., b 19 July 1840, d 31 July 1938
Darling, Charles F., b 17 Aug 1868, d 1 Jan 1892
Menard, Clara A., b 19 Aug 1876, d 5 April 1943
Jordan, Albert L., d 14 Nov 1890 aged 53 yrs
Martin, Albert H., 1876-1921
Martin, Clara E., 1876-1939

Fiske, Lovett, 1814-1906
Remington, Alma, w/o Lovett Fiske, 1815-1902
Fisk, Sewall H., b 30 Dec 1810,d 18 Sept 1862, A member of Co B 16th
Reg Mass Vols
Fisk, John, d 16 Dec 1833 aged 73 yrs
Fisk, Abigail, w/o John Fisk, d 14 April 1849 aged 76 yrs 8 mos
Fisk, Horace, d 5 June 1879 aged 78 yrs 11 os
Fisk, Melissa, w/o Horace Fisk, d 2 July 1873 aged 64 yrs 2 mos
Littlefield, Susan V., d 20 Nov 1913 aged 75 yrs 7 mos
Morgan, Jacob, d 29 Aug 1870 aged 69 yrs 9 mos
Bridges, Nathan, d 18 May 1844 aged 71 yrs
Bridges, Nabby A., w/o Nathan Bridges, d 11 May 1858 aged 76 yrs 10
mos 11 days
Whiting, Nathan, d 2 Aug 1793 aged 13 mos
Leland, Jeremiah, d 4 Oct 1808 aged 55 yrs
Leland, Mary, w/o Jeremiah Leland, d 30 Oct 1795 AE 41 yrs
Leland, Sarah, w/o Jeremiah Leland, d 4 July 1820 AE 57 yrs
Walker, Charles C., b 3 Oct 1798, d 21 July 1863
Walker, Zemina, w/o Charles C. Walker, b 15 Oct 1800, d 12 May 1863
Walker, Charles J., Killed at the Battle of Gettysburg, 2 July 1863 aged 24
yrs
Packard, Hermon, s/o Benjamin & Martha H. Packard, d 15 Dec 1856
aged 4 yrs 8 mos
Rockwood, Timothy, d 22 Feb 1806 aged 76 yrs
Rockwood, Deborah, w/o Timothy Rockwood, d suddenly (BROKEN)
Rockwood, Joanna, d/o Timothy & Deborah Rockwood, d 26 Feb 1809
Partridge, Joseph, 1814-1896
Partridge, Elizabeth S. C., w/o Joseph Partridge, 1818-1904
Partridge, Maria, d/o Joseph & Elizabeth Partridge, 1840-1840
Partridge, Sarah, d/o Joseph & Elizabeth Partridge, 1859-1860
Stedman, John, d 5 April 1800
Tidd, Daniel, d 21 June 1806 aged 46 yrs
Littlefield, Betsey, d 22 Sept 1807

Brown, Amos, s/o E. & R. Brown, d 27 Feb 1805 aged 22 yrs
Fairbanks, Joseph, d 9 Feb 1791 aged 27 yrs
Fairbanks, Mary, w/o Joseph Fairbanks, d 12 Feb 1790
Fairbanks, Mary, d 19 Feb 1801 aged 20 yrs
Fairbanks, Lieut. Drury, d 19 June 1836 aged 54 yrs
Marsh, Lydia, d 14 May 1812 aged 21 yrs
Marfh, Elifha, d 1797
Newton, Simeon, d 24 Feb 1807 aged 66 yrs
Newton, Jerusha, w/o Simeon Newton, d 23 Sept 1835 aged 94 yrs
Culter, Calvin, d 12 Nov 1831 aged 65 yrs
Culter, Ruth, w/o Calvin Culter, d 26 Oct 1835 aged 69 yrs
Ludden, Phebe Sheffield, d 12 Aug 1870 aged 84 yrs 6 mos 6 days
Sheffield, Betsey, d June 1798 aged 17 yrs
Culter, Sally, d 2 May 1803 aged 2 yrs
Mellen, Ursula, w/o John Mellen, d 25 Oct 1803 aged 24 yrs
Culter, Col. Simeon, d 13 July 1799 aged 49 yrs
Culter, Elizabeth, w/o Col. Simeon Culter, d 1 May 1849 aged 95 yrs
Nutting, Dwight, d 22 Sept 1871 aged 60 yrs
Culter, Martin, d 7 Jan 1845 aged 71 yrs
Culter, Sophia, w/o Martin Culter, d 17 May 1849 aged 66 yrs
Culter, Betsey M., d/o Martin & Sophia Culter, d 15 Dec 1877 aged 64 yrs
Parkman, Altethina, w/o Dr. Elias Parkman & d/o Captain William
    Belcher of Preston, CT, d 15 June 1792 aged 29 yrs
Wheeler, William H., A member of Co H 2nd Regt Mass Cavalry was
    taken prisoner 6 July 1864, d 30 Dec 1864 Florence, South Carolina
Wheeler, Edgar M., d 28 July 1856 aged 3 yrs 10 mos 3 days
Lealand, Lt. Asaph, d 6 Aug 1812 aged 82 yrs
Lealand, Beulah, w/o Lt. Asaph Lealand, d 25 Nov 1798
Claflin, Anna, w/o William Claflin, d 18 Oct 194 aged 20 yrs
Bullard, Otis Brigham, 1815-1905
Culter, Abigail, w/o Otis Brigham Bullard, 1820-1904
Colman, Loring, s/o E. A. & M. J. Colman, d 23 June 1854 aged 15 yrs
Stone, John, d 8 Sept 1806 aged 41 yrs
Bullard, Capt. Samuel, d 27 May 1793 aged 79 yrs
Bullard, Deborah, w/o Capt. Samuel Bullard, d 1841
Ames, Moses, d 25 May 1816 aged 30 yrs
Thayer, Alexander, d 25 Sept 1807 aged 67 yrs
Thayer, Abigail, w/o Alexander Thayer, d 9 Feb 1827 aged 74 yrs
Wheeler, Jotham Jr., d 8 May 1882 aged 64 yrs 1 mo 15 days
Pierce, Mary E., d 15 Jan 1887 aged 65 yrs 1 mo

Larkin, Peter, b 23 Aug 1785, d 11 July 1836
Larkin, Lucy, w/o Peter Larkin, b 18 Feb 1787, d 9 Aug 1872
Larkin, Charles A., 1830-1910
McLaughfin, Malachi, d 4 Nov 1827 aged 33 yrs
Cutler, Jonathan, d 8 March 1762 aged 52 yrs
Marshall, Abigail, w/o Jonathan Cutler, d 1794
Haven, Lt. John, d 6 Oct 1785 aged 74 yrs
Haven, Mary D., w/o Lt. John Haven, d 6 Oct 1796 aged 86 yrs
Beale, Alice, d 26 Dec 1824
Phipps, Lt. Aaron, d 21 Aug 1809 aged 49 yrs
Whiting, Lt. Samuel, d 5 July 1814 aged 88 yrs
Whiting, Anna, w/o Lt. Samuel Whiting, d 21 March 1842 aged 90 yrs
Phipps, Deacon Aaron, d 18 Oct 1792
Phipps, Zeruiah, d/o Joseph & Mary Phipps, d 25 Aug 1795 aged 3 yrs
Whiting, Samuel, d 16 June 1807 aged 41 yrs
Sumner, Lydia, d 3 May 1839 aged 71 yrs
Mellen, Lt. Joseph, d 12 Nov 1787 aged 49 yrs 8 mos
Mellen, Daniel, d 4 Jan 1784 aged 69 yrs
Perry, Mary, w/o Lt. James Perry & formerly w/o Lt. Joseph Mellen, d 29
    April 1813 aged 68 yrs
Mellen, William, d 4 Sept 1807 aged 41 yrs
Kinsman, Eliza A., w/o Eliphalet E. Kinsman, d 25 Oct 1851 aged 24 yrs
Johnson, Sarah E., d/o J. & H. Johnson, d 7 March 1806
Humphrey, Rev. James H., 1842-1915
Pearson, Florence A., w/o Rev. James H. Humphrey, 1851-1915
Blanchard, Horace, b 11 Sept 1807, d 13 July 1847
Blanchard, Mary Ann, w/o Horace Blanchard, d 9 Jan 1837 aged 24 yrs
Simons, James F., d 30 Aug 1877 aged 68 yrs
Simons, Nancy E., w/o James F. Simons, d 13 Feb 1899 aged 81 yrs
Blanchard, Cina M., w/o James F. Simons, d 8 Aug 1853 aged 41 yrs
Rice, Martha W., w/o Sylvanus Pond, d 8 Sept 1856 aged 28 yrs 7 mos
Rockwood, Calvin, 1792-1863
Howe, Lois, w/o Calvin Rockwood, 1792-1881
Rochwood, Nancy H., 1825-1847
Rockwood, Edwin F., 1835-1862
Rockwood, Emeline Helena, w/o Calvin Rockwood, d 13 Nov 1893 aged
    63 yrs
Bent, Emeline, w/o Hiram Bent, d 27 July 1841 aged 29 yrs
Leland, Hermon, b 22 June 1798, d 15 Jan 1868
Barrett, Sarah, w/o Hermon Leland, b 5 Jan 1798, d 22 May 1863

Littlefield, Captain Ephraim, d 13 Nov 1778 aged 66 yrs

Bellows, Asa E., b 5 Jan 1805, d 2 March 1870

Bullard, Capt. Isaac, d 12 Jan 1814 aged 88 yrs

Bullard, Miriah, w/o Capt. Isaac Bullard, d 13 July 1801 aged 57 yrs

Bullard, Beulah, w/o Capt. Isaac Bullard......

Rockwood, Thomas T., d 11 Oct 1872 aged 60 yrs 4 mos

Rockwood, Evelinal, w/o Thomas T. Rockwood, d 27 Aug 1887 aged 75 yrs

Parker, Elma F., s/o James W. & Kate C. Parker, b 1 Sept 1870, d 21 July 1875

Margan, Henry, b 9 Aug 1820, d 21 March 1900

Morgan, Sarah G., w/o Henry Morgan, b 25 Oct 1815, d 20 March 1900

Buzzell, Zeriah, w/o Edmond Buzzell, d 10 Feb 1862 aged 85 yrs

Batchelder, Millicent, w/o Odlin Batchelder, d 15 July 1859 aged 70 yrs

Batchelder, Oldin, d 30 April 1860 aged 85 yrs

Batchelder, Huldah, w/o Oldin Batchelder, d 13 Dec 1846 aged 69 yrs 6 mos

Chamberland, Eliza Jane, d/o Eliphalet & Harriet Chamberland, d 11 Oct 1833 aged 5 mos 10 days

Travis, Daniel B., d 19 May 1835 aged 21 yrs

Leland, Capt. Benuel, d 23 June 1839 aged 59 yrs

Leland, Clarissa, w/o Capt. Benuel Leland, d 22 July 1837 aged 58 yrs

Travis, Randall, d 26 Nov 1861 aged 63 ys

Travis, Abigail B., w/o Randall Travis, d 12 March 1879

Fiske, Asa, d 26 Aug 1830, also bodies of many of his children, grandchildren & great grandchildren, who d. prior to 1853

Leland, Gilbert T., d 13 July 1861 aged 48 yrs

Leland, Adeline, d 29 Dec 1905 aged 84 yrs

Howe, William, 1807-1873

Howe, Louisa, w/o William Howe, 1805-1891

Howe, Luther, 1837-1924

Howe, Isaac, d 10 March 1843 aged 86 yrs

Howe, Lois, w/o Isaac Howe, d 22 Sept 1850 aged 84 yrs

Mann, William, d 21 April 1837 aged 75 yrs

Sherman, Elisha, d 8 June 1845 aged 66 yrs

Sherman, Nancy, w/o Elisha Sherman, d 26 Jan 1850 aged 60 yrs

Cole, Merrill, d 15 Oct 1849 aged 21 yrs 4 mos

Hatten, George F. Thompson, s/o William & Eliza Hatten, d 19 Aug 1862 aged 35 yrs 6 mos

Sherman, J. N., 1817-1907

Sherman, Catherine, w/o J. N. Sherman, 1819-1845
Sherman, Irene, w/o J. N. Sherman, 1825-1905
Sherman, Willis R., 1819-1896
Sherman, Mary A., w/o Willis R. Sherman, 1820-1891
Sherman, Melissa A., 1842-1844
Sherman, Alice A., 1850-1933
Warfield, Addison, 1816-1893
Warfield, Harriet A., w/o Addison Warfield, 1821-1897
Warfield, Harriet M., d/o Addison & Harriet Warfield, 1841-1841
Warfield, Elias A., s/o Addison & Harriet Warfield, 1842-1845
Slocum, Elmira R., w/o Lewis Slocum, d 14 Dec 1836 aged 37 yrs
Morgan, Jacob, d 29 Aug 1870 aged 69 yrs 9 mos
Jones, Henry Elisha, 1804-1874
Hunstable, Lydia Hannah, w/o Henry Elisha Jones, 1803-1884
Morse, Henry, d 15 April 1766 aged 62 yrs
Morse, Sarah, w/o Henry Morse, d 17 Nov 1762 aged 64 yrs
Morse, Rebecca, w/o Ezekiel Morse, b 24 March 1729, d 19 Nov 1807
Morse, Lt. Henry, d 2 Dec 1734, d 23 June 1807
Morse, Ezekiel, 1724-....(Broken)
Fiske, Almeda W., w/o J. N. Fiske, 1849-1919
Pratt, Abigail, d 19 Sept 1896 aged 92 yrs 8 mos 28 days
Batchelder, Emily, 1837-1914
Batchelder, George, d 13 mos
Watson, Abigail, b 2 March 1778, d 19 Jan 1861
Stone, Anna W., b 23 Oct 1808, d 1 May 1872
Pond, Almira L., w/o John N. Batchelder, d 18 April 1857 aged 21 yrs
Hawes, Col. Ichabod, d 14 June 1836 aged 52 yrs
Wight, James, d 12 Oct 1853 aged 84 yrs
Wight, Irene, w/o James Wight, d 29 Nov 1849 aged 72yrs
Wight, Milton, s/o James & Irene Wight, d 1 Nov 1817
Cutler, Jason T., s/o Elihu & Rebecca Cutler, d 21 April 1843 aged 9 yrs
Cutler, Arthur E., s/o Elihu & Rebecca Cutler, d 3 Sept 1842 aged 5 yrs
Cutler, Elihu, s/o Elihu & Rebecca Cutler, d 6 Nov 1841 aged 3 days
Snells, Dexter W., 1808-1884
Morse, Mary, w/o Ebenezer Morse, d 17 Feb 1831 aged 52 yrs
Marsh, Sarah, d 19 April 1840 aged 41 yrs
Marsh, Henry A., d 18 March 1833 aged 49 yrs
Marsh, Clarissa D., w/o Henry A. Marsh, d 30 Nov 1847 aged 64 yrs
Btchelder, Charlotte D., w/o Daniel S. Batchelder, d Dec 1834 aged 21 yrs
Bemis, Peter, 1788-1869

Bemis, Sally H., 1795-1870

Fairbnks, Capt. Nathan, d 5 Sept 1825 of Typhus fever aged 36 yrs

Fairbanks, Sally, w/o Capt. Nathan Fairbanks, d 19 June 1819 AE 24 yrs

Fairbanks, Mary, w/o John Fairbanks Esq., d 25 Feb 1834 aged 76 yrs

Fairbanks, John Esq., d 1844 aged 86 yrs

Whiting, Col. Asa, d 29 Nov 1858 aged 76 yrs

Whiting, Clarissa H., w/o Col. Asa Whiting, d 5 Oct 1819 aged 60 yrs

Whiting, Mary G., d/o Asa & Clarissa Whiting, d 26 Nov 1831 aged 24 yrs

Whiting, Nathan, d 15 April 1818 aged 44 yrs

Whiting, Meletiah W. L., w/o Nathan Whiting, d 14 Jan 1859 aged 78 yrs

Brown, Ezra, d 2 April 1816 aged 58 yrs

Brown, Rhoda, w/o Ezra Brown, d 23 March 1822 aged 58 yrs

Brown, Martin, s/o Ezra & Rhoda Brown, d 3 Oct 1817 aged 25 yrs

Pierce, Nicamor, d 21 Dec 1851 aged 57 yrs

Brown, Emily, w/o Nicamor Pierce, d 16 Aug 1873 aged 68 yrs

Wilken, Dr. George, d 2 May 1826 of Consumpton aged 32 yrs

Pierce, Charles Henry, s/o Nicamor & Emily Pierce, d 9 Feb 1833 aged 3 yrs

Pierce, George Edward, s/o Nicamor & Emily Pierce, d 17 Dec 1832 aged 4 yrs 10 mos

Fisk, Timothy, b June 1804, d Jan 1899

Batchelder, Lucretia, w/o Timothy Fisk, b Dec 1806, d July 1887

Fiske, Hannah, w/o John B. Coombs, b 13 July 1806, d 20 March 1884

Eames, Hannah, w/o David Fiske, b 24 Jan 1774, d 12 Feb 1856

Fiske, David, d 24 May 1816

Wheelock, Joseph, d 28 March 1868 aged 62 yrs

Adams, Sybil, w/o John Strickland, d 11 June 1874 aged 86 yrs

Hill, Daniel S., d 24 Oct 1854 aged 67 yrs

Leland, Polly, w/o Daniel S. Hill, d 22 March 1876

Parker, Edward G., d 13 Feb 1893 aged 86 yrs 4 mos 9 days

Parker, Mary, w/o Edward G. Parker, d 31 Aug 1879 AE 71 yrs 4 mos 25 days

Leland, James Jr., d 23 Feb 1854 aged 41 yrs

Leland, Frances S., w/o James Leland Jr., d 1 March 1892 aged 76 yrs 1 mo

Leland, James, d 16 July 1854 aged 71 yrs

Hill, Whiting, d 26 July 1800 aged 52 yrs

Hill, Hannah, w/o Whiting Hill, d 7 Sept 1850 aged 96 yrs 4 mos

Whiting, Nathan, d 22 March 1869 aged 44 yrs

Whiting, Olive, w/o Nathan P. Whiting, d 14 May 1874

Whiting, William Henry, s/o Nathan & Olive Whiting, d 26 July 1849 aged 18 yrs

Whiting, Albert, s/o Nathan & Olive Whiting, d 30 Sept 1848 aged 3 mos

Whiting, William, s/o Nathan & Olive Whiting, d 22 Sept 1812 aged 6 yrs

Whiting, Rowena, d/o Nathan & Olive Whiting, d 17 March 1844 AE 17 mos

Whiting, Jason J., 1810-1888

Blanchard, Susan, d 16 Nov 1872 aged 73 yrs

Currier, Ebenezer H., d 9 May 1856 aged 60 yrs 2 mos

Currier, Betsey P., w/o Ebenezer H. Currier, d 1 March 1871 AE 73 yrs 7 mos

Currier, Lovina P., w/o Charles E. Currier, b 6 Feb 1827 Grantham, New Hampshire, d 7 Feb 1878 Chicago

Daniels, Timothy, d 2 Dec 1888

Puffer, Laura A., w/o John Puffer, b 30 Dec 1830, d 11 Aug 1877

Batchelder, Lucy, w/o Nathan Batchelder, d 4 Jan 1874 aged 84 yrs 5 mos

Tyler, David S., d 14 Nov 1868 aged 66 yrs

Tyler, Hannah K., w/o David S. Tyler, d 27 July 1833 aged 35 yrs

Tyler, Caroline B., w/o David S. Tyler, d 4 July 1877 aged 82 yrs

Tyler, Hannah M., d/o David & Caroline Tyler, d 22 March 1838 aged 3 mos

Gallott, Courtland, 1828-1911

Gallott, Amanda, w/o Courtland Gallott, 1826-1888

Smith, Isaac Jr., d 10 July 1837 aged 45 yrs

Fiske, Abner, b 5 Aug 1808, d 17 June 1880

Bellows, Loronda, b 11 Sept 1809, d 19 March 1890

Battelle, Freeman, 1837-1909, A member of Co C 16th Regt Mass Vols

Fiske, Malvina, 1834-1919

Smith, Isaac, d 7 Dec 1838 aged 86 yrs

Smith, Prudence, w/o Isaac Smith, d 10 Feb 1843 aged 75 yrs

Fiske, Dr. Timothy, 1778-1863

Daniels, Rhoda, w/o Dr. Timothy Fiske, 1782-1874

Adams, Capt. Lemuel, d 28 Aug 1833 aged 45 yrs

Travis, George C., 1828-1873

Hoffman, Walter B., 1873-1928

Pond, Hannah C., b 25 Sept 1803, d 27 March 1881

Pond, Nelson, b 9 Jan 1803, d 26 Dec 1891

Hoffman, Helen S., 1854-1924

Hoffman, Charles E., 1846-1915

Dickerson, Thomas, d 2 Nov 1844 aged 50 yrs

Dickerson, Rhoda, w/o Thomas Dickerson, d 13 Jan 1833 aged 38 yrs

Dickerson, Miranda, w/o Thomas Dickerson, d 20 Jan 1836 aged 40 yrs

Dickerson, Edward, d 28 Feb 1851

Dickerson, Susan H., w/o Edward Dickerson, d 24 Oct 1843 aged 38 yrs

Dickerson, Rev. Timothy A.M. for 24 years pastor of the Christ Church in the town, b 25 June 1761 Amherst, MA, d 6 July 1813

Wheaton, Rev. Joseph, b 16 March 1788 Rehoboth, MA, d 4 Feb 1823

Wheaton, Mary, w/o Rev. Joseph Wheaton, d 28 July 1817 aged 26 yrs

Wiswell, Jonathan, d 17 May 1835 aged 29 yrs

Smith, Mercy, w/o Jonathan Wiswell & d/o Isaac Smith, d 9 July 1836 aged 33 yrs

Smith, Ann, w/o Adam Leland & d/o Isaac & Prudence Smith, b 13 May 1796, d 2 Dec 1866

Fiske, John, b 25 July 1806, d 10 Oct 1867

Fiske, Elbridge Burnap, only s/o John & Mary M. Fiske, b 28 Oct 1832, d 9 June 1843

Fiske, Mary N., w/o John Fiske, b 25 March 1811, d 17 July 1884

Rockwood, Polly, w/o Ezra Rockwood, d 23 Jan 1817 aged 29 yrs

Rockwood, Edward, d 2 Oct 1855 aged 21 yrs

Burnap, Lydia, d 25 March 1862 aged 77 yrs

Dickerson, Elizabeth Prentiss, d/o Thomas & Susan G. Dickerson, b 30 July 1837, d 20 March 1910

Crout, Susan, w/o Thomas Dickerson, d 31 Oct 1862

Dickerson, Sarah Warren, d/o Thomas & Susan Dickerson, d 21 Dec 1841 aged 2 yrs

Littlefield, Ruth, w/o Luther Rockwood, d 1 Oct 1855 aged 74 yrs

Rockwood, Luther E., d 16 May 1862

Puffer, Susan, w/o Jonathan Puffer, d 5 Jan 1861 aged 29 yrs

Puffer, Rosella L., d/o Jonathan & Susan Puffer, d 7 Dec 1868 aged 18 yrs

Underwood, Betsey, w/o Timothy Mellen, d 18 April 1865 aged 81 yrs

Mellen, Timothy, d 26 Jan 1845 aged 65 yrs

Mellen, James Esq., d 30 May 1834 aged 81 yrs

Mellen, Deborah, w/o James Mellen Esq., d 29 Aug 1836 aged 78 yrs

Mellen, John, b 23 Feb 1766, d 3 Aug 1837

Mellen, Mary, w/o John Mellen, b 22 June 1767, d 20 Dec 1837

Rockwood, William, d 15 June 1836 aged 29 yrs

Rockwood, Timothy, d 7 March 1848 aged 70 yrs

Burnap, Mary, w/o Timothy Rockwood, d 24 Sept 1872 aged 91 yrs 6 mos

Cutler, Hon. Elihu Jr., b 6 Dec 1806, d 19 April 1855

Cutler, Rebecca, w/o Hon. Elihu Cutler Jr., b 23 March 1809, d 19 Nov 1893

Cutler, Elbridge, Professor in Harvard College, b 29 Dec 1830, d 27 Dec 1870

Stedman, John, b 17 May 1772, d 13 Jan 1818

Richardson, Mercy, w/o John Stedman & d/o Abijah & Mercy D. Richardson, (too far in ground to read)

Stedman, Josiah, d 1 Sept 1836 aged 63 yrs

Stedman, Keziah, w/o Josiah Stedman, d 17 Feb 1825 aged 44 yrs

Leland, Henry, s/o Oliver & Abigail Leland, d 4 Nov 1804 aged 17 yrs

Leland, Ambrose, s/o Oliver & Abigail Leland,d 26 Sept 1801 aged 5 mos 23 days

Cowen, Sylvia, w/o Luther Cowen, d 12 Dec 1849 aged 21 yrs

Leland, Sylvia, w/o John Leland & d/o Oliver & Abigail Leland, d 25 Dec 1846 aged 56 yrs

Leland, Oliver, d 11 June 1838 aged 78 yrs

Leland, Abigail, w/o Oliver Leland, d 11 Dec 1839 aged 72 yrs

Johnson, Nathaniel Jr., d 3 May 1840 aged 79 yrs

Johnson, Persis C., w/o Nathaniel Johnson Esq., d 4 April 1854 aged 91 yrs

Johnson, Calvin, s/o Nathaniel & Persis C. Johnson, d 12 Jan 1820 AE 32

Johnson, Nathaniel, d 18 Oct 1851 aged 52 yrs

Johnson, Eunice, w/o Nathaniel Johnson, d 23 Dec 1878 aged 80 yrs 3 mos

Cutler, Hon. Elihu, d 9 June 1857 aged 86 yrs

Cutler, Lavina N., w/o Hon. Elihu Cutler, d 19 March 1833 aged 64 yrs

Cutler, Persis P., w/o Hon. Elihu Cutler, d 18 Oct 1867 aged 63 yrs

Cutler, Betsey R., d 15 Jan 1886 aged 84 yrs

Cutler, Charles MD., d 20 Dec 1839 aged 25 yrs

Morse, Rev. Abner, b 5 Sept 1793 Medway, MA, d 16 May 1865

Morse, Thomas J. Esq., d 4 Feb 1859 aged 57 yrs

Leland, Lucy, d/o Daniel & Harriet J. Leland & w/o Thomas J. Morse, b 16 May 1793, d 25 Jan 1879

Perry, Baruch, d 13 Oct 1837 aged 44 yrs

Perry, Betsey, w/o Baruch Perry, d 13 March 1828 aged 35 yrs

Underwood, Joshua, d 15 March 1821 aged 77 yrs

Underwood, Lydia, w/o Joshua Underwood, d 2 June 1815 aged 69 yrs

Fairbanks, Joseph S., s/o Elijah & Abigail Fairbanks, d 8 Nov 1825 aged 27 yrs

Wood, Sarah, d 29 March 1820 aged 31 yrs
Marshall, Mary, d 8 March 1837 aged 71 yrs
Foster, Jeremiah, 1790-1852
Wenzell, Louisa, w/o Jeremiah Foster, 1797-1870
Wenzell, Seneca, d 18 June 1854
Blake, Polly Wenzell, d 29 May 1905 aged 95 yrs
Wenzell, Hannah, d/o Seneca & Polly Wnnzell, b 27 March 1833, d 13 Jan 1852
Wenzell, Sibble, d 4 Sept 1848 aged 78 yrs
Wenzell, Jacob, d 9 April 1823 aged 55 yrs
Wenzell, Dexter, d 30 April 1852
Bemis, Augustine, 1845-1847
Bemis, Amory L., 1848-1853
Bemis, Augustine Samuel, 1816-1896
Leland, Ophella, w/o Augustine Samuel Bemis, 1818-1907
Marsh, Deacon Charles, d 28 Oct 1845 aged 60 yrs
Marsh, Sally, w/o Deacon Charles Marsh, d 23 Dec 1865 aged 77 yrs
Marsh, Caroline S., d/o Deacon Charles & Sally Marsh, d 14 April 1821 aged 12 days
Marsh, Charles, s/o Dea. Charles & Sally Marsh, d 17 Sept 1822 AE 3 days
Marsh, Albert A., s/o Deacon Charles & Sally Marsh, d 12 June 1830 aged 21 yrs
Marsh, Emily Ann, d/o Deacon Charles & Sally Marsh, d 20 June 1833 aged 19 yrs
Leland, Capt. Daniel, d 18 Oct 1838 Ware, MA aged 32 yrs
Pond, Elvira H., w/o Newell Pond, d 14 Aug 1846 aged 43 yrs
Whiting, Sarah H., d 28 May 1843 aged 61 yrs
Marsh, Deacon Eser, d 28 Nov 1835 aged 91 yrs
Marsh, Esther, w/o Deacon Eser Marsh, d 14 April 1826 aged 77 yrs
Marsh, Betsey, 1792-1822
Marsh, Sophia, 1776-1858
Perry, Charlotte, d 11 Nov 1896 aged 72 yrs

Braggville Cemetery
Rockland Street
Holliston, Massachusetts

Bragg, Alfred, b 10 July 1811, d 19 Feb 1889

Bragg, Sarah, w/o Alfred Bragg, 1818-1912

Bragg, Nancy, w/o Ariel Bragg, b 15 May 1781 Hopkinton, MA, d 16 Nov 1865 Milford, Ma

Bragg, Elizabeth, w/o Col. Ariel Bragg, d 21 June 1816 aged 42 yrs

Bragg, Ariel, b 30 July 1772 Wrentham, MA, d 26 Oct 1855 Milford, MA

Bragg, Sibbel, w/o Ariel Bragg, d 16 July 1798

Bragg, Edna M., 1874-1891

Bragg, John F., 1856-1917

Bragg, John Fisher, 1845-1895

Bragg, Fowler, d 8 March 1889 aged 91 yrs

Bragg, Sarah Frances, w/o Fowler Bragg, d 3 March 1862 aged 40 yrs 12 days

Bragg, Emeline, d/o Fowler & Sarah Bragg, d 1 March 1856 aged 18 mos

Pierce, Lizzie C., w/o John F. Bragg, 1852-1889

Ryan, Mary A., w/o John F. Bragg, 1845-1879

Kimball, Francis, b 19 Sept 1797, d 8 April 1834

Kimball, Eunice, w/o Francis Kimball, b 31 Oct 1794, d 8 March 1869

Kimball, Joshua B., 1829-1902

Bragg, Hermon, b 19 Aug 1855, d 23 Jan 1894

Bryan, Eudora Bragg, w/o Hermon Bragg, b 17 Oct 1852, d 22 June 1922

Bragg, Hermon, b 22 Aug 1874, d 1 April 1962

Bragg, Ariel, b 24 May 1813, d 31 Dec 1866

Bragg, Sarah E., w/o Ariel Bragg, b 4 Sept 1826, d 27 Sept 1907

Bragg, George Archer, s/o Ariel & Sarah Bragg, b 19 April 1844, d 27 Dec 1844

Bragg, Charles S., b 21 March 1857, d 20 July 1882 Flagstaff

Jones, Ada L. B., 1822-1901

Jones, Appleton B., 1824-1863

Jones, George, 1802-1875

Jones, John F., 1833-1869

Garrett, Alice, d/o Thomas & Sarah Garrett, d 27 Sept 1856 aged 2 yrs 16 days

Forestall, Louisa, w/o Amasa Forestall, d 8 April 1847 aged 40 yrs
Forestall, Miraim, w/o Amasa Forestall, d 15 Jan 1858 aged 40 yrs
Cutler, Ebenezer, d 12 Dec 1828 aged 82 yrs
Cutler, Esther, d 18 July 1832
Leland, Daniel Jr., d 13 July 1822 aged 45 yrs
Leland, Hannah, w/o Daniel Leland Jr., d 21 Sept 1835 aged 56 yrs
Leland, William, d 20 June 1879 aged 78 yrs 6 mos
Leland, Sarah, w/o William Leland, d 25 Dec 1839 aged 35 yrs
Cutler, Esther, d/o Eleazer Cutler, d 18 Jan 1809 aged 33 yrs
Leland, Daniel, d 14 Dec 1835 aged 93 yrs 10 mos 23 days
Cutler, Ebenezer, d 12 Dec 1828 aged 82 yrs
Cutler, Esther, w/o Ebenezer Cutler, d 18 July 1833 aged 89 yrs
Johnson, Lydia, sister of Ebenezer Cutler, d 18 Dec 1831 aged 80 yrs
Phipps, Jackson L., s/o Josephus & Emeline Phipps, d Aug 1858
Adams, Moses, d 10 June 1850 aged 69 yrs
Brown, Nancy W., w/o James S. Brown & d/o Moses & Ruth Adams, d 12
    July 1840 aged 30 yrs
Brown, Norman H., s/o James & Nancy W. Brown, d 3 July 1840 aged 6
    mos
Miller John, d 16 June 1889
Miller, Elizabeth K., w/o John Miller, d 3 Feb 1886 aged 59 yrs
Phipps, Daniel, b 15 Oct 1827, d 28 Feb 1865
Phipps, Alice, w/o Dana Phipps, d 30 Sept 1883 aged 84 yrs 9 mos 5 days
Phipps, Dana, b 10 Aug 1796, d 17 May 1877
Miller, Warren, b 15 Feb 1797, d 11 May 1877
Miller, Jerusha, w/o Warren Miller, d 8 Jan 1836 aged 58 yrs 7 mos
Miller, Amy D., w/o Warren Miller, d 28 July 1902 aged 79 yrs
Chamberlain, Enoch, d 17 Aug 1841 aged 63 yrs
Fisk, Levi, d 20 June 1819 aged 53 yrs
Fisk, Jemima, w/o Levi Fisk, d 6 March 1819 aged 46 yrs
Watkins, Andrew, d 26 July 1805 aged 69 yrs
Watkins, Thankful, w/o Andrew Watkins, d 19 March 1811 aged 71 yrs
Watkins, Polly, w/o Elijah Watkins, d 10 May 1846 aged 74 yrs

Leland, Abner, d 17 April 1819 aged 75 yrs

Leland, Hannah, w/o Abner Leland, d 16 Nov 1847 aged 93 yrs 6 mos

Chamberlain, Caroline J., w/o Jonas Chamberlain, d 27 May 1834 AE 28 yrs

Leland, Capt. Nathan, d 29 May 1842 aged 64 yrs

Leland, Polly, w/o Capt. Nathan Leland, d 28 Jan 1821 aged 40 yrs

Bridges, Benjamin, d 26 Jan 1814 AE 74 yrs

Bridges, Esther, w/o Benjamin Bridges, d 18 Feb 1819 aged 75 yrs

Adams, Appleton, 1822-1862, A member of Co D 1st Mass Heavy Art

Adams, Julia A., w/o Appleton Adams, 1824-1905

Bridges, Lydia, w/o Nathan Bridges, d 20 July 1808 aged 34 yrs

Leland, Syrena C., w/o Erastus Leland, d 11 May 1852

Merchant, Achsah, w/o George W. Merchant & d/o Samuel & Achsah Leland, d 25 May 1839 aged 28 yrs

Chase, Mary, b 1 April 1818, d Dec 1889

Leland, Nancy......

Adams, James, d 10 July 1859 aged 78 yrs

Adams, Lydia, d 14 Nov 1875 aged 91 yrs

Adams, Edward H., 1883-1977

Adams, Elizabeth J., w/o Edward H. Adams, 1891-1971

Tower, Elizabeth, 1797-1849

Tower, Joseph, 1784-1868

Tower, Mary B., 1826-1906

Tower, Carrie E., d/o J. & E. Tower, d 5 March 1865 aged 28 yrs

Leland, Russell, d 16 Dec 1863 aged 51 yrs

Leland, Dexter M., s/o Abner & Mariah J. Leland, d 26 March 1841 aged 4 mos 8 days

Cutler, Jonathan, d 15 April 1857 aged 76 yrs

Cutler, Sarah, w/o Jonathan Cutler, d 13 Feb 1860 aged 78 yrs

Cutler, Joseph, d 23 Oct 1812 aged 11 mos

Whitney, George, 1821-1892

Whitney, Louisa P .C. L., w/o George Whitney, 1825-1889

Leland, Miriah, w/o Abner Leland & d/o David & Phebe Graves, d 8 Aug 1841

Spindel, Jane L., w/o Theodore Spindel, 1839-1921

Claflin, Samuel, b 17 Aug 1795, d 24 March 1873

Banfield, John, d 25 Feb 1875 aged 77 yrs

Banfield, Elias S., d 28 March 1880 aged 76 yrs

Banfield, Abbie, w/o Elias S. Banfield, d 20 Aug 1879 aged 68 yrs

Cozzens, William, s/o Joseph & Sally Cozzens, d 11 Sept 1845 aged 2 yrs

White, Sally, d 26 Nov 1806 AE 22 yrs
Perry, Abel H., 1811-1897
Perry, Miranda W., w/o Abel H. Perry, 1812-1848
Perry, Mary, w/o Abel H. Perry, 1806-1863
Hall, Samuel, d 16 Sept 1814 aged 89 yrs
Hall, Mary, w/o Samuel Hall, d 16 Sept 1833 aged 90 yrs

South/Hoppin River Cemetery
Washington Street
Holliston, Massachusetts

Fairbanks, Francis P., 1826-1910
Fairbanks, Miranda, w/o Francis P. Fairbanks, 1833-1878
Fairbanks, Arthur B., s/o Francis & Miranda Fairbanks, 1864-1875
Fairbanks, Clara A., d/o Francis & Miranda Fairbanks, d 12 Feb 1861
   aged 5 yrs 9 mos
Claflin, William Jr., d 17 Oct 1872 aged 75 yrs 2 mos 14 days
Claflin, Susan F., w/o William Claflin Jr., d 9 May 1870 aged 69 yrs 6
   mos 13 days
Middleton, Caroline M., w/o Jonathan Middleton, d 14 May 1861 AE 28
   yrs
Claflin, Alice B., d/o William & Susan F. Claflin, b 18 Jan 1840, d 18
   March 1841
Hill, Margaret, w/o Lt. Ebenezer Hill, d 7 June 1804 aged 69 yrs
Hill, Sergt. Ebenezer, ...
Claflin, Mary B., w/o Clavin Claflin, d 18 Aug 1866 aged 73 yrs
Claflin, Calvin, d 28 March 1871 aged 84 yrs 4 mos
Claflin, Hannah, w/o Calvin Claflin, d 11 Feb 1854 aged 66 yrs
Albee, Admiral, d 30 July 1848 aged 68 yrs
Bullard, Asa, d 2 May 1803 AE 73 yrs
Albee, Admiral, d 30 Aug 1849 AE 29 yrs
Albee, Charles, d 20 July 1854 AE 23 yrs
Hatch, Althira A., w/o William L. F. Hatch, d 16 Oct 1844 aged 27 yrs
Bullard, Hannah, w/o Walter Bullard, d 13 Oct 1825 aged 17 yrs
Messinger, Henry, d 8 July 1882 aged 61 yrs 3 mos 6 days
Hartshorn, Dennis, d 28 June 1888 aged 76 yrs 6 mos 6 days

Hartshorn, Hannah G., w/o Dennis Hartshorn, 1812-1897
Pierce, John H., d 31 July 1876 aged 28 yrs
Pierce, James M., d 14 Aug 1878 aged 24 yrs
Pond, Achsall, w/o Phillip Pond, d 10 Jan 1832 aged 32 yrs
Pond, Eliza, w/o Phillip Pond, d 21 March 1871 aged 68 yrs
Pond, Phillip, d 28 Sept 1879 aged 84 yrs
Claflin, Silence, w/o John Claflin & formerly w/o Capt. Aaron Pond, d 5
    April 1844 aged 78 yrs
Pond, Capt. Aaron, d 26 Nov 1815 AE 52 yrs
Pond, Aaron, d 25 Oct 1815 AE 80 yrs
Howard, Edwin, d 9 June 1874 aged 48 yrs 8 mos 5 days
Howard, Susan, w/o Edwin Howard, b 3 Jan 1818, d 6 Oct 1892
Littlefield, Ephraim, d 10 Jan 1828 aged 77 yrs
Littlefield, Sarah, w/o Ephraim Littlefield, d 22 Sprt 1823 aged 76 yrs
Littlefield, Loammi, d 6 March 1874 aged 90 yrs
Littlefield, Beulah, w/o Loammi Littlefield, d 8 July 1821 aged 31 yrs
Littlefield, Eliza, w/o Loammi Littlefield, d 9 Aug 1868 aged 67 yrs
Littlefield, Susannah, d/o Loammi & Eliza Littlefield, d 28 Jan 1833 aged
    20 yrs
Clark, Lydia, w/o Abijah Clark, d 30 Jan 1806 aged 27 yrs
Clark, Zilpha, w/o Nathan Clark, d 15 July 1812
Rider, Deana, w/o Asa Rider, d 6 Jan 1823 AE 58 yrs
Bullard, Huldah, d/o Daniel & Ruth Bullard, d 6 Jan 1853 aged 46 yrs
Bullard, Nathan, d 5 May 1822 aged 76 yrs
Hill, Bathsheba, w/o Nathan Bullard, d Feb 1825 AE 82 yrs
Littlefield, Tabatha, w/o John Littlefield, d 4 April 1819 AE 81 yrs
Gilmore, Nancy, w/o Patrick Gilmore, d 18 Aug 1843 aged 72 yrs
Welcomb, Jane, w/o Joseph D. Welcomb, b 13 Nov 1823, d 14 Sept 1859
Adams, Alexis, d 1 Nov 1861 aged 34 yrs
Adams, George Everett, s/o George & Susan Adams, b 14 Dec 1849, d 11
    April 1873
Holbrook, Dennis, 1799-1848
Holbrook, Elizabeth C., 1828-1830
Berns, John C., 1851-1852
Barber, Hamblet, 1751-1834
Barber, Rhoda, 1753-1824
Claflin, William, 1772-1854
Claflin, Anna J., 1774-1794
Claflin, Sarah W., 1777-1815
Claflin, Lois B., 1773-1864

Adams, Benjamin S., 1818-1822

Claflin, Samuel W., 1815-1828

Claflin, Martha M., 1817-1823

Adams, George, 1819-1900

Adams, Susan, w/o George Adams, d 26 Sept 1892 aged 72 yrs

Bartlett, William O., d 5 April 1872 aged 55 yrs 9 mos 7 days

Bartlett, Sarah, w/o William O. Bartlett, d 21 Dec 1898 aged 73 yrs 11 mos 29 days

Bartlett, William E., s/o William O. & Susan Bartlett, d 10 March 1861 aged 8 yrs 7 mos 5 days

Adams, Fanny, w/o Ethan R. Adams, d 19 July 1850 aged 40 yrs

Adams, Eatham R., d 26 Feb 1858 aged 45 yrs

Littlefield, Elial Esq., d 25 March 1865 aged 83yrs 6 mos

Littlefield, Sophia, w/o Elial Littlefield Esq., d 20 Dec 1869 aged 90 yrs 6 mos

Littlefield, Capt. Oliver Prescott, s/o Elial & Sophia Littlefield, d 3 Sept 1831 aged 30 yrs

Littlefield, Joseph Mellen, s/o Elial & Sophia Littlefield, d 6 Nov 1832 aged 11 yrs 6 mos

Lovering, Gilbert, s/o Thaddeus & Elizabeth Lovering, d 4 Dec 1805 AE 17 yrs

Adams, Horace, d 7 April 1880 aged 65 yrs

Adams, Laura A., d/o Jonathan & Hepsibeth Adams, d 9 Oct 1857 aged 29 yrs

Adams, Jonathan, d 5 Oct 1864 aged 83 yrs 4 mos

Adams, Hepsibeth, w/o Jonathan Adams, d 1 April 1852 aged 66 yrs

Hemenway, Mary, w/o Capt. Daniel Hemenway, d 3 March 1803

Parker, Lois, w/o Abner Johnson & formerlly w/o Nathaniel Pierce, b 3 Sept 1791, d 24 Oct 1873

Pierce, Nathaniel, d 13 Oct 1849 aged 59 yrs 4 mos

Claflin, John, 1750-1888

Claflin, Mary S., 1752-1821

Goff, Polly G., 1779-1846

Claflin, Hannah, 1791-1822

Claflin, Ethan O., 1808-1823

Goff, Col. Ethan, 1781-1886

Claflin, Hannah, 1825-1829

Old North Cemetery
Cedar Street
Holliston, Massachusetts

Dewing, George William, s/o Reuben & Mary Dewing, d 2 Feb 1833 aged 3 yrs 5 mos

Cozzens, Isaac, d 28 Aug 1843 aged 82 yrs

Cozzens, Sarah, w/o Isaac Cozzen, d 31 July 1839 AE 78 yrs

Cozzens, Nabbe, d/o Isaac & Sarah Cozzens, d 13 Nov 1806 AE 19 yrs

Cozzens, Abigail, w/o Joseph Cozzens, d 25 May 1806 AE 81 yrs

Haven, Deacon Jesse, d 28 Dec 1816 AE 68 yrs

Haven, Betsey, w/o Capt. John Haven, d 31 March 1821 aged 42 yrs

Bullard, Samuel H., s/o Samuel & Esther Bullard, d 11 Oct 1832 aged 1 yrs 9 mos 11 days

Bullard, Haziah, d 2 Sept 1831 aged 61 yrs

Bullard, Kezia, w/o Haziah Bullard, d 10 May 1821 aged 49 yrs

Bullard, Hannah, d/o Haziah & Kezia Bullard, d 2 June 1824 aged 14 yrs

Bullard, Benjamin, s/o Haziah & Kezia Bullard, d 21 July 1805 aged 1 week

Bullard, Ebenezer, d 18 Sept 1803 AE 60 yrs

Bullard, Patty, w/o Ebenezer Bullard, d 20 Jan 1826 AE 53 yrs

Townsend, Sarah, d 19 July 1822 aged 22 yrs

Lamb, Esther Albert, d/o Daniel & Jane S. Lamb, d 9 Aug 1829 aged 16 yrs

Whitaker, Clementina F., w/o John Whitaker, d 12 May 1851 aged 32 yrs

Whitaker, Ellen Faustina, d/o John & Clementina Whitaker, d 23 Sept 1844 aged 1 yr 3 mos 16 days

Lamb, Ellen M., d/o James H. & Sarah B. Lamb, d 8 Oct 1850 aged 14 mos

Lamb, Presis d (too far in ground)

Whittemore, Achsah, d 22 Feb 1867 aged 59 yrs 6 mos 14 days

Walland, Isaac, d 6 June 1845 aged 21 yrs 2 mos 7 days

Gallott, William, d 9 Nov 1838 aged 44 yrs

Nichols, Samuel, d 9 Oct 1808 of Fever

Bullard, Capt. Samuel, d 5 May 1839 aged 61 yrs

Bullard, Persis, w/o Capt. Samuel Bullard, d 29 Aug 1815 aged 26 yrs

Bullard, Esther H., w/o Capt. Samuel Bullard, d 19 June 1841

Bullard, Samuel, d 27 Jan 1816 aged 74 yrs

Bullard, Lydia, w/o Samuel Bullard, d 23 Dec 1833 aged 95 yrs 5 days
Eames, Lt. Reuben, d 16 May 1818 AE 75 yrs
Eames, Jane, w/o Lt. Reuben Eames, d 2 Feb 1837 AE 90 yrs 7 mos 15 days
Eames, Capt. Aaron, d 11 Feb 1827
Eames, Sarah, w/o Capt. Aaron Eames, d 23 Sept 1824 aged 67 yrs
Eames, Mary, w/o Capt. Aaron Eames, d 25 Nov 1828 aged 57 yrs
Freeland, Sally, d 13 April 1821
Bridges, Capt. Alpheus, d 6 Oct 1825 aged 39 yrs
Eames, Nathan (broken)
Eames, Emerson, (broken)
Eames, Hopestill, d 5 April 1821 aged 77 yrs
Eames, Mary, w/o Hopestill Eames, d 6 March 1821 aged 74 yrs
Eames, Cynthia H., w/o Nathan Eames, d 4 Jan 1875 aged 79 yrs 4 mos 22 days
Bullard, Joel, d 11 Jan 1827 AE 57 yrs
Bullard, Lyman, s/o Joel & Lucretia Bullard, d 3 Oct 1820 of Fever AE 19 yrs

Lake Grove Cemetery
Higland Street
Holliston, Massachusetts

Older section only

Whiting, Edwin F., b 20 June 1830, d 15 Oct 1895
Payson, Mariah R., w/o Edwin F. Whiting, b 11 June 1830, d 20 Aug 1893
Whiting, Alice P., 1870-1945
Harrison, Berthram M., 1903-1972
Phillips, Grace E., 1903-....
Gilmore, Louisa R., 1844-1889
Morse, Charles, 1817-1898
Whitmore, Isabelle M., w/o Charles Morse, 1817-1911
Rockwood, Benjamin A., b 24 Aug 1823, d 25 July 1894
Payson, Adela R., w/o Benjamin A. Rockwood, b 20 Dec 1825, d 22 April 1899

Rockwood, Annie Louise, d/o Benjamin & Adela Rockwood, b 25 June 1852, d 1 April 1892

Rockwood, Josephine Eliza, d/o Benjamin & Adelia Rockwood, b 8 Dec 1850, d 18 March 1909

Rockwood, Adelia Frances, d/o Benjamin & Adela Rockwood, b 26 March 1854, d 13 Feb 1924

Razee, Lloyd E., b 30 Sept 1861, d 15 March 1937

Rockwood, Elizabeth, w/o Lloyd E. Razee, b 12 March 1861, d 12 Oct 1927

Payson, John M., 1840-1929

Payson, Harriet M., w/o John M. Payson, b 10 Sept 1844, d 28 Sept 1873

Payson, Warren L., b 5 July 1821, d 29 April 1889

Payson, Adelia M., b 12 Aug 1827, d 25 Aug 1907

Clark, Annie E., adopted d/o Warren & Adelia Payson, b 15 Feb 1857, d 3 Aug 1871

Payson, Samuel, b 12 March 1793, d 24 Dec 1859

Pond, Adela, w/o Samuel Payson, b 14 May 1798, d 17 Feb 1823

Mellen, Beulah L., w/o Samuel Payson, b 30 Nov 1802, d 31 May 1842

Rockwood, Martin B., 1817-1892

Hill, Izanne, w/o Martin B. Rockwood, d 6 Oct 1868 aged 47 yrs 19 mos

Rockwood, Mary Ann, 1832-1900

Rockwood, Nancie Ella, d/o Martin & Izanne Rockwood, d 13 Nov 1863 aged 14 yrs 7 mos

Trevett, W. Fiske, 1833-1901

Trevett, Carrie A., w/o W. Fiske Trevett, 1840-1921

Fiske, Jonas, b 14 March 1810, d 29 April 1881

Thompson, Asenath, w/o Jonas Fiske, b 30 May 1812, d 29 April 1877

Bellows, Edward L., b 15 Oct 1841, d 1 Aug 1866

Bellows, Louisa J., b 19 July 1849, d 3 July 1854

Bellows, Walter, b 1 Nov 1851, d 17 April 1852

Bellows, Jarvis M., 1846-1902

Bellows, Sarah A., 1846-1941

Bellows, Eva H., 1859-1933

Bellows, Luther, b 1 Dec 1810, d 15 Jan 1896

Bellows, Janet T., b 23 June 1817, d 31 Jan 1893

Nichols, Mary S., 1856-1941

Nichols, Stephen S., 1828-1915

Nichols, Mary J.W., 1829-1889

Nichols, Charley S., 1861-1879

Nichols, Willie W., 1858-1859

Nichols, Grace S., 1861-1934
Nichols, H. O. B., 1859-1944
Nichols, Charley F. S., 1888-1908
Batchelder, William S., 1800-1876
Batchelder, Rhoda W., 1795-1874
Thayer, William R., b 20 March 1808, d 6 Nov 1878
Legg, Harriet, w/o William R. Thayer, b 26 April 1818, d 22 April 1880
Bridley, E. Frank, 1844-1875
Decker, John C., 1812-1879
Decker, Margaret M., w/o John C. Decker, 1813-1883
Decker, Edward L., s/o John & Margaret Decker, 1854-1931
Underwood, Martha
Byrnes, Michael, 1817-1903 C., 1844-1873
Holbrook, Rhoda, w/o Michael Byrnes, 1806-1892
Phipps, Albert E., 1856-1923
Phipps, Luther H., 1827-1906
Holbrook, Elizabeth, w/o Luther H. Phipps, 1827-1863
Darling, Harriet, w/o Luther H. Phipps, 1844-1915
Phipps, Eldred L., 1868-1920
Phipps, Abba H., 1860-1923
Mayhuse, E. Mabel, 1876-1960
Kingsbury, Elijah, d 2 Nov 1888 aged 86 yrs
Phipps, Joanna W., w/o Elijah Kingsbury, d 9 Aug 1877 aged 62 yrs 10
  mos
Kingsbury, Marie, d/o Elijah & Joanna Kingsbury & w/o B. F. Boyden, d
  27 Sept 1870
Metcalf, George S., d 24 Oct 1868 aged 33 yrs
Metcalf, Julia A., w/o Dr. A. J. Johnson, 1839-1904
Standish, Henry M., 1843-1912
Standish, Mary E., 1847-1927
Hall, Emma Standish, 1873-1918
Pond, Amelia Elizabeth, d/o Abel & Lucy Pond, 1866-1886
Pond, Abel, d 1 Feb 1882 aged 73 yrs 4 mos
Pond, Lucy A., w/o Abel Pond, 1835-1927
Pond, Elizabeth Sarah, w/o Abel Pond, d 28 April 1857 aged 46 yrs
Heaton, Amelia, w/o Abel Pond, d 27 Jund 1863 aged 38 yrs 11 mos
Pond, Gilbert Thayer, s/o Abel & Elizabeth Pond, d 17 Aug 1847 aged 14
  mos
Pond, Herbert Robinson, s/o Abel & Amelia Pond, d 16 July 1863 aged 5
  weeks

Pond, Nancy, 1804-1890
Pond, Edmund, 1825-1905
Pond, Miranda, w/o Jemitos Pond, d 15 Aug 1878 aged 83 yrs
Wheelock, William W., 1824-1896
Wheelock, Harriet L., w/o William W. Wheelock, 1830-1916
Tenney, Austin C., 1807-1881
Tenney, Lois F., w/o Austin C. Tenney, 1811-1896
Hooker, Harlow, 1824-1884
Travis, Saphronia A., w/o Harlow Hooker, 1830-1908
Hooker, Emma Jane, d/o Harlow & Saphronia Hooker, d 15 Nov 1870
Currier, Arthur M., b 26 Feb 1808 Plymouth, NH, d 21 Jan 1871
Currier, Mary Ann, w/o Arthur M. Currier, b 8 Nov 1813, d 24 Oct 1886
Currier, Mary Ann, d/o Arthur & Mary Ann Currier, b 22 Jan 1886, d 5
     April 1887
Currier, Mary Elizabeth, d/o Arthur & Mary Ann Currier, b 17 March
     1888, d 28 July 1889
Currier, Elizabeth Allen, d/o Arthur & Mary Ann Currier, b 9 Dec 1841,
     d 18 July 1843
Currier, James Whitney, s/o Arthur & Mary Ann Currier, b 10 March
     1848, d 14 Aug 1872
Bates, Ella H., w/o Dresser T. Bates, b 3 Jan 1846, d 6 April 1878
Currier, Edward M., b 19 June 1852, d 25 June 1925
Currier, Ella A., w/o Edward M. Currier, b 16 Sept 1854, d 25 April 1843
Hayes, Joseph Alvin, 1846-1914
Currier, Annie Maria, w/o Joseph Alvin Hayes, 1849-....
Merrill, Joshua, d 26 May 1876 aged 54 yrs
Merrill, Hannah M., w/o Joshua Merrill, d 10 Feb 1883 aged 57 yrs
Pike, Moses, d 9 Aug 1860 aged 46 yrs 10 mos
Pike, Octavia, w/o Moses Pike, d 9 March 1843 aged 33 yrs
Pike, Clara P., d/o Moses & Octavia Pike, d 30 Oct 1877 aged 30 yrs 1 mo
Pike, Clarissa S., w/o Moses Pike, d 11 May 1874 aged 61 yrs 11 mos
Pike, Alfred W., 1848-1921
Pike, Azelia M., w/o Alfred W. Pike, 1848-1920
Cleale, Alfred, 1818-1894
Cleale, Mary E., 1816-1891
Cleale, Addison J., 1849-1890
Cleale, Edgar A., 1857-1917
Rockwood, Edwin E., d 29 July 1880 aged 25 yrs
Spring, George E., 1879-1959
Spring, Beula E., w/o George E. Spring, 1884-1970

Spring, Charles Edward MD, 1841-1890
Adams, Viorna Minervia, w/o Dr. Charles Edward Spring, 1843-1937
Miller, John, b 21 Dec 1804, d 14 Jan 1864
Perry, Caroline, w/o John Miller, b 1 Nov 1803, d 19 Nov 1860
Miller, George, d 23 Feb 1841 aged 3 mos 6 days
Smith, Edgar N., 1847-1884
Smith, Frank E., 1877-1878
Smith, Dora H., 1848-1919
Smith, Charles J., 1877-1926
Tidd, Emma Smith, 1876-1947
Harriman, T., 1816-1880
Harriamn, S.M., 1816-1905
Harriman, Emma F., 1848-1855
Harriman, Rose E., 1858-1878
Eames, George H., 1847-1914
Eames, Jane S., w/o George H. Eames, 1849-1938
Eames, George E., 1871-1942
Eames, Mary T., w/o George E. Eames, 1878-1962
Eames, Norman E., 1870-1870
Eames, Austin K., 1873-1883
Eames, Perley E., 1877-1878
Johnson, Horatio H., b 13 March 1807, d 23 Jan 1878
Johnson, Joan D., w/o Horatio H. Johnson, b 23 July 1804, d 6 Nov 1876
Hall, Erastus D., 1834-1904, A member of Co K 6th NH Regt
Hall, Othelia K., w/o Erastus D. Hall, 1844-1929
Bellows, Samuel A. Jr., 1847-1849
Bellows, Walter, 1857-1858
Baker, Albert H., 1848-1892
Baker, Emma J., w/o Albert H. Baker, 1854-1875
Knowlton, Ebenezer, d 20 July 1872 aged 82 yrs 24 days
Knowlton, Nancy, w/o Ebenezer Knowlton, d 2 May 1876 aged 84 yrs 3
    days
Baker, Henry, 1815-1892
Baker, Lorinda, d 25 March 1877 aged 66 yrs
Whiting, George A., 1827-1903
Perry, Maria H., w/o George A. Whiting, 1834-1915
Whiting, Georgianna A., 1838-1905
Tenney, Allen Gay, 1886-1923
Tenney, Fred C., 1859-1919
Tenney, Saidee W., w/o Fred C. Tenney, 1863-1959

Tenney, Pauline, d/o Fred & Saidee Tenney, 1891-1915
Smith, Doris L., 1906-1918
Hatch, Emma L., 1891-1954
Haven, Charles T., 1860-1928
Haven, Lizzie A., w/o Charles T. Haven, 1873-1952
Phills, Ernest S., 1902-1975
Belcher, William H., 1835-1907, A member of Co B 16th Mass Inf
Belcher, Annie M., w/o William H. Belcher, 1839-1917
Brown, Frank A., 1860-1930
Brown, Nettie R., w/o Frank A. Brown, 1861-1946
Pickering, Laleita E. Brown, 1887-1976
Buckley, John, 1870-1941
Buckley, Emma A., w/o John Buckley, 1881-1913
Buckley, John J., 1909-1913
Buckley, Helen E., 1905-1906
Buckley, Florence M., 1903-1987
Austin, William H., 1830-1917
Austin, Sarah J., w/o William H. Austin, 1833-1919
Austin, William E., 1872-1954
Austin, Eva A., w/o William E. Austin, 1879-1903
Philbrook, Mary, 1860-1933
Philbrook, Honer D., 1854-1948
Philbrook, Doris S., 1895-1950
Earl, Arthur R., 1858-1950
Marshall, Etta, w/o Arthur R. Earl, 1861-1941
Leland, Charles W., 1831-1900
Leland, Abbie G., 1829-1916
Leland, Charles H., 1860-1926
Haynes, Jennie M., 1871-1958
Welch, Ella Frances, 1870-1937
Welch, Thomas H., 1866-....
Colby, Ernest G., 1896-1910
Lord, Mellard E., 1878-1941
Allen, Martha, w/o Mellard E. Lord,......
Spofford, William H., 1811-1893
Gorden, Sally, w/o William H. Spofford, 1807-1875
Scates, Abbie G., 1838-1875
Cloutman, Eliza M., 1834-1876
Spofford, James W., 1846-1875
Shelnut, Stanley Henry, 1881-1935

Shelnut, Ella Alice, 1882-1959
York, Harvey E., 1873-1924
August, John F., 1879-1962
August, Alice H., 1880-1965
Towne, Henry W., 1848-1922
Towne, Ada L., w/o Henry W. Towne, 1856-1933
Flint, Jane H., w/o George D. Flint, 1839-1890
Adams, George E., 1877-1922
Rawson, Annie L., w/o George E. Adams, 1874-1958
Adams, Esther M., d/o George E. & Annie L. Adams, 1902-1984
Adams, Everett R., 1901-1955
Adams, Vivian C., w/o Everett R. Adams, 1902-....
Lovering, Lawson, d 8 Nov 1891 aged 77 yrs
Lovering, Juliette, w/o Lawson Lovering, 1814-1906
Morse, Benaiah, 1819-1905
Fisher, Eliza A., w/o Benaiah Morse, 1818-1893
Morse, Hattie A., 1853-1910
Morse, Caroline F., 1843-1910
Morse, Willard B., 1845-1919
Bigelow, George Porter, 1843-1910
Bigelo, Ellen Harriet, w/o George Porter Bigelow, 1840-1923
Morrison, William P., 1855-1936
Morse, Walter R., 1858-1927
Gardner, Nettie L., 1863-1946
Morse, Gardner Allen, 1903-1946
Morse, Mildred Allen, 1900-1986
Morse, Lucille M., 1930-1934
Crawford, Frederick, 1903-1960
Parker, Dorothy, w/o Frederick Crawford, 1910-1957
Perkins, Francis B., b 21 Sept 1835, d 24 Dec 1918, Sergt, Co K 35th
    Regt Mass Inf
Perkins, Mary E., w/o Francis B. Perkins, b 17 Jan 1848, d 10 Dec 1883
Perkins, Elsie L., b 17 Aug 1846, d 21 Feb 1935
Perkins, Sprague H., b 6 Sept 1872, d 10 May 1945
Perkins, Leander, b 3 March 1814, d 2 March 1897
Perkins, Fanny L., w/o Leander Perkins, b 29 Aug 1813, d 1 Aug 1883
Allen, John, d 28 April 1905 aged 77 yrs
Allen, Susan Augusta, w/o John Allen, d 3 July 1880
Pond, John J., 1849-1927
Pond, Abbie J., 1851-1929

Pond, Harry J., 1888-1987
Gay, William King, 1859-1859
Gay, William, 1828-1911
Travis, Henrietta, w/o William Guy, 1828-1900
Cutler, Lorenzo, b 14 June 1845, d 2 May 1909
Cutler, Lillian M., w/o Lorenzo Cutler, b 10 March 1865, d 6 Oct 1946
Cutler, Cora W., b 25 May 1895, d.....
Cutler, Albion M., 1849-1926
Adams, Emma I., w/o Albion M. Cutler, 1853-1922
Cutler, Corporal James A., 1890-1919
Lovering, Frances I., d 23 May 1856 aged 13 yrs
Bartlett, George A., 1835-1912
Hoffman, Mary M., w/o George A. Bartlett, 1836-1885
Parmenter, Leora H., w/o George A. Bartlett, 1847-1923
Dyer, Arthur T., d 1895
Curtis, Fred E., 1858-1895
Wright, Frank B., 1871-1938
Wright, Maude C., w/o Frank B. Wright, 1871-1938
Cobb, Rufus J., 1789-1842
Cobb, Nancy, w/o Rufus J. Cobb, 1796-1874
Wiley, Edwin C., 1851-1888
Wiley, Charles, 1820-1894
Wiley, Frances E., w/o Charles Wiley, 1825-1885
Wiley, Frank E., s/o Charles & Frances Wiley, 1848-1874
Wiley, Fred M., s/o Charles & Frances Wiley, 1852-1874
Wiley, Albert M., 1846-1889
Jordan, William Thayer, 1857-1931
Cutler, Alfred, b 11 July 1824, d 12 Feb 1889
Cutler, Elizabeth J., w/o Alfred Cutler, b 20 March 1837, d 23 April 1901
Cutler, Marion N., d/o Alfred & Elizabeth Cutler, b 9 Aug 1872, d 12
    April 1886
Rawson, Edward T., b 26 March 1832, d 5 Aug 1915
Rawson, Adelaide, 1854-1946
Bateman, Charles H., 1849-....
Bateman, Catherine A., w/o Charles H. Bateman, 1853-1919
Hawes, Calvin M., 1836-1875
Hawes, Laura A., 1838-1921
Abbott, Charles, b 8 March 1835, d 31 May 1882
Waters, Rev. Simeon, d 2 March 1867, buried Ocala, Florida
Goodale, Elisabeth, w/o Rev. Simeon Waters, d 25 April 1834 aged 57 yrs

Thompson, Gaius, b 24 July 1805, d 21 Feb 1868

Thompson, Mary B., w/o Gaius Thompson, b 16 July 1812, d 15 Sept 1873

Abbott, Frederick C., b 7 Oct 1861, d 15 May 1907

Abbott, Marietta, b 26 Aug 1836, d 1 May 1910

Cutler, Abner H., b 7 May 1815, d 28 Sept 1875

Cutler, Persis W., w/o Abner H. Cutler, b 4 Feb 1810, d 27 Jan 1890

Cutler, Sophia, b 21 Feb 1840, d 3 Jan 1842

Cutler, Ita G., 1879-1958

Cutler, Martha L., 1881-1972

Holmes, S. Denzil, 1845-1899

Holmes, W. Frank, 1872-1918

Bullard, Albert Wheeler, 1846-1915

Brooks, Mary T. T., w/o Albert Wheeler Bullard, 1851-1930

Brooks, George E. W., 1862-1959

Poor, Mary M., w/o George E. W. Brooks, 1887-1979

Brooks, M. Elizabeth, d/o George & Mary Brooks, 1920-1966

Brooks, A. T. Wilson, 1854-1935

Brooks, Lizzie S., w/o A. T.Wilson Brooks, 1855-1943

Brooks, Alvan, b 12 May 1812, d 5 July 1892

Taylor, Mary T., w/o Alvan Brooks, b 13 Nov 1822, d 7 Nov 1914

Andrews, Mary Elizabeth, 1847-1918

Albert, C. Andrews, 1846-1916, A member of Co H 32nd Mass Inf

Andrews, Mabel L., 1870-1956

Holmes, Elizabeth, 1822-1882

Holmes, Stephen, 1815-1887

Gilson, Warren H., 1831-1890

Gilson, Ellen M., w/o Warren H. Gilson, 1838-1917

Wilkens, Albert F., 1889-1946

Smith, H. Madeline, w/o Albert F. Wilkins, 1891-1961

Wilkens, Dana P., s/o Albert & H. Madeline Wilkens, 1831-1994

Colvin, Romona M., w/o Dana P. Wilkens, 1931-....

Bacon, Henry, b 31 Jan 1814, d 8 Nov 1892

Eames, Ann, w/o Henry Bacon, b 11 Dec 1814, d 12 Aug 1874

Patch, George H., A member of Co I 19th Mass Vol Inf, enlisted 22 July 1861 served 3 years & 16 Battles, d 26 July 1887 aged 42 yrs 7 mos

Patch, Caroline E., w/o George H. Patch, d 11 Nov 1941 aged 91 yrs 8 mos

Howe, Alonzo L., 1841-1921

Holbrook, Abbie M., w/o Alonzo L. Howe, 1843-1914

Ware, Emma Josephine, w/o Henry Ware, b 15 May 1846, d 7 Oct 1870
Emery, Mary A., w/o Ferdinand I. Pierce, d 18 July 1902 aged 52 yrs
McKerson, Almira, w/o Israel Pierce, d 31 March 1891 aged 83 yrs
Pond, Edwin D., 1835-1903
Ware, Carrie A., w/o Edwin D. Pond, 1844-1916
Holbrook, Harlous, b 22 May 1814, d 30 Jan 1887
Holbrook, Mary W., w/o Harlous W. Holbrook, b 7 July 1817, d 9 July
   1898
Wicker, Deacon Joshua, 70 yrs
Smith, M. Helen, w/o Edward J. Smith, d 8 April 1874 aged 37 yrs
Taft, Anna L., 1832-1895
Taft, James E., 1827-1895
Taft, George F., 1856-1938
Farrington, Sophia J., w/o George F. Taft, 1858-1935
Smith, Samuel P., d 17 Feb 1867 aged 62 yrs
Smith, Persis J., d 21 Jan 1875 aged 72 yrs 6 mos
Sargent, Waldo H., 1871-1958
Thrope, Lalia E., w/o Waldo H. Sargent, 1876-1952
Sargent, Virginia, 1921-1925
Sargent, Waldo L., 1902-1975
Sargent, Grace E., 1909-1983
Eames, Willis E., 1858-1928
Eames, Mary E., w/o Willis E. Eames, 1863-1930
Eames, Leslie A., 1889-1957
Eames, Susie, w/o Leslie A. Eames, 1891-1971
Eames, Leonard, 1917-1965
Paddelford, Albert F., 1847-1905
Norris, Emma A., w/o Albert F. Paddelford, 1849-1933
Paddelford, Clara, w/o Albert F. Paddelford, 1875-1928
Paddelford, Francis O., 1824-1890
Paddelford, Harriet E., w/o Francis O. Paddelford, b 16 Feb 1826, d 26
   Jan 1873
Paddelford, Ella M., w/o Francis O. Paddelford, b 30 July 1847, d 2 Aug
   1885
Harding, Bertha M., 1899-1960
Sawin, Samuel, d 24 Dec 1858 aged 89 yrs 2 mos 26 days
Sawin, Patty, w/o Samuel Sawin, d 16 April 1847 aged 71 yrs 7 mos 14
   days
Leland, Eliza Houghton, 1859-1924
Leland, Helen Houghton, 1891-1976

Houghton, Cryus Houghton, b 12 July 1804, d 6 Dec 1868
Houghton, Eliza A., w/o Cyrus Houghton, b 25 Feb 1807, d 15 Aug 1893
Belcher, Henry T., d 30 Nov 1862 aged 47 yrs
Belcher, Mary J., d 23 Nov 1898 aged 82 yrs
Belcher, W. Abbott, 1852-1927
Belcher, Eola J., w/o W. Abbott Belcher, 1855-1924
Gilkey, Frank J., 1871-1930
Gilkey, Ida L., w/o Frank J. Gilkey, 1882-1946
Sawyer, Sarah Letitia Parker, b 17 Dec 1839, d 4 Jan 1888 Nervi, Italy
Parker, Deacon John, b 16 June 1798, d 27 March 1893
Fales, Mary Ann, w/o Deacon John Parker, b 21 Dec 1800, d 16 July 1885
Littlefield, Clark, b 21 Aug 1794, d 28 April 1864
Littlefield, Electra J., w/o Clark Littlefield, d 17 May 1879 aged 82 yrs 2
    mos
Pond, Clark J., 1830-1903
Pond, Sarah J., w/o Clark J. Pond, d 4 May 1874
Pond, Laurinda C., w/o Clark J. Pond, 1841-1907
Pond, Josephine E., b 7 Feb 1856, d 2 Oct 1857
Pond, Eustis F., 1866-1867
Bates, Herbert L., 1867-1932
Pond, Lizzie C., w/o Herbert L. Bates, 1864-1958
Bullard, Henry E., 1847-1915
Shippe, Ella M., w/o Henry E. Bullard, 1850-1906
Bullard, Edmund A., 1872-1893
Bullard, Henry, 1873-1949
Fogg, Sara S., w/o Henry A. Bullard, 1881-1917
Bullard, Appleton, 1804-1875
Harding, Hepzibah L., w/o Appleton Bullard, 1813-1893
Bullard, Lovina M., 1834-1836
Bullard, Edmund A., 1841-1853
Bullard, George Harding, 1878-1959
Litchfield, Bertha Mary, w/o George Harding Bullard, 1882-1938
Woodbury, Joseph Emerson, 1827-1893
Barker, Martha, w/o Joseph Emerson Woodbury, 1832-1901
Woodbury, Clarence Emerson, 1854-1929
Follensby, Ina, w/o Clarence Emerson Woodbury, 1860-1908
Claflin, Hamblet B., b Dec 1817, d April 1891
Curtis, Betsey, w/o Hamblet Claflin, b Sept 1817, d March 1892
Stoddard, Russell S., b 24 Feb 1828, d 3Oct 11890

Stoddard, Harriet B., w/o Russell S. Stoddard, b 26 Nov 1832, d 13 Dec 1913

Thompson, Lloyd O., MD, b 15 April 1870, d 16 July 1881

Thompson, Sally, 1796-1881

Thomson, Orrin, b 24 Oct 1821, d 4 Jan 1904

Stone, Lizzie C., w/o Orrin Thomson, b 22 Feb 1827, d 16 Sept 1905

Turner, Luther H.,....

Turner, Eliza Jane, w/o Luther H. Turner, 1837-1907

Allison, Annie Davison, 1842-1924

Curry, George W., 1844-1875

Bemis, Emma S. Curry, d 1881

Curry, Ada, 1860-1890

Horton, George P., 1846-1910

Horton, Elizabeth M., w/o George P. Horton, 1856-1910

Whiting, Daniel, b 13 June 1786, d 7 Dec 1875

Whiting, Sarah, w/o Daniel Whiting, d 14 Nov 1864 aged 77 yrs

Whiting, Nelson, s/o Daniel & Sarah Whiting, d 3 Aug 1828 aged 5 mos

Johnson, Samuel G., b 17 April 1833, d 26 Feb 1869

Johnson, Lizzie A., 1835-1897

Stone, Franklin A., b 20 March 1827, d 10 Sept 1906

Stone, Eliza J., w/o Franklin A. Stone, b 3 Nov 1825, d 20 June 1904

Stone, Marion Alfreda, b 17 Aug 1860, d 4 Sept 1881

Hunt, John L., b 6 May 1816, d 3 Dec 1869

Hunt, Julia Ann, w/o John L. Hunt, b 19 Aug 1814, d July 1903

Dewing, Joseph H., 1843-1929

Hunt, Althea M., w/o Joseph H. Dewing, 1844-1921

Dewing, Grace A., d/o Joseph & Althea Dewing, 1877-1904

Hunt, George F., 1850-1921

Fiske, Wilbur, 1834-1914

Bailey, Martha, 1801-1877

Bailey, Rozanna C., 1809-1883

Travis, Arthur, b 8 Nov 1870, d 16 Nov 1937

Travis, Mary, w/o Arthur J. Travis, b 4 June 1865, d 18 March 1932

Travis, Frank E., 1882-1955

Kenley, Cora M., w/o Frank E. Travis, 1877-1955

Thompson, Adin, b 30 Nov 1818, d 30 Nov 1888

Cozzen, Sarah, w/o Adin Thompson, b 4 Aug 1824, d 11 Jan 1912

Drake, Willis K., 1854-1887

Monroe, J. P., 1850-1894

Monroe, Zibiah F., w/o J. P.Monroe, 1843-1905

Monroe, Addie, d/o J. P. & Zibiah Monroe, d 4 Sept 1884 aged 3 mos 22 days

Monroe, Harry, s/o J. P. & Zibiah Monroe, d 27 March 1885 aged 2 yrs 5 mos

Wilder, George, 1822-1915

Wilder, Hepsibeth H., w/o George Wilder, 1822-1893

Wilder, Leora, 1845-1933

Leland, Ezra, 1825-1894

Curtis, Clarissa E., w/o Ezra Leland, 1833-1923

Harrington, Ella M., 1862-1931

Forbes, Gustavus, 1859-1937

Forbes, Amey O., w/o Gustavus Forbes, 1862-1929

Forbes, Edith, 1898-1986

Barber, Edward, d 1932

Garvin, Charles H., 1856-1927

Garvin, Nellie C., w/o Charles H. Garvin, 1858-1946

Perry, Lucinda Kimball, d/o Edwin & Sally J. Perry, b 22 March 1836, d 12 Jan 1851

Perry, James Mason, s/o Edwin & Sally J. Perry, 1850-1851

Perry, Benjamin Wisner, s/o Edwin & Sally J. Perry, b 24 Aug 1831, d 21 Jan 1863

Perry, Horace Bacon, s/o Edwin & Sally J. Perry, b 1848, d Lost at Sea 26 March 1869

Perry, Charles, 1866-1936

Perry, Frances M., w/o Charles H. Perry, 1876-1956

Perry, Elmer M., 1901-1979

Claflin, Harold O., 1889-1923

Keady, Elizabeth Perry Claflin, w/o Harold O. Claflin, 1894-1973

Claflin, Lucretia B., w/o Aaron E. Claflin, 1849-1879

Draper, Calvin, d 22 Oct 1871 aged 71 yrs

Draper, Judith, w/o Calvin Draper, d 29 Nov 1868 aged 66 yrs 3 mos

Gage, Phineas K., 1811-1882

Gage, Phebe W., 1812-1851

Gage, Harriet M., 1815-1889

Gage, Lizzie F., 1839-1859

Rockwood, Adelia M., 1838-1915

Gage, Watson P., 1841-1915

Travis, Edson P., 1856-1936

Travis, Lizzie F., 1864-1949

Fiske, George B., b 1 Feb 1868, d 11 Aug 1955

Leonard, Ida A., w/o George B. Fiske, b 10 Nov 1868, d 10 May 1956

McClary, Mary G., 1868-1894

Fiske, Francis F., 1837-1920

Burnap, Ellen L., w/o Francis F. Fiske, 1841-1904

Fiske, Anna, d/o Francis & Ellen Fiske, 1866-1866

Fiske, Ellen Frances, d/o Francis & Ellen Fiske, 1874-1875

McClary, George H., 1829-1899

McClary, Elizabeth A., w/o George H. McClary, 1838-1931

Pond, George Nelson, b 22 Aug 1829, d 10 Jan 1897

Pond, Abby M.,w/o George Nelson Pond, b 24 Nov 1840, d 15 April 1894

Paterson, Nellie B., 1871-1883

Partridge, George J., 1826-1897

Partridge, Hannah B., w/o George J. Partridge, 1825-1901

Thayer, Seth, b 5 March 1803, d 14 Nov 1896

Thayer, Clarissa H., w/o Seth Thayer, b 16 June 1811, d 22 May 1876

Thayer, Mary Whiting, d/o Seth & Clarissa H. Thayer, b 18 June 1832, d 8 Sept 1833

Thayer, Charles Henry, s/o Seth & Clarissa H. Thayer, b 29 Dec 1833, d 20 Aug 1834

Sanger, Bessie W., 1866-1873

Brown, Irving Charles, 1865-1938

Noyes, Alice, w/o Irving Charle Brown, 1869-1966

Brown, Lena Mae, 1889-1971

Wiswell, Horace A., b 1 Jan 1837, d 9 June 1966

Wiswell, Mary P., b 19 Dec 1843, d 7 June 1871

Lindsey, Sarah A., d 10 March 1852 aged 35 yrs

Door, Reuben S., 1843-1885

Ellis, Carrie L., w/o Reuben S. Dorr, d 21 Feb 1875 aged 38 yrs

Ellis, William H., d 23 May 1875 aged 34 yrs 11 mos

Ellis, Frank W., d 5 Jan 1873 aged 30 yrs 7 mos

Ellis, William, d 13 Oct 1871 aged 62 yrs 5 mos

Ellis, Louisa H., w/o William Ellis, d 21 June 1880

Ellis, Angie H., d 20 Nov 1871 aged 21 yrs 10 mos

Pond, Elbridge S., b 15 Aug 1831, d 3 Dec 1880

Spofford, Preston L., d 7 Jan 1871 aged 30 yrs 2 mos

Ellis, Louisa P., w/o Preston L. Spofford, d 18 May 1871 aged 26 yrs 2 mos

Bemis, Charles A., b 4 March 1818, d 26 March 1886

Bemis, Caroline S., w/o Charles A. Bemis, b 4 Feb 1816, d 5 March 1897

Cutler, Amos, b 3 March 1815, d 1 Feb 1895

Cutler, Sabrina M., w/o Amos Cutler, b 25 March 1823, d 29 March 1900
Baker, Richard, 1827-1892
Baker, Eleanor, w/o Richard Baker, 1837-1898
Baker, Frank S., 1874-1959
Baker, Levina M., w/o Frank S. Baker, 1880-1971
Ware, Laura L., 1830-1906
Farquhar, Pollin, b 19 May 1852, d 26 Oct 1927
Farquhar, Elizabeth, b 24 Dec 1853, d 22 Dec 1913
Farquhar, Jean Grant, w/o Henry T. Bartlett, b 5 June 1839, d 11 Sept 1924
Farquhar, Charles, b 7 Aug 1854, d 8 Feb 1935
Brown, Ida L., w/o Charles S. Farquhar, b 6 Dec 1862, d 13 April 1933
Furber, Doris E., b 24 Dec 1892, d 20 March 1904
Furber, Charles H., 1850-1926
Farquhar, Nellie E., w/o Charles H. Furber, 1856-1941
Furber, Ruth H., b 22 June 1888, d 25 June 1978
Furber, Harold F., s/o Charles & Nellie Furber, b 2 Jan 1884, d 14 July 1953
Furber, Annie M., w/o Harold F. Furber, b 23 Feb 1885, d 31 May 1975
Farquhar, Samuel, 1842-1918
Chapman, Avra Anna, w/o Samuel Farquhar, 1843-1915
Farquhar, John, 1805-1887
Farquhar, Eliza A., w/o John Farquhar, 1812-1907
Stone, Henry, 1814-1899
Stone, Sarah B., w/o Henry Stone, 1813-1891
Clapp, George I., 1843-1881
Daniels, Emma L., w/o George I. Clapp, 1843-1890
Clapp, Gracie, 1873-1873
Kett, Philis, b 25 Oct 1794, d 25 May 1878
Kett, Francis, 1794-1885
Kett, William J., b 22 Jan 1843, d 27 Dec 1922
Taylot, Elizabeth, A., w/o William J. Kett, b 15 Feb 1848, d 24 Sept 1927
Miller, Henry M., 1854-1913
Miller, Albert N., d 24 Feb 1886 aged 64 yrs
Miller, Izanna L., w/o Albert N. Miller, b 31 Aug 1826, d 20 April 1881
Miller, Eva J., w/o Albert N. Miller, d 30 Aug 1882 aged 30 yrs
Miller, Sarah B., w/o Albert N. Miller, d 4 April 1918 aged 80 yrs
Baker, William, 1822-1895
Baker, Mary A., w/o William Baker, 1822-1905
Mann, Richard, S., 1837-1909

Mann, Sylvia E., w/o Richard S. Mann, 1831-....
Walker, Charles Austin, 1842-1916
Walker, Sarah Anna, w/o Charles Austin Walker, 1849-1930
Walker, Cora Belle, d/o Charles & Sarah Ann Walker, 1870-1922
Fiske, Leslie Clark, 1873-1917
Fiske, Annie L., 1866-1953
Fiske, James F., 1841-1909
Craig, Sarah M., w/o James F. Fiske, 1844-1935
Colburn, Edwin, 1840-1932
Dickerson, Sarah F., w/o Edwin Colburn, 1843-1909
Colburn, Ruth, 1899-1991
Colburn, Prentess S., 1902-1992
Woodsum, Charles B., 1832-1918
Woodsum, Priscilla M., w/o Charles B. Woodsum, 1836-1902
Watson, Joseph D., 1902-1964
Watson, Eva M., 1897-1961
Leland, John Dana, 1867-1934
Dunbar, Gustena, w/o John Dana Leland, 1866-1946
Partridge, Albert B., 1850-1929
Temple, Mary E., w/o Albert B. Partridge, 1848-1920
Partridge, Blanche E., d/o Albert & Mary Partridge, 1890-1981
Jones, Daniel S., 1841-1920
Ayer, Ellen F., w/o Daniel S. Jones, 1840-1912
Lockhart, Jeffrey P., 1864-1891
Wayne, Benjamin F., 1847-1907
Holmes, Adelaide E., w/o Benjamin F. Wayne, 1850-1921
Harding, Oscar R., b 1 May 1852, d 25 Jan 1868
Harding, Rosanna, b 5 April 1831, d 5 Dec 1897
Wilder, Charles, 1816-1893
Johnson, Emily P., w/o Charles Wilder, 1817-1903
Wilder, Rufus M., 1844-1853
Wilder, Mary E., 1849-1934
Wilder, Sydney, 1813-1888
Wilder, Sefuantes B., w/o Sydney Wilder, 1812-1877
Wilder, Elizabeth, 1838-1925
Wilder, Alice, 1850-1926
Wilder, Anna, 1832-1866
Wilder, Sarah A., 1843-1909
Lewis, J. Edwin, b Feb 1838, d Dec 1912
Bancroft, Alice C., w/o J. Edwin Lewis, b July 1837, d Aug 1865

Leland, Hermon B., 1834-1909
Leland, Martha., w/o Hermon B. Leland, 1835-1917
White, Albert Audubon, b 6 Sept 1846, d 13 Sept 1930
Lovell, Mathetta, w/o Albert A. White, b 3 Aug 1860, d 5 March 1912
Kittridge, Harold P., 1909-1965
Stratton, Eleanor P., w/o Harold P. Kittridge, 1910-1965
Stratton, Albion W., 1848-1916, A member of Co G 16th Maine Vols
Hines, Ella, w/o Albion W. Stratton, 1849-1915
Stratton, Hadley F., 1877-1946
Farrington, Edith P., w/o Hadley F., Stratton, 1882-1956
Lasier, Isabel Claflin, b 8 May 1888, d 2 May 1963
Gallott, Lambert, 1833-1924
Gallott, Orissa M., 1835-1921
Gallott, Mary O., 1865-1960
Lapham, William C., 1831-1917
Lapham, Isabelle A., w/o William C. Lapham, 1844-1915
Johnson, Warren E., b 28 Oct 1836, d 12 Dec 1906
Johnson, Mary, w/o Warren E. Johnson, b 25 Jan 1838, d 3 Feb 1907
Putney, Emma J., 1851-1928
Perty, Elbridge F., 1823-1904
Dailey, Catherine C., w/o Elbridge F. Perry, 1830-1856
Farrington, Samantha D., w/o Elbridge F. Perry, 1831-1904
Perry, George O., 1853-1855
Perry, Katie F., 1856-1856
Perry, Stella J., 1860-1862
Hart, George H., 1860-1918
Gallott, Ella M., w/o George H. Hart, 1860-1939
Guild, Fred W., 1888-1962
Hart, Alice M., w/o Fred W. Guild, 1888-1960
Guild, Fred W. Jr., 1917-1937
Guild, George F., 1911-1980
McLean, Eli Harrison, 1877-1918
Hutchins, Mabel M., 1867-1961
Chilstrom, Robert T., 1906-1979
McLean, Dorothy, w/o Robert T. Chilstrom, 1905-....
Whitney, George, 1841-1904
Farmer, Elizabeth, w/o George Whitney, 1843-1928
Pray, Charles, 1877-1938
Mills, Charles, 1855-1855
Colby, George, 1859-1860

Marshall, Charles H., 1836-1863
Pettis, Mary J., w/o Charles H. Marshall, 1842-1912
Smart, William H., 1847-1914
Smart, Georgia A., 1851-1929
Smart, Perley H., 1878-1897
Hoffman, Ira W., 1830-1901
Putnam, Susan R., w/o Ira W. Hoffman, 1836-1916
Brown, Ezra Jr., 1790-1812
Adams, Olive, w/o Ezra Broawn Jr., 1788-1843
Burnap, Sewall G., MD, 1802-1871
Brown, Betsey A., w/o Dr. Sewall G. Burnap, 1812-1842
Blanchard, Elizabeth, w/o Dr. Sewall G. Burnap, 1817-1900
Harding, Caleb, d 29 June 1856 aged 35 yrs
Harding, R., 1797-1878
Harding, O. R. , 1801-1853
Freeman, Oliver D., 1818-1891
Freeman, Mary A., w/o Oliver D. Freeman, b 31 July 1818, d 21 April
    1889
Freeman, Mary B., b 10 Dec 1846, d 22 Sept 1881
Bullard, Lewis H., 1811-1916
Fiske, George Batchelor, 1834-1910
Rawson, Edward C., 1860-1927
Keske, Effie Louise, w/o Edward C. Rawson, 1862-1898
Fiske, M. Florence, w/o Edward C. Rawson, 1864-1936
Jordan, Willard C., 1861-1932
Jordan, Marion A., w/o Willard C. Jordan, 1859-1932
Pierce, Sophia Mayo, 1848-1891
Iwweaks, Deborah Mayo, 1860-1918
Lund, Edward A., 1888-1962
Lund, Lillian P., w/o Edward A. Lund, 1886-1979
Holmes, William E., 1865-1940
Chesmore, Adlene L., w/o William E. Holmes, 1874-1976
Dexter, Judge J. P., 1865-1942
Badger, John P., 1842-1900
Shaw, William E., 1855-1940
Shaw, Elizabeth I., w/o William E. Shaw, 1859-1942
Ball, D. W., 1869-1946
Parker, Ralph H., 1877-1932
Parker, Katherine B., 1876-1961
Parker, Alice W., 1909-1911

Robinson, W. Irving, 1849-1912

Robinson, Jennie M., w/o W. Irving Robinson, 1842-1917

Partridge, Deacon Horace, b 23 April 1805 Medway, MA, d 2 Sept 1853

Adams, Esther, w/o Deacon Horace Partridge, b 21 Feb 1806 Readfield, Maine, d 11 March 1873

Partridge, Betsey, b 6 Jan 1816 Medway, MA, d 14 March 1854

Sanger, Samuel A., 1824-1877

Sanger, Hannah M., 1832-1861

Sanger, Eliza A., 1831-1889

Taylor, Harrison, 1833-1918

Taylor, Ellen B., w/o Harrison Taylor, 1830-1925

Taylor, Nellie L., b 4 July 1861, d 3 July 1902

Taylor, Evelyn B., 1860-1928

Taylor, Emma O., 1862-1943

Batchelor, B. F., 1 Nov 1801, d 23 April 1879

Daniels, Lucinda, w/o B. F. Batchelor, b 12 July 1805, d 3 Oct 1879

Batchelder, Charles F., 1846-1891

Batchelor, Martha A., w/o Charles F. Batchelor, 1845-1893

Fitts, Charles H., 1813-1908

Fitts, Emeline A., w/o Charles H. Fitts, 1819-1901

Fitts, Charles, b 21 Feb 1849, d 1 Feb 1882

Buell, Helen Fitts, b 29 Aug 1848, d 22 March 1914

Fitts, Helen Louise, b 22 Feb 1880, d 21 Jan 1967

Taft, Ellen M., w/o William W. Taft, 1861-1894

Leland, Aaron, d 10 March 1881 Worcester, MA

Leland, Rowena W., w/o Aaron Leland, d 21 Sept 1896 aged 81 yrs

Leland, Harry, d 1867

Temple, Annah, w/o Harry Leland, d 1867

Tyler, Phebe, d 11 Nov 1862 aged 93 yrs 2 mos

Ellsworth, Willis, s/o William & Harriet M. Tyler, b 21 March 1862, d 10 Dec 1864

Tyler, W. H., MD, 1837-1931

Rice, Alice M., w/o Dr. W. H.Tyler, 1859-1938

Miller, Daniel, b 24 Oct 1813, d 12 April 1867

Adams, Persis, 1788-1859

Tyler, Leslie, 1857-1931

Mabie, Harriet L., w/o Leslie Tyler, 1856-1909

Tyler, Sylvester, b 14 March 1827, d 29 May 1911

Miller, Anna, w/o Sylvester Tyler, b 27 June 1836, d 18 Feb 1867

Crosby, Miriam Frances, w/o Sylvester Tyler, 1899-1923

Holbrook, Corp. George H., wounded at Gettysburg, d Mt. Pleasent
   Hospital Washington DC 17 April 1865 aged 19 yrs A member of Co K
   58th Reg Mass Vols
Holbrook, Moses, d 17 May 1871 aged 51 yrs
Holbrook, Anna D., w/o Moses Holbrook, 1822-1905
Wheeler, John C., 1848-1917
Wheeler, Emma A., w/o John C. Wheeler, 1861-1933
Gooch, Arthur H., 1858-1937
Gooch, Blendena E., w/o Arthur H. Gooch, 1856-1919
Parker, Jennie F., d 8 Feb 1872 aged 11 yrs 9 mos 20 days
Parker, Lorenzo, b 18 May 1812, d 11 July 1887
Parker, Mary E., w/o Lorenzo Parker, b 29 Dec 1812, d 10 Jan 1900
Parker, Mason, 1907-1915
Parker, Edward Oliver, 1868-1949
Parker, Bessie M., 1864-1952
Jones, Betsey O., d 4 June 1865 aged 64 yrs 11 mos
Frail, Sarah A., d 24 March 1866 aged 34 yrs 8 mos
Frail, Abbie B., d 14 Feb 1878 aged 59 yrs 7 mos
White, Oliver, 1797-1875
White, Betsey, w/o Oliver White, 1838-1906
Tyler, William H., 1834-1917
Tyler, Harriet M., w/o William H. Tyler, 1838-1906
Thompson, Fletcher A., b 8 May 1847, d 20 Nov 1894
Southwick, Laura A., w/o Fletcher Thompson, b 25 Nov 1849, d 18 Oct
   1932
Thompson, George Southwick, MD, 1876-1937
Claflin, John, b 5 April 1810, d 16 Sept 1888
Claflin, Angeline, w/o John Claflin, b 23 Jan 1809, d 15 Feb 1892
Claflin, Francis Everett, s/o John & Angeline Claflin, b 16 July 1839, d 3
   March 1841
Claflin, John Willard, s/o John & Angeline Claflin, b 19 March 1852, d
   26 Nov 1854
Leland, Granville, 1829-1897
Claflin, Jane M., w/o Granville Leland, b Sept 1834, d March 1879
Leland, Eddie E., b May 1869, d 4 Sept 1877
Runglman, James, 1857-1931
Runglman, Alice, w/o James Runglman, 1857-1939
Shippe, Lucilla G., d 1916
Shippe, John D., d 1911
Daniels, Ella A., d 1852

Daniels, Mary A., d 1852
Daniels, Augustus, d 1854
Shippe, Henry C., d 1873
Shippe, Lizzie C., d 1868
Shippe, Edmund F., d 1857
Shippe, Amasa G., d 1855
Shippe, Abbott I., d 1874
Shippe, Mary B., 1853-1892
Pond, Albert P., 1844-1891
Battles, George E., 1870-1933
Daniels, Betsey C., d 1860
Daniels, John, d 1843
Backshall, William J., 1892-1923
Backshall, Florence E., w/o William J. Backshall, 1897-1944
Bononno, Marion E., 1922-1973
Kennedy, John A., 1857-1915
Kennedy, Catherine E., w/o John A. Kennedy, 1868-1930
Leland, Leslie, b 13 Nov 1888, d 27 April 1954
Leland, Francis O., b 14 Sept 1849, d 13 Jan 1920
Stoddard, Anna J., w/o Francis O. Leland, b 24 Nov 1851, d 2 Sept 1928
Leland, Orlando, b 19 Jan 1807, d 30 Dec 1887
Cutler, Ursula, b 28 Oct 1811, d 13 April 1886
Leland, Lewis A., b 16 Nov 1842, d 23 Oct 1929
Leland, Frances A., w/o Lewis Leland, b 14 June 1848, d 1 Sept 1930
Britton, Lawson V., b 11 Feb 1824, d 19 Feb 1875
Britton, Edith H., only child of Lawson V. & Mary F. Britton b 8 June
    1867, d 24 Oct 1872
Whittimore, Charles S., 1860-1934
Allen, Isabella, w/o Charles S. Whittmore, 1864-1958
Bacon, Mary A., 1819-1877
Bacon, Abel H., 1812-1891
Bacon, Albert M., 1842-1895
Bacon, Sarah R., 1838-1909
Bacon, Nellie V., 1859-1902
Croom, Herbert, 1883-1968
Croom, Mary G., w/o Herbert Croom, 1885-1936
Croom, Elma E., 1885-1966
Saunders, Norman W., 1871-1942
Saunders, Laura W., w/o Norman W. Saunders, 1869-1933
Dempsey, Mildred W., d/o Norman & Laura Saunders, 1899-1987

Bridges, Alpheus, 1826-1892
Bridges, Adelia M., w/o Alpheus Bridges, 1830-1906
Turnock, Henry, 1858-1929
Sheridan, Minnie, w/o Henry Turnock, 1866-1961
Snow, Henry, 1857-1940
Snow, Eveline, w/o Henry Snow, 1849-1931
Snow, Elmer L., 1882-1953
Cutler, Uriel, 1822-1910
Lovering, Susan E., w/o Uriel Cutler, 1827-1907
Cutler, U. Herbert, 1853-1854
Cutler, S. Eliza, 1858-1917
Leland, Edmund Francis, b 30 June 1825, d 14 April 1889
Cutler, Mary Lucretia, w/o Edmund Francis Leland, b 24 March 1829, d 8
    March 1822 (dates as written on stone)
Leland, Ella A., b 19 Dec 1855, d 13 Aug 1943
Comey, Aratus, 1837-1907
Comey, Annah Leland, 1840-1934
Williams, Jane Comey, 1879-1952
Leland, Hon. Alden, d 30 Aug 1883 aged 75 yrs 9 mos
Leland, Annah W., w/o Hon. Alden Leland, d 9 July 1854 aged 41 yrs
Leland, Rhoda A., w/o Hon. Alden Leland, 1827-1899
Leland, Howard A., b 22 Aug 1898, d 24 Oct 1911
Leland, Richard C., b 23 Nov 1891, d 17 July 1956
Leland, Katharine H., b 16 June 1892, d 14 June 1971
Leland, Rev. Willis Daniels, PH.d, b 30 March 1854, d 15 May 1902
Alvord, Susan Gridley, w/o Rev Willis D. Leland, b 25 April 1860, d 4
    March 1930
Morgan, Louise Leland, w/o John P. Morgan, b 9 Aug 1920, d 24 Sept
    1977
Cutler, Uriel, 1776-1848, donated land for this cemetery
Morse, Nabby, w/o Uriel Cutler, 1783-1862
Cutler, Henry Morse, 1865-1930
Travis, Annie, w/o Henry Morse Cutler, 1873-1959
Capone, Edmund P., 1904-1980
Cutler, Newell Lovering, 1850-1930
Grimes, Lucy, w/o Newell Lovering Cutler, 1866-1936
Cutler, Uriel Waldo, 1854-1936
Cutler, Emma, w/o Uriel Waldo Cutler, 1856-1950
Walker, Timothy, 1801-1888
Turner, Louisa, w/o Timothy Walker, b 26 Aug 1801, d 18 July 1866

Holbrook, James, b Dec 1809, d 5 Sept 1871
Holbrook, Mahala, w/o James Holbrook, d 1891
Tufts, Walter, d March 1866 aged 28 yrs
Tuft, Charles, d 15 July 1859 aged 59 yrs
Tufts, Sophia, w/o Charles Tufts, d 28 April 1875 aged 73 yrs
Riley, James S., 1865-1933
MacPherson, Anne, w/o James S. Riley, 1859-1961
Simmons, J.S., 1835-1901
Bridges, Emma A., w/o J.S. Simmons, 1841-1906
Bellows, J. N., 1835-1913
Tibbetts, Hattie C., w/o H. B. Tibbetts, d 2 July 1881 aged 34 yrs 9 mos
Tibbetts, Harrison B., b Sept 1845, d 29 Dec 1925
Gove, Mattie T., w/o Harrison B. Tibbetts, b Sept 1846, d July 1881
Partridge, Eda B., w/o Harrison B. Tibbetts, b Aug 1854, d May 1930
Banniman, Susan N., b 6 Dec 1848, d 9 Jan 1849
Warfeld, Abijah B., b 30 May 1811, d 8 May 1849
Warfield, William V., 1845-1895
Warfield, Sarah Elizabeth, w/o Abijah B. Warfield, 1819-1896
Nichols, Job, b 28 Aug 1795, b 18 May 1877
Temple, Betsey, w/o Job Nichols, b 18 Dec 1798 Reading, MA, d 12 Dec
    1863
Nichols, Roswell, s/o Job & Betsey Nichols, b 26 March 1825, d 2 Oct
    1826
Nichols, Gustavus, s/o Job & Betsey Nichols, b 15 Nov 1826, d 21 Jan
    1832
Nichols, Maryianna, d/o Job & Betsey Nichols, b 23 Aug 1828, d 26 Feb
    1856
Littlefield, Amory, b 15 March 1796, d 24 June 1869
Littlefield, Marcy, w/o Amory Littlefield, b 27 Sept 1797, d 25 Aug 1881
Littlefield, Emily F., w/o John Littlefield, 1845-1889
Wiley, Benjamin, 1845-1926
Phipps, Eleanor A., w/o Benjamin Wiley, 1844-1907
Williams, Lorena C., w/o Benjamin Wiley, 1857-1928
Whiting, Susan Ann, w/o Timothy M. Whiting, d 25 June 1858 aged 22
    yrs
Sheffield, Irene, d 9 June 1875 aged 85 yrs 2 days
Evans, Thomas, d 24 April 1908 aged 68 yrs
Baker, William J., 1838-1904
Baker, Ann, w/o William J. Baker, 1837-1909
Baker, Ann, 1836-1920

Pyne, Ellen, 1862-1932
Hall, Marguerite S., 1913-1916
Kendall, Salma, b 3 Oct 1816, d 27 May 1898
Hart, John M., b May 1823, d Feb 1905
Hart, Sarah P., b April 1823, d Dec 1902
Hill, Charles F., 1856-1919
Hill, Alice F., w/o Charles F. Hill, 1856-....
Hart, Sarah L., w/o John M. Hart, d 27 Jan 1850 aged 24 yrs
Hart, Sarah E., d/o John M. & Sarah L. Hart, d 20 Dec 1874 aged 25 yrs
Fales, Almira, w/o Calvin Lincoln, 1803-1877
Lincoln, Calvin, 1800-1857
Loomis, Charles Lincoln, MD, 1859-1888
Lincoln, Esther L., w/o Lafayette C. Loomis, 1823-1870
Lincoln, Asa, 1759-1835
Lincoln, Esther, w/o Asa Lincoln, 1767-1823
Fairbanks, Joseph H., s/o Daniel & Augusta L. Fairbanks, d 2 Oct 1851
    aged 3 yrs 7 mos 6 days
Fairbanks, Frank L., s/o Daniel & Augusta L. Fairbanks, d 20 May 1855
    aged 6 mos
Carter, Henry, 1857-1918
Brown, Lilla, w/o Henry Carter, 1867-1922
Carter, Mary A., w/o Henry Carter, 1826-1895
Payne, Shadrake B., d 23 April 1879 aged 71 yrs 5 mos
Payne, Orissa, b 31 Aug 1800, d 29 Dec 1896
Willard, Abbie, d 28 Feb 1886 aged 77 yrs 8 mos 11 days
Barber, Hamlet, 1814-1901
Barber, Miranda P., w/o Hamlet Barber, d 13 July 1879 aged 59 yrs
Case, Rev. John E., b 27 Nov 1856, d 28 Feb 1928
Clarke, Lilly, w/o Rev. John E. Case, b 3 June 1857, d 13 March 1927
Bigelow, Venetta E., d/o W. L. & C. Bigelow, d 14 Aug 1876
Hodgkin, Emory, 1816-1892
Hodgkin, Maria, w/o Emory Hodgkin, d 3 Dec 1884 aged 80 yrs 5 mos
Leland, George H. B., 1874-1960
Nash, Mary, w/o George H. B. Leland, 1875-1957
Merritt, Howard A., 1857-1935
Merritt, Ella E., w/o Howard A. Merritt, 1862-1937
Thayer, Bessie Merritt, 1881-1960
Rice, Christiania, 1832-1923
Merritt, A. Maurice, 1903-1974
Carroll, Emma, w/o A. Maurice Merritt, 1905-1992

Daniels, Dan Nelson, 1875-1943
Daniels, Jessie M., w/o Dan Nelson Daniels, 1872-1958
Goodrich, Cyrus A., 1871-1951
Goodrich, Carrie I., w/o Cyrus A. Goodrich, 1865-1946
Littlefield, George Edwin, 1872-1945
Trafton, Susan J., w/o George Edwin Littlefield, 1872-1947
Wentworth, John H., 1857-1946
Wentworth, Lillian G., w/o John H. Wentworth, 1861-1941
Wentworth, Helen, d/o John & Lillian Wentworth, 1887-1983
Stone, Joseph, 1789-1853
Heald, Hannah, w/o Joseph Stone, 1794-1866
Whitcomb, Eliza, b 23 Jan 1826, d 12 Nov 1880
Whitcomb, Nellie M., d/o Alpha & Eliza Whitcomb, & w/o George F.
   Harding, d 4 March 1871 aged 21 yrs 3 mos 23 days
Whitcomb, Marinda S., d/o Samuel & Hannah Whitcomb, d 17 May 1840
   aged 28 yrs
Goodins, James M., 1868-1908
Marshall, Mary E., w/o James M. Goodins, 1859-1904
Finn, Matthew H., b 6 Jan 1865, d 6 Oct 1928
Finn, Frank B., 1862-1943
Howarth, John, 1825-1895
Howarth, Mary A., w/o John Howarth, 1825-1903
Wheeler, Warren W., 1825-1903
Wheeler, Abigail E., w/o Warren W. Wheeler, 1827-1909
Morse, Emma, 1866-1898
Wheeler, Charles H., 1882-1956
Wheeler, Grace M., w/o Charles H. Wheeler, 1884-1931
Wheeler, Warren, b 25 July 1858, d 27 June 1889
Heath, Cyrus D., b 12 April 1827, d 19 Jan 1870
Heath, Esther J., w/o Cyrus D. Heath, b 13 March 1827, d 1 March 1873
Crosby, Mark, 1813-1884
Crosby, Margaret P., w/o Mark Crosby, 1816-1848
Crosby, Louise R., w/o Mark Crosby, 1821-1881
Eames, Anna, w/o Niles Eames, d 15 Dec 1882 aged 73 yrs
Gilmore, Laura A., 1907-1956
Eames, George H., 1836-1898
Volk, E. Margaret, w/o George H. Eames, 1836-1917
Jackson, Eva Eames, d/o George & Margaret Eames, 1861-1942
Bartlett, Henry W., d 5 June 1856 aged 21 yrs
Bartlett, Charles H. M., 1854-1929

Tyler, Ida M., w/o Charles H. M. Bartlett, 1857-1934
Staples, Benjamin F., 1840-1900
Staples, Mary E., w/o Benjamin Staples, b 8 Dec 1850, d 7 Sept 1909
Whitcomb, Alpha, b 23 Dec 1825, d 18 July 1887
Cutler, S. Morse, b 13 May 1816, d 13 Jan 1885 Washington, DC
Bullard, Elmira A., w/o S. Morse Cutler, b 16 Sept 1822, d 29 Oct 1889
Hayes, Jesse, 1813-1897
Hayes, Lucy A., w/o Jesse Hayes, 1823-1896
Treen, Benjamin F., 1849-1923
Treen, Ida F., 1855-1950
Treen, Marion L., 1880-1901
Pierce, Jonas, b 25 Sept 1797, d 25 March 1870
Fairbanks, Mary, w/o Jonas Pierce, b 5 March 1803 Sudbury, MA, d 13
    March 1870
Bridges, Newell E., 1859-1904
Adams, Mary H., w/o Newell E. Bridges, 1861-1945
Bridges, Eugene A., s/o Newell & Mary Bridges, 1887-1891
Bridges, Benjamin A., 1828-1890
Johnson, Martha M., w/o Benjamin A. Bridges, 1827-1914
Wight, Mary F., 1858-1904
Eames, Newell, 1804-1887
Eames, Elizabeth C., w/o Newell Eames, 1807-1887
Shaw, Thomas Houston, 1862-1933
Shaw, Alberta V., w/o Thomas Houston Eames, 1860-1956
Shaw, Mabelle E., d/o Thomas & Alberta Shaw, 1899-1983
Shaw, Thomas Houston, 1892-1904
Farrington, Dexter, 1804-1893
Farrington, Hepsabeth, w/o Dexter Farrington, 1807-1896
Dudley, Frank E., 1863-1892
Morrill, Mima, w/o J. H. Morrill, 1860-1893
Pells, Jane Parkin, 1834-1878
Pells, Willie Ashley, 1871-1877
Pells, Josiah Boyd, 1858-1936
Fiske, Walter Henry, 1864-1893
Shefflitt, Betty G., 1823-1988
Ward, Stephen G., 1947-1991
Cutler, William B., MD, b 13 Dec 1848, d 5 March 1909
Hebard, Susan A., w/o Dr. William B. Cutler, b 28 Sept 1839, d 11 May
    1914

Hollistion Town Hall
Washington Street Route 126
Holliston, MA
01746

Carpenter Cemetery
Mendon Road
North Attleborough, Massachusetts

Carpenter, George C., b 18 Sept 1875, d 1 Nov 1930
Carpenter, Bertha L., w/o George C. Carpenter, b 26 June 1883, d 10 May 1960
Bellows, Charles A., b 7 June 1846, d 19 Dec 1918
Carpenter, Clara A., w/o Charles A. Bellows, b 17 Jan 1847, d 4 Feb 1922
Carpenter, Edwin Francis, b 26 Sept 1854, d 7 Aug 1919
Lee, M. Anna E., w/o Edwin Francis Carpenter, b 30 Nov 1859, d 29 June 1845
Carpenter, Lewis, b 12 May 1817, d 28 April 1866
Cargill, Cynthia A., w/o Lewis Carpenter, b 13 Feb 1818, d 21 July 1890
Brown, Lydia, d 1 Dec 1856 aged 61 yrs
Carpenter, John, d 18 May 1851 aged 78 yrs
Carpenter, Marcy, w/o John Carpenter, d 20 April 1863 aged 83 yrs
Carpenter, Namon B., d 7 Feb 1877 aged 69 yrs
Carpenter, Sylvia, w/o Namon B. Carpenter, d 19 May 1866 aged 61 yrs
Guild, Henry A., 1839-1901
Guild, Adaline H., w/o Henry A. Guild, 1846-1916
Guild, Flosice A., d/o Henry & Adaline Guild, 1870-1946
Brien, Ernestine E., 1860-1945
Carpenter, Joseph, 1839-1908
Carpenter, Cynthia B., 1837-1861
Carpenter, Ellen M., 1840-1895
Carpenter, Henry B., 1861-1934
Carpenter, Delia M., 1838-1840
Carpenter, W. H., d 25 Oct 1888 aged 74 yrs
Carpenter, Hannah, w/o W. H. Carpenter, d 8 Jan 1867 aged 47 yrs
Brown, David, d 16 Oct 1849 aged 98 yrs
Brown, Cloe, w/o David Brown, d 25 Jan 1841 aged 87 yrs
Carpenter, Susan C., w/o John B. Carpenter, d 9 Nov 1866 aged 31 yrs
Carpenter, Frank T., s/o John B. & Susan C. Carpenter, d 19 Oct 1868 aged 9 yrs 2 mos 21 days

Carpenter, Jesse A., b 25 Dec 1850, d 27 Jan 1923

Carpenter, Medora A., b 21 Oct 1859, d 24 Feb 1889

Carpenter, Ida M., b 9 May 1868, d 11 Aug 1942

Carpenter, Jesse L., 1905-1984

Carpenter, Ida Mae, w/o Jesse L. Carpenter, 1898-1985

Roberts, Henry P., 1904-1973

Roberts, Thelma C., w/o Henry P. Roberts, 1907-1982

Anderson, Peter V., 1959-1988

Lancaster, Dorothy L., 1934-1977

Carpenter, Jesse F., b 8 April 1930, d 23 Dec 1992, Cumberland, RI
Retired Police Chief

Anderson, Jacqueline R., w/o Jesse F. Carpenter, b 31 Dec 1932, d....

Carpenter, Chester L., 1897-1967

Carpenter, Susan M., w/o Chester L. Carpenter, 1914-1973

Durgin, William F., b 12 July 1915, d 22 June 1984

Walker, Mary L., w/o William F. Durgin, b 22 Jan 1915, d....

Clark, Ross R., b 13 Feb 1879, d 20 Dec 1958

Metcalf, Ellie C., w/o Ross R. Clark, b 6 Oct 1874, d 10 Feb 1944

Metcalf, Henry, b 3 Aug 1847, d 31 May 1928

Carpenter, Emily A., w/o Henry Metcalf, b 30 April 1848, d 27 Sept 1911

Carpenter, Noah A., d 20 April 1869 aged 60 yrs

Carpenter, Abby, w/o Noah A. Carpenter, d 30 Oct 1900 aged 93 yrs

Carpenter, Henry Albert, s/o Noah A. & Abby Carpenter, d 6 March 1847
aged 8 mos 5 days

Hixon, Edmund T., b 22 Sept 1851, d 16 June 1898

Carpenter, Nancy W., w/o Edmund T. Hixon, b 24 July 1844, d 31 Oct
1927

Hixon, Mortimer J., s/o Edmund & Nancy Hixon, b 10 Sept 1888, d 7
Sept 1890

Walker, Cynthia Hixon, b 13 Dec 1879, d 19 March 1966

Walker, Edmund Hixon, s/o Cynthia Hixon Walker, b 27 June 1916, d 30
Jan 1988

Paine Cemetery
Paine Road
North Attleborough, Massachusetts

Ryan, Martin S., WW 1, b 24 May 1900, d 15 Nov 1965

Carpenter, Sarah A., w/o William Carpenter, b 5 Nov 1826, d 10 May 1888

Blanchard, John E., d 19 April 1944 aged 75 yrs

Blanchard, Mary A., w/o John E. Blanchard, d 28 Jan 1864 aged 41 yrs

Blanchard, Elizabeth, d/o John & Mary Blanchard, d 6 Aug 1855 aged 3 yrs

Marble, Charlotte, w/o Edwin R. Marble, d 2 July 1891 aged 71 yrs

Cudworth, B., b 5 March 1781, d 22 Aug 1869

Cudworth, Susan, w/o B. Cudworth, b 1 March 1777, d 22 March 1836

Cudworth, Roxanna, d/o B. & Susan Cudorth, 1811-1829

Cudworth, B. G., b 8 July 1820, d 26 Jan 1870

Cudworth, Anjenette, w/o B. G. Cudworth, b 6 Oct 1827, d 8 Oct 1867

Blanchard, George, d 22 Feb 1861 aged 80 yrs

Blanchard, Betsey, w/o George Blanchard, d 8 Sept 1860 aged 74 yrs

Blanchard, William H., d 17 Feb 1858 aged 47 yrs 9 mos 10 days

Tewyan, William H. Jr., 1952-1975

Brailey, Erastus, 1873-1945

Brown, Mary A., 1896-1960

Brown, Nelson, 1896-1968

Dunphy, Colon V., 1927-1971

Johnson, Virginia M., w/o Colon V. Dunphy, ...

Johnson, William D., 1887-1957

Perry, Hattie L., w/o William D. Johnson, 1895-1992

Johnson, Robert P., 1925-1940

Watson, Russell A., 1912-....

Johnson, Marion R., w/o Russell A. Watson, 1917-....

Rhynard, Owen H., 1900-1935

Crum, Edward C. Sr., b 14 Oct 1892, d 13 May 1961

Ryhnard, Edward, 1869-1961

Rhynard, Annie E., w/o Edward Rhynard, ...

Crum, Ethel W. Rhynard, b 25 Dec 1903, d 9 April 1988

Paine, Anna Olny, d 1835

Paine, Arnold, d 11 day 9 mos 1853 New York

Paine, Dorcas, d 1892 aged 89 yrs

Mowry, Daniel N., s/o Daniel & Almira Mowry, d 8 Sept 1869 aged 33 yrs
Mowry, Stephen G., s/o Daniel & Almira Mowry, d 31 Aug 1865 aged 22 yrs 3 mos
Mowry, Justus, d 17 July 1840 aged 64 yrs
Mowry, Anna, w/o Justus Mowry, d 15 Aug 1857 aged 74 yrs
Mowry, Eliza, d/o Justus & Anna Mowry, d 8 Nov 1822 aged 16 yrs
Mowry, Sarah, d/o Justus & Anna Mowry, d 2 Oct 1844 aged 27 yrs
Mowry, Richard, s/o Justus & Anna Mowry, d 28 Nov 1844 aged 25 yrs
Mowry, Mary Ann, d 1856 aged 14 yrs
Johnson, John H., 1844-1915
Johnson, Elizabeth A., w/o John H. Johnson, 1848-1939
Johnson, John H., s/o John & Elizabeth Johnson, 1868-1905
Johnson, Owen L., 1869-1937
Johnson, Pauline J., w/o Owen L. Johnson, 1874-1941
Sweetland, Susan A., d 23 Feb 1881 aged 70 yrs 6 mos 11 days
Sweetland, Laura, d 3 May 1875 aged 78 yrs
Sweetland, Cynthia, d 1856
Park, Russell, d 12 Dec 1835 aged 39 yrs
Park, Calista S., w/o Russell Park, d 17 Feb 1878 aged 78 yrs
Sweetland, Olive, d 7 July 1854
Holmes, Eliphlet, d 2 May 1826 aged 78 yrs
Holmes, Amy, w/o Eliphlet Holmes, d 30 Nov 1853 aged 95 yrs
Holmes, Milton, b 29 Sept 1794, d 8 July 1863
Holmes, Betsey, w/o Milton Holmes, d 24 Dec 1868 aged 78 yrs
Holmes, George Benton, s/o Milton & Betsey, d 8 Oct 1854 aged 19 yrs
Holmes, Harriet, d/o Milton & Betsey Holmes, d 13 March 1830 aged 21 yrs
Holmes, Joanna, d 23 Dec 1876 aged 91 yrs
King, Raymond K., 1832-1892
King, Abbie E., w/o Raymond K. King, 1837-1920
King, Ida F., d/o Raymons & Abbie King, 1864-1864
King, Lizzie M., d/o Raymond & Abbie King, 1867-1888
Tucker, John S. H., d 21 Nov 1876 aged 40 yrs 7 mos 13 days
Tucker, Mary Jane, w/o James D. Tucker, d 4 March 1863 aged 27 yrs 4 mos
Tingley, William S., b 18 Oct 1830, d 15 Jan 1879 aged 48 yrs
Tingley, Susan, w/o Elisha Tingley, d 28 April 1845 aged 40 yrs
Tingley, Elisha, b 23 June 1799, d....
Sweetland, John W., d 26 Nov 1826 aged 53 yrs

Sweetland, Amy, w/o John W. Sweetland, d 28 Nov 1871 aged 87 yrs 11 mos

Tucker, Delford B., d 22 Dec 1875 aged 68 yrs 8 mos 11 days

Tucker, Amey Ann, w/o Delford B. Tucker, d 27 April 1853 aged 43 yrs

Tucker, Lydia E., w/o Delford B. Tucker, d 6 Aug 1836 aged 20 yrs

Woods, Lydia, d 14 Feb 1842 aged 81 yrs

Sweetland, Nancy, d 11 Sept 1847 aged 19 yrs

Sweetland, Phebe, d 1 Feb 1849 aged 81 yrs 15 days

Sweetland, May, d 1 Feb 1849 aged 80 yrs 3 days

Sweetland, William, d 28 Jan 1849 aged 77 yrs 10 days

Bloomingdale, Alonzo M., d 18 March 1861 aged 29 yrs 11 days

Biron, Margaret B., b 27 July 1916, d 12 July 1990

Lemieux, Arthur O., b 12 Feb 1916, d 3 Feb 1991

Hingley, Albert W., 1913-1972

Hingley, Harriet, w/o Albert W. Hingley, 1923-....

Martel, Dolores L. Demers, b 4 Oct 1936, d 23 Nov 1992

Cudworth, David A., b 29 Dec 1847, d 15 Feb 1922

Cudworth, Emeline Maria, w/o David A. Cudworth, b 22 Feb 1841, d 2 Nov 1883

Cudworth, Georgianna Thayer, d/o David A. & Emeline Maria Cudworth, b 23 Nov 1876, d 28 Dec 1877

Brien, Armand N., 1910-1985

Underwood, Albert, b 14 May 1835, d 29 Dec 1902

Underwood, Ann Frances, w/o Albert Underwood, b 5 March 1841, d 14 April 1917

Esten, John, b 15 Dec 1825, d 25 June 1898

Esten, Laura A., w/o John Esten, b 1 July 1829, d 4 Dec 1905

Bowen, Arthur E., b 20 July 1877, d 16 Dec 1906

Bowen, George, d 3 Sept 1928 aged 89 yrs

Bowen, Eudora S., w/o George Bowen, d 19 Dec 1801 aged 49 yrs

Sweetland, Samuel N., s/o Albert & Hannah Sweetland, 1845-1933

Brown, Rebecca, w/o Samuel N. Sweetland, 1843-1920

Sweetland, Robert N., s/o Samuel & Rebecca Sweetland, 1881-1907

Sweetland, Leon C., b 21 Oct 1871, d 29 Aug 1899

Sweetland, Albert D., b 16 Dec 1804, d 14 Dec 1881

Sweetland, Hannah, w/o Albert D. Sweetland, b 12 March 1809, d 23 April 1884

Sweetland, Ella Amelia, d/o Albert D. & Hannah Sweetland, d 28 Sept 1865

Robinson, Ezra C., 1808-1888

Robinson, Weltha E., w/o Ezra C. Robinson, 1804-1880
Jordan, Lorenzo Augustus, 1867-1965
Baab, Annie Maria, w/o Lorenzo Augustus Jorden, 1868-1954
Morin, Rudolph Joseph, 1897-1979
Jordan, Lillis Isabel, w/o Rudolph Joseph Morin, 1889-1981
Millard, William H., 1840-1908
Holmes, Sarah A., w/o William H. Millard, 1825-1910
Holmes, Charles F., b 9 April 1823, d 21 April 1900
Hartshorn, Julia, w/o Charles F. Holmes, b 4 Nov 1827, d 25 Aug 1898
Holmes, James, d 9 Sept 1875 aged 85 yrs 4 mos 3 days
Holmes, Nancy A., w/o James Holmes, d 19 Feb 1882 aged 89 yrs 10 days
Holmes, Elizabeth H., b 24 Jan 1821, d 9 Feb 1896
Holmes, Eleanor F., b 18 Nov 1820, d 4 April 1910
Woodward, Emma E., 1861-1950
Holmes, James Lawrence, s/o Charles F. & Julia H. Holmes, 1858-1860
Holmes, Cora Estelle, d/o Charles F. & Julia H. Holmes, 1860-1937
Holmes, Percy Gilbert, s/o Charles F. & Julia H. Holmes, 1864-1890
Holmes, Eliphelet, d 24 Oct 1867 aged 79 yrs
Holmes, Betsey, w/o Eliphelet Holmes, d 21 March 1866 aged 70 yrs
Holmes, Augustus, d 1 Aug 1874 aged 74 yrs
Holmes, Mary Ann, w/o Augustus Holmes, d 1 Feb 1829 aged 26 yrs
Holmes, Lilli G., w/o Augustus Holmes, d 31 Aug 1881 aged 78 yrs
Coolum, Liston M., 1855-1936
Littlefield, Emma M., d/o Liston M. Coolum, 1857-1942
Holmes, William A., b 3 Nov 1832, d 28 May 1859
Days, Frances A., w/o William A. Holmes & d/o George Days, b 9 Nov
    1835, d 6 Jan 1892
Jordan, Charles E., 1833-1916
Jordan, Marianne S., w/o Charles E. Jordan, 1834-1912
Jordan, Charles Davis, s/o Charles & Marianne S. Jordan, 1862-1863
Jordan, Lorenzo, 1808-1894
Jordan, Sarah B., w/o Lorenzo Jordan, 1808-1851
Dana, William H., b 29 July 1811, d 29 Aug 1884
Dana, Sophia T., w/o William H. Dana, b 23 Dec 1813, d 11 May 1892
Dana, George F., s/o William & Sophia Dana, b 20 Sept 1845, d 8 Sept
    1917
Dana, Lizzie A., 1836-1921
Ralph, Helen M., 1843-1921
Ralph, Dana A., 1890-1958
Ralph, Marion E., w/o Dana A. Ralph, 1890-1974

Kettell, George H., 1858-1936
Kettell, Edith D., w/o George H. Kettell, 1877-1956
Kettell, Orin E., s/o George & Edith Kettell, 1903-1955
Kettell, Arnold M., s/o George & Edith Kettell, 1916-1960
Kettell, Albert F., s/o George & Edith Kettell, 1898-1961
Allen, Charles J., 1854-1932
Allen, Ina I., w/o Charles J. Allen, 1859-1914
Allen, Ivan T., s/o Charles J. & Ina I. Allen, 1877-1902
Allen, Mrytle V., d/o Charles & Ina Allen, 1894-1918
Allen, Rowena C., d/o Charles & Ina Allen, 1890-1920
Allen, Charles B., 1884-1932
Landry, William J., 1885-1958
Landry, Ethel L., w/o William J. Landry, 1892-1934
Sartsaver, David N., 1954-1993
Landry, Joseph, 1854-1933
Forcier, Sophia, w/o Joseph Landry, 1860-1947
Tucker, Jennie L., 1859-1941
Dodge, Ann Carolyn Duke, d/o Stewart T. Dodge, b 9 Sept 1934, d 30
    March 1988
Dodge, Stuart T., 1905-1955
Dodge, Grover W., 1871-1957
Dodge, Ethelinda T., w/o Grover W. Dodge, 1873-1960
Tucker, Cornelius M., 1832-1903
Cobb, Mary L., w/o Cornelius M. Tucker, 1834-1923
Roberts, Robert A., 1927-1987
Roberts, Muriel M., w/o Robert A. Roberts, 1926-....
Paine, Caleb, d 1851 aged 79 yrs
Paine, Dorcas, d 1852 aged 71 yrs
Paine, Mary W., d 1825 aged 20 yrs
Paine, Senter, d 1826 aged 25 yrs
Sweetland, Mariette, d 18 Dec 1863 aged 63 yrs
Paine, Nathaniel M., d 1853 aged 1 mos
Paine, Anna Almira, d 1856 aged 5 yrs
Paine, John L., d 1856 aged 7 yrs
Paine, Susan L., d 1864 aged 22 yrs
Paine, Alfred M., d 1864 aged 14 yrs
Sweetland, Clark, d 11 Jan 1818 aged 60 yrs 11 mos
Sweetland, Elizabeth H., w/o Clark Sweetland, d 5 Dec 1798 aged 41 yrs
    1 mo 16 days
Sweetland, Hannah, d 12 May 1838 aged 61 yrs 9 mos

Sweetland, Clarinda, d 24 Aug 1863 aged 79 yrs

Sweetland, Elizabeth, d/o Clark & Elizabeth Sweetland, d 11 Oct 1790 aged 2 mos

Sweetland, Samuel, s/o Clark & Elizabeth Sweetland, d 13 March 1831 aged 50 yrs

Sweetland, Lina H., d/o Clark & Elizabeth Sweetland, d 27 Sept 1843 aged 46 yrs

Fuller, Celinda S., w/o Naaman Fuller, d 3 Jan 1857 aged 61 yrs 7 mos

Sweetland, Rowen, s/o Lieut. William & Sarah Sweetland, drowned 5 Aug 1811 aged 23 yrs

Sweetland, Arnold, s/o Lieut. Willaim & Sarah Sweetland, d 4 May 1782 aged 3 yrs

Sweetland, Charles, s/o Lieut. William & Sarah Sweetland, d 13 Oct 1789 aged 4 yrs

Sweetland, William, s/o Lieut. William & Sarah Sweetland, d 5 Oct 1866 aged 75 yrs

Sweetland, Sarah, d 30 June 1875 aged 81 yrs

Sweetland, Lucetta, d/o William & Sarah Sweetland, d 4 Aug 1864 aged 67 yrs

Moore, Deborah, w/o Comfort Moore & d/o William & Sarah Sweetland, d 1 April 1852 aged 73 yrs

Moore, Adaline, d/o Comfort & Deborah Moore, d 3 Dec 1860 aged 51 yrs

Sweetland, Lieut. William, d 9 JAn 1837 aged 82 yrs

Sweetland, Sarah, w/o Lieut. William Sweetland, (Broken)

Mowry, Daniel, d 31 May 1869 aged 62 yrs

Mowry, Almira H., w/o Daniel Mowry, d 1879 aged 76 yrs

Mowry, Daniel C., d.....

Mowry, Louisa C., w/o Daniel C. Mowry, d 16 Jan 1923 aged 52 yrs

Old North Burying Ground
Park & Washington Streets
North Attleborough, Massachusetts

Richards, Grace, d/o Nathan & Mehetable Richards, d 23 Dec 1799 aged 13 yrs

Richards, Calvin, d 10 Feb 1800 aged 37 yrs
Richards, Mehetable, w/o Nathan Richards, d 6 May 1785
Richards, Nathan, d 27 Sept 1798 aged 72 yrs
Clarke, Mehetable, d Oct 1769 aged 70 yrs
Clark, Jeremiah, d 6 Oct 1762
Everett, Mary, w/o Deacon Richard Everett, d 7 Jan 1782 aged 95 yrs
Everett, Sally, w/o Wilbur Everett, d 24 Sept 1789 aged 56 yrs
Caesar, Here lies the Best of Slaves, Now turning to Dust, Caesar the
    Ethiopean, Craves a place among the just. His faithful soul has fled to
    realms of Heavenly light, and by the Blood that Jesus shed, is changed
    from Black to White, d 15 Jan 1780 aged 77 yrs
Everett, Josiah, d 27 Oct 1893
Daggett, Mary, w/o Ebenezer Daggett, d 1 Dec 1772 aged 75 yrs
Daggett, Ebenezer, d Aug 1740
Daggett, Capt. Eliah, d 25 Jan 1808 aged 19 yrs
Daggett, Rebecca, 1709-1799
Daggett, Deacon John, d 7 Sept 1724 aged 63 yrs
Smith, Martha, w/o David Smith, d 6 May 1799 aged 58 yrs
Richardson, Royal, d 24 Nov 1797 aged 27 yrs
Swan, Ebenezer, d 30 March 1795 aged 67 yrs
Backinton, Sylvia, d/o William & Elizabeth Blackinton, d 3 March 1790
    aged 6 yrs
Guild, Ebenezer, d July 1816
Guild, Abigail, w/o Ebenezer Guild, d 20 Nov 17 (Can't read)
Butler, Mary, d/o Israel & Mary Butler, d 31 March 1730 aged 13 yrs
Ellis, Jesse, d 13 June 1863 aged 38 yrs
Whiting, Sybil, d/o Daniel & Patty Whiting, d 18 Jan 1818 aged 22 yrs
Stanley, Timothy, d 9 Oct 1776 aged 50 yrs
Stanley, Becca, w/o Timothy Stanley, d Nov (can't read)
Edwards, John,......
Maxcy, Abigail, ...
Maxcy, Abigail, d/o Lt. Josiah & Mary Maxcy, d July 1757 aged 19 yrs
Maxcy, Josiah, s/o Lt. Josiah & Mary Maxcy, d 23 Sept 1766 aged 8 yrs
Maxcy, Josiah, d 25 March 1772 aged 64 yrs
Maxcy, Sarah, w/o Benjamin Maxcy, d 19 April 1774 aged 32 yrs
Maxcy, Joseph, d 20 Oct 1757 aged 55 yrs
Maxcy, Alexander, d 2 April 1724 aged 26 yrs
Maxcy, Henry, d April 1771 aged 37 yrs
Maxcy, Hannah, d/o Josiah & Mary Maxcy, d 6 Jan 1751 aged 8 days
Maxcy, Joseph, d 31 Dec 1750 aged 5 yrs

Sweet, Naomi, w/o Ebenezer Sweet, d 22 June 1776 aged 33 yrs
Blackinton, George, d 28 March 1778 aged 59 yrs
Blackinton, Mary, w/o George Blackinton, d 9 May 1802 aged 50 yrs
Blackinton, Mary, w/o George Blackinton, d Feb 1809
Metcalf, Nathaniel, d 14 Jan 1798 aged 84 yrs
Metcalf, Ruth, w/o Nathaniel Metcalf, d 14 Jan 1796 aged 72 yrs
Blackinton, Chloe, w/o Othniel Blackinton, d 18 April 1825 aged 65 yrs
Blackinton, Patience, d 16 Nov 1744 aged 52 yrs
Blackinton, John, d 1805
Blackinton, Othniel, d 1804

Tufts, James C., d 14 April 1827 aged 27 yrs

Read, Chloe, w/o James C. Tufts & d/o Artemus & Betsey Staples, d 26 May 1827 aged 23 yrs

Tufts, Emeline A., d/o James & Chloe Tufts, d 21 July 1844 aged 22 yrs

Stanley, David T., b Sept 1801, d 3 Jan 1877

Stanley, Thomas, s/o David T. & Louisa Stanley, d Sept 1833 aged 3 yrs

Stanley, Jenckes, s/o Doct. Thomas & Mary Stanley, b 15 March 1797, d 7 May 1897

Stanley, Mary, w/o Thomas Stanley, BROKEN

Stanley, William, d 27 Jan 1806 aged 80 yrs

Stanley, Zilpha, w/o William Stanley, d 19 Oct 1807 aged 81 yrs

Price, Edward, d 4 Sept 1831

Stanley, Lieut. Amos, d 4 Jan 1810 aged 85 yrs

Stanley, Anna, w/o Lieut. Amos Stanley, d 27 Sept 1804 aged 74 yrs

Carpenter, Elizabeth, w/o John Carpenter, d 17 May 1788 aged 34 yrs

Pullen, James, d 16 Oct 1785 aged 68 yrs

Pullen, Lydia, w/o James Pullen, d 5 May 1805 aged 85 yrs

Daggett, Daniel, d 3 Dec 1796 aged 57 yrs

Daggett, Margaret, w/o Daniel Daggett, d 11 Aug 1829 aged 88 yrs

Daggett, Daniel, d 19 Aug 1838 aged 64 yrs

Daggett, Margaret, 2nd w/o Daniel Daggett, d 5 March 1828 aged 54 yrs

Daggett, Benjamin, d 11 Sept 1807 aged 44 yrs

Daggett, Polly, w/o Benjamin Daggett, d 16 March 1820 aged 52 yrs

Perry, Abigail, w/o Jacob Perry, d 20 July 1775 aged 75 yrs

Daggett, Ichabod, d 3 Sept 1780

Perry, Jacob, d 4 Nov 1810 aged 77 yrs

Perry, Freelove, d 14 Dec 1815 aged 91 yrs

Pullen, Job, s/o James & Phebe Pullen, d 31 Jan 1790

Price, Sarah Ann, d/o Edward & Sarah Price, d 8 July 1813 aged 11 yrs

Stanley, Zilphah, d 31 Jan 1816 aged 51 yrs

Stanely, Deacon Jonathan, d 5 May 1811 aged 70 yrs

Stanely, Hannah, w/o Dea. Jonathan Stanley, d 29 June 1808 aged 58 yrs
Stanely, Martha, w/o Dea. Jonathan Stanley, d 14 Aug 1770 aged 87 yrs
Kelly, William Roberts, s/o John & Mary J. Kelley, d 27 July 1840 aged
    20 yrs
Henry, Sally, d/o Benjamin Henry, b 28 Jan 1798, d 1 April 1836
Perry, Chloe, w/o Joseph Perry, d 23 Feb 1830 aged 60 yrs
Fuller, Darius, d 25 Dec 1862 aged 66 yrs
Fuller, Bebee, w/o Darius Fuller, d 19 Nov 1865 aged 77 yrs
Fuller, George Washington, s/o Darius & Bebee Fuller, b 4 July 1836, d
    13 Nov 1867
Fuller, Phebe Ann, d/o Darius & Bebee Fuller, d 11 Feb 1849 aged 23 yrs
Stanley, Anson, s/o Jesse & Bebee Stanley, d 1 Dec 1785 aged 2 yrs 1 mo
Town, Gideon, d 6 Oct 1802 aged 74 yrs
Town, Martha, w/o Gideon Town, d 5 Nov 1799 aged 76 yrs
Towne, Lucinda, w/o Abeshar Towne, d 10 April 1844 aged 76 yrs
Towne, Willard, b 25 Jan 1794, d 12 July 1830
Towne, Miranda, w/o Willard Towne, b 23 Oct 1766, d 10 Jan 1 (can't
    read)
Clark, Roseila, d 30 Sept 1887
Cushing, Charlotte Amanda, d/o Josiah & Mindwell Cushing, d 30 Jan
    1822 aged 3 yrs 7 mos
Robinson, Noah, d 30 June 1788 aged 31 yrs
Robinson, Lieut. Noah, d 27 Sept 1793 aged 89 yrs
Robinson, Deborah, w/o Zephariah Robinson, d 11 Feb 1778
Daggett, Polly, d 1820
Robinson, Henry, s/o Lt. Obed & Abigail Robinson, d 2 June 1799 aged 3
    yrs

St. Mary's Cemetery
Towne Street
North Attleborough, Massachusetts

Older section only

Bride, William Martin, 1849-1923
Bride, Annie M., w/o William Martin Bride, 1858-1928
Bride, Estelle Louise, 1885-1910

Murphy, M. Joseph, 1885-1911
Murphy, Elizabeth J., w/o M. Joseph Murphy, 1884-1936
Devlin, John, d 1915
Clarke, Mary, w/o John Devlin, d 1912
Roy, Omesime, b 18 April 1838, d 24 June 1911
Racette, Mary J., w/o Omesime Roy, b 18 Jan 1841, d....
Heon, Arthur E., 1886-1957
Doran, John, 1854-1940
Doran, Mary E., w/o John Doran, 1860-1937
Saart, Albert G., 1872-1930
Saart, Herman G., 1874-1951
Cassidy, Michael S., 1844-1922
Kenlin, Catherine, w/o Michael S. Cassidy, 1854-1932
Cassidy, Theresa V., 1884-1912
Cassidy, Gertrude M., 1894-1971
Doyle, Martin C., d 28 July 1908
Kelly, John, 1871-1933
McCarthy, Edwin E., 1884-....
McCarthy, Annie, w/o Edwin McCarthy, 1883-1954
Curtis, Owen, 1840-1912
Curtis, Mary E., w/o Owen Curtis, 1843-1913
Curtis, Owen Jr., s/o Owen & Mary Curtis, 1872-1936
Rubyck, Peter, s/o John & Sophie Rubyck, 1887-1909
Meeham, John F., 1871-1912
Meeham, Caroline, w/o John F. Meeham, 1873-1956
Poleski, Josephine, 1864-1916
Gallant, Tranquil, 1848-1913
Bourgeois, Marie, w/o Tranquil Gallant, 1853-1920
Gallant, Alice, 1877-1911
Rudolph, William, 1868-1955
Fischer, Matilda H., 1871-1951
Rudolph, William J., 1887-1910
Rudolph, Herman G., 1894-1921
Heon, Gideon, 1858-1912
Heon, Josephine A., w/o Gideon Heon, 1866-1941
Heintz, Alphonse, 1840-1898
Heintz, Stacia, w/o Alphonse Heintz, 1859-1941
Darrah, Catherine E., 1898-1945
Darrah, Vernon J., 1921-1952
Long, Elizabeth, 1873-1949

Johnson, Alice, 1903-1945
Beaulieu, Albion J., 1911-1946
Gaffney, Mabel C., 1892-1945
Armington, Arthur W.,.......
Brady, Edward T., 1873-1954
Murphy, Annie M., w/o Edward T. Brady, 1876-1951
Brady, Edward J., 1911-1980
O'Hare, Ruth, w/o Edward J. Brady, 1912-1990
Urbank, Rodney, 1942-1943
Brodeur, Eugene J., 1890-1958
Brodeur, Adrienne M. B., w/o Eugene J. Brodeur, 1888-1947
Tremblay, J. Frank, 1912-1959
Brodeur, Irene M., w/o J. Frank Tremblay, 1918-1994
Gervais, Albert J., 1880-1947
Beaulieu, Leda A., w/o Albert J. Gervais, 1881-1962
Boule, Arthur, 1885-1946
Boule, Leontine A., w/o Arthur Boule, 1887-....
Welch, Edmund T. Sr., D.M.D., 1900-1959
McMamus, Agnes V., w/o Edmund T. Welch Sr., 1898-1994
Diamond, Joseph E., 1894-1954
McManus, Anna M., w/o Joseph E. Diamond, 1896-1958
Murphy, Mabel L., 1901-1978
Shea, John P., 1869-1955
Riley, Mary L., w/o John P. Shea, 1874-1952
Guay, Omer T., 1877-1947
Labrie, Caroline, w/o Omer T. Guay, 1879-1954
Tobin, James R., d 1941
Tobin, Ozilda F., w/o James R. Tobin, d 1926
Kennedy, Mary, 1856-1938
Maguire, Hugh, 1887-1967
Maguire, Josephine, w/o Hugh Maguire, 1894-1973
Lamelin, Stanislas, 1877-1945
Lamelin, Odlie, w/o Stanislas Lamelin, 1880-1927
Nolan, Edward, 1867-1947
Nolan, C. Lillian, w/o Edward Nolan, 1890-1943
Nolan, Rita Jeannette, d/o Edward & C. Lillian Nolan, 1918-1928
Dowdall, James, 1860-1935
Dowdall, Mary Ann, w/o James Dowdall, 1850-1931
Collins, John, 1887-1984
Collins, Sarah A., w/o John Collins, 1886-1956

Collins, Joseph A., 1917-1928
McAvoy, Walter E., 1911-....
McAvoy, Mary G., w/o Walter E. McAvoy, 1909-1974
Conners, John, 1871-1956
Clancy, Annie L., w/o John Conners, 1875-1940
Conners, Catherine R., 1909-1984
Quinn, Patrick, 1870-1946
Murphy, Bridget, w/o Patrick Quinn, 1867-1944
Messier, Rudolph, 1895-1948
Quinn, Mary, w/o Rudolph Messier, 1894-1984
Roy, Phillip, d 31 March 1939
Gervais, Arthur, 1889-1934
Gervais, Eugene, 1894-1944
Gervais, Oliver, 1890-1956
Frost, Isaac W., 1858-1935
Murray, Louis C., d 14 Dec 1828
Tierney, Thomas, 1867-1931
Tierney, Bridget, w/o Thomas Tierney, 1866-1931
Tierney, Patrick Matthew, 1875-1944
Fontaine, Joseph D., 1879-1930
Fontaine, Albina, w/o Joseph D. Fontaine, 1880-1968
Kelly, Francis G., d 10 Jan 1931
Grey, Honora, w/o Francis G. Kelly, d 26 Dec 1931
Kelly, Winifred E., 1887-1969
Poirier, Ferdinand, 1856-1929
Poirier, Rosalie, w/o Ferdinand Poirier, 1855-1932
Brain, Susan, 1873-1952
King, Ovid M., 1886-1954
King, Caroline M., w/o Ovid M. King, 1884-1937
Gallant, Thomas C., 1847-1931
Smith, Julie, w/o Thomas C. Gallant, 1845-1933
Diamond, Adelaide A., 1889-1953
Diamond, Marie H., 1924-1976
O'Donnell, Francis J., Mass PVT 1 CL 302 Inf 76 Division, d 11 Jan 1942
Liebecki, Edward, 1874-1930
desJardins, Edward J., 1894-1930
desJardins, Marie L., w/o Edward J. desJardins, 1893-1986
desJardins, T. Robert, s/o Edward & Marie L. desJardins, 1924-1987
Walsh, Joseph F., 1892-1951
Reynolds, Irene M., w/o Joseph F. Walsh, 1894-1937

Walsh, Rosemarie Anne, 1931-1933
Fitzgerald, Patrick H., 1889-1942
Cox, Gertrude, w/o Patrick H. Fitzgerald, 1887-1982
Fiztgerald, Robert E., s/o Patrick & Gertrude Fiztgerald, 1920-1966
Burnham, Frank, 1885-1964
Fitzgerald, Mary, w/o Frank Burnham, 1891-1964
Jones, Alice M., w/o Thomas C. Norton, 1868-1931
Norton, Thomas C., 1850-1922
Dargis, Henry, 1903-1931
Wain, Donald J., 1939-1941
Wain, Charles B., 1907-1982
Alix, Blanche A., 1904-1989
Armille, Rocco, 1877-1942
Armille, Francesca, w/o Rocco Armille, 1876-1969
Hess, Monica, 1868-1948
Reisch, Frank, 1853-1931
Hess, Otto, 1891-1963
Reisch, Mary, w/o Otto Hess, 1888-1972
Gendron, Rosalie, d 21 Nov 1931
Gendron, Edgar J., d 1 March 1960
Lecours, Joseph, 1868-1930
Chabot, Sara, w/o Joseph Lecours, 1867-1941
Brown, Alden D., b 25 Jan 1911, d 1 March 1988
Devlin, Elsie V., w/o Alden D. Brown, b 6 July 1912, d 13 Oct 1986
McGovern, Thomas Jones, Mass Pharm. Mate, 1 CL USNRF, d 13 Nov
    1930
Blanchard, Joseph A., 1867-1929
Poirier, Henrietta, w/o Joseph A. Blanchard, 1869-1945
Beaulieu, Joseph, 1869-1949
Chabot, Constant, w/o Joseph Beaulieu, 1871-1929
Belhamer, David, d 1930
Belhamer, Esther F., w/o David Belhamer, d 1951
Roy, Emma, w/o Eugene Roy, b 10 May 1864, d 20 Dec 1911
Hyland, Margaret A., d 1948
Chabot, Louis, 1858-1919
Gagnon, Theose, w/o Louis Chabot, 1864-1923
Crossey, Michael, 1837-1919
Brown, Mary F., w/o Michael Crossey, 1844-1924
Gaffey, Ann, 1839-1910
Abbott, John Frances, 1881-1911

Abbott, Mary E., 1858-1913
Peckham, James,.....
Peckham, Catherine, w/o James Peckham, b 31 Aug 1861, d 16 July 1909
Weatherbee, Arthur, 1861-1934
Weatherbee, Catherine, w/o Arthur Weathebee, 1862-1909
Weatherbee, Frank, 1886-1940
McNulty, Jennie, w/o Frank Weatherbee, 1886-1938
Graham, Jennie, w/o Herman R. Holzner, d 7 May 1950
Byrnes, Mary K., d 1945
Sheals, Joseph, d 1960
Toner, Arthur B., 1890-1949
Emerson, Gertrude M. Toner, 1892-1976
Toner, James V., 1888-1951
Zilch, Mary A., w/o James V. Toner, 1892-1986
Thompson, Arthur F., 1889-19..
Flynn, Mary A., w/o Arthur F. Thompson, 1890-1945
McKenna, Dominic, 1896-1960
Flynn, Florence J., w/o Dominic McKenna, 1894-19..
Ryan, Francis M., 1873-1945
Legrade, Arthur E., 1883-1945
Legrade, Lillian A., w/o Arthur E. Legrade, 1887-1958
Eider, Florence A., 1881-1975
Palmer, Josephine E., 1879-1955
Eider, Edward H., 1883-1964
Smith, John J., 1870-1947
Smith, Bridget, w/o John J. Smith, d 1944
Smith, John J., 1912-1977
Sullivan, John F., 1882-1960
Wells, Ada R., w/o John F. Sullivan, 1887-1976
Sullivan, John F. Jr., s/o John F. & Ada R. Sullivan, 1920-1990
Smith, Patrick J., 1875-1963
Connelly, Roseanna, w/o Patrick J. Smith, 1875-1945
Meeham, James, d 15 Jan 1942
Meeham, Delia T., w/o James Meeham, d 2 March 1945
Smith, Francis, 1913-1989
Precourt, Omer A., 1879-1942
Perron, Olivine M., w/o Omer A. Precourt, 1880-1964
Valincourt, Theo, 1885-1943
Roy, Theodore, 1878-1943
Lafayette, Julie, w/o Theodore Roy, 1882-1973

O'Brien, Edward, 1877-1958
O'Brien, Mary, w/o Edward O'Brien, 1872-1954
Gagne, Elzear, 1871-1953
Gagne, Philomine, w/o Elzear Gagne, 1862-1925
Miner, John, 1849-1922
Miner, Adeline B., w/o John Miner, 1856-1930
Miner, Henry, 1875-1933
Murphy, Michael, 1844-1916
Wolfe, Bridget, w/o Michael Murphy, 1843-1915
Murphy, Edward F., 1880-1946
Miller, Elizabeth Murphy, 1883-1957
Sweeney, Samuel J., 1873-1916
Sweeney, Maria T., w/o Samuel Sweeney,....
Ronhoch, Anna, w/o Yves Ronhoch, 1867-1919
Chabot, Basile, 1831-1915
Lapointe, Sara, w/o Basile Chabot, 1843-1924
Chabot, Francois L., 1875-1952
Chabot, Amanda J., w/o Francois L. Chabot, 1883-1949
Hall, William, 1854-1936
Hall, Melina, w/o William Hall, 1856-1940
Hall, Henry, 1888-1916
Hall, Annie, 1890-1922
Withers, William T., 1883-1903
Coleman, Annie T., 1877-1915
Germani, Anduino, 1887-1956
Germani, Maria, w/o Anduino Germani, 1892-1915
Conefy, John T., 1857-1921
Bride, Mary E., w/o John T. Conefy,....
Leary, Michael L., 1866-1921
Doyle, Mary J., w/o Michael J. Leary, 1869-1949
Leary, Anne I., d 1954
Murphy, Vincent T., d 1962
Leary, Edna M., w/o Vincent T. Murphy, d 1963
Brennam, Mary, w/o Peter Brenman, 1859-1934
Brenman, Eugene P., s/o Peter & Mary Brenman, 1888-1918
Brenman, Joseph W., 1884-1987
Flynn, John H., 1850-1925
McLoughlin, Mary Ann, w/o John H. Flynn, 1856-1942
Flynn, James F., 1876-1950
Dunn, Christopher M., 1873-1951

Flynn, Mary Louise, w/o Christopher M. Dunn, 1880-1957
Dyer, Mary A., 1837-1924
Dyer, Joseph A., 1876-1905
Dyer, Mathilda O., 1869-1941
Beaulieu, Xavier, b 8 Aug 1874, d 1925
Roy, Adelatine, w/o Xavier Beaulieu, b 17 June 1874, d 28 June 1911
Feed, David R., 1889-1918
Ellis, John D., A member of NY Buglar 21 US Ing, d 11 Ovt 1926
Leary, John H., 1870-1929
Leary, Theresa, w/o John H. Leary, 1876-1960
Leary, James B., 1941-1943
Toner, Arthur, 1857-1914
Toner, Annie, w/o Arthur Toner, 1862-1929
Toner, Louis J., 1894-1921
Toner, Frank P., 1884-1936
Toner, Lt. Robert F., 1915-1943
Reynolds, Mildred A., 1911-1916
Gerba, Valentine, 1855-1928
Chase, Doris M., 1916-1958
Reynolds, James P., 1885-1962
Reynolds, Maria L., 1889-1972
Devlin, Jane L., d 1963
Devlin, Margaret Joyce, d 1942
Chabot, Pierre, 1864-1913
Supremant, Maria, w/o Pierre Chabot, 1865-1939
Chabot, Joseph E., 1892-1967
Andrews, James, 1862-1911
Carr, Mary, w/o James Andrews, 1861-1941
Andrews, James R., 1928-1974
Andrews, James T., (Bubbles the Clown), 1901-1972
Marshall, William, 1858-1930
Quinlon, Stasia, w/o William Marshall, 1859-1940
Renner, John, 1865-1914
Renner, Ellen, w/o John Renner, 1862-1951
Renner, Herbert L., 1896-1976
Feid, Anthony, 1868-1914
Ryan, Isabelle, w/o Anthony Fied, 1868-1960
Fied, Walter A., 1897-1978
Taft, Isabelle F., 1903-1989

Simpson, Peggy, w/o James Simpson, d 31 Jan 1816 aged 43 yrs
Bugbee, Samuel, d 23 Feb 1818 aged 64 yrs
Bugbee, Eunice, w/o Samuel Bugbee, d Sept 1781 AE 23 yrs
Bugbee, Betsey, w/o Samuel Bugbee, d 9 Dec 1821 AE 76 yrs
Shepard, Tryphena, w/o Jonathan Shepard, d 12 April 1815 AE 67 yrs
Shepard, Daniel, s/o Jonathan & Tryphena Shepard, d 22 Oct 1793 AE 9
    yrs
Blake, Rachel, d 22 Aug 1833 aged 87 yrs
Blake, Ebenezer, d 12 Sept 1819 AE 89 yrs
Blake, Polly, w/o Luther Clake, d 7 Oct 1851 aged 72 yrs
Cleale, Joseph, d May 1802 AE 38 yrs
Auty, Rachel H., d/o George & Sarah Auty, d 13 March 1869 aged 24 yrs
Auty, Mary V., w/o William Barington, 1840-1912
Auty, George, b 30 Aug 1809, d 6 June 1868 New Orleans
Auty, Sarah, w/o George Auty, 1816-1897
Knight, David B., b 9 April 1837, d 23 April 1889
Auty, Sarah E., w/o David B. Knight, b 9 Feb 1843, d March 1920
Monet, Robert, d 10 Oct 1875 aged 54 yrs, A native of Paisley, Scotland
Simpson, John, d 1 May 1809 aged 37 yrs
Coan, Shubel, s/o Benjamin & Lucy Coan, d 13 March 1829 aged 27 yrs
Coan, Peter, d 15 Dec 1869 aged 67 yrs
Hartshorn, Jeremiah, d 15 Dec 1849 aged 88 yrs
Hartshorn, Rebeckah, w/o Jeremiah Hartshorn, d 5 April 1830 aged 68 yrs
Hartshorn, Eunice, d/o Jeremiah & Rebeckah Hartshorn, d 1 Sept 1819
    aged 37 yrs
Hartshorn, Jeremiah, b 8 Aug 1784, d 29 June 1852
Hartshorn, Masadiah, w/o Jeremiah Hartshorn, b 14 July 1785, d 5 July
    1852
Cobb, Jesse, d 1827

Cobb, Caroline M., w/o Captain Artemas L. Cooper, b 28 Oct 1809, d 5 Feb 1855

Cooper, Sarah J., d/o Captain Artemas & Caroline Cooper, b 4 Dec 1841, d 5 July 1847

Cooper, William, s/o Captain Artemas & Caroline Cooper, b 1836, d 13 July (can't read)

Barrow, Lucy M., w/o Michael D. Barrow, d 28 Jan 1869 aged 51 yrs

Barrow, Harriet, d/o Michael & Lucy Barrow, d 28 Aug 1849 aged 8 mos

Barrow, Frances Gardner, s/o Michael & Lucy Barrow, d 18 Aug 1853 aged 14 mos

George, Capt. Lewis, d 11 June 1834 aged 44 yrs

George, Nancy, w/o Capt. Lewis George, d 11 Sept 1839 aged 45 yrs

Pettee, William C., b 18 Sept 1810, d 29 Dec 1891

Cobb, Sarah Eddy, w/o William C. Pettee, b 28 July 1812, d 2 May 1902

Cobb, John Jr., d 7 May 1816 aged 48 yrs

Cobb, Dudania, w/o John Cobb Jr., d 12 Oct 1846 aged 71 yrs

Cobb, John T., s/o John & Dudania Cobb, d 26 May 1818

Cobb, Zuba A., d/o John & Dudania Cobb, d 27 July 1816 aged 11 yrs

Cobb, John, d 14 Oct 1822 aged 88 yrs

Cobb, Hildah, w/o John Cobb, d 29 Dec 1816 aged 77 yrs

Grant, Elizabeth, d/o Jedson & Abigail Grant, d 10 July 1832 aged 7 yrs

Cobb, Henry W., s/o James & Lymtha Cobb, d 30 Oct 1832 aged 31 yrs

Miller, John, d 31 March 1830 aged 26 yrs

Miller, John, d 27 May 1857 aged 79 yrs

Miller, Nancy, w/o John N. Miller, d 16 Oct 1865 aged 84 yrs

Wilder, Frank W., b 17 Nov 1856, d 30 May 1898

Blake, Ezra, d 13 May 1866 aged 85 yrs 7 mos 3 days

Blake, Lowell P., 1815-1895

Blake, Betsey Y., w/o Lowell P. Blake, 1813-1901

Pond, Jabez E., 1799-1880

Porter, Elizabeth, w/o Jabez E. Pond, 1804-1862

Pond, William E., s/o Jabez & Elizabeth Pond, 1826-1904

Warren, Mary, w/o William E. Pond, 1832-1879

Pond, Mary Ellis, d/o William & Mary Pond & w/o Charles S. McCoy, 1865-1914

Rawcliffe, John, 1815-1883

Sharp, Mary, w/o John Rawcliffe, 1820-1884

Sharp, John, s/o Joesph & Mary Sharp, d 1 Sept 1852 aged 23 yrs 11 mos 26 days

Crossley, John, d 8 April 1878 aged 76 yrs

Belcher, Susnnah, w/o John Crossely, 1802-1903
Bartlett, Newell R., 1888-1942
Bartlett, Johanna, 1888-1968
Berry, Inez Patton, 1881-1940
Larson, John E., 1881-1965
Larson, M. Christine, w/o John E. Larson, 1880-1963
Orris, William, 1859-1940
Orris, Jennie, w/o William Orris, 1858-1934
Mitchell, Helenus S., 1868-1928
Carlson, Hermon, 1851-1920
Carlson, Tekia, w/o Hermon Carlson, 1853-1920
White, Eli E., d 11 Nov 1855 aged 30 yrs
Hill, Seth R., b 4 Oct 1828, d 9 Oct 1895
Hill, Abaline C., w/o Seth R. Hill, b 9 Dec 1823, d 29 June 1900
Cobb, Jennie O., w/o W. P. Cobb, b 17 April 1878, d 27 March 1908
Cobb, Martin D., b 17 May 1831, d 4 Jan 1910
Cobb, Elizabeth H., w/o Martin D. Cobb, b 23 Oct 1828, d 22 May 1890
Atkinson, George, d 23 Oct 1885 aged 66 yrs
Atkinson, Irena A., w/o George Atkinson, d 24 Aug 1914 aged 86 yrs
Atkinson, William C., s/o George & Irena A. Atkinson, d 21 July 1882
    aged 14 yrs
Hilton, Elmira F., w/o John J. Hilton, d 3 Feb 1865 aged 30 yrs 9 mos
Keith, Emma Isabel, d/o George W. & Mary A. Keith, d 10 May 1865
    aged 16 yrs 2 mos 20 days
Shepard, Benjamin, 1746-1839
Shepard, Susanna, w/o Benjamin Shepard, 1745-1835
Shepard, Oliver, 1787-1814
Shepard, Benjamin, 1775-1849
Shepard, Polly, w/o Benjamin Shepard, 1775-1837
Shepard, Charles, 1804-1825
Shepard, Benjamin, b 6 June 1801, d 3 April 1892
Shepard, Mary Ann, w/o Benjamin Shepard, b 5 Dec 1801, d 25 Dec 1879
Boutelle, Rev. Thomas, b 1 Feb 1805, d 28 Nov 1866
Shepard, Mary E., w/o Rev. Thomas Boutelle, b 7 Oct 1806, d 27 Sept
    1866
Laier, Carl, 1861-1918
Laier, Anna M., w/o Carl Laier, 1866-1956
Hill, Frank E., 1865-1944
Hill, Anna w/o Frank E. Hill, 1873-1951
Ellis, Henry, 1860-1940

Ellis, Lena, w/o Henry Ellis, 1867-1926
Blake, Erwin L., 1856-1944
Beebe, Flora M., w/o Erwin L. Blake, 1855-1940
Blake, Franklin Nelson, b 11 June 1853, d 9 Dec 1929
Blake, Mary Emma, w/o Franklin Nelson Blake, b 14 July 1856, d 25 Aug 1919
Blake, Corp. Ezra Nelson, d 12 Sept 1862 from wounds received at the Battle of Bull Run, 30 Aug 1862 aged 39 yrs
Blake, Rhoda T., w/o Corp. Ezra Nelson Blake, b 16 Oct 1832, d 4 March 1860
Wilson, Homer, 1864-1950
Ainsworth, Edith, w/o Homer Wilson, 1873-1939
Reid, Thomas, d 3 Feb 1862 aged 53 yrs
Kenyon, Ralph, d 1889
Kenyon, Susannah, w/o Ralph Kenyon, d 11 May 1862 aged 26 yrs
Prineer, Ellen, w/o James Prineer, d 5 April 1861 aged 20 yrs 6 mos
Leland, Eunice, w/o Timothy Hancock, b 5 Aug 1817, d 22 Sept 1867
Hancock, John, d 13 Feb 1842 aged 32 yrs
White, Susan, w/o Lysander White, d 21 Nov 1864 aged 61 yrs
White, Rufus, d 20 Aug 1865 aged 87 yrs
White, Betsey, w/o Rufus White, d 14 Dec 1867 aged 95 yrs
White, Stillman, d 29 Aug 1831 aged 26 yrs
Starkey, Hartford, 1788-1841
Fisher, Fannie B., w/o Hartford Starkey, 1794-1856
Starkey, Thomas, d 8 Oct 1845 aged 86 yrs
Starkey, Irene, w/o Thomas Starkey, d 26 Sept 1836 aged 75 yrs
White, Rufus, b 31 Aug 1796, d 24 April 1876
White, Marcy, w/o Rufus White, b 12 Aug 1794, d 22 Dec 1886
Tucker, Benjamin R., adopted s/o Rufus & Marcy White, b 27 Oct 1837, d 27 July 1879
Starkey, Willard T., d 21 May 1882 aged 82 yrs 5 mos
Starkey, Amelia S., w/o Willard T. Starkey, d 12 Jan 1879 aged 75 yrs
Hancock, Henry, d 1 April 1810 aged 70 yrs
Hancock, Esther, w/o Henry Hancock, d 20 Feb 1841 aged 92 yrs
Hancock, Timothy, b 28 May 1785, d 22 Dec 1872
Hancock, Abbey, w/o Timothy Hancock, b 20 April 1787, d 11 Sept 1826
Hancock, Sarah, w/o Timothy Hancock, b 24 Sept 1795, d 19 Feb 1872
Grant, Sarah, w/o Abel Grant, d 29 June 1822 aged 59 yrs
Hancock, Harriet N., b 4 Nov 1829, d 1 July 1884
Hancock, Timothy E., b 10 April 1814, d 28 Aug 1895

Hancock, Timothy E., b 10 April 1814, d 28 Aug 1895

Hancock, Harriet P., w/o Timothy E. Hancock, b 2 Nov 1816, d 8 Feb 1846

Hancock, Dorcas P., w/o Timothy Hancock, b 22 Oct 1821, d 22 Jan 1883

Shepard, Hephzibah, w/o Benjamin Shepard, d 26 Aug 1804 aged 88 yrs

Hancock, George L., b 11 May 1819, d 19 Oct 1902

Hancock, Ellen E., w/o George L. Hancock, b 29 Oct 1845, d 18 Feb 1895

Blake, Ezra, d 25 May 1838 aged 91 yrs

Blake, Abigail, w/o Ezra Blake, d 16 Nov 1783 aged 34 yrs

Blake, Melatiah, w/o Ezra Blake, d 23 Sept 1840 aged 87 yrs

Blake, Brainard, s/o Ezra & Melatiah Blake, d 11 March 1814

Barron, William, s/o Nicholas & Bathsheba Barrow, d 22 Nov 1785 AE 4 yrs

Cobb, Sarah, w/o John Cobb, d 20 April 1807 AE 96 yrs

Cobb, John, d 21 Nov 1777 AE 71 yrs

Cobb, Ebenezer, d 13 June 1807 AE 58 yrs

George, Jerusha, w/o John George, d 1831

George, John, d 12 Jan 1804 AE 90 yrs

George, Sarah, w/o John George, d 8 Jan 1789 AE 34 yrs

Messenger, Sweetser, d 21 Oct 1807 AE 74 yrs

Messenger, Elizabeth, w/o Sweetser Messenger, d 3 June 1811

Messinger, Polly, w/o Capt. George Messinger, d 2 April 1844 aged 71 yrs

South Burial Ground
W. Bacon Street
Plainville, Massachusetts

Guild, Joseph, b 5 Oct 1751, d 8 Oct 1828

Guild, Sarah, w/o Joseph Guild, b 3 June 1756, d 22 May 1849

White, Martin B. S., d 13 Dec 1851 aged 27 yrs

Richardson, Sophia W., d 23 Jan 1862 aged 65 yrs

Richardson, Comfort, w/o Royal Richardson, d 6 March 1852 aged 32 yrs

Everett, William, d 7 March 1824 aged 71 yrs

Everett, Jesse, elder s/o William & Sally Richard Everett, b 25 Aug 1770, d 20 June 1835

Sprague, Deacon John, d 13 May 1813 aged 80 yrs

Sprague, Mary, w/o Deacon John Sprague, d 2 March 1816 aged 79 yrs

Blackinton, Willard Day, 1800-1847

Baker, Keziah A., w/o Willard Day Blackinton, 1806-1886

Blackinton, Deacon Joel, d 8 Dec 1836 aged 75 yrs

Blackinton, Sarah, w/o Deacon Joel Blackinton, d 22 Dec 1833 aged 69 yrs

Cheever, Abigail, w/o George Cheever, d 15 March 1823 aged 36 yrs

Cheever, George, d 24 May 1826 aged 54 yrs

Cheever, Sally, w/o George Cheever, d 19 Feb 1816 aged 37 yrs

Blackinton, Molly, d 17 May 1808 aged 6 yrs

Maxcy, Nabby, w/o Henry Maxcy, d 26 Dec 1807 aged 25 yrs

Blackinton, Samuel, d 14 March 1815 aged 62 yrs

Blackinton, Mehitable, w/o Samuel Blackinton, d 14 July 1828 aged 73 yrs

Blackinton, George, d 1 April 1826 aged 82 yrs

Blackinton, Judith, w/o George Blackinton, b 20 Feb 1767, d 16 Nov 1853

Fairbanks, Alice, b 8 May 1775, d 18 Aug 1855

Blackinton, Cyrus, d 1 May 1851 aged 73 yrs

Blackinton, Philadelphia, w/o Cyrus Blackinton, d 27 Sept 1828 aged 40 yrs

Blackinton, John W., s/o Cyrus & Philadelphia Blackinton, d 9 Feb 1808 AE 7 weeks 3 days

Blackinton, Charles A., d 4 Jan 1873 aged 67 yrs 11 mos

Cabot, Betsey, w/o Charles A.Blackinton & d/o William & Elizabeth Cabot, d 18 Sept 1835 aged 33 yrs

Slack, Benjamin, d 1 Jan 1846 aged 51 yrs

Aldrich, Mary, w/o Benjamin Slack, d 10 Aug 1886 aged 70 yrs 10 mos

Slack, Vashti E., w/o Benjamin Slack, d 11 Oct 1828 AE 30 yrs

Walcott, Hannah, d/o Pentecast & Hannah Wallcott, d 18 July 1830 aged 58 yrs 2 mos

Riley, William....

Riley, Mary, w/o William Riley, b 19 March 1781, d 4 Dec 1859

Walcott, Moses, d 9 March 1810 aged 65 yrs

Bugbee, James R., 1817-1906

Phillips, Amanda, w/o James R. Bugbee, b 15 Aug 1821, d 27 June 1847

Bugbee, Lucy Ann, w/o James R. Bugbee, b 29 April 1855, d 6 Aug 1855

Bugbee, Chester, d 16 Nov 1876 aged 90 yrs

Blake, Jerusha, w/o Chester Bugbee, b 14 May 1788, d 5 Jan 1825

Bugbee, Lucretia, w/o Chester Bugbee, b 27 Aug 1795, d 25 Aug 1836

Bugbee, Nancy, w/o Chester Bugbee, b 7 Jan 1803, d 27 July 1869

Robinson, Ursula B., d 4 Aug 1819 aged 30 yrs

Fuller, Mary, d 26 Dec 1861 aged 84 yrs

Cabot, William, d 17 July 1832 aged 57 yrs

Cabot, Elizabeth, w/o William Cabot, d 22 Feb 1810 aged 46 yrs

Fuller, Stephen, b 18 Dec 1754, d 22 Feb 1832

Maxcy, Mary, w/o Stephen Fuller, b 30 March 1753, d 10 March 1817

Fuller, Maxcy, s/o Stephen & Mary Fuller, b 20 April 1790, d....

Richardson, James, d 2 Sept 1843 aged 70 yrs

Richardson, Anna, w/o James Richardson, d 19 Oct 1861 aged 77 yrs 8
mos 11 days

Gage, Mary A., w/o Joseph Gage, d 20 July 1858 aged 30 yrs

Whittmore, Jesse, d 24 Sept 1850 aged 84 yrs

Cook, Nancy Clark, d/o Onesimes & Lydia Cook, d 10 Jan 1818 aged 3
yrs

Fletcher, Rev. Daniel L., d 16 Sept 1842 aged 42 yrs 25 days

Hatch, George D., d 24 July 1879 aged 63 yrs 3 mos 29 days

Hatch, Deborah, w/o George D. Hatch, d 4 Jan 1872

Hatch, Israel, d 18 Dec 1875

Hatch, Mary G., w/o Isreal Hatch, d 28 Dec 1875 aged 85 yrs 10 mos

Hatch, Sarah Jane, b 10 Oct 1828, d 5 July 1868

Hatch, Israel A., 1818-1897

Maguire, Margaret M., w/o Israel A. Hatch, 1822-1895

Hatch, Thomas C., 1844-1865

Huestin, Fanny M., d/o Clark & Fanny M. Huestin, d 23 Nov 1878 aged
39 yrs

Pierce, Washington, 1782-1860

Pierce, Fanny, w/o Washington Pierce, 1786-1879

Pierce, Edwin H., b 30 May 1825, d 16 Dec 1885

Jewett, Sarah, 1769-1862

Jewett, Nancy, 1790-1868

Jewett, Ephraim, 1800-1800

Hines, Charles A., 1830-1854

Jewett, Susan A., 1830-1901

Hine, Freddie A., 1853-1854

Jewett, Ellena M., 1855-1872

Jewett, Frances E., 1857-1874

Hayward, Capt. Abraham, d 11 Aug 1872 aged 82 yrs 3 mos 1 day

Hayward, Marietta, w/o Capt. Abraham Hayward, d 31 Dec 1846 aged 51
yrs 9 mos

Dennett, Salle, d 9 Sept 1875 aged 84 yrs 7 mos 30 days

Magill, James, s/o Francis & Sally Magill, d 15 Oct 18 (Broken)

Magill, Francis, s/o Francis & Sally Magill, d 10 Oct 1841

McPherson, Daniel, b 17 Oct 1790, d 23 March 1873

McPherson, Sarah, w/o Daniel McPherson, d 31 July 1850 aged 63 yrs

McPherson, Sarah, d/o Daniel & Sarah McPherson, d 11 May 1827

McPherson, Lucy, d/o Daniel & Sarah McPherson, d 17 May 1827 aged 5 yrs

Everett, Erastus D., d 28 Feb 1881 aged 70 yrs

Shepard, Mercy, w/o Erastus Everett & d/o Ebenezer Daggett, b 14 Jan 1811 Attleboro, MA, d 23 Nov 1843 Boston, MA

Everett, Sarah L., w/o Erastus D. Everett & d/o Capt. Thomas Holden of Warwick Neck, RI, b 22 Aug 1816, d 1 May 1853 Sommerville, MA

Everett, Charles J., s/o Silas & Tryphena Everett, d 15 Nov 1838 aged 26 yrs

Everett, Deacon Silas, d 21 Dec 1845 aged 67 yrs

Shepard, Tryphena, w/o Deacon Silas Everett, b 4 May 1775 Wrentham, MA, d 22 Sept 1865

Everett, Harriet N., d/o Deacon Silas & Tryphena Everett, d 6 Oct 1843 aged 24 yrs

Everett, William, b 3 July 1797, d 3 May 1844

Peabody, Esther G., w/o William Everett, b 29 Aug 1797 Union, Maine, d 26 Oct 1875

Everett, Charles Edwin, s/o William & Esther Everett, b 29 June 1833, d 26 Aug 1838

Everett, George Homer, s/o William & Esther Everett, b 8 Dec 1836, d 20 Aug 1879

Everett, Mary, w/o Johnson Tolman, d 1839 Philadelphia, PA

Everett, William Henry, b 16 May 1831, d 26 Sept 1892

Everett, Emeline, b 25 Oct 1826, d 24 June 1882

Everett, Malinda Rebecca, b 6 May 1825, d 14 Dec 1869

Fisher, Ellis, d 30 Dec 1844 aged 53 yrs

Fisher, Hannah, w/o Ellis Fisher, d 28 Oct 1861 aged 68 yrs

Cargill, Benjamin, d 11 March 1876 aged 85 yrs

Cargill, Almira P., w/o Benjamin Cargill, b 2 July 1811, d 21 Feb 1886

Cargill, Mary Ann, w/o Benjamin Cargill, d 10 Jan 1847 aged 42 yrs

Cargill, George C., d 12 Jan 1869 aged 38 yrs 11 mos 15 days

Cargill, Calista L., w/o George C. Cargill, d 18 July 1872 aged 41 yrs 9 mos

Cheever, George Whitefield, 1803-1891

Cheever, George Whitefield, 1803-1891
Warren, Thais Davis, w/o George Whitefield Cheever, 1803-1891
Blackinton, Ellis, b 8 March 1783, d 20 May 1870
Blackinton, Mary, w/o Ellis Blackinton, b 17 Feb 1787, d 10 Feb 1859
Fuller, John, d 17 May 1843 aged 57 yrs
Fuller, Nancy, w/o John Fuller, d 26 Nov 1861 aged 77 yrs 6 mos
Horr, George W., d 20 June 1828
Everett, Joel, 1791-1876
Everett, Hannah, w/o Joel Everett, b 2 Feb 1793, d 6 July 1853
Blackinton, Allen A., d 21 Feb 1881 aged 47 yrs
Blackinton, Emeline, b Oct 1807, d 14 Jan 1905
Blackinton, Wilson, b 4 May 1810, d 1884
Cheever, John P., b 15 May 1797, d 2 July 1879
Walcott, Capt. William, d 28 July 1825
Tifft, Albert C., b 31 May 1811, d 31 March 1866
Tifft, Catherine, w/o Albert C. Tifft, b 25 Jan 1810, d 1 June 1862
Tifft, John, s/o Samuel & Mary Tifft, b 10 Sept 1800, d 29 June 1851
Blackinton, Azubah, w/o John Tifft, b 15 Dec 1807, d 9 May 1832
Tifft, Mary Ann, d/o Leonard & Charity Tifft, b 8 Oct 1825, d 12 Aug
    1818
Tifft, Samuel, b 4 May 1770, d 25 Nov 1855
Tifft, Nancy, w/o Samuel Tifft, b 24 March 1770, d 27 Sept 1849
Tifft, Leonard, s/o Samuel & Nancy Tifft, b 13 Aug 1798, d 18 May 1826
Tifft, Mary Ann, d/o Samuel & Nancy Tifft, b 5 April 1807, d 18 March
    1809
Warren, Harriet B., d 30 Dec (too far in ground to read)
Warren, Gardner.....
Fletcher, Rebecca, w/o Joseph Warren, d 26 Nov 1861

Plainville Cemetery
W. Bacon Street
Plainville, Massachusetts

King, Walter H., 1875-1950
King, Jesse E., w/o Walter H. King, 1879-1940
King, Henry C., 1903-1918

Smith, Martha, 1834-1925
Cheever, Frederick I., 1862-1937
Smiley, Catherine, w/o Frederick I. Smith, 1863-1929
Blanchard, William E., 1868-1947
Blanchard, Lillian E., w/o William E. Blanchard, 1865-1944
Blanchard, Leroy E., s/o William & Lillian Blanchard, 1889-1918
Blanchard, Russell, 1891-1923
Staples, Fannie I., 1857-1937
Staples, Annie J., 1862-1950
Abercrombie, Ralph W., 1862-1904
Staples, Isabel, w/o Ralph W. Abercrombie, 1860-1941
Grennell, Edgar G., 1864-1941
Staples, Minnie M., w/o Edgar G. Grennell, 1866-1959
Morrow, Nellie E., w/o George K. Morrow, 1870-1923
Shannan, James H., b 16 Nov 1855, d 10 Feb 1917
Shannon, Albert B., b 22 Feb 1867, d 16 June 1953
Balcom, Walter F., 1885-1920
Balcom, Marion W., w/o Walter F. Balcom, 1891-1973
Balcom, Ruth J., d/o Walter & Marion Balcom, 1919-1920
Bowder, John H., 1863-1927
Eaton, Ida M., w/o John H. Bowder, 1867-1922
Wood, Charles H., 1836-1922
Wood, Mary E., w/o Charles H. Wood, 1841-1920
Wood, Wallace E., 1878-1929
King, Annie Wood, 1864-1949
Johnston, Louise King, 1888-1931
Hartman, Frederick, 1865-1924
Hartman, Theresa M., w/o Frederick Hartman, 1867-1956
Chase, Gilson E., 1849-1933
Chase, Martha J., w/o Gilson E. Chase, 1859-1936
Gamble, Fred K., 1871-1926
Lord, Sarah O., w/o Fred K. Gamble, 1873-1925
Smith, Edwin W., 1891-1961
Jones, Edna M., w/o Edwin W. Smith, 1859-1931
Lawton, Eldon E., 1877-1940
Gilmore, Minerva Lawton, 1896-1985
Jones, Rev. Alfred W., 1891-1969
Maxcy, Virgil W., 1852-1934
Blake, Adalina, w/o Virgil W. Maxcy, 1857-1941
Maxcy, Ella E., 1883-1974

Blakney, David H., b 12 Feb 1860, d 25 March 1927
Scott, Mary L., w/o David H. Blackney, b 13 Feb 1872, d 28 Sept 1911
Blackney, Marian Louise, d/o David & Mary Blackney, b 9 July 1909, d
    17 June 1912
Wain, James Brown, 1857-1916
Spedding, Susan, w/o James Brown Wain, 1858-1933
Doland, Frederick T., 1860-1903
Doland, Carrie B., w/o Frederick T. Doland, 1860-1941
Wood, George W., 1858-1928
Whiting, Inez E., w/o George W. Wood, 1858-1914
Swanson, Walter B., b 9 March 1878 Franklin, MA, d 18 March 1952
    Providence, RI
Slack, Myra Lydia, w/o Walter B. Swanson, b 23 Nov 1874 North
    Attleboro, MA, d 7 Aug 1945 Bristol, RI
McCann, Elizabeth, 1841-1914
Blake, Sarah E., d/o Elizabeth McCann, 1877-1948
Swallow, Henry A., 1860-1911
McLeod, Jeannett A., w/o Henry A. Swallow, 1860-1936
Barrows, Harrie H., 1853-1914
Barrows, Theresa V., w/o Harrie H. Barrows, ...
Burt, Walter C., 1872-1938
Keith, Flora M., w/o Walter C. Burt, 1872-1960
Marble, Charles F., 1863-1954
Marble, Nellie M., w/o Charles F. Marble, 1869-....
Swallow, Robert C., 1883-1949
Swallow, John H., 1884-1951
Swallow, Edgar D., 1889-1956
Swallow, Roy L., 1885-1959
Stephenson, William, 1893-1978
Swallow, Elsie I., w/o William Stephenson, 1890-1981
Rowan, William, 1847-1907
Rowan, Harry B., 1884-1932
Babcock, Clara B., w/o Harry B. Rowan, 1884-1963
Blackwell, John H., 1830-1904
Blackwell, Isabella A., w/o John H. Blackwell, 1831-1914
Anderson, Seleanor M., 1867-1935
Coombs, John W., 1844-1910
Coombs, Adelaide L., w/o John W. Coombs, 1841-1931
Coombs, Ethel Lillian, d/o John & Adelaide Coombs, 1872-1954
Brock, Percy S., 1899-1956

Greve, August, 1857-1892

Klaus, Martin, b 1 March 1845, d 15 Feb 1913

Klaus, Marie, w/o Martin Klaus, b 22 Jan 1848, d 28 May 1933

Metcalf, Allen T., 1855-1913

Metcalf, Ella E., w/o Allen T. Metcalf, 1855-1931

Ford, Mae W., w/o Henry W. Ford, 1877-1924

McGregor, Duncan, 1854-1917

McGregor, Ann Maria, w/o Duncan McGregor, 1866-1959

McGregor, Barbara R, d/o Duncan & Ann Maria McGregor, 1901-1914

Anderson, Amos S., 1838-1926

Anderson, Dacie A., w /o Amos S. Anderson, 1844-1913

Anderson, Blanche, d/o Amos & Dacie Anderson, 1875-1937

Darn, Karl, 1848-1907

Bramel, Augusta, w/o Karl Darn, 1848-1932

Rhodes, Bradford C., 1850-1918

Knowlton, Hattie L., w/o Bradford C. Rhodes, 1855-1910

Rhodes, Herbert L., s/o Bradford C. & Hattie L. Rhodes, 1878-1946

Swift, William F., 1866-1920

Swift, Mabel B., w/o William F. Swift, 1868-1910

Blocksom, Laura M., 1886-1961

Barrow, Edwin S., 1849-1907

Barrow, Susan A., 1852-1919

Barrow, Shirley D., 1882-1889

Simpson, William, d 18 Oct 1888 aged 34 yrs

Simpson, Rachel, 1863-1948

Barrow, Frederick D., b 30 June 1886 aged 36 yrs

Barrow, Hope, w/o Frederick D. Barrow, b 24 June 1847, d 14 June 1937

Fales, George H. Jr., b 27 Aug 1872, d 20 April 1925

Davis, Edward P., 1838-1908

Davis, Mary A., w/o Edward P. Davis, 1836-1925

Davis, Irving A., s/o Edward P. & Mary A. Davis, 1859-1893

Olney, Charles H., 1859-1903

Olney, Lena A., w/o Charles H. Olney, 1862-1945

Patt, Albert, 1825-1906

Patt, Sarah, w/o Albert Patt, 1829-1896

Thompson, Harry B., 1879-1956

Burg, Grace E., w/o Harry B. Thompson, 1884-1980

Burg, Eliza, mother of Grace E. Burg, 1854-1941

Thompson, Herbert E., 1854-1925

Thompson, Julia, w/o Herbert E. Thompson, 1851-1924

Thompson, Earl B., 1890-1973
Slater, Bertha M., w/o Earl B. Thompson, 1888-1973
Cook, Helen S., d/o Earl & Bertha M. Thompson, 1918-1943
Breen, Joseph F., 1858-1922
Breen, Emma J., w/o Joseph F. Breen, 1860-1940
Miller, Charles W., b 10 April 1857, d 11 April 1898
Miller, Elizabeth, w/o Charles W. Miller, b 5 Dec 1862, d 6 May 1942
Cobb, Cornelia E., 1838-1923
Cobb, Lyman A., 1835-1937
Gardiner, Barton G., 1881-1936
Gardiner, Gertrude A., w/o Barton G. Gardiner, 1888-1975
Wood, Charles A., 1857-1952
Wood, Agnes, w/o Charles A. Wood, 1860-1946
Laird, Agnes, 1816-1896
Harden, Arlon S., 1834-1913
Harden, Thankful B., w/o Arlon S. Harden, 1830-1889
Harden, Fannie B., 1873-1942
Blackwell, George, 1833-1883
Cropper, Margaret, w/o George Blackwell, 1836-1916
Blackwell, John W., 1856-1911
Ware, Edna J., w/o John W. Blackwell, 1858-1895
Marble, Etta, w/o John W. Blackwell, 1875-1949
Cropper, Mary G. C., 1829-1907
Blackwell, Warren R., 1877-1905
Graham, Flora L., w/o Warren R. Blackwell, 1878-1952
Warren, George A., 1830-1915
Warren, Angenette B., w/o George A. Warren, 1832-1908
Warren, George W., s/o George & Angenette Warren, 1852-1895
Warren, Lillie J., d/o George & Angnette Warren & w/o Edson N.
    Leonard, 1850-1925
Robinson, L. Eugene, 1850-1918
Robinson, Annie Laurie, w/o L. Eugene Robinson, 1853-1901
Robinson, Anna Ida, w/o L. Eugene Robinson, 1856-1919
Miller, Everett C., 1891-1953
Butler, Lulu, w/o Everett C. Miller, 1883-1965
Croftey, Daniel, 1842-1912, A member of Co I 18th Mass Vols
Croftey, Emily A., w/o Daniel Croftey, 1845-1923
Cook, Hattie Miller, 1888-1925
Miller, James B., 1857-1909
Miller, Edna L., w/o James B. Miller, 1856-1932

Miller, Albertus D., s/o James & Edna Miller, 1884-1906
Miller, Leon, s/o James & Edna Miller, 1885-1945
Franklin, John W., 1885-1931
Emerson, Edna Arleta, w/o John W. Franklin, 1889-1923
Copeland, James C., 1859-1926
Copeland, Annie M., w/o James C. Copeland, 1872-1903
Heilborn, Leopold A., 1860-1902
Cobb, Mary A., w/o Leopold A. Heilborn, 1863-1940
Sherman, John B., b 10 Oct 1881, d 5 Aug 1905
Rhodes, Arthur D., 1871-1931
Rhodes, Emma H., w/o Arthur D. Rhodes, 1881-1970
Maxcy, Ernest L., 1906-1965
Maxcy, M. Florence Whiting, 1883-1966
Maxcy, George A., 1883-1919
Maxcy, Frank A., 1857-1932
Maxcy, Ida E., 1860-1942
Burton, Albert E., b 16 April 1861, d 24 Feb 1928
Burton, Nettie M., w/o Albert E. Burton, b 16 June 1862, d 15 Dec 1911
Whitin, Frederic C., b 31 March 1850, d 20 May 1921
Whitin, Geneva V., w/o Frederic C. Whitin, b 2 Jan 1855, d 2 Nov 1908
Jordan, Edgar L., b 24 March 1851, d 8 March 1910
Jordan, Eugene A., w/o Edgar L. Jordan, b 24 Aug 1857, d 18 Jan 1918
Rowe, G. William, 1848-1922
Morse, Annie E., w/o G. William Rowe, 1863-1931
Barrows, Earle M., 1904-1987
Miller, William, 1879-1950
Damon, Florence E., w/o William Miller, 1878-1911
Horning, Hermon, b 12 Sept 1855, d 13 July 1904
Hatch, John B., b 12 June 1841, d 10 July 1906
Mason, Hannah F., w/o John B. Hatch, b 15 Aug 1843, d 19 June 1927
Prew, Frank R., 1874-....
Prew, Mamie T., w/o Frank R. Prew, 1874-1900
Olney, Stephen W., 1834-1919
Olney, Harriet P., w/o Stephen W. Olney, 1838-1918
Munroe, Robert G., 1867-1948
Munroe, Ida L., w/o Robert G. Munroe, 1879-1951
Freeman, Elmer A., b 7 Oct 1863, d 13 Oct 1891
Clark, Stephen, b 18 Aug 1805, d 1 Dec 1857
Pierce, Chloe M., w/o Stephen Clark, b 27 Nov 1810, d 15 Jan 1907
Hoffman, Frank, 1846-1888

Hoffman, Frank, 1846-1888
Hoffman, Bertha, w/o Frank Hoffman, 1848-1935
Simpson, Julia A., d/o Frank & Bertha Hoffman, 1878-1897
Burton, Albert W., b 19 Dec 1831, d 24 July 1909
Bennett, Mary Ellia, w/o Albert W. Burton, 1836-1922
Burton, Alice W., b 24 Aug 1859, d 6 April 1885
Noble, Maria L. B., b 13 May 1866, d 25 April 1928
Hatch, Bernice E., 1877-1949
Hatch, Clarence M., 1878-1947
White, Charles H., 1858-1930
White, Lillian J., w/o Charles H. White, 1862-1938
White, Vernon O., 1883-1949
White, Arthur M., 1885-1911
Griffiths, Arthur L., 1859-1918
Griffiths, Mary E., w/o Arthur L. Griffiths, 1861-1930
Griffiths, Gertrude I., 1884-1953
Braslow, Oliver S., b 29 May 1806, d 9 April 1866
Barden, Frank Irwin, 1846-1922
Warren, Harriet, w/o Frank I. Barden, 1845-1913
Day, Anna W., 1852-1925
Warren, James F., b 1 March 1801, d 29 Dec 1890
Blackinton, Adeline D., w/o James Warren, b 5 Ferb 1806, d 21 June
    1878
Warren, George M., b 11 April 1832, d 11 Feb 1894
Jordan, Sarah L., w/o George M. Warren, b 1 Sept 1845, d 14 March
    1937
Phillips, Edward A., b 17 June 1860, d 2 July 1899
Etzenspencer, John E., 1844-1892
Etzenspencer, Amelia, w/o John E. Etzenspencer, 1857-1884
Mead, William B., 1861-1920
Stearns, George B., b 26 March 1852, d 28 March 1920
Stearns, Martha A., w/o George B. Stearns, b 29 Oct 1846, d 5 Oct 1901
Hawkins, Elizabeth G., d/o Dexter & Eliza Hawkins, d 25 Nov 1900
Semple, Joseph M., 1869-1962
Peck, Aravilla, w/o Joseph M. Semple, 1872-1942
Semple, Agnes E., 1891-1891
Graham, Clara E. C., w/o Joseph H. Semple, 1875-1947
Peck, Royal J., 1831-1914
Follett, Ellen E., w/o Royal J. Peck, 1836-1923
Peck, Lucy A., 1873-1875

Miller, Louise P., w/o William A. Miller, 1863-1929
Miller, Louise A., 1885-1868
Miller, Frederick G., 1832-1881
Miller, Johanna C., w/o Frederick C. Miller, 1837-1917
Miller, Oscar C., 1858-1899
Miller, Louisa L., 1866-1883
Miller, Henry, 1862-1864
Glidden, David, b 5 April 1866, d 27 Sept 1888
Glidden, Reuele W., b 19 Nov 1830-....
Glidden, Almy L., w/o Reuele W. Glidden, b 3 Jan 1833, d 4 June 1881
Glidden, Elizabeth H., w/o Reuele W. Glidden, b 16 Oct 1832, d....
Carpenter, Harry L., 1875-1942
Whitehill, Mirian, w/o Harry L. Carpenter, 1879-1952
Carpenter, Elizabeth, d/o Harry L. & Mirian Carpenter, 1914-1920
White, John W., 1886-1931
White, Matilda, w/o John W. White, 1871-1923
Carpenter, George H., b 24 June 1861, d 14 Feb 1904
Carpenter, Sarah G., w/o George H. Carpenter, b 12 Dec 1854, d 11 Feb
   1928
Ewer, Charles, 1840-1919
Ewer, Isabella, w/o Charles Ewer, 1844-1925
Ewer, Agnes, d/o Charles & Isabella Ewer, 1885-1922
Richards, Betsey Blake, b 6 March 1815, d 14 Sept 1888
Blake, A. Curtis, d 5 May 1871 aged 28 yrs
Jackson, Charles O., b 12 May 1829, d 13 Dec 1903
Jackson, Drucy B., w/o Charles O. Jackson, b 22 Aug 1831, d 9 June 1891
Hawkins, Laura M., 1845-1929
Hawkins, Dexter E., d 5 Dec 1894 aged 66 yrs
Hawkins, Elizabeth, w/o Dexter E. Hawkins, d 13 April 1875 aged 43 yrs
Coombs, Orrin L., b 20 Aug 1828, d 3 July 1889
Pond, Emory, 1823-1893
Wyatt, Sarah J., w/o Emory Pond, 1833-1894
Maintien, John B., 1832-1892
Maintien A., w/o John B. Maintien, 1836-1909
Jones, Thomas R., 1824-1907
Jones, Hannah, w/o Thomas R. Jones, 1828-1901
Parker, Charles Howard, b 9 Jan 1865, d 28 Feb 1932
Parker, Florence Amelia, w/o Charles Howard Parker, b 2 Aug 1868, d 8
   Sept 1936
Maintien, William F., 1863-1921

Pond, Jennie G., w/o William F. Maintien, 1862-1933
Klein, Charles 1889-1913
Greve, Albert, 1832-1913
Greve, Alvine, w/o Albert Greve, 1842-1926
Greve, Agnes, d/o Albert & Alvine Greve, 1886-1892
Bragg, Charles W., 1841-1917
Bragg, Sarah O., w/o Charles W. Bragg, 1841-1924
Bragg, Frank Arthur, s/o Charles W. & Sarah O. Bragg, 1872-1879
Tifft, Isabella J., w/o L. Crandall Tifft, b 12 Feb 1842, d 15 Aug 1894
Tifft, L. Crandall, b 19 Aug 1837, d 22 Aug 1905
Ware, Louie Erville, b 15 Nov 1869, d 1 March 1906
Price, Richard, 1836-1898
Price, Caroline, 1837-1873
Price, Caroline Bradbury, 1865-1900
Price, Elizabeth H., 1875-1904
Ware, Edmund R., b 26 Sept 1831, d 8 March 1929
Davis, Mary, w/o Edmund R. Ware, b 13 May 1840, d....
Pate, Francis G., b 13 Feb 1830, d 18 Dec 1925
White, Ellen S., w/o Francis G. Pate, b 10 April 1830, d 10 Dec 1903
Pate, Ellen Frances, d/o Francis G. & Ellen S. Pate, b 12 Aug 1861, d 24
   Aug 1861
Guild, Joseph, b 13 April 1794, d 27 Aug 1871
Warren, Rebeckah P., w/o Joseph Guild, b 27 May 1798, d 11 May 1872
Darling, Albert R., 1842-1913
Darling, Harriet A., w/o Albert R. Darling, 1842-1914
Darling, Etta G., 1863-1870
Darling, Arthur G., 1872-1900
Warren, LaBurton, b 23 July 1834, d 6 Oct 1902
Warren, L. Fidelia, w/o LaBurton Warren, b 14 Oct 1835, d 6 July 1865
Warren, Elvera A., b 19 Feb 1861, d 16 Feb 1917
Cheever, George F., 1840-1920
Cheever, Augusta M., w/o George F. Cheever, 1844-1915
Cheever, Howard G., s/o George F. & Augusta M. Cheever, 1873-1875
Cheever, Harry G., s/o George F. & Augusta M. Cheever, 1876-1885
Cheever, Warren H., b 28 Dec 1829, d 6 Jan 1881
Niles, Charles, s/o William & Harriet Niles, d 4 Oct 1864 aged 27 yrs 3
   mos 17 days
Tifft, Isabel J., 1867-1944
Tifft, Maria L., 1873-1958
Reed, David D., 1845-1891

Reed, Mary F., w/o David D. Reed, 1853-1906

Reed, Charles E., s/o David & Mary F. Reed, 1883-1908

Semple, John M., 1872-1946

Reed, Ella E., w/o John M. Semple, 1875-1947

Goundier, Charles, b 5 Jan 1832, d 28 May 1899

Hall, Betsey J., w/o Charles Goundier, b 29 April 1837, d 21 June 1920

Goundier, Charles, s/o Charles & Betsey Goundier, b 18 Nov 1856, d 12 Oct 1896

Rand, William, s/o George S. & Hannah Rand, d 11 April 1878 aged 24 yrs 7 mos

Blackinton, Nellie E., w/o David H. Blackinton, d 8 Aug 1885 aged 30 yrs 3 mos 15 days

Almy, Ruth S., d 6 March 1850 aged 22 yrs 11 mos

Blackinton, William, b 10 April 1819, d 21 July 1888

Blackinton, Lydia, w/o William Blackinton, b 10 Aug 1821, d 6 Nov 1881

Guild, Gilbert G., b 18 Oct 1831, d 14 Nov 1885

Burton, Lizzie, w/o Gilbert Guild, b 13 July 1828, d 18 July 1880

French, Benjamin, d 5 July 1835 aged 46 yrs

Tappan, Maria, d 30 Dec 1882 aged 60 yrs 1 mo 11 days

Tappan, Benjamin E. F., d 20 March 1883 aged 32 yrs 10 mos

Blackinton, Alice S., w/o Benjamin French, d 10 Aug 1881 aged 82 yrs 11 mos 27 days

Bennett, Edgar A., 1851-1919

Bennett, Emily M., w/o Edgar A.Bennett, 1850-1907

Bennett, Irving A., 1875-1880

Bennett, Elvie E., 1877-1892

Bennett, Emily A., 1889-1890

Dolly, Aravesta, 1841-1910

Corey, Elizabeth, w/o Christopher H. Corey, d 3 Sept 1875 aged 72 yrs 3 mos 8 days

Rand, James H., b 27 April 1859, d 23 Dec 1914

Rand, Samuel C., b 24 Dec 1822, d 27 May 1905

Rand, Hannah W., w/o Samuel C. Rand, b 20 Feb 1820, d 21 Jan 1900

Kinball, Bertha E., 1873-1953

Lillibridge, Lester Lewis, b 18 Oct 1825, d 1881

Reed, Walter D., 1890-1924

Wasson, Mary E., w/o Walter D. Reed, 1879-1967

Corbin, Leroy F., 1900-1974

Whiting, Katherine L., w/o Leroy F. Corbin, 1906-1986

Barton, Clinton E., b 27 Sept 1906, d 11 Feb 1986

McKechnie, Bessie, w/o Clinton E. Barton.....

Coombs, Reuben, d 28 Oct 1874 aged 80 yrs 6 mos 2 days

Coombs, Permelia M., w/o Reuben Coombs, d 26 March 1859 aged 67 yrs

Hawkins, Fred W., 1867-1948

Hawkins, Catherine J., w/o Fred W. Hawkins, 1863-1933

Coombs, Harriet S., 1823-1887

Coombs, Charles C., 1816-1899

Coombs, Horace E., 1847-1940

Davis, Caroline, w/o Horace E. Coombs, 1850-1899

Wilson, Albert C., b 10 June 1832, d 3 Oct 1886

Wilson, Sarah R., w/o Albert C. Wilson, 1829-....

Wilson, Charles Arthur, s/o Albert & Sarah Wilson, b Jan 1870, d 5 May 1889

Kent, Henry N., 1835-1919

Porter, S. Josephine, w/o Henry N. Kent, 1838-1898

Morse, Charles L., b 3 Sept 1838, d 16 July 1873

Rathburn, Albert P.,.....

Rathburn, Lucy A., w/o Albert P. Rathburn, d 15 May 1889 aged 62 yrs 5 mos 9 days

Rathburn, Albert Augustus, s/o Albert P. & Lucy A. Rathburn, d 4 July 1858 aged 5 yrs

Rathburn, Edward Albert, s/o Albert P. & Lucy A. Rathburn, d 30 Dec 1864 aged 2 yrs

Matthewson, William A., b 25 June 1870, d 24 March 1905

Matthewson, Ida W., b 28 Dec 1871, d 11 Feb 1957

Witherell, Naavan, b 21 July 1839, d 17 Jan 1912

Witherell, Caroline T., w/o Naavan Witherell, b 14 April 1849, d 22 May 1908

Whiting, James O., 1828-1903

Rhodes, Nancy J., w/o James O. Whiting, 1825-1909

Miles, James S., b 14 March 1836, d 7 May 1864

Ware, Timothy, d 30 Oct 1875

Wilde, John, 1841-1910

Wilde, Annie J., w/o John Wilde, 1851-1909

Meyer, George, 1824-1873

Meyer, Harriet A., w/o George Meyer, 1828-1907

Meyer, George, s/o George & Harriet A. Meyer, 1859-1888

Meyer, Margaret, d/o George & Harriet A. Meyer, 1861-1933

Metcalf, Abbie P., 1841-1923

Ware, Lizzie W., w/o G. Bentley Ware, d 15 Sept 1878 aged 39 yrs 8 mos

Wait, John J., 1831-1916

Wait, Ernest J., s/o John J. & Alice R. Wait, d 1 April 1879 aged 19 yrs

Gould, Sally, w/o Jonas Gould of Boston, d 22 Aug 1857 aged 90 yrs

Gould, William, d 13 April 1855 aged 55 yrs

Wayant, Louis Jacob, 1846-1924

Wayant, Helena M., w/o Louis Jacob Wayant, 1865-1926

Young, Francis, 1818-1882

Young, Louisa, w/o Francis Young, 1826-1912

Corbin, Francis O., 1874-1948

Corbin, Mary L., w/o Francis O. Corbin, 1874-1946

Corbin, Leroy F. Jr., AMM F 3 US Navy WW 2, b 13 June 1927, d 25 July 1991

Blake, Virgil, b 28 April 1799, d 22 Sept 1875

Blake, Roxanna, w/o Virgil Blake, b 18 Jan 1798, d 20 Jan 1882

Swallow, Elmer L., b 9 Aug 1861, d 17 Oct 1900

Swallow, Sarah J., b 29 Dec 1863, d 5 Nov 1922

Swallow, George, b 7 June 1833, d 30 March 1925

Swallow, Susan E., b 14 Oct 1836, d 13 Aug 1913

Chafee, Sophia, w/o Harvey Chafee, d 7 Dec 1870

Chafee, Harvey, d 23 Jan 1863 aged 58 yrs 1 mo 4 days

Borgal, James F., 1886-1925

Borgal, Mattie E., w/o James F. Borgal, 1891-1962

Ware, Thomas, b 31 May 1813, d 16 Feb 1897

Ware, Elizabeth, w/o Thomas Ware, d 23 Nov 1873

Ware, Emma Jane, d/o Thomas & Elizabeth Ware, b 14 Dec 1844, d 21 Dec 1868

Pitcher, Lyman, b 20 June 1786 Marlborough, MA, d 10 April 1871 Providence, RI

Pitcher, Mary, w/o Lyman Pitcher, (Broken)

Pitcher, Maria, d/o Lyman & Mary Pitcher, b 25 Sept 1819, d 15 May 1861

Draper, Lafayette, 1824-1905

Haskell, Sarah S., w/o Lafayette Draper, 1824-1915

Draper, Milton, b 10 July 1808, d 12 June 1884

Powers, James R., d 3 Aug 1873 aged 58 yrs 7 mos 18 days

Powers, Martha, w/o James R. Powers, d 10 Oct 1858 aged 41 yrs 15 days

Mann, Herbert, d 10 Dec 1809 aged 29 yrs

Draper, Sally, d 23 Oct 1782

Wennell, Harold R., b 16 June 1896, d 18 June 1909

Jackson, George F., 1854-1936

Jackson, Ella A., w/o George F. Jackson, 1853-1910

Jackson, Anna H., w/o George F. Jackson, 1859-1931

Chamberlain, Betsey, 1880-1953

Ware, Howard, 1901-1964

Sayles, Mary Ware, 1881-1970

Cargill, David, d 22 Dec 1858 aged 75 yrs 8 mos 14 days

Cargill, Hannah, w/o David Cargill, d 27 Sept 1870 aged 85 yrs 10 mos 10 days

Cummings, George M., 1911-....

Cummings, Agnes B., w/o George M. Cummings, 1909-1976

Cargill, David, d 22 Dec 1858 aged 75 yrs 8 mos 14 days

Cargill, Hannah, w/o David Cargill, d 27 Sept 1870 aged 85 yrs 10 mos 10 days

Whitman, Henry C., d 20 Aug 1883 aged 64 yrs 11 mos 11 days

Whitman, Julia A., d 6 Oct 1912 aged 90 yrs

Cargill, Lyman, s/o David & Hannah Cargill, d 23 April 1851 aged 40 yrs

Cargill, Harriet, w/o Lyman Cargill, d 17 Sept 1898 aged 89 yrs

Cargill, Loring, s/o Lyman & Harriet Cargill, d 19 Oct 1841 aged 2 yrs 1 mo

Cargill, Warren, s/o David & Hannah Cargill, d 17 Nov 1857 Cassville, MO aged 38 yrs 3 mos 4 days

Cargill, E. L., 1837-1908

Cargill, Hattie E., w/o E. L. Cargill, 1841-1924

Fisher, W. W., 1834-1901

Fisher, E. C., 1838-1915

Fisher, N. A., 1834-1863

Fisher, Willie, 1863-1864

Guild, Samuel, d 12 March 1857 aged 70 yrs

Guild, Huldah, d 17 Oct 1874 aged 84 yrs

Guild, Emily P., d 19 April 1866 aged 39 yrs

Guild, Maria A., w/o Samuel Guild, d 6 Sept 1819 aged 30 yrs

Guild, Elizabeth S., d 8 Dec 1854 aged 43 yrs

Witherell, Elizabeth R., b 3 July 1818, d 10 May 1901

Witherell, Shepard A., b 2 April 1815, d 7 Feb 1884

Witherell, Jane C., w/o Shepard A. Witherell, b 19 March 1814, d 20 May 1897

Witherell, Lorenzo V., 1841-1931

Witherell, Harriet A., w/o Lorenzo V. Witherell, 1844-1924

Thomas, Charles E., 1859-1940

Thomas, Cora, w/o Charles E. Thomas, 1859-1941

Meyers, Rudolph H., b 16 April 1854, d 16 Sept 1888
Meyers, Ida M., b 31 May 1857, d 24 Oct 1884
Blackinton, Leonard A., b 26 Oct 1869, d 14 Oct 1893
French, Edwin Davis, Artist/Engraver, b 19 Jan 1851, d 8 Dec 1906
Brainerd, Mary, w/o Edwin Davis French, 26 April 1849, d 8 June 1929
Black, Cyrus B., 1869-1913
Richards, Willard, d 23 May 1876
Harding, Harriet, w/o Willard Richards, d 3 Nov 1882
Guild, Charles L., 1829-1883
Guild, Nancy P., w/o Charles L. Guild, 1829-1913
Guild, Ernest A., 1855-1893
Richards, Edgar M., b 31 Jan 1840, d 15 Feb 1841
Richards, Asman, b 6 March 1842, d 25 June 1842
Richards, Jesse F., b 24 Nov 1808, d 13 May 1881
Jillson, Betsey, w/o Jesse F. Richards, b 27 Aug 1811, d 25 April 1842
Blake, Joseph, b 28 April 1810, d 30 Jan 1866
Blake, Ann E., w/o Joseph Blake, b 3 Sept 1818, d 16 July 1876
Borden, Thomas, b 2 May 1788 Wrentham, MA, d 13 Oct 1845
Borden, Rachel S., w/o Thomas Borden, b 1 March 1789, d 29 Jan 1880
Bardon, John, 1814-1905
Bardon, Rosetta, w/o John Bardon, b 15 May 1820, d 5 Oct 1893
Bardon, Jesse I., s/o John & Rosetta Bardon, d 4 Jan 1848 aged 1 yr 9 mos
Bardon, Lillie R., d/o John & Rosetta Bardon, d 20 June 1881 aged 39 yrs
Darling, Nelson B., d 3 Dec 1867 aged 42 yrs
Darling, Julia A., w/o Nelson B. Darling, d 14 Sept 1887 aged 67 yrs
Blackinton, Lemuel, 1819-1879
Guild, Susan F., w/o Lemuel Blackinton, 1823-1851
Snell, Ella F., d/o Lemuel & Susan F. Blakcinton, 1851-1928
Bragg, James, (Broken)
Bragg, Harriet A., w/o James Bragg, d 23 Dec 1881
Phillip, Mary A., w/o W. Phillip, d 14 April 1856 aged 19 yrs
Slack, Isaac W., b 7 Nov 1823, d 2 March 1889
Marton, Harriet A., w/o Isaac W. Slack, b 13 Sept 1816, Providence, RI, d
    24 April 1881
Fuller, Willis M., b 19 Jan 1857, d 2 July 1927
Fuller, Viola M., w/o Willis M. Fuller, b 28 Jan 1856, d 30 Dec 1927
Fuller, Chauncey, b May 1817, d Oct 1901
Fuller, Catherine Cecilia, w/o Chauncey Fuller, b 16 May 1815, d 11
    April 1885
Fisher, Arthur Ellis, 1845-1912

Fisher, Mary Elizabeth, w/o Arthur Ellis Fisher, 1852-1946
Hawes, Amos C., b 24 June 1794, d 5 Nov 1879
Hawes, Drusa, w/o Amos C. Hawes, b 26 Nov 1797, d 24 Dec 1870
Fisher, George E., d 31 Oct 1890 aged 69 yrs
Fisher, Sarah C., w/o George E. Fisher, d 6 June 1892 aged 71 yrs
Herring, H. Mortimer, 1850-1929
Herring, Mary Elizabeth, w/o H. Mortimer Herring, 1859-1927
Herring, Elizabeth, w/o James F. Herring, b 17 March 1834, d 18 July
    1893
Herring, Eva Emily, d/o James F. & Elizabeth Herring & w/o John Irving,
    b 9 Nov 1871, d 22 Nov 1896
Simmons, Francis W., b 15 Jan 1922, d 11 July 1982
Simmons, Grace Etter, w/o Francis W. Simmons, b 17 Nov 1919, d 9 Jan
    1987
Grosee, Frederick, d 13 Oct 1881 aged 21 yrs 7 mos 8 days
Grosee, Charlotte, w/o Frederick Grosee, b 16 Nov 1823, d 10 March
    1886
Cheever, Edson T., 1856-1926
Illingworth, Annice A., w/o Edson T. Cheever, 1856-1944
Barney, Frank E., b March 1878, d Jan 1941
Barney, Ethel E., w/o Frank E. Barney, b Nov 1878, d Jan 1948
Blackinton, Leonard, b 17 Feb 1796, d 17 Nov 1857
Blackinton, Caroline, w/o Leonard Blackinton & d/o Aaron & Sally
    Blackinton, b 20 May 1801, d 19 July 1882
Blackinton, Leonard A., s/o Leonard & Caroline Blackinton, 1820-1824
Slack, Arthur H., 1884-1945
Slack, Alma B., w/o Arthur H. Slack, 1880-1954
Slack, Benjamin, b 11 Nov 1849, d 31 Aug 1937
Slack, Lydia, w/o Benjamin Slack, b 28 May 1852, d 10 Aug 1902
Phillips, John, b 22 Nov 1813, d (Broken)
Walcott, Lydia M., w/o John Phillips, d 13 May 1860 aged 45 yrs
Phillips, Martha, w/o John Phillips, d 10 Dec 1865 aged 79 yrs
Carpenter, Lewis B., b 16 Jan 1824, d 8 Sept 1885
Carpenter, Rachel, w/o Lewis B. Carpenter, b 2 April 1833, d 18 July
    1889
Whiting, Warren C., 1849-1915
Andrews, Linda, w/o Warren C. Whiting, 1856-1913
McLeod, Hector, b 11 March 1838, d 10 June 1915
McLeod, Helen S., w/o Hector McLeod, b 19 June 1838, d 24 Dec 1889
Somes, George W., 1837-1914

Peers, Georgianna, w/o George W. Somes, 1837-1925

Somes, William M., s/o George W. & Georgianna Somes, b 29 Sept 1862, d 24 Nov 1879

Broadbent, Lilla Mary, w/o Charles W. Broadbent, b 13 Dec 1867, d 13 Dec 1911

Ware, Cyrus, d 1 March 1881 aged 74 yrs

Ware, Eliza, w/o Cyrus Ware, 1809-1890

Thompson, C. Melville, 1849-1936

Thompson, Laura F., w/o C. Melville Thompson, 1851-1937

Fisher, Samuel P., d 6 Jan 1863 aged 67 yrs

Fisher, Charlotte, w/o Samuel P. Fisher, d 1872

Fisher, Susan C., w/o Samuel P. Fisher, d 23 Jan 1881

Eaton, Amos, b 6 Oct 1815, d 20 Jan 1879

Eaton, Elizabeth, w/o Amos Eaton, b 17 April 1816, d 11 Aug 1890

McLeod, Barbara, d/o James & Isabella McLeod, b 4 June 1835, d 26 April 1884

McLeod, James, b Scotland, d 17 March 1878 aged 77 yrs

McLeod, Isabella, w/o James McLeod, b & buried in Nova Scotia, d 22 Feb 1866 aged 67 yrs

Tappan, Ella F., w/o Edward King, b 7 June 1861, d 4 March 1887

King, Martin E., 1913-1974

King, Martin L., 1837-1913

King, Martha, w/o Martin L. King, 1836-1924

King, Edward M., 1860-1924

Gleason, Kathryn, w/o Edward M. King, 1889-1943

King, Maud S., b 2 June 1868, d 4 June 1875

King, Etta, w/o John H. Tuttle, b 9 May 1858, d 31 Dec 1878

Leander, Ruth O., 1910-1986

Loughlin, Bernard, b 28 Dec 1832, d 30 Sept 1885

Hanly, Eliza, w/o Bernard Loughlin, b 6 Dec 1831, d 2 Sept 1897

Loughlin, Jane E., d/o Bernard & Eliza Loughlin, 1853-1854

Loughlin, Sylvester F., s/o Bernard & Eliza Loughlin, 1856-1863

Loughlin, Walter L., s/o Bernard & Eliza Loughlin, 1865-1869

Loughlin, Gertrude L., d/o Bernard & Eliza Loughlin, 1875-1875

Loughlin, Emily L., d/o Bernard & Eliza Loughlin, 1860-1951

Loughlin, Geroge B., b 25 May 1858, d 26 June 1939

Slade, Anna G., w/o George B. Loughlin, b 6 April 1870, d 19 Oct 1920

Pherson, Daniel R., 1828-1875

Pherson, Jerusha B., w/o Daniel R. Pherson, 1827-1894

Pherson, Albert W., 1825-1902

Pherson, Mary, w/o Albert W. Pherson, 1829-1919
Pherson, Frank, s/o Albert & Mary Pherson, 1851-1874
Black, Amos H., 1846-1924
Black, Luella M., w/o Amos H. Black, 1858-1921
Black, Frank M., 1884-1957
Black, Rose, w/o Frank M. Black, 1883-1933

Goff & Wheeler Lot
Rehoboth Historical Cemetery # 9
Moulton Road
Rehoboth, Massachusetts

Goff, Mrs. Mehitable, w/o Richard Goff & d/o Stephen Bullock Esq., b 3
    Aug 1767, d 23 June 1843
Goff, Richard, d 1 Sept 1836 aged 87 yrs
Yeaw, William, d 28 Aug 1810 aged 52 yrs
Wardell, Huldah, w/o Simeon Wheeler, d 9 May 1828 agd 72 yrs 2 mos
Wheeler, Mary Ann, w/o George J. Wheeler, d 25 Jan 1858 aged 29 yrs 1
    mo   23 days
Wheeler, Benjamin A., d 14 Aug 1855 aged 27 yrs 14 days
Wheeler, Simeon, s/o Cromwell & Olive Wheeler, d 18 Sept 1849 aged 26
    yrs 3 days
Wheeler, John D., s/o Cromwell & Olive Wheeler, d 28 July 1847 aged 22
    yrs
Wheeler, Albert F., s/o Cromwell & Abby Wheeler, d 14 Dec 1847 aged 1
    yr
Wheeler, Olive Frances, d/o Cromwell & Abby Wheeler, d June 1858
    aged 5 yrs 10 mos 22 days
Wheeler, Harriet H., d/o Cromwell & Abby Wheeler, d 29 Sept 1865 aged
    22 yrs 2 mos 16 days
Wheeler, Mary Adalaide, d/o Cromwell & Abby Wheeler, d 23 Nov 1858
    aged 13 yrs 10 mos 28 days
Wheeler, Abby Ann, d/o Cromwell & Abby L. Wheeler, d 24 Sept 1858
    aged 18 yrs 8 mos 2 days
Wheeler, George A., s/o Cromwell & Abby L. Wheeler, d 13 April 1878
    aged 31 yrs 2 mos 8 days
Wheeler, Eldora R. Barney, d/o Cromwell & Abby L. Wheeler, b 10 Nov
    1854, d 31 Dec 1884
Wheeler, Cromwell, b 12 March 1814, d 13 March 1905
Goff, Abby L., w/o Cromwell Wheeler, b 13 Feb 1818, d 11 Sept 1897
Wheeler, Cromwell, d 14 March 1884 aged 95 yrs 2 mos 14 days
Wheeler, Olive, w/o Cromwell Wheeler, d 21 Nov 1866 aged 73 yrs 10
    mos

Goff, Bathshebe, w/o Lt. Joseph Goff Jr., d March 1814 aged 35 yrs
Goff, Joseph, d 12 Sept 1840 aged 69 yrs
Goff, Abigail, w/o Horatio Goff & widow of the Late Joseph Goff, d 26
    June 1842 aged 44 yrs
Goff, Horatio, d 11 June 1856 aged 51 yrs
Goff, Joseph, d 22 Jan 1874 aged 72 yrs
Goff, Patience A., w/o Joseph Goff, b 18 Feb 1814, d 30 Oct 1862
Goff, Warren, b 18 Oct 1846, d 26 May 1910
Goff, Levi Jr., d 5 Dec 1819 aged 51 yrs 7 mos
Luther, Mahitabel, w/o Rev. Child Luther & formerly w/o Levi Goff Jr., d
    2 April 1857 aged 83 yrs 3 mos
Goff, Rebecca, d/o Joseph & Patience Goff, d 1799 aged 15 yrs
Goff, Joseph, d 18 Jan 1820 aged 95 yrs
Goff, Patience, w/o Joseph Goff, d 31 Sept 1819 aged 89 yrs

Greenwood Cemetery Historical # 26
Plain Street
Rehoboth, Massachusetts

Horton, Gerald P., 1888-1968
Horton, Jennie, w/o Gerald P. Horton, 1887-1983
Martin, Joseph W., 1914-....
Martin, Geraldine, w/o Joseph W. Martin, 1911-...
Matthews, George E., b 20 Sept 1907, d 1 April 1981
Matthews, Cora M., w/o George E. Matthews, b 30 May 1912, d 19 Nov
    1982
Reed, Raymond L., 1909-1970
Reed, Ruth V., w/o Raymond Reed, 1913-....
Horton, Frederick W., 1879-1966
Horton, Ethel E., w/o Frederick W. Horton, 1888-1967
Horton, Frederick L., 1907-1978
Horton, Selina M., w/o Frederick L. Horton, 1911-....
Ashcroft, James A., S Sgt US Army WW2, b 30 June 1917, d 20 Oct 1985
Richmond, Dorothea E. (Betty), b 16 Feb 1832, d 2 Oct 1994
Johnson, Hugh F. Sr., b 20 Feb 1935, d 28 Jan 1993
Reed, Betty L., w/o Hugh F. Johnson Sr., b 2 April 1938, d....

Pierce, Rev. James L., b 13 March 1822, d 3 May 1897

Bryant, Susan M., w/o Rev. James L. Pierce, b 2 Feb 1920, d 24 July 1893

Bryant, Henry, d 7 April 1868 aged 79 yrs 4 mos

Bryant, William H., b 25 May 1825, d 17 Feb 1899

Bryant, Anstpus, w/o Henry Bryant, d 29 June 1877 aged 94 yrs

Pierce, Lester L., 1897-1922

Pierce, Robert E., 1896-1922

Grant, Rose May, w/o Arthur D. Pierce, 1857-1903

Pierce, Arthur D., 1861-1928

Pierce, Lloyd B., b 19 Nov 1835, d 22 March 1911

Pierce, Mary J., w/o Lloyd B. Pierce, 1840-1926

Pierce, Bryon C., 1866-1945

Pierce, Caleb B., b 26 Jan 1818, d 23 Jan 1859

Pierce, Susan, w/o Caleb B. Pierce, b 6 Jan 1825, d 18 Oct 1902

Pearce, Frederick P., b 26 Dec 1820, d 1 May 1905

Pearce, Mary G., w/o Frederick P. Pearce, b 11 Dec 1819, d 7 June 1851

Pearce, Olivia, w/o Frederick P. Pearce, b 21 April 1818, d 15 April 1876

Pearce, Daniel, d 4 Nov 1860 aged 66 yrs

Pearce, Susan, w/o Daniel Pearce, d 29 Aug 1888 aged 89 yrs

Oldridge, William P., d 26 Nov 1885 aged 75 yrs

Oldridge, Almanda S., w/o William P. Oldridge, d 21 Jan 1891

Oldridge, Daniel H., 1843-1922

Oldridge, Julia, w/o Daniel H. Oldridge, d 16 May 1903 aged 57 yrs

Oldridge, John O., s/o Daniel & Julia Oldridge, d 1 Aug 1879 aged 11 mos

Nichols, Otis Henry, s/o Samuel & Mary Nichols, d 16 Nov 1855 aged 21 yrs 9 days

Nichols, Samuel, d 30 Dec 1888 aged 77 yrs 10 mos

Baker, Nancy, w/o Samuel Nichols, d 1888

Oldridge, Joseph, 1875-1954

Graham, Margaret J., w/o Joseph Oldridge, 1878-1941

Wheeler, Maria S. w/o J. Merrill Wheeler, b 13 May 1819, d 18 Jan 1882

Nichols, Charles B., b 28 Aug 1831, d 18 June 1917

Nichols, Sarah, w/o Charles B. Nichols, b 4 Feb 1833, d 24 Feb 1898

Horton, Samuel O., 1846-1917

Pierce, Janette M., w/o Samuel O. Horton, 1857-1933

Kelton, Philip, d 8 Feb 1873 aged 79 yrs 3 mos

Kelton, Lydia, w/o Philip Kelton, d 9 June 1881 aged 90 yrs 10 mos

Kelton, Jesse W., w/o Philip & Lydia Kelton, d 2 Sept 1844 aged 21 yrs

Kelton, Mary Ann, d/o Philip & Lydia Kelton, d....

Kelton, Captain John, d 23 Nov 1811 aged 88 yrs
Kelton, Rhoda, w/o Edward Kelton, d 3 May 1839 aged 78 yrs
Kelton, Edward, s/o Edward & Rhoda Kelton, d 10 Sept 1805 aged 13 yrs
Kelton, Edward, d 20 May 1848
Peppen, Solomon, 1828-1907
Mosher, Amelia, b 15 Oct 1831, d 23 May 1904
Goff, Henry H., 1848-1907
Horton, Almira E., w/o Henry H. Goff, 1858-1941
McComb, James, 1844-1934
Pierce, Charles H., 1872-1953
Copeland, Sarah, w/o Charles H. Pierce, 1873-1923
Pierce, Ralph C., 1896-1947
Pierce, Edith E., w/o Ralph C. Pierce, 1904-1992
Corey, William D., 1877-1957
Corey, Mary V., w/o William D. Corey, 1888-1954
Lyons, Manuel E., 1881-1943
Lyons, Sarah L., w/o Manuel E. Lyons, 1886-1918
Lyons, Samuel H., 1889-1935
Lyons, Laura E., w/o Samuel H. Lyons, 1887-1952
Goff, James H., 1846-1923
Horton, Isabell, w/o James H. Goff, 1860-1939
Britton, James, 1846-1937
Britton, Annie, w/o James Britton, 1843-1937
Bell, Mary Britton, d/o James & Annie Britton, 1890-1920
Vincent, Adreen H., 1885-1979
Britton, Margaret, w/o Adreen H. Vincent, 1889-1984
Russell, Olive Horton, 1925-1973
Goff, Herbert W. E., b 28 July 1879, d 4 Oct 1898
Goff, Leroy H., 1886-1946
Davis, Nathaniel B., d 13 Dec 1866 AE 83 yrs
Davis, Mary, w/o Nathaniel B. Davis, d 4 June 1867 aged 82 yrs
Davis, Anna M., d Aug 1826
Davis, Rev. Jacob, d 22 Oct 1903 aged 94 yrs 2 mos 5 days
Davis, Harriet, w/o Rev. Jacob Davis, d 29 May 1887 aged 77 yrs 9 mos
Collins, Wilbur J., 1865-1930
Hardy, Ellen L., 1868-1943
Briggs, Isaac, b 3 May 1903 aged 61 yrs 7 mos 25 days
Briggs, Ellen F., w/o Isaac Briggs, d 30 March 1883 aged 38 yrs 1 mo
Briggs, Ida M., w/o Issac Briggs, d 26 May 1898 aged 42 yrs 6 mos 27
   days

Horton, Gilbert A., 1839-1903
Horton, Rachel B., w/o Gilbert A. Horton, 18..- Broken
Horton, George N., 1867-1907
Horton, Robert C., 1889-1919

Rehoboth Village Cemetery
Est 1773
Rehoboth, Massachusetts

Marsh, George W., 1841-1897
Bowen, Ellen, w/o George W. Marsh, 1843-1920
Bowen, Edward L., 1841-1917
Pierce, Clinton A., 1889-1916
Dawson, Viola Pierce, 1902-1954
Pierce, Delmar Z., 1896-1966
Goff, Leon E., 1892-1960
Elwell, Addie M., w/o Leon E. Goff, 1891-1940
Goff, Grace M., w/o Leon E. Goff, 1896-1952
Goff, Auther, 1859-1950
Goff, Carrie F., w/o Arthur Goff, 1862-1933
Goff, Lizzie M., d/o Arthur & Carrie Goff, 1885-1949
Goff, Harold A., s/o Arthur & Carrie Goff, 1887-1974
Goff, Annie R., w/o Harold A. Goff, 1889-1987
Allen, Elizabeth Rothernel, 1890-1993
Gibbs, George E., 1878-1943
Ormsbee, Edna A., w/o George E. Gibbs, 1888-1917
Ormsbee, Albert A., b 7 Sept 1862, d 25 Feb 1931
Davis, Minnie M., w/o Albert A. Ormsbee, b 4 Aug 1874, d 19 June 1959
Kimball, Ivory W., 1872-1957
Bixby, Frances L., w/o Ivory W. Kimball, 1874-1924
Parson, Carrie L., w/o Ivory W. Kimball, 1871-1952
Lindberg, Elsie E., 1892-1966
Lindberg, Eric W., 1895-1972
Lindberg, Philly A., 1904-1930
Lindberg, Millie D., 1867-1947
Peck, Edwin G., 1843-1930

Peck, L. Augusta, w/o Edwin G. Peck, 1846-1910
Ames, Inez B., w/o Edwin G. Peck, 1858-1941
Marvel, John C., 1817-1907
Peck, Ruth N., w/o John C. Marvel, 1815-1843
Peck, Frances A., w/o John C. Marvel, 1832-1899
Marvel, R. Amelia, 1851-1871
Marvel, Mary W., 1864-1865
Marvel, William H., 1843-1909
Bowen, Harriet, w/o William H. Marvel, 1845-1872
Marvel, Harriet, 1872-1872
Bliss, Cornelius, 1833-1908
Bliss, Jane H., 1831-1926
Bliss, William E., 1866-1857
Bliss, Gertrude M., 1874-1889
Peck, Sylvanus, b 21 April 1784, d 13 Nov 1853
Peck, Charlotte, w/o Sylvanus Peck, b 17 Feb 1788, d 24 July 1878
Walden, Myron Stanley, 1890-1976
Viall, Mary Adelaide, w/o Mryon Stanley Walden, 1890-1987
Reed, Gustavus A., b 23 Dec 1811, d 22 April 1889
Reed, Electra A., w/o Gustavus A. Reed, b 25 March 1818, d 18 July 1893
MacNeil, Thomas J., 1861-1924
Reed, Delight C., w/o Thomas MacNeil, 1856-1939
Reed, Almon Augustus, 1849-1919
Reed, Harriet Amelia, 1856-1910
Lake, Hiram, MD, 1820-1898
Fuller, Olive, w/o Dr. Hiram Lake, 1820-1909
Reed, Gertrude Imogene, d/o Dr. Hiram & Olive Reed, 1850-1927
Lake, Nancy, w/o Richard Lake, d 31 Oct 1861 aged 28 yrs 6 mos 20 days
Lake, Nancy B., d/o Richard & Nancy Lake, d 4 Feb 1862 aged 5 mos 18 days
Lake, Martha, w/o Richard Lake, d 6 Feb 1877 aged 33 yrs 11 mos 22 days
Lake, Eleanor, d/o Richard & Martha Lake, d 8 Sept 1876 aged 1 yr 1 mo
Lake, Aldin R., 1906-1979
Lake, Margaret M., w/o Aldin R. Lake, 1910-1975
Lake, Richard O., b 15 Nov 1831, d 23 Nov 1909
Brines, Richard, 1842-1916
Pyne, Margaret, w/o Richard Brines, 1840-1907
Horton, Ellis, d 16 Feb 1849 aged 47 yrs
Horton, Mary E., w/o Ellis Horton, d 26 Nov 1857 aged 52 yrs

Medbery, Ebenezer A., b 3 Aug 1837, d 26 July 1907
Medbery, Ruth A., w/o Ebenezer A. Medbery, 1838-1920
Medbery, Frederick E., 1876-1933
Atkinson, Samuel Martin, 1860-1914
Atkinson, Sarah Marie, w/o Samuel Martin Arkinson, 1858-1927
Hall, Emma Bradford, 1885-1950
Sweetland, William J., 1865-1936
Pride, Alice E., w/o William J. Sweetland, 1866-1926
Risley, Ida J., w/o William J. Sweetland, 1871-....
Newton, Thomas, d 11 Feb 1848 aged 39 yrs
Reynolds, William, d 1895
Reynolds, Sarah, w/o William Reynolds, d May 1907 aged 74 yrs
Moulton, James, d 4 May 1883 aged 43 yrs 26 days
Moulton, Julia M., w/o James Maulton, d 2 Nov 1909 aged 68 yrs 3 mos
Alden, Dean W., 1896-1976
Moulton, Florence G., w/o Dean W. Alden, 1901-1963
Moulton, James, 1869-1946
Moulton, Bessie A., 1867-1914
Bliss, George B., b 26 Sept 1814, d 3 Sept 1887
Bliss, Elizabeth S., w/o George B. Bliss, b 29 Sept 1817, d 8 Sept 1889
Pierce, Jeremiah, b 29 Aug 1786, d 23 March 1837
Wheeler, Candance, w/o Jeremiah Pierce, b 30 Sept 1789, d 18 Oct 1882
Bliss, George B., 1807-1879
Walker, Ann M., w/o George B. Bliss, 1811-1887
Bliss, Julianna P., d/o George & Ann Bliss, 1838-1845
Bliss, Sarah R., d/o George & Ann Bliss, 1849-1850
Bliss, William R., s/o George & Ann Bliss, 1852-1864
Goff, Henry C., 1835-1900
Bliss, Angeline S., w/o Henry C. Goff, 1843-1926
O'Brien, William J., b 5 March 1829, d 23 Aug 1896
Mason, Mary, w/o William J. O'Brien, b 4 May 1842, d 13 Jan 1880
Myer, Henry, d 21 Dec 1881 aged 39 yrs, A member of Co L 10th Reg
    Battilion, RI Vols
Myer, Ellen, w/o Henry Myer, d 4 Dec 1907 aged 70 yrs
Black, Johnson, d 27 Nov 1908 aged 76 yrs
Black, Isabella, w/o Johnson Black, d 10 July 1883 aged 52 yrs
Black, Ada B., d 1 Nov 1906 aged 61 yrs
Black, Robert J., 1860-1912
Peckman, James Leroy, s/o James F. & Lydia Peckman, b 17 Aug 1890, d
    30 March 1913

Bowen, Otis P., b 3 March 1827, d 26 Aug 1910

Bowen, Ruth, w/o Otis P. Bowen, b 13 April 1832, d 26 Nov 1913

Bowen, Herbert, b 29 Sept 1857, d 24 Feb 1907

Viall, Christopher Carpenter, 1853-1923

Bowen, Clara G., w/o Christopher C. Viall, 1855-1938

Gilman, Annie Viall, 1885-1977

Peck, Gustavus B., b 31 Dec 1832, d 11 Dec 1900

Bliss, Sylvanus A., b 20 Dec 1834, d 9 May 1930

Wood, Alice H., w/o Sylvanus A. Bliss, b 1 Dec 1841, d 31 July 1922

Bliss, Sylvanus E., s/o Sylvanus & Alice Bliss, b 2 March 1865, d 2 Sept 1865

Bliss, Mattie A., d/o Sylvanus & Alice Bliss, b 24 Jan 1874, d 13 June 1876

Bliss, Adelbert H., s/o Sylvanus & Alice Bliss, b 13 Sept 1877, d 29 Aug 1878

Streeter, Alexander S., d 11 June 1877 Cambridge, MA

Streeter, Hannah, w/o Alexander S. Streeter, b 25 April 1822, d 15 Sept 1906

Bliss, James H., d 15 Nov 1853 aged 36 yrs 7 mos 2 days

Bliss, Sarah Jane, w/o James H. Bliss, b 19 Sept 1817 Milton, New Hampshire, d 20 April 1898 Dover, New Hampshire

Bliss, Edwin H., s/o James & Sarah Jane Bliss, d 19 Feb 1865 aged 23 yrs

Moulton, C. Maria, d/o Robert & Sarah Moulton, of Wilton, New Hampshire, d 3 April 1870 aged 64 yrs 6 mos

Lee, Samuel, d 6 May 1878 aged 70 yrs

Bowen, Rosella, w/o Samuel Lee, d 22 April 1892 aged 84 yrs

Bowen, Joseph, d 10 April 1852 aged 72 yrs

Bowen, Polly, d Sept.....

Bowen, Nancy, d/o Joseph & Polly Bowen, d 20 March 1851 aged 36 yrs

Moulton, Calvin, b 21 March 1791, d 10 April 1863

Moulton, Nancy, w/o Calvin Moulton, b 25 Jan 1797, d 18 Feb 1821

Moulton, Phebe, w/o Calvin Moulton, b 10 Oct 1797, d 23 Feb 1880

Goff, Ephraim Jr., s/o Ephraim & Hannah M. Goff, b 17 May 1814, d 17 Nov 1833

Goff, Luther, s/o Ephraim & Hannah M. Goff, b 8 Nov 1819, d 26 Nov 1896

Goff, Amy, d/o Ephraim & Hannah M. Goff, b 23 March 1829, d 24 April 1831

Morse, Fanny F., b 17 Dec 1823, d 7 Sept 1909

Goff, Ephraim Sr., b 28 Jan 1782, d 1 Oct 1865

Goff, Hannah, w/o Ephraim Goff Sr., b 19 Nov 1794, d 12 July 1844

Holmes, Roland, d 14 Aug 1932 aged 24 yrs

Watson, Bethiah, d 28 Jan 1857 aged 75 yrs

Watson, William, d 5 April 1863 aged 72 yrs

Watson, Ann, w/o William Waston, d 12 June 1855 aged 60 yrs

Watson, Sarah A., d/o William & Ann Watson, s 11 Sept 1851 aged 21 yrs

Watson, Maria, d/o William & Ann Watson, d 22 June 1856 aged 22 yrs

Watson, Joseph, d 6 June 1862 aged 37 yrs

Watson, Allen N., d 11 June 1863 aged 36 yrs

Watson, Abby W., d 23 Feb 1863 aged 25 yrs

Watson, Sarah, d 15 Aug 1866 aged 89 yrs

Watson, John William, s/o William & Ann A. Watson, b 12 Jan 1818, d 15 Sept 1899

Watson, Captain Joseph, b 16 Sept 1779 Barrington, RI, d 16 Sept 1859 Rehoboth, Ma

Watson, Mr. John, d 23 July 1831 aged 86 yrs

Watson, Sarah, w/o John Watson, d 26 Nov 1814 aged 67 yrs

Allen, Paschal, 1818-1899

Allen, Mary A., w/o Paschal Allen, 1822-1856

Allen, Eliza N., w/o Paschal Allen, 1824-1912

Smith, Ella Susan, 1856-1916

Dawley, Hattie E., d/o Joseph & Phebe W. Dawley, d 27 March 1870 aged 20 yrs

Dawley, Joseph, 1808-1875

Allen, Phebe Wheaton, w/o Joseph Dawley, 1822-1898

Peck, Calvin J., 1812-1893

Locke, Emeline, w/o Calvin J. Peck, 1821-1903

Peck, George C., 1856-1861

Peck, Fannie V., 1863-1878

Peck, Thomas J., 1845-1918, A member of Co D 59th & 5th Regt Mass Vol Inf

Sprague, Lydia H., w/o Thomas J. Peck, 1846-1925

Bowen, George L., d 16 July 1892 aged 43 yrs

Bowen, Mary, w/o George L. Bowen, d 1 May 1900 aged 49 yrs

Bowen, Ebenezer M., d 13 Feb 1855 aged 70 yrs 10 mos 22 days

Bowen, Nancy, w/o Ebenezer M. Bowen, d 9 March 1891 aged 70 yrs 4 mos

Grant, Emily Mary, 1875-1876

Grant, Henry T., 1858-1900

Reynolds, Lovina W., w/o Henry T. Grant, 1853-1925
Thatcher, Captain James J., 1848-1905
Thatcher, Eliza A., w/o Capt. James J. Thatcher, 1856-1948
Sutherland, Ida Thatcher, 1882-1912
Webber, James, d 9 Feb 1828
Webber, Molly, w/o James Webber, d 22 April 1868
Webber, Lovina, d 30 Dec 1867 aged 39 yrs
Webber, Betsey, d 11 March 1864 aged 65 yrs
Whitney, Clarence S., 1850-1913
Hunt, Martha W., w/o Clarence S. Whitney, 1849-1926
Carpenter, Samuel J., d 3 June 1894 aged 53 yrs, A member of Co D 1st
   CVA
Gould, Amos S., 1859-1924
Gould, Etta C., w/o Amos S. Gould, 1862-1927
Angell, Amos J., 1848-1914
Ballard, Mattie K., w/o Amos J. Angell, 1851-1896
Fenton, Larkin, b 15 Sept 1827, d 4 April 1891
Fenton, Mahala M., w/o Larkin Fenton, b 13 Jan 1825, d 24 Oct 1883
Lowry, James Rudd, 1854-1917
Lowry, Amelia A., w/o James Rudd Lowry, 1862-1957
Lowry, James R. Jr., 1881-1882
Hill, Thomas, 1855-1921
Hill, Annie, w/o Thomas Hill, 1861-1923
Hill, William T., 1893-1919
Hill, Thomas, b 21 Dec 1812, d 8 March 1897
Hill, Susanna, w/o Thomas Hill, d 28 Feb 1877 aged 58 yrs 4 mos 26 days
Bliss, George D., b 9 Dec 1855, d 7 June 1923
Bliss, Cyrus W., b 4 April 1823, d 4 April 1883
Munroe, Hannah T., w/o Cyrus W. Bliss, b 1 Feb 1828, d 9 May 1910
Brown, Arnold de F., 1838-1874
Horton, Amanda M., w/o Arnold de F. Brown, 1838-1929
Brown, Cora, 1871-1871
Cushing, Lorring, b 28 Jan 1815, d 19 Oct 1870
Robinson, Hannah, w/o Lorring Cushing, b 1 Oct 1818, d 3 June 1907
Lane, Amos B., b 7 June 1814, d 21 Dec 1898
Allyn, Cornelia, w/o Amos B. Lane, b 22 Oct 1805, d 4 Sept 1847
Robinson, Phebe, w/o Amos B. Lane, b 26 Oct 1816, d 13 Aug 1890
Chipman, Elizabeth, 1856-1931
Chipman, Irene C., 1858--1907
Chipman, Dr. James L., b 24 Nov 1830, d 16 Nov 1894

Chipman, Sarah, w/o Dr. James L. Chipman, b 8 April 1846, d 3 Jan 1919

Luther, Ira, 1810-1882

Luther, Nancy B., w/o Ira Luther, 1812-1904

Luther, Allen B., s/o Ira & Nancy Luther, 1843-1864

Luther, Ira W., s/o Ira & Nancy Luther, 1848-1864

Carpenter, Julia I., 1883-1913

Irons, Nelson A., d 22 Sept 1885 aged 59 yrs 2 mos

Irons, Olive, w/o Nelson A. Irons, d 7 Jan 1901 aged 68 yrs 11 mos

Rogers, Olive B., w/o Henry T. Rogers, d 24 Nov 1884 aged 68 yrs 3 mos

Irons, Sarah, d/o Nelson & Olive A. Irons, d 14 Sept 1855 aged 1 yr 17 days

Bliss, Lewis S., d 14 Oct 1870 aged 82 yrs

Bliss, Betsey, w/o Lewis S. Bliss, d 20 Dec 1863 aged 74 yrs

Luther, Rhodolphus, b 3 June 1803, d 6 May 1890

Luther, Lephe, w/o Rhodolphus Luther, b 7 March 1800, d 25 Nov 1878

Pierce, Darius, d 28 Nov 1851 aged 65 yrs

Pierce, Mason M., d 26 May 1843 aged 23 yrs

Smith, Joseph, d 17 June 1830 aged 72 yrs

Smith, Lucy, w/o Joseph Smith, d 14 July 1846 aged 72 yrs

Smith, Mary, d/o Joseph & Lucy Smith, d 22 Oct 1851 aged 21 yrs

Smith, Lucy Ann, d/o Joseph & Lucy Smith, d 30 July 1852 aged 36 yrs

Mason, Joanna Grand, d/o John & Joanna Mason, d 29 March 1864

Bliss, Zenas, s/o Zenas & Kezia Bliss, b 11 June 1806 Rehoboth, MA, d 24 May 1862 Johnston, RI

Miller, Lewis L., s/o Martha N. & Col. Z.B. Bliss, b 2 Oct 1868 Providence, RI, d 10 July 1869 Providence, RI

Bliss, Mattie, d/o Col. Z.B. & Martha Bliss, b 22 Sept 1864 Johnston, RI, d 22 May 1866 Fort Porter, Buffalo, NY

Tracy, Edward, 1845-1920

Tracy, Georgianna A., w/o Edward Tracy, d 6 April 1916 aged 67 yrs

Carpenter, Dutee, d 1 Sept 1907 aged 72 yrs

Carpenter, Royal MD., d 23 May 1849 aged 71 yrs

Carpenter, Elvira, w/o Dr. Royal Carpenter, d 1840

Bliss, John, d 12 March 1825 aged 78 yrs

Bliss, Sarah, w/o John Bliss, d 20 March 1856 aged 102 yrs 5 mos

Frost, Lois Maria, w/o William F. Frost, d 29 Nov 1853 aged 33 yrs 7 mos

Frost, Henry F., s/o William & Lois M. Frost, d 29 Feb 1864 aged 18 yrs

Grant, Herbert F., 1880-1944

Grant, Violet G., w/o Herbert F. Grant, 1896-1956

Bliss, Cromwell, d 7 Feb 1848 aged 70 yrs
Bliss, Nancy, w/o Cromwell Bliss, d 1843
Salmon, William J., 1888-1946
Salmon, Clare J., w/o William J. Salmon, 1902-....
Bliss, Sylvanus, d 15 March 1842 aged 32 yrs
Bliss, Elizabeth, w/o Sylvanus Bliss, d 2 June 1876 aged 61 yrs 5 mos
Waterman, Asa, b 25 Sept 1856, d 20 Sept 1935
Waterman, Emma E., w/o Asa Waterman, b 25 March 1860, d 23 Oct
    1904
Hannalty, Thomas J., 1880-....
Waterman, Nellie E., w/o Thomas K. Hannalty, 1883-1956
Waterman, John E., 1885-1950
Waterman, Emma, w/o John Waterman, 1886-1970
Adams, William, d 15 Feb 1899 aged 95 yrs 7 mos 6 days
Fuller, Horace Newton, b 12 July 1811, d 13 April 1848
Fuller, Candace Emily, b 4 July 1843, d 6 Oct 1843
Baker, George A. Jr., 1912-1994
Fuller, Ezra, b 6 Oct 1870 aged 78 yrs
Fuller, Hannah, w/o Ezra Fuller, d 20 March 1864 aged 67 yrs
Fuller, Hannah, d/o Ezra & Hannah Fuller, d 30 Sept 1811 aged 11 yrs
Fuller, Otis, d 5 Feb 1876 aged 51 yrs
Fuller, Nancy A., d 27 June 1890 aged 63 yrs
North, George, 1872-1924
Bliss, Noah, d 2 July 1875 aged 86 yrs 10 mos 13 days
Bliss, Deacon Asahel, d 22 May 1855 aged 83 yrs 8 mos
Martin, Deborah, w/o Dea. Asahel Bliss, d 8 June 1858 aged 81 yrs
Baker, Erwin J., 1811-188-
Bliss, Rosina, w/o Erwin J. Baker, 1816-1882
Bradbury, Samuel L., 1879-19..
Hayden, Mabel Frances, w/o Samuel L. Bradbury, 1878-1940
Bradbury, Inez Mabel, 1906-1912
Hayden, Walter H., b 1853 Quincy, MA, d 1921
Baker, Rosina, w/o Walter H. Hayden, 1859-1923
Carpenter, Abel, d 9 Oct 1852 aged 50 yrs
Smith, Samuel, d 17 Feb 1839 aged 83 yrs
Smith, Hannah, w/o Samuel Smith, d 15 Nov 1857 aged 96 yrs 6 mos
Burr, Cromwell, d May 1848
Northan, Olive, w/o Captain Joseph Northan, d 8 Dec 1861 aged 92 yrs 11
    mos
Goodall, David, 1820-1906

Carpenter, Christopher Jr., d 7 Dec 1851

Carpenter, Emeline, w/o Christopher Carpenter Jr., d 16 July 1840 aged 34 yrs

Carpenter, Ruth, w/o Christopher Carpenter Jr., d 11 Oct 1849 aged 35 yrs

Bliss, Olive, w/o Noah Bliss, d 19 Feb 1867 aged 74 yrs 2 mos

Bliss, Asahel N., d 24 July 1833 aged 25 yrs

Horton, Betsey Ann, d 13 Feb 1857 aged 44 yrs

Horton, Mary Ann, d 13 July 1851 aged 32 yrs

Bliss, William M., s/o Martin & Sophia Bliss, d 25 June 1857 Attleborough, MA aged 35 yrs 10 mos 23 days

Bliss, Lemira, w/o William M. Bliss & d/o Edward & Lemira Bliss, d 6 March 1840 aged 24 yrs

Bliss, George D., d 1 May 1856 aged 27 yrs

Bliss, Mary, w/o George D. Bliss & d/o Edward & Lemira Bliss, d 20 March 1851 aged 22 yrs

Fuller, Olive H., d/o Ezra Fuller, d 26 March 1903 aged 68 yrs

Salisbury, Earle C., 1888-1964

Fuller, Frank F., 1865-1943

Salisbury, Lizzie M., w/o Frank F. Fuller, 1879-1971

Fuller, Cyrus, b 22 Feb 1829, d 21 March 1919

Fuller, Lydia, w/o Cyrus Fuller,d June 1883

Richardson, Hallam, 1860-1907

Sprague, Lydia R., w/o Hallam Richardson, 1864-1929

Richardson, Margaret A., 1899-1907

Drown, Joshua Esq., d 13 May 1877

Luther, William, 1871-1949

Drown, William J., s/o Joshua Drown, d 9 Jan 1852 aged 24 yrs

Drown, Jonathan, d 1808 Alexandria, VA

Drown, Sarah, w/o Jonathan Drown, d 7 June 1841 aged 92 yrs

Drown, Hannah, d/o Jonathan & Sarah Drown, d 15 March 1863 aged 84 yrs

Drown, Azubah D., d 10 Nov 1873 aged 99 yrs

Guild, Walter A., 1858-1937

Guild, Mary E., w/o Walter A. Guild, 1862-1906

Guild, Harvey S., s/o Walter & Mary Guild, 1883-1894

Carpenter, Nathan, d 17 Jan 1875 aged 82 yrs

Carpenter, Mima, w/o Nathan Carpenter, d 22 March 1841 aged 37 yrs

Carpenter, Rachel, w/o Nathan Carpenter, d 2 May 1875

Drown, Hiram, 1803-1879

Goff, Miram, w/o Hiram Drown, 1804-1879

Drown, Mariam Jane, 1835-1904

Drown, Hiram Howard, 1840-1864

Opferkuch, Josephine, 1854-1929

Wilmarth, George W., 23 Sept 1870 aged 51 yrs

Wilmarth, Ruth, w/o George W. Wilmarth, d 1850

Drown, George W., s/o A. & Eliza R. Drown, d 8 Oct 1852 aged 1 yr 1 mo 11 days

Blanding, James Esq., d 28 June 1870 aged 89 yrs

Blanding, Elizabeth, w/o James Blanding Esq., d 16 Nov 1865 aged 82 yrs

Blanding, William, MD, b 7 Feb 1773 Rehoboth, MA, d 12 Oct 1857 Rehoboth, MA

Blanding, Abram O., surgeon of 20th Iowa Reg., b 28 April 1823, Rehoboth, MA, d 31 July 1892 Palmer, Florida

Blanding, Sarah, w/o Dr. Abram O. Blanding, b 11 June 1837 Zanesville, Florida, d 21 June 1912 Gainesville, Florida

Blanding, William, b 1 Nov 1820, d 17 Oct 1920

Blanding, Lephe Hunt, d/o James & Elizabeth Blanding, d 21 Nov 1864

Blanding, Juliet Maria, d/o James & Elizabeth Blanding, d 7 May 1853

Blanding, William, d 12 June 1830 aged 82 yrs

Blanding, Lydia, w/o William Blanding, d 30 Aug 1835 aged 85 yrs

Blanding, Lephe, d/o William & Lydia Blanding, d 17 Oct 1822 aged 31 yrs

King, Deacon Elisha D., d 7 Aug 1880 aged 84 yrs 8 mos 1 day

King, Mary A.C., w/o Deacon Elisha D. King, d 15 Feb 1882

King, Robert Harvey, s/o Deacon Elisha & Mary King, d 26 May 1872

King, Benjamin H., d 16 Dec 1847 aged 22 yrs

Short, William F., s/o Ebenezer & Martha Short, d 26 March 1854 aged 5 yrs

King, Freelove, d/o Robert & Freelove King, d 20 Feb 1858

King, Mary, d/o Robert & Freelove King, d 16 Dec 1867

Carpenter, Francis H., d 21 May 1881 aged 68 yrs 27 days

Carpenter, Betsey B., w/o Francis H. Carpebter, d 4 Sept 1889 aged 71 yrs 3 mos 3 days

Carpenter, Sarah E., d/o Francis & Betsey Carpenter, d 4 May 1867 aged 18 yrs 7 mos

Carpenter, Samuel B., s/o Francis & Betsey Carpwnter, d 14 Nov 1843 aged 18 mos

Carpenter, William H., s/o Francis & Betsey Carpenter, d 24 Jan 1887 aged 20 yrs 8 mos

Horton, Nancy, w/o Darius Horton, d 12 Sept 1841 aged 57 yrs

Horton, William, s/o Darius & Nancy Horton, d 14 Nov 1833 aged 12 yrs

Tanner, William Palmer, 1870-1936

Servies, Clara, w/o William Palmer Tanner, 1874-1964

Miller, Sylvester Allen, b 10 June 1849, d 23 June 1936

Miller, Gilbert M., d 8 Jan 1861 aged 50 yrs

Allen, Rebecca, w/o Gilbert M. Miller, b 16 Feb 1816, d 23 Feb 1906

Carpenter, Joseph W., d 27 Jan 1864 aged 62 yrs 2 mos 3 days

Horton, Louisa, w/o Joseph W. Carpenter, d 23 June 1889 aged 78 yrs 11 mos 26 days

Carpenter, Louisa W., d/o Joseph & Louisa Carpenter, d 3 Feb 1851 aged 1 yr 11 mos

Allen, Deacon Sylvester C., d 5 Feb 1842 aged 53 yrs

Allen, Hannah, w/o Deacon Sylvester Allen, d 8 July 1876 aged 84 yrs 9 mos

Allen, Abby Maria, d/o Deacon Sylvester & Hannah Allen, d 6 Aug 1826 aged 8 yrs

Allen, Amanda M., d/o David W. & Eliza Allen, d 10 July 1865 aged 4 yrs 5 mos 24 days

Cushing, Capt. Caleb, d 21 March 1861 aged 84 yrs 11 mos

Cushing, Horace, d 11 Aug 1851 aged 45 yrs

Bucklin, Nancy, d 9 June 1885 aged 86 yrs

Carpenter, Samuel G., d 29 Aug 1843 aged 39 yrs

Carpenter, Seraphina A., w/o Samuel G. Carpenter, d 4 Oct 1890 aged 80 yrs

Bliss, Darius, d 1 Jan 1839 aged 83 yrs

Bliss, Nathaniel, d 1825

Carpenter, Stephen, d 15 July 1850 aged 85 yrs

Carpenter, Hannah, w/o Stephen Carpenter, d 17 April 1850 aged 80 yrs

Carpenter, William M., s/o Stephen & Hannah Carpenter, d 18 Nov 1816 aged 18 yrs

Perry, William M., d 20 Jan 1881 aged 69 yrs 28 days

Wheaton, Nancy G., w/o William M. Perry, d 2 Nov 1889 aged 71 yrs

Perry, Hattie, d 16 May 1892 aged 38 yyrs 2 mos 12 days

Wilmarth, Capt. Joseph, d 29 Nov 1897 aged 82 yrs

Carpenter, Thomas, d 26 April 1805 aged 74 yrs

Carpenter, Elizabeth, w/o Thomas Carpenter, d 17 May 1804 aged 68 yrs

Carpenter, Deacon Thomas, d 31 May 1779 aged 87 yrs

Carpenter, Mary, w/o Dea Thomas Carpenter, d 28 April 1783 aged 87 yrs

Carpenter, Elizabeth, w/o Caleb Carpenter, d 21 July 1839 aged 100 yrs 2 mos 4 days

Carpenter, Milton, b 31 Jan 1798 Rehobth, MA, d 27 Jan 1874

Blanding, Susan, d 6 Sept 1809 aged 28 yr

Carpenter, Caleb, d 13 Aug 1835 aged 67 yrs

Carpenter, Hannah, w/o Caleb Carpenter & d/o Thomas George of Wrentham, MA, d 12 March 1805 aged 34 yrs

Carpenter, Mary, w/o Caleb Carpenter, d 15 Feb 1847 aged 69 yrs

Carpenter, Amanda F., d/o Caleb & Hannah Carpenter, d 25 Nov 1841 aged 41 yrs

Carpenter, Rosella, d/o James & Lucy Carpenter, b 26 Aug 1799, d 30 Oct 1806

Carpenter, James, b 15 Sept 1767, d 20 Oct 1812

Bliss, Lucy, w/o James Carpenter, b 23 June 1769, d 21 Sept 1817

Cushing, Josiah, d 15 May 1817 aged 81 yrs

Reed, W. Hodges, d 26 Dec 1888 aged 73 yrs

Reed, Amanda, w/o W. Hodges Reed, d 30 Dec 1886 aged 67 yrs 7 mos

Carpenter, Joseph, b 8 Sept 1789, d 12 Nov 1880

Carpenter, Nancy, w/o Joseph Carpenter, b 19 Dec 1793, d 4 May 1880

Reed, Mary E., w/o William H. Reed, d 15 March 1885 aged 39 yrs 3 mos

Reed, Mary L., d/o William & Mary Reed, d 22 Oct 1885 aged 8 mos 2 days

Fales, Mabel E., 1871-1958

Fales, Lester T. J., 1873-1969

Carpenter, Mary W., b 31 March 1831, d 7 July 1907

Carpenter, Thomas W., b 26 Feb 1833, d 28 Feb 1898

Carpenter, Freddie W., s/o Thomas & Mary Carpenter, d 20 Jan 1875 aged 16 yrs 1 mo 23 days

Carpenter, Thomas, s/o Thomas & Mary Carpenter, d 25 Jan 1875 aged 8 yrs 5 mos 12 days

Carpenter, Willie S., s/o Thomas & Mary Carpenter, d 1 Jan 1875 aged 6 yrs

Lane, Lydia Carpenter, d/o Isiah & Hopestill Lane, d 1 Nov 1850 aged 33 yrs

Gardner, Benjamin F., b 24 May 1814, d 13 March 1886

Lane, Lephe A., w/o Benjamin F. Gardner, b 15 March 1820, d 16 Oct 1885

Drown, Marcy, w/o Isaiah Lane, d 7 Aug 1876 aged 69 yrs 4 mos 11 days

Lane, Isaiah, d 1 Aug 1837 aged 54 yrs 2 mos 12 days

Willmarth, Hannah, w/o Samuel N. Willmarth, d 18 Dec 1814 aged 30 yrs

Wheeler, Jeremiah, d 4 Aug 1839 aged 86 yrs

Wheeler, Elizabeth, w/o Jeremiah Wheeler, d 13 April 1825 aged 71 yrs

Wheeler, Dexter, s/o Jeremiah & Elizabeth Wheeler, d 18 April 1835 aged 58 yrs

Cushing, Elizabeth, w/o Jacob Cushing, d 24 Sept 1824 aged 74 yrs

Bliss, Nelson Smith, s/o Asaph & Abigail Bliss, d 5 Sept 1839 Mobile, Alabama aged 26 yrs

Carpenter, Asaph, b 31 May 1805, d 14 July 1883

Carpenter, Caroline, w/o Asaph Carpenter, b 18 Nov 1810, d 4 June 1892

Remington, Carrie C., d/o William & Chloe Remington, d 31 March 1876 aged 20 yrs 6 mos 11 days

Remington, Chloe, w/o William A. Remington & d/o Asaph & Caroline Carpenter, d 24 Dec 1856 aged 28 yrs

Carpenter, Thomas, d 29 Oct 1822 aged 66 yrs

Carpenter, Chloe, w/o Thomas Carpenter, d 27 Jan 1813 aged 48 yrs

Carpenter, Edwin S., 1873-1904

Carpenter, Amelia A., w/o Edwin S. Carpenter, 1872-1943

Carpenter, Peter, b 5 Oct 1773, d 9 June 1814

Carpenter, Nancy, w/o Peter Carpenter, b 17 May 1778, d 21 Aug 1857

Blanding, Martha A., w/o Col. Christopher Blanding, b 28 Jan 1761, d 28 Jan 1856

Lane, Ebenezer, s/o Isiah & Marcy Lane, A member of Co H 16th Mass Vols, Killed in the Battle of Spottsylvina, Virginia, 12 May 1864 aged 36 yrs 3 mos 24 days

Bliss, Capt. Asaph, d 14 Sept 1857 aged 85 yrs

Bliss, Abigail, w/o Capt. Asaph Bliss, d 1 Nov 1825

Bliss, Sarah, w/o Capt. Asaph Bliss, d 23 Sept 1857

Cushing, Capt. Loring, d 12 Sept 1816 aged 44 yrs

Cushing, Lucy, w/o Capt. Loring Cushing, d 18 Jan 1851 aged 71 yrs

Short, Ebenezer, d 9 Jan 1815 aged 53 yrs

Short, Martha, w/o Ebenezer Short, d 2 Nov 1834

Burr, Capt. Isaac, d 3 Feb 1770 aged 46 yrs

Burr, Rachel, w/o Capt. Isaac Burr, d 20 Dec 1811 aged 82 yrs

Rogerson, Rev. Robert, d 20 March 1799 aged 78 yrs

Bliss, James, Esq., d 5 March 1842 aged 81yrs

Bliss, Tabitha, w/o James Bliss Esq., d 10 Oct 1858 aged 75 yrs 7 mos

Bliss, Mary, w/o James Bliss Esq., d 9 Aug 1828 aged 63 yrs

Bliss, Ephraim, 1699-1778

Carpenter, Rachel, w/o Lt. Ephraim Bliss, 1699-1784

Bliss, Alvah, 1730-1825

Moulton, Judith, 1734-1755

Rogerson, Capt. John, d 9 Dec 1835 aged 73 yrs 4 mos

Rogerson, Mary, w/o Capt. John Rogerson, d 30 May 1833 aged 62 yrs

Carpenter, Col. Samuel, d 10 Dec 1803 aged 50 yrs

Carpenter, Lydia F., w/o Col. Samuel Carpenter, d 10 Feb 1786 aged 40
  yrs

Carpenter, Lydia S., w/o Col Samuel Carpenter, d 11 March 1796 aged 43
  yrs

Rogerson, Alfred, s/o Capt. John & Mary Rogerson, d 3 Oct 1820 aged 23
  yrs

Smith, Capt. Samuel, d 21 May 1849 agd 59 yrs

Rogerson, Betty, w/o Rev. Robert Rogerson & d/o Thomas Bowen, d 12
  Dec 1793 aged 65 yrs

Peck, Cromwell, d 15 June 1843 aged 70 yrs

Peck, Peddy, w/o Cromwell Peck, d 18 June 1857 aged 84 yrs

Peck, Branford, d 21 June 1871 aged 63 yrs

Peck, Ann, b 25 Aug 1887, d 1 March 1890

Brown, Royal P., d 10 May 1825 aged 51 yrs

Goff, Cyrus, b 17 Nov 1793, d 15 March 1830

Weber, Mary w/o Ezekiel Weber, b 15 Aug 1795, d 26 Nov 1828

Peck, Billings, b 11 May 1801, d 25 Feb 1882

Goff, Delila, w/o Billings Peck, b 24 Feb 1807, d 26 Oct 1889

Goff, Hiram, b 18 Jan 1807, d 12 July 1887

Goff, Sylvester, b 12 Jan 1765, d 26 Jan 1837

Bliss, Rebecca, w/o Sylvester Goff, b 12 July 1771, d 9 Oct 1839

Beals, Horace E., b 21 Sept 1863, d 26 Oct 1957

Borden, Lillian C., w/o Horace E. Beals, b 5 June 1875, d 30 Dec 1953

Frost, Walter Bliss, 1852-1924

Barber, Alice Almira, w/o Walter Bliss Frost, 1858-1937

Bliss, Gilbert, d 18 May 1885 aged 67 yrs 3 mos 13 days

Bliss, Ardelia H., w/o Gilbert Bliss, d 5 Feb 1897 aged 79 yrs 2 mos 8
  days

Boyce, Justin, 1883-1932

William, Sara, w/o Justin Boyce.....

Goff, Enoch, b 20 March 1819, d 22 Feb 1899

Goff, Keziah, w/o Enoch Goff, b 9 April 1821, d 8 Oct 1904

Paull, Seth, b 17 Aug 1824, d 25 Oct 1864

Carpenter, Harriet J. Paull, b 13 March 1828, d 5 March 1893

Mansfield, Lucius R., 1874-1940

Mansfield, Evelyn B., w/o Lucius Mansfield, 1871-1938

Goff, Simeon K., b 18 Ot 1847, d 27 Aug 1922

Lawton, Louisa E., w/o Simeon Goff, b 25 Aug 1851, d 16 March 1932

Goff, Walter, b 26 Aug 1877, d 16 Oct 1879

Borden, Clark Pierce, b 22 May 1842, d 3 Oct 1927, A member of Co F 39th Mass Vols Inf US Army

Carpenter, Cynthia S., w/o Clark Pierce Borden, b 2 Jan 1849, d 3 Feb 1930

Borden, Capt. Everett Carpenter, s/o Clark & Cynthia Borden, b 18 March 1873, d 26 Sept 1930

Humphrey, Raymond W., 1893-1966

Humphrey, Irene M., w/o Raymond W. Humphrey, 1898-1972

Brown, Edwin C., 1844-1915

Brown, Emma, w/o Edwin C. Brown, 1847-1915

Brown, Charles E., 1854-1917

Angell, Henry B., 1873-1930

Latham, Laura, w/o Henry B. Angell, 1874-1965

Allen, George W. Sr. 1893-1960

Angell, Dorothy F., w/o George W. Allen Jr., 1909-1964

Cash, Alvin C., 1841-1924

Cash, Florine, w/o Alvin C. Cash, 1844-1938

Cash, Harry A., 1870-1928

Cox, John, 1866-1930

Cox, Catherine M., w/o John Cox, 1865-1943

Cox, Earl T., 1896-1957

Cox, Sophia C., w/o Earl T. Cox, 1865-1977

Hughes, Harry S., 1868-1954

Hughes, Alice, w/o Harry S. Hughes, 1866-1962

Hughes, Harry Arden, 1896-1960

Nash, Benjamin, d 23 March 1883 aged 89 yrs 2 mos

Nash, Susan D., w/o Benjamin Nash, d 29 May 1891 aged 85 yrs 7 mos

Nash, Susie P., w/o Charles Nash, d 24 April 1895 aged 31 yrs

Nash, James H., d 24 Feb 1877 aged 44 yrs

Nash, Ardelia M., w/o James H. Nash, d 7 April 1867 aged 28 yrs

Nash, Mabel Ardelia, d/o Charles & Susan P. Nash, d 14 March 1904 aged 13 yrs

Horton, Danforth C., b 2 May 1813, d 1 Nov 1890

Simmons, Mary, w/o Danforth C. Horton, b 19 Aug 1811, d 19 April 1894

Wilmarth, Capt. Daniel L., b 5 Oct 1793, d 9 Jan 1858

Wilmarth, Mary C., w/o Capt. Daniel L. Wilmarth, b 17 April 1798, d 16 Nov 1888

Lake, George C., b 24 June 1851, d 3 Nov 1906

Bliss, Mary J., w/o George C. Lake, b 22 June 1854, d 17 Aug 1906

Lake, Abby F., d/o George & Mary Lake, b 22 May 1878, d 14 Aug 1878

Bliss, Ruth, b 1 Dec 1805, d 8 April 1880

Bliss, Amanda, b 3 Oct 1798, d 21 Dec 1888

Bliss, Col. Abiah, d 12 Aug 1858 aged 90 yrs

Bliss, Rebekah, w/o Col. Abiah Bliss, d 11 April 1856 aged 84 yrs

Whiting, Rachel C., w/o James Whiting & d/o Col. Abiah Bliss, d 30 Jan 1843 Taunton, MA aged 30 yrs

Kent, George W., d 1 May 1877 aged 78 yrs

Kent, Sally, w/o George W. Kent, d 10 April 1886 aged 82 yrs

Webber, Mary, w/o Cyrus Webber, b 5 July 1807, d 11 April 1860

Goff, Cromwell, 1790-1865

Goff, Ruth, w/o Cromwell Goff, 1785-1852

Goff, Eliza, d/o Cromwell & Ruth Goff, 1821-1838

Horton, Benjamin, b 30 April 1815, d 16 July 1899

Horton, Caroline C., w/o Benjamin Horton, d 25 Oct 1885 aged 69 yrs

Horton, Seneca L., s/o Benjamin & Betsey Horton, d 30 Oct 1822 aged 16 days

Horton, Capt. Benjamin, d 21 Sept 1854 aged 69 yrs

Horton, Betsey, w/o Capt. Benjamin Horton, d 1 Dec 1855 aged 70 yrs

Goff, George L., 1829-1879

Reed, Harriet N., w/o George L. Goff, 1824-1904

Goff, Fred G., 1865-1957

Carpenter, Ellery W., 1910-1987

Goff, Ellery L., 1858-1954

Tyrell, Mary E., w/o Ellery L. Goff, 1857-1942

Carpenter, Enoch A., 1886-1964

Goff, Elsie L., w/o Enoch A. Carpenter, 1888-1985

Olsen, James C., 1885-1958

Olsen, Nellie I., w/o James C. Olsen, 1882-1954

Anthony, Agnes, 1896-1982

Wilcox, Samuel A, 1879-1963

Wilcox, Ella L., w/o Samuel A. Wilcox, 1885-1969

Goff, Charles B., 1876-1949

Gardiner, Cora H., w/o Charles B. Goff, 1877-1960
Goff, Muriel, d/o Charls & Cora Goff, & w/o Alfred B. Roberts, 1910-1946
Roberts, Alfred B., 1909-1967
Kammerer, Eugene, 1885-1965
Quint, Clara S., w/o Eugene Kammerer, 1896-1968
Cohen, Leon, 1916-1969
Kammerer, Margaret, w/o Leon Cohen, 1918-....
Koerner, C. Henry, 1890-1964
Koerner, Sigrid A., w/o C. Henry Koerner, 1892-1966
Knight, Frank F. W., 1902-1953
Knight, Mildred E., w/o Frank F. W. Knight, 1902-19..
Waterman, Albert D., 1881-1954
Waterman, Lillian R., w/o Albert D. Waterman, 1881-1955
Viall, Carlton G., Tec 5 US Army WW2, 1910-1976
Gilbert, Walter, 1898-....
Viall, Charles Carpenter, b 28 Jan 1917, d 13 Nov 1989
Hundt, Grace M., w/o Charles Carpenter Viall, b 7 Nov 1920, d....
Davidson, Helen E., w/o Walter E. Gilbert, 1897-1985
Viall, Harriet E., 1908-1972
Viall, William B., 1904-1969
Freethey, Rebecca, w/o William B. Viall, 1904-1955
Viall, Richard E., 1934-1979
Mutter, Harry C., 1909-1988
Viall, Etta L., w/o Harry C. Mutter, 1914-1968
Sarkisian, Simeon, 1868-1942
Waters, Mary, 1889-1949
Sutherland, Robert, 1859-1945
Smith, Bert C., 1885-1947
Pray, Mary E., w/o Bert C. Smith, 1884-1961
Smith, D. Bertrand, 1909-1992
Peck, Bernice H., w/o D. Bertrand Smith, 1907-....
Carpenter, G. W., 1876-1966
Carpenter, Ethel S., w/o G. W. Carpenter, 1883-1970
Mute, Laura F., 1895-1943
Randall, Horace H., 1871-1943
Bowen, Phebe A., w/o Horace H. Randall, 1873-1967
Randall, Horace Jr., 1911-1985
Jordan, Lorine, w/o Horace H. Randall Jr., 1909-....
Goff, Harold C., 1895-1963

Randall, Leah M., w/o Harold C. Goff, 1897-1985
Goff, William O., 1875-1942
Goff, Ruth, w/o William O. Goff, 1878-1951
Goff, Earl N., 1900-1979
Goff, Barbara F., w/o Earl N. Goff, 1900-1983
Stromberg, Otto S., 1884-1941
Erickson, Frida, w/o Otto S. Stromberg, 1890-1967
Carpenter, Joseph Allen, 1880-1963
Peck, Bessie, w/o Joseph Allen Carpenter, 1891-1965
Bliss, Charles S., 1884-1985
Browning, Eola E., w/o Charles S. Bliss, 1890-1976
Bliss, Martha B., 1871-1955
Kinne, John T., 1872-1939
Tootill, Sarah T., w/o John T. Kinne, buried Canterbury, CT
Hass, John, 1860-1935
Hass, Irene P., w/o John Hass, 1866-1957
Hass, Elvira P., 1893-1976
Hass, Joseph P., 1896-1992
Hass, Marian A., w/o Joseph P. Hass, 1903-1977
Morgan, Annice Hass, 1894-....
Moulton, Margaret, b 2 Aug 1910, d 27 July 1954
Moulton, Lenora M., b 13 Sept 1875, d 4 May 1941
Smith, Samuel E., 1866-1945
Smith, Ruth E., w/o Samuel E. Smith, 1868-1947
Smith, Samuel S., 1902-1989
Smith, Nellie R., w/o Samuel S. Smith, 1888-1973
Smith, Margaret, w/o Samuel S. Smith, 1908-1973
Smith, Edward E., 1907-....
Smith, Florence M., w/o Edward E. Smith, 1912-1975
Swanson, Andrew, 1874-1940
Swanson, Ingrid, w/o Andrew Swanson, 1873-1979
Bennett, Samuel L., 1886-1944
Bennett, Mary R., w/o Samuel L. Bennett, 1894-1987
Parant, Aurele A., 1877-1941
Parant, Corine B., w/o Aurele A. Parant, 1882-1972
Allen, Thomas T., 1883-1961
Munroe, Mabel I., w/o Thomas T. Allen, 1886-1947
Allen, Barbara, d/o Thomas & Mabel Allen, 1919-1961
Watson, Hezekiah Horton, 1871-1943
Jonah, Jesse B., w/o Hezekiah Horton Watson, 1874-1968

Watson, Frederick H., s/o Hezekiah & Jesse Watson, 1814-1992
Lindopp, Dorothy H., w/o Frederick H. Watson, 1914-....
Trenin, Anthony B., 1869-1945
Smith, Ruth A., w/o Anthiny B. Trenin, 1874-1940
Smith, David F., 1885-1955
Stevenson, Thomas, 1855-1941
Stevenson, James, 1885-1970
Kennedy, Agnes, w/o James Stevenson, 1883-1958
Gardiner, Kenneth R., 1899-1994
Atkins, Helen, w/o Kenneth R. Gardiner, 1904-1935
Ormsbee, Stanley B., 1885-1958
Ormsbee, Helena Z., w/o Stanley B. Ormsbee, 1887-1969
Fitts, Clark D., 1917-1975
Fitts, Harriet B., w/o Clark D. Fitts, 1920-....
Grovsor, Carl A., 1872-1951
Grovsor, Emma C., w/o Carl A. Grovser, 1880-1951
Grovser, Albert G., 1911-1978
Grovser, Jean G., w/o Albert G. Grovser, 1905-1973
Grovser, Allen H., 1918-....
Grovser, Pauline E., w/o Allen H. Grovser, 1917-....
Booth, James R., 1879-1944
Turner, Loretta F., w/o James R. Booth, 1883-1947
Booth, Charles H., 1882-1957
Turner, Grace G., w/o Charles H. Booth, 1882-1960
Willis, Jesse Booth, 1887-1939
Turner, Susan A., 1874-1966
Booth, Philip C., 1905-1959
Parker, Richard R., 1936-1936
Parker, Jean E., 1943-1944
Parker, Hope G., 1900-1986
Parker, Reginald, 1911-1987
Parker, Raymond F., Sr., US Army WW2, b 30 Sept 1911, d 20 Aug 1993
Bennett, Caroline O., 1923-1975
Viall, Harvey K., 1858-1940
Viall, Mirian J., 1860-1939
Viall, Aaron S., 1894-1937
Crowther, Wilfred, 1870-1939
Crowther, Bertha, w/o Wilfred Crowther, 1878-1964
Watson, James D., 1898-1982
Watson, Gladys, w/o James D. Watson, 18999-1956

Hill, Georgie, mother of Gladys Watson, d 1941
Crowther, Kenneth, 1904-1987
Crowther, Alice M., w/o Kenneth Crowther, 1905-1972
Gorman, James Edward, 1910-1965
Jessop, Fred, 1873-1941
Graham, Clara, w/o Fred Jessop, 1873-1969
Barker, Ella L., 1880-1959
Hunt, Capt. Robert, b 7 Dec 1883, d 26 Nov 1967
Williams, Carl G., 1874-1936
Williams, Cora E., w/o Carl G. Williams, 1877-1959
Barker, James H., 1883-1953
Moore, Humphrey W., 1874-1942
Garside, Sarah G., w/o Humphrey W. Moore, 1877-1963
Whittaker, Charles, 1892-1941
Coggeshall, Bartha M., w/o Charles Whittaker, 1891-1974
Hathaway, Horace, 1890-1979
Shaw, Mildred A., w/o Horace C. Hathaway, 1895-....
Hathaway, Merrill, s/o Horace & Mildred Hathaway, 1917-....
Pearson, Viola D., w/o Merrill Hathaway, 1920-....
Hathaway, Elton B., d 20 Jan 1943, Mass Pvt 302 Inf 76 Div
Howard, John H., 1862-1944
Stackpole, Ida W., w/o John H. Howard, 1871-1960
Angell, Arthur K., 1882-1969
Angell, Mary L., w/o Arthur K. Angell, 1890-1983
Allard, Thomas T., 1868-1942
Allard, Esther V., 1868-1948
Allard, Roger V., 1895-1966
Allard, Ethel R., w/o Roger V. Allard, 1894-1966
Braun, Charles H., 1876-....
Rieo, Flora B., w/o Charles H. Braun, 1889-1954
Clark, Newton A., 1868-1945
Deming, Grace, w/o Newton A. Clark, 1875-1945
Carpenter, Horace W., b 24 Oct 1907, d 20 Oct 1950
Carpenter, George W., 1877-1955
Carpenter, Grace R., w/o George W. Carpenter, 1878-1966
Ward, Frank M. Sr., 1872-1948
Hague, Emma B., w/o Frank M. Ward Jr., 1871-1958
Catlow, George, 1879-1964
Gilbert, Alice, w/o George Catlow, 1879-1957
Crawford, John W., 1879-1945

Crawford, Mary E., w/o John W. Crawford, 1880-1965
Morgan, Charles E., 1867-1948
Morgan, Della M., w/o Charles E. Morgan, 1875-1945
Morgan, Edward L., 1910-1947
Lloyd, William W. Sr., 1897-1970
Olsen, Ellen T., w/o William W. Lloyd Sr., 1899-1979
Ward, Frank M., Jr., 1910-....
Catlow, Isabella F., w/o Frank M. Ward Jr., 1915-1991
Hall, Jesse C., 1897-1990
Hall, Mary V., w/o Jesse C. Hall, 1900-1978
Drahan, William J., 1895-1980
Drahan, Ellen A., w/o William Drahan, 1894-....
Talbot, John C., 1874-1956
Lord, Harriet, w/o John C. Talbot, 1878-1965
Lord, John W., 1876-1944
Buskane, William J., 1861-1952
Kershaw, Alice M., w/o William J. Buskane, 1864-1951
Buskane, Ethelwyn, d/o William & Alice Buskane, 1885-1978
Thayer, Oman G., 1897-1975
Thayer, Marion H., w/o Oman G. Thayer, 1898-1969
Thayer, Oman G., Jr., 1925-1944
Goyette, David N., 1879-1943
Horton, Amelia M., w/o David N. Goyette, 1882-1979
Horton, Elmer D., 1884-1955
Tilton, Thaddeus F., 1898-1951
MacRury, Louise, w/o Thaddeus F. Tilton, 1902-....
Coates, Hartley, 1881-1953
Coates, Elsie, w/o Hartley Coates, 1887-1961
Williams, John S. Sr., 1874-1951
Bownes, Josephine, w/o John . Williams Sr., 1873-1959
Williams, Richard, s/o John & Josephine Williams, 1910-1964
Bushnell, Fred M., 1884-1975
Bushnell, Marion W., w/o Fred M. Bushnell, 1886-1964
Johnson, John J., 1894-1969
Johnson, Lillian, w/o John J. Johnson, 1905-1993
Johnson, Lydon Amelia, 1936-1953
Whitfield, William H. G., 1888-1959
Whitfield, Mabel Frost, 1884-1952
Pray, Charles W., 1890-1955
Williams, Mary, w/o Charles W. Pray, 1891-1995

Dangnon, Ethelyn, d/o Charles & Mary Pray, 1913-1995
Carpenter, Robert E., 1877-1951
Peck, Mary F., w/o Robert E. Carpenter, 1888-1972
Corser, Lester J., 1912-1966
Freeman, Audrey Corser, 1935-1979
Harman, Ethelbert, 1880-1951
Harmon, Edna M., 1882-1955
Moore, George H., 1903-1985
Moore, Ruth L., w/o George H. Moore, 1904-1955
Gray, Lester R., 1901-1976
Flaherty, Elizabeth A., w/o Lester R. Gray, 1901-1964
Gray, Chester E., 1910-1988
Craft, Dodothy W., w/o Chester E. Gray, 1913-1994
Meagher, John J., 1917-1972
Carlson, Carl A., 1903-1964
Carlson, Dennis C., 1927-1986
Angell, Edgar L., 1885-1976
Angell, Dorothy M., w/o Edgar L. Angell, 1900-1982
Fowler, Marshall M., 1908-1979
Chamilland, Edith, w/o Marshall M. Fowler, 1910-1987
Fisher, Edith J., 1884-1983
Gingrich, Madeline C., 1916-1987
Bliss, Fred C., 1888-1971
Bliss, Henry F., 1886-1971
Bliss, Nina J., w/o Henry F. Bliss, 1884-1971
Read, Kenneth, 1899-1988
Higgins, Isabelle C., w/o Kenneth Read, 1904-1981
MacDonald, Walter, b 28 Oct 1900, d 17 Oct 1976
Jarvus, Mae S., w/o Walter MacDonald, b 16 June 1901, d 9 Sept 1971
Ramspott, Robert H., b 5 Jan 1895, d 29 Nov 1979
Parker, Ruth, b 21 Aug 1898, d 30 Dec 1991
Higgins, Everett D., 1888-1955
Winters, Gracie, w/o Everett D. Higgins, 1891-1990
Trim, Horace S., 1878-1947
Trim, Harriet E., w/o Horace S. Trim, 1886-1976
Jones, William L., 1908-1974
Jones, Ella V., w/o William L. Jones, 1907-1987
Synder, Matilda A., 1886-1946
Hubbard, Mrytle H., 1911-1974
Hubbard, William H., 1908-1978

Logan, William F., 1881-1950
Faust, Mabel, w/o William F. Logan, 1882-1947
Phelan, Walter, 1883-1963
Phelan, Ada C., w/o Walter Phelan, 1890-1968
Mitchell, Edgar J., 1887-1958
Gradwell, Grace G., w/o Edgar J. Mitchell, 1888-1982
Maddock, John F., 1897-1962
Mitchell, Grace M., w/o John F. Maddock, 1895-1979
Lacey, D. Grant, 1922-1968
Lacey, Gladys C., w/o D. Grant Lacey, 1922-1981
Hinnam, Chauncey J., 1872-1948
Liddle, Katherine B., w/o Chauncey J. Hinnam, 1874-1957
Hinnam, Harold S., 1896-1963
Wilkins, Lorena J., w/o Harold S. Hinnam, 1894-1972
Weaver, Harry F., 1875-1963
Fradd, Edith M., w/o Harry F. Weaver, 1873-1961
Richardson, Lloyd S., 1897-1955
Hubbert, Winslow L., 1868-1950
Bowers, Dr. Frederick, 1904-1952
Wyatt, Helen B., 1908-....
Bowers, Susan, 1845-1977
Balland, Norman P., 1902-1969
Richardson, Carl A., 1901-1956
Richardson, Rachel, w/o Carl A. Richardson, 1894-1970
West, Henry Evans, 1870-1957
Kent, Lillian, w/o Henry Evans West, 1876-1948
Peck, Harold E., 1895-1977
Peck, Emma C., w/o Harold E. Peck, 1895-1973
Saunders, Clarence A., b 12 May 1888, d 14 Jan 1968
Saunders, Lizzie M., w/o Clarence A. Saunders, b 30 April 1888, d 18
    Oct 1976
Saunders, Ralph W., b 14 Aug 1921, d 14 Oct 1978
Sargeant, Edgar L., 1875-1950
Sargeant, Priscilla T., w/o Edgar L. Sargeant, 1885-1945
Bowen, Fred R., 1911-1983
Bowen, Gracie M., w/o Fred R. Bowen, 1915-....
Thompson, Herbert, 1908-1976
Thompson, M. Inez, w/o Herbert Thompson, 1917-1969
Ellis, Theodore I., 1906-1963
Cottrele, Irene G. Ellis, 1909-1983

Bennett, Amos, 1900-1975
Armstrong, Flora B., w/o Amos Bennett, 1905-1979

Bosworth Cemetery
Rehoboth Historical # 49
Hornbine Street
Rehoboth, Massachusetts

West, James C., d 27 Nov 1876 aged 67 yrs 2 mos 19 days
West, Ann M., w/o James C. West, d 13 Feb 1883 aged 74 yrs 9 mos 18 days
West, Charles Henry, s/o James & Ann West, d 13 Jan 1856 aged 13 yrs 11 mos 22 days
Horton, Gideon J., 1813-1899
Horton, Laura, w/o Gideon Horton, d 29 June 1874 aged 57 yrs 8 mos 22 days
West, Edward, Fell in Battle of the Wilderness Virginia, 6 May 1861 aged 26 yrs 6 mos 3 days
Horton, Lovina, d/o Gideon & Lovina Horton Jr., d 5 Sept 1853 aged 69 yrs 19 days
Bosworth, Levi, d 15 Sept 1872 Providence, RI, aged 52 yrs
Bullock, Patience, w/o Joseph West, d 30 April 1877 aged 88 yrs
Wilmarth, Dan, d 4 Nov 1842
Wilmarth, Mary Ann, w/o Dan Wilmarth & d/o Joseph & Patience West, d March 1838 aged 19 yrs
West, Charles R., s/o Joseph & Patience West, d 12 April 1862
Jones, Simpson, d 21 July 1874 aged 81 yrs
Jones, Sarah W., w/o Simpson Jones, d 9 Nov 1869 aged 72 yrs
Jones, Elizabeth, w/o Simpson Jones, d 29 Jan 1845 aged 53 yrs
Bosworth, Deacon Lloyd, d 27 Feb 1858 aged 71 yrs
Bosworth, Elizabeth, w/o Dea Lloyd Bosworth, d 27 Sept 1836 aged 52 yrs
Bosworth, Jane, w/o Levi Bosworth & d/o Samuel & Jane Pierce, d 1863?
Bosworth, Lloyd, s/o Rev. Lloyd & Elizabeth Bosworth, d 27 Nov 1837 aged 26 yrs
Bosworth, Deacon David, d 12 March 1834 aged 67 yrs

Bosworth, Elizabeth, w/o Dea David Bosworth, d 31 July 1851 aged 86 yrs

Bosworth, Pardon, d 4 Jan 1803 aged 28 yrs

Bosworth, Gardner, d 3 Aug 1821 aged 28 yrs

Buffington, Hail, d 25 Aug 1841 aged 40 yrs

Buffington, Patience, w/o Hail Buffington, d 29 March 1841 aged 38 yrs

Bosworth, Matilda, d/o Dea David Bosworth, d 2 Sept 1844 aged 45 yrs

Bosworth, Julia, w/o Gardner Bosworth, d 11 Aug 1864 aged 65 yrs 8 mos

Bosworth, Gardner, s/o Gardner & Julia Bosworth, d 13 Feb 1821 aged 1 yr

Bosworth, Irena, d/o Gardner & Julia Bosworth, d 28 July 1833 aged 15 yrs

Simmons, Deacon Josiah, d 13 July 1871 aged 86 yrs

Simmons, Betsey, w/o Dea. Josiah Simmons, d 22 Jan 1877 aged 81 yrs

Simmons, Nancy, w/o Dea. Josiah Simmons, d 30 July 1835 aged 54 yrs

Simmons, William W., s/o Dea. Josiah & Nancy Simmons, d 18 Nov 1853 aged 37 yrs

Simmons, Clarissa, w/o William W. Simmons, d 1842

Simmons, Martha, w/o William W. Simmons, d 6 Oct 1852 aged 49 yrs

Simmons, Earl T., s/o William & Martha Simmons, d 18 Jan 1853 aged 4 yrs

Simmons, George Henry, s/o William & Martha Simmons, d 23 Feb 1846

Goff, Samuel, d 18 Nov 1810 aged 29 yrs

Goff, Crumel, d 26 June 1826 aged 40 yrs

Salisbury, Polly, w/o Levi Goff & widow of Cromwell Goff, d 4 June 1864 aged 78 yrs 5 mos 16 days

Horton, Chloe, w/o Abiel Horton, d 16 April 1810 aged 87 yrs

Horton, Abiel, d 8 Dec 1833 aged 86 yrs

Goff, Elder Nathan, d 23 June 1819 aged 69 yrs

Goff, Betsey, w/o Elder Nathan Goff, d 29 Jan 1832 aged 70 yrs

Horton, Daniel, d 6 Oct 1819 aged 69 yrs

Goff, Ephraim, s/o Ephraim & Hannah Goff, d 17 Nov 1832 aged 19 yrs

Goff, William, d 14 Oct 1834 aged 49 yrs

Goff, Sally, w/o William Goff, d 1 Nov 1844 aged 55 yrs

Goff, Olive, d 16 April 1848 aged 26 yrs

Goff, Lydia Ann, d/o William & Sally Goff, d 5 Jan 1839 aged 23 yrs

Goff, Sylvanus, b 6 Feb 1794,

Lovell Goff Cemetery
Rehoboth Historical # 16
Elm Street
Rehoboth, Massachusetts

Hix, Deacon Benjamin, d 24 March 1762 aged 47 yrs
Hix, Lydia, w/o Deacon Benjamin Hix, d 1 Feb 1820 aged 72 yrs
Goff, Ariel, d 16 Jan 1836 aged 83 yrs
Goff, Sally, w/o Ariel Goff, d 27 Nov 1853 aged 93 yrs
Goff, Lovell, d 13 July 1822 aged 70 yrs
Woodcock, Polly, d 21 Oct 1880 aged 83 yrs
Goff, Constant, d 29 June 1790
Goff, Nancy, w/o Constant Goff, d 1803 aged 79 yrs
Wheeler, William, d 5 May 1827 aged 63 yrs
Wheeler, Samuel, d 21 July 1847 aged 89 yrs
Wheeler, Sarah, w/o Samuel Wheeler, d Nov 1798 aged 40 yrs
Goff, Edwin M., d 18 Oct 1873 aged 60 yrs 4 mos 21 days
Goff, Darius, d 20 Aug 1835 aged 42 yrs 11 mos 13 days
Payne, Olive, formerly w/o Samuel Goff, d 30 Nov 1858 aged 94 yrs
    d 7 Nov 1856
Goff, Constant, d 18 May 1832 aged 68 yrs
Millard, Martha, d 20 Jan 1832 aged 73 yrs
Colvin, Julia A., w/o Draper Colvin, d 21 July 1812 aged 35 yrs 3 mos
Goff, Zenas, s/o Israel & Sarah Goff, d 15 July 1841 aged 31 yrs
Goff, Israel, Soldier of the Revolution, d 25 March 1849 aged 90 yrs
Goff, Sarah, w/o Israel Goff, d 5 Sept 1842 aged 78 yrs
Goff, Mercy, w/o Bayles Goff, d 18 June 1845 aged 42 yrs 2 mos 23 days
Goff, Lucina, d/o Bayles & Mercy Goff, d 4 Feb 1852 aged 26 yrs 11 mos
    2 days
Goff, William Henry, s/o Alfred B. & Mary P. Goff, b 16 July 1841,
    Drowned in Connecticut River at Windsor, 20 July 1861
Goff, Mary P., w/o Alfred B. Goff, d 14 April 1888 aged 83 yrs
Salisbury, William, d 26 Feb 1857 aged 87 yrs
Peck, Josephus, d 8 Oct 1847 aged 46 yrs
Horton, Nancy, d/o Daniel Horton, d 29 Dec 1824 aged 54 yrs
Peck, Gordon Spencer, s/o Josephus & Lemira Peck, d 19 Oct 1839 aged 1
    yr

Peck, Horace Chandler, s/o Josephue & Lemira Peck, d 21 Sept 1836 aged 1 yr 3 mos
Peck, Ezra Mason, s/o Josephus & Lemira Peck, d 28 Sept 1833 aged 1 yr
Horton, Hannah, w/o Sylvanus Horton, d 7 March 1843 aged 62 yrs
Horton, Nathan B., s/o Sylvanus & Hannah Horton, d 9 Sept 1827 aged 4 yrs 2 mos 26 days
Horton, Nancy, d/o Daniel Horton, d 29 Dec 1824
Salisbury, Levi, b 16 Oct 1894, d 10 Sept 1882
Salisbury, Philander, w/o Levi Salisbury, d 28 Dec 1834 aged 36 yrs 3 mos 8 days
Salisbury, Sally, w/o Henry Austin & d/o Levi & Philander Salisbury, d 12 May 1859 aged 30 yrs
Salisbury, Lemira, w/o George Wilson & d/o Levi & Philander Salisbury,d 1 July 1856 aged 24 yrs 2 mos 13 days

Baker Cemetery
Rehoboth Historical # 43
Spring Street
Rehoboth, Massachusetts

Davis, Joseph L., d 21 Nov 1889 aged 63 yrs 7 mos 21 days
Shaw, Susan, w/o Joseph L. Davis, b 3 Dec 1824, d 28 April 1898
Martin, Earl P., b 26 Nov 1810, d 7 July 1892
Martin, Phebe, w/o Earl P. Martin, b 25 May 1810, d 29 June 1884
Wheaton, Jason N., b 10 June 1836, d 29 June 1914
Wheaton, Esther P., w/o Jason N. Wheaton, b 9 Dec 1840, d 15 May 1919
West, Samuel, b 5 May 1790, d 13 Dec 1866
West, Mary, w/o Samuel West, d 30 May 1858 aged 71 yrs
Reed, William B., 1849-1936
Reed, Betsey J. H., w/o William B. Reed, 1851-1917
West, Horace, b 9 Jan 1824, d 7 Dec 1861
West, Betsey, w/o Horace M. West, b 6 July 1823, d 11 Feb 1911
West, Horace R., 1857-1942
West, Louisa J., w/o Horace R. West, 1858-1916
Ried, Alfred W., 1872-1961
Ried, Susan, w/o Alfred W. Ried, 1869-1910

Ried, Estella D., w/o Alfred W. Ried, 1888-1920

West, Ann Frances, d/o Horace & Betsey West, d 19 April 1859 aged 12 yrs

Horton, John E., b 14 July 1836, d 19 Feb 1911

Horton, Sarah J., w/o John E. Horton, d 13 April 1886 aged 43 yrs 8 mos

Horton, Eliza, b 15 May 1836, d 6 Aug 1910

Horton, Hiram, d 25 Sept 1896 aged 83 yrs 9 mos 22 days

Horton, Eliza S., w/o Hiram Horton, d 15 May 1882 aged 73 yrs

Martin, Charles W., 1844-1910

Martin, Anne E., w/o Charles W. Martin, 1857-1932

Reed, Otis M., 1874-1907

Martin, Hiram L., b 10 Oct 1842, d 14 Oct 1916

Kelton, John, b 4 July 1818, d 6 Aug 1899

Kelton, Hannah M., w/o John Kelton, b 24 Sept 1819, d 8 May 1899

Kelton, Gardner, s/o John & Hannah Kelton, b 2 Sept 1848, d 6 May 1849

Chase, Charles L., 1879-1948

Chase, Mabel, w/o Charles L. Chase, 1878-1952

Chase, Merrill E., s/o Charles & Mabel Chase, 1902-1956

Chase, John W., 1856-1946

Chase, Annie W.B., w/o John W. Chase, 1861-1942

Chase, John Edson, s/o John & Annie Chase, 1884-1886

Brown, Ossian Ripley, 1893-1949

Chase, Abbie, w/o Ossian Ripley Brown, 1888-1957

Baker, Levi, b 10 Jan 1824, d 22 March 1909

Horton, Angelina, w/o Levi Baker, b 6 Dec 1824, d 15 Dec 1895

Baker, John, b 18 Nov 1846, d 31 May 1860

Baker, Charles L., b 16 Sept 1862, d 16 Feb 1864

Horton, John, d 22 Nov 1865 aged 83 yrs 8 mos

Horton, Susanna, w/o John Horton, d 25 April 1875 aged 94 yrs 1 mo 11 days

Horton, James 2nd, d 28 May 1862 aged 56 yrs

Horton, Almira, w/o James Horton 2nd, d 26 March 1876 aged 72 yrs

Horton, Harriet, d/o John & Susan Horton, d 2 May 1847 aged 30 yrs

Horton, James N., d/o James & Almira Horton, d 13 Oct 185 (Broken)

Horton, Darius, d 24 Dec 1872 aged 63 yrs 11 mos 24 days

Horton, Harriet, w/o Darius Horton, d 3 June 1886 aged 78 yrs

Horton, Edwin R. M., d 17 Jan 1862, A member of Co A 3rd Reg RI Heavy Art

Horton, Lydia, d 15 April 1831 aged 3 yrs 2 mos 16 days

Horton, Darius, d 12 March 1831 aged 1 yr 7 mos

Baker, Mason, d 21 Jan 1890 aged 85 yrs
Baker, Rosina, w/o Mason Baker, d 9 Sept 1848 aged 43 yrs
Davis, John A., d 22 June 1896
Davis, Melinda, w/o John A. Davis, d 4 Aug 1887 aged 75 yrs 11 mos
Baker, Charles M., d 6 Oct 1855 aged 23 yrs
West, Dexter, b 8 Dec 1834, d 20 April 1913
West, Julia E., w/o Dexter West, b 6 Nov 1839, d June 1907
Eastherbrook, Elizabeth, w/o John Eastherbrook, d 30 May 1915 aged 73
   yrs
Horton, Betsey, b 10 July 1803, d 14 Oct 1894
Davis, Nathaniel, 1820-1905
Wood, Elizabeth, w/o Nathaniel Davis, ...
Perry, Frederick, 1895-1971
Horton, Abbie M., w/o Frederick Perry, 1895-1971
Horton, Josephus W., 1838-1916
Horton, Mary E., w/o Josephus W. Horton, 1847-1926
Dank, Rev. Frederick J., 1868-1943
Dank, Ethel L., w/o Rev. Frederick J. Dank, 1883-1968
Pierce, William L., d 14 Aug 1885 aged 48 yrs
Pierce, Sarah, w/o William L. Pierce, b 13 July 1842, d....
Pierce, John W., 1862-1932
Kelton, Mary E., w/o John W. Pierce, 1855-1923
Horton, Charles F., 1831-1882
Horton, Waity A., w/o Charles F. Horton, 1821-1900
Horton, George M., 1885-1949
Horton, Jane C., w/o George M. Horton, 1900-1967
Tschirch, Suzanne Ganswohl, 1885-1915
Reese, John, 1880-1963
Reese, Anna L. Selma, w/o John Reese, 1879-1942
Bullock, Ann Maria, d/o Levi & Suzanne Bullock, d 2 Oct 1845 aged 8
   yrs
Bullock, Levi, d 19 Feb 1836 aged 47 yrs
Bullock, Rosannah, w/o Levi Bullock, d 29 Aug 1878 aged 89 yrs
Baker, Matilda, d 19 April 1898 aged 88 yrs
Baker, John, b 3 Dec 1789, d 8 Aug 1836
Martin, Mary K., w/o John Baker, b 18 Feb 1799, d 15 Feb 1866
Manchester, Hannah, w/o John Baker, 1752-1837
Baker, Julia A., w/o Mason Baker, d 18 Feb 1884 aged 72 yrs
Baker, Nathaniel, d 11 Jan 1881 aged 51 yrs 4 mos 14 days
Eddy, Sarah A., w/o Nathaniel Baker, d 21 Sept 1886 aged 54 yrs 11 mos

Baker, John, d 8 July 1883 aged 49 yrs
Chase, Mary J., w/o John Baker, b 12 Sept 1853, d 1 April 1932
Swanson, John H., 1877-1948
Baker, Grace J., w/o John H. Baker, 1876-1960
Horton, Norman M., 1886-1949
Horton, Ann Maude, w/o Norman M. Horton, 1894-1976

Wheeler Lot
Rehoboth Historical # 12
Wheeler Street
Rehoboth, Massachusetts

Wheeler, Deacon Jonathan, d 13 Sept 1869 aged 76 yrs 10 mos 23 days
Wheeler, Rachel, w/o Deacon Jonathan Wheeler, d 6 Nov 1869 aged 80
  yrs 3 mos
Wheeler, Nancy A., d/o Rev. Jonathan & Rachel Wheeler, d 8 Dec 1897
  aged 78 yrs
Green, George, b 10 Dec 1825, d 13 Jan 1900
Green, Sarah J., w/o George Green, b 9 Oct 1824, d 24 July 1905
Martin, James, b 22 Nov 1816, d 9 Jan 1869
Martin, Mary A., w/o James Martin, b 24 Dec 1818, d 5 Aug 1895
Wheeler, Nathan G., b 26 Nov 1826, d 10 Jan 1897
Wheeler, Julia, w/o Nathan G. Wheeler, b 10 April 1830, d 4 July 1892
Searle, Ella A., w/o Albertus Searle, d 1 April 1895 aged 43 yrs
Walker, Rev. Charles, d 31 Dec 1877 aged 45 yrs
Hendrick, Benjamin, d 24 March 1866 aged 33 yrs 4 mos
Hendrick, Rachel, w/o Benjamin Hendrick, d 13 Sept 1864 aged 41 yrs 3
  mos
Mann, Emma F., w/o George A. Mann & d/o Benjamin & Rachel
  Hendrick, d 8 July 1876 aged 20 yrs
Harris, Betsey, w/o William Harris, d 15 Aug 1874 aged 57 yrs 9 mos 5
  days

Moulton, Elihu, d 31 March 1844 aged 62 yrs 5 mos

Moulton, Nancy, w/o Elihu Moulton, 11 Sept 1856 aged 76 yrs

Moulton, Mary A. Pierce, d/o Elihu & Nancy Moulton, d 31 March 1866 aged 61 yrs 1 day

Moulton, Elihu Jr., b 25 Feb 1803, d 15 Oct 1845

Moulton, Fanny Babbett, d/o Elihu & Mercy G. Moulton, b 6 Aug 1838, d 20 Sept 1831

Davis, Joseph, d 11 Oct 1859 aged 79 yrs 3 mos 13 days

Davis, Betsey, w/o Joseph Davis, d 13 May 1857 aged 67 yrs 8 mos 15 days

Nichols, Elizabeth J., b 31 Jan 1879, d 21 June 1963

Nichols, Gallen E., b 18 Oct 1877, d 20 March 1962, RI Pvt, Battry B 1 Regt Art, Spanish/American War

Nichols, Stephen L., b 7 Jan 1903, d 21 May 1970, Col US Army WW 2

Nichols, Ruth A., b 18 May 1906, d 16 June 1968

Nichols, Galen Laird, PFC US Army WW 2, b 25 May 1928, d 9 June 1971

Nichols, Charlotte M., b 17 July 1830, d 29 Jan 1910

Nichols, Frank M., b 10 June 1882, d 27 April 1980

Nichols, Stephen M., b 13 Oct 1844, d 1 Feb 1920

Brown, Jeanette, w/o Stephen M. Nichols, b 12 Feb 1845, d 18 Oct 1894

Nichols, Jennie, b 1 June 1887, d 7 July 1887

Nichols, Galen E., 1877-1962

Laird, Elizabeth, w/o Galen E. Nichols, 1879-1963

Nichols, Galen, s/o Israel & Joanna Nichols, d 2 March 1877 aged 78 yrs

Martin, Huldah, w/o Galen Nochols, d 27 April 1855 aged 77 yrs

Cole, Albert A., d 24 May 1885 aged 65 yrs

Cole, Betsey N., w/o Albert A. Cole, d 11 Dec 1906 aged 83 yrs

Nichols, Capt. Joseph Esq., d 9 June 1862 aged 91 yrs

Nichols, Polly, w/o Capt. Joseph Nichols Esq., b 15 Feb 1776, d 8 Sept 1850

Nichols, Israel Esq., d 16 Nov 1822 aged 55 yrs

Nichols, Joanna, w/o Israel Nichols Esq., d 28 March 1850 aged 83 yrs

Nichols, Comfort, s/o Israel & Joanna Nichols........

Nichols, Otis, d 2 Feb 1888 aged 92 yrs 19 days
Walker, Betsey, w/o Otis Nichols, d 17 Nov 1824 aged 23 yrs 9 mos 1 day
Walker, Hannah, w/o Otis Nichols, d 27 Aug 1886 aged 80 yrs 11 mos 4
  days

Joseph S. Pierce Lot
Rehoboth Historical # 16
Kelton Street
Rehoboth, Massachusetts

Reed, William, 1873-1953
Reed, Dora M., w/o William Reed, 1879-1972
Goff, Clifton D., 1885-1948
Goff, William, 1840-1926
Pierce, Ellen, w/o William Goff, 1847-1936
Pierce, Charles E., 1851-1923
Blackmar, Ida A., w/o Charles E. Pierce, 1857-1927
Barney, James, s/o Daniel & Mary G. Barney, d 23 April 1851 aged 10
  mos
Barney, Mary G., w/o Daniel B. Barney, d 23 May 1854 aged 30 yrs
Pierce, Childs L., d 27 Sept 1845 aged 25 yrs
Pierce, Joseph S., 1814-1897
Pierce, Sybil, w/o Joseph S. Pierce, 1810-1897
Larson, Karl Victor, 1894-1981
Pierce, Lucy E., w/o Karl Victor Larson, b 13 Dec 1895, d 22 Sept 1978
Pierce, George Reuben, s/o Reuben & Mary Pierce, d 10 Sept 1843 aged 2
  yrs 6 mos
North, Mabel, 1884-1968
Pierce, Nathan, d 11 March 1861 aged 85 yrs
Pierce, Rhoda, w/o Nathan Pierce, d 3 Feb 1858
Pearce, Rebecca, w/o Jonathan Pearce, d 20 Sept 1802 aged 21 yrs
Adams, Susan Emily, d/o Warren & Eliza Adams, d July 1842 aged 8 yrs
Adams, Rebecca, d/o Warren & Eliza Adams, d 20 Feb 1835 aged 2 mos
  20 days
Pierce, Eliza, w/o Nathaniel B. Pierce & formerly w/o Warren Adams, d
  14 May 1877 aged 75 yrs 6 mos 3 days

Adams, Warren, d 25 Aug 1836 aged 29 yrs
Pierce, Laura Ann, w/o Joseph S. Pierce, d 2 April 1842 aged 19 yrs
Pierce, Lydia Ann, w/o Joseph S. Pierce, d 5 Feb 1844 aged 19 yrs
Gentle, James Milton, 1925-1980

Bosworth Lot
Rehoboth Historical Cemetery # 24
Purchase Street
Rehoboth, Massachusetts

Pierce, Aricom, d 10 Oct 1820 aged 30 yrs
Pierce, Abigail, w/o Aricom Pierce, d 26 March 1853 aged 58 yrs
Pierce, Abby Ann, d/o Aricom & Abigail Pierce, d 25 Oct 1839 aged 16 yrs
Luther, Abigail, w/o Theophilus Luther, d 8 March 1863 aged 90 yrs 6 mos
Pierce, Nathan W., d 29 Nov 1877 aged 58 yrs 8 mos 25 days
Earl, Rebecca, w/o Nathan W. Pierce & d/o Stephen & Rebecca Earl, d 16 Nov 1860 aged 13 yrs
Pierce, Isaac N., d 21 July 1852 aged 36 yrs

Several broken and unreadable stones

Joshua Pierce Lot
Rehoboth Historical # 45
Spring Street
Rehoboth, Massachusetts

Pierce, Sarah, d/o Joshua & Betsey Pierce, d 30 April 1867 aged 22 yrs 8 mos

Pierce, Frank H., 1848-1920

Pierce, Hannah J., w/o Frank H. Pierce, 1852-1941

Rounds, Nathaniel, A Soldier & Pensioner of the Revolutionary War, d 25 Feb 1850 aged 91 yrs

Pierce, Wheaton, killed at the Battle of Coal Harbor, 6 June 1864

Pierce, Leonard W., 1878-1936

Goff, Emma F., w/o Leonard W. Pierce, 1881-19..

Pierce, Wilson D., b 22 July 1842, d 19 Dec 1904, RI Hosptial Guard, Civil War

Essex, Susanna E., w/o Wilson D. Pierce, b 19 Feb 1866, d....

Pierce, Arthur W., b 25 Aug 1899, d 29 April 1900

Pierce, Howard F., 1882-1883

Pierce, Joshua, d 19 Nov 1875 aged 78 yrs 8 mos 7 days

Wheaton, Betsey, w/o Joshua Pierce, 1804-1890

Pierce, Ardelia, w/o Henry Clark, 1835-1923

Robertson, James, 1835-1918

Pierce, Elmira, w/o James Robertson, 1828-1910

Pierce, Charles M., b 18 March 1834, d 21 Feb 1918, A member of Co D 3rd Regt RI Heavy Art

Pierce, Joshua, d 26 Nov 1801 aged 49 yrs 8 mos

Pierce, Susanna, w/o Joshua Pierce, d 9 Dec 1850 aged 97 yrs

Pierce, Harold L., 1885-1965

Horton Lot
Rehoboth Historical Cemetery # 44
Spring Street
Rehoboth, Massachusetts

West, Benjamin, b 30 Sept 1807, d 5 Feb 1887
Payson, Lucinda, w/o Benjamin West, b 14 April 1804, d 15 June 1884
West, Martha, w/o Benjamin West, b 23 June 1780, d 9 Jan 1866
West, Eliza, b 29 April 1803, d 1 March 1899
West, Lydia, w/o Cromwell West, d 9 May 1864 aged 70 yrs
Colvin, J. D., 1842-1882
West, Ann Eliza, w/o J. D. Colvin, 1845-1921
Colvin, Benjamin, s/o J. D. & Ann Eliza West, 1866-....
Bowen, Freelove, w/o Benjamin Bowen, d 17 Nov 1825 aged 75 yrs 7 mos

Medbury Lot
Rehoboth Historical Cemetery #5
Old Pine Street
Rehoboth, Massachusetts

Medbury, Ebenezer, d 24 Jan 1825 aged 68 yrs
Medbury, Elizabeth, w/o Ebenezer Medbury, d 5 Sept 1851 aged 84 yrs

Hunt Cemetery
Rehoboth Historical # 6
Broad & Salisbury Streets
Rehoboth, Massachusetts

3 small black slate stones....no names or dates & 1 large broken black
slate stone with an American flag

Ingalls Lot
Rehoboth Historical Cemetery # 22
Cedar Street
Rehoboth, Massachusetts

Ingalls, Elkanah, d 1806 aged 63 yrs
Ingalls, Elkanah, d 7 Feb 1807 aged 61 yrs
Ingalls, Rebecca, d 1806

Millard Yard
Rehoboth Historical Cemetery $ 21
Cedar Plain Road
Rehoboth, Massachusetts

Millard, Henry, d 25 Aug 1828 aged 57 yrs
Millard, Sarah, w/o Henry Miller, d July 1848
Millard, Cynthia, d July 1840
Millard, Capt. Ezra, b 16 July 1796, d 3 Sept 1844
Millard, Mary, w/o Capt. Ezra Millard, b 16 Sept 1793, d 23 Sept 1860

Wright, Israel R., s/o Samuel & Rachel Wright, b 28 Sept 1800, d 7 May 1822

Bliss Cemetery
Agricultural Ave
Rehoboth, Massachusetts

Bliss, Lucy, w/o Abel Bliss, d 3 May 1835 aged 66 yrs
Lord, Mary, w/o Jason P. Lord, d 5 Nov 1838 aged 25 yrs
Tripp, Huldah B., d 12 March 1891 aged 87 yrs
Bliss, Lucy,....

Several Broken Stones

Eneas Rounds Lot
Annawan Street
Rehoboth, Massachusetts

Rounds, Olive, d/o Eneas & Mary Rounds, d April 1806 AE 64 yrs 21
    days
Rounds, Mary, w/o Eneas Rounds, d 13 Feb 1866 AE 93 yrs 22 days

James Horton Lot
Pleasant Street
Rehoboth, Massachusetts

Wheeler, Clara J., 1853-1917
Holden, George W., b 13 Sept 1870, d 29 May 1959
Peirce, Millie, w/o George W. Holden, b 16 Nov 1866, d 24 Oct 1958
Holden, W. Luther, 1893-1965
Holden, Florence I., 1900-1961
Peirce, Samuel L., b 13 April 1828, d 31 Aug 1911
Horton, Ann Eliza C., w/o Samuel L. Peirce, b 26 March 1832, d 5 Oct 1911
Horton, James, d 10 Jan 1875 aged 83 yrs
Horton, Sophia W., w/o James Horton, d 28 Feb 1849 aged 53 yrs

Wheeler Cemetery
Pleasant Street
Rehoboth, Massachusetts

Brown, Harrison T., b 20 Feb 1840, d 20 Aug 1866
Horton, Mary A. W., w/o Harrison T. Borwn, b 3 Nov 1832, d....
Horton, Emma A., b 28 March 1852, d 19 March 1900
Horton, John W., b 18 Nov 1808, d 10 April 1889
Wheeler, Mary A., w/o John Horton, b 22 Jan 1873, d 9 March 1900
Wheeler, Samuel T., d 14 Nov 1864 aged 81 yrs
Wheeler, Chloe, w/o Samuel T. Wheeler, d 27 Jan 1859 aged 72 yrs
Wheeler, Samuel C., d 8 Nov 1867 aged 42 yrs 4 mos
Wheeler, Rebecca, w/o Samuel C. Wheeler, d 20 Jan 1901 aged 68 yrs 3 mos 14 days
Wheeler, George T., d 3 Dec 1882 aged 74 yrs 1 mo 20 days

Wheeler, Nancy M., w/o George T. Wheeler, d 1 May 1882 aged 73 yrs 2 mos 9 days
Horton, Rachel, d/o Nathan Horton, d 4 Dec 1835 aged 22 yrs

Burial Place Hill
Peckham Street
Rehoboth, Massachusetts

Sweet, Jonathan, d 11 Sept 1874 aged 89 yrs
Sweet, Sarah, w/o Jonathan Sweet, d 1 Feb 1852 aged 65 yrs
Sweet, Phebe, w/o John Sweet, d 22 March 1840 aged 83 yrs
Tren, Mary, d/o Samuel & Nancy Tren, d 24 June 1841 aged 3 yrs 8 mos
Martin, Hale, d 1 Sept 1851
Martin, Polly, w/o Hale Martin, d 17 Feb 1846 aged 75 yrs
Martin, Cyril, s/o Hale & Polly Martin, d 6 Dec 1863 aged 71 yrs 10 mos
Drown, Col. Frederick, b 31 Jan 1743, d 6 Sept 1804 Reveolution Soldier
Martin, Hannah, w/o Ephraim, d 17 Feb 1874 aged 89yrs 9 mos
Martin, Maria L., d/o Ephraim & Hannah Martin, d 19 Aug 1845 aged 17 yrs 22 days
Whitney, William K., b 30 July 1804, d 8 May 1889
Whitaker, Asa, d 30 May 1838 aged 59 yrs
Whitaker, Nancy, w/o Asa Whitaker, d 4 May 1870 aged 89 yrs 8 mos 13 days
Whitaker, Asa, d 23 July 1848 aged 39 yrs
Draper, Maria, w/o Goerge A. Draper & d/o Asa & Nancy Whitaker, d 28 Nov 1847 aged 20 yrs
Thurber, Benjamin, d 21 April 1793 aged 24 yrs
Peck, Gideon, d 20 Dec 1843 aged 78 yrs
Peck, Lydia,w/o Gideon Peck, d 30 Nov 1846 aged 82 yrs
Peck, Candace, d/o Gideon & Lydia Peck, d 21 March 1878 aged 76 yrs 9 mos
Peck, Capt. Noah, d 12 Jan 1856 aged 58 yrs
Peck, Emma H., w/o Capt.Noah Peck, d 1 April 1868 aged 52 yrs 6 mos
Peck, Abby H., w/o Capt. Noah Peck, d 27 Aug 1886 aged 33 yrs
Peck, Hannah, w/o William Peck, d 28 June 1840 aged 57 yrs
Peck, Martha W., w/o Capt. Edwin Peck, d 23 April 1849 aged 47 yrs

Mason, Horace D., s/o Aaron & Patsey Mason, d 15 Jan 1867 aged 33 yrs

Peck, William M., s/o Capt. Noah & Abby Peck, d 18 Nov 1846 aged 19 yrs 6 mos 13 days

Peck, Jonathan W., s/o Capt. Noah & Abby Peck, d 24 July 1842

Peck, Abby H., d/o Capt. Noah & Abby Peck, d 15 Sept 1836 aged 13 weeks

Peck, William M., s/o Capt. Noah & Abby Peck, d 1826 aged 4 mos 9 days

Mason, Aaron T., d 17 Aug 1848 aged 71 yrs

Bullock, Mary B., w/o Aaron T. Mason & d/o Stephen Bullock, d 25 May 1818 aged 41 yrs

Wheeler, Capt. Jeremiah, d 3 Sept 1832 aged 48 yrs

Wheeler, Lydia w/o Capt. Jeremiah Wheeler, d 16 Aug 1863 aged 73 yrs

Wheeler, Barnard Esq., d 1 Jan 1836 AE 73 yrs

Wheeler, Emma, w/o Barnard Wheeler Esq., d 1 Feb 1830 aged 73 yrs

Wheeler, Jeremiah, d 25 Feb 1811 AE 86 yrs

Wheeler, Elizabeth, w/o Jeremiah Wheeler, d 9 April 1788 aged 46 yrs

Wheeler, Darius Esq., d 23 Nov 1869 aged 75 yrs

Mason, Sally, w/o Darius Wheeler Esq., d 30 Nov 1861 aged 67 yrs 10 mos

Wheeler, Darius, d 31 March 1872 aged 40 yrs

Wheeler, Albert D., d 1 Sept 1887 aged 65 yrs

Thurber, Daniel, 66 yrs

Thurber, Lois, 71 yrs

Thurber, Eliza, d/o Capt. William C. Thurber, d 20 Dec 1822 AE 18 yrs

Wheeler, Henry, s/o Jeremiah & Lydia Wheeler, d 26 Sept 1838 aged 23 yrs

Wheeler, Capt. Philip, d Sept 1765

Wheeler, Martha, w/o Capt. Philip Wheeler, d 14 Aug 1745 AE 47 yrs

Rounds, Juliana, w/o Isaac Bennett & d/o James B. & Elizabeth Rounds, d 15 Jan 1897 aged 86 yrs 2 mos 20 days

Rounds, Betsey, d/o James & Elizabeth Rounds, d 21 July 1883 aged 80 yrs

Rounds, Susan, d/o James B. & Elizabeth Rounds, d 1 Oct 1861 aged 64 yrs

Rounds, James B., d 25 March 1854 aged 85 yrs

Rounds, Elizabeth, w/o James B. Rounds, d 26 Sept 1822 aged 53 yrs

Rounds, Arnold B., s/o James B. & Elizabeth Rounds, d 9 Sept 1815

Rounds, Marion, d 4 April 1810 aged 66 yrs

Millard, Ruth, w/o Zedekiah Millard, d 14 Aug 1824 aged 40 yrs

Millard, Hezekiah, d May 1840 aged 89 yrs

Miller, Patience, w/o Hezekiah Millard, d 1790 AE 69 yrs

Millard, Huldah, w/o Nathaniel Millard, d 15 Aug 1876 aged 85 yrs 1 mo 10 days

Davis, Barney, d 30 April 1822 aged 89 yrs

Davis, Anna, w/o Barney Davis, d 6 Feb 1823 aged 82 yrs

Bullock, Doct. Samuel, d 31 July 1860 agd 91 yrs 6 mos 22 days

Bullock, Hon. Stephen Esq., d 2 Feb 1816 AE 81 yrs

Bullock, Lydia, d/o Dr. Stephen & Betsey Bullock, d 21 Nov 1833 aged 26 yrs

Pierce, Elisha, d 20 July 1851 aged 42 yrs

Pierce, Capt. Perserved, d 3 April 1829 aged 43 yrs

Davis, John M., d 12 Jan 1870 aged 83 yrs

Davis, William, d 23 Feb 1823 AE 67 yrs

Davis, Mary, w/o William Davis, d 1816

Davis, Thomas, s/o John M. & Ruth Davis, d 3 Aug 1835 aged 6 yrs

Bullock, Capt. Samuel, d 10 March 1821 aged 84 yrs

Bullock, Silence, w/o Capt. Samuel Bullock, d 22 Nov 1825 aged 81 yrs

Bullock, Nancy, d/o Capt. Samuel & Silence Bullock, d 18 Dec 1802 aged 27 yrs

Bullock, Dorothy, d/o Capt. Samuel & Silence Bullock, d 27 July 1788

Martin, Anga, d May 1836

Martin, Sally, w/o Anga Martin, d 13 Sept 1861 aged 67 yrs

Martin, Luther, d 28 Feb 1834 aged 47 yrs

Martin, Nancy M., d/o Luther & Nancy Martin, d 23 Jan 1859 aged 42 yrs

Martin, Mary E., d/o Anga & Sally Martin, d 26 April 1852 aged 17 yrs 6 mos 4 days

Nichols, Caroline W., w/o William E. Nichols, d 10 Oct 1877 aged 44 yrs

West, Darius,....

West, Martha, w/o Darius West, d 4 Aug 1874 aged 80 yrs

West, James H., s/o Darius & Martha West, d....

Miller, Capt. Jacob, d 24 May 1870 aged 92 yrs 2 mos 22 days

Miller, Betsey, w/o Capt. Jacob Miller, d 14 April 1868 aged 85 yrs 6 mos

Miller, Seth, s/o Capt. Jacob & Betsey Miller, d 30 May 1848 aged 47 yrs

Miller, Sally W., d/o Capt. Jacob & Betsey Miller, d 16 Oct 1823 aged 17 yrs 4 mos

Bowers, Capt. Jonathan, d 12 Jan 1864 aged 79 yrs 4 days

Bowers, Hannah, w/o Capt. Jonathan Bowers, b 27 July 1791, d 25 March 1884

Bowers, Maria E., d/o Capt. Jonathan & Hannah Bowers, d 26 July 1843 aged 19 yrs

Bowers, Hannah, d/o Capt. Jonathan & Hannah Bowers, d 1843 aged 17 yrs

Martin, Ethan Esq., d 5 July 1806 at Troy aged 36 yrs

Carpenter, Deborah, w/o Capt. Samuel Carpenter, d 2 Nov 1787 aged 41 yrs

Martin, Calvin, MD, d 24 March 1843 aged 76 yrs

Martin, Rachel, w/o Dr. Calvin Martin, d 30 Aug 1848 aged 57 yrs

Martin, Susan, 2nd d/o Calvin & Susannah Martin, d 18 Jan 1824 aged 25 yrs

Martin, Susannah, w/o Dr. Calvin Martin, d 3 March 1821 aged 52 yrs

Martin, Hon. Simeon, s/o Silvanus & Martha Martin, b 20 Oct 1754 Rehoboth, d 30 Sept 1819

Comer, John, d 23 May 1734 aged 30 yrs

Barney, Alice, w/o Capt. Daniel Barney, d 3 July 1766 aged 66 yrs

Barney, Capt. Daniel, d 2 Feb 1784 aged 71 yrs

Miller, Amos, d 19 Sept 1821 East Bloomfield, NY aged 41 yrs

Miller, Philip, d 11 Feb 1824 aged 73 yrs

Miller, Caleb, MD, d 13 Nov 1826 Bristol, RI aged 40 yrs

Goff, Samuel Jr., d 30 Aug 1775 AE 46 yrs

Miller, Capt. Joshua, b 18 Jan 1789, d 24 Feb 1850

Millard, Philip, d 28 June 1844 aged 56 yrs

Millard, Rebeckah, w/o Philip Millard, d 20 Sept 1879 aged 83 yrs

Millard, Hannah, d/o Philip & Rebeckah Millard, d 24 March 1833

Millard, Mary Ann, d/o Philip & Rebeckah Millard, d 24 March 1833 aged 4 yrs 9 mos

Miller, Nathan, d 28 Feb 1839 aged 54 yrs

Miller, Sally, w/o Nathan Miller, d 10 Feb 1841 aged 54 yrs

Miller, Rhobe, w/o Philip Miller & d/o Caleb Mason, d 30 April 1811 aged 60 yrs

Martin, Abby, w/o Hon. Samuel Martin, b 26 July 1750 Newport, RI, d 24 March 1832 Seekonk, MA

Stephens, Susan, w/o Capt. Joseph Stephens, & d/o Simeon & Abby Martin, d 1821

Watson, John, d 17 Sept 1871 aged 88 yrs 17 days

Watson, Lydia, w/o John Watson, d 20 Oct 1874 aged 80 yrs 5 mos

Watson, William H., d 22 June 1876

Wheaton, Ephraim, d 1734

Martin, Joseph B., d 19 March 1872 aged 73 yrs 11 mos 22 days

Martin, Harriet, w/o Joseph B. Martin, d 28 March 1882 aged 74 yrs 23 days

Bullock, Abel, d 26 Dec 1832 aged 63 yrs

Bullock, Lois, w/o Abel Bullock, d 8 March 1839 aged 64 yrs

Bullock, Albert, s/o Abel & Lois Bullock, b 21 Jan 1819, d 13 June 1851

Martin, Patience, w/o Seth Martin, d 1807

Franklin, Betsey, w/o Elisha Franklin, d 19 Jan 1798 AE 25 yrs

Wheaton, Robert, d 1793 aged 86 yrs

Wheaton, Lucas, d 17 April 1874 aged 82 yrs

Wheaton, Deacon Robert, s/o Eld. Ephraim Wheaton, d 22 Nov 1780 AE 92 yrs

Wheaton, Susannah, w/o Deacon Robert Wheaton, d 17 March 1777 AE 85 yrs

Wheaton, Andrew, d 10 April 1796 AE 75 yrs

Wheaton, Lydia, w/o Andrew Wheaton, d 23 May 1815 AE 91 yrs

Wheaton, Betsey, d/o Lucas Wheaton & Elizabeth Short, d.....

Wheaton, Lucas, d 7 May 1833 aged 85 yrs

Wheaton, Louisa, w/o Lucas Wheaton & d/o Daniel Horn Esq., of Barrington, RI d 31 May 1832 aged 23 yrs

Wheaton, Elizabeth, w/o Lucas Wheaton, d 10 April 1840 aged 84 yrs

Horn, Daniel, s/o Job & Mary Ann Wheaton, d 23 Jan 1836 aged 19 yrs

Martin, Job, d 25 Jan 1875 aged 86 yrs

Martin, Mary Ann, w/o Job Martin, d 22 May 1846 aged 43 yrs

Horn, Daniel Esq., d 21 Aug 1823 aged 47 yrs

Horn, Alathea, w/o Daniel Horn Esq., d 8 Nov 1861 aged 85 yrs

Wheaton, Maria F., w/o Edward R. Wheeler & d/o Job & Mary Ann Wheaton, d 29 Dec 1856 aged 25 yrs

Bullock, Col. William, d 10 Dec 1810 AE 95 yrs

Bullock, Susannah, w/o Col. William Bullock, d 20 July 1780 AE 645 yrs

Angell, Hiram, d 1829

Bullock, Betsey, w/o Lovell Bullock, & d/o Major Allen Munroe of Seekonk, MA., d 24 June 1842 aged 36 yrs 1 mo 16 days

Bullock, Joseph, s/o Calvin Bullock, d 30 Aug 1828 aged 40 yrs

Bullock, Jerusha, w/o Calvin Bullock, d 30 Sept 1739 aged 20 yrs

Bullock, William Henry, s/o Joseph Bullock, d 29 Oct 1739 aged 20 yrs

West, Amos, d 1 May 1835

West, Zedekiah, s/o Amos & Judith West, d 28 Feb 1804 aged 25 yrs

West, Mary, d/o Amos & Judith West, d 7 May 1807 aged 26 yrs

Stephens Corners Cemetery
Annawan Street
Rehoboth, Massachusetts

Bowen, Allen, 1825-1903
Bowen, Sarah W., w/o Allen Bowen, 1831-1909
Bowen, Ellen A., d/o Allen & Sarah Bowen, 1863-1876
Bowen, Saba M., d/o Allen & Sarah Bowen, 1875-1966
Waterman, James A., d 19 July 1879 agd 59 yrs 5 mos
Waterman, Sarah, w/o James A. Waterman, d 23 July 1881 aged 51 yrs 7 mos 11 days
Keith, Emily A. Bullock, w/o Herbert C. Howes, b 29 May 1872, d 28 Jan 1937
Keith, Cephas, b 24 April 1827, d 16 Feb 1913
Godding, Sallie, w/o Cephas Keith, b 7 Jan 1832, d 1 June 1911
Keith, Orem H., b 29 Aug 1859, d 20 April 1940
Fuller, Mary A., w/o Orem H. Keith, b 18 Sept 1860, d 15 Jan 1901
Keith, Mary Ethel, b 25 Dec 1890, d 17 Dec 1972
Keith, Chester W., b 26 June 1887, d 24 Feb 1920
Keith, O. Hermon, 1889-1971
Crook, Alva, w/o O. Hermon Keith, 1896-1984
Bliss, Horace, d 1 June 1887 aged 80 yrs 17 days
Bliss, Dan, b 27 April 1801, d 11 March 1887
Bliss, Rhoda, w/o Dan Bliss, d 8 Feb 1885
Bliss, Charles W., s/o Dan & Rhoda Bliss, d 25 July 1838 aged 3 yrs
Bullock, Randall B., b 22 July 1824, d 24 April 1900
Bullock, Elizabeth, w/o Randall B. Bullock, b 13 July 1823, d 4 Nov 1904
Cole, Daniel, b 13 Oct 1819, d 27 May 1896
Cole, Nancy, w/o Daniel Cole, b 16 Oct 1815, d 27 Sept 1896
Cole, Otis, d 29 Dec 1857
Smith, Remember, b 21 Feb 1822, d 14 April 1891
Sanford, Sarah B., w/o Remember Smith, b 1 April 1824, d 29 Sept 1896
Smith, Richard C., b 1 May 1860, d 18 Aug 1935
White, Louise A., w/o Richard C. Smith, b 12 Feb 1877, d 14 March 1909
Smith, Wendell A., b 21 Feb 1909, d 7 Sept 1946

Smith, Richard R., 1905-1981
Donahue, Margaret, w/o Richard R. Smith, 1912-....
Smith, Richard T., d 5 July 1851
Smith, Sarah S., b 11 July 1852, d 28 Nov 1881
Adams, Harrie W., b 13 Feb 1876, d 15 Jan 1881
Wheeler, Arunah, b 31 March 1800, d 13 March 1890
Wheeler, Melinda, w/o Arunah Wheeler, b 18 March 1806, d 13 April....
Bullock, Barnard, b 5 May 1805, d 28 May 1865
Bullock, Mary E., w/o Barnard Bullock, b 17 June 1815, d 22 April 1871
Bullock, Mary E., d/o Barnad & Mary Bullock, b 18 Oct 1846, d 19 Jan 1871
Wilbur, Everett C., 1863-1917
Wilbur, Royal, d 29 April 1893 aged 87 yrs
Wilbur, Julia B., w/o Royal Wilbur, d 16 Feb 1874 aged 48 yrs
Wilbur, Polly, w/o Roayl Wilbur, 48 yrs
Hicks, Hezekiah, b 15 May 1777, d 2 June 1858
Hicks, Deborah, w/o Hezekiah Hickes, b 24 Sept 1777, d 5 Nov 1862
Hicks, Capt. Hezekiah, b 28 Jan 1801, d 24 July 1882
Hicks, Pamela A., w/o Capt. Hezekiah Hicks, b 18 July 1807, d 19 Sept 1882
Hicks, Jotham C., b 27 July 1789, d 25 Sept 1820 Columbia, South Carolina
Round, George, b 11 Jan 1821, d 1 Jan 1894
Round, Martha A., w/o George Round, b 18 Dec 1820, d 18 Dec 1861
Round, Arthur Edgar, s/o George & Martha A. Round, b 17 May 1855, d 26 June 1857
Round, Sarah E., d/o George & Martha A. Round, b 20 Dec 1842, d 10 May 1858
Round, Emily J., d/o George & Martha A. Round & w/o George Thomson, b 1 Oct 1840, d 4 June 1863
Wallace, Rev. George W., b 19 Feb 1814, d 11 Sept 1880
Luther, Caroline, w/o Rev. George W. Wallace, b 5 Aug 1816, d 7 Nov 1886
Wallace, George F., d 24 Sept 1872 aged 28 yrs
Short, Hezekiah P., d 12 Aug 1883 aged 86 yrs 10 mos 25 days
Short, Olive S., w/o Hezekiah P. Short, d 7 April 1890 aged 79 yrs 11 mos
Short, William, 1849-1928
Muce, Mary E., w/o William Short, 1850-1913
Mason, Deacon Edmund, d 17 April 1833 aged 52 yrs
Mason, Polly, w/o Deacon Edmund Mason, d 20 June 1816 aged 36 yrs

Mason, Bathsheba, w/o Deacon Edmund Mason, d 22 June 1865 aged 69 yrs

Luther, Adda, d/o Everett & Caroline Luther, d 31 May 1855 aged 2 yrs

Luther, Caroline, w/o Everett Luther, d 26 Oct 1853 aged 22 yrs 5 mos

Dean, Calvin G., d 17 Dec 1902 aged 78 yrs 10 days

Dean, Nancy J., w/o Calvin G. Dean, d 15 Jan 1871 aged 44 yrs 5 mos

Hicks, Job Tisdall, b 25 Dec 1816, d 23 Aug 1849 Panama

Peck, Cyril C. Jr., 1812-1886

Bliss, Hannah H., w/o Cyril C. Peck Jr., 1814-1861

Peck, William H., w/o Cyril C. & Hannah H. Peck, 1850-1832

Dexter, Horace L., 1843-1917

Peck, Hannah M., w/o Horace L. Dexter, 1845-1924

Hicks, Hannah, w/o Jotham C. Hicks, b 25 March 1785, d 5 MAy 1817 Rehoboth, MA

Hicks, Jotham C. Jr.,b 15 June 1814, d 2 April 1852 Sacramento, CA

Bullock, Dorcas, w/o Capt. James Bullock, d 8 Nov 1820 aged 90 yrs

Cole, Hannah, w/o Capt. Simon Cole, d 14 May 1802 aged 77 yrs

Short, Philip, d 22 April 1805

Short, Lydia, w/o Philip Short, d 27 Nov 1798 aged 76 yrs

Bullock, Oliver, d 10 Oct 1832 aged 66 yrs

Bullock, Susanna, w/o Oliver Bullock, d 20 Feb 1847 aged 73 yrs

Wheeler, Mason, d 25 Jan 1815 aged 45 yrs

Davis, Elisha, d 28 Oct 1877 aged 58 yrs

Davis, Leafy, w/o Elisha Davis, d 20 Oct 1838 aged 23 yrs

Davis, Peter.....

Hicks, Jotham 2nd, d 25 March 1849 aged 76 yrs

Hicks, Nancy, w/o Jotham Hicks, d 23 Nov 1866 aged 85 yrs

Peck, Betsey, w/o Arnold Peck, d 20 July 1810 aged 32 yrs

Penno, Vashti F., d 18 Dec 1868 aged 65 yrs 5 mos

Bowen, Betsey, d 15 March 1849 aged 57 yrs

Cole, Simon, d 4 Oct 1842 aged 54 yrs

Bowen, Stephen H., d 16 Feb 1843 aged 47 yrs

Bowen, Priscilla, w/o Stephen H. Bowen, d 30 Oct 1843 aged 73 yrs

Bowen, Stephen, d 11 July 1825 aged 61 yrs

Davis, Joseph, d 25 Oct 1825 aged 76 yrs

Davis, Sarah, d/o Joseph Davis, d 12 Sept 1834 aged 84 yrs

Davis, John, d 23 Jan 1871 aged 77 yrs 3 mos 23 days

Davis, Polly, w/o John Davis, d 31 May 1825 aged 24 yrs 3 mos 26 days

Davis, Cynthia, w/o John Davis, d 20 Nov 1874 aged 73 yrs 10 mos 23 days

Randall, Dr. M. R., d 23 July 1882 aged 88 yrs

Randall, George H., b 10 March 1852, d 6 May 1915

Randall, Lillian B., w/o George H. Randall, d 13 Feb 1930

Mills, William Randall, 1878-1940

Mills, Gladys Randall, 1883-1958

Peck, Deacon Cyril C., d 1 April 1871 aged 82 yrs 2 mos

Peck, Cynthia, w/o Deacon Cyril C. Peck, d 1 March 1860 aged 66 yrs 10 mos 2 days

Peck, Serephina Adelene, d/o Dea. Cyril & Cynthia Peck, d 25 Aug 1833 aged 5 yrs 5 mos 7 days

Peck, Ruth A., d/o Dea. Cyril & Cynthia Peck, d 17 May 1891 aged 55 yrs 2 mos 21 days

Peck, Sarah W., d/o Josephus & Lucinda Peck, d 8 Aug 1861 aged 77 yrs 2 mos

Parker, Lydia, b 20 Oct 1811, d 21 Oct 1848

Parker, Sarah B., b 10 May 1816, d 15 Feb 1871

Parker, Frances H., b 25 Jan 1850, d 21 Oct 1878

Parker, Lydia, b 7 Nov 1835, d 7 Nov 1842

Davis, Loring F., d 25 Aug 1847 aged 10 mos

Davis, Edward F., d 28 Feb 1854 aged 2 yrs

Peck, Royal C., d 18 March 1901 aged 64 yrs 3 mos

Peck, Lois M., w/o Royal C. Peck, d 5 May 1890 aged 60 yrs 2 mos 4 days

Peck, Nancy M., w/o Oliver C. Peck, d 1 July 1862 aged 81 yrs 4 mos 19 days

Peck, John M., d 3 July 1887 aged 78 yrs 1 mo 22 days

Peck, Oliver C., d 12 Sept 1872 aged 88 yrs

Codding, Augustus F., d 30 Dec 1843 aged 71 yrs

Codding, Eunice, d 25 Nov 1880 aged 68 yrs 4 mos 2 days

Wheeler, Dexter, 26 July 1869 aged 55 yrs

Luther, Capt. Joseph, b 22 April 1792, d 15 Feb 1870

Luther, Jerusha, w/o Capt. Joseph Luther, b 5 Aug....

Davis, Hiram, d 1 April 1885 aged 79 yrs

Pettis, Almeda, w/o Hiram Davis, b 29 Nov 1815, d 5 Dec 1898

Davis, George L., s/o Hiram & Almeda Davis, d 25 July 1864 aged 21 yrs 4 mos 15 days

Davis, Emily Frances, w/o William Davis, b 12 June 1844, d 6 Nov 1899

Rounds, Jotham B., d 1 March 1877 aged 72 yrs 24 days

Rounds, Melinda, w/o Jotham B. Rounds, d 1 May 1886 aged 76 yrs

Fuller, Arthur W., b 9 May 1866, d 25 Feb 1900

Rounds, Marcus M., s/o Jonathan & Melinda Rounds, b 1 July 1842, d 19 Feb 1914

Rounds, Harriet M., w/o Marcus M. Rounds, b 2 Aug 1842, d 14 Oct 1929

Rounds, Enos Jr., d 12 Nov 1847 aged 48 yrs

Rounds, Mary, w/o Enos Rounds Jr., d 9 June 1879 aged 83 yrs

Cole, Francis C., 1844-1915

Peck, Josephine B., w/o Francis C. Cole, 1848-1927

Cole, George C., d 25 April 1869 aged 52 yrs

Cole, Mary A., w/o George C. Cole, d 20 May 1881 aged 59 yrs 4 mos 8 days

Hix, Hezekiah, d 15 Nov 1813 aged 70 yrs

Fuller, Harold Goff, b 29 Aug 1893, d 16 Nov 1963

Kelly, Camilla F., w/o Harold Goff Fuller, b 9 March 1904, d 19 Sept 1984

Fuller, Delia A., d/o Jason W. & Phebe A. Fuller, d 19 July 1819 aged 19 yrs 5 mos 1 day

Fuller, Jason W., b 27 June 1825, d 30 May 1890

Fuller, Phebe Ann, w/o Jason W. Fuller, d 4 June 1872 aged 37 yrs 9 mos 21 days

Rounds, Gilbert W., d 26 Oct 1877 aged 58 yrs 10 mos 5 days

Rounds, Submit M., w/o Gilbert W. Rounds, d 10 Oct 1851 aged 34 yrs

Rounds, Charles H., 1845-1923

Hicks, Ira W., d 6 Sept 1838 aged 31 yrs

Rounds, Henry L., b 14 May 1817, d 16 Aug 1882

Rounds, Angeline, w/o Henry L. Rounds, b 23 Sept 1816, d 29 March 1892

Rounds, Mary Ann, d/o Henry L. & Angeline Rounds, d 1 May 1865 aged 14 yrs 5 mos 25 days

Snow, Joseph, d 11 Sept 1868 aged 80 yrs

Snow, Ellen, w/o Joseph Snow, d 1 April 1831 aged 37 yrs

Snow, Nancy, w/o Joseph Snow, d 11 Nov 1878 aged 73 yrs 4 mos 24 days

Haskins, John, 1784-1824

Haskins, Lydia, w/o John Haskins, 1758-1844

Haskins, Lewis, s/o John & Lydia Haskins, b Sept 1785, d 8 Nov 1806

Haskins, David, s/o John & Lydia Haskins, b 31 May 1785, d 24 March 1813

Haskins, John, s/o John & Lydia Haskins, b 20 May 1778, d 10 April 1820

Lane, Loring, d 27 Dec 1872 aged 68 yrs

Lewis, Albert R., 1850-1913

Lewis, Alma E., w/o Albert R. Lewis, 1854-1933

Smith, William, b 21 Jan 1810, d 8 Aug 1896

Smith, Eliza J. W., w/o William Smith, b 25 Dec 1811, d 1 Jan 1903

Smith, Clara E., b 8 Feb 1839, d 23 Aug 1820

Smith, Albert Franklin, s/o William & Eliza Smith, A member of Co G 4th Reg Mass VM, b 27 June 1842, d 12 Aug 1863 on passage from Port Hudson to Cario, Illinois

Peck, Jathniel, d 23 March 1812 aged 87 yrs

Waterman, Timothy, 1826-1911

Davis, Ruth Ann, w/o Timothy Waterman, 1838-1898

Waterman, Emily Ann, d/o Timothy & Ruth Ann Waterman, 1875-1879

Cavalier, George E., d 20 Sept 1887 aged 64 yrs

Trafford, Martha E., w/o George E. Cavalier, d 20 March 1919 aged 83 yrs

Goff, Walter H., b 7 Feb 1864 aged 10 Aug 1933

Cavalier, Nellie C., w/o Walter H. Goff, b 24 Jan 1865, d 14 Jan 1934

Wheeler, Olive, d/o Cromwell & Olive Wheeler, & w/o Marcus Read & former w/o George Bullock, d 14 Sept 1872 aged 37 yrs 6 mos

Bullock, George, s/o Jotham & Betsey Bullock, d 23 Sept 1843

Hicks, Joseph, d 14 Aug 1835 aged 56 yrs

Hicks, Betsey, w/o Joseph Hicks, d 31 Aug 1848 aged 64 yrs

Stevens, Francis W., 1833-1918

Crane, Sophia, w/o Francis W. Stevens, 1835-1921

Stevens, Othneil C., b 30 Sept 1830, d 3 Jan 1913

Morse, Abby M., w/o Othneil C. Stevens, b 29 March 1830, d 6 Feb 1888

Stevens, Ella Fay, 1854-1857

Cole, Simeon 3rd, d 13 Oct 1865 aged 70 yrs

Cole, Nancy, w/o Simeon Cole 3rd, d 24 March 1882 aged 88 yrs

Cole, Fanny, 1812-1869

Cole, Deacon W. M., b 26 Nov 1784, d 27 Nov 1855

Cole, Alice A., w/o Deacon W. M. Cole, d 22 Jan 1880 aged 77 yrs

Waterman, Franklin Wheaton, 1864-1919

Rounds, Hezekiah H., b 18 Dec 1807, d 21 May 1871

Rounds, Lucena W., w/o Hezekiah H. Rounds, b 11 March 1806, d 2 Oct 1882

Wilmarth, Louisa, b 1 March 1800, d 21 Sept 1822

Wilmarth, Charles F., b 17 July 1844, d 19 Nov 1925

Wilmarth, Annie J., w/o Charles F. Wilmarth, b 15 Sept 1847, d 11 April 1925

Wilmarth, Florence Z., b 21 Nov 1887, d 14 April 1902

Johnson, Jane H., b 25 Dec 1810, d 14 Dec 1887

Bowen, Charles, 1818-1904

Kinnecumb, Sarah G., w/o Charles Bowen, 1825-1882

Pierce, Elizabeth, w/o Charles Bowen, 1825-1904

Selleck, Viola A. Bowen, b 13 Jan 1877, d 17 Feb 1922

Bowen, Louis F., 1883-1932

Potts, William, 1855-1934

Potts, Nanette, w/o William Potts, 1854-1936

Peck, Alfred, b 30 July 1833, d 28 Sept 1893

Peck, Mary L., w/o Alfred Peck, b 21 July 1833, d 6 Sept 1897

Stevens, Francis G., b 10 Aug 1861, d 14 Feb 1897

Smith, Clarence A., 1876-1951

Davis, Clara C., w/o Clarence A. Davis, 1882-1965

Lane, Sybil, 1808-1909

Smith, Daniel, d 26 Aug 1829 aged 26 yrs

Taber, Leander H., b 9 Dec 1811, d 24 Sept 1876 Burnswick, Georgia

Allen, Sarah, w/o Leander H. Taber, d 15 May 1889 aged 79 yrs 4 mos 2 days

Pratt, Captain Seth, d 4 Aug 1832 aged 63 yrs

Pratt, Lydia, w/o Captain Seth Pratt, d 2 Feb 1861 aged 83 yrs 9 mos

Pratt, Lydia, d/o Captain Seth & Lydia Pratt, b 12 Oct 1807, d 22 June 1882

Milles, Araunah, d 8 Dec 1830 aged 45 yrs

Pratt, Aaron, d 4 March 1817 aged 85 yrs

Pratt, Lydia, w/o Aaron Pratt, d 18 Nov 1771 aged 29 yrs

Pratt, John, b 4 March 1694 Hingham, MA, d 1780

Thurber, Priscilla, w/o John Pratt, b 3 Feb 1697, d 1746

Knap, Mehitable (Stacy), w/o John Pratt, b 1712 Taunton, MA, d 1778

Perry, Eliza W., w/o Dan Perry, d 10 Aug 1853 aged 42 yrs 7 mos

Morse, Elijah, d 20 Aug 1808 aged 43 yrs

Morse, Ruth, w/o Elijah Morse, d 3 May 1824 aged 55 yrs

Round, Abner, d 27 March 1842 aged 73 yrs

Morse, Lemuel Esq., d 30 March 1869 aged 54 yrs

Morse, Abigail, w/o Lemuel Morse Esq., d 5 Oct 1869 aged 73 yrs 3 mos 28 days

Morse, Eliza J., d/o Lemuel & Abigail Morse, d 3 June 1865 aged 29 yrs 3 mos 6 days

Round, Stephen, b 12 Feb 1777, d 18 Feb 1851

Round, Esther, w/o Stephen Round, b 6 April 1783, d 26 April 1864

Round, Hiram, b 23 April 1807, d 24 Aug 1881
Round, Amelia A., w/o Hiram Round, b 21 May 1820, d 30 May 1841
Round, Sybil C., d/o Hiram & Amelia A. Round, b 16 Nov 1804, d 25
    May 1825
Round, Simeon, d 22 Sept 1860 aged 79 yrs
Round, Clarissa, w/o Simeon Round, d 26 July 1839 aged 53 yrs
Round, Nancy, d/o Simeon & Clarissa Round, b 16 Nov 1794, d 28 Nov
    1875
Churchill, William, d 15 May 1870 aged 89 yrs 5 mos
Churchill, Sally, w/o William Churchill, d 16 May 1823
Round, Simeon, d 29 July 1831 aged 77 yrs
Round, Anna, w/o Simeon Round, d 18 April 1838 aged 82 yrs
Round, Samuel, b 2 Nov 1785 North Rehoboth, MA, d 28 Feb 1861,
    North Dighton, MA
Round, Nedocia, w/o Samuel Round, b 22 April 1792 Taunton, MA, d
    1861
Round, Mercy Ann, d/o Samuel & Nedocia Round, d 27 Oct 1843 aged 20
    yrs
Packard, Amelia, b 27 Dec 1852, d 28 March 1915
Packard, Dexter, d 25 Oct 1876 aged 28 yrs
Packard, Sarah, w/o Dexter Packard, d 13 April 1885 aged 74 yrs 4 mos
Packard, William D., b 16 March 1838, d 4 May 1900
Davis, Deacon John, d 20 Nov 1883 aged 70 yrs
Davis, Alathea, w/o Deacon John Davis, d 20 Oct 1857 aged 41 yrs
Davis, Mary, w/o Deacon John Davis, d 27 Jan 1876 aged 48 yrs
Davis, John, d 18 Feb 1860 aged 81 yrs
Davis, Polly, w/o John Davis, d 23 June 1859
Round, Jabez, d 8 Jan 1891 aged 68 yrs
Round, Lucretia J., w/o Jabez Round, d 15 March 1889 aged 55 yrs
Pratt, George, b 4 Sept 1803, d 27 July 1865
Pratt, Hannah, w/o George Pratt, d 13 June 1904 aged 92 yrs
Rounds, James, b 29 July 1858, d 13 Aug 1909
Rounds, Willliam,d 11 Feb 1895 aged 79 yrs 11 mos
Rounds, Lydia, w/o William Rounds, d Nov 1876 aged 42 yrs 7 mos 23
    days
Dean, Benjamin, d 27 Nov 1890 aged 75 yrs 1 mo 7 days
Dean, Polly F., w/o Benjamin Dean, d 17 June 1896 aged 63 yrs 2 mos 18
    days
Dean, Nathan W., s/o Benjamin & Polly Dean, d 26 Nov 1871 aged 19 yrs
    7 mos 17 days

Dean, Simon, d 16 Dec 1848 aged 70 yrs

Dean, Mary, w/o Simon Dean, d 13 Sept 1850 aged 67 yrs

Field, Seth L., d 12 Dec 1861 aged 36 yrs 1 mo

Rounds, Ann E., w/o Seth L. Field, 1826-1909

Rounds, Benjamin, b 30 March 1780, d 7 Dec 1858

Rounds, Devena, w/o Benjamin Rounds, b 29 Dec 1788, d 19 July 1861

Rounds, Abner Jr., d 12 July 1848

Lincoln, Nancy P., w/o Calvin Lincoln & former w/o Abner Rounds, d 26 May 1873 aged 75 yrs

Rounds, John, b 8 Oct 1820, d....

Rounds, Leban, d 6 Aug 1888 aged 71 yrs 6 mos

Rounds, Deborah, d 18 Sept 1887 aged 68 yrs

Rounds, Joseph, d 26 Oct 1841 aged 59 yrs

Rounds, Polly, w/o Joseph Rounds, d 30 Jan 1871 aged 84 yrs 6 mos 28 days

Round, Deacon Zima, d 27 Feb 1842 aged 63 yrs

Fuller, Bertha J., w/o Jeremiah Fuller, 1831-1904

Cooper, Betsey, w/o Benjamin Cooper, d 13 Nov 1862 aged 88 yrs 8 days

Smith, John, d 4 March 1878 aged 77 yrs

Smith, Hannah, w/o John Smith, d 2 Dec 1855 aged 51 yrs

Smith, Jarvis B., 1801-1894

Smith, Patty I., w/o Jarvis B. Smith, 1803-1883

Rounds, Nelson, b 22 Aug 1817, d 15 Feb 1895

Rounds, Martha R., w/o Nelson Rounds, b 1 March 1818, d 30 March 1859

Rounds, Charles, s/o Nelson & Martha R. Rounds, d 18 March 1846 aged 2 yrs

Rounds, Cyrenes B., b 13 Oct 1791, d 14 June 1862

Rounds, Mercy P., w/o Cyrenes B. Rounds, b 2 Feb 1799, d 13 Oct 1871

Round, Almon H., s/o Cyrenes B. & Mercy Round, d 27 Oct 1894 aged 75 yrs 6 mos 13 days

Round, Sally, w/o Almon H. Round, d 1 Sept 1864 aged 45 yrs 17 days

Rounds, Frank E., b 6 April 1859, d 23 Feb 1905

Cheney, Mary, w/o Joseph Harvey, d 19 May 1867 aged 58 yrs

Morrison, Martha, 1837-1917

Guild, Abbie Rounds, 1849-1915

Morrison, Joseph, 1830-1898

Perry, George, 1819-1865

Perry, Mary E., 1863-1932

Chace, Chester M., 1869-1920

Sherburne, Frank W., 1848-1910
Sherburne, Cora, w/o Frank W. Sherburne, 1852-....
Rounds, George E., 1858-1939
Rounds, Grace E., w/o George E. Rounds, 1865-1942
Smith, Fred M., 1874-1954
Smith, Luella, w/o Fred M. Smith, 1876-1950
Smith, Harold C., 1902-....
Rounds, Bessie B., b 13 Dec 1888, d 3 Nov 1965
Rounds, George A., 1868-1941
Rounds, Annie F., w/o George A. Rounds, 1873-1945
Rounds, George Lewis, s/o George A. & Annie F. Rounds, 1899-1903
Barney, Francis W., 1845-1929
Rounds, Julia A., w/o Francis W. Barney, b 16 Aug 1849, d 5 May 1898
Matthews, Lena L., 1873-1943
Moorhouse, James S., 1833-1902
Moorhouse, Martha, w/o James S. Moorhouse, 1826-1910
Field, Frederick E., 1856-1936
Field, Stella A., w/o Frederick E. Field, 1863-1918
Field, Amey A., d/o Frederick & Stella Field, b 19 Aug 1895, d 17 Oct
    1896
Field, Lester C., 1887-1948
Field, Florence M., w/o Lester C. Field, 1897-1993
Cole, Samuel R., d 27 Jan 1892 aged 51 yrs
Danforth, Mary Augusta, b 28 March 1841, d 10 April 1910
Danforth, Mary A., w/o Thomas Danforth, d 16 March 1882 aged 73 yrs
    11 mos 8 days

Oak Knoll Cemetery
Tremont Street
Rehoboth, Massachusetts

Fiske, Leprelet P., b 20 Dec 1816, d 24 Jan 1890
Fiske, Abigail, w/o Leprelet P. Fiske, d 14 Dec 1879 aged 60 yrs 7 mos 5
    days
Fisher, Albert L., b 31 May 1843, d 12 Oct 1894
Porter, Emma, d 13 June 1864

Kent, Nathaniel, d 18 April 1832, Rehoboth, MA
Kent, Elizabeth, w/o Nathaniel Kent, d 58 yrs
Kent, Orinda, d 1855
Fuller, Dr. George, d 3 Oct 1834 aged 46 yrs
Richmond, Benjamin, d 30 June 1825 aged 73 yrs
Richmond, Betsey, w/o Benjamin Richmond, d 2 March 1850 aged 99 yrs
Kent, Deacon Ezekiel, d 17 May 1842 aged 98 yrs
Kent, Ruth, w/o Deacon Ezekiel Kent, d 8 Dec 1818 aged 74 yrs
Kent, Betsey, w/o Lewis Cranston & d/o Nathaniel & Onenda Kent, d 10
    Nov 1855 aged 36 yrs
Sanford, John, d 12 Oct 1812 aged 57 yrs
Sanford, Sarah, w/o John Sanford, d 7 Dec 1820 aged 42 yrs
Sanford, Paul, d 13 Dec 1815
Sanford, Lydia, d 5 Sept 1847
Sanford, Sarah, d 1797
Sanford, Seneca Esq., b 9 Nov 1799, d 27 April 1852
Sanford, Julana, w/o Seneca Sanford Esq, b 7 Feb 1798, d 2 Aug 1865
Ingalls, Benjamin, b 18 April 1783, d 4 Jan 1860
Ingalls, Sarah, w/o Benjamin Ingalls, b 17 Aug 1779, d 31 May 1860
Ingalls, Lydia R., d/o Benjamin & Sarah Ingalls, d 7 Jan 1831 aged 17 yrs
Deenham, Joseph, d 27 Jan 1829 aged 50 yrs
Deenham, Esther W., w/o Joseph Deenham, d 17 Sept 1825 aged 43 yrs
Jones, Alsa, b 8 Oct 1781 Rehoboth, MA, d 1 March 1858
Willis, Zebina, d 7 Feb 1805 aged 31 yrs
Bellows, Dr. Seth, d 1 May 1824 aged 43 yrs
Macomber, John, d 10 May 1821 aged 69 yrs
Macomber, Olive, w/o John Macomber, d 5 April 1816 aged 64 yrs
Macomber, John Jr., d 17 Dec 1839
Dryer, William, d 7 June 1816 aged 97 yrs
Dryer, Ruth, w/o William Dryer, d 18 Sept 1819 aged 91 yrs
Northup, Samuel, d 22 July 1812 aged 58 yrs
Bullock, Candace E., d/o Timothy & Phebe Bullock, d 4 Sept 1840 aged
    17 yrs
Bullock, Alva L., s/o Timothy & Phebe Bullock, d 21 Sept 1840
Macomber, Lemuel Jr., d 28 April 1849 aged 69 yrs
Macomber, Hannah, d 2 March 1857 aged 71 yrs 1 mo 17 days
Macomber, Sylvanus B., s/o Lemuel & Hannah Macomber, d 23 Feb 1857
    aged 35 yrs
Macomber, Samuel C., b 23 Dec 1813, d 29 April 1876
Perry, Mary M., w/o Ezra Perry, d 17 Oct 1861 aged 39 yrs

Draper, Samuel, d 21 April 1851

Draper, Polly, w/o Samuel Draper, d 22 Feb 1855 aged 69 yrs

Peck, Caleb S., d 7 Dec 1891 aged 66 yrs

Barrows, Nancy, w/o Caleb S. Peck, d 29 Oct 1920 aged 90 yrs 7 mos

Perry, George B. M., b 5 Sept 1868, d 16 June 1886

Paine, Jane M., d 4 April 1848 aged 27 yrs

Macker, Simeon, d 13 Feb 1873 aged 86 yrs

Macker, Mary, w/o Simeon Macker, d 20 Jan 1822 aged 37 yrs

Macker, Simeon, s/o Simeon & Mary Macker, d Nov 1834

Macker, Betsey, w/o Simeon Macker, d 17 Dec 1874 aged 88 yrs

Newell, Gustavus, d 21 July 1861 aged 54 yrs

Newell, Patience, w/o Gustavus Newell, d 4 Feb 1857 aged 50 yrs

Briggs, Col. Elkanah, 1788-1867

Briggs, Dolly, w/o Col. Elkanah Briggs, 1781-1874

White, Ernest E., 1881-1961

White, Zelma D., w/o Ernest E. White, 1882-1957

Briggs, Nelson, 1822-1891

Briggs, Eliza, w/o Nelson Briggs, 1826-1908

Briggs, Mary Alice, d/o Nelson & Eliza Briggs, b 9 Jan 1849, d 1 Sept 1850

Briggs, Elkanah, s/o Nelson & Eliza Briggs, b 18 Nov 1850, d 6 July 1890

Briggs, Alden Clark, s/o Nelson & Eliza Briggs, b 25 May 1852, d....

Briggs, Horatio, b 31 Aug 1854, d 29 Dec 1925

Dorrance, Addah, w/o Horatio Briggs, b 1 April 1855, d 31 Aug 1919

Perry, Edward E., 1870-1912

Briggs, Mabel E., w/o Edward E. Perry, 1874-1939

Barrows, Col. Rufus, d 25 May 1863 aged 69 yrs

Barrows, Nancy B., w/o Col. Rufus Barrows, d 14 Dec 1876 aged 79 yrs

Perry, Captain Ezra, d 1 March 1821 aged 80 yrs

Perry, Patty, w/o Capt. Ezra Perry, d 24 Oct 1836 aged 68 yrs

Perry, Jemima, w/o Capt. Ezra Perry, d 1 Feb 1808 aged 61 yrs

Perry, Horatio M., d 20 Feb 1853 aged 42 yrs

Perry, Lucy, w/o Horatio M. Perry, d 25 May 1869 aged 80 yrs

Perry, Othniel S., s/o Horatio & Lucy Perry, d 17 Oct 1876

Wilson, Malvina, w/o Othniel S. Perry, d 24 Jan 1904 aged 82 yrs

Perry, David, d 14 May 1806 aged 87 yrs

Perry, Margaret, w/o David Perry, d 13 Jan 1806

Perry, Timothy, d 1774 aged 31 yrs

Perry, Huldah, w/o Timothy Perry, d 19 Dec 1806 aged 57 yrs

Hill, Elizabeth, w/o James Hill, d 16 April 1789 aged 65 yrs

Perry, Timothy, d 28 March 1829 aged 59 yrs

Perry, Rebecca, w/o Timothy Perry, d 1 June 1834 aged 55 yrs

Sumner, Sarah M., d 18 Oct 1822

Macomber, Lemuel, d 27 Nov 1843 aged 89 yrs

Macomber, Tabitha, w/o Lemuel Macomber, d 30 Oct 1825 aged 68 yrs

Wilmarth, Jonathan, A patroit of the Revolutionary War, d 26 Oct 1839 aged 78 yrs

Wilmarth, Sally, w/o Jonathan Wilmarth, d 20 March 1843 aged 78 yrs

Horr, George, d 17 May 1860 aged 85 yrs

Horr, Elizabeth, w/o George Horr, d 8 March 1857 aged 82 yrs

Horr, Almond, s/o George & Elizabeth Horr, d 19 Nov 1824

Horr, Jacob, d 12 Dec 1845 aged 84 yrs

Horr, Abigail, w/o Jacob Horr, d 26 May 1825 aged 64 yrs

Horr, Abie, b 7 March 1793, d 19 Oct 1871

Horr, Wealthy, w/o Abie Horr, ...

Knapp, Freeman, d 23 Oct 1893 aged 90 yrs

Martin, Lydia, w/o Freeman Knapp, d 10 Oct 1880 aged 64 yrs

Howland, Isaac, d 24 Feb 1859 aged 64 yrs

Mugg, Sarah, w/o Francis McCann & d.o James & Hannah Mugg, d 14 June 1865 aged 32 yrs

Trasher, George H., Sergt Co B 58th Mass Vols, d 11 Dec 1911 aged 86 yrs

Lincoln, Eliza, w/o George H. Trasher & d/o Joseph & Sally Lincoln, d 28 Feb 1871 aged 33 yrs

Pierce, Abraham, d 1 Dec 1890 aged 62 yrs

Pierce, Harriet E., w/o Abraham Pierce, d 9 April 1902 aged 69 yrs

Pond, William F., 1852-1940

Pond, Evelyn A., w/o William F. Pond, 1856-1930

Pond, Stephen H., s/o William F. & Evelyn A. Pond, 1879-1945

Merz, Arthur E., 1894-1975

Pond, Ina G., w/o Arthur E. Merz, 1895-1989

Millard, Arthur S., 1893-1969

Kenson, Samuel, 1886-1968

Woodward, Raymond C., 1864-1947

Greene, Gladys M., w/o Raymond C. Woodward, 1896-1988

Woodward, Hazelfern M., d/o Raymond & Gladys Woodward, 1923-1943

Monner, Charles A., 1862-1931

Hoag, Harriet, w/o Charles A. Monner, 1871-1930

Fisher, James I., 1894-1955

Fisher, Matilda, w/o James I. Fisher, 1895-1983

Fisher, Alice S., 1860-1950

Larson, Axel J., 1898-1978

Fisher, Flora I., w/o Axel J. Larson, 1896-1994

Money, John H., 1861-1950

Money, Abbie O., w/o John H. Money, 1865-1944

Money, Lloyd J., 1900-1972

Torrey, John L., 1829-1910

Torrey, Martha A., w/o John L. Torrey, 1826-1885

Brown, Daniel J., b 24 March 1815, d 9 April 1893

Brown, Abby M., w/o Daniel J. Brown, b 16 Feb 1818, d 18 Sept 1895

Brown, Isadora J., d/o Daniel J. & Abby M. Brown, b 28 Jan 1846, d 9 Oct 1882

Thayer, Harriet I., 1892-1976

Cash, Samuel W., 1869-1962

Aitcheson, Augusta N., w/o Samuel W. Cash, 1867-1932

Cash, Charles H., 1881-1945

Rudolph, Agnes W., w/o Charles H. Cash, 1902-1969

Johnson, Simon J., 1840-1903

Johnson, Hannah C., w/o Simon J. Johnson, 1854-1927

Whittaker, Frederick A., 1875-1935

Whittaker, Sarah Jane, w/o Frederick A. Whittaker, 1875-1954

Whittaker, John H., 1850-1940

Whittaker, Martha, w/o John H. Whittaker, 1852-1913

Worrel, George R., 1838-1914

Biggens, Margaret, w/o George R. Worrel, 1852-1944

Metters, George H., 1887-1946

Johnson, Gertie M., w/o George H. Metters, 1890-1983

Hewitt, Anne E., w/o Alfred W. Hewitt, & d/o James & Hannah Mugg, d 14 Feb 1858 aged 22 yrs

McCann, Sarah, w/o Frank McCann, & d/o James & Hannah Mugg, d 14 June 1866

Mugg, John, s/o James & Hannah Mugg, d 3 April 1883 aged 57 yrs

Perry, Edward Payson, 1856-1915

Smith, Nettie, w/o Edward Payson Perry, 1863-1934

DuWors, Robert J., MD, 1920-1949

Brigham, Carl A., 1884-1957

Jenkins, E. Ethel, w/o Carl A. Brigham, 1887-1959

Smith, William, d 31 Jan 1880 aged 69 yrs

Smith, Mary J., w/o George Pass, d 16 June 1924 aged 75 yrs

Smith, Mary, w/o William Smith, d 29 March 1877 aged 53 yrs

Smith, Ida L., w/o Robert Smith, b 7 Sept 1868, d 6 April 1888
Smith, Thomas, 1852-1914
Smith, Florence E., 1848-1917
Cole, Zemas, 1808-1887
Briggs, Fanny W., w/o Zemas Cole, 1807-1886
Cole, George, 1850-1885
Brigham, Sabra L., w/o George Cole, 1853-1923
Randall, Allen, 1879-1927
Mitchell, Edith Cole, w/o Allen Randall, 1870-1949
Cole, Ralph, 1878-1959
Maddox, Kate, w/o Ralph Cole, 1879-1953
Hicks, Otis F., 1868-1916
Hicks, Hattie J., w/o Otis F. Hicks, 1870-....
Pell, Isabella, 1864-1923
Knight, Albert H., b 12 Sept 1830, d 24 Aug 1905
McConnell, Sarah, w/o Albert H. Knight, b 8 Dec 1865, d....
Barnett, Eli, 1835-1908
Barnett, Mary F., w/o Eli Barnett, 1838-1905
Torrey, Samuel, 1786-1869
Torrey, Martha A., w/o John L. Torrey, b 3 Dec 1826, d 28 April 1885
Torrey, Damon A., s/o John L. & Martha A. Torrey, d 24 Jan 1879 aged
    11 yrs 7 mos 24 days
Reynolds, Joseph E., 1877-1946
Reynolds, Margaret L., w/o Joseph E. Reynolds, 1876-1940
Reynolds, Caleb E., 1858-1932
Reynolds, Harriet, w/o Caleb E. Reynolds, d ....
Hicks, Asa T., b 13 Oct 1835, d 15 Jan 1891
Hicks, Phoebe, b 23 March 1841, d 11 May 1913
Torrey, George B., 1823-1901
Torrey, Maria, w/o George B. Torrey, 1827-1982
Perry, Rev. Thomas, d 29 Aug 1852 aged 70 yrs
Perry, Sally, w/o Rev. Thomas Perry, d 30 Dec 1843 aged 65 yrs
Perry, Caroline N., d 11 April 1883 aged 75 yrs 10 mos 11 days
Perry, Sera, d 17 April 1881 aged 67 yrs 9 mos
Perry, Deborah G., w/o Sera Perry, d 23 Jan 1861 aged 50 yrs
Perry, Harriet N., w/o Sera Perry, d 20 Aug 1899 aged 85 yrs
Mugg, Thomas W., b 17 Sept 1847, d 7 July 1929
Mugg, Sara E. W., w/o Thomas W. Mugg, b 27 May 1846, d 16 Feb 1922
Mugg, Annie W., d 18 Dec 1879 aged 10 yrs 4 mos 19 days
Mugg, James, d 14 May 1884 aged 77 yrs

Mugg, Hannah, w/o James Mugg, d 10 May 1880 aged 73 yrs
Munyan, Charles E., 1878-1942
Dean, Lois, w/o Charles E. Munyan, 1885-1957
Peck, Amos E., 1875-1944
Rider, Angelina I., w/o Amos E. Peck, 1877-1975
Baker, Herbert, 1874-1966
Watson, Cora M., w/o Herbert Baker, 1873-1955
Evans, Albert W., 1883-1944
Evans, Mildred C., w/o Albert W. Evans, 1901-1986
Anderson, Frances R., 1908-1947
Dorrance, John A., 1885-1951
Carpenter, Bertha E., w/o John A. Dorrance, 1901-1947
Sprigg, Marshall T., 1872-1934
VanAmburgh, Clara, w/o Marshall T. Sprigg, 1874-1952
Sprigg, Alice Clara, 1906-1965
Slate, Fred B., 1877-1949
Slate, Eva I., w/o Fred B. Slate, 1880-1973
Banks, Robert A., 1861-1927
Banks, Emma J., w/o Robert A. Banks, 1863-1938
Banks, Olive P., 1896-1985
Balkcom, Captian Jacob, d 16 Nov 1854 aged 86 yrs
Balkcom, Matilda, w/o Capt. Jacob Balkcom, d 8 Sept 1855 aged 81 yrs
Briggs, Stephen, d 30 Jan 1850 aged 88 yrs
Briggs, Lydia, w/o Stephen Briggs, d 24 Sept 1843 aged 69 yrs
Briggs, Polly, w/o Stephen Briggs, d 16 Oct 1829 aged 61 yrs
Briggs, Silvanus, s/o Stephen Briggs, d 15 Dec 1812 aged 10 yrs
Balkcom, Daniel, d 1 Sept 1834 aged 70 yrs
Balkcom, Lydia, w/o Daniel Balkcom, d 8 Aug 1830 aged 63 yrs
Balkcom, Rebeccah, d 1822
Perry, Hon. David Esq., d 18 July 1827 aged 79 yrs
Perry, Sarah, w/o Hon. David Perry Esq., d 4 Dec 1845
Perry, David, b 8 Aug 1780, d 26 April 1854
Barrows, Wheaton, d 3 Oct 1842 aged 53 yrs
Barrows, Abigail, w/o Wheaton Barrows, d 14 May 1871 aged 82 yrs
Barrows, Joseph, d 13 Feb 1825 aged 79 yrs
Barrows, Nancy, d 3 Feb 1856 aged 75 yrs
Freeman, Deacon Milton, d 3 Jan 1873 aged 70 yrs
Freeman, Eliza A., w/o Dea. Milton Freeman, d 30 Dec 1884 aged 78 yrs
Armstrong, Cinda, d 27 March 1855 aged 62 yrs
Wilmarth, Stephen, d 25 Aug 1829 aged 63 yrs

Wilmarth, Mary, w/o Stephen Wilmarth, d 26 July 1822 aged 55 yrs 7 mos

Ring, Rufus W., b 19 Dec 1808, d 25 May 1849

Ring, L. Frances, b 16 Aug 1838, d 9 April 1853

French, Lucretia, b 16 June 1818, d 13 Sept 1870

Ring, William R., b 21 May 1843, d 1 April 1853

French, Ephraim, d 11 Nov 1819 aged 57 yrs

French, Wealthy, w/o Ephraim French, d 8 June 1852 aged 88 yrs

Trasher, Simmons, d 17 April 1856 aged 69 yrs

Perry, Rhoda, w/o Simmons Trasher & d/o David Perry Esq., d 29 Jan 1832 aged 46 yrs

Perry, Ebenezer, s/o David & Sarah Perry, d 19 Sept 1801 aged 29 yrs

Perry, David, d 14 May 1806 aged 87 yrs

Perry, Margaret, w/o David Perry, d 13 Jan 1806

Groves, Davis, b 12 May 1835, d 25 Aug 1901

Henry, Annie, w/o Davis Groves, b 21 April 1832, d 12 May 1917

Groves, Ezra D., b 23 Feb 1871, d 9 Feb 1908

Reynolds, Levi M., 1839-1916

Reynolds, Hannah, w/o Levi M., 1846-1926

Slater, William, b Jan 1802, d 20 Sept 1888

Slater, Betsey, w/o William Slater, b 4 Nov 1804, d 12 March 1891

Rouse, George W., 1880-1950

Rouse, Daisy B., w/o George W. Rouse, 1885-1959

Shaw, Lucretia, 1810-1897

Ingalls, George J., d 3 Aug 1874 aged 49 yrs

Ingalls, Marie L., w/o George J. Ingalls, d 29 Dec 1891

Ingalls, Hannah, w/o George J. Ingalls, d 7 Nov 1850 aged 20 yrs

Rounds, Eugene B., 1846-1917

Rounds, H. Emma , w/o Eugene B. Rounds, 1854-1924

Rounds, Elizabeth M., d/o Eugene & H. Emma Rounds, 1887-1952

Rounds, Ethel W., d/o Eugene & H. Emma Rounds, 1884-1942

Rounds, Harriet A., d/o Eugene & H. Emma Rounds, 1881-1952

Rounds, Gertrude E., d/o Eugene & H. Emma Rounds, 1889-1974

Miller, George E., 1839-1904

Miller, Julia A., w/o Geroge E. Miller, 1839-1910

Perry, Edward B., b 12 March 1883, d 2 July 1908

Perry, Oscar S., 1884-1885

Perry, George S., 1866-1940

Gage, Harriet E., w/o George S. Perry, 1869-1932

Perry, Winona M., d/o George S. & Harriet E. Perry, 1890-1969

Wilmarth, William A., b 26 July 1795, d 3 Dec 1873
Perry, Osborn, b 13 Sept 1821, d 24 Feb 1902
Seagrave, Harriet E., w/o Osborn Perry, b 7 May 1833, d 5 Dec 1904
Wilmarth, William A., b 23 Aug 1822, d 27 Aug 1893
Wilmarth, Joanna S., w/o William A. Wilmarth, d 5 Feb 1879 aged 59 yrs
   9 mos 14 days
Carpenter, Benjamin, 1822-1853
Carpenter, Nancy, w/o Benjamin Carpenter, 1819-1908
Carpenter, Louisa Esther, 1848-1927, Founder & Benefactress of the Oak
   Knoll Cenetery
Carpenter, Eustace V., 1848-1924

First Baptist Church Cemetery
Baptist Road
Swansea, Massachusetts

Peck, Deacon Thomas, d Feb 1770
Peck, Mary, w/o Deacon Thomas Peck, d 27 May 1804
Fisher, Constant, w/o Augustus Mason, d 19 Nov 1764 AE 33 yrs
Barney, Jacob, d 10 May 1777 AE 28 yrs
Cole, Elizabeth, w/o Benjamin Cole, d March 1748 AE 39 yrs
Kingsley, Aaron, d 19 June 1785
Kingsley, Mary, w/o Deacon Jonathan Kingsley, d March 1756
Kingsely, Benjamin, d 9 April 1767
Sanders, Joseph, d 2 Jan 1783 aged 49 yrs
Sanders, Anne, w/o Joseph Sanders, d 22 Dec 1765
Harding, Richard, d 14 Dec 1748 AE 67 yrs
Luther, Judith, w/o John Luther, d Dec 1751
Martin, Marcy, w/o John Martin, d 1760
Fox, Efther d Aug 1737
Martin, John, of Rehoboth, d 6 Feb 1730 AE 61 yrs
Pearce, Jonathan, s/o Jeremiah & Submit Pearce, d 29 June 1731
Cole, Nathaniel, d 1755 AE 53 yrs
Cole, Sarah, w/o Nathaniel Cole, d 19 Oct 1787 AE 83 yrs
Kingsley, Capt. Hezekiah, d 1769

Several more black slate stones, but unable to read

Peleg Slade Cemetery
Hortonville Road
Swansea, Massachusetts

Slade, Col. Peleg, d 28 Dec 1813 AE 87 yrs

Slade, H., d 9 Oct 1817 AE 36 yrs

Chace Cemetery
Sharp's Lot Road
Swansea, Massachusetts

Chace, Abigail, w/o John Chace, d 3 June 1852 aged 50 yrs
Lewis, Joanna, w/o Timothy Chace, d 21 Feb 1880 aged 86 yrs
Chace, Elizabeth, d 9 May 1883 aged 81 yrs
Chace, Barney, d 13 Oct 1816 aged 20 yrs
Chace, Betsey, d 2 Sept 1811 aged 38 yrs
Chace, Deliverance, d 30 Dec 1819 aged 88 yrs
Chace, Enoch, d Sept 1805 aged 80 yrs

Pierce Cemetery
Swansea, Massachusetts

Pierce, Alvar, s/o Jabez M. & Mary K. Pierce, d 20 July 1842 aged 20 yrs
Pierce, Ira, s/o Jabez M. & Mary Pierce, d 26 Jan 1828 aged 1 yr 1 mo
Kelton, Mary, w/o Jabez M.Pierce, d 8 Jan 1831 aged 33 yrs
Pierce, Jabez M., d 22 July 1837 aged 44 yrs

Cole Cemetery
Swansea, Massachusetts

Cole, Desire, w/o Constant Cole,d 3 Jan 1826 aged 92 yrs
Cole, Betsey, d 7 May 1808 aged 41 yrs
Cole, Capt. Constant, d 30 Jan 1807 aged 37 yrs

Peck, James, s/o Thomas & S. Peck of Seekonk, d 25 May 1822 aged 30 yrs

Cole, Constant, d 26 Oct 1832 aged 99 yrs

Brown, Betsey, w/o Aaron Cole & d/o William & Lettice Brown, b 1 Aug 1767, d 7 May 1808

Cole, Jemima, d/o Constant & Desire Cole, d 21 Jan 1866 aged 90 yrs 11 mos

Cole, Aaron, d 2 Oct 1847 aged 70 yrs

Cole, Elmira, w/o Thomas Cole & d/o Aaron & Betsey Cole, d 13 Feb 1868 aged 70 yrs

Salisbury, Ruth, widow of Caleb Salisbury, d 7 May 1832 aged 92 yrs

Cole, Aaron, s/o Constant & Desire Cole, b 9 Oct 1768, d 2 Oct 1847

Peck, Thomas, s/o Thomas & Rebecca Peck, d 9 May 1871 aged 76 yrs 8 mos 7 days

Christ Church Cemetery
Main Street
Swansea, Massachusetts

Bridge, Roger, 1929-1989

Ferguson, Arnzen Sr., 1916-1993

Ferguson, Harriet, w/o Arnzen Ferguson Sr., 1921-....

Gray, Franklin Sr., 1897-1988

Gray, Hattie W., w/o Franklin Gray Sr., 1906-1975

Gray, Charles D., b 30 May 1909, d 15 Oct 1985

Glidden, Elizabeth, w/o Charles D. Gray, b 3 Dec 1906, d 20 March 1988

Stirrup, Robert, 1889-1981

Stirrup, Mary A., w/o Robert Stirrup, 1890-1968

Chace, Leonard A., 1891-1971

Chace, Mary W., w/o Leonard A. Chace, 1894-1976

Sunderland, Bertha Moss, b 26 July 1901, d 12 July 1981

Griffiths, G. W., 1857-1937

Dodson, George B., b 5 Dec 1881, d 27 Nov 1959

Lynch, Josephine C., w/o George B. Dodson, b 19 July 1886, d 19 Jan 1987

Field, Leonard, 1891-1958

Gray, Elizabeth, w/o Leonard Field, 1896-1987

Traynor, Joseph Chadwick, 1901-1989

Richardson, Ivah, w/o Joseph Chadwick Traynor, 1905-1988

Traynor, Joseph, b 18 April 1868, d 14 Dec 1954

Traynor, Mary, w/o Joseph Traynor, b 8 March 1868, d 6 June 1944

Traynor, Richard, b 23 Feb 1872, d 19 Oct 1952

Gray, Lewis S., 1860-1932

Gray, Henriettta, w/o Lewis S. Gray, 1862-1943

Gray, Clarence W., s/o Lewis S. & Henrietta Gray, 1886-1933

Gray, Avis Mabel, d/o Lewis S. & Henrietta Gray, 1833-1903

Gray, Jeremiah, 1818-1898

Gray, Alice C. C., w/o Jeremiah Gray, 1829-1863

Gray, Kate, d/o Jeremiah & Alice C. C. Gray, 1858-1860

Gray, Lizzie, d/o Jeremiah & Alice Gray, 1854-1860

Gray, Mary, d/o Jeremiah & Alice Gray, 1855-1871

Gray, Lydia B., w/o Samuel Gray, d 21 May 1869 aged 26 yrs 9 mos

Mitchell, William, 1806-1880

Mitchell, Emelikem, w/o William Mitchell, 1815-1863

Eddy, Frank R., b 30 Aug 1871, d 10 Aug 1950

Eddy, Mabel Augusta, w/o Frank R. Eddy, b 4 Aug 1870, d 27 March
1956

Gray, William A., 1825-1884

Carr, Ruth H., w/o William A. Gray, 1825-1879

Gray, Mima C., d/o William & Ruth Gray, 1860-1872

Gray, Ada R., d/o William & Ruth Gray, 1855-1922

Cobb, Charles M., 1852-1918

Gray, Elizabeth J., w/o Charles M. Cobb, 1853-1915

Norton, Laura Duncan, b 31 Aug 1909, d 4 May 1982

Norton, Elizabeth R., b 4 Sept 1872, d 2 June 1925

Norton, Michael S., b 26 Nov 1868, d 18 July 1934

Adams, Samuel S., b 21 April 1904, d 9 Nov 1959

Eddy, Edith E., w/o Samuel S. Adams, b 25 Feb 1908, d 22 March 1995

Chace, Reuben, b 3 Feb 1790, d 5 Aug 1864

Chace, Phebe, w/o Reuben Chace, b 25 July 1797, d 13 Feb 1864

Chace, David, s/o Reuben & Phebe Chace, b 31 Jan 1822, d 6 Sept 1839

Chace, Reuben F., s/o Reuben & Phebe Chace, b 6 Feb 1839, d 16 Sept
1839

Gray, William, 1831-1836

Holcomb, Betsey B., w/o Henry Holcomb & d/o Reuben & Phebe Chace, d
22 Aug 1852 aged 26 yrs 9 mos

Purington, Clark, b 23 Nov 1815, d 16 Dec 1889

Purington, Bethany B., w/o Clark Purington, b 25 April 1819, d 11 Oct 1851

Purington, Clark, s/o Clark & Bethany B. Purington, b 31 Aug 1844, d 1 Oct 1844

Mason, Frances A., w/o Jacob P. Barstow, b 24 Sept 1837, d 4 April 1916

Barstow, Jacob P., b 29 June 1839, d 24 Oct 1916

Mason, John Esq., d 8 Jan 1871 aged 89 yrs

Mason, Frances B., w/o John Mason Esq., d 12 Nov 1869 aged 69 yrs 11 mos 2 days

Mason, Elizabeth, w/o John Mason Esq. d 27 March 1835 aged 47 yrs

Mason, Nancy M., d/o John & Elizabeth Mason, d 8 July 1844 aged 20 yrs

Mason, John Jr., b 23 Jan 1812, d 28 Oct 1885

Mason, Phebe R., w/o John Mason Jr., d 7 Nov 1847 aged 28 yrs

Mason, Parthenia A., w/o John Mason Jr., b 18 April 1820, d 26 March 1909

Jones, Alice A. Wynne, 1863-1944

Jones, Eleanor Wynee, 1832-1917

Jones, John Wynne, 1857-1938

Attwell, Nancy B., w/o Benjamin F. Attwell & d/o John & Mary Winslow, d 13 April 1864 aged 40 yrs

Attwell, Joseph, b 3 July 1817, d 3 July 1817

Attwell, Benjamin F., b 3 July 1817, d 5 April 1866 Lung Fever

Gray, John, 1771-1854

Shearman, Elizabeth, w/o John Gray, 1771-1830

Cotton, Elizabeth, w/o John Gray, 1788-1837

Shearman, Col. Peleg, 1747-1811

Heath, Mary, w/o Col. Peleg Shearman, 1746-1837

Shearman, Zoviah, d/o Peleg & Mary Shearman, 1790-1826

Brayton, John C., s/o Stephen & Mary H. Gray Brayton, 1822-1903

Case, Joseph, 1817-1893

Gray, Eliza S., w/o Joseph Case & d/o John & Elizabeth Gray, 1806-1895

Gray, Richmond C., 1861-1919

Gray, Etta M., w/o Richmond C. Gray, 1863-1943

Gray, Majorie L., 1889-1947

Gray, Horace, 1850-1921

Gray, Clara F., w/o Horace Gray, 1855-1929

Sears, Francis Richmond, 1906-1974

Sears, Elmer Snow, 1874-1957

Gray, Mima C., w/o Elmer Snow Sears, 1883-1961

Wood, Herbert A., b 9 Oct 1838, d 2 Sept 1918

Wood, Almedia C., w/o Herbert A. Wood, b 20 Dec 1847, d 6 May 1879

Eddy, Estelle W., b 7 May 1892, d 29 April 1912

Eddy, Della A., b 18 April 1890, d 4 Sept 1913

Wood, Daniel B., b 27 Sept 1809, d 5 Jan 1891

Wood, Mary Ann,, w/o Daniel B. Wood, b 6 Aug 1815, d 26 June 1889

Wood, Fannie E., d/o Daniel & Mary Wood, b 13 July 1854, d 13 May 1922

Davis, Leroy A., 1871-1938

Davis, Gertrude A., w/o Leroy A. Davis, 1873-1957

Chace, Charles Frederick, s/o Joseph & Betsey W. Chace, b 13 Feb 1828, d 7 Feb 1891

Chace, Frank M., b 16 April 1856, d 6 Aug 1921

Chace, Amanda L., w/o Frank M. Chace, b 17 Sept 1858, d 19 May 1938

Chace, Hollister R., 1898-1965

Chace, Mildred, w/o Hollister R. Chace, 1899-1967

Chace, Richard S., d April 1841 Swansea, MA aged 31 yrs 10 mos

Chace, Rev. Benjamin H., d 31 May 1897 aged 85 yrs 3 mos

Slade, Sarah, w/o Rev. Benjamin Chace, d 27 March 1906 aged 89 yrs 4 mos

Chace, Orville Slade, s/o Rev. Benjamin H. & Sarah Chace, d 30 Dec 1848 aged 5 yrs 6 mos 20 days

Chace, Royal, d 5 Feb 1850 Sacremento, California

Austin, George, b 27 March 1799, d 6 Dec 1867

Austin, Betsey B., w/o George Austin, b 28 July 1800, d 14 Nov 1877

Wellington, Dr. James Lloyd, 1818-1916

Sisson, Charlotte, w/o Dr. James Lloyd Wellington, 1825-1881

Wellington, William H., s/o Dr. James & Charlotte Wellington, 1861-1928

Wellington, Ethelyn R., w/o William H. Wellington, 1870-1965

Stevens, Lucinda, d/o Frank S. & Julia A. B. Stevens, b 14 June 1859, d July 1859

Stevens, Frank S., b 6 Aug 1827, d 25 April 1898

Stevens, Elizabeth B., w/o Frank S. Stevens, b 2 April 1849, d 14 Feb 1936

Birch, James E., b 30 Nov 1827, d 12 March 1857

Birch, Frank S., b 1 Oct 1856, d 12 March 1836

Wood, John A., b 22 Feb 1807, d 19 May 1867

Winslow, Sarah, w/o John A. Wood & d/o Dr. Ebenezer Winslow, b 18 Sept 1807, d 16 Dec 1867

Wood, Helen Maria, d/o John & Sarah Wood, d 16 July 1849 aged 16 yrs

Wood, Henry O., 1837-1925

Ingalls, Ann A., w/o Henry O. Wood, 1839-1923

Wood, Helen M., d/o Henry & Ann Wood, 1865-1865

Wood, Hattie, d/o Henry & Ann Wood, 1868-1871

Winslow, Katharine, w/o Dr. Ebenezer Winslow, d 16 April 1841 aged 77 yrs

Slade, William Esq., d 17 May 1842 aged 67 yrs

Brown, Elizabeth, w/o William Slade Esq., d 4 March 1856 aged 66 yrs

Slade, William, d 2 Aug 1883 aged 63 yrs

Mason, James H., b 18 Aug 1817, d 11 June 1893

Mason, Mary E., w/o James H. Mason, b 6 Feb 1822, d July 1889

Mason, Frederick A., s/o James H. & Mary E. Mason, b 13 Aug 1844, d 23 Nov 1872

Wellington, Arthur W., b 4 Nov 1846, d 24 Feb 1918

Wellington, Ellen R., w/o Arthur Wellington, b 23 Dec 1849, d 19 March 1923

Chace, Joseph S., d 26 Feb 1903 aged 65 yrs 3 mos

Chace, Ellen F., w/o Joseph Chace, d 19 Sept 1919 aged 76 yrs

Chace, Ellen Frances, d/o Joseph & Ellen Chace, b 19 Jan 1870, d 4 July 1956

Ripley, Francis N., b 14 Jan 1898, d 20 July 1927

Chace, James E., d 12 Feb 1869 aged 63 yrs 1 mo 12 days

Chace, Hannah E., w/o James E. Chace, d 12 Aug 1896 aged 87 yrs 7 mos

Chace, Margaret C., d/o James E. & Hannah E. Chace, d 25 Sept 1859 aged 17 yrs 8 mos 15 days

Chace, Philip S., s/o James E. & Hannah E. Chace, d 27 Sept 1885 aged 49 yrs 6 mos

Chace, Earle, b 5 April 1784 Swansey, MA, d 8 Oct 1877

Chace, Lydia, w/o Earle Chace, b Sommerset, MA, d 11 April 1873 aged 93 yrs 25 days

Monroe, James, d 8 Oct 1854 aged 66 yrs

Monroe, Betsey, w/o James Monroe, d 13 Aug 1863 aged 73 yrs

Monroe, Clara, d/o James & Betsey Monroe, d 25 Sept 1843 aged 18 yrs

Earle, Amos E., b 2 Dec 1894, d 4 Jan 1919

Maxam, Annie B., w/o Benjamin F. Earle, b 2 May 1857, d 17 Nov 1898

Winslow, William, s/o Doct. Ebenezer Winslow, d 1 Jan 1861 aged 79 yrs 8 mos

Wheeler, Ann, w/o William Winslow & d/o Barnet & Ann Wheeler, d 4 Jan 1867 aged 73 yrs 11 mos 19 days

Winslow, Mary Ann, w/o Enoch Chace & d/o William & Ann Winslow, d 29 Oct 1853 aged 26 yrs

Maxam, William E., d 19 Feb 1888 aged 68 yrs 11 mos

Maxam, Willard, b 19 Feb 1866, d 9 June 1942

Wilmarth, Mary, w/o Clement Wilmarth, d 4 Jan 1869 aged 33 yrs

Chace, Joseph F., b 25 Aug 1797, d 3 May 1878

Winslow, Betsey, w/o Joseph Chace & d/o Ebenezer & Katherine Winslow, b 31 Oct 1802, d 7 June 1879

Gardiner, Katherine F., w/o Benjamin B. Gardiner, b 11 April 1836, d 16 April 1914

Chace, Elias D., b 10 Dec 1815, d 27 Aug 1875

Chace, Chloe L., w/o Elias D. Chace, b 7 July 1815, d 27 Feb 1880

Chace, Walter A., b 13 March 1846, d 30 March 1915

Chace, Josephine E. S., w/o Walter A. Chace, b 20 Aug 1853, d 15 July 1905

Chace, Mabel W., b 8 May 1882, d 17 Feb 1938

Robinson, Mary, d 18 Oct 1844 aged 65 yrs

Chace, Thomas C., b 20 Dec 1827, d 24 June 1891

Chace, Josephine A., w/o Thomas C. Chase, b 19 April 1836, d 10 May 1903

Altham, Jonas, b 26 Feb 1815, d 10 Oct 1885

Altham, Mary, w/o Jonas Altham, b 7 Sept 1821, d 7 Dec 1903

Altham, George J., b 27 May 1862, d 22 March 1932

Altham, Nellie J., w/o George J. Altham, b 6 July 1876, d 31 Aug 1976

Wood, Levi 2nd, b 14 May 1802, d 7 May 1843

Sanders, Ardella A., w/o Levi Wood 2nd, b 31 Jan 1806, d 12 Sept 1864

Major, Capt. William, d 15 July 1851 Providence, RI

Major, Mehitable, w/o Capt. William Major, d 15 Feb 1864 aged 90 yrs

Major, Mary R., d/o Capt. William & Mehitable Major, d Sept 1844

Trafton, Elias D., b 6 May 1792, d 10 May 1869

Perry, Sophronia R., w/o Elias D. Trafton & d/o Capt. Jonathan Perry of Nantucket, MA, 1799-1894

Trafton, Jonathan P., s/o Elias & Sophronia Trafton, b 5 Jan 1829, d 17 April 1856

Gardiner, Harold W., 1902-1979

Ford, Edith H., w/o Harold W. Gardiner, 1908-....

Hodges, John R., d 24 Oct 1879 Washington, DC

Hodges, Sophronia E., w/o John R. Hodges, b 13 May 1821, d 5 Nov 1899

Pierce, Isaiah, 1833-1906
Trafton, Betsey O., w/o Isaiah Pierce, 1825-1883
Baker, Henry Clinton, 1898-1955
Ratcliffe, Gertrude, w/o Henry Clinton Baker, 1898-1967
Brown, Rev. Edgar D., 1889-1961
Brown, Beulah W., w/o Rev. Edgar D. Brown, 1894-1976
Hunt, Stanley, 1891-1967
Whittaker, Esther E., w/o Stanley Hunt, 1893-1985
Pierce, Richard F., US Army WW2, b 2 May 1906, d 9 Feb 1994
Tucker, Charles I., 1st Lt. US Army WW2, b 12 July 1913, d 25 Feb 1987
Wilcox, Reginald H., 1903-1991
Traynor, Grace R., w/o Reginald H. Wilcox, 1901-1994

Kingsley Cemetery
Old Fall River Road
Swansea, Massachusetts

Mason, Gardner, d 18 May 1808 aged 40 yrs
Captain Daniel Salisbury, d 7 April 1809 aged 95 yrs
Hale, Anne, w/o Capt. Daniel Salisbury, d 20 May 1770 aged 46 yrs
Cole, Patience, w/o Capt. Daniel Salisbury, d 16 Jan 1820 aged 91 yrs
Ormsbee, Rachel, w/o Jonathan Ormsbee, d 24 Dec 1788 aged 42 yrs
Mason, Patience, w/o Elder John Mason, d 22 Oct 1798 aged 73 yrs
Mason, Zeriah, w/o John Mason, d 26 July 1765 aged 18 yrs
Mason, Ruthy, w/o Aaron Mason, d 6 Oct 1753 aged 47 yrs
Mason, Elder John, d 27 June 1801 aged 85 yrs
Mason, Aaron, d 5 Nov 1751 aged 3 mos
Mason, Phebe, d/o Aaron & Ruth Mason, d 27 March 1745 aged 19 yrs
Mason, Dr. James, of Swansey, d 18 Sept 1785 aged 40 yrs
Mason, Alice, w/o Dr. James Mason, d 10 Nov 1779 aged 31 yrs
Mason, Phebe, w/o Dr. James Mason, d 15 March 1792 aged 34 yrs
Mason, James, s/o Nathan & Candace Mason, d 16 Dec 1776 aged 2 yrs
Mason, Rev. Russell, d 11 Jan 1799 aged 85 yrs
Mason, Aaron, d 25 Dec 1731 aged 29 yrs
Kingsely, Charles Edwin, s/o Elisha & Mary Kingsley, d 20 March 1845
    aged 5 yrs 20 days

Rounds, Mary, w/o Benjamin K. Rounds, & d/o John & Patience Rounds, d 17 Aug 1880 aged 65 yrs 1 days

Bushee, Sally, d/o John & Patience Bushee, d 1 Nov 1881 aged 76 yrs 26 days

Bushee, Betsey, w/o Eastc Pierce & d/o John & Patience Bushee, d 24 Dec 1881 aged 80 yrs 9 mos 4 days

Bushee, Patience, w/o John Bushee, d 21 Jan 1874 aged 99 yrs

Bushee, Levi, s/o John & Patience Bushee, d 18 Dec 1875 aged 73 yrs 6 mos 14 days

Kinglsey, Mary A., w/o ......Peck, b 22 June 1834, d 5 April 1907

Peck, Charles H., s/o ......& Mary Peck, 1865-1930

Pierce, George D. W., d 27 Oct 1874 aged 38 yrs 2 mos 24 days

Pierce, Julia A., w/o George D. W. Pierce, d 16 Nov 1873 aged 37 yrs 1 mo 16 days

Pierce, Julia, d/o George & Julia Pierce, b 19 April 1865, d 9 July 1865

Pierce, George, s/o George & Julia Pierce, b 9 April 1865, d 10 April 1865

Baker, Hale, d 11 Dec 1875 aged 86 yrs 4 mos 3 days

Baker, Mary M., w/o Hale Baker, d 27 Aug 1884 aged 88 yrs 6 mos 2 days

Baker, Phebe, w/o Hale Baker, d 19 Jan 1834 aged 40 yrs

Baker, Sarah, w/o Francis Baker, d 8 Nov 1849 aged 84 yrs

Mason, Gardner, s/o Job & Martha C. Mason, d 18 May 1803 aged 40 yrs

Vinicum, Susannah, w/o Gardner Mason & d/o John & Susannah Vinicum, d 9 May 1872 aged 95 yrs 4 mos 25 days

Kingsley, Elisha, s/o Hezekiah & Mima Kingsley, d 7 Jan 1868 aged 69 yrs 10 mos 22 days

Kingsley, Allen N., s/o Elisha & Mary Kingsley, drowned 9 July 1861 aged 30 yrs 20 days

Martin Cemetery
Locust Street
Swansea, Massachusetts

Martin, Phebe, w/o Melatiah Martin, d 3 Sept 1787 aged 41 yrs 1 mo 29 days

Martin, Melatiah, d 9 Sept 1794 aged 58 yrs 3 mos 17 days

Martin, Ann, d 28 Sept 1800 aged 22 yrs

Martin, John, d 14 Jan 1834 aged 61 yrs

Martin, Lydia, w/o John Martin, d 27 Sept 1858 aged 85 yrs

Martin, Job, d 8 April 1838 aged 36 yrs

Martin, Ardella A., d/o John & Lydia Martin, d 26 July 1830 aged 23 yrs

Martin, Lemira, d/o John & Lydia Martin, d 9 March 1828 aged 23 yrs

Mason, Mary Sisson, d/o Harding & Nancy Mason, d 4 Sept 1833 aged 20 yrs

Mason, Lydia, d/o Harding & Nancy Mason, d 19 July 1836 aged 28 yrs 18 days

Martin, Lucinda E., w/o Nevalentine B. Martin, d 28 May 1848 aged 40 yrs

Martin, Nevalentine B., d 20 Nov 1879 aged 71 yrs

Kingsley, Margaret P., w/o John H. Martin, d 8 June 1864 aged 25 yrs 6 mos

Martin, Eliza Jane, d/o Job & Hannah B. Martin, d 22 Aug 1833 aged 6 yrs 1 mo 28 days

Martin, Angeline, w/o William H. Martin, d 26 Aug 1860 aged 26 yrs

Martin, William H., b 24 Oct 1820, d Feb 1866

Hale Cemetery
Locust Street
Swansea, Massachusetts

Hale, Bethiah, w/o Deacon John Hale, d 7 Sept 1815 aged 86 yrs

Hale, Deacon John, d 9 Jan 1810 aged 84 yrs

Mason, Mary, w/o Benajah Mason, d 25 Oct 1784 aged 82 yrs

Hale, Lieut. John Jr., d 27 Feb 1790 aged 40 yrs

Mason, Lurana, w/o John Hale Jr., & d/o Simeon & Hannah Mason, d 1 June 1825 aged 71 yrs

Hale, Betsey, w/o Levi Hale, d 29 July 1801 aged 25 yrs

Hail, John, s/o Job & Mary Hail, d 11 April 1800 aged 11 yrs

Hale, Phebe, w/o John Monroe & d/o Daniel Hale Esq., d 12 Nov 1834 aged 53 yrs

Monroe, John, d 23 Sept 1867 aged 88 yrs

Monroe, Lydia, w/o John Monroe, d 19 March 1872 aged 79 yrs

Mason, John, d 7 Jan 1834 aged 57 yrs

Mason, Benajah of Swansey, d 20 Aug 1823 aged 72 yrs

Hale, Daniel, s/o William J. & Mary A. Hale, b 23 Aug 1897, d 1 Aug 1974

Hale, William J., b 30 March 1866, d 12 Feb 1936

Hale, Mary, b 13 July 1855, d 7 May 1932

Hale, Mary, b 1 Dec 1837, d 20 March 1928

Hale, Daniel M., b 19 April 1862, d 16 Aug 1874

Hale, Daniel, b 9 Oct 1832, d 9 July 1896

Hale, Daniel Esq., d 5 Sept 1830 aged 73 yrs

Hale, Cynthia, w/o Daniel Hale Esq., d 1 Oct 1822 aged 62 yrs

Horton, Alfred, s/o Gideon & Mercy Horton, d 24 June 1849 aged 25 yrs

Horton, Lydia, w/o Alfred M. Horton, d 1 Dec 1875 aged 65 yrs

Monroe, Phebe R., d/o John & Phebe Monroe, d 16 Nov 1867 aged 49 yrs

Hale, Daniel, s/o Daniel & Cynthia Hale, d 5 Feb 1867 aged 73 yrs

Hale, Sarah, w/o Daniel Hale & d/o David & Sarah Mason, d 23 Jan 1833 aged 39 yrs

Hale, Luther B., s/o Daniel & Cynthia Hale, d 20 July 1828 aged 26 yrs

Hale, Slade, s/o Daniel & Cynthia Hale, d Havana aged 23 yrs

Hale, Jonathan B., b 28 Sept 1800, d 4 Nov 1858
Hale, Rosanna, w/o Jonathan B. Hale, b 20 Oct 1812, d 26 July 1904
Hale, Elizabeth, b 17 April 1838, d 29 Sept 1908
Hale, Mason, b 4 Feb 1845, d 21 June 1845
Mason, Mary, w/o Mason Hale & d/o Barnibus & Hannah Mason, d 30
    Oct 1853 aged 83 yrs 11 mos 4 days
Hale, Daniel, s/o Daniel & Sarah Hale, d 18 Sept 1822 aged 11 mos

Mason Chace Cemetery
Baker Road
Swansea, Massachusetts

Chace, Leroy J., 1857-1923
Blanchard, Mary E., w/o Leroy J. Chace,......
Chace, Andrew W., 1855-1941
Chace, Mary E., w/o Andrew W. Chace, 1864-1932
Chace, Mabel M., d/o Andrew & Mary Chace, b 22 Nov 1887, d 13 May
    1902
Chace, Rachel, d/o Andrew & Mary Chace, b 21 Aug 1891, d 16 Oct 1892
Chace, Elias B., 1836-1908
Chace, John E., 1847-1920
Chace, Lavina, w/o Elias Chace, d 10 June 1888 aged 84 yrs
Chace, Elias, d 14 June 1875 aged 78 yrs
Chace, Barney, s/o Reuben & Betsey Chace, d 13 Oct 1816 aged 20 yrs
Chace, Betsey, w/o Reuben Chace, d 2 Sept 1811 aged 38 yrs
Chace, Reuben, d 27 March 1851 aged 80 yrs 9 mos 12 days
Chace, Elizabeth, w/o Reuben Chace, d 29 Oct 1858 aged 89 yrs
Chace, Enoch, d Sept 1805 aged 80 yrs
Chace, Deliverance, w/o Enoch Chace, d 30 Dec 1819 aged 88 yrs
Chace, Emeline, 1845-1922
Chace, James W., s/o Elias & Lavina Chace, d Sept 1842 aged 6 mos
Chace, Mason, b 18 Feb 1871 aged 54 yrs 6 mos 6 days
Chace, Lorana P., w/o Mason Chace, d 19 April 1895 aged 72 yrs
Chace, Sylvanus, s/o Mason & Lorana Chace, d 29 March 1847 aged 11
    mos
Chace, Laroy, s/o Mason & Lorana P. Chace, d 19 April 1857 aged 5 yrs

Chace, Joseph H., s/o Mason & Lorana P. Chace, d 26 Nov 1868 aged 24 yrs

Chace, Reuben, s/o Mason & Lorana P. Chace, d 8 Nov 1866 aged 22 yrs, A member of Co D 7th Mass Vol

Chace, Sylvanus J., d 22 March 1914 aged 65 yrs 26 days

Walker, Mary Ella, w/o Sylvanus J. Chace, & d/o George E. & Lucinda D. Walker, d 7 Nov 1880 aged 25 yrs 6 mos 22 days

Chace, Clarabell, d/o Sylvanus & Mary E. Chace, d 18 Dec 1875 aged 3 mos

Chace, Cora M., d/o Sylvanus & Mary Chace, b 1 Nov 1873, d 14 Feb 1895

Chace, Henry C., s/o Sylvanus & Fannie G. Chace, d 16 Dec 1915 aged 15 yrs 1 mo 17 days

McNeil, Frank L., 1878-1947

Eddy Family Cemetery
Swan Finishing Co., Parking Lot
Swansea, Massachusetts

To honor and Perpetuate the Memory of Eddy, Zachariah 1639-1718, One of the purchasers of Swansea, 29 Dec 1696. He set aside this spot, which is to live and remain as a burying place for the families of said Eddys and for such of their neighbors as the said Eddys shall admitt forever. To mark the resting place of his parents, Samuel & Elizabeth Eddy.

Eddy, Samuel, s/o Rev. William Eddy, Vicar of St. Dunstan's Church in Cranbook, Co. Kent, England and came on the "Handmaid" in 1630 to Plymouth, where he resided for fifty years. d 12 Nov 1687 Swansea, MA

Eddy, Elizabeth, w/o Samuel Eddy, d 24 May 1689 aged 82 yrs

Greenman, Esther, w/o William Greenman, d 1746 aged 54 yrs

Eddy, Ruth, d/o Captain Jeremiah Eddy, d 14 Nov 1756 aged 20 yrs

Eddy, Captain Jeremiah, d 9 Feb 1758 Maryland, aged 61 yrs

Eddy, Peleg, s/o Capt. Jeremiah & Elizabeth Eddy, d 18 March 1758 Surinam aged 32 yrs

Eddy, Amey, w/o Deacon William Eddy, d 11 Aug 1829 aged 78 yrs
Eddy, Caleb, d 21 Nov 1748 aged 71 yrs
Winslow, Nancy J., d/o John & Mary Winslow, d 24 April 1807 aged 13
    mos
Winslow, Nathan R., s/o Doct. William & Bethany Winslow, d 16 Oct
    1832

Town Hall Cemetery
Main Street
Swansea, Massachusetts

Winslow, Bethany, w/o Doct. John Winslow, d 29 Aug 1801 aged 26 yrs
Winslow, Doct, John, d 5 May 1838 aged 72 yrs
Winslow, Anna, d/o Dr. Ebenezer & Elizabeth Winslow, d 12 June 1781
    aged 5 yrs 5 mos
Winslow, Betty, w/o Capt. Ezekiel Winslow, d 7 March 17-4 aged 80 yrs
Winslow, Dr. Ebenezer, d 5 March 1832 aged 90 yrs
Winslow, Sarah, w/o Humphrey Winslow, d 29 Oct 1818 aged 46 yrs
Nichols, Caroline A., d/o Joseph P. & Parthenia Nichols, d 8 Sept 1830
    aged 1 yr 5 mos
Handy, Mary A., w/o Silas H. Handy, d 19 Nov 1886 aged 64 yrs 3 mos
    22 days
Handy, Silas H., d 18 Oct 1878 aged 63 yrs 6 mos 11 days
Kingsley, Bethania C., w/o Erastus T. Kingsley, d 3 July 1882 aged 78 yrs
    11 mos 15 days
Kingsley, Erastus T., d 8 Oct 1875 aged 74 yrs 11 mos
Chace, Betsey, w/o Philip Chace, d 17 March 1849 aged 72 yrs
Trott, Edward, d 21 July 1842 AE 37 yrs
Howard, George W., d 12 Nov 1883 aged 77 yrs 11 mos 25 days
Howard, Betsey, w/o Goerge W. Howard, d 6 Nov 1899 aged 67 yrs 2 days
Lincoln, Phienia, d 6 Jan 1850 aged 47 yrs 1 mo
Stebbins, Frank R., 1847-1912
Stebbins, William H., b 5 May 1823, d 20 Nov 1907
Stebbins, Harriet N., w/o William H. Stebbins, b 4 March 1823, d 26 Oct
    1903

King, Edward S., s/o Henry S. & Adeline B. King, b 11 Nov 1884, d 20
   Aug 1891
Sturtevant, Wilbur Lee, s/o Rev. James T. & Lousa C. Sturtevant, d 10
   April 1840 aged 9 mos 25 days
Balch, Aaron L., b 17 June 1802, d 1 Nov 1839
Trott, Martha, w/o Capt. James Trott, d 28 June 1839 aged 68 yrs
Stebbins, Mary A., d/o Dr. Artemas & Caroline R. Stebbins.....
Stebbins, Content R., w/o Dr. Artemas Stebbins, & d/o Dr. John Winslow,
   d 2 Feb 1842 aged 49 yrs
Chace, Susan M., w/o Reuben Chace 2nd, b 14 April 1842, d 7 Sept 1915
Chace, Reuben 2nd, b 1 Dec 1833, d 8 March 1919, A member of Co C
   22th Reg
Chace, Mary, w/o Samuel Chace, d 23 Oct 1860 aged 65 yrs
Chace, Samuel d 26 Oct 1872 aged 93 yrs 5 mos 14 days
Stebbins, Bethania B., d 20 March 1812 aged 20 yrs
Stebbins, Artemas T., s/o Dr. Artemas & Content H. Stebbins, d 9 March
   1857 aged 27 yrs
Trott, Ellen A., d 27 Aug 1810 aged 24 yrs 1 mo
Hill, Parshan, w/o Caleb Hill, d 7 Jan 1786 aged 37 yrs
Hill, Mary, d/o Jonathan & Elizabeth Hill, d 19 June 1757
Hill, Ruth, d/o Jonathan & Elizabeth Hill, d 5 June 1759 aged 22 yrs
Hill, Jonathan, d 9 Feb 1737 aged 53 yrs
Hill, Elizabeth, w/o Jonathan Hill, d 9 Sept 1756 aged 73 yrs
Trott, John, d 25 June 1824 aged 90 yrs
Weaver, Hannah, w/o John Trott, & d/o Peter Weaver, d 9 Oct 1819 aged
   75 yrs
Trott, Capt. James, d 26 Oct 1808 aged 70 yrs
Winslow, Charles B., d 6 May 1845 aged 38 yrs
Winslow, Betsey E., w/o Charles B. Winslow, d 2 Jan 1892 aged 74 yrs
Winslow, Amanda, w/o Charles B. Winslow, d 13 April 1835 aged 21 yrs
Winslow, William Brown, s/o Charles B. & Betsey E. Winslow, d 2 Jan
   1842 aged 11 mos
Slade, Caroline B., w/o Jonathan Slade, d 1 Feb 1845 aged 33 yrs
Slade, Caroline Winslow, d/o William Walter & Ida W. Slade, b 22 Dec
   1872, d 13 Nov 1932
Baker, Philip, b 11 Aug 1797 Lynn, MA, d 28 Jan 1881 Swansea, MA
Winslow, Eliza E., w/o Philip Baker & d/o Dr. John Winslow, d 6 Oct
   1848 aged 43 yrs 6 mos
Winslow, Francis B., b 13 Dec 1813, d 5 March 1888
Winslow, Hannah B., b 23 May 1820, d 1 Oct 1894

Winslow, Frances, d/o Francis B. & Hannah B. Winslow, b 25 June 1854, d 16 June 1918

Winslow, John H., MD, s/o John & Mary Winslow, d 13 July 1836 aged 32 yrs

Baker, Caroline F., d/o Philip & Eliza E. Baker, b 21 Jan 1830, d 29 Jan 1905

Baker, Adeline M., d/o Philip & Eliza Baker, d 29 May 1845 aged 20 yrs

Baker, Henry, 1840-1917

Baker, Anna E., w/o Benjamin W. Sherman, b 18 Dec 1841, d 24 Nov 1888

Thomas Cemetery
Rte 6
Swansea, Massachusetts

Smith, Constant, d 7 Feb 1835 aged 89 yrs 3 mos

Barney, Peleg, Revolutionary Pensioner, d 15 Feb 1838 aged 75 yrs

Barney, Lucinda, w/o Peleg Barney & d/o Israel Barney, d 22 Sept 1844 aged 74 yrs

Martin, Benjamin Alvin, 1844-1939

Read, Fannie M., w/o Benjamin Alvin Martin, 1851-1928

Haynes, Benjamin G., 1882-1907

Franklin, Shubael, d 16 Jan 1821 aged 66 yrs

Franklin, Betsey, w/o Shubael Franklin, d 7 March 1827

Franklin, Lemuel W., s/o Reuben & Betsey W. Franklin, d 6 May 1819 aged 35 yrs 6 mos

Barney, Patience, d 2 Dec 1849 aged 82 yrs

Child, Henry L., d 23 Nov 1870 aged 49 yrs 10 mos 23 days

Child, Frank T., 2nd s/o Daniel & Elizabeth M. B. Child, b 13 July 1858, d 20 April 1860

Grant, Daniel, d 25 April 1868 aged 93 yrs 9 mos

Grant, Rachel, w/o Daniel Grant, d 22 May 1861 aged 86 yrs 6 mos

Luther, Samuel, d 20 Nov 1843 aged 75 yrs 2 mos

Luther, Abigail, w/o Samuel Luther, d 9 May 1859 aged 88 yrs

Beers, Daniel, d Aug 1782 aged 35 yrs

Kingsley, Huldah, d 15 Sept 1810 aged 78 yrs

Peck, Col. Robert, d 5 Feb 1832 aged 38 yrs 26 days
Peck, Polly, w/o Col. Robert Peck, d Aug 1860 aged 77 yrs
Jennings, Freelove, w/o James Jennings, d 8 Sept 1820 aged 83 yrs
Kingsley, Benjamin, d 1 Feb 1852 aged 93 yrs
Martin, John E., b 4 March 1805, d 25 May 1888
Smith, Elizabeth B., w/o John E. Martin, b 12 May 1815, d 13 April 1897
Kingsley, Sally, d/o James & Annie Kingsley, b 25 Nov 1807, d 23 Dec 1891
Peckham, Aaron, d 16 March 1842 aged 87 yrs
Kingsely, Henry P., b 9 May 1809, d 8 Feb 1897
Kingsely, Lydia C., w/o Henry P. Kingsley, b 10 Feb 1819, d 10 March 1883
Peckham, Marie, d/o Mason & Esther Peckham, d 22 Nov 1834 aged 16 yrs
Peckham, Almira B., w/o Giles Peckham, d 27 April 1847 aged 29 yrs
Luther, Gilbert, b 27 July 1813, d 4 April 1889
Luther, Elizabeth, w/o Gilbert Luther, b 16 April 1821, d March 1888
Barney, Emily F., w/o George S. Barney, d 24 Sept 1864 aged 27 yrs
Daggett, Deacon James, b 1 April 1769, d 21 July 1844 aged 75 yrs
Barney, Dexter, d 11 June 1859 aged 55 yrs 7 mos
Barney, Eliza, w/o Dexter Barney, d Sept 1876
Carpenter, Eliza Peck Barney, b 10 Dec 1835, d 11 April 1910
Peck, Peleg, b 5 May 1776, d 25 May 1809
Peck, Abigail, w/o Peleg Peck, b 2 July 1777, d 3 July 1846
Peck, Henry, b 23 Nov 1805, d 12 March 1832
Kingsley, Margaret, b 11 Dec 1838, d 8 June 1884
Truesdale, William E., 1881-1957
Camac, Margaret Z., w/o William E. Truesdale, 1882-1965
Kimball, Hazen B., 1900-1977
Kimball, Virginia E., w/o Hazen B. Kimball, 1913-....
Tasiner, Charles Earl, 1875-1956
Tasiner, Mary Ann, w/o Charles Earl Tasiner, 1875-1942
Mason, Gideon Peck, 1822-1905
Luther, Ruth Ann, w/o Gideon Peck Mason, 1832-1907
Mason, Lyman Mason, s/o Gideon Peck & Ruth Ann Mason, 1866-1930
Mason, Thomas Luther, s/o Gideon Peck & Ruth Ann Mason, 1859-1931
Reed, Ida May, w/o Thomas Luther Mason, 1868-1932
Mason, Albert Thomas, s/o Gideon Peck & Ruth Ann Mason, 1901-1943
Adam, Lydia Lillian, w/o Albert Thomas Mason, 1900-1970
Peckham, Giles, b 21 Sept 1816, d 22 Feb 1904

Peckham, Sally M., w/o Giles Peckham, d 3 July....(can't read)

Pierce, George M., 1823-1903

Pierce, Mary Ann, w/o George M. Pierce, 1825-1901

Peckham, Mason, d 8 Jan 1872

Peckham, Esther, w/o Mason Peckham, d 9 Dec 1858 aged 63 yrs

Bailey, William, d 19 Dec 1874 aged 66 yrs 7 mos 5 days

Sheldon, Susan H., w/o William Bailey, b 22 Feb 1826, d 1 July 1915

Simmons, Amanda, w/o William Bailey & d/o Seth & Rebekah Simmons,
   d 27 Sept 1818

Bailey, Archibald, d 5 Nov 1833 Aged 62 yrs

Bailey, Elizabeth, w/o Archibald Bailey, d 20 Jan 1865 aged 90 yrs 11
   mos 14 days

Bailey, John, d 3 Jan 1862 aged 59 yrs

Peck, Eliza S., w/o John Bailey & d/o Thomas Peck Esq., d 27 Aug 1834
   aged 29 yrs

Simmons, Esek B., b 31 March 1809, d 3 Nov 1886

Simmons, Phebe B., w/o Esek B. Simmons, b 29 Dec 1814, d 24 Dec 1893

Simmons, Bradford B., b 22 Jan 1848, d 11 Sept 1865

Burr, Captain Caleb, d 23 Jan 1856 aged 83 yrs

Burr, Martha, w/o Capt. Caleb Burr, d 24 Feb 1856 aged 82 yrs

Burr, Julia, d/o Capt. Caleb & Martha Burr, d 15 March 1831 aged 22 yrs

Luther, Ruth, w/o Samuel Luther, b 11 Oct 1774, d 8 Jan 1850

Burr, Simeon, b 4 July 1776, d 24 Oct 1844

Adams, Abby, w/o Albert S. Adams, d 3 March 1839 aged 29 yrs

Sylvester, Abby, w/o Joseph B. Sylvester, d 3 Sept 1864 aged 86 yrs

Bosworth, David, d 25 Sept 1903 aged 81 yrs

Bosworth, Catie H., d 1 Feb 1895 aged 67 yrs

Bosworth, Elizabeth, w/o David Bosworth & d/o John & Hopestill
   Thurber, d 1 April 1865 aged 40 yrs

Bowker, Daniel O., b 10 April 1890, d....

Simmons, Louisa B., w/o Daniel O. Bowker, b 22 March 1892, d 25 Aug
   1962

Bosworth, William E., 1862-1942

Pratt, Hester M., w/o William E. Bosworth, 1870-1959

Barney, Wheaton, b 4 March 1816, d 23 April 1897

Barney, Betsey W., w/o Wheaton Barney, b 23 Nov 1819, d 6 Oct 1904

Read, Chester, b 23 July 1804 Lewiston, Maine, d 13 Aug 1876

Barney, Willard, d 11 July 1856 aged 64 yrs 5 mos

Barney, Polly, w/o Willard Barney, d 15 March 1873 aged 78 yrs 10 mos
   28 days

Corbin, William F., b 11 Dec 1841, d 17 AUg 1905

Whitten, Imogene A., w/o William F. Corbin, b 15 March 1858, d 8 Aug 1912

Lovell, Maria O., w/o William F. Corbin, 1852-1875

Corbin, Elizabeth M., b 28 Feb 1875, d 12 Aug 1875

Peck, Captain Salisbury, s/o Captain Peleg & Mary Peck, d 10 Aug 1818 Havana aged 31 yrs

Kingsley, Eliza, w/o David Kingsely, & w/o Capt. Salisbury Peck & d/o Cyrenes & Patience Barney, d 21 March 1831 aged 36 yrs

Kingsley, Deacon David, d 31 Dec 1866 aged 83 yrs

Kingsley, Nancy T., w/o Deacon David Kingsley, d 2 July 1875 aged 76 yrs

Kingsley, Mary P., d/o David & Olive Kingsley, d 12 Oct 1836 aged 22 yrs

Luther, Thomas P., d 20 May 1884 aged 80 yrs

Peck, Adaline, w/o Thomas P. Luther & d/o Col. Robert T. Peck, d 16 Dec 1840 aged 31 yrs

Wood, Warren W., b 22 Dec 1855, d 3 Feb 1895

Roberts, Rose Peckham Wood, w/o Warren W. Wood, 1867-1957

Peckham, Darius N., b 9 Feb 1830, d 22 July 1909

Peckham, Olive B., b 7 July 1831, d 14 Jan 1892

Peck, George, s/o Thomas & Elizabeth Peck, d 1 July 1841

Peck, Mary, w/o George Peck, d 26 Dec 1838 aged 36 yrs

Peck, Thomas Esq., d 18 Oct 1851 aged 85 yrs

Peck, Elizabeth, w/o Thomas Peck Esq., d 24 Nov 1844 aged 80 yrs

Peck, General William, s/o Thomas & Elizabeth Peck, b 12 April 1795, d 25 May 1839

Peck, Lemira, w/o General William Peck & d/o Job & Chloe Mason, b 30 April 1803, d 12 Nov 1856

King, William, b 18 Jan 1794, d 8 Aug 1859

King, Lydia, w/o William King, d 4 Oct 1868 aged 67 yrs

Simmons, Seth, 18 Jan 1863 aged 83 yrs

Simmons, Rebekah, w/o Seth Simmons, d 27 Oct 1864 aged 81 yrs 6 mos 5 days

Barney, Samuel, s/o Willard & Polly Barney, d 25 Oct 1849 aged 20 yrs 7 mos 5 days

Barney, Otis, b 8 Nov 1804, d 11 Aug 1888

Barney, Betsey, w/o Otis Barney, b 16 May 1800, d 14 Feb 1879

Barney, Mary A., b 20 Aug 1841, d 7 Aug 1844

Munroe, George J., b 14 Feb 1833, d 7 Jan 1872

Munroe, Julia F., w/o George J. Munroe, b 26 Aug 1845, d 19 July 1918

Thurber, John 2nd, b 11 Oct 1822, d 18 June 1865

Thurber, Sarah, w/o John Thurber 2nd, d 8 Sept 1894 aged 71 yrs

Barney, William R., b 10 Oct 1816, d 8 Jan 1894

Barney, Mary, w/o William R. Barney, b 13 May 1818, d 15 Jan 1894

Martin, Benjamin F., b 24 Aug 1834, d 14 Aug 1800

Barney, Mary Ann, w/o Benjamin Martin, b 15 March 1846, d 11 Jan 1925

Peck, Laura, b 10 Dec 1829, d 13 Dec 1895

Peck, Peleg, b 19 Feb 1817, d 2 April 1882

Allen, Ezra, b 24 May 1786, d 22 March 1865

Barney, Harriet, w/o Ezra Allen, b 9 Dec 1800, d 13 June 1883

Allen, Albert E., b 24 Aug 1840, d 24 Nov 1922

Davis, Captain Daniel, Lost at Sea 27 Feb 1840 aged 42 yrs 8 mos

Davis, Betsey W., w/o Captain Daniel Davis, d 1 March 1870 aged 69 yrs

Cornell, Captain James, 1782-1848

Rounds, Amey, w/o Capt. James Cornell, 1788-1845

Cornell, Ruth R., 1820-1841

Thurber, Samuel, 1805-1891

Thurber, Phebe, w/o Samuel Thurber, 1809-1891

Mahony, Minerva P., d/o Samuel & Phebe Thurber, b 8 Nov 1828, d 20 Jan 1893

Thurber, John, d 29 Oct 1876 aged 77 yrs

Thurber, Hopestill, w/o John Thurber, d 11 July 1873 aged 70 yrs

Thurber, Jeremiah, s/o John & Hopestill Thurber, d 29 Aug 1858 aged 61 yrs

Thurber, Betsey, w/o Jeremiah Thurber, d 27 Oct 1861 aged 63 yrs

Thurber, Sarah, d/o Jeremiah & Betsey Thurber, d 13 Feb 1855 aged 28 yrs

Barney, William M., d 23 Oct 1849

Barney, Annie, w/o William M. Barney, d 4 April 1858 aged 87 yrs

Rounds, Nathaniel, 1788-1834

Rounds, Phebe K., w/o Nathaniel Rounds, 1794-1872

Rounds, Sarah E., d/o Nathaniel & Phebe Rounds, 1826-1896

Rounds, Martha, d/o Nathaniel & Phebe Rounds, 1820-1837

Hathaway, Gilbert W., b 19 June 1849, d 26 Jan 1914

Hathaway, Charles F., 1860-1940

Hathaway, Lemuel, d 10 Dec 1896 aged 72 yrs

Hathaway, Lydia A., w/o Lemuel Hathaway, d 28 Dec 1895 aged 71 yrs

Norton, Benjamin F., 1818-1880

Norton, Sarah, w/o Benjamin F. Norton, 1840-1931
Norton, Benjamin, d 20 Aug 1855 aged 75 yrs
Norton, Sarah, w/o Benjamin Norton, d 19 Nov 1860 aged 73 yrs
Eddy, Charles, 1849-1892
Eddy, Mary O., w/o Charles Eddy, 1847-1935
Eddy, Charles Henry, d 25 July 1897 aged 19 yrs
Barney, Caleb, d 11 June 1857 aged 82 yrs 6 mos
Barney, Roby W., w/o Caleb Barney, d 24 Feb 1885 aged 95 yrs 9 mos 5
    days
Wood, William F., s/o William & Polly Wood, d 7 Feb 1895 aged 43 yrs
    10 mos
Fowler, Henry N., 1889-1951
Grant, William, d 25 Nov 1863 agd 47 yrs
Clarney, Ernest J., 1850-1931
Peck, Frances E., w/o Ernest J. Clarney, 1851-1930
Peck, Salisbury, b 11 Oct 1818, d 27 Feb 1885
Peck, Alice, d/o Salisbury & Ruth M. Peck, 1852-1865
Peck, Emory Arthur, s/o Salisbury & Ruth M. Peck, d 12 Aug 1846 aged
    6 mos
Handy, Thomas P., b 9 Sept 1803, d 14 Aug 1877
Handy, Esther H., w/o Thomas P. Handy, d 11 May 1882 aged 75 yrs 8
    mos 24 days
Barney, Jacob, b 15 July 1780, d 3 Sept 1862
Barney, Rebecca, w/o Jacob Barney, d 15 April 1858 aged 80 yrs
Barney, Herbert T., 1884-1956
Andrea, George H., 1855-1908
Andrea, Louisa A., w/o George H. Andrea, 1857-1945
Chase, Gardner, d 30 July 1851 aged 66 yrs
Chase, Rebecca C., w/o Gardner Chase, d 6 July 1843 aged 52 yrs
Wheeler, Cyril C., d 14 Feb 1849 aged 51 yrs
Buffington, David F., 1850-1910
Buffington, Emily J., w/o David F. Buffington, 1854-1914
Wood, William H., d 19 April 1885 aged 78 yrs 5 mos
Wood, Polly H., w/o William H. Wood, d 23 Oct 1902 aged 84 yrs 8 days
Thurber, Stephen, 1802-1868
Thurber, Joanna, w/o Stephen Thurber, 1802-1867
Thurber, John, 1776-1861
Wood, Eleanor, w/o John Thurber, 1776-1855
Graham, Henry, d 11 March 1873 aged 80 yrs

Porier, Sarah, w/o Henry Graham & d/o Hugh & Bette Porier, d 21 Aug
    1895 aged 101 yrs
Greer, Margaret, d 16 March 1880 aged 89 yrs
Graham, Charlotte A., d/o Henry & Sarah Graham, d 3 Aug 1858 aged 35
    yrs
Walker, Allen C., b 13 Aug 1811, d 18 Dec 1902
Walker, Bethia K., b 1 March 1822, d 27 May 1898
Handy, Albert M., d 17 Dec 1881 aged 34 yrs 4 mos
Handy, Martin, d 11 Nov 1852 aged 75 yrs
Mason, Elizabeth, w/o Joseph Mason, d 4 June 1820
Mason, Ann D. C., d/o Joseph & Elizabeth Mason, d 20 Nov 1830 aged
    45 yrs 1 mo
Mason, Eliza, d/o Joseph & Elizabeth Mason, d 10 April 1821 aged 26 yrs
Mason, Esther, d/o Joseph & Elizabeth Mason, d 16 Nov 1808 aged 19 yrs
Barney, Wheaton, d 4 Aug 1784
Barney, Comfort, d 18 March 1820 aged 51 yrs
Barney, Mary, w/o Nathaniel Barney, d 8 March 1838 aged 64 yrs
Barney, Annah, formerly w/o Daniel Davis & late widow of Jonathan
    Barney, b 1 July 1776, d 16 June 1850
Davis, Nancy, w/o John Davis, b 18 July 1795, d 12 Feb 1879
Short, Simeon, b 30 May 1770, d 28 March 1848
Short, Submit W., w/o Simeon Short, b 10 May 1778, d 8 Aug 1848
Short, Eunice, w/o Jonathan Paine & d/o Simeon & Submit Short, d 1836
Short, Nancy, d/o Simeon & Submit Short, d 17 Dec 1832 aged 12 yrs
Short, Clarissa, w/o Henry S. Short, b 1 Feb 1807, d 20 April 1841
Short, Henry S., b 3 July 1805, d 12 Sept 1867
Short, Ezra P., d 4 May 1884 aged 74 yrs 11 mos 2 days
Short, Hannah G., b 14 Aug 1832, d 20 June 1909
Peck, Patience, w/o Ebenezer Peck & d/o Ebenezer & Patience Short, b 10
    Oct 1787, d 20 Sept 1803
Mason, Joshua, b 4 March 1797, d 17 Dec 1850
Short, Lydia, w/o Joshua Mason & d/o Simeon & Submit Short, d 2 Feb
    1833 aged 26 yrs
Burr, James W., s/o James & Elizabeth Burr, d 18 Oct 1841 aged 35 yrs
Burr, James, d 10 Sept 1811 aged 47 yrs
Burr, Betsey, w/o James Burr, d 15 Jan 1861 aged 86 yrs
Burr, Lydia Child, w/o Rev. Ethan Allen, b 3 June 1801, d 16 Feb 1888
Burr, Lydia, w/o Elisha Burr, d 7 March 1799 agd 59 yrs
Burr, Martha, w/o Elisha Burr, d 1797
Burr, Elisha, d Nov 1815

Pearce, Benjamin, ...

Kingsley, Nicholas, d 19 April 1863 aged 83 yr

Brown, William, d 8 April 1810 aged 83 yrs

Brown, Freelove, w/o William Brown, d 11 Nov 1855 aged 75 yrs

Brown, Nathan, s/o William & Freelove Brown, d 9 July 1838 aged 30 yrs

Brown, Marcia W., d/o William & Freelove Borwn, d 15 Oct 1840

Mason, James, s/o Joseph Mason, d 9 March 1861 aged 66 yrs

Mason, Ann, w/o James Mason, d 15 June 1867 aged 75 yrs

Bullock, Mary, w/o Stephen Bullock, d 12 March 1839 aged 64 yrs

Bullock, Stephen, d 8 June 1838 Columbia, PA aged 66 yrs

Bullock, Darius, d 7 Sept 1825 aged 25 yrs

Bullock, Mary, d/o Stephen & Mary Bullock, d 2 Feb 1809 aged 4 yrs

Kingsley, Deacon Hezekiah, d 16 Jan 1842 aged 74 yrs

Kingsley, Mima, w/o Deacon Hezekiah Kingsley, d 19 Dec 1857 aged 84 yrs

Kingsley, Mary, w/o Dea. Hezekiah Kingsley, d 3 Oct 1824 aged 88 yrs

Thurber, Benjamin, of Seekonk, d 13 Sept 1837 aged 77 yrs

Wood, Jonathan, d 23 Sept 1823 aged 78 yrs

Barney, Laura Ann, d 24 April 1859 aged 59 yrs

Norton, George G., d 13 March 1868 aged 50 yrs

Norton, Anne W., w/o George G. Norton, d 15 May 1877 aged 61 yrs

Lovell, Edward R., b 28 May 1826, d 31 Jan 1916

Lovell, Eliza A., w/o Edward R. Lovell, d 25 Feb 1892 aged 60 yrs

Wickham, James, b 10 June 1804, d 27 Jan 1883

Hard, Sybil, w/o James Wickham, d 25 Aug 1877 aged 65 yrs 4 mos 20 days

Pierce, Ezra, d 28 Aug 1875 aged 75 yrs

Pierce, Joanna, w/o Ezra Pierce, d 6 Nov 1891 aged 90 yrs

Graham, Josiah Wilson Jr., b 28 May 1857, d 1 Dec 1885

Graham, Julia M., d 16 Dec 1868 aged 35 yrs 6 mos

Barney, Edwin, 1804-1834

Barney, Abby, 1806-1901

Barney, Captain Charles, d 17 Nov 1874 aged 45 yrs

Barney, Alice, w/o Capt. Charles Barney, d 15 March 1882 aged 45 yrs

Wood, Sally, w/o Alba Wood, d 21 Nov 1868 aged 64 yrs

Jayne, Jerusha B., d 3 July 1876 aged 50 yrs

West, Lydia, w/o Joseph Jayne, b 22 Oct 1793, d 16 July 1872 Havana, Cuba

Lawton, Hiram, b 20 Nov 1821, d 14 April 1898

Lawton, Maribah M., w/o Hiram Lawton, b 10 Feb 1822, d 1 Jan 1891

Lawton, Maribah M., b 9 Oct 1857, d 7 Nov 1862
Lawton, Luther, b 11 June 1859, d 11 Jan 1860
Lawton, John B., b 14 Sept 1862, d 5 Jan 1878
Hawkins, Sanford, 1857-1915, Organist of Cranston Baptist Church
Martin, Laura C., w/o Sanford Hawkins, 1869-1946
Horton, Welcome F., b 20 May 1865, d 25 May 1901
Barney, Henrietta E., w/o Welcome F. Horton & d/o Henry W. & Eliza A.
  Barney, b 23 April 1864, d 5 Feb 1938
Garruthers, Alexander, 1845-1920
Schultz, Sophia A., w/o Alexander Garruthers, 1848-1935
Norton, Emma E., d 1 Oct 1930
Franklin, George C., 1830-1895
Norton, Annie, w/o George C. Franklin, 1850-1927
Franklin, Rowena A., 1878-1929
Eddy, Frank, b 3 June 1848, d 28 June 1916
Powers, Della A., w/o Frank Eddy, b 31 Aug 1844, d 11 Jan 1880
Healy, Alonzo, b 1 Jan 1835, d 13 Dec 1900
Case, Mary Jane, w/o Alonzo Healy, b 14 April 1840, d 17 April 1920
Gammons, S. Addie, w/o Benjamin P. King & d/o Zemi T. & Laura A.
  Gammons, d 29 Dec 1870 aged 21 yrs 5 mos
Healy, Stafford, d 12 Dec 1878 aged 86 yrs
Healy, Ann, w/o Stafford Healy, d 4 Sept 1871 aged 72 yrs
Horton, Rev. Josephus, 1816-1885
Horton, Ann A., w/o Rev. Josephus Horton, 1818-1890
Horton, George W., s/o Rev. Josephus & Ann Horton, d 25 Oct 1871 aged
  21 yrs 9 mos
Horton, John F., 1864-1923
Horton, Gilbert M., 1827-1903
Horton, Sarah F., w/o Gilbert M. Horton, 1826-1906
Horton, Welcome, b 20 May 1865, d 25 May 1901
Healy, Ellen M., w/o Fernando Healy, b 10 March 1839, d 6 July 1890
Sedgwick, Lydia A., d/o Elisha D. & Lydia P. Pierce, b 16 June 1844, 25
  May 1870
Pierce, Elvira M., d/o Elisha D. & Lydia P. Pierce & w/o Charles G. A.
  Peterson, b 21 Aug 1847. d 6 Sept 1878
Davis, Elisha, b 27 Nov 1831, d 22 April 1904
Munroe, Etherrinda, w/o Elisha Davis, b 22 March 1830, d 9 Dec 1924
Mason, George, d 1 May 1869 aged 68 yrs
Mason, Sarah E., w/o Geoge Mason, d 15 March 1871 aged 68 yrs

Cleaveland, William R., d 28 Jan 1889 aged 59 yrs

Cleaveland, Sarah G., w/o William R. Cleaveland, 1829-1901

Cleaveland, Joscar, 1853-1923

Barney, Jonathan, b 6 Dec 1815, d 2 Dec 1858

Barney, Esther G., b 27 Dec 1825, d 19 July 1944

Barney, Mason, b 4 Sept 1782, d 1 April 1868

Smith, Martha, w/o Mason Barney, b 7 Aug 1784, d 21 Dec 1806

Grant, Polly, w/o Mason Barney, b 20 Oct 1787, d 6 Jan 1864

Barney, Rodman S., b 7 Feb 1823, d 15 Sept 1866

Barney, Rachel M., w/o Jonathan Barney, d 4 Aug 1886 aged 25 yrs

Barney, Laura Ann, of Seekonk, d 27 Nov 1867 aged 60 yrs

Thatcher, Rev. James, d 11 March 1871 aged 62 yrs 8 mos 22 days

Collin, Rebecca W., w/o Rev. James Thatcher, d 26 April 1888 aged 84
    yrs 7 mos 26 days

Brown, Capt. Gardner, d 24 May 1868 aged 63 yrs

Brown, Sophia, w/o Capt. Gardner Brown, d 9 Oct 1872 aged 60 yrs 5
    mos

Brown, James A., s/o Capt. Gardner & Sophia Brown, d 12 April 1875
    aged 26 yrs

Brown, Dr. William C., d 15 Sept 1882 aged 35 yrs 9 mos

Horton, Seth S., b 29 Aug 1800, d 9 Nov 1869

Horton, Olive, w/o Seth S. Horton, b 5 Dec 1800, d 14 March 1882

Horton, Nathan B., s/o Seth S. & Olive Horton, b 28 Jan 1842, d 19 Oct
    1864

Peckham, Allen M., b 3 Sept 1826, d 14 Oct 1895

Allen, Harriet B., w/o Allen M. Peckham, b 26 Feb 1838, d 29 Aug 1906

Peckham, Mahala L., d 12 Feb 1887 aged 71 yrs

Peckham, Almira, d/o Aaron Peckham, d 4 Sept 1876 aged 74 yrs

Bixby, Fred E., b 8 Dec 1862, d 6 Aug 1925

Davis, Lydia B., w/o Fred E. Bixby, b 1 Aug 1864, d 4 May 1951

Martin, Benjamin, d 16 May 1873 aged 64 yrs

Martin, Sarah, w/o Benjamin Martin, d 26 Jan 1892 aged 77 yrs

Horton, Horace D., d 3 May 1894 aged 76 yrs

Horton, Martha C., w/o Horace D. Horton, b 7 March 1824, d 17 Feb
    1907

Manchester, Henry, d 12 Feb 1883 aged 69 yrs 9 mos

Manchester, Deborah P., w/o Henry Manchester, d 31 July 1876 aged 45
    yrs 6 mos

Manchester, George H., s/o Henry & Deborah Manchester, d 30 July 1873
    aged 19 yrs 9 mos 27 days

Manchester, Mathew C., s/o Henry & Deborah Manchester, d 31 Aug 1876 aged 20 yrs 9 days

Manchester, William F., s/o Henry & Deborah Manchester, d 3 Oct 1876 aged 16 yrs 8 mos 14 days

Place, Ruth Eddy, d/o John B. & Ann Place, b 3 May 1885, d 3 March 1961

Eddy, Seth, b 22 Jan 1836, d 1 Dec 1916

Bosworth, Ruth P., w/o Seth Eddy, b 17 Nov 1839, d 19 May 1916

Eddy, Jesse, s/o Seth & Ruth Eddy, b 9 Jan 1868, d 12 Jan 1868

Thatcher, William, b 9 Aug 1839, d 8 May 1908

Horton, Ellen L., w/o William Thatcher, b 1 May 1839, d 12 April 1934

Barney, Welcome, b 8 June 1821, d 11 Aug 1896

Barney, Abby W., w/o Welcome Barney, b 4 March 1825, d 12 May 1868

Barney, Rodman S. Jr., 1904-1990

Nichols, Mildred E., w/o Rodman S. Barney, 1908-....

Norton, George J., b 28 March 1848, d....

Norton, Emma C., w/o George J. Norton, b 16 July 1848, d 13 Oct 1897

Barney, James M., b 23 Feb 1822, d 30 Sept 1895

Barney, Esther B., w/o James M. Barney, b 2 March 1828, d 1 March 1920

Barney, Ida O., d/o James M. & Esther B. Barney, b 12 Dec 1856, d 26 Nov 1883

Grant, Arel, 1789-1873

Luther, Hannah, w/o Arel Grant, 1804-1890

Grant, Henry H., s/o Arel & Hannah Grant, 1834-1918

Grant, Albert, s/o Arel & Hannah Grant, 1838-1914

Grant, Benjamin, s/o Arel & Hannah Grant, 1840-1912

Barney, Edith, w/o David Barney, 1874-1931

Barney, Ella, w/o David Barney, b 29 July 1870, d 10 June 1901

Horton, James S., b 14 April 1825, d 18 Jan 1894

Kelton, James F., b 19 Jan 1852, d 6 Sept 1911

Munroe, Ellen, w/o James F. Kelton, b 10 Oct 1864, d 23 March 1917

Brown, Nancy, w/o Jabez Brown, b 13 Dec 1806, d 1 Nov 1890

Belle, Ethel Barney, b 4 June 1879, d 18 Nov 1959

Barney, Algernon H., b 12 Aug 1850, d 18 April 1926

Brayton, Madora, w/o Algernon H. Barney, b 14 Feb 1852, d 30 Dec 1904

Sampson, Jessie E., w/o Algernon H. Barney, b 28 March 1878, d 7 Aug 1978

Norton, Welcome Leroy, b 16 Jan 1887, d 11 Feb 1908

Barney, Rodman S., b 16 Jan 1875, d 26 Aug 1917

Merewether, Augusta, w/o Rodman S. Barney, b 21 April 1879, d 23 Feb 1962

Norton, William, b 7 Oct 1857, d 4 June 1902

Barney, Gertrude B., w/o William Norton, b 17 May 1856, d 5 Oct 1934

Grant, Herbert M., 1852-1924

Bowen, Daniel P., b 1 Sept 1838, d 2 Nov 1916

Campbell, Annie C., w/o Daniel P. Bowen, b 17 Aug 1862, d 11 Feb 1930

Lathrop, Philip N., s/o Henry H. & Annie M. Lathrop, 1862-1902

Champlin, Mary A., w/o Philip N. Lathrop, 1861-....

Horton, Otis H., b 4 June 1819, d 17 June 1896

Horton, Elizabeth, w/o Otis H. Horton, b 30 Jan 1824, d 5 May 1891

Horton, Jeremiah, b 28 Dec 1824, d 20 Aug 1902

Mason, Mary Jane, w/o Jeremiah Horton, b 6 March 1829, d 29 Jan 1904

Peck, Abby W., d 4 March 1892 aged 73 yrs 11 mos 4 days

Peck, Irene B., d 8 March 1888 aged 84 yrs 10 mos 2 days

Case, Isaiah, d 14 April 1877 aged 63 yrs

Case, Mary Ann, w/o Isaiah Case, d 2 Jan 1860 aged 49 yrs

Case, Ann Maria, d/o Isaiah & Mary Ann Case, d 10 Dec 1854 aged 17 yrs 6 mos 16 days

Horton, John M., b 29 April 1810, d 12 Feb 1894

Bailey, Eliza, w/o John M. Horton, b 5 Nov 1813, d 15 Oct 1900

Horton, Jonathan M., d 29 July 1888 aged 42 yrs 2 mos 11 days

Horton, Elizabeth, d/o John M. & Eliza Horton, d 17 Nov 1881 aged 32 yrs 3 mos 11 days

Horton, Elisha W., d 20 Feb 1868 aged 48 yrs

Pierce, Caroline M., w/o Elisha W. Horton, d 5 June 1895 aged 81 yrs

Watson, Abbie C., d/o Gilbert R. & Abbie E. Watson, 1875-1959

Horton, Elisha C., b 28 May 1856, d 14 Nov 1902

Bosworth, Carrie A., w/o Elisha C. Horton, b 24 June 1851, d 25 Feb 1908

Horton, Lydia, w/o James Marton & d/o Lt. James & Freelove Horton, d 23 Dec 1861 aged 93 yrs

Horton, Jervis, s/o Lt. James & Freelove Horton, b 9 Sept 1781, d 9 April 1849

Martin, Elizabeth, w/o Jervis Horton & d/o Meltiah & Phebe Martin, b 14 July 1782, d 29 March 1849

Kelton, John F., s/o Philip & Betsey Kelton, d 18 Nov 1859 aged 4 yrs 3 mos 8 days

Kelton, Lizzie S., w/o Thomas S. Delane & d/o Philip & Betsey Kelton, d 25 Sept 1881 aged 23 yrs 1 mo 20 days

Lathrop, Henry H., 1838-1865

Wood, Annee M., w/o Henry H. Lathrop, 1837-1864

Horton, Jacob H., b 12 Jan 1810, d 15 July 1887

Horton, Sarah A., w/o Jacob H. Horton, b 6 Oct 1812, d 3 May 1889

Mason, Daniel, d 18 Feb 1877 aged 80 yrs 16 days

Mason, Mary, w/o Daniel Mason, d 2 March 1876 aged 74 yrs 11 mos 2 days

Mason, Daniel T., s/o Daniel & Mary Mason, d 3 Oct 1866 aged 19 yrs 28 days

Mason, James, s/o Daniel & Mary Mason, d 18 Sept 1820 aged 9 days

Millard, Nancy T., w/o Gardner P. Millard, b 9 April 1828, d 8 May 1892

Millard, Ara Adna, w/o Asa Bosworth, b 24 Dec 1846, d 18 Dec 1895

Millard, Henry W., b 8 Jan 1820, d 13 April 1897

Millard, Zeruah G., w/o Henry W. Millard, b 12 April 1816, d 5 March 1894

Millard, Gardner P., b 17 Jan 1825, d 1 Dec 1906

Millard, Ann M., w/o Gardner P. Millard, 1825-1891

Kelton, Edward F., s/o Philip & Betsey Kelton, b 19 June 1848, d 1 Jan 1900

Kelton, Betsey, b 29 May 1821, d 23 April 1894

Kelton, Philip P., d 2 Jan 1867 aged 46 yrs 21 yrs

Horton, Halsey E., s/o John M. & Eliza B. Horton, d 28 Sept 1807 aged 83 yrs

Leade, Katie H., w/o Halsey E. Horton & d/o Rev. S. & Rebecca Leade, d 12 Jan 1881 aged 29 yrs

Barney, Anson L., b 4 May 1833, d 28 Sept 1907

Barney, Anna W., b 6 Oct 1833, d 2 Oct 1896

Barney, Jerome A., b 14 May 1863, d 10 Oct 1888

Barney, William W., b 2 April 1858, d 19 Nov 1883

Barney, Frank I., 1869-1916

Barney, Gertrude W., 1872-1961

Watson, John W., d 29 April 1872 aged 66 yrs 6 mos 29 days

Watsn, Martha B., w/o John W. Watson, d 2 Oct 1893 aged 80 yrs 2 mos

Wood, Sarah L., 1844-1844

Wood, William H., 1836-1872

Wood, Emily F., 1840-1883

Horton, Rev. Geroge H., 1862-1930

Horton, Carrie E., w/o Rev. George H. Horton, 1865-1946

Horton, Seth A., b 12 Nov 1834, d 2 April 1867, A member of Co H 40th Reg Mass Vols

Horton, Rebecca E., w/o Seth A. Horton, b 2 Oct 1834, d 19 March 1908
Fish, Mary E., 1846-1923
Horton, Andrew L., 1862-1890
Horton, Annie R., w/o Andrew L. Horton, 1864-1933
Horton, Levi, b 28 Jan 1801, d 24 Jan 1868
Steinbrick, Charles, b 27 Dec 1839, d 9 April 1915
Gill, George, 1872-1954
Steinbrick, Minnie, w/o George Gill, 1873-1958
Millard, Mary A., w/o Joseph W. Sweet, 1837-1924
Sweet, Warren M., 1872-1950
Sweet, Alice B., 1880-1961
Schobel, Hope M., b 9 June 1924, d 6 April 1987
Peck, Cassandana F., b 9 Sept 1846, d 30 July 1848
Wheeler, Mary E., d/o P. W. & F. J. Peck, b 3 July 1853, d 3 Feb 1875
Peck, Philip W., b 21 Sept 1819, d 15 June 1894
Barney, Frances F., w/o Philip W. Peck, b 6 Dec 1823, d 28 Jan 1900
Peck, Thomas W., b 20 Aug 1844, d 28 Feb 1900
Wheeler, Mary E., w/o George A. Wheeler, d 3 Feb 1875 aged 21 yrs 6 mos
Peckham, Horace M., 1860-1939
Kelton, Lydia L., w/o Horace Peckham, 1861-1926
Peckham, Betsey L., d/o Horace & Lydia Peckham, d 20 Oct 1913 aged 20 yrs 20 days
Barney, Horace W., b 3 Feb 1831, d 10 Sept 1897
Barney, Annie M., w/o Horace W. Barney, d 24 Nov 1879 aged 42 yrs 3 mos
Burgess, Frank F., 1865-1922
Fenner, Henry, d 9 July 1888 aged 27 yrs 15 days
West, Charles F., d 14 Jan 1880 aged 31 yrs 1 mo 27 days
Martin, John C., b 20 Nov 1855, d 15 Aug 1927
Martin, Abbie C., w/o John C. Martin, b 28 Oct 1853, d 4 Feb 1902
Fenner, Thomas R., b 30 Aug 1816, d 19 Nov 1896
Fenner, Marcella, w/o Thomas R. Fenner, b 1821, d 12 Sept 1894
Bixby, Albert L., b 28 Feb 1807, d 13 Jan 1897
Horton, Mary A., w/o Albert L. Bixby, b 15 Oct 1867, d 4 April 1900
Mohurter, Samuel R., 1881-1937
Mohurter, Loretta, w/o Samuel R. Mohurter, 1883-1954
Mitchell, Louisa W., 1868-1924
Easterbrook, William H., b 14 Aug 1857, d 7 Sept 1886

King, Mary, w/o William H. Eastherbrook, b 14 Nov 1857, d 20 June 1939

Munroe, Stephen F., 1846-1908

Munroe, Rufina M. E., w/o Stephen F. Munroe, 1850-1908

Peck, William, s/o Captain Peleg Peck, d April 1778 aged 20 yrs

Peck, Peleg, b 19 Feb 1817, d 22 April 1882

Peck, Laura A., w/o Peleg Peck, b 10 Dec 1821, d 16 Dec 1895

Peck, Laura W., d/o Peleg & Laura Peck, b 19 June 1844, d 22 Sept 1842

Peck, Benjamin, b 3 June 1790, d 29 Oct 1825

Peck, Mary, w/o Benjamin Peck, b 30 April 1786, d 23 Sept 1825

Peck, Martha D., d/o Benjamin & Mary Peck, b 12 Oct 1819, d 23 Jan 1821

Thornton, Mary, w/o Lt. Michael J. Higgins, & d/o Peleg & Laura A. Peck, b 11 March 1846, d 16 Sept 1917

Thurston, Benjamin P., 1810-1898

Thurston, Lydia L., w/o Benjamin P. Thurston, d 21 April 1880 aged 69 yrs 10 mos

Martin, Deacon Gideon, b 19 March 1803, d 16 June 1886

Bixby, Walter B., b 14 Jan 1897, d 15 June 1900

Bixby, Joseph A., b Feb 1832, d Aug 1899

Bovel, Elizabeth R., w/o Joseph A. Bixby, b Dec 1829, d July 1900

Barney, Beriah S., b 12 Feb 1873, d 26 April 1914

Barney, Fannie H., w/o Willard E. Severence, b 21 Aug 1864, d 17 Feb 1914

Scott, Winifield B., 1863-1915

Horton, Albert L., d 2 July 1899

Horton, Ida, w/o Albert L. Horton, d 13 Dec 1892 aged 18 yrs 1 mo

Horton, Cora, w/o Albert L. Horton, d 24 Dec 1943 aged 71 yrs 11 mos 5 days

Bowen, Ira B., 1813-1885

Bowen, Nancy, w/o Ira B. Bowen, 1819-1902

Horton, Jarvus Scott, b 26 March 1851, d 29 Dec 1934

Horton, Ida Frances, w/o Jarvus Scott Horton, b 30 Dec 1857, d 9 Feb 1916

Horton, Gilbert R., 1854-1910

Horton, Josephine M., w/o Gilbert R. Horton, 1851-1943

Horton, Clarence Alden, b 8 Jan 1882, d 12 July 1884

Martin, Emerson E., b 29 Aug 1876, d 8 Feb 1915

Peck, Albert G., d 26 Nov 1886 aged 82 yrs

Peck, Patience, w/o Albert G. Peck, d 8 March 1879 aged 52 yrs

Peck, Mary C., d/o Albert & Patience Peck, d 13 March 1893 aged 26 yrs 5 mos 16 days

Wallen, George, 1848-1920

Wallen, Clara B., w/o George Wallen, 1851-1941

Wallen, Ruth Naomi, d/o George & Clara B. Wallen, 1887-1936

Horton, Peter Nelson, b 22 Sept 1854, d 24 Dec 1948

Horton, Ida Marietta, w/o Peter Nelson Horton, b 3 Feb 1860, d 12 Jan 1927

Martin, Albert, b 3 April 1873, d 17 May 1929

Martin, Arthur H., 1871-1938

Buffington, Walter Smith, s/o John & Anne E. W. Buffington, d 7 July 1870 aged 19 yrs 6 mos

Buffington, Frank, b 9 Feb 1841, d 1 Nov 1912

Buffington, Priscilla C., w/o Frank Buffington, b 6 March 1840, d 13 Dec 1908

Buffington, John A., b 21 Aug 1810, d 22 Aug 1893

Bosworth, Ann Eliza, w/o John A. Buffington, b 7 Aug 1815, d 20 Dec 1902

Kenfield, Amentha, w/o H. A. Bosworth, d 18 Oct 1885 aged 55 yrs

Bosworth, H. Alonzo, d 21 Aug 1869 aged 47 yrs

Bosworth, Margaret, w/o H. Alonzo Bosworth, d 22 May 1847 aged 25 yrs

Bosworth, Peleg, b 28 Sept 1805, d 12 Feb 1887

Bosworth, Peleg, d 29 April 1829 aged 51 yrs

Bosworth, Susanna, w/o Peleg Bosworth, d 7 Aug 1863 aged 82 yrs

Bosworth, George S., b 2 July 1824, d 26 July 1881

Bosworth, Mary A., w/o George S. Bosworth, b 11 July 1824, d 12 July 1902

Bosworth, Peleg, 1753-....

Smith, Mary, w/o Peleg Bosworth, 1749-1818

Peck, Edgar H., 1849-1918

Peck, Emily O., w/o Edgar H. Peck, 1854-1922

Martin, J. Elbridge, b 1 Feb 1841, d 28 Jan 1914

Read, Mary Elizabeth, w/o J. Elbridge Martin, b 14 June 1845, d 20 April 1882

Duncan, Emily P., w/o J. Elbridge Martin, b 6 Oct 1854, d 31 May 1939

Wheeler, Jeremiah A., 1867-1921

Goff, Josephine B., w/o Jeremiah A. Wheeler, 1873-1915

West, Herbert E., 1892-1975

West, Louisa M., w/o Herbert E. West, 1896-1970

Burns, Helen, sister of Louisa M. West, 1900-1985

West, Herbert E. Jr., 1925-1990

Adams, Walter A., 1896-1967

Adams, Eva M., w/o Walter A. Adams, 1896-1961

Allen, Everett, 1890-1960

Richmond, Louisa, w/o Everett Allen, 1891-1969

Horton, Everett L., 1897-1968

Kelton, Emma, w/o Everett L. Horton, 1898-1959

Jones, Douglas Scott, b 10 Nov 1961, d 31 July 1982

Horton, Leland R., 1891-....

Horton, Ellen A., w/o Leland R. Horton, 1893-....

Healing, Malcolm L., b 7 Oct 1910, d 6 July 1976

Pearson, Doris, w/o Malcolm L. Healing, b 24 April 1920, d ....

Jones, Harry C., 1898-1988

Marfiat, Barbara V., w/o Harry C. Jones, 1902-1994

Peckham, Edith E., 1884-1973

Reed, Theodore, 1908-1957

Miller, Charles H., 1880-1971

Brown, Margaret, w/o Charles H. Miller, 1880-1921

Dean, Anna, w/o Charles H. Miller, 1879-1961

Whittmore, Royce W., 1913-1986

West, Madeline, w/o Royce W. Whittmore, 1910-....

Lindberg, Alfred B., 1909-1989

Lindberg, Dorothy H., w/o Alfred B. Lindberg, 1918-....

Martin, Leonard H., S. Sergt. US Army Korea, b 18 Feb 1926, d 17 Jan
    1977

Carpenter, Charles A., 1903-1975

Martin, Grace E., w/o Charles A. Carpenter, 1902-1964

Duckworth, Walter Jr., PVT US Army WW2, 1903-1983

Saunders, Bessie M., w/o Walter Duckworth Jr., 1898-1987

Adams, B. Herbert, 1915-1983

Ormsbee, Dorothy, w/o B. Herbert Adams, 1918-....

Chace, Charles D., 1898-1969

Chace, Clara, w/o Charles D. Chace 1904-1989

Bruce, Dana H., 1877-1966

Peckham, Flora M., w/o Dana H. Bruce, 1901-1975

West, Harold B., 1899-1950

Wood, Mildred L., w/o Harold B. West, 1829-1993

Grant, Marcus M., 1839-1922

Grant, Ruth K., w/o Marcus M. Grant, 1844-1943

Grant, Harrie L., 1867-1949

Grant, Annie M., w/o Harrie L. Grant, 1866-1938
Vinnicum, George W., 1854-1930
Barker, Sidney, 1844-1926
Barker, Emeline F., w/o Sidney Barker, 1844-1940
Child, Moses Tyler, s/o Henry William & Betsey Bowen Child, 1826-1911
Wood, Abby Amy, w/o Moses Tyler Child, 1846-1930
Luther, George F., 1836-1911
Luther, Martha A., w/o George F. Luther, 1834-1913
Luther, Ira H., 1865-1940
Aldrich, Emma E., w/o Ira H. Luther, 1866-1942
Aldrich, Annie B., sister of Emma E. Aldrich, 1871-1952
Luther, Carlisle H., 1897-1970
Jolin, Lillian E., w/o Carlisle H. Luther, 1901-1955
Martin, Susan Amelia, w/o Isaac P. Martin, 1849-1924
Martin, Issac P., 1857-1939
Morris, Thomas E., 1852-1917
Morris, Cora E., w/o Thomas E. Morris, 1861-1925
Seymour, James H., 1858-1922
Oldfield, Ida M., w/o James H. Seymour, 1870-1938
Wood, Thomas D., 1877-1941
Wood, Mary A., w/o Thomas D. Wood, 1878-1964
Crandall, Henry B., b 29 Jan 1810, d May 1909
Crandall, Hannah E., w/o Henry B. Crandall, d 26 Sept 1908 aged 56 yrs
    19 days
Ormsbee, Daniel, s/o Otis & Sarah Ormsbee, d 20 Dec 1896 aged 81 yrs
Crandall, Daniel Henry, s/o Henry B. & Hannah C. Crandall, d 10 July
    1898 aged 23 yrs
Crandall, Harriet Elizabeth, d/o Henry B. & Hannah C. Crandall, d 10
    Oct 1898 aged 18 yrs
Crandall, Edward Hicks, s/o Henry & Hannah Crandall, d 10 Nov 1898
    aged 21 yrs
Crandall, Julia A. F., d/o Henry & Hannah Crandall, d 9 Sept 1905 aged
    20 yrs
Lindberg, Nils E., 1872-1943
Olsen, Caroline, w/o Nils E. Lindberg, 1876-1956
Rabbitt, Helen L., 1920-1955
Lindberg, John W., 1918-1927
Blackledge, Joseph, 1833-1914
Warburton, Sarah B., w/o Joseph Blackledge, 1838-1918
Cady, Charles J., 1854-1931

Davis, Julia E., w/o Charles J. Cady, 1851-1915
Thurber, Luther, 1854-1921
Davis, Fanny M., w/o Luther Thurber, 1860-1936
Davis, Harley E., 1887-1934
Davis, Marybelle C., w/o Hartley E. Davis, 1882-1951
Maker, Amos F., 1867-1951
Favor, Emma A., 1873-1960
Burlingame, Everett B., 1861-1967
Burlingame, Minnie C., w/o Everett B. Burlingame, 1875-1969
Conyers, Clarence J., 1891-1951
Acker, Elric, 1892-1965
Edwards, Ethel, w/o Elric Acker, 1894-1967
Edwards, David, 1869-1939
Bowen, Ruth A., w/o David Edwards, 1869-1933
Ormsbee, Arthur R., 1894-1978
Ormsbee, Effie A., w/o Arthur Ormsbee, 1896-1976
Peck, Lloyd F., 1880-1943
Smith, Mary L., w/o Lloyd F. Peck, 1881-1946
Douglas, David, 1858-1931
Oatley, Mary F., w/o David Douglas, 1862-1957
Sunman, Andrew W., 1886-1925
Luther, Ethel A., w/o Andrew W. Sunman, 1894-1903
Sunman, Richard A., 1920-....
Gardner, Irving J., 1885-1953
Horton, Bertha L., w/o Irving J. Gardner, 1888-1982
Gardner, Russell H., s/o Irving & Bertha Gardner, 1909-1934
Whittaker, Thomas J., 1856-1945
Horton, Susan M., w/o Thomas J. Whittaker, 1857-1947
Orrall, George J., 1886-1946
Orrall, Grace S., w/o George J. Orrall, 1904-....
Wood, Elisha J., 1878-1960
Wood, Edna A., w/o Elisha J. Wood, 1879-1952
Wood, Evelyn, 1912-1956
Nichols, George L., 1895-1965
Mitchell, Izelia R., w/o George L. Nichols, 1906-1948
Thomas, Charles L., 1875-1950
Brewer, Etta C., w/o Charles L. Thomas, 1880-1960
Johnson, George F., 1882-1950
Johnson, Mary E., w/o George F. Johnson, 1880-1960

Chace Cemetery
Baker Street
Swansea, Massachustts

Chase, Leroy J., 1857-1923

Blanchard, Mary E., w/o Leroy J. Chace.....

Chace, Andrew, 1855-1941

Chace, Mary E., w/o Andrew Chace, 1864-1932

Chace, Mabel M., d/o Andrew & Mary Chace, b 22 Nov 1887, d 13 May 1902

Chace, Rachel, d/o Andrew & Mary Chace, b 21 Aug 1891, d 16 Oct 1892

Chace, Sylvanus J., d 22 March 1914

Walker, Mary Ella, w/o Sylvanus Chace & d/o George & Lucinda D. Walker, d 7 Nov 1880 aged 25 yrs 6 mos

Chace, Cora M., d/o Sylvanus & Mary Ella Chace, b 1 Nov 1873, d 14 Feb 1895

Chace, Emeline, 1845-1922

Chace, Reuben, s/o Mason & Lorana M. Chace, d 8 Nov 1866 aged 22 yrs

Chace, Mason, d 18 Feb 1871 aged 54 yrs 6 mos

Chace, Lorana P., w/o Mason Chace, d 19 April 1893 aged 72 yrs

Chace, Enoch, d Sept 1805 AE 80 yrs

Chace, Deliverance, w/o Enoch Chace, d 30 Dec 1819 AE 88 yrs

Chace, Reuben, d 2 March 1854 aged 80 yrs 9 mos 12 days

Chace, Elizabeth, w/o Reuben Chace, d 29 Oct 1858 aged 79yrs

Chace, Betsey, w/o Reuben Chace, d 2 Sept 18.......38 yrs 8 mos

Chace, Barney, s/o Reuben & Betsey Chace, d 13 Oct 1816 aged 20 yrs 2 mos

Chace, Elias, d 14 June 1875 aged 78 yrs

Chace, Louisa, w/o Elias Chace, d 10 June 1888 aged 84 yrs

Chace, Elias B., 1836-1908

Chace, John F., 1847-1920

Monroe Cemetery
Burnside Street
Swansea, Massachusetts

Monroe, Herziah M., w/o Albert N. Monroe & d/o Captain Valentine & Mary A. Mason, d 26 Oct 1856 aged 36 yrs 9 mos 4 days

Monroe, Thomas, s/o Jonathan & Susan Monroe, d 22 March 1855 aged 15 yrs

Monroe, Nancy A., d/o Jonathan & Susan Monore, d 30 Jan 1848 aged 20 yrs

Monroe, Jonathan, s/o Stephen & Momibah Monroe, d 13 Nov 1860 aged 78 yrs 5 mos

Peck, Susannah, w/o Jonathan Monroe & d/o Thomas S. & Rebecca Peck, d 31 Dec 1852 aged 55 yrs 3 mos 11 days

Mason Read Cemetery
Hortonville Road
Swansea, Massachusetts

Martin, James, d 8 Nov 1839 aged 68 yrs 1 mo 6 days

Martin, Mason, s/o Elisha & Amy Martin, d 13 April 1872 aged 83 yrs

Martin, Amos, s/o Elisha & Amy Martin, b Swanzey, MA, d 3 Dec 1860 Providence, RI aged 73 yrs

Mason, Amy Gibbs, w/o Elisha Martin & d/o Simeon & Hannah Mason, d 1 Oct 1847 aged 81 yrs

Read, Mason, d 25 Oct 1871 aged 82 yrs

Read, Amey, w/o Mason Read, d 19 Feb 1860 aged 68 yrs 14 days

Eddy Lot
St. Louis de France Cemetery
Buffington Street
Swansea, Massachusetts

Eddy, Robert S., b 24 Oct 1833, d 29 Sept 1901

Brichtman, Edwin, of Fall River, MA, b 14 April 1812, d 22 Aug 1885

Eddy, Lydia E., d/o Charles B. & Lydia H. Eddy, d 18 Sept 1869 aged 23 yrs 8 mos 25 days

1 large stone...can't read

Hortonville Road
Swansea, Massachusetts

Cornell, Lydia L., d 8 Jan 1834 aged 38 yrs

Sherman, Robert, d 22 June 1859 aged 86 yrs

Sherman, Rebecca, w/o Robert Sherman, d 20 April 1859 aged 88 yrs

Sherman, Edward, s/o Robert & Rebecca Sherman, d 1846

Sherman, William W., 1852-1926

Sherman, D. Nelson, d 28 July 1889 aged 57 yrs 4 mos 5 days

Sherman, Julia W., w/o D. Nelson Sherman, d 9 March 1917 aged 87 yrs 2 mos 23 days

Sherman, John, d 9 Oct 1879 aged 79 yrs

Rounds, Lovina, w/o John Sherman, d 21 April 1887 aged 89 yrs 5 mos 4 days

Eddy, Joseph, d 6 Feb 1882

Eddy, Nancy, w/o Joseph Eddy, d Feb 1895 aged 88 yrs

Eddy, Jabish, d 27 Dec 1871 aged 62 yrs

Mason, Mary W., w/o Nathaniel Mason, d 14 April 1830 aged 26 yrs

Lewis, Jonathan, d 7 March 1871 aged 68 yrs 4 mos

Lewis, Louisa, w/o Jonathan Lewis & w/o Gideon Horton, d 1 Jan 1892 aged 87 yrs 3 mos 15 days

Swansey, Stephen S., d 9 Oct 1881 aged 85 yrs 6 mos 1 day

Swansey, Sarah R., w/o Stephen S. Swansey, d 6 July 1875 aged 73 yrs 4 mos 16 days

Cowing, Matilda, w/o Peter Cowing, d 28 April 1845 aged 45 yrs

Cowing, Peter, d 5 May 1873 aged 61 yrs

Marvel, Ann L., d/o Jesse & Abigail Marvel, d 17 March 1867 aged 49 yrs 7 mos 21 days

Rounds, William, d 30 Aug 1862 aged 49 yrs 8 days. He was killed by falling of a derrick in Taunton, MA

Rounds, Almira, w/o William Rounds, d 4 Jan 1878 aged 68 yrs

Rounds, Joshua, d 1856 aged 65 yrs

Rounds, Meribah, w/o Joshua Rounds, d 11 March 1871 aged 82 yrs

Bliss, George E. W., 1831-1903

Marvel, Phebe J., w/o George E.W. Bliss, 1828-1916

Graves, Z. Walso, b 2 June 1880, d 25 May 1920

Graves, Maria B., w/o Z. Waldo Graves, b 23 March 1856, d 15 May 1922

Eddy, George A., b Nov 1850, d May 1917

Humphrey, Maria, w/o George A. Eddy, b July 1846, d May 1926

Eddy, Alice Emma, w/o George A. Eddy, d 25 Nov 1878

Edson, Jeremiah P., b Sept 1821, d Nov 1911

Pierce, Alice M., w/o Jeremiah P. Edson, b June 1822, d Aug 1912

Eddy, George L., d 7 July 1862 aged 32 yrs

Edson, Lucy, w/o Geoge L. Eddy, d 1 Jan 1910 aged 93 yrs

Marvel, Sarah, w/o William Marvel 2, d 22 Sept 1869

Rounds, Joshua, d 5 April 1875 aged 57 yrs 3 mos 21 days

Rounds, Mary Ann, w/o Joshua Rounds, d 20 March 1883 aged 64 yrs 5 mos

Baker, Nathan, d 26 Oct 1856 aged 69 yrs 9 mos

Baker, Nancy, w/o Nathan Baker, d 24 Jan 1851 aged 60 yrs 9 mos 12 days

Luther, Eben, d.....

Luther, Lovina, w/o Eben Luther, d 4 July 1836 aged 66 yrs

Chase, Daniel, d 21 Nov 1821 aged 78yrs

Chase, Isabel, w/o Daniel Chase, d 29 Sept 1833 aged 77 yrs

Mason, Rosmond, d/o Peleg & Roby Mason, d 16 Feb 1842 aged 79 yrs

Bosworth, Lorana, w/o Ichabod Bosworth, d 15 Aug 1857 aged 87 yrs 5 mos

Mason, Elder Benjamin, d Feb 1818
Mason, Anna, w/o Elder Benjamin Mason, d 5 Sept 1838 aged 90 yrs
Mason, Mary, w/o Caleb Mason, d 18 Dec 1805
Edson, William, d 7 Dec 1886 aged 74 yrs 6 days
Allen, Sarah M., d/o Daniel & Sarah Edson, d 15 Jan 1904 aged 88 yrs 10 mos 21 days
Edson, Sarah, w/o Daniel Edson, d 8 May 1869 a ged 73 yrs 9 mos
Chase, Sarah, w/o Elisha Chase, d 16 Oct 1835 aged 43 yrs
Luther, Ezra, b 20 Nov 1805, d 15 May 1882
Luther, Lovice M., w/o Ezra Luther, b 11 May 1813, d 20 Jan 1877
Luther, Charles, s/o Ezra & Lovice M. Luther, d 7 Dec 1858
Davis, John......
Marvel, John, b 22 Nov 1803, d 22 June 1890
Fowler, Julia, w/o John Marvel, d 28 Dec 1873 aged 70 yrs 2 mos 1 day
Marvel, John H., d 10 Aug 1833
Marvel, Albert, d 8 Dec 1843 aged 2 yrs
Doris, James, d 14 March 1888 aged 74 yrs 8 mos 11 days
Doris, Lydia B., d/o James & Charlotte Davis, d 12 June 1838 aged 1 yr 4 mos
Chace, Marcy, w/o Weston Chace, d 28 Jan 1870 aged 85 yrs 3 mos

Old Warren Road Cemetery
Old Warren Road
Swansea, Massachusetts

Davis.....
Davis, Franklin, 1858-1922
Davis, Harriet E., w/o Captain George Davis, 1825-1905
Davis, Captain George B., 1829-1915
Davis, Job Luther, 1862-1948
Wilson, Brigham, d 13 Aug 1874 aged 84 yrs
Bosworth, Patience M., b 13 June 1832, d 22 June 1903
Bosworth, Joseph T., s/o Jonathan & Mary Bosworth, who was killed in the Battle of Antietram & also buried there 17 Sept 1862 aged 27 yrs
Bosworth, Jonathan C., d 5 April 1878 aged 77 yrs 3 mos 26 days

Bosworth, Mary, w/o Jonathan C. Bosworth, d 27 July 1881 aged 86 yrs 1 day

Mason, Hannah, w/o Marmaduke Mason, d 13 Sept 1874 aged 93 yrs 2 mos 11 days

Mason, Elisha H., s/o Hannah Mason, d 28 Jan 1856 aged 47 yrs

Woodmansee, Mary, d 1818

Luther, Anna C., d/o Job & Parthany Luther, d 16 Oct 1821 AE 20 yrs

Luther, Hezekiah, d 23 Sept 1796

Luther, Job, d 25 Aug 1846 AE 81 yrs

Luther, Parthenia, w/o Job Luther, d 6 May 1851 aged 81 yrs

Boomer, Thomas, d 18 Dec 1848 aged 29 yrs 6 mos

Boomer, Mary E., w/o Thomas Bommer & Job Luther, d 26 July 1893 aged 85 yrs 11 mos 9 days

Luther, Abby, w/o Henry Luther, d 26 Jan 1890 aged 86 yrs 3 mos 9 days

Luther, Benjamin T., s/o Henry & Abby Luther, d 2 Jan 1865 Cuba aged 28 yrs

Gardiner, Anna, d 17 July 1835 aged 77 yrs

Wilbur, James, d 6 Oct 1848 aged 75 yrs

Wilbur, Elizabeth, w/o James Wilbur, d 24 March 1823 aged 47 yrs

Hull, Sarah b., 1834-1918

Hull, Manton F., 1863-1916

Gardiner, Alexander, d 28 April 1861 aged 80 yrs

Gardiner, Elizabeth, w/o Alexander Gardiner, d 18 Jan 1867 aged 82 yrs

Luther, Joseph, b 22 Sept 1837, d 13 Jan 1925

Luther, Elizabeth G., b 14 Dec 1824, d 20 May 1909

Luther, Captain Joseph G., b 31 Dec 1789, d 13 June 1857

Luther, Tamer, w/o Captain Joseph G. Luther, b 2 Dec 1800, d 24 Sept 1892

Luther, Captain Joseph G., d 1854

Brown, David, d 1822

Brown, Anne, d/o Captain Elisha & Anne Brown, d 5 Nov 1802 aged 20 yrs

Brown, Caprain Elisha, d 23 Sept 1846 aged 91 yrs

Brown, Sarah, d/o Captain Elisha Brown, d 27 Nov 1842 aged 56 yrs

Brown, James, d 4 May 1836 aged 71 yrs

Brown, James, d 19 Jan 1862 aged 92 yrs 11 mos 25 days

Brown, Susan, w/o James Brown, d 25 Oct 1869 aged 83 yrs

Brown, Jonathan, b 5 April 1801, d 19 Feb 1879

Hunter, Elizabeth K., d/o J.K. & Sally Brown, b 25 Nov 1836, d 5 Nov 1872 New York

Mason, Sally, w/o Jonathan K. Brown, b 26 Dec 1806, d 24 Jan 1897

Hull, Sarah, w/o Samuel S. Hull, d 17 June 1863 aged 64 yrs

Hull, Samuel S., d 23 Aug 1862 aged 74 yrs

Wilbur, Sarah E., b 11 March 1842, d 27 Oct 1896

Wilbur, Elizabeth, d/o James & Elizabeth Wilbur, d 29 Aug 1878 aged 63 yrs 5 mos 17 days

Wilbur, Mary, d/o James & Elizabeth Wilbur, d 9 Dec 1881 aged 82 yrs

Wilbur, James, s/o James & Elizabeth Wilbur, d 19 Feb 1874 aged 90 yrs 3 mos 23 days

Wilbur, William, s/o James & Elizabeth Wilbur, b 1 May 1810, d 10 April 1857

Wilbur, Zephaniah S., s/o James & Elizabeth Wilbur, d 3 March 1843 aged 35 yrs

Gardner, Zerviah, w/o William Gardner, d 13 Sept 1824 aged 63 yrs

Gardner, Francis, d 14 Feb 1843 aged 72 yrs

Gardner, Joseph, d 20 Oct 1829 aged 29 yrs

Wood, John B., d 16 March 1888 aged 83 yrs 6 mos 9 days

Wood, Lydia L., w/o John B. Wood, d 29 Sept 1875 aged 77 yrs 11 mos 11 days

Maney, Mary, d/o Catherine Maney, d 24 Jan 1879 aged 24 yrs 5 mos 1 day

Mount Hope Cemetery
Hortonville Road
Swansea, Massachusetts

Reeves, Ida Miller, 1855-1908

Mason, Daniel C., d 18 Dec 1879 aged 56 yrs 1 mo

Mason, John B., s/o Capt. John & Zerviah Mason, d 20 Nov 1865 aged 30 yrs 27 days

Gardner, Jerome B., 1832-1906

Esther, Carrie E., w/o Jerome B. Gardner, 1835-1891

Gardner, Israel, d 29 Aug 1882 aged 85 yrs 3 mos 24 days

Gardner, Elizabeth H., w/o Israel Gardner, d 23 Sept 1882 aged 85 yrs 4 mos 8 days

Gardner, Stephen M., d 22 July 1911 aged 73 yrs 20 days

Gardner, Fannie M., w/o Stephen M. Gardner, d 29 Dec 1896 aged 53 yrs 20 days

Arnold, Ida M., w/o George W. Arnold, b 16 May 1875, d 8 Jan 1900

Gardner, Frank M., b 4 March 1865, d 25 Dec 1939

Gifford, Minnie M. Gardner, w/o Frank M. Gardner, b 5 June 1867, d 24 Jan 1938

Gardner, Andrew J., b 1 Nov 1836, d 4 Jan 1908

Mason, Elizabeth S., w/o Andrew J. Gardner, b 5 Sept 1845, d 22 Aug 1919

Mason, Samuel C., b 4 June 1838, d 11 Dec 1865

Baker, George E., 1872-1956

Baker, Ella C., w/o George E. Baker, 1875-1943

Baker, Gertrude A., 1896-1896

Baker, Andrew W., 1839-1920

Baker, Mary J., w/o Andrew Baker, 1839-1926

Cummings, Levi L., 1840-1916

Cummings, Rebecca H., w/o Levi Cummings, 1840-1920

Nichols, Capt. Philip, d 17 June 1842 aged 38 yrs

Nichols, Rebecca W., w/o Capt. Philip Nichols, d 16 Oct 1895 aged 88 yrs

Mason, William V., b 21 June 1848, d 9 Nov 1891

Mason, Samson, b 4 Feb 1854, d 15 March 1898

Mason, Valentine, b 7 Oct 1825, d 12 March 1908

Mason, Deborah, w/o Valentine Mason, b 9 May 1827, d 30 Nov 1900

Miller, Martin, d in service of his Country in Emory Hospital, Washington DC, 22 Oct 1862 aged 40 yrs

Miller, Susan M., w/o Martin Miller, d 5 Nov 1886 aged 63 yrs

Marden, Marietta Frances, b 10 June 1848, d 5 June 1924

Cleaveland, John, d 17 ept 1898 aged 73 yrs

Mason, Adaline Lydia, w/o John Cleaveland & d/o Joshua & Lydia Short Mason, 1831-1916

Cleaveland, John M., 1872-1952

Cleaveland, Benjamin, d 5 Feb 1867 aged 68 yrs 10 mos 4 days

Cleaveland, Hannah, w/o Benjamin Cleaveland,...Broken

Cleaveland, Eliza, d/o Benjamin & Hannah Cleaveland, d 11 Dec 1873 aged 31 yrs 5 mos 21 days

Cleaveland, Edwin, d 2 July 1862 at the Chesapeake Hospital in the service of his Country AE 27 yrs 6 mos 4 days

Cleaveland, Sarah, d/o Benjamin & Hannah Cleaveland, 1837-1918

Cleaveland, Benjamin, 1863-1911

Lewis, Joseph, b Jan 1846, d 27 April 1920

Lewis, Mary A., w/o Joseph Lewis, b Oct 1856, d 17 Dec 1897

Lawton, John J., b 29 Nov 1829, d 8 May 1913

Lewis, Caroline C., w/o Christpher Lewis, d 20 April 1893 aged 59 yrs 3 mos 29 days

Lewis, Frank, b 17 Jan 1860, d 18 April 1890

Potter, John S., d 29 Dec 1881 aged 65 yrs

Potter, Delia, w/o John S. Potter, 1853-1925

Dabney, Elizabeth, 1890-1914

Davis, Henry d 27 March 1886 aged 70 yrs

Sissons, George Esq., d 15 Sept 1857 aged 62 yrs 1 mo 24 days

Sissons, Eliza A., w/o George Sisons Esq., d 28 Dec 1889 aged 74 yrs 10 mos 7 days

Snow, Jeannette M., d/o George & Eliza A. Sissons, d 7 June 1917 aged 83 yrs 6 mos 24 days

Miller, Rev. William, d 1 Sept 1903 aged 86 yrs 4 mos 9 days

Buffington, Anna, w/o Rev. William Miller, d 16 Sept 1901 aged 88 yrs 4 mos

Marden, James Frank, b 19 March 1838, d 14 March 1906

Grey, Elizabeth Y., d/o Samuel & Elizabeth Grey, d 2 May 1840 aged 24 yrs

Grey, Jane, d/o Samuel & Elizabeth Grey, d 29 March 1838 aged 18 yrs

Cotton, John S., d 23 Dec 1872 aged 77 yrs 9 mos 28 days

Gardner, Anice, w/o John S. Cotton & d/o Samuel & Anice Gardner, b 29 March 1796, d 6 Jan 1843

Cotton, Manly K., w/o Franklin L. Alny, b 24 June 1846, d 12 March 1939

Cotton, John S. Jr., b 26 April 1826, d 28 Sept 1885

Cotton, Ellen A., d/o Hiram & Catherine A. Horton & w/o James M. Cotton, b 20 Aug 1858, d 3 March 1925

Cotton, James M., b 9 Oct 1848, d 22 Dec 1933

Grey, Horace, s/o David & Betsey P. Grey, d 22 Oct 1815 aged 77 yrs

Grey, Mary, d/o Joseph & Avis Grey, d 24 Jan 1822 aged 22 yrs

Grey, Sarah, d/o Joseph & Avis Grey, d 15 Aug 1821 aged 26 yrs

Buffington, George D., 1843-1946

Buffington, Elizabeth, w/o George D. Buffington, 1849-1914

Gardner, Frank H., 1869-1943

Gardner, Edith, w/o Frank H. Gardner, 1874-1982

Chace, Ephraim, d 15 Feb 1835 aged 67 yrs

Chace, George R., 1822-1901

Chace, Arzilia R., w/o George R. Chace, 1830-1915

Chace, Emma L., 1851-1925

Buffington, Patience, d 12 Jan 1847 aged 27 yrs 7 mos 19 days

Gray, Joseph, d 6 April 1812 aged 80 yrs

Gray, Sarah, d 21 Sept 1832 aged 67 yrs

Hatch, Mary, w/o Hervey Hatch, b 8 Aug 1827, d 9 Nov 1851

Buffington, Stephen, d 17 Sept 1892

Buffington, Susan, w/o Stephen Buffington, d 8 Aug 1893 aged 77 yrs 5 mos 11 days

Gardner, Job, d 27 Nov 1907 aged 80 yrs 11 mos

Sanders, Marietta, w/o Job Gardner, b 14 Dec 1832, d 5 Jan 1901

Lockhart, Lloyd B., 1925-....

Trimms, Thomas J., 1865-1931

Lockhart, George B., 1891-1958

Bosworth, Mildred B., w/o George B. Lockhart, 1899-....

Craig, Mathew W., 1863-1943

Peirce, Rebecca G., w/o Mathew W. Craig, 1867-1951

Craig, Howard, s/o Mathew & Rebecca G. Peirce, 1892-1919

Holmes, Alton C., 1888-1939

Holmes, Gertrude, w/o Alton C. Holmes, 1890-1967

Holmes, Alton C., Jr., 1910-1968

Chapman, Samuel S., 1886-1940

Mercer, James, 1856-....

Mercer, Jennie, w/o James Mercer, 1864-....

Buffington, Carl, 1886-....

Buffington, Annette B., w/o Carl Buffington, 1889-1949

Gendron, Clara, 1863-1931

Emery, Arthur R., 1887-1955

Emery, L. May, w/o Arthur R. Emery, 1887-1970

Hilton, Dr. John D., 1862-1952

Hilton, Elizabeth, w/o Dr. John D. Hilton, 1874-1958

Peck, Dorothy Hilton, 1897-1984

Goss, Edward, b 17 Sept 1862, d 17 Jan 1937

Lord, Emma, w/o Edward Goss, b 2 March 1867, d 4 April 1938

Goss, Henry E., s/o Edward & Emma Goss, b 14 Nov 1898, d 3 Nov 1960

Gardner, Lois, w/o Henry E. Goss, b 18 Jan 1899, d....

Kellogg, Emery C., 1879-1972

Kellogg, Edith M., 1882-....

Woodward, Ellsworth S., b 22 Sept 1888, d 2 March 1947

Goss, Annie W., w/o Ellsworth Woodward, b 18 Dec 1889, d 13 Jan 1962

Martin, Frank N., 1855-1943

Martin, Mary M., w/o Frank N. Martin, 1857-1940
Hayes, John, 1845-1913
Hayes, Sarah E., w/o John Hayes, 1852-1928
Hayes, Cora, 1889-1892
Sherman, Charles M., 1850-1921
Sherman, Anna J., w/o Charles M. Sherman, 1855-1934
Sherman, Annie M., 1887-1948
Sherman, David M., 1878-1956
Milne, J.W., 1872-1932
Milne, Etta J., w/o J.W. Milne, 1884-1957
Horton, Mary E., 1876-1950
Sands, John A., 1889-1955
Sands, Edith, w/o John A. Sands, 1873-1952
Sands, Marion L., d/o John & Edith Sands, 1907-1918
Fisk, Walter S., 1882-1944
Fisk, George W., 1854-1935
Fisk, May/Mary L., w/o George W. Fosk, 1854-1924
Abbe, Martha J., 1859-1937
Sadler, George E., 1863-1937
Sadler, Esther J., w/o George E. Sadler, 1865-1922
Sadler, George M., s/o George E. & Esther J. Sadler, 1898-1963
Sadler, Jennie M., w/o George M. Sadler, 1902-1990
Nye, Caleb R., 1861-1928
Walker, Mary J., w/o Caleb R. Nye, 1858-1925
Nye, Harriet Evelyn, w/o Caleb R.Nye, 1863-....
Giunte, Casper, 1860-1943
Giunti, Joseph, 1890-1979
Smith, James T., 1865-1946
Smith, Sarah, w/o James T. Smith, 1865-1938
Lee, Edward P., 1898-1930
Lee, Sarah, w/o Edward P. Lee, 1896-....
Smith, William C., Mass CPL 47th Co 153 Depot Brigade WWI, b 15 March 1892, d 6 April 1956
Mayo, Ruth S., 1890-1936
Mayo, Irvin L., 1886-1961
Franklin, Clara Irene, 1896-1951
Strange, William T., 1873-1962
Strange, Mary E., w/o William T. Strange, 1886-1939
Kerns, John A., 1872-1941
Arnzen, Cynthia, w/o John A. Kerns, 1882-1973

Kerns, John Paige, 1917-1974
Varley, Sarah, 1847-1925
Ormerod, Charles, 1868-1933
Ormerod, Florence V., w/o Charles Ormerod, 1874-1948
Ormerod, Charles Varley, 1893-1961
Pilkington, John Edwin, 1881-1944
Pilkington, Constance Maud, 1881-1959
Negus, George H., 1855-1942
Hunt, Thomas H., 1880-....
Hunt, Minnie, 1880-1942
Lingard, R. David, 1930-1954
Gill, Walter, 1884-....
Gill, Alice J., w/o Walter Gill, 1896-1955
Bolton, James, Mass PFC Co H 39th Inf WWI, b 14 May 1890, d 14 Nov 1959
Gregory, Alice, 1895-1959
Bishop, Joseph S., 1894-1959
Bishop, Olive, w/o Joseph S. Bishop, 1907-1959
Cook, Thomas, 1880-1960
Parker, Christina, w/o Thomas Cook, 1888-1959
Yeaton, Isabelle M., 1897-1986
Yeaton, Geoffrey D., 1898-1945
Caldwell, Charles R., 1892-1951
Caldwell, Jessie A., w/o Charles R. Caldwell, 1897-1945
Hall, Edgar S., 1883-1944
Hall, Annie, w/o Edgar S. Hall, 1887-1963
Baker, F. Preston, 1892-1943
Baker, Grace A., w/o F. Preston Baker, 1898-1978
Knight, Alfred E., 1864-1945
Knight, Jemima, w/o Alfred E. Knight, 1864-1947
Martin, Frank, 1899-1987
Martin, Florence, w/o Frank Martin, 1898-1978
Dana, Albert J., 1869-1946
Dana, Julia, w/o Albert J. Dana, 1862-1933
Easterbrooks, Walter E., 1872-1936
Easterbrooks, Louise S., w/o Walter E. Easterbrooks, 1866-1934
Bosworth, Ichabod, 1856-1934
Horton, Addie F., w/o Ichabod Bosworth, 1863-1959
Wood, George E., 1839-1926
Rounds, Harriet N., w/o George E. Wood, 1842-1920

Wood, Ervin F., s/o George & Harriet Wood, 1867-1941
Gardner, Edith B., w/o Ervin F. Wood, 1868-1942
Wood, Mary B., d/o Ervin & Edith Wood, 1893-1974
Gardiner, Eugene Willis, 1866-1937
Lyon, Libbie Jane, w/o Eugene Willis Gardiner, 1869-1944
Gardiner, Clarence Eugene, s/o Eugene & Libbie Gardiner, 1894-1940
Flynn, Hazel G., d/o Eugene & Libbie Wood, 1891-1962
Shaw, Alton K., 1901-1960
Shaw, Eleanor G., w/o Alton K. Shaw, 1901-1989
Fiske, Norman Royal, b 28 June 1897, d 4 Sept 1954
Robinson, Rose Cecelia, w/o Norman Royal Fiske, b 18 Sept 1890, d 20
   Oct 1970
Fiske, Gertrude C., w/o Frank R. Fiske, 1878-1941
Fiske, Frank R., 1876-1949
Chace, Frank H. 1861-1937
Chace, Carrie, w/o Frank H. Chace, 1867-1946
Chace, Bessie F., 1884-1954
Chace, Charles F., 1887-1956
Lewis, Frank K., 1881-1936
Lewis, Emma, w/o Frank K. Lewis, 1882-1949
Springer, Arthur C., 1884-1953
Choate, George H., Mass PVT 28th Co Coast Artillery WWI, b 25 Aug
   1895, d 26 Oct 1958
Choate, William H., 1853-1945
Choate, Isabella M., w/o William H. Choate, 1867-1938
Simcock, J. Raymond, 1889-1963
Wells, Rhoda E., w/o J. Raymond Simcock, 1887-1937
Henry, George W., 1862-1935
Henry, Edna L., w/o George W. Henry, 1888-1964
Henry, James W., 1862-1928
Henry, Anna M., w/o James W. Henry, 1872-1939
Chace, Charles H., 1854-1943
Chace, Annie R., w/o Charles H. Chace, 1859-1942
Shea, John, 1858-1927
Shea, Margaret, w/o John Shea, 1865-1920
Weeden, Robert H., 1871-1930
Weeden, Esther A., w/o Robert H. Weeden, 1875-1969
Weeden, Demaris, d/o Robert & Esther Weeden, 1900-1926
Weeden, Robert H., s/o Robert & Esther Weeden, 1901-1986
Weeden, Doris, w/o Robert H. Weeden, 1905-1984

Weeden, Mabel C., 1869-1925
Murphy, George P., 1873-1924
Rothwell, William H., 1849-1924
Rothwell, Myoh A., w/o William H. Rothwell, 1849-1932
Maddox, William, 1876-1936
Maddox, Betsey A., w/o William Maddox, 1876-1957
Rothwell, Arthur, 1892-1977
Rothwell, Lila, w/o Arthur Rothwell, 1892-1959
Rothwell, Pauline, d/o Arthur & Lila Rothwell, 1928-1932
Gardner, Charles H., d 8 June 1907 aged 54 yrs 5 mos 8 days
Hazen, George E., 1829-1891
Hazen, Anna M., w/o George E. Hazen, 1856-....
Hazen, Nathan F., 1893-....
Hazen, George W., 1879-1918
Hazen, Mabel C., w/o George W. Hazen, 1887-....
Hazen, George E., 1911-1911
Gardner, Raymond Cleaveland, s/o Chester R. & Alice C. Gardner, b 12
    April 1904, d 25 Feb 1905
Cleaveland, Alice, b 29 Dec 1874, d 25 Aug 1942
Gardner, Chester R., b 10 Nov 1875, d 23 Sept 1963
Manchester, Philip H., 1850-1922
Manchester, Nancy J., w/o Philip H. Manchester, 1829-1904
Manchester, Bertha M., w/o Philip H. Manchester, 1883-1936
Gardner, John C., 1871-1942
Mason, Emma M., w/o John C. Gardner, 1875-1907
Monroe, Ida A., w/o John C. Gardner, 1880-1940
Gardner, John M., s/o John C. & Ida A. Gardner, 1904-1959
Allen, Catherine C., w/o John M. Gardner, 1907-1979
Gardner, Emma, w/o Charles H. Gardner, d 9 March 1933 aged 78 yrs 11
    mos 9 days
Hayes, Helen R. Gardner, 1893-1957
Morse, Edward G., 1878-1931
Morse, Alice R., w/o Edward G. Morse, 1882-1972
Morse, Edward K., b 28 Aug 1852, d 22 March 1903
Morse, Alice W., w/o Edward K. Morse, b 3 March 1856, d 13 Aug 1949
Luther, John, d 3 Jan 1914 aged 54 yrs
Luther. Jeremiah, d 8 Oct 1901 aged 80 yrs
Luther, Catherine, w/o Jeremiah Luther, d 22 Dec 1921 aged 93 yrs 9 mos
    7 days
Walker, Sarah S., 1870-1942

Walker, Rufus R., 1873-1921
Walker, Thomas Bentley, infant s/o Rufus R. & Sarah S. Walker, d 27
Sept 1908
Williams, Benjamin, 1829-1964
Williams, Abby E., 1830-1903
Williams, Annette, 1860-1938
Gardner, David B., 1888-1957
Williams, Grace R., w/o David B. Gardner, 1893-1954
Mason, Oliver, b 19 Jan 1894, d 20 Aug 1968
Mason, Sarah E., w/o Oliver Mason, b 26 April 1899, d 4 Feb 1984
Wilbur, Dorothy, d/o Henry & Jennie Wilbur, b 29 July 1900, d 24 Aug
1901
Wilbur, Henry E., b 31 March 1864, d 31 Dec 1951
Wilbur, Jennie B., w/o Henry E. Wilbur, b 10 July 1865, d 20 March 1947
Brown, Mason, 1815-1882
Brown, Ann P., w/o Mason Brown, 1822-1902
Brown, Charles I., 1848-1905
Brown, John P., 1857-1877
Stevens, Thomas H., 1846-1930
Stevens, Annie A., w/o Thomas H. Stevens, 1855-1914
Stevens, Charles C., 1872-1901
Stevens, Gladys A., 1879-1949
Campbell, Daniel W., b 22 Nov 1846, d 13 Aug 1901
Campbell, Emma, w/o Daniel W. Campbell, b 19 Aug 1855, d....
Welshman, Agnes J., 1875-1923
Lewin, George W., b 22 Feb 1836, d 10 Feb 1923
Thurston, Sarah B., b 20 Aug 1865, d 13 July 1945
Richardson, Wallace Sr., 1894-1965
Davis, Mildred G., w/o Wallace Richardson Sr., 1896-1986
Davis, Grace Goff, 1870-1901
Howard, M. Ethel, 1891-1942
Fritch, Marion Davis, 1900-1982
Mitchell, John R., 1854-1933
Mitchell, Minnie M., 1866-1934
Mason, Job, b 6 May 1851, d 18 March 1910
Mason, Mary, w/o Job Mason, b 11 Jan 1856, d 8 Dec 1902
Bowler, George B., 1846-1905
Bowler, Lydia C., 1846-1915
Midwood, Ellen, b 10 Dec 1847, d 31 May 1927
Midwood, John, b 23 Oct 1831, d 29 June 1898

Gardner, Willard C., 1869-1961

Barney, Carolyn, w/o Willard C. Gardner, 1872-1918

Gardner, Marcia E., d/o Williard & Carolyn Gardner, 1898-1913

Gardner, Madora A., d/o Willard & Carolyn Gardner, ...

Chace, Nathan, 1862-1938

Chace, Adelaide L., w/o Nathan Chace, 1865-1953

Chace, George M., s/o Nathan & Adelaide Chace, 1888-1969

Chace, Marion, w/o George M. Chace, 1892-1981

Weaver, Arthur, 1859-1926

Peck, Lura R., w/o Arthur Weaver, 1860-1934

Macomber, William Penn, b 18 Jan 1832, d 15 Feb 1918

Dean, Esther, w/o William Penn Macomber, b 21 April 1839, d 31 Dec 1910

Easterbrooks, Preston B., 1876-1931

Easterbrooks, Nora Clara, 1848-1921

Easterbrooks, Ezra Otis, 1847-1917

Easterbrooks, Frank D., 1874-1946

Easterbrooks, George C., b 25 July 1845, d 15 June 1910

Easterbrooks, Kesia M., w/o George C. Easterbrooks, b 15 Aug 1849, d 20 April 1917

Easterbrooks, George Clarence, s/o George C. & Kesia M. Easterbrooks, b 19 Aug 1871, d 15 July 1932

Easterbrooks, Frank Lester, s/o George C. & Kesia M. Easterbrooks, b 6 Jan 1877, d 13 Aug 1895

Law, Maria F., w/o Stephen C. Johnson, b 6 Feb 1849, d 10 March 1935

Johnson, Edith Finette, d/o Stephen C. & Maria F. Law Johnson, b 17 Jan 1884, d 29 Jan 1934

Macomber, Richard R., d 17 March 1884 aged 52 yrs 1 mo 29 days

Macomber, Sarah J., w/o Richard R. Macomber, d 4 Jan 1898 aged 67 yrs

Peckham, Louise S. M., 1871-1953

Chace, Benjamin, 1820-1896

Pierce, Rachel, w/o Benjamin Chace & d/o Barzillan & Ruth Buffington, 1826-1913

Weaver, Stephen, b 9 Dec 1826, d 29 Jan 1900

Weaver, Ruth A., w/o Stephen Weaver, b 8 April 1830, d 10 Aug 1917

Easterbrooks, Charles C., 1855-1935

Goff, Carrie E., w/o Charles C. Easterbrooks, 1857-1916

Easterbrooks, Elmer, s/o Charler C. & Carrie E. Easterbrooks, b 29 Aug 1886, d 3 Jan 1900

Case, Alfred, d 5 Oct 1861 aged 41 yrs

Case, Eleanor, w/o Alfred Case, d 31 Dec 1858

Case, Addie L., d/o Alfred & Eleanor Case, d 11 Oct 1855 aged 1 yr 2 mos 1 day

Case, Daniel H., s/o Frederick & Angeline Lewis Case, b 12 Oct 1842 Swansea, MA, d 7 Nov 1925 Rehoboth, MA

Kelton, Rev. George, d 21 Nov 1862 aged 76 yrs

Kelton,Hannah, w/o Rev. George Kelton, d 7 Dec 1864 aged 73 yrs 5 mos 13 days

Kelton, Gardner B., b 14 Aug 1822, d 30 March 1903

Kelton, Mary C., w/o Gardner B. Kelton, b 8 Sept 1838, d 17 Oct 1916

Kelton, Minnie B., d/o Gardner & Mary Kelton, b 12 Feb 1865, d 8 March 1903

Slade, LeRoy E., 1857-1930

Slade, Cassandra M., w/o LeRoy E. Salde, 1863-1945

Slade, Lida W., 1892-1905

Cleveland, Calvin, b 19 Dec 1861, d 4 Jan 1904

Cleveland, Henrietta M., w/o Calvin Cleveland, b 17 July 1861, d 11 Jan 1937

Mason, Henry N., b 23 Feb 1836, d 25 May 1889

Mason, Nancy T., b 15 Sept 1835, d 29 April 1904

Doe, Arnold R., b 23 Sept 1874, d 31 Aug 1923

Wilbur, Mary E., w/o Arnold R. Doe, b 21 Nov 1886, d 4 Jan 1955

Wilbur, Daniel, s/o James & Elizabeth Wilbur, b 22 Oct 1817, d 24 Sept 1896

Lee, Nancy, w/o Daniel Wilbur & d/o George & Nancy Lee, b 30 March 1828, d 19 March 1915

Wilbur, William, b 21 Sept 1863, d 12 Feb 1941

Eddy, Caroline E., w/o William Wilbur, b 12 Sept 1863, d 3 Dec 1947

Lee, James H., b 26 Feb 1832, d 16 Oct 1910

Brown, Marcus A., b 19 Dec 1819, d 10 Feb 1894

Brown, Maria F., w/o Marcus A. Brown, b 10 July 1828, d 18 Jan 1900

Brown, Clarence A., b 3 June 1850, d 14 May 1924

Brown, Emma L., w/o Clarence A. Brown, b 20 March 1850, d 14 Jan 1912

Simcock, George Allen, 1854-1922

Simcock, Sarah, w/o George Allen Simcock, 1866-1925

Simcock, David, 1902-1985

Simcock, Eliza A., w/o David Simcock, 1906-1934

Simcock, Lyman, 1900-1988

Simcock, Sovina, 1892-1898

Simcock, C. Royal, 1887-1923

Ferguson, Maria B., 1859-1930

Clayton, Margaret, 1836-1926

Simcock, William, 1838-1906

Simcock, Margaret, w/o William Simcock, 1839-1893

Simcock, John, d 8 March 1888 aged 73 yrs 6 mos 22 days

Simcock, Annie, w/o John Simcock, d 1 Nov 1898 aged 86 yrs 3 mos 18 days

Simcock, Annie, w/o Manuel Vote, d 26 March 1881, aged 30 yrs 3 mos 26 days

Sherman, Asa, d 25 Nov 1905, aged 87 yrs 11 mos 21 days

Sherman, Lois, w/o Asa Sherman, d 1 Aug 1907

Sherman, William P., s/o Asa & Lois Sherman, d 29 Oct 1870 aged 23 yrs

Case, Aaron, d 27 March 1871 aged 82 yrs 7 mos 21 days

Case, Lovina, w/o Aaron Case, d 5 March 1876 aged 77 yrs 9 mos 22 days

Case, Isaac, b 25 April 1823, d 4 June 1898

Case, Mercy A., w/o Isaac Case, b 19 Feb 1828, d 6 Aug 1850

Case, Hannah, w/o Isaac Case, b 14 May 1815, d 22 Feb 1903

Easterbrooks, Levi, b 15 April 1805, d 21 Nov 1886

Easterbrooks, Eliza, w/o Levi Easterbrooks, d 23 July 1842 aged 37 yrs

Easterbrooks, Jane, w/o Levi Easterbrooks, b 26 March 1817, d 26 Jan 1889

Johnson, Ernest Law, 1885-1955

Easterbrooks, Eugene B., 1882-1936

Easterbrooks, Gertrude L., 1882-1946

Eddy, David F., b 18 Oct 1867, d 15 Feb 1946

Borden, Minnie F., w/o David F. Eddy, b 27 Nov 1866, d 13 Aug 1952

Eddy, Hiram F., s/o David & Minnie Eddy, b 18 Sept 1895, d 16 Oct 1946

Eddy, Ruth Bordon, b 15 July 1897, d 13 Oct 1990

Mason, Samuel W., b 3 July 1865, d 3 Oct 1947

Roth, Frances, w/o Samuel W. Mason, b 22 Feb 1870, d 6 Oct 1963

Mason, Frederick W., b 10 Aug 1885, d 10 Aug 1885

Mason, Roswell E., b 8 Nov 1891, d 12 Sept 1909

Wilson, Oliver M., 1880-1947

Wilson, Louise, w/o Oliver M. Wilson, 1883-1942

May, John T., b 16 Oct 1885, d 2 April 1919

Coupe, Ralph E., 1856-1930

Coupe, Sarah L., w/o Ralph E. Coupe, 1859-1941

Coupe, PVT Clarence R., 306th Inf Killed in Action 27 Aug 1918, Buried in Oise Aisme Cemetery, France

Brown, Henry C., 1848-1927
Brown, Florence G., w/o Henry C. Brown, 1855-1909
Brown, Elizabeth, 1879-1941
Brown, Agnes L., 1888-1955
Davis, Sarah E., w/o Benjamin H.Jackson, 1823-1911
Sias, George W., 1856-1935
Sias, Lizzie E., w/o George W. Sias, 1860-1929
Cole, Louis H., 1874-1953
Whitehead, Edith S., w/o Louis H. Cole, 1870-1930
Cole, Frank C., 1878-1918
Whitehead, Jennie L., w/o Frank C. Cole, 1874-1959
Cole, Lois A., 1907-....
Cole, William H., b 1 May 1835, d 2 Jan 1913
Cole, Sarah A., w/o William H. Cole, b 2 Nov 1844, d 19 May 1924
Cowings, William H., 1837-1908
Cowings, Harriet M., w/o William H. Cowings, 1842-1908
Cowings, Edgar F., 1870-1953
Cowings, Hannah M., w/o Edgar F. Cowings, 1869-1953
Wood, Alpheus H., 1849-1934
Wood, Helen F., w/o Alpheus H. Wood, 1856-1910
Wood, Henry B., s/o Alpheus & Helen F. Wood, 1881-1970
Muller, Camille, 1878-1946
Muller, Amelia Sophia, w/o Camille Muller, 1873-1928
Davidson, Lester, 1899-1964
Davidson, Louise S., w/o Lester Davidson, 1899-1990
Tattersall, Henry, 1885-1952
Tattersall, Olive I., w/o Henry Tattersall, 1893-1985
Osbaldston, Albert, 1877-1936
Osbaldston, Hannah E., w/o Albert Osbaldston, 1878-1943
Livesy, Elizabeth J., b 23 Feb 1845, d 11 March 1923
Brown, Gertrude F., w/o Isaac Brown, 1849-1919
Andrews, George Morton, b 3 Aug 1864, d 23 June 1916
Andrews, Bessie, w/o George Morton Andrews, d 7 Feb 1956
Arnold, Frank Johnston, b 31 Oct 1858, d 3 March 1939
Tripp, Alice Read, w/o Frank Johnston Arnold, b 20 July 1859, d 11 April
    1942
Gardner, Henry N., 1896-1958
Gardner, Annie H., w/o Henry N. Gardner, 1897-1960
Archibald, Isaac, 1843-1919
Archibald, Annie, w/o Isaac Archibald, 1843-1937

Archibald, Ethel, d/o Isaac & Annie Archibald, 1875-1916
Archibald, Edmund, s/o Isaac & Annie Archibald, 1872-1933
Archibald, William D., s/o Isaac & Annie Archibald, 1876-1953
Archibald, Elizabeth M., w/o William D. Archiblad, 1879-1952
Bowen, Augusta R., 1886-1935
Allen, Ruth A., w/o Ira Allen, 1829-1914
Hewitt, Robert E., 1874-1943
Hewitt, M. Elizabeth, w/o Robert E. Hewitt, 1881-1964
Thurston, Henry B., 1883-1914
Marvel, Helen C., w/o Henry B. Thurston, 1884-1962
Burnham, George H., husband of Helen C. Marvel, 1886-1960
Peck, Mary D., w/o Cyril C. Peck, 1823-1901
Douglas, Huldah E., w/o William M. Douglas, d 16 April 1892 aged 76
    yrs 3 mos 26 days
Pierce, William H., 1858-1933
Douglas, Martha S., w/o William H. Pierce, 1855-1939
Gardner, Carrie M., 1882-1961
Pierce, Edith D., 1887-1967
Pierce, Andrew T., 1821-1913
Pierce, Eliza A., w/o Andrew T. Pierce, 1824-1851
Pierce, Mary E., w/o Andrew T. Pierce, 1832-1892
Pierce, Silas A., 1860-1946
Baker, Sarah F., w/o Silas A.Pierce, 1860-1940
Pierce, Nathan F., 1846-1909
Nichols, Dexter, 1834-1923
Nichols, Emma A., w/o Dexter Nichols, 1853-1925
Martin, Howard, 1878-1942
Brightman, Hattie M., w/o Howard Martin, 1880-1957
Mitchell, Frank M., 1870-1935
Mitchell, Lucy B., 1873-1949
Mitchell, F. Carl, 1894-1903
Mitchell, William, 1836-1918
Mitchell, Margaret, 1842-1892
Mitchell, Josephine, 1855-1911
Weaver, Thomas, d 14 Feb 1874 aged 59 yrs
Bosworth, Otis, d 13 April 1914 aged 77 yrs 3 mos 21 days
Bosworth, Ella A., w/o Otis Bosworth, d 22 Aug 1912 aged 61 yrs 4 mos
    14 days
Borrows, Emma A., w/o Parker Weaver, 1857-1936

Weaver, Parker, s/o Thomas & Martha Weaver, b 6 June 1854, d 12 April 1915

Sherman, Martha, w/o Thomas A. Weaver, d 1 March 1867 aged 49 yrs

Weaver, Benjamin T., s/o Thomas A. & Martha Weaver, d 6 June 1867 aged 19 yrs

Weaver, Parker, d 14 March 1870 aged 85 yrs 7 mos 14 days

Weaver, Lydia, w/o Parker Weaver, d 3 March 1869 aged 82 yrs

Weaver, Benjamin B., s/o Parker & Lydia Weaver,d 18 Feb 1843 aged 23 yrs

Weaver, John R., s/o Parker & Lydia Weaver, d 19 Feb 1840

Weaver, Nancy, d/o Parker & Lydia Weaver, d 7 May 1826 aged 7 yrs

Weaver, Lydia, d 11 May 1853 aged 42 yrs 10 mos 16 days

Chace, Sarah, w/o Gilbert Chace, b 27 Oct 1792, d 31 Oct 1858

Easterbrooks, James E., b 22 Nov 1832, d 8 Sept 1896

Easterbrooks, Lauretta G., w/o James Easterbrooks, d 26 Nov 1893 aged 60 yrs

Currie, Mary E., w/o James Easterbrooks, d 26 Nov 1921 aged 65 yrs

Anthony, Walter F., b 25 Oct 1860, d 29 Oct 1939

Anthony, Aleena G., w/o Walter F. Anthony, b 24 Nov 1861, d 3 April 1898

Easterbrooks, Caleb, d 25 Aug 1855 aged 70 yrs

Easterbrooks, Parthenia, w/o Caleb Easterbrooks, d 26 Aug 1864 aged 74 yrs

Easterbrooks, Lydia P., d 29 Oct 1853 aged 43 yrs

Easterbrooks, Edward, d 20 Dec 1832 aged 20 yrs

Easterbrooks, Nelson G., d 29 Sept 1846 aged 30 yrs

Easterbrooks, Susan, w/o Nelson G. Easterbrooks, d 3 June 1861 aged 42 yrs

Easterbrooks, Fanny L., d 27 Aug 1847 aged 20 yrs

Easterbrooks, Mary F., d 3 Oct 1848 aged 18 yrs

Easterbrooks, John, d 13 July 1852 aged 33 yrs

Gardner, Preserved S., d 1873

Mason, Capt John, d 20 Nov 1881 aged 84 yrs 5 mos 20 days

Mason, Zerviah, w/o Capt. John Mason, d 6 May 1882 aged 85 yrs 8 mos 7 days

Gardiner, Ira Mason, b 2 Sept 1836, d 22 May 1901

Braman, Mary F., w/o Ira Mason Gardiner, d 4 June 1880 aged 36 yrs

Richmond, Mercie, w/o Ira Mason Gardiner, b 26 May 1837, d 16 June 1913

Wilbour, Harum, s/o Daniel Wilbour, d 18 Sept 1845 aged 61 yrs

Wilbour, Esther, w/o Harum Wilbour, d 11 April 1866 aged 78 yrs
Anthony, David, 1844-1905
Anthony, Anna S., 1844-1917
Anthony, Bessie M., 1902-1944
Anthony, Marcus M., 1854-1929
Chase, Stephen, d 17 Sept 1904 aged 84 yrs
Chase, Betsey J., d 6 Aug 1910 aged 83 yrs
Henry, Clifford, 1895-1946
Chace, Eunice, w/o Clifford Henry,......
Cutshal, Joseph C., 1888-....
Baker, Elizabeth F., w/o Joseph C. Cutshal, 1884-1932
Gardner, James S., b 23 Aug 1824, d 26 April 1886
Gardner, Lydia A., w/o James S. Gardner, b 10 Sept 1822, d 15 Dec 1910
Marvel, George, b 23 Aug 1853, d 18 May 1926
Marvel, Mavina R., w/o George Marvell, b 19 Jan 1855, d 17 Sept 1887
Marvel, Sarah, w/o George Marvel, b 2 Dec 1855, d 26 June 1936
Marvel, Florence E., d/o George & Sarah Marvel, b 20 Feb 1882, d 29 Oct
    1942
Tallman, Asa, d 25 Oct 1879 aged 81 yrs 3 mos 16 days
Marvel, James H., b 3 Oct 1848, d 29 Dec 1929
Jenney, Ellen M., w/o James H. Marvel, b 8 June 1849, d 26 July 1933
Eddy, Phebe, d 3 July 1868 aged 74 yrs
Webster, Elizabeth B., d 5 Sept 1891 aged 65 yrs
Marvel, Bennanuel, b 26 Sept 1823, d 28 Dec 1906
Marvel, Harriet E., w/o Bennanuel Marvel, b 19 Nov 1823, d 25 May
    1893
Marvel, Mary E., b 28 July 1856, d 12 Aug 1903
Baker, Elisha, d 24 Oct 1857 aged 60 yrs
Baker, Maria, w/o Elisha Baker, d 2 March 1875 aged 73 yrs 8 days
Stanley, Charles, d 17 May 1852 aged 24 yrs 7 mos
Eddy, David B., b 1 Jan 1797, d 26 May 1868
Baker, Harriet H., w/o David B. Eddy, b 21 Feb 1805, d 7 Feb 1892
Eddy, Hiram Baker, b 22 Jan 1829, d 19 OCt 1909
Simmons, Nancy M., w/o Hiram Baker Eddy, b 4 April 1838, d 12 Jan
    1927
Eddy, Charles Brown, s/o Hiram Baker & Nancy M. Baker, b 23 May
    1863, d 24 May 1876
Arnold, Samuel C., b 9 Feb 1835, d 5 Jan 1902
Arnold, Hannah H., b 27 Dec 1836, d 26 July 1915
Usher, Willard, b 22 May 1813, d 5 Sept 1845

Usher, Sarah A., w/o Willard Usher & w/o Alexander Gardner, b 31 March 1815, d 29 July 1898

Frances, Angennette, b 9 June 1840, d 25 Oct 1841

Sherman, George C., 1867-1942

Sherman, Herbert L., 1863-1920

Sherman, William H., b 26 May 1830, d 25 June 1890

Peck, Elizabeth B., w/o William H. Sherman, b 27 Dec 1827, d 28 April 1905

Sherman, Ellen F., d/o William H. & Elizabeth Sherman, b 8 Aug 1858, d 6 Sept 1935

Sherman, Sanders, 1795-1868

Sherman, Phebe, 1793-1861

Sherman, Catherine, 1820-1863

Sherman, George, 1822-1841

Sherman, Nancy, 1824-1841

Sherman, Rachel, 1835-1836

Sherman, Charles H., 1836-1911

Sherman, Solomon, 1757-1838

Sherman, Sybil, w/o Solomon Sherman, 1768-1818

Sherman, Amanda, 1792-1842

Sherman, Jane, 1804-1831

Sherman, Atherton, 1792-1868

Sherman, Rachel, w/o Atherton Sherman, 1795-1823

Luther, Samuel, 1760-1828

Luther, Patience, w/o Samuel Luther, 1766-1816

Young, Elmer D., 1853-1932

Courtney, Ruth M., w/o Elmer D. Young, 1856-1895

Chace, Caroline A., w/o Elmer D. Young, 1851-1918

Young, Harry D., 1876-1941

Young, George G., 1876-1942

Caswell, Ruth Y., 1899-1954

Young, John W., 1848-1940

Courtney, Charlotte, 1819-1895

Caswell, Florence M., 1877-1937

Mason, Abbie A., 1812-1865

Mason, Warren B., 1822-1823

Mason, Mary B., 1824-1845

Mason, Olney, 1787-1851

Mason, Lillis, 1788-1854

Mason, Gardner, 1810-1844

Mason, Lydia T., 1815-1882
Mason, Francis Gardner, 1840-1928
Mason, Kezia M., 1834-1897
Mason, Martha E., 1839-1927
Mason, Mary E., 1842-1928
Pettis, Caroline G., M., 1836- 1902 Vallejo, California
Hirsch, Isabella A., 1844-1891
Shove, Elmer E., 1883-1929
Shove, Elsie, w/o Elmer E. Shove, 1881-1941
Finch, Ella J., 1860-1934
Puffer, Joseph W., 1819-1893
Puffer, Mary C., w/o Joseph W. Puffer, 1818-1895
Puffer, Charles G., 1846-1912
Puffer, Miriam, w/o Charles G. Puffer, 1849-1927
Puffer, Frank A., 1857-1916
Rounds, George O., 1860-1930
Puffer, Ida L., w/o George O. Rounds, 1855-1948
Arnold, Howard S., b 13 July 1889, d 10 Jan 1973
Gifford, Meriba A., w/o Howard S. Arnold, b 2 Dec 1888, d 27 Nov 1986
Wood, Nathan 16 Jan 1825, d 6 July 1904
Kingsley, Abba M., w/o Nathan Wood, b 10 April 1828, d 8 April 1889
Wood, Nathan H., w/o Nathan & Abba M., Wood, b 15 Feb 1851, d 3
   Sept 1853
Arnold, Arthur E., b 29 April 1860, d 20 Feb 1940
Wood, Eloise K., w/o Arthur E. Arnold, b 19 Aug 1861, d 3 Oct 1938
Arnold, Edmund K., b 27 June 1884, d 23 Nov 1955
Goodrich, Icsa A., w/o Edmund K. Arnold, b 30 June 1887, d 6 June 1965
Arnold, Dorothy B., d/o George & Alyce B. Arnold, b 21 Dec 1920, d 18
   Aug 1925
Pierce, Chauncey, 1845-1918
Wood, Benjamin N., 1842-1918
Wood, Margaret E., w/o Benjamin N. Wood, 1858-1928
Wetherell, Lloyd T., b 20 Dec 1817, d 15 Feb 1894
Wetherell, Eliza, w/o Lloyd T. Wetherell, b 28 June 1818, d 20 Feb 1894
Wood, Benjamin A., s/o Benjamin & Madgie E. Wood, d 19 Aug 1890
   aged 3 yrs 7 mos
Read, Jennie S., 1868-1919
Read, Alton E., 1894-1950
Wood, Col. Haile, d 6 May 1860 aged 71 yrs 56 mos 13 days

Wood, Mary, w/o Col. Haile Wood, d 30 Oct 1872 aged 87 yrs 7 mos 8 days

Wood, William, s/o Col. Haile & Mary Wood, d 17 Aug 1840 aged 29 yrs

Wood, Miss Laura, d/o Col. Haile & Mary Wood, b 17 April 1823, d 20 Oct 1853

Wood,John, b 4 Dec 1765, d 24 March 1829

Wood, Seth, d 4 April 1815, on same stone, his wife, d 17 June 1784 (no Name written on stone)

Champlin, Laura, 1864-1940

Tallaksen, Lars, 1871-1951

Brown, Mary, d/o William & Clara B. Brown, b 28 Nov 1879, d 13 Feb 1945

Sampson, John J., 1881-1972

Brown, Lavenia S., w/o John J. Sampson, 1888-1937

Eddy, Sarah M., 1836-1925

Eddy, Arra, 1857-1929

Chace, Howard L., 1862-1946

Davis, Catherine, w/o Howard L. Chace, 1862-1945

Chace, Walter L., 1872-1938

Place, Linnie M., w/o Walter L. Chace, 1881-1970

Cobb, Jason H., d 23 July 1885 aged 77 yrs

Luther, James, d 1 Jan 1859 aged 78 yrs

Luther, Lydia, w/o James Luther, d 2 May 1836 aged 48 yrs

Luther, Joseph, s/o James & Lydia Luther, b 4 Jan 1828, d 3 Dec 1853

Luther, Lydia, d/o James & Lydia Lutehr, 1820-1896

Arnold, Franklin G., b 11 Sept 1858, d 5 Jan 1940

Wood, Angeline H., w/o Franklin G. Arnold, b 30 June 1859, d 1 Dec 1916

Arnold, Mary W., b 30 Oct 1886, d 8 April 1967

Simmons, Charles A., 1879-1964

Simmons, Josephine H., w/o Charles A. Simmons, 1888-....

Simmons, Louis A., s/o Charles & Josephine Simmons, 1909-1927

Weeks, Maria, w/o William Weeks, b 9 March 1830, d 3 Dec 1890

Lawton, Perry, d 1 June 1885 aged 58 yrs

Lawton, Mary A., w/o Perry Lawton, d 8 April 1896 aged 48 yrs

Brown, William W., d 17 May 1892 aged 37 yrs 9 mos 17 days

Brown, Clara B., w/o William W. Brown, 1859-1945

Gardner, Earle R., b 19 July 1896, d 1 Sept 1896

Bailey, Robert, b 26 Dec 1832, d 9 Nov 1907

Bailcy, Pluma A., w/o Robert Bailey, b 17 Feb 1857, d 24 Sept 1897

Bailey, Helen G., d/o Robert & Pluma Bailey, 1888-1964
Simmons, William A., 1854-1896
Simmons, Mary A., w/o William A. Simmons, 1862-1903
Simmons, George A., s/o William A. & Mary A. Simmons, 1877-1878
Eddy, Stephen, 1813-1900
Eddy, Mary, w/o Stephen Eddy, 1820-1896
Eddy, Isaac W., s/o Stephen & Mary Eddy, 1857-1862
Eddy, Mary E., d/o Stephen & Mary Eddy, 1852-1862
Eddy, Andrew J., s/o Stepehn & Mary Eddy, 1850-1862
Eddy, George A., s/o Stephen & Mary Eddy, 1846-1862
Hope, John R., d 30 Nov 1897 aged 44 yrs 3 mos
Hope, Charles E., d 30 Aug 1935 aged 72 yrs
Bullock, Mary K., 1871-1958
Chace, Enoch, b 20 Feb 1828, d 7 Dec 1904
Gardner, Mary S., w/o Enoch Chace, b 17 Dec 1829, d 17 Sept 1911
Iacoma, Shirley B., 1895-1948
Pierce, Lydia A., b 6 March 1839, d 26 June 1927
French, Nancy J., b 22 May 1841, d 29 Oct 1915
Gardner, Frederick L., b 2 Sept 1875, d 23 Dec 1958
Lake, Isabel W., w/o Frederick L. Gardner, b 3 March 1874, d 24 March
    1959
Gardner, Andrew G., s/o Frederick & Isabel Gardner, b 11 July 1911, d 21
    June 1919
Chace, James T., 1820-1893
Chace, Elizabeth, w/o Jame T. Chace, 1834-1904
Hope, Henry, d 22 April 1886 aged 72 yrs 10 mos
Hope, Susan, w/o Henry Hope, d 30 Nov 1895 aged 74 yrs 1 mo
Chase, Elijah Pitts, b 1 Oct 1822, d 13 Dec 1910
Edson, Jane, w/o Elijah Pitts Chase, b 2 Jan 1819, d 9 Jan 1903
Hope, Sarah, d/o ELijah & Jane Hope, b 1 June 1859, d 17 Dec 1937
Ormerod, James, 1843-1906
Ormerod, Ellen, w/o James Ormerod, ...
Ormerod, Elizabeth, 1873-1948
Ormerod, George, 1875-1912
Ormerod, Mary E., w/o George Ormerod, 1872-1947
Ormerod, Riley, 1841-1883
Ormerod, Harriet, w/o Riley Ormerod, 1842-1921
Ormerod, Ida, 1878-1912
Ormerod, Jane, 1870-1934
Spraque, John T., b 1816, d 12 March 1889

Sprague, Cynthia B., w/o John T. Sprague, d 19 May 1887 aged 72 yrs
Sprague, Cynthia E., d 28 April 1873 aged 26 yrs
Hibbard, John E., 1869-....
Hibbard, Susan A., w/o John E. Hibbard, 1871-....
Phillips, James L., 1848-1913
Phillips, Mercy, w/o James L. Phillips, 1851-1923
Phillips, Charlie L., 1878-1884
Parkes, Anna, w/o William L. Phillips, 1867-1934
Beette, Frank W., 1871-1940
Phillips, Susan, w/o Frank W. Beette, 1874-1955
Sherman, Howard N., 1893-1975
Phillips, Jennie, w/o Howard N. Sherman, 1875-1950
Robinson, Stephen W., b 12 Oct 1845, d 6 July 1920
Daley, Eliza J., w/o Stephen W. Robinson, b 7 April 1849, d 1 May 1920
Daley, Anson S., b 19 July 1820, d 28 June 1884
Earle, Lydia S., w/o Anson S. Daley, b 6 June 1826, d 11 Jan 1907
Daley, Abbie E., b 23 June 1846, d 6 Feb 1906
Earle, Edward S., 1795-1883
Sherman, Eleanor D., w/o Edward S. Earle, 1793-1879
Earle, Clarissa D., d/o Edward & Eleanor Earle, 1821-1841
Earle, James S., s/o Edward & Eleanor Earle, 1828-1856
Earle, William H., s/o Edward & Eleanor Earle, 1833-1846
Slade, Rufus S., 1813-1884
Slade, Mercy, w/o Rufus S. Slade, 1811-1891
Slade, Mary S., d/o Rufus & Mercy Slade, 1844-1911
Sisson, Martha, 1779-1863
Burt, Esther, 1795-1832
Jones, Thomas J., 1848-1935
Slade, Ella, w/o Thomas J. Jones, 1843-1931
Phillips, LaRoche, b 20 May 1812, d 29 April 1883
Phillips, Sarah B., w/o LaRoche Phillips, b 27 Nov 1812, 2 May 1884
Howe, George W., d 2 March 1900 aged 66 yrs 2 mos 16 days
Howe, Eliza S., w/o George W. Howe, d 4 Nov 1886 aged 47 yrs 6 mos 8
    days
Henriken, Edwin J., 1888-1957
Moody, Essie L., ...
Moody, Sarah B., 1843-1928
Moody, Edward S., 1846-1931
Kossoi, Hattie, d/o Abraham & Sony Kossoi, b 9 Oct 1885, d 6 Oct 1894
Briggs, James, b 8 June 1822, d 17 April 1899

Briggs, Hannah, b 6 Feb 1818, d 1 June 1894

Sherman, Daniel, b 21 April 1784, d 24 Dec 1877

Sherman, Nancy, b 20 Nov 1780, d 4 Nov 1859

Briggs, Abel, b 19 Dec 1822, d 9 Oct 1904

Briggs, Charles A., MD, b 25 Dec 1863, d 14 Dec 1942

Briggs, Mary F., w/o Dr. Charles A. Briggs, 1864-1957

Briggs, Edith A., d/o Dr. Charles & Mary Briggs, 1895-1969

Sherman, Eben, d 12 Aug 1874 aged 87 yrs 5 mos 6 days

Sherman, Silence B., w/o Eben Sherman, d 5 Feb 1869 aged 67 yrs

Mason, Evelyn E., b 11 Nov 1830, d 19 Sept 1923

Sherman, Elmima A., b 13 Jan 1837, d 5 Feb 1916

Osborn, Sarah M., b 11 Dec 1870, d 13 Jan 1963

Osborn, Mattie S., b 19 Oct 1868, d 31 Jan 1871

Kingsley, Julia, b 2 Feb 1905-....

Kingsley, Esther, b 23 Sept 1913-....

Kingsley, Gardner, b 21 Feb 1825, d 12 Nov 1897

Rogers, Rhoda C., w/o Gardner Kingsley, b 3 Feb 1830, d 8 Oct 1900

Kingsley, Edwin G., b 2 Sept 1855, d 22 Feb 1865

Kingsley, Martha G., b 11 May 1866, d 4 July 1954

Kingsley, Charles E., b 20 Nov 1867, d 6 Jan 1954

Peckham, Lena A., w/o Charles E. Kingsley, b 29 Dec 1874, d 29 Aug
1961

Luther, John, d 11 Dec 1850 aged 55 yrs 6 mos 28 days

Luther, Partheria G., w/o John Luther, d 21 Sept 1870 aged 68 yrs 5 mos
18 days

Wilbur, Daniel W., b 13 Nov 1845, d 16 Oct 1923

Brown, Marion F., w/o Daniel W. Wilbur, b 14 Sept 1848, d 17 Oct 1918

Pearse, William H., b 28 July 1871, d 4 Feb 1923

Wilbur, Bertha F., w/o William H. Pearse, b 7 Sept 1871, d 28 May 1902

Pearse, Elizabeth, d/o William & Bertha Pearse, b 29 Aug 1890, d 17 Oct
1911

Wilbur, Daniel, b 14 Nov 1818, d 19 June 1896

Wilbur, Nancy O., w/o Daniel Wilbur, b 25 Sept 1822, d 22 March 1860

Wilbur, Sarah E., w/o Daniel Wilbur, b 20 Nov 1833, d 2 Aug 1896

Wilbur, William B., s/o Daniel & Nancy O. Wilbur, d 3 Sept 1893 aged
43 yrs 2 mos 3 days

Wilbur, Roswell, s/o Daniel & Nancy O. Wilbur, d 20 Sept 1876 aged 22
yrs 8 mos

Osborn, Rev. Joseph W., Ph.D, b 23 July 1836, d 4 Jan 1889

Osborn, Martha A., w/o Rev. Joseph W. Osborn, b 23 Feb 1834, d 6
   March 1914
Osborn, Mary G., b 24 Oct 1863, d 20 March 1941

Swansea Town Hall
Main Street
Swamsea, MA
02777

Swansea Public Library
Main Street
Swansea, MA
02777

Bennett, Aaron A., 1842-1918
Bennett, Ellen, w/o Aaron A. Bennett, 1840-1880
Dupee, Sarah F., 1844-1925
Bennett, Frank A., 1869-1890
Bennett, Geogre E., 1867-1893
Murphy, James, 1863-1928
Tate, Elizabeth, w/o James Murphy, 1856-1927
Bennett, Willard H., b 20 Feb 1857, d 19 Nov 1939
Powers, Ida L., w/o Willard H. Bennett, b 25 Feb 1856, d 13 Feb 1920
Folger, Arlington A., 1858-1929
Hunt, Johanna, w/o Arlington A. Folger, 1864-1952
Procter, Braman, 1896-1937
Stewart, Florence Mary, w/o Braman Procter, 1886-1969
Whiting, Lewis L., 1864-1920
Whiting, S. Annabelle C., w/o Lewis L. Whiting, 1857-1913
Tillson, Joseph, b 11 March 1801, d 10 Aug 1882
Tillson, Captain Nehemiah, b 6 Feb 1768, d 25 Aug 1846
Morse, Abigail, w/o Capt. Nehemiah Tillson, b 15 Aug 1768, d 26 June
    1852
Fales, Frederick, 1855-1917
Fales, A. Isabel, w/o Frederick Fales, d 9 May 1895 aged 37 yrs
Fales, Walter R., 1846-1927
Briggs, Alden C., b 25 Aug 1852, d 14 March 1923
Peck, Sarah Jane, w/o Alden C. Briggs, b 5 March 1847, d 28 Feb 1892
Willard, Elijah, b 17 May 1813, d 3 June 1881
Jackson, Mary A., w/o Elijah Willard, b 27 May 1815, d 4 June 1873
Willard, Artemas, s/o Elijah & Mary A. Willard, b 21 June 1851, d 8
    April 1913
Willard, Mary Ballem, d/o Elijah & Mary A. Willard, b 14 July 1849, d
    25 April 1924
Porter, Samuel King, MD, b 14 Dec 1822, d 25 Feb 1899
Gilman, Sarah Ann, w/o Dr. Samuel King Porter, b 27 Jan 1824, d 17 Feb
    1892
Coleman, John F., b 3 March 1816, d 15 April 1888

Coleman, Clarissa M., w/o John F. Coleman, b 2 Nov 1818, d 4 July 1895
Coleman, Albert W., b 16 March 1844, d 13 Nov 1905
Nash, John A., 1857-1939
Nash, Nellie M., w/o John A. Nash, b 13 Dec 1858, d 13 Nov 1889
Ware, John E., 1874-1947
Johnston, Lily, w/o John E. Ware, 1886-1963
Ware, E. Burnett, 1919-1968
Ware, John, 1912-1973
Fiske, Rev. Frederick Augustus, 1816-1879
Nelson, Anna, w/o Rev. Frederick A. Fiske, 1812-1848
Woods, Abbie, widow of Rev. Frederick A. Fiske, 1834-1925
Ward, Francis E., b Dec 1862, d Feb 1924
Ward, Elizabeth N., w/o Francis E. Ward, b Feb 1856, d Sept 1895
Cook, Alonzo, 1828-1917
Cook, Cordelia M., w/o Alonzo Cook, 1830-1913
Cook, Jessie E., 1851-1880
Guild, Florence Cook, 1858-1939
Guild, Arthur C., 1887-1977
Guild, Gertrude C., w/o Arthur C. Guild, 1895-1967
Fales, Francis L., d 7 Feb 1868 aged 8 yrs
Fales, Dixon D., d 13 Aug 1882 aged 77 yrs
Fales, David M., d 18 Sept 1879 aged 74 yrs
Fales, Susan Helen, w/o David M. Fales, d 24 June 1890 aged 64 yrs
Brown, Alexander, 1813-1889
Brown, Margaret, 1814-1896
Brown, Daniel, 1841-1904
Brown, Hester A., 1844-1933
Gerould, Joseph B., d 27 Nov 1875 aged 74 yrs
Gerould, Fanny C., w/o Joseph B. Gerould, d 9 Jan 1884 aged 76 yrs
Warren, Frances E., w/o Issac B. Warren, d 26 July 1870 aged 39 yrs
Warren, Arthur C., s/o Isaac B. & Frances E. Warren, d 30 Sept 1857
    aged 9 mos
George, William E., b 1824 Wrentham, MA, d 1885, Petersham, MA
Goddard, Lucy Augusta, w/o William E. George, 1836-1900
Ware, Hiram, 1827-1904
Kemp, Nancy, w/o Hiram Ware, 1833-1906
Ware, Emily J., 1880-1929
George, Edson W., b 16 July 1848, d 23 Nov 1935
George, Nettie M., w/o Edson W. George, b 1 April 1848, d 26 Nov 1884
George, Nellie F., w/o Edson W. George, b 15 Jan 1853, d 9 Aug 1897

George, Fannie L., b 20 July 1872, d 9 July 1875

George, J. Edson, b 27 April 1876, d 5 April 1896

Ware, John, d 2 Jan 1796 aged 62 yrs

Ware, Ezra, d 2 Feb 1815 aged 74 yrs

Ware, Oliver, d Jan 18 (broken)

Smith, William D., 1816-1881

Lenkfield, Adelaide, w/o William D. Smith, 1836-1907

Smith, Laura M., d/o William & Adelaide Smith, 1860-1862

Smith, William, s/o William & Adelaide Smith, 1862-1937

Smith, Mary A., d/o William & Adelaide Smith, 1866-1939

Smith, Maria F., d/o William & Adelaide Smith, 1869-1953

Smith, Colonel Samuel, 1789-1854

Dupee, Polly, w/o Col. Samuel Smith, 1791-1857

Smith, Charles, s/o Col. Samuel & Polly Smith, 1811-1835

Smith, Samuel, s/o Col. Samuel & Polly Smith, 1813-1841

Pond, Mary S., d/o Col. Samuel & Polly Smith, 1814-1846

Smith, Laura A., d/o Col. Samuel & Polly Smith, 1822-1848

Gay, Almeda, w/o William S. Gay, d 18 July 1837 aged 29 yrs

Pierce, John, d 30 May 1846 aged 37 yrs

Lawson, Christina, 1849-1911

Hamilton, Charles Jr., b 10 Aug 1856, d 11 Feb 1935 Wrentham, MA

Fuller, Bertha M., w/o Charles Hamilton Jr., b 6 Sept 1859, d 17 Nov 1931

Hamilton, Charles, Master Mariner, b 1 Nov 1826 Boston, MA, d 25 Dec 1887 Wrentham, MA

Fisher, Martha E., w/o Charles Hamilton, b 25 Sept 1828, d 8 May 1911

Kendall, Charles, 1840-1935, A member of Co 11, 45th Regt. MVM

Kendall, Emily M., 1840-1884

Kendall, Jennie A., 1868-1942

Love, Charles E., b 10 May 1834, d 25 Nov 1891

Procter, Thomas, b 14 Jan 1811, d 22 March 1885

Braman, Zeolyde A.H., w/o Thomas Proctor, b 29 Sept 1816, d 10 Feb 1887

Proctor, William Melville, b 7 Nov 1849, d 26 March 1925

Ware, Alice Pamela, w/o William M. Proctor, b 22 Feb 1851, d 7 Dec 1928

Coleman, Erwin N., s/o Harvey B. & Abby Coleman, d 20 July 1862 aged 3 yrs 2 mos 16 days

Coleman, Harvey, d 11 Oct 1865 aged 80 yrs 10 mos 4 days

Coleman, Job, d 14 Nov 1830 aged 70 yrs

Coleman, Anne, d 15 Oct 1844

Force, Lyman, s/o Elijah & Hannah Force, d 1 June 1812 aged 25 yrs

Force, Sophia, d/o Elijah & Hannah Force, d 20 Dec 1812 aged 10 yrs

Bennett, Edward H., b 20 Oct 1806, d 9 April 1896

Bennett, Susan D., w/o Edward H. Bennett, b 7 Feb 1805, d 13 Nov 1885

Dale, John, d 15 Feb 1813 aged 73 yrs

Dale, Catherine, w/o John Dale, d 10 May 1825 aged 62 yrs

Farrington, Bradford, b 12 May 1812 Wrentham, MA, d 31 July 1869
   Boston, MA

Barnes, Henry, d 30 April 1867 aged 27 yrs

Barnes, Norman K., d 22 April 1864 Camp Mead, RI, aged 34 yrs

Mayshaw, Henry, b 29 March 1843, d 28 Jan 1920

Mayshaw, Leon, b 26 May 1876, d 30 June 1900

Barnes, Adaline, b 4 Dec 1808, d 5 May 1885

Barnes, Amory, b 18 Feb 1806, d 28 Oct 1893

Fairfield, George Rex, 1824-1896

Starkey, Charlotte I., w/o George Rex Fairfield, 1832-1912

Guild, Charles T., 1842-1919, A member of Co G 40th NY Vols

Fairfield, Irene, w/o Charles T. Guild, 1855-1940

Hartshorn, Henry A., 1847-1925

Cobb, Ida May, w/o Henry A. Hartshorn, 1854-1898

Fiske, David F., b 22 Feb 1828, d 17 Sept 1841

Fiske, William D., b 4 Jan 1829, d 23 April 1872

Coleman, Abigail, w/o Harvey Coleman, b 31 Oct 1821, d 9 Dec 1900

Coleman, Harvey, d 17 June 1894 aged 72 yrs 2 mos

Mann, Amherst, d 20 May 1840 aged 80 yrs

Mann, Polly, w/o Amherst Mann, d 29 March 1847 aged 89 yrs

Mann, Timothy, d 23 June 1826 aged 31 yrs

Fales, Mary W., d 22 Dec 1859 aged 21 yrs

Fales, William, d 29 Sept 1856 aged 58 yrs

Willard, Ashbal, 1837-1916, A member of Co D 40th Regt Mass Vols

Willard, Harriet E., w/o Ashbal Willard, 1838-1928

Young, Horace J., 1878-1955

Willard, Florence L., w/o Horace J. Young, 1879-1965

Rand, Samuel, d 21 Aug 1852 aged 82 yrs

Farrington, David S., b 12 Sept 1829, d 9 Feb 1899

Farrington, Phebe A., w/o David S. Farrington, b 6 Dec 1837, d 24 Feb
   1898

Fisher, Eliza A., w/o George W. Fisher, d 17 Nov 1880 aged 8 yrs 7 mos
   4 days

Fisher, George W., d 23 Feb 1858 aged 48 yrs 2 mos 1 day

Fisher, James, d 12 March 1866 aged 82 yrs

Fisher, Rebecca, w/o James Fisher, d 6 Nov 1846 aged 56 yrs

Fisher, Harrison Jones, d 24 Feb 1816 aged 3 weeks

Fisher, Hon. Josiah J., d 15 Aug 1838 aged 52 yrs

Norton, Jerusha, w/o Hon. Josiah Fisher, b 5 April 1789, d 1 April 1867

Fisher, Elizabeth Stanley, d/o Hon. Josiah & Jerusha Fisher, b 16 Oct
    1822, d 8 Aug 1903

Fisher, Josiah Jones, s/o Josiah J. & Jerusha Fisher, d 17 March 1854
    aged 25 yrs

Fishe, George J., b 4 Aug 1829, d 4 Dec 1868 Nice, France

Fiske, Maria J., w/o George J. Fiske, b 5 Dec 1817, d 8 Feb 1876

Fisher, F. Angenette, w/o George H. Fisher, b 19 July 1829, d 9 Oct 1884

White, Henry M., 1818-1898

White, Harriet, w/o Henry M. White, 1818-1897

White, Emma H., d/o Henry & Harriet White, 1849-1907

George, William E., 1817-1886

Lewis, Cornelia D., w/o William H. George, 1824-1886

Metcalf, Frank E., 1852-1880

George, Anna M., w/o Frank E. Metcalf, 1846-1886

George, Captain Artemas, 1783-1848

Grant, Anne, w/o Capt. Artemas George, 1785-1840

George, Artemas A., s/o Capt. Artemas & Ann George, 1810-1829

George, Thomas A., s/o Capt. Artemas & Anne George, 1815-1903

George, Hannah M., d/o Capt. Artemas & Anne George, 1821-1826

Cowell, Martha, w/o Captain Artemas George, 1786-1865

Cook, Oliver, b 3 Dec 1838, d 4 March 1879

Cook, Amelia T., w/o Oliver Cook, b 19 May 1835, d 5 Aug 1877

Cook, Daniel A., b 28 March 1801, d 4 Aug 1877

Cook, Eunice E., w/o Daniel A. Cook, b 25 June 1810, d 13 Dec 1886

Cook, Eunice Frances, b 30 Nov 1843, d 3 Sept 1845

Helfron, Calista, w/o John G. Helfron, d 31 Dec 1861 aged 20 yrs

Hawes, Ebenezer, b 25 May 1800, d 10 Nov 1890

Hawes, Eliza, w/o Ebenezer Hawes, b 30 March 1800, d 7 Sept 1840

Bennett, Laura, w/o Ebenezer Hawes, 1816-1907

Stone, David T., 1835-1926

Stone, Sarah J., w/o David T. Stone, 1840-1912

Stone, David Stanley, 1881-1916

Stone, Helen J., 1861-1944

Cobb, William., 1807-1865

Cobb, Jane T., 1808-1878

Cobb, William Jr., 1844-1844

Bean, Rev. Joseph, d 12 Dec 1784 aged 66 yrs

Messenger, Rev. Henry, d 30 March 1750 aged 55 yrs

Mann, Rev. Samuel, d 22 May 1719 aged 72 yrs

Porter, William G., d 17 Feb 1868 aged 65 yrs

Porter, Hannah M., w/o William G. Porter, d 22 Feb 1882 aged 79 yrs 9 mos 10 days

Hawes, Cynthia, d/o Daniel & Jemima Hawes, d 21 Feb 1878 aged 77 yrs

Hawes, Jemima, d/o Daniel & Jemima Hawes, d 23 March 1891 aged 94 yrs

Ide, James A., d Feb 1888

Ide, Betsey, w/o James A. Ide, d 14 May 1853

Ide, James, d 23 Aug 1844 aged 75 yrs

Markham, Chester, 1793-1881

Day, Martha, w/o Chester Markham, 1791-1864

Standish, Lewis H., 1828-....

Markham, Martha, w/o Lewis H. Standish, 1827-1895

Ober, George Hawes, b 2 Oct 1841, d 29 May 1863

Ober, Horace B., 1849-1933

Deming, Clara L., w/o Horace B. Ober, d 28 Nov 1914

Ware, William D., 1815-1888

Ware, Betsey A., d/o William & Betsey Ware, d 7 Feb 1857 aged 27 yrs

Harding, Lydia R., 1805-1878

Darling, Anna, b 6 Oct 1790, d 24 Oct 1878

Heminway, E. Dexter, 1817-1896

Scott, Catherine Fleming, w/o E. Dexter Heminway, 1825-1892

Pond, Charles R., b 14 Feb 1827, d 27 Nov 1905

Pond, Rebecca, w/o Charles R. Pond, b 23 July 1827, d 4 Sept 1854

Pond, Helen L., b 27 Dec 1832, d 18 May 1878

Aldrich, Charles M., b 22 July 1847, d 10 Nov 1906

Aldrich, Eva F., w/o Charles M. Aldrich, b 27 Sept 1857, d 19 Dec 1906

George, Catherine A., d/o Jesse & Hannah George & w/o Lafayette Bates, b 26 July 1826, d 22 April 1879

Felt, Daniel Ide, b 28 June 1816, d 3 March 1870

Rawson, Harriet, w/o Daniel Ide Felt, b 9 Jan 1805, d 1 Dec 1866

Ober, Rev. Benjamin, b 4 April 1805, d 8 Sept 1883

Hawes, Nancy, w/o Rev. Benjamin Ober, b 27 Sept 1814, d 6 July 1867

Gilmore, Warren K., 1836-1917

Gilmore, Ellen M., w/o Warren K. Gilmore, 1845-1937

Gilmore, Evelyn C., w/o Warren K. Gilmore, 1831-1862
Dart, Gustavus F., 1831-1905
Dart, Adiliza, w/o Augustus F. Dart, 1833-1934
Pond, Gilbert W., 1816-1874
Markham, Phebe A., w/o Gilbert W. Pond, 1823-1887
Markham, Jane A., 1831-1912
Everett, Oliver, 1817-1900
Everett, Delia, w/o Oliver Everett, 1860-1910
Everett, Captain George, b 22 April 1785, d 11 June 1804
Everett, Nancy, w/o Capt. George Everett, b 22 Jan 1782, d 16 May 1867
Shaw, Maria, w/o Latimer R. Shaw, b 2 Sept 1799, d 20 June 1841
Shaw, Louisa Baldwin, b 15 March 1835, d 6 Dec 1836
Stanton, Frank A., b 25 June 1867, d 24 Jan 1890
Aldrich, Sarah Jane, d/o Artemas & Janet Aldrich, b 17 July 1832, d 24
    June 1868
Stanton, Hattie, w/o George A. Stanton & d/o Artemas & Janet Aldrich, b
    24 Dec 1844, d 4 June 1883
Aldrich, Artemas, b 3 Jan 1809, d 9 Sept 1887
Mann, Janet T., w/o Artemas Aldrich, b 23 March 1808, d 20 Jan 1893
Aldrich, Amos, b 10 Feb 1785, d 26 April 1871
Aldrich, Sally, w/o Amos Aldrich, b 10 Jan 1782, d 10 Oct 1865
Holmes, Robert P., d 1 June 1850
Holmes, Anna Maria, w/o Robert P. Holmes, 1822-1905
Farrington, Charles Edward, b 4 March 1831, d 9 April 1834
Farrrington, Nelson A., b 31 Dec 1832, d 13 April 1904
Farrington, Charles, b 28 Oct 1838, d 17 July 1906
Farrington, Annie Louise, MD, b 30 Aug 1871, d 2 Oct 1897
Farrington, Daniel Sumner, b 9 Nov 1865, d 31 May 1935
Farrington, Charles Wilde, b 12 Aug 1802, d 6 Feb 1894
Butts, Ann C., w/o Charles Wilde Farrington, b 30 Oct 1799, d 30 Jan
    1893
Hitchcock, Sarah G., b 6 Dec 1820, d 19 March 1896
Hawes, John A., b 1 July 1838, d 3 June 1875
Hawes, Ellen S., w/o John A. Hawes & d/o Artemas & Ann George, b 18
    April 1826, d 6 April 1858 Richmond VA
Cowell, Horace, s/o Hiram & Susan Cowell, d 5 March 1870 Santa Cruz,
    California aged 26 yrs
Cowell, Hiram, b 27 Oct 1804, d 31 May 1845
Fisher, Susan, w/o Hiram Cowell, b 17 June 1813, d 12 Dec 1887
Fisher, Preston, 1785-1849

Lovell, Huldah, w/o Preston Fisher, 1785-1870
Phinney, Alfred, 1862-1926
Ide, Mary, w/o Alfred Phinney, 1860-1938
Cowell, William, 1777-1867
Cowell, Ruth, 1788-1867
Cowell, Jemima M., 1817-1846
Cowell, Elizabeth H., 1829-1854
Cowell, Leonidas, 1811-1894
Cowell, Nancy L., 1823-1904
Blake, George E., b 28 Oct 1859, d 16 Aug 1947
Blake, Deacon George, 1833-1920
Day, Harriet A., w/o Deacon George Blake, 1831-1909
Fisher, Harriet P., w/o Charles Messenger, b 12 July 1812, d 15 April
    1894
Felt, Annie B., 1824-1896
Felt, Col. Oliver, 1787-1846
Shepard, Almira, w/o Col. Oliver Felt, 1787-1873
Felt, Martha B., d/o Oliver & Almira Felt, 1814-1858
Felt, Almira S., d/o Oliver & Almira Felt, 1816-1860
Felt, Edmund J., 1812-1892
Whitney, Adeliza T., w/o Edmund J. Felt, 1811-1861
Felt, Emma W., d/o Edmund & Adeliza Felt, 1848-1848
Felt, James M., s/o Edmund & Adeliza Felt, 1841-1858
Felt, Oliver, 1853-1925
Owen, Carrie B., w/o Oliver Felt, 1863-1892
Cowell, John, b 11 Nov 1809, d 29 Aug 1898
Carpenter, Laura A., w/o John Cowell, b 3 May 1811, d 4 May 1888
Lane, Edith Cowell, eldest d/o Nathan & Ellen M. Lane, b 16 Feb 1876, d
    23 Sept 1941
Lane, Nathan, b 31 Aug 1845, d 23 Nov 1931
Cowell, Ellen M., w/o Nathan Lane & d/o John & Laura Cowell, b 14 Feb
    1848, d 30 May 1909
Fisher, Josiah C., b 15 Feb 1836, d 10 May 1836
Fisher, Isabella M., w/o Josiah C. Fisher, b 11 March 1834, d 19 Nov
    1852
Fisher, Abigail W., b 13 Nov 1831, d 6 Jan 1874
Fisher, Carlo M., b 12 May 1800, d 13 Aug 1872
Sayles, Dutee, d 3 Dec 1851 aged 57 yrs
Sayles, Nancy, w/o Dutee Sayles, d 25 Aug 1825 aged 26 yrs
Sayles, Betsey, w/o Dutee Sayles, d 9 April 1881 aged 80 yrs

Sayles, Horatio F., d 9 June 1854 aged 32 yrs

Pond, Hollis, 1804-1886

Williams, Abigail W., w/o Hollis Pond & Ebenezer & Abigail Williams, b 12 Sept 1799 Mansfield, MA, d 25 July 1871

Pond, Charles, s/o Hollis & Abigail Pond, d 11 Aug 1840 aged 1 yr 10 mos

Kellock, Henry, s/o Calvin & Jerusha K. Fisher, d 18 Sept 1843 aged 9 1/2 mos

Fisher, Anna Brastow, 1836-1924

Payson, Nabby, b 8 Oct 1786, d 13 Aug 1869

Fales, Samuel, d 8 June 1843 aged 84 yrs 10 mos

Fales, Abigail, w/o Samuel Fales, d 2 Nov 1824 aged 63 yrs

Fairbanks, Sophia C., b 22 March 1802, d 4 Jan 1849

Pond, Huldah, w/o Increase Pond, d 11 April 1825 aged 71 yrs

Pond, Increase, 1742-1807

Metcalf, Ellenor, d/o David & Ann S. Metcalf, d Sept 1827 aged 4 yrs

Craige, Moses, d 20 March 1850 aged 95 yrs

Craige, Annah, w/o Moses Craige, d 16 May 1820 aged 63 yrs

Williams, Rebecca, d/o Rev. William Williams & w/o Captain Lewis Fisher, d 12 May 1860 aged 87 yrs

Fisher, Lewis, d 23 April 1832 aged 69 yrs

Fisher, Mary A., b 17 April 1803, d 26 July 1857

Fisher, Emily J., b 2 April 1826, d 13 Jan 1847

Hawes, Timothy, b 25 Dec 1808, d 18 Dec 1842

Cobb, Ethan, b 17 Oct 1817, d 13 March 1896

Dean, Louisa C. H., w/o Dr. Oliver Dean, 1815-1902

Hawes, Sally, w/o Ebenezer Hawes, d 17 March 1853 aged 83 yrs 2 mos

Hawes, Ebenezer, d 17 Sept 1837 aged 69 yrs

Fisher, Abby V., 1832-1914

Hawes, Warren, d 7 Aug 1888 aged 81 yrs 11 mos 16 days

Hawes, Cynthia, w/o Warren Hawes, d 23 May 1893 aged 83 yrs 10 mos 16 days

Fairbanks, John, s/o Ebenezer & Sally Hawes, d 1 Sept 1825 aged 24 yrs

Fisher, Luther, s/o Luther & Abigail Fisher, b 13 June 1829 Wrentham , MA, d 17 Sept 1848, Harvard MA

Fisher, Luther, d 27 June 1836 aged 37 yrs 11 mos

Whiting, Captain Timothy, d 25 July 1818 aged 57 yrs

Whitaker, Margaret, w/o Richard Whitaker Jr., d 27 Dec 1827 aged 24 yrs

Cobb, Joseph, d 14 Jan 1868 aged 66 yrs

Cobb, Cecilla, w/o Joseph Cobb, d 30 Aug 1853 aged 40 yrs

Messenger, Adeline, w/o Thomas N. Wood, d 21 Feb 1884 aged 54 yrs 3
mos 23 days
Messenger, Horatio N., d 8 March 1877 aged 76 yrs 8 mos 17 days
Messenger, Pelitiah, d 19 Oct 1814 aged 45 yrs
Messenger, Polly, w/o Pelitiah Messenger, d 20 May 1827 aged 56 yrs
Messenger, Charles H., s/o Horatio & Lois Messenger, d 28 Nov 1828
aged 2 yrs 3 mos 24 days
Ruggles, Calvin D., 1840-1929
Bullard, Harriet E., w/o Calvin D. Ruggles, 1841-1867
Furber, Sarah, w/o Calvin D. Ruggles, 1828-1921
Ruggles, Fred, s/o Calvin & Sarah Ruggles, 1873-1874
Ruggles, Oliver, 1793-1859
Ruggles, Lucinda J., w/o Oliver Ruggles, 1797-1881
Ruggles, David, s/o Oliver & Lucinda Ruggles, 1827-1838
Ruggles, Henry, s/o Oliver & Lucinda Ruggles, 3 mos
Ruggles, Gilbert Fuller, s/o Oliver & Lucinda Ruggles, 1830-1853
Ruggles, Adelaide S., w/o Gilbert F. Ruggles, 1833-1869
Bugbee, William B., MD, b 25 May 1822, d 2 April 1856
Parker, Emily S., b 3 June 1832, d 17 Nov 1884
Mann, Howard, b 30 July 1799, d 14 Jan 1864
Mann, Betsey I., w/o Howard Mann, b 25 Sept 1798, d 13 Aug 1828
Mann, Susan I., b 2 Oct 1802, d 28 Feb 1897
Mann, Elizabeth G., b 29 Dec 1826, d 15 March 1846
Mann, Susan I., b 4 Aug 1823, d 20 March 1837
Mann, James H., b 4 April 1841, d 12 Nov 1856
Mann, Albert H., b 5 May 1831, d 26 Oct 1903
Cobb, Captain Hermon, b 24 Nov 1776, d 19 Aug 1845
Cobb, Polly, w/o Capt. Hermon Cobb, b 1 Oct 1780, d 19 Nov 1867
Cobb, Hermon Jr., b 5 Oct 1807, d 20 Dec 1860
Cobb, Lucy, w/o Hermon Cobb Jr., b 26 May 1807, d 22 June 1887
Fisher, Elias, 1793-1869
Wyman, Frances, w/o Elias Fisher, 1797-1878
Fisher, Susan Frances, d/o Elias & Frances Fisher, 1834-1835
Fisher, Ann Louise, d/o Elias & Frances Fisher, 1823-1837
Fisher, Abby Maria, d/o Elias & Frances Fisher, 1831-1866
Fisher, Calvin Jr., d 13 Nov 1869 aged 72 yrs
Fisher, Ann Eliza, w/o Calvin Fisher Jr., d 14 Dec 1838 aged 35 yrs
Kellock, Jerusha, w/o Calvin Fisher Jr., d 17 Dec 1870 aged 60 yrs
Bugbee, Samuel S., MD, b 8 Dec 1813, d 3 May 1844
Bugbee, Oliver, b 7 Dec 1815, d 10 July 1835

Bugbee, Samuel, MD, b 4 June 1781, d 14 July 1841
Bugbee, Eliza D., w/o Dr. Samuel Bugbee, b 5 June 1786, d 17 July 1859
Blackburn, Nancy H., b 24 Oct 1808, d 22 Dec 1868
Bryant, Eliza D., b 2 Oct 1826, d 1 March 1870
Bugbee, Harriet F., b 14 Sept 1818, d 9 May 1837

Cook Cemetery
West Street
Wrentham, Massachusetts

Ballou, Levi, d 14 June 1836 aged 53 yrs
Ballou, Hepza, w/o Levi Ballou, d 20 Nov 1860
Ballou, Levi Thompson, b 13 March 1816, d 22 Jan 1899
Ballou, Louisa Seymour, w/o Levi Thompson Ballou, b 24 Aug 1815, d 14
    Jan 1899
Ballou, George Ripley, b 3 April 1846, d 30 July 1890
Ballou, Julius Stanley, b 30 May 1851, d 6 Nov 1881
Fisher, Charles, b 22 Sept 1808, d 20 April 1892
Fisher, Julia A., w/o Charles Fisher, b 25 Jan 1809, d 18 July 1896
Fisher, Otis, d 29 Dec 1864 aged 73 yrs 7 days
Fisher, Aaron, d 16 Nov 1862 aged 69 yrs 5 mos 10 days
Wilder, Louisa B., w/o Aaron Fisher, b May 1811, d 1889
Fisher, Electra R., w/o Jason Tower & d/o Charles & Julia Fisher, d 13
    June 1857 aged 23 yrs
Fisher, Francis B., b 22 May 1843, d 1 March 1890
Fisher, Henry, b 10 May 1835, d 18 Jan 1910
Comsett, James F., 1830-1870
Hopkins, Mary M., w/o James F. Comsett, 1836-1867
Jaber, Mary A., d 29 Jan 1883 aged 74 yrs 9 mos 22 days
Haskel, Cynthia E., b 18 Oct 1843, d 6 Nov 1922
Hopkins, Betsey J., w/o Thomas R. Hopkins & d/o Caleb & Rachel
    Jefferson, d 2 Nov 1856 aged 48 yrs 11 mos
Curley, James A., s/o James & Mary Curley, d 15 Feb 1859 aged 4 yrs
Thompson, Addison, d 2 Oct 1873 aged 65 yrs 2 mos 3 days
Hancock, Sally, w/o Addison Thompson & d/o Samuel & Amey Hancock,
    d April 1838 aged 27 yrs

Cook, Martha A., w/o Addison Thompson, b 18 Dec 1814, d 7 Jan 1892
Thompson, Eugene W., d 9 Sept 1868 aged 23 yrs 10 mos 1 day
Follett, Chester B., 1875-1939
Emery, Agnes, w/o Chester B. Follett, 1875-1927
Metcalf, Amy, d 8 June 1892 aged 61 yrs 3 mos
Cook, George M., s/o Philander & Mary Cook, d 14 Aug 1861 aged 2 yrs
Cook, Frank L., s/o Philander & Mary Cook, d 14 April 1858 aged 2 yrs
Cook, Alice M., d/o Philander & Mary Cook, d April 1859
Cook, Sarah M., d/o Philander & Mary Cook, d 5 Jan 1847 aged 4 yrs
Cook, Mary F., d/o Philander & Mary Cook, d 17 Aug 1849 aged 5 weeks
Cook, Philander P., d 10 Feb 1880 aged 62 yrs
Cook, Mary F., w/o Philander P. Cook, d 8 Oct 1897 aged 74 yrs 3 mos
Metcalf, Silas....
Metcalf, George H., 1820-1906
Metcalf, Hattiet A., w/o Silas Metcalf, 1825-1899
Fisher, Eliab W., b 9 Sept 1825, d 13 May 1853
Fisher, Lewis, b 31 May 1784 Franklin, MA, d 6 June 1858
Fisher, Miriam, w/o Lewis Fisher, b 14 Nov 1787, d 27 Oct 1875
Fisher, Elizabeth M., d/o Lewis & Miriam Fisher, b 29 Jan 1819, d 31
    Dec 1895
Fisher, Abigail G., w/o William Chamberlain, b 10 May 1820, d 31 Aug
    1898
Ray, George E., d 10 March 1888 aged 71 yrs 3 mos 23 days
Ray, Sophronia C., w/o George E. Ray, d 10 June 1879 aged 62 yrs 10 ms
Adams, Eunice M., d/o George & Sophronia Ray, d 12 April 1888 aged
    47 yrs 9 mos 25 days
Cook, Horace, b 18 Jan 1790, d 3 May 1843
Cook, Lucretia, w/o Horace Cook, b 15 Feb 1782, d 15 Aug 1868
Burt, Nellie, w/o Evarad R. Cook, b 12 Dec 1859, d 13 May 1904
Cook, Myrtle Louise, d/o Evarad & Nellie Cook, b 29 March 1892, d 1
    March 1916
Gilmore, William, s/o William & Mary Gilmore, b 11 Dec 1772, d 4 Feb
    1847
Gilmore, Nancy, w/o William Gilmore & d/o Peter & Avis Fales, b 18
    Sept 1775, d 1 Oct 1826
Clark, Betsey, w/o William Gilmore & d/o Onesimus & Lydia Cook, b 4
    Feb 1801, d 10 Jan 1870
Cook, Horace Lyman, b 26 Aug 1816, d 1 Feb 1909
Hawkins, Lucy Ann Esther, w/o Horace Lyman Cook, b 8 Sept 1826, d 29
    Oct 1911

Cook, Eldora Lucretia, d/o Horace & Lucy Cook, b 7 Dec 1845, d 1 Aug 1847

Cook, Frederic Horace, s/o Horace & Lucy Cook, b 15 Dec 1848, d 23 Jan 1869

Guild, Deacon Samuel of Franklin, MA, d 25 Dec 1840 aged 78 yrs

Guild, Ruth, w/o Deacon Samuel Guild, d 28 Sept 1839 aged 75 yrs

Guild, John C.,.....

Guild, Ebenezer, d 26 Sept 1822 aged 76 yrs

Guild, Lydia, w/o Ebenezer Guild, d 9 April 1819 aged 69 yrs

Atwood, Emily, d/o Timothy & Esther Guild, d 18 July 1811 aged 23 yrs

Ray, Frank, s/o George & Sophronia C. Ray, d 19 Aug 1884 aged 39 yrs 11 mos 2 days

Crowinshield, James, d 3 Aug 1806 aged 26 yrs

Crowinshield, Anna, w/o James Crowinshield, d 21 July 1852 aged 79 yrs

Crowinshield, Richard, d 12 April 1819 aged 80 yrs

Crowinshield, Mary w/o Richard Crowinshield, d 9 June 1807 aged 70 yrs

Crowinshield, Mary, d 20 April 1816 aged 49 yrs

Cooke, Deacon Abner, d 23 April 1817 aged 82 yrs

Cooke, Rhoda, w/o Deacon Abner Cooke, d 9 Sept 1816 aged 78 yrs

Haskell, Grace, w/o Abner Haskell, d May 1799 AE 74 yrs

Haskell, Abner, d 1799 AE 78 yrs

Haskell, John, d 16 June 1833 aged 81 yrs

Haskell, Mary, w.o John Haskell, d 1821

Smith, Benjamin, b 11 Feb 1792 Taunton, MA, d 19 Aug 1855 aged 63 yrs 6 mos 8 days

Smith, Nancy, w/o Benjamin Smith, d 27 Sept 1865 aged 71 yrs

Grant, Elery, d 10 Jan 1856 aged 70 yrs 5 mos 10 days

Grant, Mary, w/o Elery Grant, d 12 Oct 1855 aged 67 yrs 1 mo 13 days

Ray, Gideon, d 1808

Ray, Eunice, w/o Gideon Ray, d 2 Dec 1819 aged 59 yrs

Ray, Chloe, w/o Robert Ray, d Sept 1797

Ray, Robert, d 1845 AE 80 yrs

Heaton, Benjamin, s/o Nathaniel & Margaret Heaton, b 23 Feb 1775, d 8 June 1800

Cady, Letisa, d 28 May 1821 aged 73 yrs

Grant, Capt. Joshua, d 1810 AE 43 yrs

Grant, Lois, w/o Capt. Joshua Grant, d 16 Feb 1857 aged 87 yrs

Groosman, Sanger, s/o Elder Zephannah & Polly Grossman, 1811-1902

Groosman, Polly, w/o Elder Zephannah Grossman, d 1836

Picket, Calista, w/o John Picket & d/o David & Hannah Hawes, d 4 Nov 1825 aged 27 yrs

Hawes, David, d 24 March 1842 aged 83 yrs

Hawes, Hannah, w/o David Hawes, d 1865

Tillinghast, Mary, d/o Joseph & Eliza Ann Torrey, d 22 April 1847 aged 24 yrs

Tillinghast, Allen, b 28 Feb 1768, d 28 April 1854

Tillinghast, Patience, w/o Allen Tillinghast & d/o Rev. William Williams, b 28 Aug 1774, d 8 Oct 1861

Hawes, Darius, d 24 March 1864 aged 63 yrs 10 mos

Hawes, Mary, w/o Darius Hawes, b 5 Feb 1815, d 2 May 1872

Hawes, Lewis, d of Small Pox

Hawes, Elizabeth Caroline, d/o Darius & Mary Hawes, b 6 May 1847, d 29 Jan 1849

Holmes, Robert W., s/o Lewis & Mary J. Holmes, 1849-1931

Hawes, Hannah C., w/o Robert W. Holmes, 1842-1929

Blake, Ira F., d 7 Aug 1880 aged 48 yrs 3 mos 21 days

Blake, Sarah, w/o Ira F. Blake, d 5 May 1894 aged 52 yrs

Follett, Benjamin R., b 7 Dec 1831, d 30 June 1882

Follett, Rachel F., w/o Benjamin R. Follett, b 6 Aug 1837, d 29 Nov 1915

Holmes, Arthur E., 1877-1929

Holmes, Bertha Maria, 1878-1939

Holmes, Carrie Bell, 1881-1881

Williams, Betsey, widow of William Williams, d 3 Aug 1850 aged 63 yrs

Gilmore, George A., b 4 June 1798, d 18 May 1872

Sherburne, Sarah, w/o George A. Gilmore, b 10 July 1797, d 30 Aug 1873

Borden, Martha Jane, w/o George A. Gilmore & d/o Stephen & Phebe Borden, b 9 Feb 1838, d 11 Oct 1869

Gilmore, Edward S., s/o George & Martha Jane Gilmore, b 17 Aug 1862, d 12 March 1862

Gilmore, George H., s/o George & Sarah Gilmore, b 6 Oct 1820, d 5 April 1903

Hawkins, Mary Ann, w/o Mortimer C. Cook, & d/o Amos & Mary Ann Hawkins, d 11 Nov 1843 aged 18 yrs 8 mos 1 day

Fuller, Job, d 23 Feb 1817 aged 76 yrs

Fuller, Mary, w/o Job Fuller, d April 1816 AE 66 yrs

Grant, George, d 16 March 1865 aged 66 yrs 2 mos

Grant, Miranda C., w/o George Grant, d 16 June 1872 aged 69 yrs 10 mos

Grant, Joanna S., w/o George Grant, d 24 Nov 1825

Grant, George William, s/o George & Miranda C. Grant, d 15 Oct 1857 aged 24 yrs 1 mo

Grant, Zeolde, d/o George & Miranda C. Grant, d 21 May 1885 aged 53 yrs

Grant, Adeliza, d/o George & Miranda C. Grant, d Dec 1850 aged 20 yrs

Sherburne, William, d 15 Srpt 1816

Sherburne, Sarah, w/o William Sherburne, b 9 Jan 1769, d 5 Dec 1858

Sherburne, Eleanor, d/o William & Sarah Sherburne, b 2 March 1800, d 23 July 1868

Aldrich, Asa, d 10 July 1825 aged 81 yrs

Aldrich, Lucy, w/o Asa Aldrich, d April 1829

Aldrich, Anson T., s/o Amos & Sarah Aldrich, d 25 Feb 1833 aged 19 yrs

Hawkins, Betsey, w/o Alvah Hawkins, d 26 June 1857 aged 56 yrs

Hawkins, David, d 1852

Hawkins, Mary, w/o David Hawkins, d 28 July 1860 aged 88 yrs

Hawkins, Almira, d/o David & Mary Hawkins, d 2 Sept 1842 aged 27 yrs 2 mos

Ray, Elias, d 26 April 1855

Ray, Sally Ann, w/o Elias Ray, d 22 Sept 1842

Metcalf, Reuben G., d 26 Dec 1875 aged 81 yrs 6 mos

Metcalf, Hannah, w/o Reuben G. Metcalf, d 15 Nov 1820 aged 31 yrs

Metcalf, Sarah Ann, w/o Reuben G. Metcalf, d 29 March 1834

Metcalf, Lieffy, w/o Reuben G. Metcalf, d 18 March 1875 aged 83 yrs

Metcalf, Elias, b 20 April 1790, d 1 May 1874

Metcalf, Melansa, b 27 Nov 1799, d 12 June 1879

Ray, Charles A., s/o Charles & Eunice E. Ray, d 8 Nov 18....

Ray, Charles, d 14 Nov 1854 aged 74 yrs

Ray, Eunice E., w/o Charles Ray, d 17 June 1836 aged 50 yrs

Sheldon, Ruth A., d 13 Aug 1833 aged 34 yrs

Alexander, Betsey, eldest d/o John & Ruth Whipple Alexander, d 10 April 1838 aged 58 yrs

Metcalf, Thomas, 1749-1832

Ray, Jemima, w/o Thomas Metcalf, 1756-1830

Grant, Benjamin, d 31 Dec 1812 AE 84 yrs

Grant, David, d 5 April 1853 aged 85 yrs

Grant, Rachel, w/o David Grant, d 1817

Grant, Milton, d 3 May 1834 aged 34 yrs

Sheldon, Huldah, w/o Milton Grant, & d/o Rhodes & Prusha Sheldon, d 1 April 1835 aged 25 yrs

Grant, William, d 2 March 1870 aged 75 yrs

Grant, Charlotte L., w/o William Grant, d 5 March 1887 aged 83 yrs
Cook, Warren Foster, b 4 July 1824, d 7 July 1895
Cook, Sarah Ellen, w/o Warren Foster Cook, b 6 Aug 1826, d 3 Sept 1902
Whipple, Fenner E., b 21 Feb 1863, d 17 April 1898
Evans, Maurice A., 1851-1926
Whipple, Idella P., w/o Maurice A. Evans, 1863-1933
Peck, Henry C., 1830-1916
Peck, Lottie F., w/o Henry C. Peck, 1841-1926
Peck, Bertha T., d/o Henry & Lottie F. Peck, 1876-1909
Hawes, Nelson, b 2 Oct 1872, d 4 July 1892
Childs, Catherine S., w/o Nelson Hawes, b 5 March 1830, d 23 April
    1916
Hawes, Olive, w/o Nelson Hawes, b 11 Aug 1804, d 15 Sept 1849
Jenckes, Arnold A., 1847-1908
Jenckes, Ruth E., w/o Arnold A. Jenckes, 1846-1939
Morrell, Mary V., 1826-1909
Bates, Charles H., 1866-1947
Eldridge, Willett, 1855-1917
Eldridge, Mimmie, 1869-1962
Gaskill, George, 1864-1919
Baston, Elizabeth, 1872-1958
Kellogg, Alice, w/o George Reginald Kellogg, 1896-1932
Kellogg, George Reginald, 1893-1984
Forester, George W., 1847-1920
Forster, Sarah A., w/o George W. Forester, 1848-1917
Forster, Howard Douglas, 1886-1911
Stedman, Simeon, d 19 March 1877 aged 80 yrs
Stedman, Ardelia C., w/o Simeon Stedman, d 4 Aug 1874 aged 70 yrs 2
    mos 8 days
Cook, George M., b 12 Jan 1851, d 17 Aug 1922
Cook, Emma Clare, w/o George M. Cook, b 17 Aug 1856, d 2 Jan 1897
Freeman, Willard O., b 2 Feb 1792, d 6 Jan 1869
Freeman, Ruth, w/o Willard O. Freeman, b 6 Oct 1795, d 7 June 1859
Freeman, Milly, w/o Willard O. Freeman, b 2 Aug 1796, d 10 Feb 1869
Mason, George, b 6 Sept 1797, d 1 Dec 1828
Mason, Sally F., w/o George Mason, b 7 June 1793, d 7 Feb 1870
Scott, Thomas E., 1842-1892
Metcalf, Mary E., w/o Thomas E. Scott, 1848-1925
Scott, Edwin I., 1869-1935
Campbell, Lillian D., w/o Edwin I. Scott, 1872-1956

Wheaton, Sarah, w/o Eliab D. Whipple, b 30 Sept 1831, d 1 Jan 1919

Whipple, Eliab D., b 6 April 1831, d 15 Oct 1908

Hawkins, Darius, d 28 May 1849 aged 90 yrs

Hawkins, Esther, w/o Darius Hawkins, d 11 May 1825 aged 65 yrs

Grant, Samuel, d 20 July 1815 aged 62 yrs

Grant, Experience, w/o Samuel Grant, d 15 Jan 1849 aged 95 yrs

Ray, Ellen C., w/o George Ray, b 19 April 1843, d 5 Sept 1921

Grant, Joseph, d 11 April 1860 aged 74 yrs

Hawes, Cynthia, w/o Joseph Grant & d/o Elisha & Margaret Hawes, d 27 June 1827 aged 38 yrs

Grant, Samuel, d 28 Oct 1870 aged 67 yrs

Grant, Alpha A., w/o Samuel Grant, d 18 June 1902 aged 94 yrs

Salla, Alfred, d 18 Sept 1847 aged 35 yrs 10 mos 5 days

Salla, Prudence, w/o Alfred Salla, b 10 April 1811, d 3 Aug 1872

Salla, Ruxa T., d/o Alfred & Prudence Salla, d 29 Aug 1848 aged 6 yrs

Salla, Mary, d 11 Feb 1840 aged 67 yrs

Grant, Agnes M., b 23 July 1870, d 18 June 1960

Grant, Samuel Esq., d 12 March 1815 aged 39 yrs

Grant, Urania, w/o Samuel Grant Esq., d 15 May 1845 aged 67 yrs

Grant, Fenner, d 28 Feb 1878 aged 76 yrs 5 mos

Grant, Mary Ann, w/o Fenner Grant, d 20 April 1838 aged 82 yrs 9 mos 11 days

Tucker, Suzanne, w/o Whipple Tucker, d 4 May 1832 aged 52 yrs 11 mos

Tucker, Whipple, d 1816

Tucker, Louisa, d/o Whipple & Suzanne Tucker, d 1821

Follett, Benjamin, d 11 May 1878 aged 67 yrs 2 mos 9 days

Packard, Charles W., b 8 Jan 1833, d 4 Oct 1854

Haskell, Mary, w/o Charles Packard, b 8 Oct 1831, d....

Austin, George, b 16 Nov 1821, d 16 Jan 1912

Austin, Sarah G., w/o George Austin, b 6 Feb 1824, d 8 June 1890

Austin, George W., s/o George & Sarah Austin, d 9 Nov 1849 aged 2 yrs

Austin, Annie E., d/o George & Sarah Austin, d 15 Nov 1861 aged 16 yrs

Haskell, John, b 23 Aug 1787, d 2 April 1866

Aldrich, Asenath, w/o John Haskell, b 14 Aug 1789, d 21 Dec 1868

Hawkins, Rufus, d 28 April 1869 aged 82 yrs

Hawkins, Anna, w/o Rufus Hawkins, d 16 Oct 1852 aged 67 yrs

Mellen, Frank R., b 25 Nov 1853, d 3 March 1941

Jencks, Flora, w/o Frank R. Mellen, b 1 Nov 1858, d 26 Jan 1935

Comstock, Cyrus, d 1827

Comstock, Abigail, w/o Cyrus Comstock, d 10 April 1848 aged 77 yrs

Day, Susan, w/o Fisher Day, d 14 May 1821 aged 28 yrs 4 mos 17 days

Follett, Alzada, w/o James J. Newman, b 31 March 1867, d 7 Oct 1896

Follett, William, 1806-1889

Jencks, Lydia C., w/o William Follett, 1812-1859

Darling, John E., b 28 March 1838, d 25 Jan 1906

Mellen, Robert E., 1827-1891

Mellen, Emma E., w/o Robert E. Mellen, 1826-1916

Mellen, Harry W., 1860-1862

Clark, Peter, d 17 Sept 1855 aged 50 yrs

Esty, Martin H., d 23 Sept 1880 aged 82 yrs

Esty, Hannah M., w/o Martin H. Esty, d 12 April 1870 aged 73 yrs 3 mos

Esty, Ann Frances, d/o Martin & Hannah Esty, d 31 Dec 1896 aged 63 yrs 8 mos

Metcalf, Dr. Paul, b 19 April 1775, d 28 Nov 1852

Guild, Rachel, w/o Reuben Guild, d 4 June 1793 aged 20 yrs

Metcalf, Silas, d 4 July 1822 aged 76 yrs

Metcalf, Marcy, w/o Silas Metcalf, d 30 April 1835 aged 81 yrs

Guild, Deacon Joseph, d 12 Jan 1819 aged 71 yrs

Guild, Margaret, d/o Joseph & Rebekah Guild, d 18 April 1833 aged 62 yrs

Gorton, John A., 1819-1879

Gorton, Emeline C., w/o John A. Gorton, 1826-1869

Clark, John W., d 27 Jan 1885 aged 62 yrs 27 days

Clark, Olive T., w/o John W. Clark, d 1 April 1882 aged 51 yrs 6 mos

Clark, Onesemus, d 16 Nov 1839 aged 65 yrs

Clark, Lydia, w/o Onesemus Clark, d 3 June 1861 aged 78 yrs

Clark, Mirian, w/o Stephen Clark & d/o Josiah Thayer, d 27 Aug 1824 aged 78 yrs

Clark, Rhoda, d/o Stephen & Thankful Clark, d 9 June 1805 aged 16 yrs

Williams, Betsey, d/o Rev. William Williams, b 27 May 1868, d 3 June 1868

Williams, Mary, w/o Nathan Williams, d 19 May 1872 aged 78 yrs 1 mo

Butterworth, Noah, d 2 April 1850 aged 89 yrs

Butterworth, Rachel, w/o Noah Butterworth, d 31 Dec 1832 aged 71 yrs

Williams, Rev. William, d 22 Sept 1823 aged 75 yrs

Williams, Dolly, w/o Rev. William Williams, d 24 April 1833 aged 76 yrs

Haskell, Comfort, d 28 March 1804 aged 57 yrs

Haskell, Zepha, w/o Comfort Haskell, d 12 March 1859 aged 91 yrs

Haskell, Mary, w/o Comfort Haskell, d 3 Oct 1784 aged 35 yrs

Howard, Capt. John, Lost at Sea 1797 aged 86 yrs

Howard, Lydia, w/o Capt. John Howard, d 6 March 1843 aged 86 yrs
Howard, Welcome, s/o Capt. John & Lydia Howard, d 11 May 1815
   Norfolk, VA aged 20 yrs
Howard, Lucy, d/o Capt. John & Lydia Howard, d 5 Dec 1880 aged 89 yrs
Ware, Timothy, d 30 May 1799 AE 52 yrs
Guild, Deacon Ebenezer, d 29 May 1790 aged 66 yrs
Guild, Margaret, s/o Deacon Ebenezer Guild, d 11 Aug 1810 aged 86 yrs
Lane, Rebecca, w/o David M. Lane, d 23 April 1791 aged 15 yrs
Ballou, Sally, w/o Caleb Ballou, d 20 Jan 1849 aged 46 yrs
Miller, Deacon Joseph, d 30 April 1832 aged 91 yrs
Miller, Thankful, w/o Deacon Joseph Miller, d 6 Feb 1823 aged 86 yrs
Thain, Thomas, d 23 Oct 1858 aged 55 yrs
Thain, Maranda, w/o Thomas Thain, d 22 June 1893 aged 94 yrs 2 mos
Thain, Ellen A., d/o Thomas & Maranda Thain, d 11 Nov 1863 aged 21
   yrs 7 mos
Thain, Eugene A., 1839-1922
Thain, Samuel B., 1837-1917
Thain, William W., d 16 July 1881 aged 52 yrs 3mos
Chauvey, Aime J., 1854-1949
Sinney, Celesta M., w/o Aime J. Chauvey, 1869-1887
Burlingame, Lewis W., b 22 April 1867, d 12 May 1941
Grant, Margaret A., w/o Lewis W. Burlingame, b 29 June 1817, d 9 Dec
   1924
Gurney, Rev. Preston, s/o Ichabod & Clarissa Gurney of Whitman, MA,
   1843-1921
Hawes, Maria S., w/o Rev. Preston Gurney & d/o Darius & Mary Hawes,
   1843-1928
Metcalf, Edgar H., b 6 Feb 1846, d 5 Dec 1906
Worden, Francena A., w/o Edgar H. Metcalf, b 13 July 1846, d 27 Jan
   1927
Roberts, James Eli, 1861-1944
Grant, Edith M., w/o James Eli Roberts, 1861-1907
Grant, Joseph, 1836-1888
Grant, Sarah, 1838-1905
Grant, Wilfrid P., 1856-1866
Grant, Annie F., 1877-1880
Cook, Conrad W. Jr., 1894-1965
Jencks, Margaret L., w/o Conrad W. Cook Jr., 1903-1980
Cook, Franklyn C., 1935-....

Comstock, Walter, s/o Martin & Betsey Comstock, b 21 March 1843, d 1867

Comstock, Nathan, s/o Cyrus & Abigail Comstock, b 19 Oct 1806, d 11 June 1858 Iowa

Comstock, Betsey C., w/o Nathan Comstock, b 9 Oct 1805, d 12 March 1887

Mellen, Charles C., b 15 Dec 1857, d 4 June 1935

Mason, Mary L., w/o Charles C. Mellen, b 1 Sept 1858, d 14 Sept 1920

Grant, Patience, d/o Beriah & Elizabeth Grant, d 12 June 1830

Grant, Moses, d 14 April 1816 aged 67 yrs

Grant, Parley, w/o Moses Grant, d 7 Jan 1824 aged 72 yrs

Grant, Olive, d/o Benjamin & Sufanna Grant, d 1793

Grant, Moses, d 15 Dec 1804 AE 96 yrs

Grant, Thankful, w/o Moses Grant, d 19 Oct 1793 AE 82 yrs

Fisher, Betty, d 18 Nov 1840 aged 89 yrs

Fisher, Betty, w/o Jonathan Fisher, d 12 March 1825 AE 99 yrs 9 mos 12 days

Fisher, Jonathan, d 24 Sept 1798 AE 77 yrs

Fisher, Jonathan, s/o Jonathan & Betty Fisher, d 1 March 1792 aged 24 yrs

Fisher, Cornelius, s/o Jonathan & Betty Fisher, d 1 Dec 1790 AE 30 yrs

Grant, Justus, d 31 July 1811 aged 31 yrs

Coor, Cynthia, d 10 Feb 1817 AE 25 yrs

Grant, Esther, d 11 Sept 1815 AE 28 yrs

Williams, Patience, w/o Rev. William Williams, & d/o Col. Martin Miller of Warren, RI, d 18 June 1803 AE 50 yrs

Read, G. L., 1847-1933

Gorton, Ellen, w/o G. L. Read, 1847-1924

Cheever, Elias, d 5 April 1837 AE 68 yrs

Cheever, Phebe, w/o Elias Cheever, d 20 Oct 1821 aged 58 yrs

Cheever, Elias Jr., s/o Elias & Phebe Cheever, d 9 Sept 1813 aged 19 yrs

Jenckes, Wheaton, s/o Job & Sarah Jenckes, d 4 Sept 1803 aged 1 yr

Jenckes, William, d 5 Nov 1815 AE 91 yrs

Ray, Levi, d 8 March 1839 aged 54 yrs

Ray, Cynthia, w/o Levi Ray, d 20 July 1819 aged 24 yrs

Cheever, Clarissa, d/o Elias & Phebe Cheever, d 28 March 1831 AE 33 yrs

Cheever, Otis G., b 1 Nov 1801, d 24 April 1872

Cheever, Susan, w/o Otis G. Cheever, b 9 Feb 1801, d 15 Nov 1882

Ray, James, d 7 Oct 1826 aged 60 yrs

Ray, Thankful, w/o James Ray, d 4 Sept 1862 aged 93 yrs

Ray, Sally, d/o James & Thankful Ray, d 5 Jan 1822 aged 21 yrs

Grant, Welcom, s/o Jeremiah & Elizabeth Grant, d 8 Oct 1791

Sherburne, Marion, b 11 April 1844, d 1 July 1896

Grant, Mabelle W. Miller, d/o Charles & Eliza E. Grant, b 30 May 1863, d 3 Nov 1926

Sherburne, William J., b 27 Dec 1837, d 5 Nov 1872

Sherburne, Urania C., b 20 March 1846, d 16 July 1893

Hawes, Albert E., 1843-1907

Hawes, Helen A., w/o Albert E. Hawes, 1843-1913

Hawes, Frederick W., 1869-1910

Hawes, Charles, b 5 April 1802, d 29 Jan 1894

Hawes, Susan, w/o Charles Hawes, d 8 July 1872 aged 66 yrs

Ray, Selina, w/o James Ray, d 29 March 1829 aged 30 yrs

Hawes, Elisha, d 24 May 1818 AE 68 yrs

Hawes, Margaret, w/o Elisha Hawes, d 9 Dec 1837 aged 67 yrs

Hawes, Eliab, d 23 Jan 1825 aged 20 yrs

Hawes, Lyman, d 7 Feb 1864 aged 65 yrs

Jenckes, Luke, s/o William Jenckes, d 13 Oct 1848 aged 74 yrs 3 mos

Packard, Ephraim C., d 29 Apeil 1852 aged 27 yrs 4 mos

Haskell, John, b 24 Nov 1824, d 24 May 1873

Haskell, Louisa M., w/o John Haskell, b 16 Jan 1842, d 6 July 1897

Fisher, Nelson M., 1814-1890

Thayer, Eunice, w/o Nelson M. Fisher, 1818-1898

Fisher, Alvira M., w/o R. Albert Fisher & d/o Emery & Bathsheba K. Fisher, d 26 Aug 1860 aged 20 yrs

Fisher, Mary E., w/o R. Albert Fisher & d/o Lucian & Eliza A. Kendall, d 4 July 1868 aged 27 yrs

Sloan, James G., d 25 Dec 1876 aged 61 yrs 3 mos 6 days

Freeman, Olive H., w/o James G. Sloan & d/o Willard & Ruth Freeman, d 18 Feb 1851 aged 36 yrs

Johnson, Lucy C., d 13 March 1874 aged 59 yrs

Cargill, Frances E., d 8 Feb 1898 aged 69 yrs 4 mos

Cargill, Harvey, d 7 Nov 1890 aged 60 yrs

Grant, Addie J.C., 1858-1955

Sherburne, Alice, b 18 June 1840, d 25 April 1863

Burnt Swamp Cemetery
Burnt Swamp Road
Wrentham, Massachusetts

Sheldon, Francis, b 18 April 1839, d 15 Nov 1917

Sheldon, Olive E., w/o Francis Sheldon, b 12 Jan 1839, d 27 Feb 1907

Sheldon, Donald R., b 7 June 1900, d 23 June 1979

Sheldon, Nina B., w/o Donald R. Sheldon, b 12 March 1893, d 24 Sept 1965

Belisle, Edith Sheldon, b 13 March 1903, d 5 Sept 1976

Sheldon, George F., b 13 Nov 1896, d 25 Oct 1967

Sheldon, Fredericka S., w/o George F. Sheldon, b 26 May 1896, d 10 May 1966

Belsile, Rector, b 31 Jan 1891, d 16 April 1969

Sheldon, Berton E., b 21 Aug 1861, d 5 March 1941

Sheldon, Mary P., w/o Berton E. Sheldon, b 20 May 1871, d 27 Aug 1939

Sheldon, Arthur F., b 13 May 1897, d 22 Jan 1972

Pond, Horace, d 12 Nov 1883 aged 65 yrs

Pond, Lucy G., w/o Horace Pond, d 25 July 1900 aged 76 yrs 2 mos 19 days

Pond, Edgar A., 1851-1910

Hancock, Harriet E., w/o Edgar A. Pond, 1850-1934

Miller, Whipple M., 1799-1882

Salusbury, Mehitable, w/o Whipple M. Miller, 1814-1899

Stearns, Emma E., 1856-1931

Newell, Charles E., b 14 Feb 1861, d 22 Feb 1931

Newell, Emma F., w/o Charles E. Newell, b 9 Dec 1865, d 10 April 1917

Guild, Eliza H., 1808-1866

Ray, John H., b 10 July 1820, d 11 May 1903

Ray, Elizabeth, w/o John H. Ray, d 2 July 1869 aged 43 yrs 6 mos

Miller, Lorenzo, d 16 Aug 1858 aged 42 yrs 2 mos 15 days

Miller, Lauritta W., w/o Lorenzo Miller, 1811-1904

Barker, Lyman, 1814-1865

Buell, Amelia, w/o Lyman Barber, 1818-1893

Mason, Frank W., 1856-1950

Mason, Sarah W., w/o Frank W. Mason, 1854-1928

Mason, James B., b 22 Nov 1841, d 15 Sept 1887

Mason, Laurinda, w/o James B. Mason, b 23 Jan 1817, d 25 Dec 1882

Mason, Bradford A., b 16 Dec 1848, d 14 Feb 1903

Aldrich, Nathan, d 16 July 1862 aged 89 yrs 4 mos

Aldrich, Lois, w/o Nathan Aldrich, d 19 Oct 1861 aged 87 yrs

Pierce, Washington, b 19 Oct 1810, d 10 Oct 1892

Pierce, Nancy C., w/o Washington Pierce, d 9 Sept 1862 aged 48 yrs 2 mos 25 days

Harris, Alexander, 1804-1880

Cheever, Harriet, w/o Alexander Harris, 1811-1890

Harris, Frank, s/o Alexander & Harriet Harris, 1856-1941

Weatherhead, Preston, d 29 June 1848 aged 57 yrs

Weatherhead, Sally, w/o Preston Weatherhead, d 1 March 1854 aged 65 yrs 8 mos

Darling, Eleanor M., w/o Alfred O. Darling, d 13 April 1854 aged 24 yrs

Allen, Julia A., w/o Sanford W. Allen, d 10 June 1851 aged 34 yrs 2 mos

Allen, Sanford W., d 27 Feb 1893 aged 79 yrs 25 days

Duval, Antionette, w/o Sanford W. Allen, d 5 Oct 1902 aged 70 yrs 10 mos 23 days

Allen, Mary, w/o James W. Thompson, d 8 April 1914 aged 76 yrs 4 mos

Clark, Sarah Ann, w/o William A. Clark, d 22 Jan 1860 aged 36 yrs 2 mos

Pierce, John, b 12 Sept 1790, d 25 May 1876

Pierce, Caroline F., w/o John Pierce, b 27 Feb 1808, d 26 April 1881

Darling, Elias, d 27 Oct 1833 aged 72 yrs

Darling, Nancy, w/o Elias Darling, d 12 Sept 1853 aged 93 yrs 6 mos

Harrington, Joseph F., d 22 June 1857 aged 57 yrs

Harrington, Rosina, w/o Joseph F. Harrington, d Aug 1862 aged 61 yrs

Darling, Silas Jr., d 17 Feb 1843 aged 27 yrs

Darling, Sarah Jane, d/o Silas & Phebe Darling, d 6 March 1842 aged 23 yrs

Darling, Louisa, d/o Silas & Phebe Darling, d 3 Dec 1845 aged 19 yrs

Darling, Allen, d 12 July 1877 aged 57 yrs 10 mos

Darling, Maria, w/o Allen Darling, d 15 Aug 1883 aged 68 yrs

Grant, Harlous, d 15 May 1862 aged 51 yrs 5 days

Gilmore, Joseph, d 15 Oct 1859 aged 68 yrs

Gilmore, Sarah S., w/o Joseph Gilmore, d 30 May 1861 aged 71 yrs

Gilmore, Mary Abby, d/o Joseph & Sarah Gilmore, d 16 April 1821 aged 1 yr

Mason, Deacon George, d 24 May 1845 aged 69 yrs

Mason, Mary, w/o Deacon George Mason, d 4 Jan 1862 aged 85 yrs

Brown, Almira, d 24 Nov 1893 aged 87 yrs

Brown, Marianne, d/o John & Almira Brown, d 10 July 1845 aged 16 yrs

Rhodes, Silas, d 23 April 1849 aged 56 yrs 10 mos 29 days

Rhodes, Patience, w/o Silas Rhodes, d 25 Dec 1866 aged 73 yrs 7 mos

Rhodes, Amos S., d 7 Sept 1882 aged 65 yrs 11 mos 5 days

Rhodes, Laura, w/o Amos S. Rhodes, d 20 April 1867 aged 49 yrs 1 mo

Rhodes, Silas Bernard, s/o Amos & Laura Rhodes, d 11 Sept 1851 aged 1
yr 2 mos

Rhodes, Herbert, d 13 Oct 1855 aged 24 yrs 5 mos

Rhodes, Charlotte E., b 15 Aug 1821, d 22 Dec 1893

Rhodes, Warren, 1829-1884

Rhodes, Rachel, w/o Warren Rhodes, 1833-1917

Rhodes, Stillman M., s/o Warren & Rachel Rhodes, 1854-1885

Rhodes, Jonathan, d 11 Nov 1872 aged 76 yrs

Rhodes, Almira, w/o Jonathan Rhodes, d 24 April 1881 aged 89 yrs

Rhodes, Wilson, d 18 Dec 1872 aged 44 yrs

Rhodes, Edson, d 23 Sept 1870 aged 32 yrs

Rhodes, Cindarilla, w/o Emulous Rhodes, d 1 Sept 1857 aged 37 yrs

Whiting, Harriet R., w/o Emulous Rhodes & d/o Otis & Polly Whiting, d
1 May 1845 aged 45 yrs

Newell, Emily F., d 1 June 1903 aged 72 yrs 9 mos

Follett, William, d 22 Nov 1867 aged 68 yrs 5 mos 16 days

Follett, Fanny, w/o William Follett, d 17 June 1887 aged 83 yrs 5 mos 10
days

Follett, Julia, d/o William Fanny Follett, d 22 July 1844 aged 21 yrs

Rogers, Nathaiel W., d 6 Aug 1905 aged 80 yrs 11 mos

Rogers, Cynthia, w/o Nathaniel W. Rogers, b 4 July 1824, d 24 March
1898

Newell, Emor A., b 8 Sept 1851, d 22 July 1893

Newell, Lydia, b 22 Feb 1853, d 29 Oct 1910

Newell, Wilbur O., 1857-1936

Newell, Rose A., w/o Wilbur O. Newell, 1866-1958

Parker, Caroline K., b 18 Aug 1826, d 21 Dec 1904

Sheldon, William Alonzo, s/o Nathaniel & Avilda J. Sheldon, b 30 April
1844, d 13 Jan 1885

Harris, Mary E., w/o William Alonzo Sheldon, b 23 April 1844, d 27 Jan
1919

Thayer, Davis, b 17 Sept 1823, d 7 April 1893

Thayer, Lavina M., w/o Davis Thayer, d 24 Jan 1890 aged 61 yrs

Thayer, Emma B., 1876-1918

Thayer, Sumner Davis, 1856-1904

Thayer, Josephine, w/o Sumner Davis Thayer, 1856-1910

Craig, John A., d 16 July 1869 aged 64 yrs

Craig, Sophia A., w/o John A. Craig, d 8 Jan 1876 aged 69 yrs 4 mos

Miller, Susan, w/o Jesse Miller, d 7 Jan 1870 aged 58 yrs 3 mos 13 days

Nash, Frederick, b 18 Nov 1851, d 28 Sept 1934

Burlingame, Charlotte A., w/o Frederick Nash, b 5 May 1860, d 22 June 1901

Nash, Frederick A., s/o Frederick & Charlotte Nash, b 17 April 1880, d 11 Feb 1948

Hancock, Samuel, d 15 May 1843 aged 59 yrs

Hancock, Amey, w/o Samuel Hancock, d 18 Feb 1858 aged 76 yrs

Guild, Benjamin H., b 31 Oct 1829, d 18 July 1902

Cheever, Ann E., w/o Benjamin H. Guild, b 7 May 1860, d 24 April 1880

Guild, Frank H., b 31 Aug 1856, d 26 Oct 1891

Bagnell, Nancy L., w/o Frank H. Guild, 1859-1922

Guild, Elmer F., 1879-1932

Grant, Joshua L., b 28 July 1815, d 3 Nov 1898

Grant, Clarissa, w/o Joshua L. Grant, b 13 Aug 1820, d 2 April 1904

Williams, Rounseville, b 8 Jan 1821, d 19 April 1891

Williams, Lydia, w/o Rounseville, b 8 Jan 1821, d 19 April 1891

Ray, Lydia H., w/o Rounseville Williams, 1823-1906

Williams, Rounseville L., 1848-1927

Willaims, Louisa Ella, w/o Rounseville Williams, 1854-1926

Miller, Sarah, w/o David Miller, d 28 Jan 1856 aged 89 yrs 8 mos

Hawes, Silas M. M., b 27 May 1799, d 26 Dec 1879

Hawes, Nancy B., w/o Silas M. M. Hawes, d 8 Oct 1857 Providence, RI aged 43 yrs

Rhodes, Willie E., b 8 Sept 1863, d 1 Dec 1899

Wilson, James E., 1874-1917

Crowinshield, Hannah, d 9 April 1876 aged 68 yrs

Crowinshield, Richard, d 31 Jan 1883 aged 80 yrs

Peck, Naomi, w/o Richard Crowinshield, d 16 Jan 1845 aged 78 yrs

Crowinsheild, J. A., b 10 June 1818, d 7 March 1896

Crowinshield, Ida, w/o J.A. Crowinshield, d 1883

Fairbanks, Charles A., b 19 July 1842, d 6 Jan 1892

Crowinshield, Abigail, d 31 May 1857 aged 70 yrs

Follett, Susan, b 8 Sept 1811, d 23 March 1900

Lucas, John, 1845-1915

Lucas, Eliza Mary, w/o John Lucas, 1848-1932

Follett, Homer A., b 29 June 1836, d 3 April 1917

Follett, Merilla A., w/o Homer A. Follett, b 2 Aug 1844, d 9 Nov 1928

Follett, Charles, b 23 Sept 1810, d 18 March 1886

Follett, Alonzo, b 30 March 1823, d 25 Oct 1894

Follett, Catherine J., w/o Alonzo Follett, b 26 July 1827, d 1 Dec 1862

Miller, Rhoda T., w/o Gilmore Miller, d 21 July 1843 aged 25 yrs

Miller, Jesse T., s/o Gilmore & Rhoda Miller, d 3 Aug 1842 aged 14 mos

Miller, Horace, s/o Gilmore & Rhoda Miller, d 6 June 1844 aged 4 yrs 6 mos 14 days

Miller, Jesse, d 14 Sept 1845 aged 73 yrs

Miller, Levina, w/o Jesse Miller, d 21 Aug 1837 aged 63 yrs

Miller, Nancy, w/o Jesse Miller, d 3 Aug 1854 aged 71 yrs

Hancock, Deacon Philip, d 9 Aug 1832 aged 52 yrs

Hancock, Daniel M., d 13 Dec 1883 aged 75 yrs

Hancock, Rachel J., w/o Daniel Hancock, d 21 April 1882 aged 73 yrs

Hancock, Reuben, s/o Daniel & Rachel J. Hancock, d 16 Sept 1830 aged 14 mos

Hancock, Joseph Stillman, d 11 Jan 1839 aged 29 yrs

Rhodes, Julia A., b 1 Jan 1830, d 31 May 1903

Rhodes, Clementine M., w /o Thomas Rhodes & former w/o Joseph S. Hancock, d 11 Nov 1886 aged 74 yrs

Rhodes, Earl Murdock, 1888-1918, 165th US Inf, d Chateau Thienry, France 28 July 1918

Outhouse, Edmund, b 28 June 1823, d 16 July 1898

Outhouse, Lucy A., w/o Edmund Outhouse, b 17 July 1828, d 6 July 1909

Rhodes, Thomas R., d 17 March 1811 aged 70 yrs

Rhodes, Sarah, w/o Thomas R. Rhodes, d 14 April 1814 aged 39 yrs

Aldrich, David, d 23 May 1879 aged 98 yrs

Aldrich, Jemima, w/o David Aldrich, d 8 Feb 1876 aged 92 yrs

Chase, William Converse, b 17 Sept 1860, d 30 Sept 1922

Aldrich, Sarah Samantha, w/o William Converse Chase, b 20 Dec 1854, d 24 March 1924

Huntley, Sarah H., w/o David B. Aldrich & d/o Rev. Leland Huntley, d 26 April 1892 aged 67 yrs 10 mos

Clark, Moses R., b 29 Jan 1847, d 5 Jan 1914, A memner of Co K 5th Mass Vols & Co E 15th Us Inf

Aldrich, Flora M., w/o Moses R. Clark, b 12 March 1855, d 3 April 1941

Sheldon, Joanna, w/o Orin Sheldon, b 1820, d 9 Sept 1869

Wellman, Marilla, b 24 April 1812, d 8 Feb 1890

Sheldon, Col. Rhodes, b 21 July 1786, d 15 Dec 1867

Sheldon, Prusha, w/o Col. Rhodes Sheldon, b 5 Jan 1783, d 6 June 1849

Sheldon, Orin, b 10 March 1820, d 22 Feb 1893

Sheldon, Nathaniel, b 13 Dec 1814, d 27 Jan 1884

Sheldon, Avilda J., w/o Nathaniel Sheldon, b 30 Nov 1818, d 12 July 1904

Sheldon, Merton R., b 11 March 1857, d 3 Oct 1859

Sheldon, Emily A., w/o Merton R. Sheldon, b 14 Aug 1857, d 11 Sept 1845

Darling, Lyman W., 1851-1890

Hancock, George S., d 22 Jan 1911 aged 76 yrs

Hancock, M. Louise, w/o George S. Hancock, d 3 Oct 1889 aged 56 yrs

McEwen, James W., 1857-1925

McEwen, Maria L., w/o James W. McEwen, 1854-1926

Ray, Barton J., b 11 Jan 1826, d 8 March 1906

Ray, Jane A., w/o Barton J. Ray, b 10 Jan 1829, d 21 Aug 1902

Ray, Allen R., 1829-1915

Grant, Mary E., w/o Allen R. Ray, 1833-1910

Belcher, Melansa J., w/o Abner Belcher, d 11 June 1862 aged 60 yrs 4 mos

Belcher, Abner, d 6 Jan 1868 aged 73 yrs 4 mos 20 days

Clark, Joshua S., d 28 April 1880 aged 56 yrs

Clark, Cynthia A., w/o Joshua S. Clark, 1826-1904

Darling, Wilson, b 20 April 1829, d 26 Feb 1886

Darling, Eliza J., w/o Wilson Darling, d Oct 1908

Clark, Aaron, d 20 Dec 1847 aged 38 yrs

Clark, Maria, w/o Aaron Clark, ...

Caselton, William J., 1851-1919

Caselton, Johanna K., w/o William Caselton, 1871-1958

Forbush, Sarah Elizabeth, d/o Rev. Jonathan & Sally Forbush, d 26 April 1840 aged 17 yrs

Wrentham Town Hall
West Street
Wrentham, MA
02093

Index

Allen, Amanda, 243
Allen, Asa, 14
Allen, Barbara, 250
Allen, Benjamin, 12
Allen, Catherine, 342
Allen, Charles, 191
Allen, Cynthia, 14
Allen, Deacon Sylvester, 243
Allen, Eleanor, 86
Allen, Eliza, 237
Allen, Elizabeth, 12, 17, 233
Allen, Emma, 69
Allen, Esther, 86
Allen, Eunice, 83
Allen, Everett, 326
Allen, Ezra, 314
Allen, George, 22, 23, 247
Allen, Gladys, 20
Allen, Grace, 22
Allen, H, 18
Allen, Hannah, 243
Allen, Harriet, 319
Allen, Ina, 191
Allen, Isabella, 178
Allen, Ivan, 191
Allen, John, 83, 164
Allen, Josiah, 12, 17
Allen, Julia, 380
Allen, Julitta, 108
Allen, Lucy, 85
Allen, Mae, 99
Allen, Martha, 163
Allen, Mary, 118, 237, 380
Allen, Mrytle, 191
Allen, Nellie, 23
Allen, Paschal, 237
Allen, Phebe, 237
Allen, Rebecca, 243
Allen, Rhoda, 108
Allen, Rowena, 191
Allen, Ruth, 348
Allen, Samue, 108
Allen, Samuel, 125
Allen, Sanford, 380
Allen, Sarah, 282, 333
Allen, Squire, 86
Allen, Susan, 164
Allen, Thoma, 250
Allison, Annie, 169
Allyn, Cornelia, 238
Almy, Ruth, 221
Altham, George, 301
Altham, Jonas, 301
Altham, Mary, 301
Altham, Nellie, 301
Alvord, Susan, 179
Ames, Inez, 234
Ames, Moses, 142
Amesbury, Ann, 65
Amesbury, Charles, 65
Amesbury, Ellen, 65
Amesbury, Ruth, 65
Amesbury, Samuel, 65
Amesbury, Vianna, 65
Amos, Esther, 82
Amos, William, 82
Amsden, Lucy, 74
Anderson, A, 26

Anderson, Amos, 215
Anderson, Blanche, 215
Anderson, Charles, 26
Anderson, Dacie, 215
Anderson, E, 76
Anderson, Edna, 62
Anderson, Effie, 26
Anderson, Frances, 291
Anderson, Jacqueline, 186
Anderson, Johanna, 26
Anderson, John, 26
Anderson, Julia, 22
Anderson, Peter, 186
Anderson, Seleanor, 214
Andrea, George, 315
Andrea, Louisa, 315
Andrew, Elizabeth, 80
Andrew, William, 80
Andrews, Bessie, 347
Andrews, Etta, 93
Andrews, George, 347
Andrews, Hattie, 37
Andrews, James, 203
Andrews, Linda, 226
Andrews, Mabel, 166
Andrews, Mary, 166
Angell, Amos, 238
Angell, Arthur, 252
Angell, Charlotte, 32
Angell, Cyril, 32
Angell, Dorothy, 247, 254
Angell, Edgar, 254
Angell, Gladys, 28
Angell, Henry, 247
Angell, Hiram, 275
Angell, Mary, 252
Angell, Thomas, 32
Angevine, Alice, 56
Annis, Alice, 77
Annis, James, 77
Annis, Susan, 73
Anthony, Agnes, 248
Anthony, Aleena, 349
Anthony, Anna, 350
Anthony, Bessie, 350
Anthony, David, 350
Anthony, Marcus, 350
Anthony, Walter, 349
Archibald, Annie, 347
Archibald, Edmund, 348
Archibald, Elizabeth, 348
Archibald, Ethel, 348
Archibald, Isaac, 347
Archibald, William, 348
Argus, Arno, 28
Argus, Herman, 28
Armille, Francesca, 200
Armille, Rocco, 200
Armington, Arthur, 198
Armitage, Elizabeth, 23
Armitage, John, 23
Armitage, Joseph, 23
Armstrong, Cinda, 291
Armstrong, Flora, 256
Arnold, Alice, 24
Arnold, Annie, 21
Arnold, Arthur, 352
Arnold, Austin, 135

388

Batchelder, Lucretia, 146
Batchelder, Lucy, 147
Batchelder, Millicent, 144
Batchelder, Oldin, 144
Batchelder, Rhoda, 160
Batchelder, William, 160
Batchelor, B, 176
Batchelor, Martha, 176
Batchelor, Sarah, 17
Batchford, George, 212
Bateman, Catherine, 165
Bateman, Charles, 165
Bates, Addie, 63
Bates, Annie, 58
Bates, Charles, 58, 373
Bates, Ella, 161
Bates, Frank, 58
Bates, Herbert, 168
Bates, Howard, 58
Bates, James, 81
Bates, Joseph, 58
Bates, Kate, 58
Bates, Mary, 58
Bates, Sarah, 58, 81
Bath, William, 62
Batson, Emma, 39
Battelle, Freeman, 147
Battenshall, Frances, 30
Battenshall, Jesse, 30
Battenshall, Joseph, 30
Battenshall, Mary, 30
Battles, George, 178
Bauer, Albert, 87
Bauer, Christopher, 78
Bauer, Johanna, 78
Bauer, Lorenz, 88
Beale, Alice, 143
Beals, Horace, 246
Bean, Lizzie, 46
Bean, Rev. Joseph, 363
Bears, Louisa, 62
Bearse, William, 55
Beaulieu, Albion, 198
Beaulieu, Joseph, 200
Beaulieu, Leda, 198
Beaulieu, Xavier, 203
Becker, Emile, 76
Becker, Louis, 76
Beebe, Flora, 207
Beers, Courtland, 45
Beers, Daniel, 310
Beers, Ella, 35
Beers, Leonora, 45
Beette, Frank, 355
Belcher, Abner, 384
Belcher, Annie, 163
Belcher, Charles, 55
Belcher, Cora, 55
Belcher, Cynthia, 55
Belcher, Eola, 168
Belcher, Henry, 168
Belcher, Mary, 55, 168
Belcher, Melansa, 384
Belcher, Rose, 55
Belcher, Susnnah, 206
Belcher, W, 168
Belcher, William, 163
Belhamer, David, 200

Belhamer, Esther, 200
Belisle, Edith, 379
Bell, Mary, 232, 258
Belle, Ethel, 320
Bellows, Asa, 144
Bellows, Charles, 185
Bellows, Dr. Seth, 286
Bellows, Edward, 159
Bellows, Eva, 159
Bellows, J, 180
Bellows, Janet, 159
Bellows, Jarvis, 159
Bellows, Loronda, 147
Bellows, Louisa, 159
Bellows, Luther, 159
Bellows, Samuel, 162
Bellows, Sarah, 159
Bellows, Walter, 159, 162
Belot, Barbara, 59
Belsile, Rector, 379
Bemis, Amory, 150
Bemis, Augustine, 150
Bemis, Caroline, 171
Bemis, Charles, 118, 171
Bemis, Emma, 169
Bemis, Evelyn, 118
Bemis, Henry, 118
Bemis, Nancy, 118
Bemis, Peter, 145
Bemis, Sally, 146
Benedict, Newton, 128
Benjamin, Ina, 28
Bennett, Aaron, 358
Bennett, Amos, 256
Bennett, Caroline, 251
Bennett, Edgar, 221
Bennett, Edward, 361
Bennett, Ellen, 358
Bennett, Elvie, 221
Bennett, Emily, 221
Bennett, Frank, 358
Bennett, Geogre, 358
Bennett, Irving, 221
Bennett, Laura, 362
Bennett, Mary, 218, 250
Bennett, Samuel, 250
Bennett, Susan, 361
Bennett, Willard, 358
Benson, Annie, 31, 70
Benson, Muriel, 63
Benson, Richard, 31
Benson, Septimus, 31
Bent, Emeline, 143
Benton, E, 48
Benton, Edward, 48
Benton, Gladys, 55
Benton, James, 47
Benton, Jane, 47
Bergevine, Edna, 29
Berns, John, 155
Berry, Inez, 206
Berthold, Elden, 49
Berthold, Herman, 49
Besse, Louisa, 138
Best, Jean, 99
Betts, Rev. Jacob, 31
Bickley, Cecilia, 112
Bickley, John, 112

Briggs, Walter, 62
Briggs, Wheaton, 36
Briggs, William, 37
Brigham, Carl, 289
Brigham, Sabra, 290
Bright, Edna, 127
Bright, Edwin, 51
Bright, Elizabeth, 135
Bright, Elvira, 137
Bright, Harry, 127
Bright, Henry, 127
Bright, Ida, 51
Bright, Ina, 127
Bright, Mabel, 127
Bright, Mary, 127
Bright, Warren, 127
Brightman, Charles, 19
Brightman, Hattie, 348
Brines, Richard, 234
Bristol, Charles, 23
Bristol, Edgar, 23
Bristol, Eliza, 23
Bristol, Ellen, 23
Bristol, Emily, 23
Bristol, Emma, 23
Britton, Annie, 232, 258
Britton, Edith, 178
Britton, James, 232, 258
Britton, Lawson, 178
Britton, Margaret, 232, 258
Broadbent, Elizabeth, 51
Broadbent, Hugh, 51
Broadbent, James, 51
Broadbent, Lilla, 227
Broadley, Sarah, 80
Brock, Albert, 138
Brock, Arthur, 138
Brock, Mary, 138
Brock, Percy, 214
Brodeur, Adrienne, 198
Brodeur, Eugene, 198
Brodeur, Irene, 198
Bromeley, Adelaide, 52
Bromeley, Nancy, 52
Bromeley, Samuel, 52
Bronson, Emma, 34
Bronson, Gladys, 29
Bronson, John, 34
Brooks, A, 166
Brooks, Alvan, 166
Brooks, George, 166
Brooks, Julia, 121
Brooks, Julian, 121
Brooks, Lizzie, 166
Brooks, M, 166
Brooks, Mary, 166
Broomhead, Charles, 81
Broomhead, Walter, 71
Brown, Abby, 289
Brown, Agnes, 347
Brown, Alden, 200
Brown, Alexander, 359
Brown, Almira, 380
Brown, Amelia, 30
Brown, Amos, 142
Brown, Andrew, 68
Brown, Ann, 343
Brown, Anne, 334

Brown, Arnold, 238
Brown, Benjamin, 99
Brown, Betsey, 175, 296
Brown, Beulah, 302
Brown, Captain Elisha, 334
Brown, Capt. Gardner, 319
Brown, Charles, 247, 343
Brown, Clar, 353
Brown, Clarence, 345
Brown, Cloe, 185
Brown, Cora, 238
Brown, Daniel, 289, 359
Brown, David, 185, 334
Brown, Della, 15
Brown, Dr. William, 319
Brown, Edwin, 247
Brown, Elizabeth, 300, 347
Brown, Emily, 146
Brown, Emma, 247, 345
Brown, Ezra, 146, 175
Brown, Florence, 347
Brown, Frank, 163
Brown, Freelove, 317
Brown, George, 31
Brown, Gertrude, 347
Brown, Harrison, 270
Brown, Hazel, 27
Brown, Henry, 347
Brown, Hester, 359
Brown, Ida, 172
Brown, Irving, 171
Brown, Isadora, 289
Brown, James, 319, 334
Brown, Jeanette, 263
Brown, Jesse, 15
Brown, John, 343
Brown, Laveruia, 353
Brown, Lena, 171
Brown, Lewis, 137
Brown, Lilla, 181
Brown, Lorinda, 20
Brown, Lucy, 31
Brown, Lydia, 99, 185
Brown, Marcia, 317
Brown, Marcus, 31, 345
Brown, Margaret, 326, 359
Brown, Maria, 345
Brown, Marianne, 380
Brown, Marion, 356
Brown, Martha, 31, 125
Brown, Martin, 146
Brown, Mary, 187, 200, 353
Brown, Mason, 343
Brown, Minerva, 38
Brown, Nancy, 152, 320
Brown, Nathan, 317
Brown, Nelson, 187
Brown, Nettie, 163
Brown, Norman, 152
Brown, Ossian, 260
Brown, Percy, 30
Brown, Phebe, 21
Brown, Rebecca, 189
Brown, Rev. Edgar, 302
Brown, Rhoda, 146
Brown, Royal, 246
Brown, Sarah, 68, 334
Brown, Sophia, 319

398

Coan, Shubel, 204
Coates, Elsie, 253
Coates, Hartley, 253
Cobb, Albert, 46
Cobb, Amaziah, 46
Cobb, Bertha, 46
Cobb, Bessie, 125
Cobb, Captain Hermon, 367
Cobb, Caroline, 204
Cobb, Cecilla, 366
Cobb, Charles, 44, 297
Cobb, Cornelia, 216
Cobb, Dudania, 205
Cobb, Ebenezer, 208
Cobb, Edwin, 49
Cobb, Elizabeth, 206
Cobb, Ellis, 50
Cobb, Ethan, 366
Cobb, Frederick, 50
Cobb, George, 49
Cobb, Henry, 205
Cobb, Hermon, 367
Cobb, Hildah, 205
Cobb, Ida, 361
Cobb, Jane, 363
Cobb, Jason, 353
Cobb, Jennie, 206
Cobb, John, 205, 208
Cobb, Joseph, 366
Cobb, Lucy, 367
Cobb, Lyman, 216
Cobb, Martin, 206
Cobb, Mary, 46, 191, 217
Cobb, Nancy, 165
Cobb, Olava, 50
Cobb, Polly, 367
Cobb, R, 46
Cobb, Rufus, 165
Cobb, S, 46
Cobb, Sarah, 205, 208
Cobb, Thomas, 46
Cobb, William, 46, 362, 363
Cobb, Z, 50
Cobb, Zuba, 205
Coburn, John, 82
Coburn, Maria, 82
Cochrane, Dana, 134
Cochrane, I, 134
Cochrane, Samuel, 64
Cochrane, Walter, 134
Cockell, Henry, 136
Codding, Augustus, 279
Codding, Eunice, 279
Cody, Marion, 61
Coe, Edward, 29
Coggeshall, Bartha, 252
Coggsell, Mary, 5
Coggsell, Thomas, 5
Cohen, Leon, 249
Colburn, Edson, 56
Colburn, Edwin, 173
Colburn, Prentess, 173
Colburn, Ruth, 173
Colby, Ernest, 163
Colby, George, 174
Colby, Herbert, 61
Cole, Aaron, 296
Cole, Albert, 263

Cole, Alice, 281
Cole, Arvil, 46
Cole, Betsey, 263, 295
Cole, Capt. Constant, 295
Cole, Constant, 296
Cole, Daniel, 276
Cole, Deacon W, 281
Cole, Desire, 295
Cole, Elizabeth, 38, 294
Cole, Elmira, 296
Cole, Fanny, 281
Cole, Francis, 280
Cole, Frank, 347
Cole, George, 280, 290
Cole, Hannah, 278
Cole, Jemima, 296
Cole, Lois, 347
Cole, Louis, 347
Cole, Lucy, 118
Cole, Mary, 44, 280
Cole, Merrill, 144
Cole, Nancy, 276, 281
Cole, Nathan, 118
Cole, Nathaniel, 294
Cole, Otis, 276
Cole, Patience, 302
Cole, Perle, 46
Cole, Polly, 92
Cole, Ralph, 290
Cole, Retta, 34
Cole, Samuel, 46, 285
Cole, Sarah, 294, 347
Cole, Seneca, 38
Cole, Simeon, 281
Cole, Simon, 278
Cole, William, 347
Cole, Zemas, 290
Coleman, Abigail, 361
Coleman, Albert, 359
Coleman, Anne, 361
Coleman, Annie, 202
Coleman, Clarissa, 359
Coleman, Erwin, 360
Coleman, Harvey, 360, 361
Coleman, Job, 360
Coleman, John, 358
Coles, Chester, 63
Coles, William, 63
Collin, Rebecca, 319
Collingwood, Ethel, 29
Collingwood, Fred, 29
Collingwood, Harold, 29
Collingwood, Lenora, 29
Collins, Jessie, 69
Collins, John, 198
Collins, Joseph, 199
Collins, Sarah, 198
Collins, Wilbur, 232, 258
Colman, Lorin, 142
Colson, George, 138
Colvin, Benjamin, 267
Colvin, J, 267
Colvin, Julia, 258
Colvin, Romona, 166
Comer, John, 274
Comey, Annah, 179
Comey, Aratus, 179
Comey, Ethel, 102

402

Comey, Frank, 101
Comey, Ophelia, 101
Comey, William, 101
Comsett, James, 368
Comstock, Abigail, 374
Comstock, Betsey, 377
Comstock, Cyrus, 374
Comstock, Nathan, 377
Comstock, Walter, 377
Conefy, John, 202
Connelly, Roseanna, 201
Conners, Catherine, 199
Conners, John, 199
Connor, Olive, 106
Conway, Eliza, 120
Conway, James, 120
Conyers, Clarence, 328
Cook, Abbie, 119
Cook, Alice, 369
Cook, Alonzo, 359
Cook, Amelia, 362
Cook, Conrad, 376
Cook, Cordelia, 359
Cook, Daniel, 362
Cook, Eldora, 370
Cook, Eliza, 105
Cook, Emma, 373
Cook, Eunice, 362
Cook, Francis, 82
Cook, Frank, 369
Cook, Franklyn, 376
Cook, Frederic, 370
Cook, George, 32, 369, 373
Cook, Gertrude, 114
Cook, Goerge, 32
Cook, Hattie, 216
Cook, Haze, 114
Cook, Helen, 216
Cook, Herbert, 114
Cook, Horace, 369
Cook, Jessie, 359
Cook, John, 61
Cook, Lucretia, 369
Cook, Lucy, 113
Cook, Martha, 46, 369
Cook, Mary, 82, 114, 369
Cook, Myrtle, 369
Cook, Nancy, 210
Cook, Oliver, 362
Cook, Philander, 369
Cook, Sarah, 61, 369, 373
Cook, Thomas, 340
Cook, Warren, 373
Cooke, Deacon Abner, 370
Cooke, Jennie, 116
Cooke, Lucy, 116
Cooke, Mary, 116
Cooke, Rena, 116
Cooke, Rhoda, 370
Cooke, Winslow, 116
Coolum, Liston, 190
Coombs, Adelaide, 214
Coombs, Charles, 222
Coombs, Ethel, 214
Coombs, Harriet, 222
Coombs, Horace, 222
Coombs, John, 214
Coombs, Orrin, 219

Coombs, Permelia, 222
Coombs, Reuben, 222
Cooper, Betsey, 284
Cooper, Earl, 64
Cooper, Elizabeth, 42
Cooper, Herbert, 64
Cooper, Sarah, 205
Cooper, Thomas, 87
Cooper, William, 205
Cooper. Alvin, 45
Coor, Cynthia, 377
Copeland, Annie, 217
Copeland, James, 217
Copeland, Sarah, 232, 258
Corbett, Abigail, 139
Corbett, James, 128
Corbin, Daniel, 110
Corbin, Elizabeth, 313
Corbin, Francis, 223
Corbin, Leroy, 221, 223
Corbin, Mary, 223
Corbin, Otis, 110
Corbin, William, 313
Corey, Ada, 84
Corey, Charles, 135
Corey, Elizabeth, 221
Corey, Martin, 85
Corey, Mary, 232, 258
Corey, William, 232, 258
Cornell, Captain James, 314
Cornell, Lydia, 331
Cornell, Ruth, 314
Corser, Lester, 254
Corson, David, 126
Corson, Fred, 127
Corson, Hannah, 126
Cosseboom, Amanda, 129
Cosseboom, Frances, 129
Cosseboom, Minnie, 129
Cotton, Abby, 134
Cotton, Daniel, 134
Cotton, Elizabeth, 298
Cotton, Ellen, 337
Cotton, James, 337
Cotton, John, 337
Cotton, Manly, 337
Cotton, William, 134
Cottrele, Irene, 255
Coupe, Ellen, 19
Coupe, Elsie, 22
Coupe, Ernest, 9
Coupe, PVT Clarence, 346
Coupe, Ralph, 346
Coupe, Sarah, 346
Coupe, William, 18
Courtney, Charlotte, 351
Courtney, Gertrude, 39
Courtney, Ruth, 351
Cowell, Elizabeth, 365
Cowell, Ellen, 365
Cowell, Hiram, 364
Cowell, Horace, 364
Cowell, Jemima, 365
Cowell, John, 365
Cowell, Leonidas, 365
Cowell, Martha, 362
Cowell, Mary, 139
Cowell, Nancy, 365

Daniels, Albert, 113
Daniels, Annie, 120
Daniels, Arvilla, 112
Daniels, Augustus, 178
Daniels, Betsey, 178
Daniels, Cyrus, 102
Daniels, Dan, 182
Daniels, Dora, 102
Daniels, Ella, 177
Daniels, Ellen, 110
Daniels, Elvira, 110
Daniels, Emma, 172
Daniels, Fisher, 116
Daniels, Freda, 132
Daniels, Harry, 112
Daniels, Hattie, 136
Daniels, Henry, 132
Daniels, Jessie, 182
Daniels, John, 107, 178
Daniels, Joseph, 113
Daniels, Julian, 77
Daniels, Lois, 124
Daniels, Louisa, 107
Daniels, Lucinda, 176
Daniels, Lucius, 136
Daniels, Lucretia, 105
Daniels, Lucy, 117
Daniels, Mary, 120, 135, 136, 178
Daniels, Milcah, 124
Daniels, Myrtle, 112
Daniels, Nahum, 117
Daniels, Nathan, 107
Daniels, Olive, 114
Daniels, Pauline, 77
Daniels, Rhoda, 147
Daniels, Sabin, 110
Daniels, Sally, 117
Daniels, Sarah, 107, 136
Daniels, T, 102
Daniels, Timothy, 147
Daniels, Waldo, 112
Daniels, Walter, 120
Dank, Ethel, 261
Dank, Rev. Frederick, 261
Darey, George, 24
Dargis, Henry, 200
Darling, Albert, 220
Darling, Allen, 380
Darling, Anna, 363
Darling, Annice, 137
Darling, Arthur, 220
Darling, Charles, 140
Darling, Dora, 113
Darling, Edward, 74, 113
Darling, Eleanor, 380
Darling, Elias, 380
Darling, Eliza, 384
Darling, Etta, 220
Darling, Fenner, 140
Darling, Harriet, 113, 160, 220
Darling, Herbert, 113
Darling, John, 375
Darling, Julia, 225
Darling, Kenneth, 113
Darling, Louisa, 380
Darling, Lyman, 384
Darling, Marcia, 134
Darling, Maria, 380

Darling, Mayo, 113
Darling, Nancy, 380
Darling, Nelson, 225
Darling, Sadie, 140
Darling, Sarah, 140, 380
Darling, Silas, 380
Darling, Wilson, 384
Darn, Kar, 215
Darrah, Catherine, 197
Darrah, Vernon, 197
Dart, Adiliza, 364
Dart, Gustavus, 364
Dauphinee, George, 127
Davidson, Elizabeth, 139
Davidson, Emma, 54
Davidson, Helen, 249
Davidson, Lester, 347
Davidson, Louise, 347
Davis, Alathea, 283
Davis, Anna, 232, 258, 273
Davis, Barney, 273
Davis, Betsey, 263, 314
Davis, Captain Daniel, 314
Davis, Captain George, 333
Davis, Caroline, 222
Davis, Catherine, 353
Davis, Clara, 282
Davis, Cora, 29
Davis, Cynthia, 278
Davis, Deacon Aaron, 1
Davis, Deacon John, 283
Davis, Edward, 215, 279
Davis, Elisha, 278, 318
Davis, Ellen, 125
Davis, Emily, 279
Davis, Eunice, 2
Davis, Fanny, 328
Davis, Franklin, 333
Davis, Fred, 127
Davis, George, 279
Davis, Gertrude, 112, 299
Davis, Grace, 343
Davis, Harley, 328
Davis, Harriet, 232, 333
Davis, Henry, 337
Davis, Hiram, 279
Davis, Irving, 215
Davis, Job, 333
Davis, John, 125, 261, 273, 278, 283, 333
Davis, Joseph, 259, 263, 278
Davis, Julia, 328
Davis, Julius, 112
Davis, Leafy, 278
Davis, Leroy, 299
Davis, Loring, 279
Davis, Lydia, 319
Davis, Margaret, 1, 258
Davis, Mary, 215, 220, 232, 273, 283
Davis, Marybelle, 328
Davis, Melinda, 261
Davis, Mildred, 343
Davis, Minnie, 233
Davis, Nancy, 316
Davis, Nathaniel, 232, 258, 261
Davis, Peter, 278
Davis, Polly, 278, 283
Davis, Rev. Jacob, 232, 258
Davis, Richard, 35

407

411

414

Goff, Andrew, 98
Goff, Anna, 96
Goff, Annie, 233
Goff, Ariel, 258
Goff, Asenath, 94
Goff, Auther, 233
Goff, Barbara, 250
Goff, Bathshebe, 230
Goff, Benjamin, 92, 94, 99
Goff, Betsey, 257
Goff, Carrie, 233, 344
Goff, Charles, 92, 248
Goff, Chester, 98
Goff, Clifton, 264
Goff, Col. Ethan, 156
Goff, Constant, 258
Goff, Cromwell, 248
Goff, Crumel, 257
Goff, Cynthia, 81
Goff, Cyrus, 246
Goff, Darius, 258
Goff, Deborah, 93
Goff, Delila, 246
Goff, Earl, 250
Goff, Edwin, 258
Goff, Elder Enoch, 92
Goff, Elder Nathan, 257
Goff, Elenor, 94
Goff, Eliza, 248
Goff, Elizabeth, 30
Goff, Ellery, 248
Goff, Elsie, 248
Goff, Emerson, 98
Goff, Emma, 266
Goff, Enoch, 93, 246
Goff, Ephraim, 96, 98, 99, 236, 257
Goff, Eudora, 92
Goff, Flora, 81
Goff, Fred, 248
Goff, George, 99, 248
Goff, Gilbert, 66
Goff, Grace, 233
Goff, Hannah, 92, 94, 237
Goff, Harold, 233, 249
Goff, Harriet, 99
Goff, Hattie, 40
Goff, Henry, 81, 92, 232, 235, 258
Goff, Herbert, 232, 258
Goff, Hiram, 246
Goff, Horatio, 230
Goff, Howard, 100
Goff, Isaiah, 94
Goff, Israel, 258
Goff, James, 30, 232, 258
Goff, Jane, 92
Goff, Jefferson, 94
Goff, Jesse, 94
Goff, Joseph, 230
Goff, Josephine, 325
Goff, Judith, 92
Goff, Keziah, 246
Goff, Leon, 233
Goff, Leroy, 232, 258
Goff, Levi, 92, 230
Goff, Lillas, 92
Goff, Lillian, 92
Goff, Lizzie, 233
Goff, Louis, 97

Goff, Lovell, 258
Goff, Lucina, 258
Goff, Luther, 236
Goff, Lydia, 257
Goff, Mabel, 31
Goff, Mary, 93, 258
Goff, Mercy, 258
Goff, Miram, 242
Goff, Mrs. Mehitable, 229
Goff, Muriel, 249
Goff, Nancy, 92, 94, 97, 258
Goff, Nathan, 30, 94, 95
Goff, Olive, 257
Goff, Pamela, 94
Goff, Patience, 230
Goff, Polly, 94, 156
Goff, Priscilla, 92
Goff, Rebecca, 230
Goff, Richard, 229
Goff, Ruth, 95, 248, 250
Goff, Sally, 257, 258
Goff, Samuel, 94, 257, 274
Goff, Sarah, 66, 81, 95, 99, 258
Goff, Simeon, 247
Goff, Sybil, 94
Goff, Sylvanus, 257
Goff, Sylvester, 246
Goff, Truman, 92, 99
Goff, Walter, 247, 281
Goff, Warren, 230
Goff, William, 81, 94, 99, 250, 257, 258, 264
Goff, Zenas, 97, 258
Goghreaurn, William, 78
Gonia, Annie, 27
Gooch, Arthur, 177
Gooch, Blendena, 177
Goodale, Elisabeth, 165
Goodall, David, 240
Goodins, James, 182
Goodrich, Carrie, 182
Goodrich, Cyrus, 182
Goodrich, Icsa, 352
Goodwin, William, 101
Gorden, Sally, 163
Gorman, James, 252
Gorton, Ellen, 377
Gorton, Emeline, 375
Gorton, Jennie, 113
Gorton, John, 375
Gorton, Rebecca, 98
Gorton, Thomas, 98
Goss, Annie, 338
Goss, Edward, 338
Goss, Henry, 338
Gould, Albert, 129
Gould, Alice, 126
Gould, Amos, 238
Gould, Etta, 238
Gould, Marcy, 126
Gould, Mira, 129
Gould, Nina, 129
Gould, Priscilla, 105
Gould, Sally, 223
Gould, William, 126, 223
Goundier, Charles, 221
Gousie, Marie, 79
Gove, Mattie, 180
Gowen, Deacon Charles, 113

Gowen, Elvira, 113
Gowen, Horace, 113
Gowen, Luther, 113
Gowen, Polly, 113
Gowen, Sarah, 113
Goyette, David, 253
Gradwell, Grace, 255
Graham, Charlotte, 316
Graham, Clara, 218, 252
Graham, Flora, 216
Graham, Henry, 315
Graham, Jennie, 201
Graham, Josiah, 317
Graham, Julia, 317
Graham, Margaret, 231, 258
Graham, Mary, 81
Grant, Addie, 378
Grant, Adeliza, 372
Grant, Agnes, 374
Grant, Albert, 320
Grant, Alpha, 374
Grant, Anne, 362
Grant, Annie, 327, 376
Grant, Arel, 320
Grant, Benjamin, 320, 372
Grant, Campbell, 62
Grant, Capt. Joshua, 370
Grant, Carrie, 131
Grant, Charlotte, 373
Grant, Clarissa, 382
Grant, Daniel, 310
Grant, David, 372
Grant, Edith, 376
Grant, Edna, 72
Grant, Elery, 370
Grant, Elizabeth, 205
Grant, Emily, 237
Grant, Esther, 377
Grant, Experience, 374
Grant, Fenner, 374
Grant, George, 371, 372
Grant, Harlous, 380
Grant, Harrie, 326
Grant, Helen, 25
Grant, Henry, 237, 320
Grant, Herbert, 239, 321
Grant, Joanna, 371
Grant, Joseph, 374, 376
Grant, Joshua, 382
Grant, Justus, 377
Grant, Lois, 370
Grant, Mabelle, 378
Grant, Marcus, 326
Grant, Margaret, 376
Grant, Mary, 370, 374, 384
Grant, Milton, 372
Grant, Miranda, 371
Grant, Moses, 377
Grant, Olive, 377
Grant, Parley, 377
Grant, Patience, 377
Grant, Polly, 319
Grant, Rachel, 310, 372
Grant, Rose, 231, 258
Grant, Ruth, 326
Grant, Samuel, 374
Grant, Sarah, 207, 376
Grant, Thankful, 377

Grant, Urania, 374
Grant, Violet, 239
Grant, Walter, 72
Grant, Welcom, 378
Grant, Wilfrid, 376
Grant, William, 315, 372
Grant, Zeolde, 372
Graves, Maria, 332
Graves, Z, 332
Gray, Ada, 297
Gray, Alice, 297
Gray, Avi, 297
Gray, Charles, 296
Gray, Chester, 254
Gray, Clara, 298
Gray, Clarence, 297
Gray, Eliza, 298
Gray, Elizabeth, 297
Gray, Etta, 298
Gray, Franklin, 296
Gray, Hattie, 296
Gray, Henriettta, 297
Gray, Horace, 298
Gray, Jeremiah, 297
Gray, John, 298
Gray, Joseph, 21, 338
Gray, Kate, 297
Gray, Lester, 254
Gray, Lewis, 297
Gray, Lizzie, 297
Gray, Lula, 65
Gray, Lydia, 297
Gray, Majorie, 298
Gray, Mary, 297
Gray, Mima, 297, 299
Gray, Richmond, 298
Gray, Sarah, 338
Gray, William, 297
Green, George, 262
Green, Lois, 121
Green, Sarah, 262
Greene, Glady, 288
Greene, Henry, 119
Greene, Lois, 119
Greene, Martin, 119
Greene, Mary, 76
Greene, Myrtle, 76
Greene, Nabbi, 68
Greene, William, 76
Greenman, Esther, 307
Greenwood, Alonzo, 128
Greenwood, Cora, 129
Greenwood, James, 25
Greenwood, Margaret, 25
Greenwood, Martha, 25
Greenwood, Thomas, 25
Greer, Margaret, 316
Gregory, Alice, 340
Grennell, Edgar, 213
Greve, Agnes, 220
Greve, Albert, 220
Greve, Alvine, 220
Greve, August, 215
Grey, Elizabeth, 337
Grey, Honora, 199
Grey, Horace, 337
Grey, Jane, 337
Grey, Mary, 337

417

418

Hall, Melina, 202
Hall, Othelia, 162
Hall, Ruana, 5
Hall, Ruth, 33
Hall, Samuel, 154
Hall, Thomas, 110
Hall, Uberto, 74
Hall, William, 48, 202
Hallam, Eliza, 105
Hallam, Flora, 101
Hallam, Samuel, 104
Hallam, Thomas, 105
Halleburton, William, 137
Halliday, Ella, 66
Halliday, Emma, 76
Halliday, Rena, 76
Halliday, Thomas, 76
Hamant, Francis, 114
Hamant, Helen, 114
Hamilton, Ann, 42
Hamilton, Charles, 360
Hamilton, James, 42
Hamilton, John, 42
Hamilton, Joseph, 42
Hamilton, Margaret, 42
Hamilton, Nancy, 42
Hamlin, George, 73
Hamlin, Maria, 73
Hammond, Edward, 41
Hammond, Ellen, 41
Hammond, Hen, 41
Hammond, Josephine, 41
Hammond, Sophia, 41
Hammond, William, 41
Hancock, Abbey, 207
Hancock, Amey, 382
Hancock, Annie, 65
Hancock, Daniel, 383
Hancock, Deacon Philip, 383
Hancock, Dorcas, 208
Hancock, Ellen, 208
Hancock, Esther, 207
Hancock, Eva, 111
Hancock, Francis, 111
Hancock, George, 208, 384
Hancock, Hannah, 111
Hancock, Harriet, 130, 207, 208, 379
Hancock, Henry, 207
Hancock, John, 207
Hancock, Joseph, 383
Hancock, M, 384
Hancock, Rachel, 383
Hancock, Reuben, 383
Hancock, Sally, 368
Hancock, Samuel, 382
Hancock, Sarah, 207
Hancock, Timothy, 207
Hancock, Walter, 111
Handy, Albert, 316
Handy, Bertha, 38
Handy, Esther, 315
Handy, George, 38
Handy, Gladys, 38
Handy, Martin, 316
Handy, Mary, 308
Handy, Silas, 308
Handy, Stella, 38
Handy, Thomas, 315

Handy, Willard, 38
Hanly, Eliza, 227
Hannalty, Thomas, 240
Hanson, Anna, 28
Hanson, Henry, 79
Hanson, Mary, 79
Hanway, Mary, 33
Hard, Sybil, 317
Harden, Arlon, 216
Harden, Fannie, 216
Harden, Thankful, 216
Harding, Annie, 48
Harding, Bertha, 167
Harding, Caleb, 175
Harding, Harriet, 225
Harding, Hepzibah, 168
Harding, Lydia, 363
Harding, Moses, 48
Harding, O, 175
Harding, Oscar, 173
Harding, R, 175
Harding, Richard, 294
Harding, Rosanna, 173
Harding, Russ, 128
Hardley, Ellen, 258
Hardon, Alcott, 47
Hardon, Anna, 66
Hardy, Ellen, 232
Hardy, Eunice, 103
Harlow, Clifford, 100
Harlow, John, 99
Harlow, Nellie, 99, 100
Harman, Ethelbert, 254
Harmon, Edna, 254
Harriamn, S, 162
Harriman, Emma, 162
Harriman, Rose, 162
Harriman, T, 162
Harrington, Ella, 170
Harrington, Frances, 26
Harrington, Joseph, 380
Harrington, Rosina, 380
Harris, Alexander, 380
Harris, Betsey, 105, 262
Harris, Electra, 136
Harris, Elisha, 105
Harris, Elizabeth, 55
Harris, Ellen, 10
Harris, Emma, 55
Harris, Eunice, 10
Harris, Frank, 380
Harris, George, 73
Harris, Mary, 381
Harris, Nancy, 136
Harris, Ralph, 55
Harris, Robert, 73
Harris, Sarah, 73
Harris, Vera, 73
Harrison, Berthram, 158
Hart, Alice, 174
Hart, George, 174
Hart, John, 181
Hart, Sarah, 181
Hartman, Frederick, 213
Hartman, Theresa, 213
Hartmann, Edward, 124
Hartmann, Elizabeth, 124
Hartmann, Rose, 124

419

Hill, Hannah, 146
Hill, Izanne, 159
Hill, Jonathan, 309
Hill, Lucretia, 111
Hill, Margaret, 154
Hill, Mary, 309
Hill, Parshan, 309
Hill, Ruth, 309
Hill, Sergt. Ebenezer., 154
Hill, Seth, 206
Hill, Susanna, 238
Hill, Thomas, 238
Hill, Whiting, 146
Hill, William, 238
Hills, Abigail, 118
Hills, Edward, 113
Hills, Eudora, 113
Hills, George, 118
Hills, Harvey, 118
Hills, Joseph, 137
Hills, Mary, 118, 137
Hills, Sanford, 113
Hilton, Dr. John, 338
Hilton, Elizabeth, 338
Hilton, Elmira, 206
Hinds, Abbie, 25
Hinds, Clara, 73
Hinds, Edward, 73
Hinds, Hannah, 73
Hinds, Harry, 73
Hinds, Leonard, 73
Hine, Freddie, 210
Hines, Charles, 210
Hines, Ella, 174
Hingley, Albert, 189
Hingley, Harriet, 189
Hinnam, Chauncey, 255
Hinnam, Harold, 255
Hirsch, Isabella, 352
Hitchcock, Sarah, 364
Hix, Deacon Benjamin, 258
Hix, Hezekiah, 280
Hix, Lydia, 258
Hixon, Edmund, 186
Hixon, Mortimer, 186
Hoag, Harriet, 288
Hobigand, Martha, 114
Hodge, James, 71
Hodge, Mary, 71
Hodge, Nellie, 71
Hodge, Rhoda, 71
Hodge, William, 71
Hodges, Bebe, 42
Hodges, Gardner, 42
Hodges, Harold, 25
Hodges, Howard, 42
Hodges, John, 301
Hodges, Josephine, 42
Hodges, Nellie, 25
Hodges, Orville, 42
Hodges, Sophronia, 301
Hodges, William, 25
Hodgkin, Emory, 181
Hodgkin, Maria, 181
Hoffman, Bertha, 218
Hoffman, Charles, 148
Hoffman, Frank, 217
Hoffman, Helen, 147

Hoffman, Ira, 175
Hoffman, Mary, 165
Hoffman, Robert, 39
Hoffman, Walter, 147
Hogdes, Helen, 25
Hoit, Ellen, 66
Holbrook, Abbie, 166
Holbrook, Anna, 177
Holbrook, Bernice, 81
Holbrook, Caroline, 82
Holbrook, Cora, 82
Holbrook, Corp. George, 177
Holbrook, Dennis, 155
Holbrook, Elizabeth, 51, 155, 160
Holbrook, Ella, 78
Holbrook, Ezekiel, 82
Holbrook, Franklin, 82
Holbrook, Frederick, 81
Holbrook, George, 78
Holbrook, Gertrude, 81
Holbrook, Harlous, 167
Holbrook, Harry, 61
Holbrook, Horace, 51
Holbrook, James, 180
Holbrook, John, 82
Holbrook, Josephine, 82
Holbrook, Julia, 82
Holbrook, Mahala, 180
Holbrook, Maria, 82
Holbrook, Marion, 50
Holbrook, Mary, 51, 167
Holbrook, Minnie, 51
Holbrook, Moses, 177
Holbrook, Rhoda, 160
Holcomb, Betsey, 297
Holden, Alfred, 23
Holden, Dr. Charles, 36
Holden, E, 23
Holden, Florence, 270
Holden, George, 270
Holden, W. Luther, 270
Holley, Albert, 68
Holley, Alonzo, 68
Holley, Harriet, 68
Holley, Harry, 68
Holley, Richmond, 68
Holmes, Adelaide, 173
Holmes, Alton, 338
Holmes, Amy, 188
Holmes, Anna, 364
Holmes, Annie, 26
Holmes, Arthur, 129, 371
Holmes, Asenath, 4
Holmes, Augustus, 190
Holmes, Bertha, 371
Holmes, Betsey, 188, 190
Holmes, Carrie, 371
Holmes, Charles, 190
Holmes, Cora, 190
Holmes, Eleanor, 190
Holmes, Eliphelet, 190
Holmes, Eliphlet, 188
Holmes, Eliza, 22
Holmes, Elizabeth, 166, 190
Holmes, George, 67, 106, 188
Holmes, Gertrude, 338
Holmes, Hannah, 4
Holmes, Harriet, 188

422

Holmes, Ida, 129
Holmes, James, 190
Holmes, Joanna, 188
Holmes, John, 22
Holmes, Leander, 22
Holmes, Lilli, 190
Holmes, Maria, 22
Holmes, Mary, 61, 190
Holmes, Milton, 188
Holmes, Nancy, 190
Holmes, Oliver, 22
Holmes, Percy, 190
Holmes, Robert, 364, 371
Holmes, Roland, 237
Holmes, S, 166
Holmes, Samuel, 4
Holmes, Sarah, 190
Holmes, Stephen, 166
Holmes, W, 166
Holmes, William, 175, 190
Holt, Annie, 135
Holt, Mary, 64
Holton, Hilma, 65
Hooker, Emma, 161
Hooker, Harlow, 161
Hooper, Ethel, 130
Hooper, Henrietta, 130
Hooper, Irene, 130
Hooper, William, 130
Hope, Charles, 354
Hope, Henry, 354
Hope, John, 354
Hope, Sarah, 354
Hope, Susan, 354
Hopkins, Betsey, 368
Hopkins, L, 22
Hopkins, Mary, 368
Hopwood, James, 75, 76
Horn, Alathea, 275
Horn, Daniel, 275
Horne, Bessie, 33
Horne, J, 33
Horne, Walter, 33
Horning, Hermon, 217
Horr, Abie, 288
Horr, Abigai, 288
Horr, Almond, 288
Horr, Elizabeth, 288
Horr, George, 212, 288
Horr, Jacob, 288
Horr, Wealthy, 288
Horton, R, 36
Horton, Aaron, 94
Horton, Abbie, 261
Horton, Abby, 16
Horton, Abiel, 257
Horton, Abigail, 94
Horton, Adaline, 97
Horton, Addie, 340
Horton, Albert, 324
Horton, Alfred, 96, 305
Horton, Almira, 232, 258, 260
Horton, Amanda, 238
Horton, Amelia, 253
Horton, Andrew, 323
Horton, Angelina, 260
Horton, Ann, 94, 262, 270, 318
Horton, Annie, 323

Horton, Augustus, 22
Horton, Benjamin, 248
Horton, Benson, 96
Horton, Bertha, 328
Horton, Betsey, 241, 248, 261
Horton, Caleb, 104
Horton, Capt. Benjamin, 248
Horton, Caroline, 98, 248
Horton, Carrie, 322
Horton, Charles, 97, 98, 261
Horton, Charlotte, 97
Horton, Chloe, 257
Horton, Clara, 98
Horton, Clarence, 324
Horton, Constant, 94
Horton, Cora, 324
Horton, Danforth, 247
Horton, Daniel, 257
Horton, Darius, 260
Horton, Edwin, 36, 260
Horton, Eldora, 93
Horton, Elisha, 321
Horton, Eliza, 260
Horton, Elizabeth, 169, 321
Horton, Ellen, 320, 326
Horton, Ellis, 234
Horton, Elmer, 253
Horton, Emma, 98, 270
Horton, Esther, 97
Horton, Ethel, 230, 258
Horton, Everett, 326
Horton, Fannie, 97
Horton, Fred, 258
Horton, Frederick, 230
Horton, George, 69, 94, 169, 233, 261, 318
Horton, Gerald, 230, 258
Horton, Gideon, 36, 256
Horton, Gilbert, 233, 258, 318, 324
Horton, Gunge, 258
Horton, Halsey, 322
Horton, Hannah, 22, 63, 259
Horton, Harriet, 260
Horton, Helen, 36
Horton, Herbert, 92
Horton, Hiram, 260
Horton, Horace, 319
Horton, Howard, 98
Horton, Ida, 324, 325
Horton, Isabe, 258
Horton, Isabell, 232
Horton, Jacob, 322
Horton, James, 16, 37, 94, 260, 270, 320
Horton, Jane, 261
Horton, Jarvus, 324
Horton, Jemima, 258
Horton, Jennie, 230
Horton, Jeremiah, 321
Horton, Jervis, 321
Horton, Joannah, 94
Horton, John, 97, 260, 270, 318, 321
Horton, Jonathan, 321
Horton, Josephine, 324
Horton, Josephus, 261
Horton, Laura, 256
Horton, Leland, 326
Horton, Levi, 323
Horton, Lindly, 97
Horton, Louisa, 243

Horton, Lovina, 256
Horton, Lucretia, 97
Horton, Lucy, 96
Horton, Lydia, 260, 305, 321
Horton, Major Everett, 37
Horton, Martha, 104, 319
Horton, Mary, 94, 234, 241, 261, 270, 323, 339
Horton, Nancy, 97, 243, 258, 259
Horton, Nathan, 259, 319
Horton, Nelson, 98
Horton, Norman, 262
Horton, Olive, 319
Horton, Orrin, 97
Horton, Otis, 321
Horton, Pamela, 96
Horton, Patience, 94
Horton, Peter, 325
Horton, Rachel, 233, 258, 271
Horton, Raymond, 36
Horton, Rebecca, 323
Horton, Rev. Geroge, 322
Horton, Rev. Josephus, 318
Horton, Robert, 233
Horton, Samuel, 231, 258
Horton, Sarah, 69, 96, 260, 318, 322
Horton, Selena, 258
Horton, Selina, 230
Horton, Seneca, 248
Horton, Seth, 319, 322
Horton, Shubael, 94, 95
Horton, Sophia, 270
Horton, Susan, 94, 328
Horton, Susanna, 260
Horton, Waity, 261
Horton, Welcome, 318
Horton, Welcome F., 318
Horton, Wheeler, 97
Horton, William, 243
Hosie, Clara, 126
Hosie, George, 126
Hosie, Jean, 129
Hosie, John, 129
Houghton, Cryus, 168
Houghton, Eliza, 168
Howard, Annie, 137
Howard, Apollo, 102
Howard, Betsey, 308
Howard, Capt. John, 375
Howard, Caroline, 102
Howard, Edwin, 155
Howard, Franklin, 102
Howard, George, 308
Howard, Hattie, 102
Howard, Henry, 102
Howard, Huldah, 108
Howard, John, 44, 252
Howard, Lucy, 376
Howard, Lydia, 376
Howard, M, 343
Howard, Mary, 5
Howard, Susan, 155
Howard, Welcome, 376
Howarth, Florence, 29
Howarth, James, 29
Howarth, John, 182
Howarth, Mary, 182
Howe, Alice, 113
Howe, Alonzo, 166

Howe, Benjamin, 132
Howe, Edwin, 21
Howe, Eliza, 355
Howe, Ella, 113
Howe, George, 355
Howe, Isaac, 144
Howe, Lois, 143, 144
Howe, Louisa, 144
Howe, Luther, 144
Howe, Ruth, 21
Howe, W, 113
Howe, William, 144
Howland, Isaac, 288
Hoxie, Charles, 80
Hoxie, Jennie, 80
Hoyle, William, 56
Hoyt, Edith, 82
Hoyt, William, 82
Hubbard, Elisha, 132
Hubbard, Ethel, 109
Hubbard, Joshua, 125
Hubbard, Mary, 109
Hubbard, Mrytle, 254
Hubbard, Nathaniel, 109
Hubbard, Sabin, 132
Hubbard, Sarah, 121
Hubbard, William, 254
Hubbert, Winslow, 255
Huestin, Fanny, 210
Hughes, Alice, 247
Hughes, Harold, 80
Hughes, Harry, 247
Hughes, May, 12
Hulbowan, Mary, 65
Hull, Manton, 334
Hull, Samuel, 335
Hull, Sarah, 334, 335
Humbold, Margaret, 73
Humes, Marybelle, 67
Humphrey, Irene, 247
Humphrey, Maria, 332
Humphrey, Raymond, 247
Humphrey, Rev. James, 143
Humphreys, Mary, 112
Hundt, Grace, 249
Hunstable, Lydia, 145
Hunt, Abby, 6, 7
Hunt, Abigail, 3
Hunt, Althea, 169
Hunt, Ann, 3
Hunt, Capt. Robert, 252
Hunt, Carlos, 7
Hunt, Caroline, 3
Hunt, Charlotte, 3
Hunt, Daniel, 20
Hunt, Deacon Richard, 3
Hunt, Edward, 3
Hunt, Elist, 7
Hunt, Fanny, 41
Hunt, George, 169
Hunt, Johanna, 358
Hunt, John, 169
Hunt, Joseph, 3
Hunt, Julia, 39, 169
Hunt, Martha, 238
Hunt, Mary, 7
Hunt, Minnie, 340
Hunt, Rev. Samuel, 6

427

429

431

Mason, John, 298, 305, 335
Mason, Joshua, 316
Mason, Kezia, 352
Mason, Laurinda, 379
Mason, Lillis, 351
Mason, Lurana, 305
Mason, Lydia, 304, 352
Mason, Lyman, 311
Mason, Margaret, 13
Mason, Martha, 352
Mason, Mary, 74, 132, 235, 300, 304, 305, 306, 321, 322, 331, 333, 343, 351, 352, 377, 380
Mason, Nancy, 298, 345
Mason, Narzette, 75
Mason, Noah, 34
Mason, Oliver, 343
Mason, Olney, 351
Mason, Parthenia, 298
Mason, Patience, 302
Mason, Phebe, 298, 302
Mason, Polly, 277
Mason, Rev. Russell, 302
Mason, Rosmond, 332
Mason, Roswell, 346
Mason, Ruthy, 302
Mason, Sally, 272, 335, 373
Mason, Samson, 336
Mason, Samue, 346
Mason, Samuel, 336
Mason, Sarah, 77, 318, 343, 379
Mason, Thomas, 311
Mason, Valentine, 336
Mason, Warren, 75, 351
Mason, William, 65, 336
Mason, Zeriah, 302
Mason, Zerviah, 349
Mathewson, Carra, 44
Mathewson, Charles, 26, 63
Mathewson, Eunice, 66
Mathewson, John, 66
Matteson, Catherine, 28
Matteson, James, 70
Matteson, Muriel, 28
Matthews, Cora, 230, 258
Matthews, George, 230, 258
Matthews, Lena, 285
Matthewson, Ida, 222
Matthewson, William, 222
Mattson, Sandra, 64
Maxam, Annie, 300
Maxam, Willard, 301
Maxam, William, 301
Maxcy, Abigail, 193
Maxcy, Alexander, 193
Maxcy, Ella, 213
Maxcy, Ernest, 217
Maxcy, Frank, 217
Maxcy, George, 217
Maxcy, Hannah, 193
Maxcy, Henry, 193
Maxcy, Ida, 217
Maxcy, Joseph, 193
Maxcy, Josiah, 193
Maxcy, M, 217
Maxcy, Mary, 210
Maxcy, Nabby, 209
Maxcy, Sarah, 193
Maxcy, Susan, 17

Maxcy, Virgil, 213
May, Catherine, 2
May, John, 346
May, Lemuel, 16
May, Tilly, 2
Mayhuse, E, 160
Mayo, Irvin, 339
Mayo, Ruth, 339
Mayshaw, Henry, 361
Mayshaw, Leon, 361
McAvoy, Mary, 199
McAvoy, Walter, 199
McCann, Elizabeth, 214
McCann, Sarah, 289
McCarthney, Alice, 56
McCarthney, Bertram, 56
McCarthney, Ella, 56
McCarthney, Samuel, 56
McCarthy, Annie, 197
McCarthy, Edwin, 197
McClary, Elizabeth, 171
McClary, George, 171
McClary, Mary, 171
McComb, James, 232, 258
McConnell, Sarah, 290
McCormick, Thomas, 102
McCrea, Sara, 70
McCulloch, William, 21
McCutchen, Anna, 133
McDougall, Elizabeth, 132
McDougall, Julia, 133
McDougall. Charles, 133
McEwen, James, 384
McEwen, Maria, 384
McFadden, Andrew, 130
McFadden, Kate, 130
McGhee, James, 23
McGovern, Thomas, 200
McGregor, Ann, 215
McGregor, Barbara, 215
McGregor, Duncan, 215
McGregor, Una, 36
Mchalik, John, 12
McIsaac, James, 51
McIsaac, Veronica, 51
McKechnie, Bessie, 222
McKenna, Dominic, 201
McKenzie, Peter, 10
McKerson, Almira, 167
McKim, Lena, 62
McKim, Mabel, 63
McLane, Albert, 34
McLane, Chester, 34
McLane, Eliza, 60
McLane, Eugene, 34
McLane, Florence, 30
McLane, James, 60
McLane, Lucy, 34
McLaughlin, Malachi, 143
McLean, Dorothy, 174
McLean, Eli, 174
McLeod, Barbara, 227
McLeod, Hector, 226
McLeod, Helen, 226
McLeod, Isabella, 227
McLeod, James, 227
McLeod, Jeannett, 214
McLoughlin, Mary, 202

438

442

445

447

Richardson, Ivah, 297
Richardson, James, 210
Richardson, Jean, 27
Richardson, John, 107
Richardson, Lilla, 128
Richardson, Lloyd, 255
Richardson, Lt. Daniel, 68
Richardson, Lydia, 68
Richardson, Margaret, 241
Richardson, Maria, 40
Richardson, Mary, 103
Richardson, Matilda, 107
Richardson, Mehitabel, 107
Richardson, Mercy, 149
Richardson, Orville, 44
Richardson, Rachel, 255
Richardson, Roger, 27
Richardson, Royal, 193
Richardson, Ruth, 107, 108
Richardson, Sarah, 68, 69
Richardson, Sophia, 208
Richardson, Stephen, 103
Richardson, Wallace, 138, 343
Richardson, William, 40, 137
Richarson, Orville, 40
Richmond, Benjamin, 286
Richmond, Betsey, 286
Richmond, Dorothea, 230, 258
Richmond, Louisa, 326
Richmond, Mercie, 349
Rider, Angelina, 291
Rider, Deana, 155
Riding, Margaret, 7
Ried, Alfred, 259
Ried, Estella, 260
Ried, Susan, 259
Rieo, Flora, 252
Riley, Ethel, 44
Riley, James, 180
Riley, Mary, 198, 209
Riley, William, 209
Ring, L, 292
Ring, Rufus, 292
Ring, William, 292
Ripley, Francis, 300
Risley, Ida, 235
Robbins, Charles, 31
Robbins, Ethel, 75
Robbins, Ezekiel, 12
Robbins, Francis, 75
Robbins, Freeman, 39
Robbins, Lydia, 12
Robbins, Mary, 22
Robbins, Seth, 39
Roberts, Alfred, 249
Roberts, Deliah, 73
Roberts, Hattie, 67
Roberts, Henry, 186
Roberts, James, 376
Roberts, Loretta, 71
Roberts, Muriel, 191
Roberts, Robert, 191
Roberts, Rose, 313
Roberts, Thelma, 186
Roberts, William, 67
Robertson, James, 266
Robin, Captain Samuel, 9
Robins, Susan, 9

Robinson, Lieut. Noah, 196
Robinson, Ann, 15
Robinson, Anna, 216
Robinson, Annie, 216
Robinson, Asahel, 1
Robinson, Betsey, 16
Robinson, Clara, 16
Robinson, Cynthia, 10
Robinson, Daniel, 16
Robinson, Deborah, 196
Robinson, Dr. Stephen, 1
Robinson, Elijah, 1
Robinson, Ezekiel, 10
Robinson, Ezra, 189
Robinson, George, 1
Robinson, Hannah, 10, 15, 238
Robinson, Harriet, 82
Robinson, Henry, 29, 196
Robinson, Jane, 114
Robinson, Jennie, 176
Robinson, John, 114
Robinson, L, 216
Robinson, Lewis, 1, 15
Robinson, Lucy, 1
Robinson, Martha, 10
Robinson, Mary, 57, 301
Robinson, Nathaniel, 2
Robinson, Noah, 196
Robinson, Phebe, 238
Robinson, Rodger, 114
Robinson, Rose, 341
Robinson, Samuel, 10
Robinson, Sarah, 1
Robinson, Stephen, 355
Robinson, Ursula, 210
Robinson, W, 176
Robinson, Weltha, 190
Rochardson, Chloe, 68
Roches, Catherine, 18
Rochwood, Nancy, 143
Rockwood, Adelia, 159, 170
Rockwood, Albert, 119
Rockwood, Anne, 122
Rockwood, Annie, 159
Rockwood, Benjamin, 122, 158
Rockwood, Calvin, 143
Rockwood, Capt. Erastus, 119
Rockwood, Deborah, 141
Rockwood, Edmund, 119
Rockwood, Edward, 148
Rockwood, Edwin, 143, 161
Rockwood, Elizabeth, 159
Rockwood, Emeline, 143
Rockwood, Evelinal, 144
Rockwood, Joanna, 141
Rockwood, Josephine, 159
Rockwood, Luther, 148
Rockwood, Margaret, 121
Rockwood, Martin, 159
Rockwood, Mary, 159
Rockwood, Mehitable, 126
Rockwood, Nancie, 159
Rockwood, Polly, 148
Rockwood, Sarah, 123
Rockwood, Seth, 121
Rockwood, Thomas, 144
Rockwood, Timothy, 123, 141, 148
Rockwood, William, 148

448

Rockwood, William, 148
Roddell, Avis, 19
Roder, Anna, 88
Roder, Anthon, 88
Roder, Barbara, 88
Roder, John, 81, 88
Rodgers, Mina, 78
Rogers, Ann, 38
Rogers, Cynthia, 381
Rogers, Edwin, 73
Rogers, James, 33
Rogers, Lois, 63
Rogers, Nathaiel, 381
Rogers, Olive, 239
Rogers, Rhoda, 356
Rogerson, Alfred, 246
Rogerson, Betty, 246
Rogerson, Capt. John, 246
Rogerson, Dr. Robert, 2
Rogerson, Lucy, 2
Rogerson, Mary, 246
Rogerson, Rev. Robert, 245
Rollen, John, 66
Rollen, Sarah, 66
Ronhoch, Anna, 202
Rose, Catherine, 129
Rose, James, 129
Ross, Charles, 87
Ross, Clara, 78
Ross, Edgar, 54
Ross, Frank, 87
Ross, Lizzie, 87
Ross, Margaret, 21
Roth, Frances, 346
Rothwell, Arthur, 342
Rothwell, Lila, 342
Rothwell, Myoh, 342
Rothwell, Pauline, 342
Rothwell, Richard, 38
Rothwell, William, 342
Round, Abner, 282
Round, Almon, 284
Round, Amelia, 283
Round, Anna, 283
Round, Arthur, 277
Round, Clarissa, 283
Round, Deacon Zima, 284
Round, Emily, 277
Round, Esther, 282
Round, George, 277
Round, Hiram, 283
Round, Jabez, 283
Round, Lucretia, 283
Round, Marth, 277
Round, Mercy, 283
Round, Nancy, 283
Round, Nedocia, 283
Round, Sally, 284
Round, Samuel, 283
Round, Sarah, 277
Round, Simeon, 283
Round, Stephen, 282
Round, Sybil, 283
Rounds, H, 292
Rounds, Abner, 284
Rounds, Almira, 332
Rounds, Amanda, 134
Rounds, Amey, 314

Rounds, Angeline, 280
Rounds, Ann, 284
Rounds, Annie, 285
Rounds, Arnold, 272
Rounds, Benjamin, 284
Rounds, Bessie, 285
Rounds, Betsey, 272
Rounds, Charles, 280, 284
Rounds, Cyrenes, 284
Rounds, Deborah, 284
Rounds, Devena, 284
Rounds, Elizabeth, 54, 272, 292
Rounds, Enos, 280
Rounds, Ethel, 292
Rounds, Eugene, 292
Rounds, Frank, 284
Rounds, George, 285, 352
Rounds, Gertrude, 292
Rounds, Gilbert, 280
Rounds, Grace, 285
Rounds, Harriet, 280, 292, 340
Rounds, Henry, 280
Rounds, Herbert, 72
Rounds, Hezekiah, 281
Rounds, James, 272, 283
Rounds, John, 284
Rounds, Joseph, 284
Rounds, Joshua, 332
Rounds, Jotham, 279
Rounds, Julia, 285
Rounds, Juliana, 272
Rounds, Leban, 284
Rounds, Lovina, 331
Rounds, Lucena, 281
Rounds, Lydia, 283
Rounds, Marcus, 280
Rounds, Margaret, 72
Rounds, Marion, 272
Rounds, Martha, 284, 314
Rounds, Mary, 269, 280, 303, 332
Rounds, Melinda, 279
Rounds, Mercy, 284
Rounds, Meribah, 332
Rounds, Nathaniel, 266, 314
Rounds, Nelson, 284
Rounds, Olive, 269
Rounds, Phebe, 314
Rounds, Polly, 284
Rounds, Sarah, 314
Rounds, Submit, 280
Rounds, Susan, 1, 272
Rounds, Sylvanus, 134
Rounds, William, 332
Rounds, Willliam, 283
Rounseville, Atherton, 25
Rounseville, Chester, 25
Rounseville, Lucius, 25
Rouse, Daisy, 292
Rouse, George, 292
Rowan, Harry, 214
Rowan, William, 214
Rowe, G, 217
Rowe, Mary, 64
Roy, Adelatine, 203
Roy, Emma, 200
Roy, Irene, 12
Roy, Omesime, 197
Roy, Phillip, 199

453

Smith, Laura, 44, 360
Smith, Leland, 39
Smith, Lincoln, 38
Smith, Lucy, 44, 239
Smith, Luella, 285
Smith, M, 167
Smith, Mabel, 31
Smith, Margaret, 250
Smith, Maria, 360
Smith, Marilyn, 79
Smith, Martha, 193, 213, 319
Smith, Mary, 63, 128, 239, 289, 325, 328, 360
Smith, Mercy, 148
Smith, Mildred, 99
Smith, Minnie, 134
Smith, Myra, 44
Smith, N, 39
Smith, Nancy, 370
Smith, Nellie, 250
Smith, Nettie, 289
Smith, Noyes, 83
Smith, Ophelia, 39
Smith, Patrick, 201
Smith, Patty, 284
Smith, Persis, 167
Smith, Prudence, 147
Smith, Remember, 123, 276
Smith, Richard, 276, 277
Smith, Robert, 28
Smith, Rue, 44
Smith, Ruth, 39, 250, 251
Smith, Samuel, 167, 240, 250, 360
Smith, Sarah, 53, 277, 339
Smith, Stella, 133
Smith, Stephen, 53, 96
Smith, Thomas, 290
Smith, Tom, 51
Smith, Wendell, 276
Smith, William, 28, 29, 84, 127, 281, 289, 339, 360
Smith, Willim, 64
Snead, Florence, 27
Snell, Charles, 51
Snell, Ella, 225
Snell, George, 75
Snell, Helen, 51
Snell, Ida, 75
Snells, Dexter, 145
Snitko, Nicky, 30
Snodgrass, Joseph, 130
Snodgrass, Selina, 130
Snow, Ellen, 280
Snow, Elmer, 179
Snow, Eveline, 179
Snow, Florence, 138
Snow, Henry, 179
Snow, Jeannette, 337
Snow, Joseph, 280
Snow, Nancy, 280
Snyder, Elizabeth, 115
Snyder, Ruth, 114
Solomon, Dr. S, 41
Somes, George, 226
Somes, William, 227
Sommers, Fritz, 76
Southa, Margaret, 133
Southa, Robert, 133
Southwick, Chester, 22
Southwick, Laura, 177

Southwick, Nettie, 22
Spatcher, George, 26
Spear, Arthur, 59
Spear, Charlotte, 59
Spear, William, 59, 135
Specht, Christof, 88
Specht, Jackob, 88
Specht, Nicholas, 88
Spedding, Susan, 214
Spence, Catherine, 120
Spence, Hephzibah, 120
Spence, Thomas, 120
Spencer, Eunice, 1
Spinall, Isabella, 70
Spindel, Jane, 153
Spofford, James, 163
Spofford, Preston, 171
Spofford, William, 163
Sprague, Cynthia, 355
Sprague, Deacon John, 208
Sprague, Lydia, 237, 241
Sprague, Mary, 134, 209
Spraque, John, 354
Sprigg, Alice, 291
Sprigg, Marshall, 291
Spring, Beula, 161
Spring, Charles, 162
Spring, George, 161
Springer, Arthur, 341
Springer, Elizabeth, 11
Squire, Rev. Salmon, 111
Stabbs, Alice, 36
Stack, Beatrice, 102
Stack, Margaret, 102
Stack, Robert, 101
Stackpole, Ida, 65, 252
Stafford, Charles, 78
Stafford, Grace, 78
Stafford, Julia, 78
Stafford, Mary, 85
Stafford, Ruth, 78
Standish, Henry, 160
Standish, Lewis, 363
Standish, Mary, 160
Stanely, Deacon Jonathan, 195
Stanely, Hannah, 196
Stanely, Martha, 196
Stanhope, Virginia, 28
Stanley, Abbie, 132
Stanley, Anna, 195
Stanley, Anson, 196
Stanley, Becca, 193
Stanley, Charles, 350
Stanley, Clara, 59
Stanley, Daniel, 5
Stanley, David, 195
Stanley, J, 15
Stanley, Jabez, 5
Stanley, James, 132
Stanley, Jenckes, 195
Stanley, Julette, 132
Stanley, Lieut. Amos, 195
Stanley, Lyman, 59
Stanley, Mary, 8, 132, 195
Stanley, Nancy, 5
Stanley, Rebecca, 117
Stanley, Seneca, 8
Stanley, Thomas, 195

454

455

Suttis, Minnie, 72
Swallow, Edgar, 214
Swallow, Elmer, 223
Swallow, Elsie, 214
Swallow, George, 223
Swallow, Henry, 214
Swallow, John, 214
Swallow, Robert, 214
Swallow, Roy, 214
Swallow, Sarah, 223
Swallow, Susan, 223
Swan, Ebenezer, 193
Swan, Evelyn, 79
Swan, Howard, 78
Swansey, Sarah, 332
Swansey, Stephen, 332
Swanson, Andrew, 250
Swanson, Ingrid, 250
Swanson, Jane, 139
Swanson, John, 262
Swanson, Walter, 214
Swanson, Wyman, 139
Swayer, Eliza, 112
Sweeney, Edward, 65
Sweeney, George, 50
Sweeney, Leonilda, 56
Sweeney, Lucy, 65
Sweeney, Maria, 202
Sweeney, Samuel, 202
Sweeney, William, 56
Sweet, Ada, 66
Sweet, Alice, 323
Sweet, Amos, 39
Sweet, Benjamin, 66
Sweet, Charles, 42
Sweet, Clara, 37
Sweet, Dorothy, 61
Sweet, Eleanor, 38
Sweet, Ervin, 42
Sweet, Frank, 27, 39
Sweet, Frankie, 39
Sweet, Gardner, 98
Sweet, George, 64
Sweet, Henry, 68
Sweet, John, 68
Sweet, Jonathan, 271
Sweet, Laurette, 68
Sweet, Lou, 44
Sweet, Naomi, 194
Sweet, Phebe, 271
Sweet, Sarah, 271
Sweet, Warren, 323
Sweet, William, 27
Sweetland, Albert, 189
Sweetland, Amy, 189
Sweetland, Arnold, 192
Sweetland, Charles, 192
Sweetland, Clarinda, 192
Sweetland, Clark, 191
Sweetland, Cynthi, 188
Sweetland, Elizabeth, 191, 192
Sweetland, Ella, 189
Sweetland, Hannah, 189, 191
Sweetland, John, 188
Sweetland, Laura, 188
Sweetland, Leon, 189
Sweetland, Lieut. William, 192
Sweetland, Lina, 192

Sweetland, Lucetta, 192
Sweetland, Mariette, 191
Sweetland, May, 189
Sweetland, Nancy, 189
Sweetland, Olive, 188
Sweetland, Phebe, 189
Sweetland, Robert, 18, 189
Sweetland, Rowen, 192
Sweetland, Samuel, 189, 192
Sweetland, Sarah, 192
Sweetland, Susan, 188
Sweetland, William, 189, 192, 235
Swent, Minnie, 31
Swift, David, 71
Swift, Howard, 26
Swift, Levi, 26
Swift, Mabel, 215
Swift, William, 215
Sylvester, Abby, 312
Synder, Matilda, 254
T
Taber, Carrie, 136
Taber, Leander, 282
Tabor, Harrison, 135
Tabor, Susan, 46
Taft, Ann, 130
Taft, Anna, 167
Taft, Daniel, 130
Taft, Ellen, 176
Taft, George, 167
Taft, Isabelle, 203
Taft, James, 167
Talbot, Deacon Seth, 96
Talbot, Esther, 111
Talbot, Henry, 111
Talbot, John, 253
Talbot, Mary, 96
Talbot, Sally, 96
Talbot, Sarah, 111
Tallaksen, Lars, 353
Tallman, Asa, 350
Tanner, William, 243
Tappan, Benjamin, 221
Tappan, Ella, 227
Tappan, Maria, 221
Tarbox, Fay, 24
Tasiner, Charles, 311
Tasiner, Mary, 311
Tate, Elizabeth, 358
Tattersall, Henry, 347
Tattersall, Olive, 347
Taylor, Annie, 73
Taylor, Bertha, 87
Taylor, Cora, 127
Taylor, Elenor, 67
Taylor, Ellen, 176
Taylor, Emma, 176
Taylor, Ethel, 67
Taylor, Evelyn, 176
Taylor, Forrest, 67
Taylor, George, 61, 67
Taylor, Hannah, 29
Taylor, Harrison, 176
Taylor, Herbert, 127
Taylor, Mabel, 49
Taylor, Mary, 32, 166
Taylor, Nellie, 176
Taylor, Sarah, 127

Taylor, Thomas, 49
Taylor, William, 73
Taylot, Elizabeth, 172
Temple, Annah, 176
Temple, Betsey, 180
Temple, Mary, 173
Tennant, Edward, 13
Tennant, Louisa, 13
Tenney Saidee, 162
Tenney, Allen, 162
Tenney, Austin, 161
Tenney, Fred, 162
Tenney, John, 102
Tenney, Lois, 161
Tenney, Mary, 102
Tenney, Pauline, 163
Tewyan, William, 187
Thacher, John, 43
Thain, Ellen, 376
Thain, Eugene, 376
Thain, Maranda, 376
Thain, Samuel, 376
Thain, Thomas, 376
Thain, William, 376
Thatcher, Captain James, 238
Thatcher, Eliza, 238
Thatcher, Rev. James, 319
Thatcher, William, 320
Thayer, Abigail, 142
Thayer, Alexander, 142
Thayer, Bessie, 181
Thayer, Betsey, 109
Thayer, Charles, 171
Thayer, Clarissa, 171
Thayer, Davis, 109, 381
Thayer, Eliza, 110
Thayer, Elmer, 139
Thayer, Emery, 110
Thayer, Emma, 110, 381
Thayer, Eunice, 378
Thayer, Harriet, 289
Thayer, Herbert, 74
Thayer, Isalene, 119
Thayer, John, 53
Thayer, Josephine, 381
Thayer, Lavina, 381
Thayer, Lorenzo, 74
Thayer, Margaret, 109
Thayer, Margery, 53
Thayer, Marion, 253
Thayer, Mary, 41, 53, 109, 110, 171
Thayer, Oman, 253
Thayer, Rebecca, 110
Thayer, Rev. William, 110
Thayer, Seth, 171
Thayer, Sumner, 381
Thayer, Susanna, 122
Thayer, William, 110, 160
Theobald, Florence, 58
Theobald, Jean, 58
Theobald, Norman, 58
Thomas, Charles, 224, 328
Thomas, Cora, 224
Thomas, Edgar, 118
Thomas, Emma, 47
Thomas, Henry, 21
Thomas, Lena, 21
Thomas, Walter, 27

Thompson, Abbie, 42
Thompson, Addison, 368
Thompson, Adin, 169
Thompson, Arthur, 201
Thompson, Asenath, 159
Thompson, C, 227
Thompson, Clelland, 42
Thompson, Earl, 216
Thompson, Elmer, 45
Thompson, Eugene, 369
Thompson, Fletcher, 177
Thompson, Francis, 45
Thompson, Frederick, 45
Thompson, Gaius, 166
Thompson, George, 177
Thompson, Harry, 215
Thompson, Herbert, 215, 255
Thompson, Julia, 215
Thompson, Laura, 227
Thompson, Lloyd, 169
Thompson, M, 255
Thompson, Mary, 45, 69, 166
Thompson, Sally, 169
Thompson, Samuel, 45
Thomson, Orrin, 169
Thornton, Mary, 324
Thrasher, Mary, 39
Thrasher, Sarah, 39
Thrope, Lalia, 167
Thurber, Albert, 86
Thurber, Arthur, 60
Thurber, Benjamin, 271, 317
Thurber, Bertha, 83
Thurber, Betsey, 314
Thurber, Charles, 50
Thurber, Crawford, 69
Thurber, Daniel, 272
Thurber, Edwin, 60
Thurber, Eliza, 272
Thurber, Eva, 25
Thurber, Francis, 50
Thurber, Harriet, 86
Thurber, Hopestill, 314
Thurber, Jennie, 84
Thurber, Jeremiah, 314
Thurber, Joanna, 315
Thurber, John, 314, 315
Thurber, Joseph, 84
Thurber, Lois, 272
Thurber, Louis, 50
Thurber, Luther, 328
Thurber, Mary, 66, 69, 84
Thurber, Phebe, 314
Thurber, Priscilla, 282
Thurber, Samuel, 314
Thurber, Sarah, 50, 314
Thurber, Stephen, 315
Thurber, Thomas, 84
Thurber, William, 66
Thurston, Benjamin, 324
Thurston, Daniel, 116
Thurston, Henry, 348
Thurston, Lydia, 324
Thurston, Sarah, 343
Tibbetts, Harrison, 180
Tibbetts, Hattie, 180
Tidd, Daniel, 141
Tidd, Emma, 162

460

Whiting, Georgianna, 162
Whiting, Harietta, 134
Whiting, Harriet, 381
Whiting, Herbert, 109
Whiting, Inez, 214
Whiting, James, 222
Whiting, Jannette, 110
Whiting, Jason, 147
Whiting, Joseph, 110, 116
Whiting, Katherine, 221
Whiting, Lewis, 358
Whiting, Lt. Samuel, 143
Whiting, Lucy, 117
Whiting, Lydia, 120
Whiting, Martha, 134
Whiting, Mary, 146
Whiting, Meletiah, 146
Whiting, Nathan, 141, 146
Whiting, Nelson, 169
Whiting, Olive, 147
Whiting, Peter, 120
Whiting, Rachel, 248
Whiting, Rowena, 147
Whiting, Ruth, 116
Whiting, Samuel, 143
Whiting, Sarah, 150, 169
Whiting, Sila, 72
Whiting, Susan, 180
Whiting, Sybil, 193
Whiting, Warren, 226
Whiting, William, 110, 147
Whiting, Zeolide, 110
Whitman, George, 37
Whitman, Hattie, 37
Whitman, Henry, 224
Whitman, Julia, 224
Whitmarsh, Louis, 64
Whitmore, Isabelle, 158
Whitney, Adeliza, 365
Whitney, Clarence, 238
Whitney, Cora, 35
Whitney, George, 153, 174
Whitney, Harriet, 71
Whitney, Louisa, 153
Whitney, William, 271
Whittaker, Charles, 252
Whittaker, Esther, 302
Whittaker, Frederick, 289
Whittaker, John, 289
Whittaker, Martha, 289
Whittaker, Sarah, 289
Whittaker, Thomas, 328
Whittemore, Achsah, 157
Whitten, Imogene, 313
Whittimore, Charles, 178
Whittmore, 326
Whittmore, Jesse, 210
Wicker, Deacon Joshua, 167
Wickham, James, 317
Widing, Edwin, 12
Wiggin, Harriet, 77
Wiggin, Shepard, 103
Wiggins, Shepard, 103
Wight, Charles, 77
Wight, Elizabeth, 77
Wight, Irene, 145
Wight, James, 145
Wight, Mary, 183

Wight, Milton, 145
Wikman, Emma, 27
Wilbour, Esther, 350
Wilbour, Harum, 349
Wilbur, Bertha, 356
Wilbur, Caroline, 66
Wilbur, Daniel, 345, 356
Wilbur, Dorothy, 343
Wilbur, Elizabeth, 334, 335
Wilbur, Everett, 277
Wilbur, Frank, 23
Wilbur, Henry, 343
Wilbur, James, 334, 335
Wilbur, Jennie, 343
Wilbur, Julia, 277
Wilbur, Mary, 335, 345
Wilbur, Nancy, 356
Wilbur, Polly, 277
Wilbur, Roswell, 356
Wilbur, Royal, 277
Wilbur, Sarah, 335, 356
Wilbur, William, 335, 345, 356
Wilbur, Zephaniah, 335
Wilcox, Ella, 248
Wilcox, Henry, 36
Wilcox, Reginald, 302
Wilcox, Ruth, 82
Wilcox, Samuel, 248
Wilde, Annie, 222
Wilde, Eben, 25
Wilde, John, 222
Wilde, Mary, 27
Wilder, Alice, 173
Wilder, Anna, 173
Wilder, Betsey, 10
Wilder, Charles, 173
Wilder, Eliza, 16
Wilder, Elizabeth, 173
Wilder, Esther, 10
Wilder, Frank, 205
Wilder, George, 170
Wilder, Hepsibeth, 170
Wilder, Julia, 10
Wilder, Leora, 170
Wilder, Louisa, 368
Wilder, Mary, 173
Wilder, Rev. John, 10
Wilder, Rufus, 173
Wilder, Sarah, 173
Wilder, Sefuantes, 173
Wilder, Sydney, 173
Wildes, Harriet, 77
Wilding, Mary, 12
Wiley, Albert, 165
Wiley, Benjamin, 180
Wiley, Charles, 165
Wiley, Edwin, 165
Wiley, Frances, 165
Wiley, Frank, 165
Wiley, Fred, 165
Wilken, Dr. George, 146
Wilkens, Albert, 166
Wilkens, Dana, 166
Wilkins, Lorena, 255
Wilkinson, Edgar, 67
Wilkinson, Sarah, 39
Willaims, Louisa, 382
Willard, Abbie, 181